GOD AT RISK

THE COST OF FREEDOM
IN THE GREAT CONTROVERSY

BY
HERBERT E. DOUGLASS

GOD AT RISK:

THE COST OF FREEDOM IN THE GREAT CONTROVERSY BETWEEN GOD AND SATAN

Freedom; svoboda; vrijheid; libertate; wolność; laisve; liberté; freiheit; libertà; libertad; liberdada; kalayaan; merkeka; özgürlük; vryheid; mukti; frihed; volia; azaadi; su tu do; frihet; toimintavapaus; szótár; nidhasa; slobada; freedom

Herbert E. Douglass

AMAZING FACTS

Roseville, CA

"But what matter," said Charmides, "from whom I heard this?"
"No matter at all," I [Socrates] replied: "for the point is not
who said the words, but whether they are true or not."
—*The Dialogues of Plato,* Jewett, vol. 1, 11 (161).

Printed in United States of America
All Rights Reserved

Published by Amazing Facts, Inc.
P. O. Box 1058
Roseville, CA 95678-8058
800-538-7275

The author assumes full responsibility for the accuracy of all facts and quotations as cited in this book.

Unless otherwise indicated, Scripture quotations are taken from the New King James Version, Copyright © 1979, 1980, 1982. Thomas Nelson, Inc., Publishers.

References not attributed were authored by Ellen G. White

Cover Design by Haley Trimmer
Text Editing by Barry Champion and Anthony Lester
Text Design and Layout by Greg Solie – Altamont Graphics

Typeset: 12/13 Minion

Additional copies of this book may be purchased at www.amazingfacts.org

Library of Congress Cataloging-in-Publication Data

Douglass, Herbert E.
    God at risk : the cost of freedom in the great controversy between God and Satan / Herbert E. Douglass.-- 1st ed.
        p.   cm.
    Includes bibliographical references.
    ISBN 1-58019-172-X   (pbk. : alk. paper)
    1. Liberty--Religious aspects--Christianity.   2. Devil--Christianity.
3. Economy of God.   I. Title.

    BT810.3.D68 2004
    233'.7--dc22

                                                    2004003215

04 05 06 07 08 • 5 4 3 2 1

DEDICATION

For
Jan, Michael, Herb, Mavis, Reatha, Randy, Vivienne Sue, Donna,
Chip, Judy, Vannessa, Jon, Vivyan, Jimmy, Emily, Cady, Cliff,
Kristin, Candy, Britney, Ryan, Randy, Kelli,

And for Lady Douglass,
who has been most patient during the four years
we have been developing this book together.

All Fellow Travelers on the Road to Forever.

ACKNOWLEDGEMENTS

Many tributaries flow into the river of thought that eventually becomes a book. I am merely that river that now carries the wisdom of early teachers at Atlantic Union College, Seventh-day Adventist Theological Seminary and the Pacific School of Religion (Graduate Theological Union).

In that same current are life experiences that my students shared with me at Pacific Union College, Atlantic Union College, Weimar Institute and Amazing Facts College of Evangelism.

Enriching the flow are my colleagues without number—fellow teachers and pastors, publishing house confrères in both the Pacific Press Publishing Association and the Review and Herald Publishing Association, and the multitude of churches and conferences where keen minds sharpened mine.

Mere words of gratitude could never carry the weight of thanks that I have for all these gifted people, professional and lay. I wish I could figure out how to truly compensate each one of them—but maybe on the other side.

But when I think of those who have read this book in manuscript form without balking for a moment, I am beyond the ability to register my appreciation. They sharpened my mind, caught errors and non sequiturs, and forced me to ask the right questions.

Perhaps noting them at this time might help, but the published mistakes are all mine, not theirs!

I list them alphabetically but each one could be at the head of the list: Jack Blanco, Barry Champion, Gerald Grimaud, Oliver Jacques, Malcolm Maxwell, Jim Nix, Robert Nixon, Neal Wilson, Ted Wilson, and Kenneth Wood. They shall "shine as the stars forever."

TABLE OF CONTENTS

SECTION ONE

The underlying issue in the Great Controversy between God and Satan is "freedom." Over that mysterious word, that word that has summoned unspeakable courage, honor, and unselfishness in its defense, the well being of the universe has been wrenched and jeopardized. Why did God risk all on freedom?

SECTION TWO

The issues that led angels in heaven to rebel against God, the Creator, are the same reasons created beings on earth continue to rebel against God, consciously or unconsciously. What were Satan's accusations that could persuade one-third of the angels to distrust God? Why did God risk all on letting Satan live?

SECTION THREE

God responded to Satan's charges in such a way that the unfallen angels and worlds could see that He is not the kind of God that Satan had made Him out to be. What has been God's long-range plan to tell His side of the story? How does Jesus as our Substitute ("atoning Sacrifice"), High Priest ("all-powerful Mediator"), and our Example tell the truth about God and about the destiny of men and women of faith? Why did God risk all in allowing Jesus to become truly man, exposing Himself to possible failure and eternal loss?

SECTION FOUR

God created human intelligences on this planet to be His laboratory in which the principles of His government and those of Satan's could be fully displayed. How do men and women of faith respond to God's plan for them and how do they help to vindicate God's character and government? Why did God risk all in putting His case before the universe in the hands of men and women who professed to be followers of Jesus?

SECTION FIVE

God will have a people who will rightly represent Him. They will present His final appeal before the forces of Good and Evil come to their final clash and Jesus returns. Is it possible that God would risk all in placing the future of the universe on the final generation who will be the targets of Satan's fiercest attacks?

SECTION SIX

What will be Satan's last-day deceptions and assaults as He furiously challenges God's plan to have a special people with a special message for the endtime? How will God's people thwart Satan's final attempt to wrest this planet from God's control?

SECTION SEVEN

How will Satan use the United States, the beacon of freedom for more than two centuries, as his laboratory and launching pad for world domination, not militarily but through religious legislation? What will be his decoy thrusts that will obscure his primary goals in bringing on the Sunday laws and ultimately their enforcement?

SECTION EIGHT

How will God's loyalists respond to Satan's last-day deceptions and vindicate His judgment in their favor? What are the related events involving God's loyalists that will help determine the timing of the Second Advent? How will these events more fully vindicate God's wisdom and patience when He risked giving freedom to created intelligences?

SECTION NINE

The controversy will end after both God and Satan have had sufficient time to display the consequences of their plans for governing the universe. What is the core issue that will make the universe eternally secure? How will the evidence before the universe of 1) the consequences of evil and

2) the rewards of loyalty to God provide this eternal security? How do the mental/physical habits of the redeemed, who have become so settled that sin will never arise again, add to this eternal security and demonstrate God's wisdom in granting freedom to created intelligences?

SECTION TEN

The Great Controversy embraces all aspects of the Christian's life. This includes his or her approach to the Bible, the study of all intellectual areas of interest, personal relationships with family and others, and to the way that his or her church reflects the Great Controversy Theme. This church reflection will be seen in such areas as humanitarian concern, educational institutions, health-related institutions, youth concerns, and methods to reach the unchurched.

PRELUDE

T his book is about the cost of freedom. Freedom is never free![1]

I remember well those darkening clouds over America and the Free World in 1941, when President Franklin Delano Roosevelt gave his State of the Union address to Congress at the beginning of his third term in office. The thunder of war and its horror had already embraced Europe with a death grip. The president closed his speech with a description of four essential freedoms—freedom of speech and expression; freedom of worship; freedom from want; and freedom from fear. With moral clarity, the president told the world why America was committed to assisting the Free World in its defense against totalitarian regimes that were driving Planet Earth into a long night of grief.

His speech ended with: "This nation has placed its destiny in the hands, heads and hearts of its millions of free men and women, and its faith in freedom under the guidance of God. Freedom means the supremacy of human rights everywhere. Our support goes to those who struggle to gain those rights and keep them. Our strength is our unity of purpose. To that high concept there can be *no end save victory*."[2]

Inspired by Roosevelt's speech, Norman Rockwell devoted six months in 1943 to his four paintings—the *Four Freedoms*. They illustrated the reasons why brave men and women on all continents were fighting the war machines of three dictators. Rockwell chose to express the complex ideas of the *Four Freedoms* through simple, everyday scenes using his Vermont neighbors as models. "Freedom of Speech," for example, depicts a New England town meeting where a citizen stands up to express his opinions freely. These four pictures quickly became the best-known and most appreciated paintings of that era.[3]

It is one thing to talk freedom and paint its blessings. But paying the cost of these freedoms is incalculable. Ask those of the Second Ranger Battalion who climbed more than 100 feet under constant fire up the cliff

---

[1] I often wear my favorite T-shirt imprinted with "Freedom is Never Free" when writing these pages.

[2] Robert Cowley, ed., *No End Save Victory* (New York: G. P. Putnam's Sons, 2001). Emphasis supplied.

[3] I have prized these paintings ever since. They appeared at a time when the war was going against the Free World on all battlefronts. The free world needed the inspirational message that the paintings conveyed so forcefully and beautifully. They became the centerpiece of one of the many war-bond campaigns that raised millions of dollars for the war effort. The "Freedom of Religion" painting focused on several heads, young and old, in solemn thought and worship. "Freedom from Want" pictured Rockwell's own family's Thanksgiving with the turkey as the focus for his message, explaining, "Our cook cooked it, I painted it, and we ate it. That was one of the few times I've ever eaten the model." "Freedom from Fear" depicted two parents tucking their sleeping children into a quiet night's rest, the father holding the newspaper filled with the tide of war.

at Pointe-du-Hoc on June 6, 1944. They silenced the guns and saved many lives on Utah and Omaha beaches. But it cost the Rangers. At the end of that "longest day," only 50 of the more than 200 who had landed were still able to fight (see page 28). The risk and cost of freedom is incalculable.

Ask those 19-year-old teenagers (the average age of the First U. S. Marine Division) who landed August 7, 1942, on the north shore of Guadalcanal, a small tropical island not far from Australia (see page 236).

Think of the 56 signers of the Declaration of Independence in 1776. Each signer, and his family, became marked men, pursued relentlessly by the British retribution. None who had property or family were spared (see page 22) The cost of freedom is incalculable.

COST OF FREEDOM ALWAYS HIGH

I also remember well October 22, 1962. On that day I gave the chapel message at the Pacific School of Religion when Russian ships with missile capabilities were nearing Cuba. Ringing in my ears was President John F. Kennedy's address to the nation: "The path we have chosen for the present is full of hazards, as all paths are; but it is the one most consistent with our character and courage as a nation and our commitments around the world. The cost of freedom is always high—but Americans have always paid it. And one path we shall never choose, and that is the path of surrender or submission.

"Our goal is not the victory of might but the vindication of right—not peace at the expense of freedom, but both peace and freedom, here in this hemisphere and, we hope, around the world. God willing, that goal will be achieved."

Why does freedom cost so much? Because throughout history, and long before this world was created, another principle has been warring against the elegant flower of freedom. We call that principle—"evil." Evil is the underside of freedom—the misuse of freedom. Evil is the flowering of the bitter weed we call "rebellion." Evil stands freedom on its head because it substitutes so-called "independence" for genuine freedom. In addition, evil does not distinguish freedom from liberty.[4]

We call this conflict between freedom and evil "the Great Controversy." This is not a philosophical term. We are talking about real life, real persons, real choices, and real consequences.[5] This book unfolds the beginning and the end of this Great Controversy and who the main characters are in the drama of the ages. And how every reader is playing his or her part.

---

[4] See "Appendix A: How We Define Freedom"

[5] In Abraham Lincoln's reply to Douglas in their seventh and last debate, October 15, 1858, he said that both he and Douglas were in "the eternal struggle between these two principles—right and wrong—throughout the world. They are the two principles that have stood face to face from the beginning of time; and will ever continue to struggle." —*Bartlett's Familiar Quotations* (Thirteenth Edition), 538.

BEYOND CALCULATION

The power of freedom is also beyond calculation. In one generation, freedom turned Germany around. Shortly after September 11, 2001, on NATO maneuvers, the German Navy destroyer *Lutjens* requested permission to pass close by a United States guided-missile destroyer, the *Churchill*. In the middle of the Atlantic, the request seemed odd, but the captain acquiesced. As they were making their approach, the conning officer, using binoculars, announced that the *Lutjens* was flying not only the German flag, but also the American flag. As the *Lutjens* came alongside, the American sailors saw the American flag flying at half-mast and the *Lutjens'* entire topside standing at silent, rigid attention in their dress uniforms.

They had also made a sign that was displayed on her side that read, "We Stand By You." Not a dry eye on the *Churchill* as they stayed alongside for a few minutes and saluted. The German Navy gave the Americans an incredible message—the power of freedom in one generation.

THE THIN RED LINE

The fire of freedom might sometimes flicker, but it has never gone out. Rudyard Kipling called it "a thin red line of 'eroes.'"[6] But that "thin red line" has been all that was necessary in the big moments when freedom's light was dimming. Wherever one looks, the human cry for freedom has stitched the fabric of history.

On August 19, 480 B.C., a small force of 300 Spartans, that "thin red line," under Leonidas died defending Greece against nearly 200,000 Persians. Thermopylae (Hot Gates), that narrow mountain pass in central Greece, would never have been remembered if not for those valiant 300 who paid the cost of freedom. They held the pass long enough for their countrymen to organize a defense that eventually saved Greece's legacy to the world. One month later at the Battle of Salamis, the Greek navy of fewer than 400 ships under Themistocles lured 1,000 Persian ships into a trap within the Bay of Salamis, sending Xerxes packing back to Persia.

At the Thermopylae pass today is a monument with these words: "Go tell the Spartans, stranger passing by, that here obedient to their laws, we lie." The cost of freedom!

But such stories of valor and commitment to freedom are being written virtually every day. Most everybody reading this book can remember when Eastern Europe was under the heavy hand of Communism, locked within a system that we called evil.[7] We remember the courage of many through the years who gave their lives to raise freedom's flag.

---

[6] *Tommy*, Stanza 3.

[7] President Ronald Reagan called Communism a "totalitarian evil" in his speech before England's House of Commons, June 8, 1982. Most of his advisors deleted his references that branded the Soviet Union as "evil." However, he slipped his famous "evil empire" line into the final draft of his speech before the National Association of Evangelicals, March 8, 1983.

But not many know of how Romania, under the iron grip of Nicolae Ceausescu and his dreaded Securitate (the secret police), became free almost over night! I remember well watching on television the ocean wave of courage sweep over Romania in December 1989. For some time, ruthless Ceausescu had been ordering anti-government protests put down by bullets and torture.

THE SPARK THAT IGNITED A REVOLUTION

On December 10, the spark that ignited Romania's revolution began in a most unlikely place—in Timişoara, 400 kilometers from Bucharest, and by a minister of the little-known Reformed Hungarian Church, Laszlo Tokes. The brave pastor, speaking out against the horrible abuses of Ceausescu's regime, told his people that his battle with the authorities was lost and that he would be leaving the next Sunday. The mayor had threatened to physically evict Tokes and his family if he defied them longer.

To Tokes's surprise, his congregation began a permanent vigil. On December 15, a small crowd encircled the church, brandishing candles and calling on the authorities to halt their persecution of Tokes. By evening, the crowd has grown to 1,000. The next few days, the crowd included people who belonged to all denominations and national communities. Shouts of "Freedom!" echoed throughout the city. The "thin red line" was forming.

Then the massacre began. The officers who refused to shoot were themselves shot. But the revolution had begun. The news of Timişoara spread throughout Romania. In only a few days we watched this fresh wind of freedom topple the tyrant Ceausescu, who was swiftly executed. The fanaticism of Ceausescu's Securitate, 180,000 strong, was not able to restrain the wind of freedom encouraged by Tokes in Timişoara, a modern member of that "thin red line."

Freedom costs. The cost of freedom is incalculable.

REVIEWING THE ULTIMATE COST OF FREEDOM

In this book we will trace the creation of freedom back to the wisdom and love of God. We will review the cost He alone chose to bear in giving freedom—this awesome endowment—to His created intelligences. And we will quickly trace the cost of freedom borne by men and women through the centuries.

We will listen to God's Word, which describes the beginning of evil and how all suffering, pain, heartbreak and junked dreams flow from that Evil One's determination to destroy God's trustworthiness.

Then we will sketch out God's plan to tell the truth about Himself and Satan's charges. We will detail God's good news as to how men and women can find peace and power to thwart Satan's strategies. We will focus on why

God put His character and government at great risk when He gave freedom to created intelligences. We will note that throughout history, the frontiers of freedom have had to be protected against "anarchy and caprice on one side and from regimentation and suffocation by rules on the other."[8]

Not only will we highlight the Great Controversy between God's people and Satan's followers through the centuries, we will especially focus on what we all should expect in the endtime—a time when Satan will focus all his practiced expertise on destroying God's people.

This Great Controversy is far different than Hollywood's portrayal of a galactic clash of heavenly warriors with their shining swords. The Great Controversy is over the question of who can best govern the universe, who presents the best principles by which created intelligences can find hope, health, happiness and the assurance of living on a planet sanitized from all the evil that Satan is responsible for.

NOT A SPECTATOR SPORT

The Great Controversy is not a spectator sport. It does not give anyone the luxury of sitting in the bleachers. You and I are actors on the stage of the universe. How we play our part will determine not only our eternal futures but also help significantly in vindicating the integrity of God's order in the universe.

We will note how the rules and scripts are being changed constantly. We have to be alert at all times to the underhanded unfairness of our opponent, "your adversary, the devil [who] walks about like a roaring lion, seeking whom he may devour" (1 Peter 5:8).

Satan is the master of the universe's "spin zone."[9] You will follow his many deceptions in the pages to follow. This book will become your "no-spin zone"! It will be a great place to get your balance because it will be your truth-detector as well as lie-detector. The CIA calls it "disinformation"; politicians call it "spin." Words become lethal weapons when moral compasses are compromised, when immoral acts are called "gaining experience" or "youthful indiscretions."

We will focus on Jesus, who came to earth to set up His "no-spin zone." He plunged into the middle of Evil's spin zone and showed us how to expose the mendacity, pretensions, and lies that most of the world has lived by for many centuries. Jesus said, in many ways, "There can be no end save victory!"

---

[8] Joost A. M. Meerloo, M.D., *The Rape of the Mind* (New York: Grosset & Dunlap, 1961), 297.

[9] The "no-spin zone" concept first came to me with the publication of Bill O'Reilly's *The No Spin Zone* (New York: Broadway Books, 2001).

My "Liberal" And "Conservative" Friends

I am writing these pages for my "liberal" friends as well as my "conservative" friends—and for all those who want to be in the "middle," wherever that is. (I hate labels!) My "liberal" friends invigorate me with their prodding, for their concern for reasonable answers and relevance, for the value of tentativeness, for honesty in checking out the validity of "authoritative" statements, for emphasizing the individual in a world that tends to overlook or even ignore individual freedoms, for freedom of expression, no matter how unpopular. Liberal friends will see what I mean by the time they finish this book!

My "conservative" friends remind me of the power of order and coherence, for the value of rootage and the rule of law, for the security in listening to transcendence when thinking in religious terms, for their appreciation for hard-fought victories that have given us so much to prize today, such as the Mayflower Compact, the U.S. Constitution, etc! (While they turn these pages, my "conservative" friends will also discover fresh insights for which "liberals" are willing to die.)

I say all this because I believe that the thesis of this book transcends the liberal/conservative antitheses. For if God be God, then He embraces the highest concerns of both "liberals" and "conservatives." He wants from each of us an honest heart! And a will to act on wherever that honest heart leads us!

I say to both my "liberal" and "conservative" friends (and all those in the so-called "middle"), "there can be no end save victory!" Let's read on!

INTRODUCTION:
WHY THIS BOOK IS NECESSARY AS WELL AS TIMELY

T he time is ripe for a fresh look at spiritual warfare and the why of suffering. We live in a new day. For at least three centuries, the word has gone out, especially from academic circles, that modern men and women could no longer believe in the supernatural.

Few doubt today that the academic landscape has radically changed into what has been called the "postmodern" period. What once was ridiculed as irrelevant has now been overtaken by a world awash in all kinds of interest in spirituality, such as angels and otherworldly interventions, surrounded by a remarkable surge of interest in Eastern thought and religions. That there is reality beyond the physical realm is becoming a plausible notion. For the general public at least, the idea of a universe inhabited with spiritual beings that affect the affairs of this world is becoming as axiomatic as the law of gravity.

Take the local bookstore in the nearby mall. Compare the space given today to supernaturalism, to the spirit world, to angels and demons, even to Satan, with the bookstore of even 20 years ago! Observe the television and Hollywood shows, appearing like snowflakes, that feature the intervention of angels, extra-worldly beings, and interplanetary travel.[10] Or the best-selling books, such as Frank Peretti's novels and the *Left Behind* series that have become blockbuster Hollywood movies. Add to all that the Harry Potter series and Tolkien's revival. Note how the secular media have given prominent space to articles on angels.[11] And on it goes.

EMERGENCE OF THE NEW AGE MOVEMENT

Probably the most prominent phenomenon of the past 40 years has been the emergence of the New Age Movement—a sort of takeover of the West by Eastern thought and religion. Gardens supposedly grow supernaturally, exorcisms are given more credulity, "channelers" bring together past and present generations, miracle healings on television mesmerize thousands, large groups everywhere find social bonding in the "harmonics" of the universe. All the conventional categories of thought that seemed to serve well since Plato and Aristotle are definitely not "in"—supernaturalism is!

---

[10] *Star Wars, ET, Touched by an Angel, Spacehunter, Millennium, Star Trek, Close Encounters of the Third Kind, The Sixth Sense, Dragonfly, Joan of Arcadia, Tru Calling, Wonderfalls,* HBO's *Carnivàle, Dead Like Me, Buffy, the Vampire Slayer,* etc.

[11] K. L. Woodward, "Angels," *Newsweek,* Dec. 27, 1993; N. Gibbs, "Angels Among Us," *Time,* Dec. 27, 1993. Neither magazine wanted to be outdone by the other in the same week!

One example: the phenomenon of Oprah Winfrey! To her television audience of more than 22 million "she has become a post-modern priest-ess—an icon of church-free spirituality."[12] Her former pastor says that Oprah "has this sort of 'God is everywhere, God is in me, I don't need to go to church, I don't need to be a part of a body of believers, I can meditate. I can do positive thinking' spirituality. It's a strange gospel. It has nothing to do with the church Jesus Christ founded."[13] As Oprah said: "One of the biggest mistakes humans make is to believe there is only one way. Actually, there are many diverse paths to what you call God."[14]

One of those "diverse paths," of which there are many today, is the rec-ognition of Avatar Adi Da Samraj as the Divine Person, the Promised God-Man, the final Revelation of God. "I Am That One," he intones, and a sig-nificant group around the world, composed of well-known authors, musi-cians, and scholars, submit to his teachings.[15]

SINCE SEPTEMBER 11, 2001

But now, in a different direction: Since September 11, 2001, the wraps are off public discussion regarding the dimensions of Evil and its causes.[16] The horrific impact of sudden death within the safety of the best buildings built, orchestrated by religious fanatics who valued "life" on a different level than most everyone else in the Western world, has flooded the media of the world with a fundamental question: Why? Further, how does one com-bat such ghastly minds that can turn beauty and order and kindness upside down with demonic joy? How does one explain all this?[17]

Every time I have visited the Tomb of the Unknowns[18] at Arlington National Cemetery on the heights across the Potomac from Washington, D.C., I want to read again the inscription: "Here rests in honored glory an American soldier known but to God." Paying honor too is the sentry, a member of the 15-man honor guard, who walks his post, day and night, in sun or storm. All the guards are volunteers, chosen for their soldierly bear-ing and outstanding military records from among the thousands who apply for the honor. Freedom is not free! Good and evil are in heavy combat.

---

[12] LaTonya Taylor, "The Church of O," *Christianity Today,* April 1, 2002, 40.

[13] *Ibid.,* 45.

[14] *Ibid.,* 45.

[15] http://adidam.org Devotees include Elizabeth Kubler-Ross, M.D., Jeffrey Mishlove, Ph.D., and Ray Lynch, platinum recording artist.

[16] Note President Bush's speech the day after the WTC and Pentagon attacks: "This will be a monumental struggle of good versus evil, but good will prevail." And his speech before Congress, September 21, 2002: "Freedom and fear, justice and cruelty, have always been at war. And we know that God is not neutral between them."

[17] Think of Egypt's independent weekly *al-Maydan* reporting after the brutal crash at New York's World Trade Center, "Millions across the world shouted in joy: 'America has been hit!'" (Cited by Lance Morrow, *Time,* December 10, 2001, 122.)

[18] Often called "The Tomb of the Unknown Soldier."

Only God knows the weight of horror, pain, and disappointment that the "unknown soldier" experienced in his lonely fight for freedom. But multiply that weight millions and millions of times and we begin to sense what evil has done since time began.

For many, September 11, 2001 (9/11), was a wake-up call for the United States. But for those countries enduring horror such as Japan's Rape of Nanking, Stalin's USSR, Hitler's Nazi Germany, Idi Amin's Uganda, Pol Pot's Cambodia, Sadam Hussein's Iraq, and the slaughter houses of Rwanda, Bosnia, Congo, for starters—unspeakable evil has been around for a long time. The twentieth century became the catastrophic tectonic-plate shift for philosophical and religious liberalism that had promised the world it could only get better and better, that evil would be eradicated through education and social reform, that the "devil" was a myth from the Dark Ages, and that a parliament of nations could outlaw war. Such talk can be found now only in old newspapers and yellowed class lectures. Biblical themes such as demonic evil and personal devils have now become believable entities, or at least reasonable options.[19]

Lance Morrow wrote, "One of the consequences of 9/11 has been to revive, so to speak, the belief in evil. Evil is hard to define, but it's there all right. It's like pornography: you know it when you see it."[20] A few days earlier, he wrote that before 9/11 "the concept of evil as being an ignorant demonstration of cultural differences;" after 9/11, "evil is evil." He then likened evil as "a current that passes through the world, and through the human heart. It manifests itself sometimes in violent acts; it often makes itself invisible, like an electromagnetic flow, a dark humming force field. Evil is much more active and surprising than gravity, but like gravity, it is mysterious."[21]

For all these reasons and more, it is not too much to believe that many more people are ready today to think in terms of a personal Satan, fallen angels, otherworldly agents, and a personal God who has long-range solutions to the problem of evil and pain and suffering and death.[22]

---

[19] Mortimer B. Zuckerman, "In the Face of Pure Evil," (*U.S. News & World Report*, March 25, 2002), wrote: "The Israelites know that yielding to Arafat's blackmail would be an act of suicide, paving the way to a national collapse of will and meaning, and igniting another intifada on the tinder of perceived weakness, with Israel even more exposed to terrorism than it is now. The Jews remember Amalek. The lead of a tribe that attacked the Jews when they made their way out of Egypt over 3,000 years ago, he fell on the rear of a column of Israelites, just after the miraculous parting of the Red Sea. Why Amalek did this, in the face of God's preserving hand, is not great mystery. Understanding it requires only the simple acknowledgement that there is, in our world, such a thing as simple evil. The Amalek massacre confounds the notion that everyone is motivated by self-interest. Evil cannot be explained by reason. It can only be confronted."

[20] *Time*, "Awfully Ordinary," December 24, 2001.

[21] *Time*, "Has Your Paradigm Shifted?" November 19, 2001.

[22] I remember my focus on Emil Brunner in the 1960s He was a profound Swiss theologian who lived through the madness of World War II. In his classic Dogmatics, II, he wrote an amazingly clear chapter on "Angels, Spirits and the Devil." One of his insights: "A generation which has produced

THE GREAT CONTROVERSY THEME EXPLAINS THE BIG PICTURE

Stephen Hawking, that remarkable Cambridge University mathematician and cosmologist, in his 1988 book *A Brief History of Time*, wrote that were scientists to discover the long-sought "theory of everything" to explain the varying mechanisms of the universe, "we would truly know the mind of God."[23] Seventh-day Adventists have been given just that—the "theory of everything" that truly introduces us to the "mind of God." We didn't discover it; it was given to us. We call it the Great Controversy Theme, the unified field of clarity as to what is going on in this wonderful universe.[24]

The Great Controversy Theme is the organizing principle of what has come to be known as the distinctive message of Seventh-day Adventists.[25] It provides the glue of coherency to all of its teachings–theology, health principles (health maintenance plus the prevention and cure of disease), education, missiology, ecclesiology, social relations, environmental stewardship, etc.

So many in the world generally wonder why an all-powerful, all-wise, always-good God seems so distant in the presence of pain, suffering, and death. So many wonder why evil, in all of its malignancies, seems only to metastasize with each new generation. In the Great Controversy Theme,

---

two World Wars, and a totalitarian State with all its horrors, has very little cause to designate the Middle Ages as 'dark.' ... On the contrary, it is just because our generation has experienced such diabolical wickedness that many people have abandoned their former 'enlightenment' objection to the existence of a 'power of darkness', and are now prepared to believe in Satan as represented in the Bible." *The Christian Doctrine of Creation and Redemption* , translated by Olive Wyon. (Philadelphia: The Westminster Press, 1952), 135.

[23] New York: Bantam Books, 1988, 193. Hawking is the Lucasian Professor of Mathematics in the Department of Theoretical Physics at Cambridge University, the chair formerly held by Sir Isaac Newton.

[24] Oliver Sacks, M.D. (neurologist, 1933–) was intrigued with chemistry in early childhood and wrote about his utter fascination with the periodic table, especially as clarified by Dmitr Ivanovich Mendeleev. In his article, "Mendeleev's Garden" (*The American Scholar,* Autumn 2001, 21–32), Sachs wrote: "I could scarcely sleep for excitement the night after seeing the periodic table—it seems to me an incredible achievement to have brought the whole, vast, and seemingly chaotic universe of chemistry to an all-embracing order. ... To have perceived an *overall* organization, a superarching principle uniting and relating *all* the elements, had a quality of the miraculous, of genius. And this gave me, for the first time, a sense of the transcendent power of the human mind, and the fact that it might be equipped to discover or decipher the deepest secrets of nature, to read the mind of God." This was precisely my experience when I "discovered" the implications of the Great Controversy Theme.

[25] John Cobb (Claremont), among others, recognized "that any developed position is understood best when it is grasped in terms of its essential structure. This structure in turn can be understood only as the immediate embodiment of the controlling principles of a man's thoughts." After reviewing several seminal thinkers of the twentieth century, he wrote: "In each case we have seen that the philosophy employed profoundly affected the content as well as the form of the affirmation of faith. Furthermore, the implication of the whole program is that Christian faith depends for its intelligibility and acceptance upon the prior acceptance of a particular philosophy. In our day, when no one philosophy has general acceptance among philosophers, and when all ontology and metaphysics are widely suspect, the precariousness of this procedure is apparent." —*Living Options in Protestant Theology* (Philadelphia: The Westminster Press, 1962), 12, 121.

Seventh-day Adventists have a clear biblical picture of why evil exists and how it will end. This worldview focuses on Jesus Christ—how He explained evil and how we are to relate to it. In so doing, we are light years from the organizing presuppositions that frame all forms of predestination, naturalism, idealism, or existentialism. The Great Controversy Theme clearly defines the differences that separate Seventh-day Adventists from other churches.

We are not atheists who face life's tragedies and never ask "why."[26] We do not resign ourselves to *karma* with its endless cycle of fate—each tragedy merely the "merited results for the misdeeds of a former life." We do not suffer heroically as a result of *kismet,* where God decrees every misfortune.[27]

Nor are we quick to blame God for our own choices. For example, I think of a story that Oliver Jacques passed on to me regarding a patient that his physician father had during America's depression years in the 1930s. The struggling husband with 11 children complained to Dr. Jacques that his wife was expecting again. Then he cried, "How could God do this to me?"

GOD DOESN'T LOOK GOOD

God gets blamed for more than pregnancies! I hear it from sobbing parents at the death of a child: "Where was God when we needed Him?" Houses burn down, a lifetime of treasures lost, and the insurance companies say, "It was an act of God!" Mothers kill their children and blame it on God who was speaking to them. We could write chapters on how God doesn't look good to many who have never understood the kind of God who sent Jesus to this world to save it from their despair in times of grief and confusion. But God isn't the Great Heartbreaker![28]

From another angle, God is not the Grand Manipulator. On August 24, 2003, an ex-priest was strangled to death in a Shirley, Massachusetts, prison where he was serving 10 years for child molestation. One mother of three sons whom the priest had molested was truly confused by this murder: "He lived as a criminal and died as a criminal, but I don't know why God allowed this to happen."[29] With these mixed emotions, God surely is not looking good!

---

[26] It is easy to understand why many are turned off on classical Christian explanations for evil and death. In his syndicated column, January 4, 2002, Crispin Sartwell, chairman of humanities and sciences at the Maryland Institute College of Art, wrote, "The other day my wife attended a funeral of an acquaintance who had committed suicide. The minister who preached the funeral sermon recounted the story of a period of despair in her own life when she had thought about killing herself. But God intervened, she said, and saved her. I suppose the man she was burying wasn't good enough to be saved by God, or perhaps it just wasn't God's whim to stop him from blowing his brains out. ... The world just doesn't eyeball to me like the creation of an all-powerful and perfectly good being who saves ministers from suicide and condemns family men to utter despair and self-destruction and their children to live through it. If you believe that, more power to you. But why should you?" *Orlando Sentinel* (FL).

[27] John M. Fowler, *The Cosmic Conflict Between Christ and Satan* (Nampa, ID: Pacific Press Publishing Association, 2001), 7, 8. Hereafter, PPPA.

[28] See Roland Hegstad's *God's Got to Look Good* (PPPA, 1986), 13.

[29] *New York Times,* August 25, 2003.

Neither is He the Cosmic Executioner. A few days after the Twin Towers disaster, two world-renown religious broadcasters declared that the terrorist attacks came because America had been insulting God and lost divine protection.[30] Such comments do not make God look good! Neither did other comments—those who escaped death, saying, "God was looking after me!" What did those words mean to those who ask, "Why did they get a miracle and we didn't?" Another comment that I shuddered to hear: "9/11 was God's wakeup call to the Adventist Church." God surely doesn't look good with all this foolish thinking!

So I write this book for one purpose: to tell the truth about God. I hope when you finish you will say that God looks good, perhaps better than you have ever "seen" Him!

Some call our study of how God relates to evil and suffering a "theodicy." Theologians have used the word "theodicy" to describe many attempts to explain evil—especially how an all-wise and all-powerful God could be "justified" in permitting a universe shot through with evil, pain, suffering, and death to exist. The following pages could be considered an Adventist theodicy.[31]

Let's start at the beginning. Let's start before the angels or any inhabited world was created. That's really before the beginning! Read on!

---

[30] "Robertson, Falwell: U.S. Vulnerable," Associated Press, September 14, 2001.

[31] Theodicy (*theos* and *dike*—God and *justice*, or, *the justification of God*) is a term used by theologians and philosophers to refer to attempts that seek to justify how an all-powerful and good God could or should permit or cause evil to exist. Perhaps John Milton said it best when he stated the purpose of his classic, *Paradise Lost*, bk. 1, "I may assert Eternal Providence, And justify the ways of God to men." (Harvard Classics, vol. 4, 91). It could be argued that Milton provided a clearer "theodicy" in *Paradise Lost* (1658–1663) than can be found in most any theological attempt since his day. The first use of the term, "theodicy," was used by G. W. Leibnitz (1710) in the title of his first work of importance in modern times on this subject. But attempts to solve the problem are ancient as reflected in the religio-secular literature of the Near East and in biblical literature, such as the Book of Job. The chief Christian arguments flow from 1) the Augustinian tradition which posits a Sovereign God who determines (predestines) all events, including pain and suffering; 2) the Arminian tradition which counters with a Sovereign God who has created self-determining intelligent beings with freedom to be responsible for their decisions. However, in this position, though evil happens to good and responsible people, it happens for some "greater purpose" that God is orchestrating; 3) The third alternative explicitly recognizes spiritual warfare between evil forces and the will of God, on one hand, and the will of responsible human beings, on the other. Satan, the leader of all evil agencies, is in deadly conflict with God's purposes, doing his fiendish best through all manner of human trial and suffering in order to misrepresent the truth about a loving, powerful God who one day will compensate all those who remain faithful to Him in this cosmic struggle. This is the position of this study.

THE COST OF FREEDOM—NATHAN HALE

On August 27, 1776, George Washington, General and Commander in Chief of the Continental Army on Brooklyn Heights, watched the developing Battle of Long Island. Though the Continentals were woefully outnumbered their tactics almost won the day, but only almost. Their position was over run, their backs against the East River. But in one of history's confounding mysteries, General Howe, the British commander, refused to capitalize on his success, believing that he had cornered Washington's army and scuttled the Revolution. That night, under a fog of Providence as so many said, the beaten Colonists escaped across the river.

Washington now knew that he had to employ a new method of resisting the overpowering British. He would organize a spy system to keep tabs on his opponents, or all was lost— The Declaration of Independence and its signers were doomed. The Commander asked Lt. Col. Thomas Knowlton, probably America's first CIA chief, to send a spy back into Long Island. Washington desperately needed to know where General Howe would strike next.

Captain Nathan Hale, age 21, of Connecticut, volunteered in the face of his many friends who tried to talk him out of it. Knowlton's orders were vague. Even though invisible ink had been invented three years before, Hale was not even given a codebook! He chose the role of a Dutch schoolmaster and carried with him his Yale diploma as he wandered through the British army camps in Brooklyn.

Before Hale had anything to report, the British had attacked New York City. The intrepid young officer followed with them, taking copious notes. But when Continentals set much of New York ablaze in September, the British in their fury checked every young American they could find. And Hale was caught.

Before Nathan Hale was hanged, he chatted with a Captain John Montresor, who was "moved by his gentle dignity, the consciousness of rectitude and high intentions." Asked if he had anything to say, the British officer said later that young Hale's last words were, "I only regret that I have but one life to lose for my country." Hale paid the cost of freedom!

Rod Paschall, "George Washington, the Father of U.S. Intelligence" *Spies and Secret Missions, A History of American Espionage,* 20; Thomas Fleming, *Liberty! The American Revolution* (New York: Viking, the Penguin Group, 1997), 200.

The underlying issue in the Great Controversy between God and Satan is "freedom." Over that mysterious word—that word that has summoned unspeakable courage, honor, and unselfishness in its defense—the well being of the universe has been wrenched and jeopardized. Why did God risk all on freedom?

CHAPTER ONE:
LOVE WINS BUT ALSO LOSES

The big view of the cosmic conflict between God and Satan can be reduced to one word: *freedom*. And perhaps reduced to one mysterious text: "the Lamb slain from the foundation of the world" (Revelation 13:8; compare 1 Peter 1:19, 20). If God had not given freedom to created intelligences, we would not have had evil arise in a perfect universe. Nor would the Lamb have been "slain from the foundation of the world!"

Philip Yancey saw it clearly: "That risky act of rescue —'the Lamb that was slain from the creation of the world'—lies at the heart of Christian belief."[32]

God put His character and government at risk when He decided that love was worth the risk! So as far back as anyone can possibly think, God began to pay the cost of freedom.[33] This decision to give freedom to created intelligent beings is probably a decision no created being would have dared to make! Why? Who would want to give freedom to anyone when it could be seen in advance how it would be abused?

So why did God go ahead? Because He knew there was no other way to have a loving universe wherein trust and appreciation would flourish! Does anyone think that I have been forced to love my wife all these years? That somehow we have been programmed to "love" and that we did not have any choice in the matter? Hardly!

---

[32] *Rumors of Another World* (Grand Rapids, MI: Zondervan, 2003), 116.
[33] See "Appendix A: How We Define Freedom."

FREEDOM AND LOVE NEED EACH OTHER

Freedom is the atmosphere in which love flourishes. The *ability to choose* one's highest desires and the *ability to pursue* one's personal potential is an atmosphere that only an incredibly loving person could provide. Freedom and genuine love coexist, as do the two sides of a windowpane—one can't have one without the other![34]

I have performed many weddings. I have seen love's mystical chemistry create new dreams, fresh hopes, and noble commitments—sometimes out of unlikely material (as I looked at some of those star-gazing couples through my limited perspective). However, I later rejoiced to see men and women give up well-worn habits in order to adjust to life together, not because they were forced to do so but because they were in love. But this freedom to love has its risks.[35]

LOVE, A GREAT RISK

Why is this so? Why did organizing the universe on the principle of love become such a risk for God? Because the gift of freedom also means freedom not to love—the freedom to say either "yes" or "no." Saying yes without the freedom to say "no" is not love but the response of a robot. And there is no joy, no mutual trust and appreciation, in a robot even if the robot is a perfect angel. God did not start us off with a wind-up key in our back that always said, "I love You, I love You." Freedom is God's greatest gift to His creation—certified by Jesus Christ on Calvary![36]

But the cost! What if one loves, but is not loved back? That is probably the greatest hurt! Some men and women never get over the heartache of watching sweethearts or spouses walk away to someone else's arms. Parents never get over the anguish of watching their children go down dead-end roads and suffering the pain of unintended consequences. So the question: if parents saw it all in advance, would they want children?

Yet God saw it all in advance. And He has been paying the cost ever since. If we want to get a peek at how much freedom has cost God, watch Jesus die! But the Cross is only a momentary peek! The Cross is forever

---

[34] See "Appendix A: How We Define Freedom."

[35] "If God's providential program for our world involved the immediate destruction of creatures when they freely turned against God, the decision not to turn against God would basically be coerced. The choice to follow God would be a matter of *survival,* not of *morality.* The choice to love God or not (as well as every other choice between godly and ungodly alternatives) would have the same moral character as the 'choice' to breathe or not. God's design to have creatures who are capable of *moral* decision-making requires a sort of covenant of noncoercion with each of them." —Gregory Boyd, *Satan and the Problem of Evil* (Downers Grove, IL: InterVarsity Press, 2001), 183.

[36] "Supreme of gifts, which God creating, gave of His free bounty, sign most evident of goodness, and in His account most prized was liberty of will; the boon, wherewith all intellectual creatures, and them sole, He had endow'd." —Dante, *The Divine Comedy* (Harvard Classics, edited by Charles W. Eliot, translated by Henry F. Cary, vol. 20), Paradise, Canto V, 304.

the symbol of freedom and of what has been happening to God since the "foundation of the world."

GOD'S FOREVER HEARTACHE

When God gave the universe freedom, He gave Himself a forever heartache. Measure His heartache by thousands of holocausts, such as the Jewish horror in Nazi Germany. Think of the agony wrapped in millions of tornadoes, earthquakes, tidal waves, and zillions of wars. How many parents have watches their children die, many from awful diseases or accidents! What was their anguish? Multiply it by billions! God saw all that and felt it all and still thought you and I and the angels were worth it! Worth all that divine heartache that has been piling up "from the foundation of the world"! Amazing hurt is built into love and freedom!

Could there have been any other way? Not if freedom was worth the cost! Not if God wanted a universe that could respond to His love and share His glory. God is the Cosmic Lover (1 John 4:8, 16). The reason why He reveals Himself is because He is love and love is constantly self-communicating, seeking out those He loves, rejoicing in those who love back. Emil Brunner said it so well: "He is the One who wills to have from me a free response to His love, response which gives back love for love, a living echo, a living reflection of His glory."[37]

Love can happen only when intelligent beings can respond, without coercion and in perfect freedom.[38] No one can be forced to love. Love must be free to choose. And lovers must be free to respond. That's why freedom and love exist only when created beings are able to respond (that is, responseable); human beings, however, can be *ir*responsible, but never *un*responsible. If they respond in love to a loving God and His will (the New Testament attitude of "faith"[39]), they, whether angels or humans, are truly responsible, fulfilling their destiny; if they say "no" to God, they are irresponsible, not unresponsible.[40]

But there is nothing in the Bible that even hints that the ability to say "no" is part of God's design for this universe; the "no" is simply the dark

---

[37] Brunner, *op. cit.*, 55.

[38] C. S. Lewis said it well: "Free will is what has made evil possible. Why, then, did God give [created intelligences] free will? Because free will, though it makes evil possible, is also the only thing that makes possible any love or goodness or joy worth having." —*Mere Christianity* (San Francisco: HarperCollins*Publishers*, 1952, 1980), 48.

[39] In a later chapter, we will note that one's concept of faith will determine how one understands predestination and the plan of salvation (including justification and sanctification), among other topics. For now, the clearest definition of faith is one's response of "yes" to whatever God has willed for us. But this "yes" of faith is never understood in the Bible to be human merit, such as the "works" that Bible writers reject. See "Appendix J: Faith, the Word that Describes Everything."

[40] "The fact that man must respond, that he is responsible, is fixed; no amount of human freedom, nor of the sinful misuse of freedom, can alter this fact. He may deny his responsibility, and he may misuse his freedom, but he cannot get rid of his responsibility. Responsibility is part of the unchangeable structure of man's being." —Brunner, *op. cit.*, 57.

side of freedom.[41] God frequently is interpreted in the Bible as the Church's lover (Hosea 2:16; Ephesians 5:25-27), that He [Christ] is longing for His bride to "make herself ready" for "the marriage supper of the Lamb" (Revelation 19:7–9). Yet a lover, even God, can be rejected. How else to understand the Lover's lament: "How can I give you up, Ephraim? How can I hand you over, Israel?" (Hosea 11:8)

GOD DID WHAT LOVERS DO

If the God of love can be no other than what He is (and He can't lie either) He did what lovers do—He granted freedom to those He loves. In giving freedom, He created intelligent beings that were able to respond to love—they could respond with "yes" and they could respond with "no."[42]

Freedom said, "It could be done."	Love said, "It should be done."
Freedom said, "I can do it."	Love said, "I want to do it."
Freedom said, "It will cost plenty."	Love said, "I will pay the cost."

And that is God's risk—a universe of people divided between those who would say "yes" and those who would say "no." To make the risk even more painful and scary, He had to risk watching even His "bride" misuse His love, misrepresent His intentions, and "make love" with His rival—Satan himself![43]

It was a test of persuasion against coercion. God being Love could never coerce. Satan being evil had all the weapons of coercion at his service. Relying on persuasion, God took the risk of being unpersuasive.

Even though He saw it all in advance, as soon as He created Lucifer there was no turning back! He was willing to be "slain from the foundation of the world" (Revelation 13:8) in order that His grand design of a universe, populated with trusting, loving individuals, could eventually be realized—an eternally secure universe that, one day, would never again have a rebel say "No" to the overtures of love.[44]

---

[41] The philosophical concept of "dualism," that Good and Evil, Light and Darkness are fundamental elements of the universe, is certainly extra-biblical.

[42] "Love presupposes complete freedom. Enforced loved is not love at all. To be anything else except free contradicts the nature of love—precisely that love depicted in the Bible as the right kind of love. Love presupposes an even higher degree of freedom than the acknowledgement (in obedience) of God as Lord. Love is the most freely willed of any activity of which we are able to think. Love is actually the essence of free will, and contrariwise, the essence of free will is love." —Emil Brunner, *Truth as Encounter,* translated by Olive Wyon (Philadelphia: The Westminster Press, 1943), 98.

[43] Hosea 2:14–20; Revelation 19:7–9. See "Appendix B: Who was Lucifer, now known as Satan?"

[44] "It was God's purpose to place things on an eternal basis of security, and in the councils of heaven it was decided that time must be given for Satan to develop the principles which were the foundation of his system of government." —*The Desire of Ages,* 759.

Further, God, the Cosmic Lover, will not give up wooing His reluctant bride—His chosen people who wanted His name but not the responsibility of love. God would not give up on His restless, wayward bride. He does everything He can to help her get herself ready for the "wedding"![45] Imagine that! The Creator and Sustainer of the universe motivated by a love more personal and intense than that of a human lover, more tender than a nursing mother—all that boggles my mind. And to think that you and I are unique objects of His astonishing love! What could be a greater reason to help Him get us ready for the wedding?

GOD WILL HAVE HIS WEDDING

God knows three things: 1) He knows His own ability to be patient and 2) He knows that some in every generation will say "yes" to His overtures and will rightly represent Him in their profession and character. Further, 3) He knows that with the accumulated record of such people flooding the world of later generations, who also are being constantly wooed by His Spirit, eventually He will have a significant witness (Matthew 24:14) through whom and on whom He will rest His case. He will not rest until He has "sealed the servants of our God on their foreheads" (Revelation 7:3), those who have "the Father's name written in their foreheads ... . These are the ones who follow the Lamb wherever He goes ..., And in their mouth was found no guile, for they are without fault before the throne of God" (Revelation 14:1, 4, 5; see also Revelation 22:4).[46] Such people indeed help secure the universe forever!

Love wins, but also loses. Love remains, but some angels and human beings will turn away their faces forever. Such spurning of God's love has been His risk from the beginning. Perhaps Jesus revealed the heart of God most clearly when shortly before His own people murdered Him He said: "O Jerusalem, Jerusalem, ... How often I wanted to gather your children together, as a hen gathers her chicks under her wings, but you were not willing! See! Your house is left to you desolate" (Matthew 23:37, 38).

The risk of granting freedom was not only that God should have a forever heartache. He would also put Himself on trial! He would be charged with the meanest, most unfair accusations that could be leveled against anyone! For millennia, it has seemed that Satan with his accusations has been winning. More people, it seems, have believed Satan's lies about God than those who have had faith in His Word, His promises and His trustworthiness.

What were these accusations? How has God defended Himself? Read on!

---

[45] "Love never gives up" (1 Corinthians 13:7, TEV).

[46] As C. S. Lewis said so well regarding the future of good and evil: "Finality must come some time, and it does not require a very robust faith to believe that omniscience knows when." —*The Problem of Pain* (London: Collins, Fontana Books, 1957), 112.

The cost of freedom is incalculable. Ask those of the Second Ranger Battalion who climbed up the 90 feet cliff at Pointe-du-Hoc on June 6, 1944, under constant fire. This natural fortress jutted into the English Channel like a dagger between Omaha Beach and Utah Beach. Had those Rangers not taken their objective, German guns on Pointe-du-Hoc would have rained unobstructed death and destruction on the Allied forces on the land and their ships offshore with impunity.

Lt. Col. James Rudder, CO of the Ranger Force (2nd and 5th Ranger battalions) included Companies A, B, C, D, E and F of the 2nd Battalion. Because of sea currents and the lateness of their arrival, the Germans were soon aware of their approach and nothing went according to plan. Of the 68 Rangers in lead Company C, only 31 men made it to the base of the cliff; 19 were dead and 18 severely wounded. Machine guns, mortar fire and grenades rained on them from the top. Some climbed by using bayonets dug into the rocky wall, some tried to climb ropes propelled to the top.

Within the hour, those 31 reached the top only to face the entrenched defenders. They could see the carnage on Omaha Beach especially. Their next task was to silence those guns. Up until noon, those few Rangers thought the invasion had failed. Their radios were lost in the sea; they had no contact with anybody. Through the day, elements of Companies A, B, D and E gunned their way to the cliffs from the rear. The only other reinforcements that Rudder received in the next 48 hours were three paratroopers from the 101st Airborne who had been misdropped. By the end of the second day, only 50 of the more than 200 Rangers who had landed were still capable of fighting. But they never lost Pointe-du-Hoc.

But D-Day was only the beginning. Through the summer and autumn, the rain and mud and fierce German counterattacks, the reconstituted 2nd Battalion fought through northern France, Rudder still leading. Then came December and Hill 400 (named for height in meters) on the eastern edge of the Hurtgen Forest. The Germans had strongly fortified the hill. The First Army had thrown four divisions at Hill 400, accompanied by concentrated artillery and air support. Hundreds had been sacrificed but no gain.

On December 6, the commander of the 8th Division asked for the Rangers. Doing what Rangers do best, by stealth through the night, attacking at first light, they surprised the Germans. Those who were at Pointe-du-Hoc on D-Day called Hill 400 worse. After the Rangers captured the hill, the Germans poured artillery on the 2nd Battalion and counterattacked five times. At the end of two days and relief, the combined strength of the three companies left on top was five officers and 86 men. The Rangers had suffered 90 percent casualties. The cost of freedom is incalculable!

Stephen E. Ambrose, *Citizen Soldiers* (New York: Simon & Schuster, 1997), 173-177; Ambrose, *D-Day* (New York: Simon & Schuster, 1994), 398-417; Robert W. Black, *Rangers in World War II* (Ballantine Publishing Group, 1992), 186-219.

SECTION TWO

The issues that led angels in heaven to rebel against God, the Creator, constitute the same reasons why created beings on earth continue to rebel against God, consciously or subconsciously. What were Satan's accusations that could persuade one-third of the angels to distrust God? Why did God risk all on letting Satan live?

CHAPTER TWO:
WHO WAS LUCIFER (ALIAS SATAN) —THE FIRST REBEL?

L ucifer (the "light bearer") was created "full of wisdom and perfect in beauty"—"the seal of perfection" (Ezekiel 28:12, 13). Mentally, physically, emotionally, socially, spiritually—he had it all![47]

The first of all created intelligences, he was the "anointed cherub" (Ezekiel 28:14). He was "anointed" for a special purpose; he was God's Minister of Cosmic Communications—the "bearer of God's light of truth"— the angel closest to the Godhead.[48] *Nothing* was hid from his gaze.

Think about it! Lucifer was immensely qualified to accurately represent the truth about God to all created intelligences who would eventually inhabit the universe. Did he not "[walk] up and down in the midst of the stones of fire" (Ezekiel 28:14)? Surely he was aware of the mysterious force that emanated throughout the universe, that foundational principle of love that would ensure freedom of thought and action for all created beings. Surely, he saw and felt it all!

He would be God's authorized communicator—that first link between the Creator and His creation. As God's light/truth bearer, his highest

---

[47] See "Appendix B: Who Was Lucifer, Now Known as Satan?"
[48] "Satan's position in heaven had been next to the Son of God. He was first among the angels." —*Selected Messages*, bk. 1, 341.

responsibility was to make God look good. Whenever a question would arise, Lucifer had the qualifications and the job description to represent God's position fully and correctly. Could any created being ever have a more important, fulfilling responsibility?

The divine record says: "You were perfect in your ways ... till iniquity was found in you" (Ezekiel 28:15).[49] How can anyone understand this proto-iniquity? Isaiah noted that Lucifer "said in his *heart*" (Isaiah 14: 13, emphasis added) that he desired a still higher position, still more power! Did emotion prevail over reason? Did he allow his pride and ambition to erode the divine bonding between love, reason, and freedom?

Apparently, Lucifer grew weary of making God look God—he wanted some of that honor! He became less satisfied with his peerless privileges and wanted to become the executive vice president of the universe! However it happened, and as preposterous as it now seems, he began to lay plans to also "sit on the mount of congregation on the farthest sides of the north"[50] and be recognized "like the Most High."

POWER LEADS TO CONTROL AND THE TWILIGHT OF FREEDOM.

And so, for the first time in the universe of free intelligences, the craving for "power," the "desire for self-exaltation," emerged.[51] How such feelings and thoughts could possibly arise in one so close to God is beyond human understanding. Paul called it "the mystery of iniquity" (2 Thessalonians 2:7). Though it is unfathomable, we have been given the time and place—and its implications engulf us today. The lust for power sows seeds of coercion and control—somebody, somewhere will lose freedom.

Whenever the passion for power emerges in history or in our own hearts we hear Satan's words: "I will ascend ... I will exalt ... I will be like the Most High" (Isaiah 14:13, 14). The religion of power (it becomes the passion of all lives that are not committed to the power of God) is the antithesis of genuine Christianity. The desire for power not only permeates secular philosophies,

---

[49] "Iniquity" [*avlah*] denotes "the want of integrity and rectitude ... the essential part of wrong doing." Robert Girdlestone, *Synonyms of the Old Testament* (Grand Rapids, MI: Wm. B. Eerdmans Publishing Company, 1956), 79.

[50] "Mount of congregation," see the parallel chapter, Ezekiel 28:16, "mountain of God." "Sides of the north" would easily be recognized by Isaiah's contemporaries as a reference to heathen mythology that often "represented the gods as meeting in council on a mountain far to the north. ... The name Baal-zephron of Exodus 14:2 means literally, 'Baal of the North.'" —*Seventh-day Adventist Bible Commentary (SDABC)*, vol. 4, 171.

[51] "But a change came over this happy state. There was one who perverted the freedom that God had granted to his creatures. Sin originated with him, who, next to Christ, had been most honored of God, and was highest in power and glory among the inhabitants of heaven. ... Little by little, Lucifer came to indulge the desire for self-exaltation. ... Not content with his position, though honored above the heavenly host, he ventured to covet homage due alone to the Creator. ... And coveting the glory with which the infinite Father had invested his Son, this prince of angels aspired to power that was the prerogative of Christ alone." —*Patriarchs and Prophets*, 35.

it unfortunately pervades much of what we call Christian aspirations and service. To be considered "somebody," to have a name that sets one apart or above another, to be recognized as important (as symbolized with the corner office or the designated parking place), becomes the primary, overriding passion in life, rising even above one's commitment to responsibility and integrity.[52]

Fueling Satan's lust for power were mysterious feelings we now call jealousy, envy, and inevitable hatred.[53] This prototype scenario is played out daily in those who have never been converted to Christ's way of looking at power and His example of how to use it.

Ezekiel wrote that Lucifer's iniquity, his vanishing rectitude, was also rooted in vanity—"Your heart was lifted up because of your beauty; You corrupted your wisdom for the sake of your splendor" (Ezekiel 28:17). Jealousy is the other side of vanity.

Slowly, imperceptibly, jealousy became envy and Lucifer began to rationalize (justify) his strange feelings. And his feelings became words—sly, devious, deceptive words. Lucifer, the brightest of all creation, was slowly, imperceptibly becoming Satan, the beginning of entropy[54] in a perfect universe.

Jesus said that Lucifer became "the devil ... a murderer from the beginning ... no truth in him ... a liar, and the father of it" (John 8:44). John wrote that "he who sins is of the devil, for the devil has sinned from the beginning" (1 John 3:8). Hard to believe that Satan wanted to "be like the Most High" (Isaiah 14:14); actually he wanted to murder God and take His place as Ruler of the universe (How else could he take God's place?) He proved this by murdering Jesus!

John later wrote about this awful war that developed "in heaven" when "Michael and his angels fought against the dragon; and the dragon and his angels fought, but they did not prevail, nor was a place found for them in heaven any longer. So the great dragon was cast out, that serpent of old, called the Devil and Satan, who deceives the whole world; he was cast to the earth, and his angels were cast out with him" (Revelation 12:7–9).

Could all this trouble, even war in heaven, arise out of jealousy or envy? Envy has a well-deserved place as one of the Seven Deadly Sins.[55] Why? Because this list has summed up what philosophers and theologians for many centuries have seen as invasive spiritual viruses that, if not curtailed, are self-destructive.[56]

---

[52] See "Appendix C: The Heart of 'Power.'"

[53] "When God said to His Son, 'Let us make man in our image,' Satan was jealous of Jesus. He wished to be consulted concerning the formation of man, and because he was not, he was filled with envy, jealousy, and hatred."—*Early Writings, 145.*

[54] "Entropy ... the steady degradation or disorganization of a system or society." —Webster's *Ninth Collegiate Dictionary.*

[55] In English: envy, sloth, gluttony, anger, pride, lust, greed (or covetousness).

[56] See "Appendix D. The Devolution of Envy."

Some distinguish between jealousy and envy. Although there are obvious similarities, certain distinctions should be made. Some see jealousy in terms of covetousness; that is, "I like what you have and I want it. If I had it, I'd be happy. Maybe I can steal it. Or perhaps I can get Congress to raise taxes on those who have it and share those taxes with me so I can have what they have."[57] And on it goes.

ENVY MORE DAMAGING THAN JEALOUSY

But envy is more damaging. It works like this: "He's got it and I don't and I don't know how to get it! It's not fair for him to have it if others can't have it. I will destroy what 'they' have in order to make things equal." Envy becomes that grinding resentment, rarely placated. Envy is a destroyer!

The wise man said: "Wrath is cruel, and anger is outrageous; but who is able to stand before envy?" (Proverbs 27:4, KJV). James echoes this insightful look at probably the most baleful trait of the human heart: "Where envying and strife is, there is confusion and every evil work" (James 3:16, KJV).

What did Lucifer want? Why was he jealous, then envious? What drove him into such resentment that could not be placated by his infinitely gracious Creator? For starters, he was jealous—especially of the honor and privileges associated with one particular member of the Godhead. We know Him today as Jesus; the angels knew Him then as that member of the Godhead who performed the mysteries of creation throughout the universe (see Colossians 1:16).

In the course of events, Lucifer, being the first of created beings, actually saw all other angels and created beings *as they were being created!* In some way, his mind began to muse, perhaps wondering if he had been told the truth about his own beginning. Perhaps he had not been created! Perhaps he was equal to this member of the Godhead who had the special job description of being the universe's Creator—but he was being denied his rightful privileges for some mysterious reason! Whatever the case, Lucifer's heart became "lifted up," and he began to formulate his "reasons" for wanting to "be like the Most High" (Isaiah 14:14). Somehow, he would build his case!

The Godhead did all that Goodness and Love could do to present the facts before Lucifer and the rest of the angels; but Lucifer "allowed his jealousy of Christ to prevail."[58] "A strange, fierce conflict" enveloped Lucifer's heart; "truth, justice and loyalty struggl[ed] against envy and jealousy. ... But ... he was filled with pride in his own glory."[59]

---

[57] Gary North, *Successful Investing In An Age of Envy* (Sheridan, IN: Steadman Press, 1982), 4.

[58] *Patriarchs and Prophets*, 36.

[59] *Ibid.*, 37. We are devoting space to Satan's development of envy against Christ because it has much to do with the ensuing Great Controversy on earth, wherein Satan's fury intensified against the human Jesus and all those who pledge their loyalty to Him (Revelation 12:4, 5, 17).

C. S. Lewis nailed pride as *"essentially* competitive. ... Pride gets no pleasure out of having something, only out of having more of it than the next man. We say that people are proud of being rich, or clever, or good looking, but they are not. They are proud of being richer, or cleverer, or better-looking than others. ... Power is what pride really enjoys. Pride is competitive by its very nature ... If I am a proud man, then as long as there is one man in the whole world more powerful, or richer, or cleverer than I, he is my rival and my enemy."[60]

With white-hot heat, the issue focused on why Christ (as we now know this Creator member of the Godhead) "should have the supremacy? Why is he honored above Lucifer"?[61]

FREEDOM FOR ALL!

How did Lucifer go about charming and captivating other angels into understanding the rightness of his grievances? "With mysterious secrecy" he "insinuate[d] doubts that though laws might be necessary for the inhabitants of the worlds, angels, being more exalted, needed no such restraint." He promised "freedom for all" if angels would follow his lead.[62] He "presented the purposes of God in a false light—misconstruing and distorting them, to excite dissent and dissatisfaction." And then when angels did begin to murmur, believing that their leader indeed had been improperly dealt with, Lucifer stepped in "with consummate craft" and "caused it to appear as his sole purpose to promote loyalty, and to preserve harmony and peace."[63]

Master of pretense and deception, Lucifer now appeared to be the advocate of "harmony and peace" while doing all he could behind the scenes to foment rebellion. We see this characteristic of evil dividing families, neighborhoods, churches, and nations today.

This "spirit of discontent and disaffection" was new to angels as well as to the entire inhabited universe. God bore patiently with this "new element, strange, mysterious, unaccountable."[64] And when God compassionately and patiently tried to reason with Lucifer before he plunged into the "abyss of ruin," Lucifer used the "long-suffering of God as an evidence of his own superiority" and as a sign, perhaps, that God was negotiating from weakness.[65] In his persistence, deeply set habits were forming and Lucifer "became Satan, 'the adversary' of God."[66]

---

[60] Lewis, *Mere Christianity,* 122, 123.
[61] See *Patriarchs and Prophets,* 37.
[62] *Ibid.*
[63] *Ibid.,* 38.
[64] *Ibid.,* 39.
[65] *Ibid.*
[66] *Ibid.* 40.

Not all the angels bought into Satan's devious scheme to establish a better universe.[67] Angels pleaded with angels; one-third, however, caved in to Satan's delusions, mesmerized with the illusions of "unrestricted freedom,"[68] the freedom to set his own standards and control his own destiny.[69]

Why didn't God stop this rebellion before it went any further? Could He not foresee the horrific future for all concerned? Was God blindsided as to the risk and cost to Himself as well as to everyone else in the universe?

WHY DIDN'T GOD STOP LUCIFER?

At this point, we enter the scene behind the scenes and it helps explain the multitude of questions that men and women would ask throughout human history. After all, as the questions go, if God is omnipotent, He could do anything and everything—so why didn't He stop Lucifer before he went too far? If God is Love and Goodness, He would not want pain, suffering and death to exist—so why didn't His loving heart dam up all the envy and hatred of Satan before he could deceive even the angels, never mind the inhabitants of earth?[70]

The issue in the Satan-God standoff was over the fairness and goodness of God's mind, intent, and character: *Satan had challenged the integrity of God, the Creator of the universe.* Satan's charges were "artfully" disguised in "sophistry and fraud," gloved in unbelievable deceit with which he "had gained an advantage"[71] Deceit always gains miles before calm reason and truth has a chance to get the attention of thoughtful bystanders. Some say, "Now was the time for God to zap Satan." But if He did, new questions and new fears would arise throughout heaven and the other worlds: "Maybe

---

[67] Interesting, but the conflict in heaven was actually begun by loyal angels who would not take it any more! A wise writer wrote, "A note of discord now marred the celestial harmonies. The service and exaltation of self, contrary to the Creator's plan, awakened forebodings of evil in minds to whom God's glory was supreme. The heavenly councils pleaded with Lucifer." —*The Great Controversy,* 494. The loyal angels took the initiative! And ever since, it has been the privilege of all who have seen and grasped the goodness of God to take the initiative against evil.

[68] *Ibid.,* 41.

[69] "How appalling it is to realize that the very self-qualities which are today sought, taught, and highly prized among men were conceived by Satan! ... Even more distressing is the fact that a large percentage of the church has bought the same lies. Self-esteem, self-image, and the other selfisms which Satan originated are the pillars of Christian psychology."—Dave Hunt, *How Close Are We?* (Eugene, OR: Harvest House Publishers, 1993), 121.

[70] "If God were good, He would wish to make His creatures perfectly happy, and if God were almighty He would be able to do what He wished. But the creatures are not happy. Therefore God lacks either goodness, or power, or both. ... Omnipotence means power to do the intrinsically possible, not to do the intrinsically impossible. ... If you choose to say 'God can give a creature free-will and at the same time withhold free-will from it,' you have not succeeded in saying *anything* about God: meaningless combinations of words do not suddenly acquire meaning simply because we prefix to them the two other words 'God can.'" Lewis, *The Problem of Pain,* 14–16. Lewis followed with a chapter on "Divine Goodness" wherein He develops the kind of love that God has for created intelligences to whom He gave freedom of the will.

[71] *Patriarchs and Prophets,* 41.

Satan was right? Maybe God is the smiling Tyrant who allows no real disagreement! Maybe it doesn't pay to cross God!"

So God "permitted Satan to carry forward his work until the spirit of disaffection ripened into active revolt. It was necessary for his plans to be fully developed, that their true nature and tendency might be seen by all."[72] Satan had so turned the minds of the deluded angels that they now believed that God's responses to the devil's proposals were the cause of the "discord" in heaven! Amazing artfulness!

As the shadows darkened, God could not use Satan's weapons of "flattery and deceit." God needed time to let truth unfold and to allow Satan's "own work [to] condemn him."[73] Infinite wisdom knew that truth would always defend itself without force and that love (unforced loyalty) "must rest upon a conviction of [God's] justice and benevolence… Had he [Satan] been immediately blotted out of existence, some would have served God from fear rather than from love."[74]

WHY GOD DID NOT DESTROY SATAN

No matter how loyal the unfallen angels were, even they could not understand that rebellion ends in self-destruction, the absence of life. All this confusion had never happened before—a thought never thought. The law of cause and effect, for example, had never occurred to them. They had no conception of how their God of love could become a "consuming fire" to those who placed themselves completely out of harmony with Him. If Satan and his rebel angels were eliminated, loyal angels would see the act as probably necessary, but not the "inevitable result of sin." It surely would appear to be an arbitrary act of an offended God. "A doubt of God's goodness would have remained in their minds as evil seed, to produce its deadly fruit of sin and woe."[75]

We now have the background for 1) Satan's horrific experiment and 2) God's grand response—a confrontation that we now call "*the Great Controversy.*" Ellen White chiseled out the scope of the "controversy":

> "Satan's rebellion was to be a lesson to the universe through all coming ages—a perpetual testimony to the nature of sin and its terrible results. … For the good of the entire universe … he must more fully develop his principles, that his charges against the divine government might

---

[72] *Ibid.*

[73] *Ibid.*, 42.

[74] *Ibid.* "It was God's purpose to place things on an eternal basis of security, and in the councils of heaven it was decided that time must be given for Satan to develop the principles which were the foundation of his system of government. He had claimed that these were superior to God's principles. Time was given for the working of Satan's principles, that they might be seen by the heavenly universe." —*The Desire of Ages,* 759.

[75] *The Desire of Ages,* 764.

be seen in their true light by all created beings, and that the justice and mercy of God and the immutability of his law might be forever placed beyond all question."[76]

When the controversy ends, all "the inhabitants of the universe, both loyal and disloyal, will one day understand" all the issues, all the motives, all the principles and good and evil—for God has nothing to hide![77]

Lewis Walton—in his remarkable book *The Lucifer Diary*—in allegorical form, allows the reader to "look inside" Lucifer/Satan's mind as the great deceiver writes his "journal." We "listen" to his thoughts beginning with his first ambitious feelings to the last moments when he surveys the unspeakable damage for which he is responsible.[78] The Great Controversy is spelled out in a most graphic manner.

All of us may trace the main players in the drama, not by reading an allegory (helpful as it may be) but by reading the history as unfolded in the Bible and anywhere else that God has seen fit to reveal Himself. We now ask, what has been Satan's highest goal, actually his mission statement, ever since he was removed from heaven? Read on

---

[76] *Patriarchs and Prophets*, 42, 43.

[77] *Ibid.* "One of the things that surprised me when I first read the New Testament seriously was that it talked so much about a Dark Power in the universe—a mighty evil spirit who was held to be the Power behind death and disease, and sin. The difference is that Christianity thinks this Dark Power was created by God, and was good when he was created, and went wrong. Christianity agrees with Dualism that this universe is at war. But it does not think this is a war between independent powers. It thinks it is a civil war, a rebellion, and that we are living in a part of the universe occupied by the rebel." —Lewis, *Mere Christianity*, 45.

[78] Lewis R. Walton, *The Lucifer Diary* (Glennville, CA: Aralon Press, 1997), 1–433.

CHAPTER THREE:
SATAN'S HIGHEST GOAL
SINCE HE REBELLED

Jonathan Gallagher, in his perceptive book *Is God to Blame?*, coined the phrase OPERATION GODSMEAR to describe Satan's fiendish goal to convince intelligent beings throughout the universe that God could not be trusted.[79]

Satan's compelling passion, "under a thousand disguises" has been "to misrepresent the character and government of God." Possessing the master-mind of the first created being, Satan developed his passion "with extensive, well-organized plans and marvelous power."[80]

Part of his strategy, along with misrepresenting the character of God, Satan misrepresented "the nature of sin, and the real issues at stake in the Great Controversy. His sophistry lessens the obligation of the divine law, and gives men license to sin." One of his highest goals in causing angels and men to "cherish false conceptions of God" is "that they regard Him with fear and hate, rather than with love."[81]

One of the clearest evidences of Satan's success is to review the conceptions of God that men and women have invented since the earliest days of human history, beginning with Cain's misunderstanding of God.[82] At the core of these misconceptions, many men and women have sought to get God's attention and His favor either 1) by doing something (even great self-denial) and/or 2) by visiting some sacred place to feel "forgiven." Often, these choices lead to horrible cruelties done in the name of their "god."[83]

WHAT ARE SATAN'S ACCUSATIONS THAT STILL ECHO THROUGHOUT THE UNIVERSE TODAY?

- Hard for us to believe today, but one of Satan's chief charges against God was that He was basically self-centered, that God was the Divine Paramour who wanted the adoration and submission of everyone—for selfish reasons.

- We all have discovered that self-centered men and women still have diffi-culty appreciating genuine love; they think that what appears to be unal-

---

[79] Jonathan Gallagher, *Is God To Blame?* (Grantham, England: The Stanborough Press, 1992), 9.
[80] *Ibid.*, 78
[81] *The Great Controversy*, 569.
[82] See "Appendix E: The Cosmic Conflict Imbedded in Extra-Biblical Materials."
[83] *Ibid.* In the Christian world, misconceptions have led to two human speculations: "the transgressor shall not die, that salvation may be secured without obedience to the law of God." —*Patriarchs and Prophets*, 124.

loyed, unselfish love must have a hook in it. Here Satan found some response in certain angels because "from the beginning of the Great Controversy he has endeavored to prove God's principles of action to be selfish."[84] As we will soon see, our Creator's incarnation and sacrifice, a giving to humanity (John 3:16) that never gives up, proves Satan wrong, very wrong.

- To further justify his terrible charges, Satan pictured God (and still does) as "severe and unforgiving"—a "being whose chief attribute is stern justice, —one who is a severe judge, a harsh, exacting creditor."[85]

- Satan takes delight in suggesting reasons why created intelligences should mistrust God, to "doubt His willingness and power to save us," that, in some way "the Lord will do us harm by His providences." He seeks to picture "the religious life as one of gloom. He desires it to appear toilsome and difficult; and when the Christian presents in his own life this view of religion, he is, through his unbelief, seconding the falsehood of Satan."[86]

- Underneath all that Satan has said about God is his passionate hatred for law, the basic structure of the universe. Relationships between responsible people are by definition built on clear understandings that govern uncoerced relationships. Husbands and wives, melded in undivided loyalties, know instinctively that their relationship has built-in understandings. They know, without even expressing their mutual understanding, that "there shall be no other lovers except themselves." They know, without reciting their understanding every day, that they will not speak evil of each other, that they will honor each other's highest, warmest thoughts, that they will uphold each other's honor, allowing no lie or disrespect to divide their mutual loyalty.

- Unfallen angels realized that something similar existed throughout the universe, that there was an unspoken structure that described the well-being of the relationship existing between them and with God. In

---

[84] "Unselfishness, the principle of God's kingdom, is the principle that Satan hates; its very existence he denies. To disprove Satan's claim is the work of Christ and of all who bear His name." —*Education*, 154.

[85] *Steps to Christ*, 11. "Those whom he [Satan] had thus deceived imagined that God was hard and exacting. They regarded Him as watching to denounce and condemn, unwilling to receive the sinner so long as there was a legal excuse for not helping him." —*Prophets and Kings*, 311. "The Creator has been presented to their minds as clothed with the attributes of the prince of evil himself,—as arbitrary, severe, and unforgiving,—that he might be feared, shunned, and even hated by men,"—*Testimonies*, vol. 5, 738. "Christ came to this earth to reveal the Father, to place Him in a correct light before men. Satan had aroused the enmity and prejudice of the race against God. He had pointed to Him as exacting, overbearing, and condemnatory, the author of suffering, misery, and death. He charged upon God the attributes of his own character." —*Manuscript Releases*, vol. 18, 331.

[86] *Ibid.*, 116.

fact, when Lucifer's charges raised questions about God's laws being so oppressive, the idea of "law" seemed like a new thought because it had been taken for granted by those who loved one another.[87]

• But just as disaffected husbands or wives seek to justify their erring ways, Satan argued "from the first ... that God was unjust, that his law was faulty, and that the good of the universe required it to be changed."[88]

• As one would expect, Satan included in his attack against God that God is "the author of sin, and suffering, and death."[89]

• Another one of "Satan's most successful devices to cast reproach upon purity and truth" has been his amazing skill in getting even Christians to misunderstand the nature of holiness. This surely must be one of his crowning deceptions: "Counterfeit holiness, spurious sanctification, is still doing its work of deception. Under various forms it exhibits the same spirit as in the days of Luther, diverting minds from the Scriptures, and leading men to follow their own feelings and impressions rather than to yield obedience to the law of God."[90]

• As part of his charge that created beings did not really have freedom in view of God's magisterial appeal for his obedience, Satan simply charged, "self-denial was impossible with God and therefore not essential in the human family." Of course, Christ's life and death "broke forever the accusing power of Satan over the universe" on this and other accusations.[91]

• Probably one of the most amazing charges Satan made against God's character and government has been echoing since humans began to ask questions: If God were really fair and good, He would never have "permitted man to transgress His law" and thus "to sin, and bring in misery

---

[87] *Steps to Christ*, 69. "The law of love by which heaven is ruled, had been misrepresented by the arch-deceiver as a restriction upon men's happiness, a burdensome yoke from which they should be glad to escape. He declared that its precepts could not be obeyed, and that the penalties of transgression were bestowed arbitrarily."—*Prophets and Kings*, 311. "The same hatred of the principles of God's law, the same policy of deception, by which error is made to appear as truth, by which human laws are substituted for the law of God, and men are led to worship the creature rather than the Creator, may be traced in all the history of the past. Satan's efforts to misrepresent the character of God, to cause men to cherish a false conception of the Creator, and thus to regard Him with fear and hate rather than with love; his endeavors to set aside the divine law, leading the people to think themselves free from its requirements; and his persecution of those who dare to resist his deceptions, have been steadfastly pursued in all ages." —*The Great Controversy*, x. "Men are freest when they are most unconscious of freedom." —D. H. Lawrence, *Studies in Classic American Literature* [1923], Ch.1.

[88] *Patriarchs and Prophets*, 69.

[89] *The Desire of Ages*, 24.

[90] *The Great Controversy*, 193. Perhaps one of Satan's greatest achievements has been to redefine the gospel so that it is limited to primarily forgiveness.

[91] *Selected Messages*, vol. 1, 341.

and death." This "rebellious complaint against God" fails to understand that "to deprive man of the freedom of choice would be to rob him of his prerogative as an intelligent being, and make him a mere automaton.[92]

- Another charge that Satan has succeeded in getting men and women through the millennia to accept is that created beings can't keep the laws of God. Thus, the Lawmaker was unfair in His dealings with created intelligences: "In the opening of the Great Controversy, Satan had declared that the law of God could not be obeyed, that justice was inconsistent with mercy, and that, should the law be broken, it would be impossible for the sinner to be pardoned."[93]

MISUNDERSTANDING GOD LEADS TO MANY THEOLOGICAL ERRORS

Fritz Guy has clearly shown how misunderstanding the character of God has led to many theological errors: "One of the most serious ways in which the course of Christian theology has been misled by its classical and medieval heritage has been the assumption that the primary fact about God is omnipotent sovereignty and that the evidence of this sovereignty is the exercise of power to control events, including the actions of all of humanity. This assumption has kept a large part of the Christian tradition, both Catholic and Protestant, from hearing the gospel with clarity, because it has misunderstood the character of God."[94]

Summing up, these charges have become Satan's modus operandi, from the beginning of his subtle deceptions to this present day. The seed of evil has borne bitter fruit. Note the following recap:

> "It is Satan's constant effort to misrepresent the character of God, the nature of sin, and the real issues at stake in the Great Controversy. His sophistry lessens the obligation of the divine law and gives men license to sin. At the same time he causes them to cherish false conceptions of God so that they regard Him with fear and hate rather than with love. The cruelty inherent in his own character is attributed to the Creator; it is embodied in systems of religion and expressed in modes of worship. Thus the minds of men are

---

[92] *Patriarchs and Prophets*, 331.

[93] *The Desire of Ages*, 761. "Satan represents God's law of love as a law of selfishness. He declares that it is impossible for us to obey its precepts. The fall of our first parents, with all the woe that has resulted, he charges upon the Creator, leading men to look upon God as the author of sin, and suffering, and death." —*The Desire of Ages*, 24; see 117, 309. "Since the fall of Adam, men in every age have excused themselves for sinning, charging God with their sin, saying that they could not keep His commandments. This is the insinuation Satan cast at God in heaven." —*Review and Herald*, May 28, 1901.

[94] Fritz Guy, "The Universality of God's Love," in *The Grace of God and the Will of Man*, ed., Clark H. Pinnock (Minneapolis, MN: Bethany House Publishers, 1989), 33. However, Pinnock and others work within the context that God has no knowledge of the immediate future because of man's freedom, etc.

blinded, and Satan secures them as his agents to war against God. By perverted conceptions of the divine attributes, heathen nations were led to believe human sacrifices necessary to secure the favor of Deity; and horrible cruelties have been perpetrated under the various forms of idolatry."[95]

I know this is all hard to believe that a perfectly created angel, the first among all created intelligences, could ever think these thoughts. What is there about evil that makes it *so evil!*

---

[95] *The Great Controversy,* 569.

CHAPTER FOUR:
BASIC CHARACTERISTICS
OF EVIL

Throughout this book we will be discussing ultimate Evil—the full-blown personification of self-centeredness, void of any concept of what unselfish love is. Lucifer-turned-Satan, the prototype of Evil, has demonstrated what happens when freedom is betrayed by narcissistic pride that would not submit, the will that would not bow, the desire to be willful rather than willing.[96]

Satan became skilled in (1) the use of consistent, destructive lies (pretense); (2) blaming others for the damage he was doing (scapegoating); (3) clouding the issues; changing the meaning of words—the substitution of opinion for absolute truths (confusion); and (4) the use of power to control or destroy others (coercion).[97]

Those who have been infected with his self-centeredness develop intolerance to criticism, a bottomless hate for the reprover (whether God or man), an intellectual deviousness that glorifies the means rather than the end, and a ghastly use of power to coerce others. All the while, those on the pathway of evil learn ways to pretend they are respectable, trustworthy, deeply concerned about the feelings of others, and, yes, the champions of individual rights and "freedom."

The end of all this evil (and all that Satan represents) is "to kill life."[98] That is exactly the framework in which events in the last acts of the Great Controversy prior to our Lord's second advent will take place—"He was granted power to give breath to the image of the beast, that the image of the

---

[96] M. Scott Peck, M.D., *People of the Lie* (New York: Simon & Schuster, Inc., 1983), 43. Peck highlights the words "pretense" and "scapegoating" as common characteristics of evil—those who consistently lie.

[97] One of the most remarkable books of the twentieth century, *1984*, by George Orwell (Eric Hugh Blair), published first in 1949 (hardback), later in paperback (Hammondsworth, England: Penguin Books, 1954, reprinted at least 26 times), this prescient book describes the totalitarian state where Doublespeak reverses language, obliterates or revises history to suit the state, where freedom of thought is allowed to the masses because they don't think! Three chapters are entitled "War is Peace", "Ignorance is Strength", and "Freedom is Slavery." Freedom is the "freedom to say two plus two equals five." Ministry of Peace is actually the Ministry of War; joycamp is really the labor camp—examples that words mean the exact opposite of what they appear to mean. Orwell got some of his inspiration from Nazi Germany and Communist Russia, which had employed some of the methods of *1984*. Yet much of the book can be thought of as an overview of the endtime when the world generally will believe the Big Lie and falsified history, leading to the attempted extinction of those guilty of Thoughtcrimes.

[98] Peck, *op. cit.*, 79. Interesting, evil is only "live" spelled backwards.

beast should both speak and cause as many as would not worship the image of the beast to be killed" (Revelation 13:15).[99]

NO THEOLOGICAL THEORY

I am not speaking of theological theory. Nor of otherworldly, unseen deviltry. Satan's character has been incarnated many times throughout human history. Consider Josef Stalin. On November 7, 1937 (Revolutionary Day), after the military parade in Red Square, at the feast in Marshal Kliment Voroshilov's home, Stalin gave a toast that is remarkably honest and chilling—and everyone there knew exactly what he was saying for they all had lived through a ghastly bloodletting when tens of thousands of Russian military leaders had been murdered:

"I would like to say a few words, perhaps not festive ones. The Russian tsars did a great deal that was bad. They robbed and enslaved the people. They waged wars and seized territories in the interests of landowners. But they did one thing that was good—they amassed an enormous state. ... We have united the state in such a way that if any part were isolated from the common-socialist state, it would not only inflict harm on the latter but would be unable to exist independently and would inevitably fall under foreign subjugation. Therefore, whoever attempts to destroy that unity of the socialist state ... is an enemy, a sworn enemy of the state and of the peoples of the USSR. And we will destroy each and every such enemy, even if he is an Old Bolshevik; we will destroy all his kin, his family. We will mercilessly destroy anyone who, by his deeds or his thoughts—yes, his thoughts— threatens the unity of this socialist state. To the complete destruction of all enemies, themselves and their kin!" Approving exclamations followed: "To the great Stalin!"[100]

---

[99] See 276, 326.
[100] The Diary of Georgi Dimitrov, the Bulgarian head of the Comintern, kept from 1933–1949. Cited in *The Wilson Quarterly,* Summer 2003, 114.

Freedom is never free. The cost of freedom is incalculable. Ask the 56 signers of the Declaration of Independence in 1776 who put in peril not only their material assets but also their lives and those of their loved ones. Their signatures followed these closing words: *"And for support of this Declaration, with its firm reliance on Divine Providence we mutually pledge to each other our Lives, our Fortunes, and our sacred Honor."*

This pledge is far more than rhetorical flourish—it was the way of life of these most remarkable men from the 13 colonies. But each signer knew they were signing their "own death warrants," as Benjamin Rush reminded John Adams on July 20, 1811.

Eleven of the signers were merchants or businessmen, 14 were farmers, and 4 were physicians. Twenty-two were lawyers—although William Hooper of North Carolina was "disbarred" when he spoke against the Crown—and nine were judges. Stephen Hopkins had been Governor of Rhode Island. John Witherspoon, president of Princeton, was the only active clergyman to sign. Seven of the signers were educated at Harvard, four each at Yale and William & Mary, and three at Princeton.

Fifteen had their homes ransacked and burned, including William Ellery, Thomas McKean, Lyman Hall, George Clymer, Thomas Heyward, Jr., Arthur Middleton, Thomas Nelson, Jr., Francis Lewis, John Hart, Lewis Morris, Philip Livingston, William Floyd, William Hooper, Richard Stockton and Francis Hopkinson.

Five signers were captured as traitors (Heyward, Rutledge, Walton, Middleton) and endured miserable imprisonment. Ten of the 56 were wounded during the war though none died. A number lost their fortunes.

One example: John Hart, a prosperous New Jersey farmer, was among the first to feel the wrath of the British. Driven from his dying wife's bedside, he and their 13 children fled for their lives. His fields and gristmill were wasted. For more than a year he lived in forests and caves, not daring to remain two nights under the same roof. Returning home he found his wife dead and his children vanished. Hart soon died from exhaustion and a broken heart.

These men and their families were not wild-eyed rabble-rousers. They all enjoyed remarkable material security, but they valued freedom more. The world has never witnessed a more brilliant exhibition of political wisdom, or a brighter example of individual and collective firmness and courage. Their chance of success was at best dicey. Less than 3 million people scattered over a widely extended territory, no overflowing treasuries, they looked at each other and *volunteered their own wealth and integrity.* Not one of them had second thoughts; none defected or failed his pledge. They paid the cost of freedom. They trusted in Him whom they believed planted their forefathers in the New World and pledged themselves to give birth to a new country free from the oppression of either the Church or the King. The cost of freedom is incalculable.

B. J. Lossing, *Biographical Sketches of the Signers of the Declaration of American Independence* (New York: George F. Coolidge & Brother, 1848; reprinted, Aledo, TX: WallBuilder Press, 1998).

God responded to Satan's charges in such a way that the unfallen angels and worlds could see that He is not the kind of God that Satan has made Him out to be. What has been God's long-range plan to tell His side of the story? How does Jesus, as our Substitute ("atoning Sacrifice"), our High Priest ("all-powerful Mediator"), and as our Example, tell the truth about God and about the destiny of men and women of faith? Why did God risk all in allowing Jesus to become truly man, exposing Himself to possible failure and eternal loss?

CHAPTER FIVE:
GOD MEETS SATAN'S CHARGES

How God responded to Satan's devious charges reflects in dazzling brilliance how fair and trustworthy He really is. Obviously God could not use "flattery and deceit" in the controversy such as Satan could use.[101]

As we review the working of Divine intervention in the affairs of men and women since creation, we see:

"God's purposes move steadily forward to their accomplishment; to all created intelligences He is making manifest His justice and benevolence. Through Satan's temptations the whole human race have become transgressors of God's law; but by the sacrifice of His Son a way is opened whereby they may return to God. Through the grace of Christ they may be enabled to render obedience to the Father's law. Thus in every age, from the midst of apostasy and rebellion, God

---

[101] *Patriarchs and Prophets*, 42.

gathers out a people that are true to Him—a people 'in whose heart is his law' (Isaiah 51:7)."[102]

During the initial period of the controversy, God decided that one of His best laboratories for the working out of His "side" of the conflict as well as Satan's "side" would be a new world of responsible intelligences. Far from the center of the universe, past billions of starry galaxies, each hundreds of millions of light years across, our Creator picked out a small solar system with nine circling planets. On the one exactly positioned, not too far or too near its source of light and heat, He made his move to create "human beings ... a new and distinct order."

HUMANS, A NEW AND DISTINCT ORDER

Apparently this new world was the "talk" of the universe: "All heaven took a deep and joyful interest in the creation of the world and of man. ... They were made 'in the image of God' and it was the Creator's design that they should populate the earth."[103]

So we ask, why does this "new and distinct order" of creation become a part of God's answer to Satan's charges? Ellen White suggests that one of God's purposes in creating human beings was ...

"... that the longer man lived, the more fully he should reveal this image [Genesis 1:27],—the more fully reflect the glory of the Creator. ... Throughout eternal ages he would have continued to gain new treasures of knowledge, to discover fresh springs of happiness, and to obtain clearer and yet clearer conceptions of the wisdom, the power, and the love of God. More and more fully would he have fulfilled the object of his creation, more and more fully have reflected the Creator's glory."[104]

Further, God planned that in the development of the human race He would "put it in our power, through co-operation with Him, to bring this

---

[102] *Ibid.*, 338. John Milton perceived well how this ensuing conflict reflected more clearly the differences between Good and Evil:

"... But that the will
And high permission of all-ruling Heaven
Left him at large to his own dark designs,
that with reiterated crimes he might
Heap on himself damnation, while he sought
Evil to others, and enraged might see
How all his malice served but to bring forth
Infinite goodness, grace, and mercy, shewn
On Man by him seduced, but on himself
Treble confusion, wrath, and vengeance poured."
—Milton, *Paradise Lost*, bk. 1 (Harvard Classics, vol. 4, *op. cit.*, 95).

[103] *Review and Herald*, Feb. 11, 1902.

[104] *Education*, 15. One of the clearest concepts of what eternal life will be like!

scene of misery to an end."[105] This thought should make you pause and con-sider how you are helping God to bring "this scene of misery to an end." Or if you are frustrating God's plan to bring all this to an end. What a pity!

Isaiah reflected God's original plan in saying: "Everyone who is called by My Name, Whom I have created for My glory ... You are My witnesses." (Isaiah 43:7, 10). Later, Isaiah quoted God as He emphasized why human beings were created: "Who formed the earth and made it, Who has estab-lished it, Who did not create it in vain, Who formed it to be inhabited" (Isaiah 45:18).

It might be useful to ask how the creation of men and women is truly a "new and distinct order" in the universe. What is there about men and women being created "in the image of God"—in such a way that they became a "new and distinct order"—that becomes a lesson book to the universe as to how fair, trustworthy, and loving God really is? Apparently, it seems to me, that God had something very special for Planet Earth (and for the Great Controversy) when He created our Edenic parents differently then inhabitants on other worlds—especially when God created men and women "for My glory," to be "My witnesses."

WHY THE RESPONSIBILITIES OF PROCREATION

We could begin by asking why God made men and women with the responsibilities of procreation. Could it be that men and women through marriage and family relations provide insight into the character of God that angels could not?[106] Is there any clue in watching parents love children—especially when they disobey—and then think of how God relates to sinners?[107] Is there not something significant in this "new and distinct order"—this human laboratory of parents and children, from the standpoint of character development—that could not be observed otherwise, anywhere else in the universe?

Other ways, in this "new and distinct order," besides family relation-ships, shed light on the government of God. An example is freedom and order. How is that eternal balance worked out best in the communities and nations?

---

[105] *Ibid.,* 264.

[106] "The doctrine that children will be born in the new earth is not a part of the 'sure word of prophecy' (1 Peter 1:19). The words of Christ are too plain to be misunderstood. They should forever settle the question of marriages and births in the new earth. ... They will be as the angels of God, members of the royal family." —*Selected Messages,* bk. 1, 172, 173.

[107] God's primary reason for creating men and women was to demonstrate to the entire universe that Satan was wrong about his charges that created intelligences would lose their freedom if they tried to remain obedient. But after Adam and Eve failed to prove God right regarding freedom and obedience, God continued to work through them and their posterity in proving that Satan was wrong. The universe soon found out that even sinners could choose obedience and find genuine freedom by trusting in God's promises to supply all their needs—pardon and power in developing loyal sons and daughters.

Over the centuries, the whole universe has seen more clearly how satanic principles of government produce self-destructive systems in their attempts to organize a home or neighborhood or nation. Painful experiments of either totalitarian dictatorships or anarchic "democracies" continue to prove Satan wrong regarding how best to govern the universe. When at times we find groups trying to live under the rule of law governed by Christian principles, the universe can see, though perhaps only faintly, how wise God's rule of law governed by His principles really can be.[108]

GOD'S PERSONAL RISK

God surely was taking a risk when He put so much of His own future on the line in creating this "new and distinct order" of beings who could just as easily rebel as did one-third of the bright, intelligent angels! How long would it take for the universe to see God's purpose in this creation of a "new and distinct order" work out? One generation? One thousand years? Seven thousand years? One million years?

Through it all, God has made it very plain that His government, His character, would not and could not force the respect and loyalty of His created intelligences. He made them for His "glory" (Isaiah 43:7) and there would be no glory (that is, no reflection of His character) or joy in His relationship with them if they were robots or puppets.

God's fundamental principle of reason in place of force has probably never been better expressed by anyone than the following:

> "The government of God is not, as Satan would make it appear, founded upon a blind submission, an unreasoning control. It appeals to the intellect and the conscience. 'Come now, and let us reason together' is the Creator's invitation to the beings He has made (Isaiah 1:18). God does not force the will of His creatures. He cannot accept an homage that is not willingly and intelligently given. A mere forced submission would prevent all real development of mind or character; it would make man a mere automaton. Such is not the purpose of the Creator. He desires that man, the crowning work of His creative power, shall reach the highest possible

---

[108] Probably the "last great hope" for a political system that would offer "freedom and order" has been the American experiment, beginning with the Declaration of Independence (1776) and its Constitution (1787). John Adams, one of the driving forces for both documents, considered the conceptual framer of both, wrote to his son John Quincy, Ambassador to Russia, at the time of the death of his granddaughter (after the death of other children and many friends): The universe "was inscrutable and incomprehensible. ... While you and I believe that the whole system is under the constant and vigilant direction of a wisdom infinitely more discerning than ours and a benevolence to the whole and to us in particular greater even than our own self love, we have the highest consolation that reason can suggest or imagination conceive. ... Sorrow can make no alternative, afford no relief to the departed, to survivors or to ourselves." —See David McCullough, *John Adams* (New York; Simon & Schuster, 2001), 611.

development. He sets before us the height of blessing to which He desires to bring us through His grace. He invites us to give ourselves to Him that He may work His will in us. It remains for us to choose whether we will be set free from the bondage of sin, to share the glorious liberty of the sons of God."[109]

Really, we are touching thoughts that are almost beyond words. God made zillions of various animals, insects, and birds on Planet Earth, but only men and women had the ability to rebel against their Creator. In other words, of all His creation on this planet, we alone could and would spoil the magnificent place called Planet Earth.

In giving us the freedom to choose, to say No to His wishes, God was actually imprisoning Himself in a history that He could have avoided—if He wanted to!

Philip Yancey even entitled chapter six in his remarkable book, *Disappointment With God*, "Risky Business."[110] He asked: "Nearly everything theologians say about human freedom sounds somehow right and somehow wrong. How can a sovereign God take risks or imprison Himself. Yet God's creation of man and woman approached that kind of astonishing self-limitation ... And as Adam and Eve soon learned, rebellion, which also seems like freedom, involves limitation as well."

Let us read on as we watch the drama of rebellion unfold in the Garden!

---

[109] *Steps to Christ*, 43, 44. "God does not force any man into his service. Every soul must decide for himself whether or not he will fall on the Rock and be broken. Heaven has been amazed to see the spiritual stupidity that has prevailed. You need individually to open your proud hearts to the Spirit of God. You need to have your intellectual ability sanctified to the service of God. The transforming power of God must be upon you, that your minds may be renewed by the Holy Spirit, that you may have the mind that was in Christ." —*Review and Herald*, December 24, 1889.

"God does not force the will or judgment of any. He takes no pleasure in a slavish obedience. He desires that the creatures of His hands shall love Him because He is worthy of love. He would have them obey Him because they have an intelligent appreciation of His wisdom, justice, and benevolence. And all who have a just conception of these qualities will love Him because they are drawn toward Him in admiration of His attributes." —*The Great Controversy*, 541. "God might have created man without the power to transgress His law; He might have withheld the hand of Adam from touching the forbidden fruit; but in that case man would have been, not a free moral agent, but a mere automaton. Without freedom of choice, his obedience would not have been voluntary, but forced. There could have been no development of character. Such a course would have been contrary to God's plan in dealing with the inhabitants of other worlds. It would have been unworthy of man as an intelligent being, and would have sustained Satan's charge of God's arbitrary rule."—*Patriarchs and Prophets*, 49. "Rebellion was not to be overcome by force. Compelling power is found only under Satan's government. The Lord's principles are not of this order. His authority rests upon goodness, mercy, and love; and the presentation of these principles is the means to be used. God's government is moral, and truth and love are to be the prevailing power." —*The Desire of Ages*, 759.

[110] Philip Yancey, *Disappointment With God* (Grand Rapids, MI: Zondervan Publishing House, 1988), 57–62.

CHAPTER SIX:
THE GREAT CONTROVERSY THEATER MOVED TO PLANET EARTH

I s it not obvious now as to why Satan focused his hellish attentions on Planet Earth and on the newly created couple made in the "image of God"? That "image" he once envied and now hated. With the creation of humans, Satan could immediately see that God had set forth a clear challenge to all his accusations: Men and women would be God's Exhibit A of how created beings, not even possessing the prerogatives of angels, could respond to His overtures of love with spontaneous gratitude, respect, and a love that would mature forever. What a laboratory to prove Satan wrong in a way that mere argument could never do![111]

The broad scenario of why Satan focuses his attack on Planet Earth is found in Revelation 12. In typical apocalyptic fashion, John describes the war that "broke out in heaven" (verses 7, 8), how Satan was "cast to the earth, and his angels were cast out with him" (verse 9), that his purpose for coming to earth was to "deceive(s) the whole world" (verse 9), that his role as "accuser of the brethren" would bring great persecution on those who resisted him (verse 10), that he knows, after the coming of Jesus and the promise of His power to help the accused "brethren," that he has "a short time" to hold the world hostage before the "war" with the Church becomes super-heated in the last days, especially with those "who keep the commandments of God and have the testimony of Jesus Christ" (verses 12–17).

FIRST SHOTS IN A VERY LONG WAR

The first shots in this very long war on earth were heard in the Garden of Eden (Genesis 3). Here we see again some of the same tactics that he used in heaven to deceive one-third of the angels.[112] The only difference is that all the angels saw and heard God, the Accused One, face-to-face (that is, as much as created beings could "see" their Creator). As much as words can describe it, the angels sinned in the full light of Truth and Love. No further incarnation of God's character could have been made than what they were already clearly familiar since time for them began. No "savior" could be given to win them back because the only Mediator (1 Timothy 2:5) the universe has had was the One the rebels rejected, face to face!

---

[111] Ken McFarland's *The Lucifer Files* (Boise, ID: PPPA, 1988) imagines Satan's thinking throughout the Great Controversy.
[112] See **30–36**.

But for men and women of earth, the conflict is on a different level. They could live forever but only if they continued to receive "the vigor imparted by the tree of life."[113] Adam and Eve "received instruction from the all-wise Creator" perhaps directly and certainly through face-to-face visits with angels.[114]

But that one mysterious tree around which God set limits! The other worlds and the angels knew well why God placed "the tree of the knowledge of good and evil" (Genesis 2:17) in the perfect Garden of Eden.[115] These watching universes knew that freedom could be understood only when choices exist. Without a focus to their choices, Adam and Eve would not understand the power of freedom! *Even if Satan did not exist, that forbidden tree would serve its valuable purpose.* Further, loyal angels, we can be sure, were determined that Adam and Eve should know the horrific story of the war in heaven and the existence of a host of many angry, jealous angels who would trouble them in their perfect home—and the dreadful result of choosing not to trust their Creator.[116]

It is not difficult for us today to role-play what was going on in Satan's mind. The old green monster of envy really had something to hate when he saw how wonderful God's masterpiece—Adam and Eve—were! That brilliant mind, beyond any human being's capacity, was now bent on changing our first parents' "love to distrust." His crafty mind, skilled in deception, "chose to employ as his medium the serpent—a disguise well adapted for his purpose of deception."[117]

SATAN'S PLAN BEGINS TO JELL

After reviewing his own mad slippage from trust to distrust, his plan began to jell. He knew that free minds would always think and think; they could no more stop thinking than to stop breathing. But he knew well that there was a dark side to free-thinking, and he knew how to find it. He designed his schemes to take advantage of this wonderful capacity of the human mind to think. He would use his warped understanding of "freedom" to test the limits of free thought, and then take the next step—"to excite a spirit of irreverent curiosity, a restless, inquisitive desire to penetrate the secrets of divine

---

[113] *Patriarchs and Prophets*, 47, 50, 60.

[114] *Ibid.*, 50.

[115] When God warned Adam and Eve about "that tree," He did not say, "In the day that you eat of it I will surely kill you." No, only, "you shall surely die." Neither did Jesus say in John 3:16, "God so loved the world that He gave His only begotten Son, that whosoever does not believe in Him I shall destroy with everlasting punishment." No, Jesus said that whosoever believes in Him shall not commit spiritual suicide [lit. Greek]." Sin destroys the sinner—such are its wages. "God does not stand toward the sinner as an executioner of the sentence against transgression; but He leaves the rejectors of His mercy to themselves, to reap that which they have sown." —*The Great Controversy*, 36.

[116] *Patriarchs and Prophets*, 53.

[117] *Ibid.*

wisdom and power. ... Satan tempts men to disobedience, by leading them to believe they are entering a wonderful field of knowledge."[118]

Philip Yancey, in his latest book, described the Eden Paradise wherein "a great severing took place. Adam and Even reached too far, trusting themselves rather than God to set the rules."[119]

One of the most prevailing themes in all literature and poetry is the fate of stretching the pursuit of knowledge into the "forbidden"—the fruit of insatiable curiosity.[120]

Well, what happened in the beautiful Garden, unmarred by contradiction or rebel thought? The master deceiver played his Ace card—he would separate Eve from her husband![121] The concerned angels had already "cautioned Eve to beware of separating herself from her husband. ... with him she would be in less danger from temptation than if she were alone."[122]

Her second mistake was to wander in her flush of freedom, the thrill of "being on her own." That tree, that "forbidden" tree, enticed her. Chaucer expressed this profound insight, this human drivenness, in his *Canterbury Tales*. Each pilgrim tells not only why he or she is going to the cathedral but also something about themselves. One of the most insightful dialogues has been remembered as the "Wife of Bath's Tale." He had this shrewd widow, wife of several husbands, confessing a deep human mystery: *Forbid a thing, and that thing covet we.*[123] Earlier, Bernard of Clairvaux nailed it when he wrote: "Curiosity is the beginning of all sin."[124]

James outlined the anatomy of sin: "But each one is tempted when he is drawn away by his own desires and enticed. Then when desire has conceived, it gives birth to sin; and sin, when it is full-grown, brings forth death" (1:14, 15).

---

[118] *Ibid.*, 52–55. Milton saw it clearly:
"Say first what cause
Moved our grand Parents, in that happy state,
Favoured of Heaven so highly, to fall off
From their Creator, and transgress his will
For one restraint, lords of the World besides
Who first seduced them to that foul revolt?
The infernal Serpent; he it was whose guile,
Stirred up with envy and revenge, deceived
The mother of mankind. ..."
—*Paradise Lost*, bk. 1 (Harvard Classics), 91.

[119] *Rumors of Another World* (Grand Rapids, MI: Zondervan, 2003) 101.

[120] See "Appendix F: 'Wife of Bath Principle.'" "It is a masterpiece of Satan's deceptions to keep the minds of men searching and conjecturing in regard to that which God has not made known, and which He does not intend that we shall understand." —*The Great Controversy*, 523.

[121] A basic marriage principle here seems to be unfolding that both husbands and wives should strongly consider.

[122] *Patriarchs and Prophets*, 53.

[123] *Internet Medieval Source Book*, Geoffrey Chaucer, *Canterbury Tales* [Modern Version], gopher://gopher.vt.edu

[124] Cited in Roger Shattuck, *Forbidden Knowledge* (New York: St. Martin's Press, 1996), 70.

What was Eve's desire? No one knows the initial murmurings that inched Eve into wandering. The flush of freedom to be herself, apart from her husband, apart from God's restrictions (imagined, of course) that would restrain her full potential.[125]

But in Eve's desire to be "free," she was walking away from her Lord's counsel, in what Milton called "the instinct of waywardness." In her walk to what she thought was real freedom, desire led into enticement. But enticement soon leads (if not halted by a clear recognition that the Holy Spirit is speaking truth and a warning) into desire conceived—"the birth of sin."

She perceived the fruit of the forbidden tree with "curiosity and admiration."[126] Her next step, though, still unperceived as her next step into forbidden knowledge, was the thought: "Why [would] God ... withhold it [knowledge] from them?" Now she was on her own!

Satan could sense her new excitement. He moved in with his charm and deceit and affirmed her self-serving reasoning about God's restriction. And, to top it off, she was thrilled with this new experience of speaking with an "intelligent" animal!

In her new boldness, she responded to the Satan-serpent with the fling of irritated independence—she said that God not only told them not to eat the forbidden fruit, but that they should not even touch it![127] Or they would die! (Genesis 3:3). The most sympathetic Evil Counselor now joined her in questioning God's unreasonableness: "You will not surely die" (Genesis 3:4). "Look, my dear, I have eaten this fruit and I am surely not dead! Listen to me, Honey, since the day I ate this fruit, I have gained new insights, new powers, even the ability to speak! Right?"

"Eve, my dear, I don't know just why God would want to keep so much knowledge and new capabilities from you but, believe me, 'your eyes will be opened, and you will be like God, knowing good and evil'" (Genesis 3:5).

WIFE OF BATH PRINCIPLE

So together they played with the forbidden until the Wife of Bath principle took over—"*forbid a thing, and that thing covet we.*" And so true was Satan's prophecy—Eve, then Adam, and then all the rest of us, surely discovered the knowledge of evil. The deceiver must have smirked his most fiendish smile because he knew what that first couple were in for.

Still today, men and women feel the same Wife of Bath principle. We spurn the warning of our All-wise God, that the pursuit of knowledge does

---

[125] Nothing is wrong in one's desire to reach his or her potential—unless one ignores basic responsibilities that always should outweigh the desire for self-actualization. In God's plan, reaching one's potential is always found in fulfilling one's responsibilities, whatever they may be.

[126] *Patriarchs and Prophets*, 54.

[127] God did not tell Adam and Eve explicitly that they should not touch the fruit. But when we begin the trip down the slippery slope toward forbidden knowledge, all kinds of self-assurance, self-pity, and rationalization take over.

have its limitations (as men and women learned in the Tower of Babel experience). Is it possible that in our pursuit of knowledge we find more problems than we find solutions for?[128] The lesson of Genesis 3 and of most all classic literature is that experience does not necessarily equal wisdom. Milton seemed to say it best: "Be lowly wise."[129] The pursuit of knowledge and experience is one of God's greatest gifts, *but there are limitations.*

Another principle we learn from Eve's experience is that honest belief "did not save her from the penalty of sin."[130] In the final judgment, we will not be lost because we were sinners but because we "did not believe the truth, because [we] neglected the opportunity of learning what is truth."[131]

Lewis has one of his "ghosts," a religious rationalist, visiting heaven but not yet a resident. He was defending himself by saying that "it's not a question of how the opinions are formed. The point is that they were my honest opinions, sincerely expressed." One of the Solid People answered: "Of course. Having allowed oneself to drift, unresisting, unpraying, accepting every half-conscious solicitation from our desires, we reached a point where we no longer believed the Faith. Just in the same way, a jealous man, drifting and unresisting, reaches a point at which he believes lies about his best friend: a drunkard reaches a point at which (for the moment) he actually believes that another glass will do him no harm. The beliefs are sincere in the sense that they do occur as psychological events in the man's mind. If that's what you mean by sincerity they are sincere, and so were ours. But errors which are sincere in that sense are not innocent."[132]

Basically, we see in Eve's experience that the fundamental "essence of sin [is] to allow ourselves to become a contradiction of God's will."[133] We may describe how this "contradiction" developed but it is not possible "to explain [that is, give reasons, or justifications] for its existence."[134]

Alexander Pope, in his *Essay on Man,* seems to describe well how these flights of what we mistakenly call "freedom" become life choices:

---

[128] Studying the atom and the genetic code has good and bad consequences. Does our knowledge of cloning promise only good results? Etc.

[129] *Paradise Lost,* bk. 8, 173.

[130] *Patriarchs and Prophets,* 55.

[131] *Ibid.* See John 3:17–21.

[132] Lewis, *The Great Divorce* (San Francisco: HarperCollins*Publishers,* 1946, 1973), 37, 38.

[133] *Manuscript Releases,* vol. 5, 348 (Letter 22, 1896 to Colcord).

[134] "It is impossible to explain the origin of sin so as to give a reason for its existence. Yet enough may be understood concerning both the origin and the final disposition of sin, to make fully manifest the justice and benevolence of God in all His dealings with evil. Nothing is more plainly taught in Scripture than that God was in no wise responsible for the entrance of sin; that there was no arbitrary withdrawal of divine grace, no deficiency in the divine government, that gave occasion for the uprising of rebellion. Sin is an intruder, for whose presence no reason can be given. It is mysterious, unaccountable; to excuse it, is to defend it. Could excuse for it be found, or cause be shown for its existence, it would cease to be sin. Our only definition of sin is that given in the word of God; it is 'the transgression of the law'; it is the outworking of a principle at war with the great law of love which is the foundation of the divine government." —*The Great Controversy,* 493.

"Vice is a monster of so frightful mien,
As to be hated, needs but to be seen;
Yet seen too oft, familiar with her face,
We first endure, then pity, then embrace."[135]

And John Milton, examines with shuddering analysis what is ahead for all those who do not retreat from their "contradiction" with God's will, using the template of Satan's fatal choices that applies to all who make him their example:

"The mind is its own place, and in itself
Can make a Heaven of Hell, a Hell of Heaven.
What matter where, if I be still the same,
And what I should be, all but less than he
Whom thunder hath made greater? Here at least
We shall be free; the Almighty hath not built
Here for his envy, will not drive us hence:
Here we may reign secure; and, in my choice,
To reign in Hell than serve in Heaven"[136]

GOD DOES NOT WAIT FOR SINNERS TO SEEK HIM

We all know how God responded to this awful moment in the history of Planet Earth: "The Lord God called to Adam and said to him, 'Where are you?'" (Genesis 3:9). Haunting call, and every one of us has heard it more than once!

God took the initiative to restore this broken relationship—He didn't wait for Adam or Eve to seek Him! That thought alone is astounding! God seeking men and women, not men and women somehow seeking God—even though they were burdened with remorse! We shall say more about this later.

In spite of all their self-justifications, first blaming each other and then God Himself (Genesis 3:12, 13), God revealed His plan whereby they could be assured that not all was lost. He first told the deceptive Satan-serpent that he might have won the first battle but not the war: "I will put enmity between you and the woman, and between your seed and her Seed; He shall bruise your head, and you shall bruise His heel" (Genesis 3:15). And so the Great Controversy burst into new dimensions on Planet Earth.

---

[135] *Epistle II*, Line 135, (*Harvard Classics*, vol. I).

[136] *Paradise Lost*, (*Harvard Classics*, vol. IV, 96–97; Lewis, in *The Great Divorce*, has the Teacher saying: "Milton was right, the choice of every lost soul can be expressed in the words, 'Better to reign in Hell than serve in Heaven.' There is always something they insist on keeping even at the price of misery. There is always something they prefer to joy—that is, to reality. Ye see it easily enough in a spoiled child that would sooner miss its play and its supper than say it was sorry and be friends. Ye call it the Sulks. But in adult life it has a hundred fine names—Achilles' wrath and Coriolanus' grandeur, Revenge and Injured Merit and Self-Respect and Tragic Greatness and Proper Pride.'" 71, 72.

What could this veiled promise mean? The Christian church generally understands these words to be a prediction of the coming of Christ, the sinner's only Deliverer. Here is pictured the coming conflict between Satanic forces (John 8:44; Acts 13:10; 1 John 3:10) and those who are loyal to God's will (Revelation 12:1–3; Galatians 3:16, 19). Jesus came "to destroy the works of the devil" (Hebrews 2:14; 1 John 3:8).[137]

The Seed is Jesus, the "true Light which gives light to every man who comes into the world" (John 1:9). Everyone who has ever been born has been spoken to through the Spirit of Jesus: "As through Christ every human being has life, so also through Him every soul receives some ray of divine light. Not only intellectual but spiritual power, a perception of right, a desire for goodness, exists in every heart."[138]

Yet coupled with this Good News was God's warning—a dire warning we all have seen worked out in our own lives: "Against these principles there is struggling an antagonistic power. The result of the eating of the tree of knowledge of good and evil is manifest in every man's experience. There is in his nature a bent to evil, a force which, unaided, he cannot resist."[139] That force may be called Chaucer's Wife of Bath principle or Milton's "instinct of waywardness."

Our only hope as we contend with the malignity of the Evil One is to call on the Seed! We will "find help in but one power. That power is Christ. Cooperation with that power is man's greatest need."[140]

GOD'S LINE IN THE SAND

Did Satan understand the implication of God's "line in the sand" drawn between the powers of those who chose the Seed and his own devilish plans to completely overtake this world? He may not have known exactly *how* God planned to intervene, but obviously He got the point. He now knew "that his work of depraving human nature would be interrupted; that by some means man would be enabled to resist his power."[141]

Of course, some may still ask, why didn't God simply stop Adam and Eve from eating the fruit and thus spare this earth from the horror of sin? (Same question we heard earlier, "Why didn't God destroy Satan at the first indication of his rebellion in heaven?") Obviously, God could have made it impossible for Satan to ventriloquize through the charming serpent. Obviously,

---

[137] "The 'seed' is put in the singular, indicating, not that a multitude of descendants of the woman jointly shall be engaged in crushing the serpent's head, but rather that a single individual will accomplish this. These observations clearly show that in this pronouncement is compressed the record of the Great Controversy between Christ and Satan, a battle that began in heaven (Revelation 20:10)." —SDABC, vol. 1, 233.

[138] *Education*, 29; compare *Patriarchs and Prophets*, 64. See also Romans 1:18–32; 2:14–16.

[139] *Patriarchs and Prophets*, 64.

[140] *Ibid.*

[141] *Ibid.*, 66.

God could have barred Eve from reaching for the fruit, from talking with Satan! But if He did, God would be making a universe of robots or puppets. He would not have a universe of potentially loving, free-willed individuals who would enjoy life and its thrills almost as much as He does. *One cannot have love and freedom and also no choice at the same time!*[142]

How did Satan's initial victory in the Great Controversy immediately affect Planet Earth? First, after experiencing guilt for the first time, after refusing to take responsibility for their own actions, after blaming each other and then the serpent, an innocent animal was slain to provide garments for Adam and Eve (Genesis 3:21). Soon, the plant kingdom revealed the blight of Satan's touch, perhaps because his brilliant, but deranged intelligence messed up his plans to clone and/or manipulate each plant's genetic pool.[143]

The animal world also began to show the effects of Satan's laboratory experiments, perhaps as now seen in the remnants of dinosaurs and other exotic pre-flood animals.[144]

What has been God's response? It gets exciting!

---

[142] "God had power to hold Adam back from touching the forbidden fruit; but had He done this, Satan would have been sustained in his charge against God's arbitrary rule. Man would not have been a free moral agent, but a mere machine." —*Review and Herald,* June 4, 1901.

[143] "Not one noxious plant was placed in the Lord's great garden, but after Adam and Eve sinned, poisonous herbs sprang up. In the parable of the sower the question was asked the Master, 'Didst not thou sow good seed in thy field? How then hath it tares?' The Master answered, 'An enemy hath done this.' All tares are sown by the evil one. Every noxious herb is of his sowing, and by his ingenious methods of amalgamation he has corrupted the earth with tares." —Manuscript 65, 1899, *Manuscript Releases,* vol. 16, 247.

[144] "Every species of animal which God had created were preserved in the ark. The confused species which God did not create, which were the result of amalgamation, were destroyed by the flood." —*Spiritual Gifts,* vol. 3, 5.

CHAPTER SEVEN:
GOD TELLS HIS SIDE
OF THE CONTROVERSY

We now face the big question: What do we learn about God's character (which is precisely Satan's target in the Great Controversy) as He reveals Himself throughout human history? How did He go about telling His side of the story?

- *Through nature.* Of course, we are not placing these "ways in which God is seeking to make Himself known to us"[145] in any special order. Each person may say that the Bible is the first way he or she first sensed the truth about God. Others would say it was the moving of the Holy Spirit, or nature itself. Yet for many people the truth of Paul's observation was true for them: "For since the creation of the world His invisible attributes are clearly seen, being understood by the things that are made, even His eternal power and Godhead, so that they are without excuse" (Romans 1:20).

Ellen White often amplified Paul's words: "If we will but listen, God's created works will teach us precious lessons of obedience and trust. ... The poet and the naturalist have many things to say about nature, but it is the Christian who enjoys the beauty of the earth with the highest appreciation, because he recognizes his Father's handiwork, and perceives His love in flower and shrub and tree."[146]

The Psalmist reminds us that "the heavens declare the glory of God; and the firmament shows His handiwork" (19:1).

- *Through God's interventions in history.* He "speaks to us through His providential workings, ... In our circumstances and surroundings, in the changes daily taking place around us, we may find precious lessons, if our hearts are but open to discern them."[147]

Can you remember the many times when "circumstances and surroundings" were directly affected by answered prayer? I should write a book about the many mundane, some intensely personal, interventions that helped me through difficult moments, times without number. Each occasion may have appeared to others too trivial for God to have time for, but for me, it was a big solution at the moment! And answers to specific prayers!

My problem, however, is that I thought I could remember them all. But memory is not that good. I should have kept a daily journal like some

---

[145] *Steps to Christ*, 85.
[146] *Ibid.*, 85–87.
[147] *Ibid.*, 87.

of my more disciplined friends! One of those promises that has kept me moving forward has been shared with many others: "Those who decide to do nothing in any line that will displease God, will know, after presenting their case before Him, just what course to pursue. And they will receive not only wisdom but strength. Power for obedience, for service, will be imparted to them, as Christ has promised."[148] That promise is for everyone!

Further, high school students and others who have read their history books can think of great moments in the history of this world when monumental decisions or changes in national affairs "happened," the "happenings" not foreseen immediately by any of the participants—"happenings" that decidedly changed the course of history. Many of these special times in history made possible, as never before, the spread of the gospel, when the unpredictable happened, thus thwarting Satan's studied schemes.

For starters, think of the amazing Battle of Tours, France, in A.D. 732, when Charles Martel and his few stopped the northward sweep of the great Muslim army; the unrelenting wind that helped defeat the Spanish Armada in 1588;[149] the "providential fog" over Brooklyn Heights and the besieged American army in August, 1776; the remarkably calm English Channel and the covering fog that made possible the amazing escape of 335,000 British and French troops at Dunkirk, June 4, 1940.[150]

Of course, every historian writes from his own point of view.[151] For example, that's what makes the reading of the French Revolution most interesting—if one reads an English historian and then a French historian. Such is true for biographies, each written by different authors. This is not something to be alarmed about, just something to be aware of.

But when one surveys the history of humanity earliest times to the present through the spectacles of the Great Controversy Theme, fresh insights and connections arise most anywhere one looks.[152]

- *Through God's direct conversations with us through His Holy Spirit.* God speaks "through the influence of His Spirit upon the heart."

- *Through the Holy Scriptures.* Jesus said that the Old Testament Scriptures testified of Him (John 5:39). We have in both Old and

---

[148] *The Desire of Ages*, 668.

[149] The English and their Dutch allies were jubilant after a devastating attack by the much smaller Royal Navy coupled with severe storms that "destroyed perhaps one-half of the ships and at least one-third of the men." —Geoffrey Parker, *Success is Never Final* (New York: Basic Books, 2002), 41. "Flavit deus et dissipati sunt" ("God blew and they were scattered") was inscribed on the commemorative medal.

[150] See McCullough, *op. cit.*, 132, for an insightful glimpse of the timely shift of wind that prevented British ships from moving up the East River, the "cold, drenching rain," day and night (in August!) and then the "providential fog." For an overview of what seems to the author to be providential moments in world history, see "Appendix G: Providential Moments in World History."

[151] John Clive, *Not By Fact Alone* (New York: Alfred A. Knopf, 1989), ix–9. See also the introduction to James M. McPherson, ed., *To the Best of My Ability"* (New York: Dorling Kindersley Publishing, Inc., 2000), 7–10.

[152] *Education*, 125, 174–180. See "Appendix G: Providential Moments in World History."

New Testaments the many occasions when God actually spoke to men and women, most often through the prophets. We see how men and women responded to His leadings and how well life went when they followed His leadings. Throughout the Bible we see God's grace at work, providing the forgiveness for the penitent and the grace that helped men and women conquer personal weaknesses and the "fiery darts of the wicked one" (Ephesians 6:16).[153]

- *And, most important, through Jesus.* Paul spelled it out clearly in the first chapter of Hebrews that God had spoken in and through Jesus who was "the brightness of [God's] glory and the express image of His person."[154]

JESUS TELLS GOD'S SIDE OF THE CONTROVERSY

Here we are entering into the most wonderful, most exhilarating, world of thought that I know anything about: Why did Jesus become man?[155] Why did He come to die?[156]

We will look first at the big picture: He came to tell the truth about God! Beautiful trees, swirling galaxies, and gorgeous butterflies—they all can say something wonderful about God (Romans 1:20). But they tell us very little about Him personally. Above all else, Jesus came to give us a clear picture of how God thinks about men and women in their weaknesses, their fears and anxieties (Matthew 11:28–30). We now know how God feels about death (John 11), about hungry people (Mark 8:2), and about suffering (John 9:3, "Let the works of God be revealed").

The Bible describes Jesus as God from the beginning of beginnings and the Creator of all things (John 1:1–3; Colossians 1:15–17). He became the God-man, reflecting the glory of God through His life and works. Our Father in heaven endorsed Him for whom He said He was (John 1:14, 18). Our heavenly

---

[153] See "Appendix H: The Bible Reveals the Cosmic Conflict Between God and Satan."

[154] "God, who at various times and in different ways spoke in time past to the fathers by the prophets, has spoken to us by His Son, whom He has appointed heir of all things, through whom also He made the worlds; who being the brightness of His glory and the express image of His person, and upholding all things by the word of His power, when He had by Himself purged our sins, sat down at the right hand of the Majesty on high, having become so much better than the angels, as He has by inheritance obtained a more excellent name than they" (Hebrews 1:1–4). "As a personal being, God has revealed Himself in His Son. 'The outshining of the Father's glory,' 'and the express image of His person,' Jesus, as a personal Savior, came to the world. ... Christ, the light of the world, veiled the dazzling splendor of His divinity, and came to live as a man among men, that they might, without being consumed, become acquainted with their Creator. ... Christ came to teach human beings what God desires them to know. ... Yet not from the stars or the ocean or the cataract can we learn of the personality of God as it was revealed in Christ. God saw that a clearer revelation than nature was needed to portray both His personality and His character. He sent His Son into the world to manifest, so far as could be endured by human sight, the nature and the attributes of the invisible God." —*The Ministry of Healing*, 418–419.

[155] See "Appendix I: Why Jesus Came."

[156] See "Appendix J: Why Jesus Died."

Father works through Jesus and has granted to Him that honor and responsibility of being the Judge of all humanity (Mark 9:7; John 5:19–23; 14:10).

Jesus said of Himself that whoever "has seen Me has seen the Father" (John 14:9); that whoever truly knows Him as Savior will have "eternal life" (John 17:3). He told Pilate that the chief reason for coming to this world was to "bear witness to the truth" (John 18:37).

In other words, Jesus came to reveal what God is like in terms we can understand. In a way, He came as Heaven's Teacher and we all are His students. In addition to His role as humanity's Savior, coming as a Teacher is perhaps the clearest, most defining role as Jesus who "bears witness to the truth."[157]

As our "great Teacher" Jesus came "not only to atone for sin, but to be a teacher both by precept and example." What did He teach us? "He came to show man how to keep the law in humanity, so that man might have no excuse for following his own defective judgment. We see Christ's obedience. His life was without sin. His lifelong obedience is a reproach to disobedient humanity."[158] What a Teacher and what a lesson plan!

How did our "great Teacher" specifically tell God's side of the controversy? In the big picture Jesus came to prove Satan a liar—that God was not "severe, exacting, revengeful," or One who "could take pleasure in the sufferings of His creatures." God knew that "angels could not fully portray the character of God, but Christ, who was a living impersonation of God, could not fail to accomplish the work."[159]

So how did He do it?[160] What a plan! It galvanized the universe!

---

[157] See "Appendix I: Why Jesus Came."

[158] *Selected Messages,* bk. 3, 135. "The Great Teacher came to our world to stand at the head of humanity, to thus elevate and sanctify humanity by His holy obedience to all of God's requirements, showing it is possible to obey all the commandments of God. He has demonstrated that a lifelong obedience is possible." —Manuscript 1, 1892, cited in *Ibid.,* 139.

[159] *Signs of the Times,* January 20, 1890; In that same illuminating article, we find a special magnification of the big picture, especially regarding how our Lord's coming to earth directly affected our salvation: "The only way in which He could set and keep men right was to make Himself visible and familiar to their eyes. That men might have salvation He came directly to man and became a partaker of his nature. The Father was revealed in Christ as altogether a different being from that which Satan had represented Him to be." This paragraph needs to be read and reread often, for in these few words we have the rationale for what theologians call "justification" and "sanctification." The only way we can be justified (*"set right"*) and sanctified (*"kept right"*) is to keep our focus on why Jesus came to earth.

[160] C. S. Lewis saw all this from his World War II window: "Enemy-occupied territory—that is what this world is. Christianity is the story of how the rightful king has landed, you might say landed in disguise, and is calling us all to take part in a great campaign of sabotage. When you go to church you are really listening to the secret wireless from our friends: that is why the enemy is so anxious to prevent us from going. He does it by playing on our conceit and laziness and intellectual snobbery. I know someone will ask me, 'Do you really mean, at the time of day, to re-introduce our old friend the devil—hoofs and horns and all?' ... My answer is 'Yes, I do.' I do not claim to know anything about his personal appearance. If anybody really wants to know him better I would say to that person, 'Don't worry, If you really want to, you will. Whether you'll like it when you do is another question.'" —*Mere Christianity* (San Francisco: HarperCollins*Publishers,* 1952, 1980), 46.

CHAPTER EIGHT:
JESUS PROVES SATAN TO BE A LIAR

E ven to contemplate this question, we must get on our knees. I have found through the years that one thought leads to another even as the Great Controversy tree grows—one limb leading to another, smaller branches off the bigger ones, but each most necessary in the maturing of the tree. And frankly, it seems as if each new branch of thought comes best after prayerful consideration of what one has already learned about the growth of the developing Great Controversy tree and how one branch leads to another.[161] Further, one cannot graft an apple tree to an oak tree and expect it to grow! In the same way, when one tries to attach *error* to the Great Controversy tree, bells, whistles, and red lights should go off immediately.

Further still, understanding the Great Controversy is not a matter of lining up last-day events. The Great Controversy is *more Christ-centered than crisis-centered.* Understanding the truth about who Jesus is, why He came the way He did and why He died, provides the anatomy of truth that each crisis in the controversy unfolds. Let's keep our eyes on Jesus.

John makes it clear that Jesus is the Word of God; that is, even as I use words to express my thoughts in writing this book, so God used the Word (Jesus) to make His thoughts "audible" (John 1:1–3, 14). And what He is saying is not only for us on Planet Earth; "our little world is the lesson book of the universe."[162]

NOT A TEMPORARY GIFT!

Nicodemus learned that God was the Cosmic Lover who gave up One of the Godhead, Jesus Himself, to be linked with Planet Earth forever—not just for 33 years. And that a sinner's response of faith to this Gift would open up life forevermore. He learned further that God would not condemn men and women because they are sinners, but because they "loved darkness

---

[161] Some may liken the developing truths of the Great Controversy Theme to the links in a strong chain. That's helpful, but I find the linkage, the logical connection, of branches on a maturing oak tree to be more useful. Small branches extend from the larger branches, each one a logical, consistent, cohering extension of what it means to be an oak tree—all unfolding in logical sequence the distinctive, fundamental principle of being an oak once wrapped up in the fructifying acorn. The Great Controversy Theme develops like a grand oak out of the acorn. The acorn contains God's plans to vindicate His fairness and trustworthiness. The developing branches of interrelated truths unfold what God wants clearly understood by everyone!

[162] *The Desire of Ages,* 19.

rather than light" (John 3:1–21). That put the whole problem of human destiny squarely on a person's response to the "light" of truth, whether one says "yes" or "no." God would flood a person with light, but He would not force anyone to love the light. However, resisting "light" leads to unintended consequences, and that's something Satan has been learning the hard way!

Jesus told several parables that highlighted what our Heavenly Father is like. He is the Faithful, Persistent Shepherd of His sheep—no matter how far a sheep wanders, the sheep will be found, even though it doesn't know it is lost (Luke 15). This is another way of saying that God in Jesus is that Light which gives light "to every man who comes into the world," (John 1:9) even before a person knows that he needs the Light! And He will keep shining that Light on us, even when we drift into a "far country."

In the next parable, God is the Persevering Housewife who searches for the lost coin, never resting until the coin is found because the coin is still valuable, no matter how lost. This was another way of saying that God in Jesus "is able to save to the uttermost" all those who may feel they are worthless, but in God's sight, not so! (Hebrews 7:25).

THE WAITING FATHER

In the third parable, God is the Waiting Father[163] who never gives up on His wayward children. This is another way of saying that God in Jesus always has His everlasting arms outstretched to everyone, saying in words that all can understand: "Come unto Me, all you who labor and are heavy laden, and I will give you rest" (Matthew 11:28). No man or woman can ever say that God's front door was shut and that there was no light left on for him or her. Ever!

Paul reminded Timothy that Jesus is the "one Mediator between God and men"—the only Person in the universe who could reveal the truth about God in the face of Satan's accusations (1 Timothy 2:5). As a loyal follower, an angel could try to "mediate" the goodness of God but the testimony would at best be only a "character witness." Only God could reveal God, and that is why He became a baby boy and went through all the stress of a teenager and young adulthood—so that teenagers and young adults could understand that they are experiencing nothing that He has not gone through.[164] He identified with them 100 percent!

---

[163] Helmut Thielicke's neat phrase.

[164] In a letter to her young nephew Frank Belden, Ellen White wrote: "You have not a difficulty that did not press with equal weight upon Him, not a sorrow that His heart has not experienced. … Jesus once stood in age just where you now stand. Your circumstances, your cogitations at this period of your life, Jesus have had. He cannot overlook you at this critical period. He sees your dangers. He is acquainted with your temptations. He invites you to follow His example." —*Review and Herald*, May 8, 1975.

Let's keep remembering how the Great Controversy between God and Satan began and how God is willing to take the time for the universe to have all the evidence needed to prove that He can be trusted. And only God can reveal what God is like. That is why Jesus became a baby and grew to young manhood under the same rules of heredity and under the same encounters with Satan that we all must face. The message from Genesis to Revelation is that God can be trusted. But real trust comes only when you know very well the person you can trust. That is the open secret, the real deal God wants to make with each one of us: Listen to Jesus, let Him prove He can be your closest friend. That means He wants us to think clearly about why He came to earth and how His 33 years answered all the questions we could ask, and some we never thought of! Especially how Jesus made the Great Controversy more personal.[165]

Let's get specific: *Let's examine how Jesus silenced Satan's accusations that God was unfair to make laws that created beings could not keep.* Satan was right that sinners could not obey the law of God, but "Christ came in the form of humanity ('in the likeness of sinful flesh,' not unlikeness—Romans 8:3), and by His perfect obedience He proved that fallen humanity and divinity *combined* can obey every one of God's precepts."[166]

In fact, Jesus "showed that it is possible for man perfectly to obey the law" and that "through the merits of Christ, man is to show by his obedience that he could be trusted in heaven, that he would not rebel."[167] Now that is making a mighty statement to the universe! That God's plan to save the universe was involved in the saving of everyone who has faith in the promises of God. In developing men and women of faith, God is taking the risk out of His plan to restore the universe to a future without jeopardy![168]

Remember how we noted earlier that Satan had accused God of demanding "self-denial" and sacrifice from His created beings but would not exercise such unselfishness toward His created beings?[169] How did Jesus respond? Think about the circumstances that led up to His death and then all the

---

[165] One of the clearest explanations for the issues in the Great Controversy is A. Graham Maxwell's *Can God Be Trusted?* (Nashville, TN: Southern Publishing Association, 1977).

[166] *Christ's Object Lessons,* 314, emphasis supplied. "By His life and His death, Christ proved that God's justice did not destroy His mercy, but that sin could be forgiven, and that the law is righteous, and can be perfectly obeyed. Satan's charges were refuted. God had given man unmistakable evidence of His love." —*The Desire of Ages,* 762; see also 24.

[167] *The Faith I Live By,* 114.

[168] See "Appendix K: Faith, The Word That Decides Everything." "It was in order that the heavenly universe might see the conditions of the covenant of redemption that Christ bore the penalty in behalf of the human race. The throne of Justice must be eternally and forever made secure, even tho [sic] the race be wiped out, and another creation populate the earth. By the sacrifice Christ was about to make, all doubts would be forever settled, and the human race would be saved if they would return to their allegiance. Christ alone could restore honor to God's government." —*Signs of the Times,* July 12, 1899.

[169] See 38–40.

terrible aspects of Calvary. The whole universe saw that "His death had answered the question whether the Father and the Son had sufficient love for man to exercise self-denial and a spirit of sacrifice. Satan had revealed his true character as a liar and a murderer."[170]

JESUS DID NOT SATISFY AN OFFENDED GOD

From another viewpoint, Jesus did not die to pay the penalty demanded by an offending God as men and women have believed for thousands of years. He lived and died to show how God related to human disobedience—which is the purpose of the gospel and of His defense in the Great Controversy: "By a life of perfect obedience to God's law, Christ redeemed man from the penalty of Adam's disgraceful fall. Man has violated God's law. Only for those who return to their allegiance to God, only for those who obey the law that they have violated, will the blood of Christ avail. ... Bearing the penalty of the law, He gives the sinner another chance."[171]

What about the charge that God was severe, exacting, and harsh? Jesus came "to remove this dark shadow by revealing to the world the infinite love of God. ... He went about doing good, and healing all who were oppressed by Satan. ... He exercised the greatest tact, and thoughtful, kind attention, in His intercourse[172] with the people. He was never rude, never needlessly spoke a severe word, never gave needless pain to a sensitive soul. He did not censure human weakness. ... He denounced hypocrisy, unbelief, and iniquity; but tears were in His voice as He uttered His scathing rebukes. ... His life was one of self-denial and thoughtful care for others. ... Such is the character of Christ as revealed in His life. This is the character of God."[173]

In the next chapter, we will see the importance of all this humiliation in the development of the Great Controversy.

---

[170] *Patriarchs and Prophets,* 70. "The victory gained at His death on Calvary broke forever the accusing power of Satan over the universe and silenced his charges that self-denial was impossible with God and therefore not essential in the human family." —*Selected Messages,* bk. 1, 34; "Unselfishness, the principle of God's kingdom, is the principle that Satan hates; its very existence he denies. From the beginning of the Great Controversy he has endeavored to prove God's principles of action to be selfish, and he deals in the same way with all who serve God. To disprove Satan's claim is the work of Christ and of all who bear His name. It was to give in His own life an illustration of unselfishness that Jesus came in the form of humanity. And all who accept this principle are to be workers together with Him in demonstrating it in practical life" —*Education,* 154.

[171] *SDABC,* vol. 6, 1092.

[172] Common word in the 19th Century for exchanging thoughts or feelings.

[173] *Steps to Christ,* 11, 12.

CHAPTER NINE:
JESUS IDENTIFIED WITH HUMAN BEINGS

Paul obviously had the facts straight regarding how human Jesus had become when He was a baby boy in Bethlehem. Paul used language that the average person could understand. When church members in Rome, Colosse, or Corinth read Paul's letters, no one needed a theologian or a Greek teacher to explain what he was writing. To the Romans, Jesus "was born of the seed of David, according to the flesh" (Romans 1:3). In fact, Jesus came in the "likeness [not the unlikeness] of sinful flesh, on account of sin" (Romans 8:3).[174]

To the Philippians, Paul focused on Christ's magnificent cascade of humility (another insight into the character of God) when He became a human being. The first 11 verses of the second chapter give us one of the most glorious sweeps of the plan of salvation. Plumbing their depths, along with similar passages elsewhere, brings forth tears of amazement as well as thankfulness. Where in human history has anyone ever given up so much

---

[174] C. E. B. Cranfield, *The International Critical Commentary, The Epistle to the Romans* (Edinburgh: T & T Clark Limited, 1975), 380–382. Cranfield rejects "the traditional solution" which asserts that Paul "introduced ὁμοίωμα [likeness] in order to avoid implying that the Son of God assumed *fallen* human nature, the sense being: like our fallen flesh, because really flesh, but only like, and not identical with it, because unfallen. This … is open to the general theological objection that it was not unfallen, but fallen, human nature which needed redeeming. … The word ὁμοίωμα does have its sense of "likeness;" but the intention is not in any way to call in question or to water down the reality of Christ's σὰρξ ἁμαρτίας but to draw attention to the fact that, while the Son of God truly assumed σὰρξ ἁμαρτίας He never became σὰρξ ἁμαρτίας and nothing more, nor even σὰρξ ἁμαρτίας indwelt by the Holy Spirit and nothing more (as a Christian might be described as being), but always Himself." Then Cranfield quotes Barrett approvingly who understands Paul as thinking that "Christ took precisely the same fallen nature that we ourselves have" and yet "remained sinless because he constantly overcame a proclivity to sin." … The difference between Christ's freedom from actual sin and our sinfulness is not a matter of the character of His human nature (of its being not quite the same as ours), but of what He did with His human nature. … We … understand Paul's thought to be that the Son of God assumed the selfsame fallen human nature that is ours, but that in His case that fallen human nature was never the whole of Him—He never ceased to be the eternal Son of God." H. C. G. Moule, in *The Epistle to the Romans*, 211, wrote that Jesus overcame "in our identical nature, under all those conditions of earthly life which for us are sin's vehicles and occasions, … making man's earthly conditions the scene of sin's defeat." Karl Barth wrote in his massive *Church Dogmatics*, vol. 1, pt. 2, under the section entitled "Very God and Very Man": "He is a man as we are, … equal to us in the state and condition into which our disobedience has brought us. … He was not a sinful man. But inwardly and outwardly His situation was that of a sinful man. … Freely He entered into solidarity and necessary association with our lost existence. Only in this way "could" God's revelation to us, our reconciliation with Him, manifestly become an event in Him and by Him. … But there must be no weakening or obscuring of the saving truth that the nature, which God assumed in Christ, is identical with our nature as we see it in the light of the Fall. If it were otherwise, how could Christ be really like us? What concern would we have with Him?"

for so many ungrateful people—all the while, knowing in advance that billions of human beings would reject Him!

Look at Jesus, equal with God—His divinity (Philippians 3:6). Observe Him as He "emptied himself, taking the form of a servant, being born in the likeness (ὁμοώματι) [that is, not the 'unlikeness'] of men" (verse 7)—His real humanity.

Watch Him grow up as any baby boy must, maturing into a servant-leader—humanity's Example. Contemplate Him on the cross—His sacrificial atonement and humanity's Savior. Turn your eyes to the future, to His glorious exaltation when "every knee" (verse 10) shall bow—still in His humanity, but forever the answer to all misapprehensions, false charges, and lies about the character of God. The big picture—it's all there in Paul's second chapter to the Philippians.[175]

In writing to the Hebrews, Paul emphasized Christ's divinity as well as His humanity in order to make clear that the Galilean Jesus was exactly what was needed to prove Satan wrong in the Great Controversy. We noted earlier that Jesus was "the express image of God" and since His ascension now sits on the "right hand of the Majesty on High" (Hebrews 1:3). In chapter 2, the apostle emphasized our Lord's humanity by stating categorically that Jesus "likewise shared in the same" humanity that all men and women have.[176] Paul went further: Jesus did not take unto himself the status of angels but took on himself "the seed (sperm—σπέρματος) of Abraham" (verse 16).

JESUS "RISKED" EVERYTHING

Paul answered the question, why Jesus risked "everything," knowing that He would "fight the battle as every child of humanity must fight it, at the risk of failure and eternal loss."[177]

Or to put it another way, why did Jesus have to be made like human beings "in all things" (Hebrews 2:17; "in every respect," RSV)? For two reasons: 1) so that He could face Satan as any other human being must face him, and to Satan's face, prove him a liar! He would "destroy [Gr. 'paralyze'] him who had the power of death, that is, the devil" (verse 14) and thus release "those who through fear of death were all their lifetime subject to

---

[175] See Herbert E. Douglass, *Rediscovering Joy* (Hagerstown, MD: Review and Herald Publishing Association, 1994), Chapter 5, "Knowing Why Jesus Became Human," 54–63.

[176] The "likewise" of Hebrews 2:14 can be compared with "likeness" of Romans 8:3 and Philippians 2:7.

[177] *The Desire of Ages*, 49. In a telling moment in the video, *Black Hawk Down*, during the tragic Battle of the Bakara Market in Mogadishu, Somalia, in October 1993, an Army Ranger Colonel is in charge of a small convoy of humvees trying to return to base amidst heavy gun and rocket fire. He stops the convoy, drags a dead driver out of his seat and barks at a bleeding sergeant standing in shock: "Get into that truck and drive." The sergeant replied, "But I'm shot, Colonel." Colonel's reply: "Everybody's shot, get in and drive." Jesus came down into the worst firefight in history. But He was no bystander. He too was shot, like everyone else. With that kind of experience, He surely knows how to encourage the rest of us—because we all have been shot!

bondage" (verse 15); 2) so that He might earn the right to become humanity's "merciful and faithful High Priest" (verse 17).[178]

In every sense of the word, He had to become like men and women "in every respect" (not merely "like them" in the sense he was not like a zebra or a dog), so that He could become our High Priest *because* "he was in all points tempted as we are, yet without sin" (Hebrews 4:15).

Paul's thundering logic is overwhelming! Only after becoming a human being "in every respect (yet without sin)," could Jesus have genuine empathy and compassion, not mere sympathy, when He became our High Priest "since he himself is also beset by weakness" (Hebrews 5:2).[179]

What kind of human experience did our Lord share with us? First of all, prayer was a necessity: "In the days of His flesh ... He had offered up prayers and supplications, with vehement cries and tears to Him who was able to save Him from death." Jesus did not have an easy life, somehow living above the common, normal struggles of all men and women. He needed the grace (inflowing power) of God to endure loneliness, bitter hostility and misunderstanding—as we all do. And His prayer life was not always sweet exchanges; prayers were wrenched from His mouth with "cries and tears" (verse 7).

JESUS LEARNED OBEDIENCE

Further, Jesus "learned obedience" (verse 8); He did not automatically, spontaneously, respond to all occasions, whether with men or face-to-face with Satan, with a heavenly built-in brain that could never fail, give in, or sin.

On the contrary, Jesus grew as any other child would develop. The powers of his mind and body "developed gradually, in keeping with the laws of childhood."[180] He "gained knowledge as we may do."[181] Day after day, He faced the same "risk of failure" as every child or adult must.[182] As today's teenagers would say, Jesus' life on earth was not a "slam-dunk."

---

[178] On Calvary, "Jesus was earning the right to become the advocate of men in the Father's presence." —*The Desire of Ages*, 745.

[179] "He put off His crown, and divested Himself of His royal robe, to take upon Him human nature, that humanity might touch humanity. As the world's Redeemer, He passed through all the experiences through which we must pass." —*Signs of the Times*, July 12, 1899.

[180] *Ibid.*, 68.

[181] *Ibid.*, 70.

[182] "Jesus accepted humanity when the race had been weakened by four thousand years of sin. Like every child of Adam He accepted the results of the working of the great law of heredity. What these results were is shown in the history of His earthly ancestors. He came with such a heredity to share our sorrows and temptations, and to give us the example of a sinless life. ... Yet into the world where Satan claimed dominion God permitted His Son to come, a helpless babe, subject to the weakness of humanity. He permitted Him to meet life's peril in common with every human soul, to fight the battle as every child of humanity must fight it, at the risk of failure and eternal loss." —*The Desire of Ages*, 49.

He "increased in wisdom and stature, and in favor with God and men" (Luke 2:52) as every other boy or girl could and should.

He taught us how to mature, to become "perfected" (Hebrews 5:9) so that Satan could find nothing in Him to throw up triumphantly before the universe (John 14:30) that even Jesus couldn't keep God's laws and still be joyful.[183] Jesus nailed Satan at every opportunity!

Everyone has the same road to walk as Jesus: "The positiveness and energy, the solidity and strength of character, manifested in Christ are to be developed in us, through the same discipline that He endured. And the grace that He received is for us."[184]

We have just read a remarkable promise—Jesus needed the grace of God to live the life of faith even as we do today. In fact, the grace of God provided daily *enabled* Jesus to live the life of faith. And the life of faith kept Jesus from sinning. Such is the description that will identify Christians in the end-time (Revelation 14:12).[185]

Philip Yancy saw it well: "When a light is brought into a room, what was a window becomes also a mirror reflecting back the contents of that room. In Jesus not only do we have a window to God, we also have a mirror of ourselves, a reflection of what God had in mind when he created this 'poor, bare, forked animal.' Human beings were, after all, created in the image of God; Jesus reveals what that image should look like. ... By enacting what we ought to be like, he showed who we were meant to be and how far we miss the mark."[186]

SUMMARY

"In every respect" (Hebrews 2:17) Jesus became the benchmark for what men and women are called to be. The divine grace that helped Jesus to become our benchmark is the same grace promised to all men and women of faith.

In the middle of an otherwise unremarkable and deserted road on the Kansas-Nebraska border in north central Kansas is located the surveyor's benchmark from which all property in Kansas, Nebraska, and parts of South Dakota, Wyoming, and Colorado are referenced. Soon after the passing of the Kansas-Nebraska Act in 1854, a survey was commissioned by the United

---

[183] "He had kept His father's commandments, and there was no sin in Him that Satan could use to his advantage. This is the condition in which those must be found who shall stand in the time of trouble. It is in this life that we are to separate sin from us, through faith in the atoning blood of Christ. ... It rests with us to co-operate with the agencies which Heaven employs in the work of conforming our characters to the divine model." —*The Great Controversy*, 623.

[184] *Ibid.*, 73.

[185] See "Appendix K: Faith, The Word That Decides Everything."

[186] Philip Yancey, *The Jesus I Never Knew* (Grand Rapids, MI: Zondervan Publishing House, 1995), 269, 270.

States government so that the lands newly opened for settlement could be properly and legally plotted out for the homesteaders.

Today, that original surveyor's benchmark—"Red Sandstone Marker"— can be seen under a manhole cover in the middle of that deserted road made by Charles Manners in 1856. In recent times, a brass surveyor's benchmark has been placed on that special stone.

Jesus became that model man, the Example that shut Satan's mouth. His life became the universe's Benchmark from which all created intelligences can be referenced. Of course, such an exposé of Satan's lies drove Satan to destroy Jesus. But in so doing, Jesus fulfilled His other reason for becoming a man—to pay the cost of man's salvation.

How did the Benchmark highlight God's side of the Great Controversy? Read on!

CHAPTER TEN:
JESUS REVEALED THE BEAUTY AND IMMUTABILITY OF GOD'S LAW

A s we noted earlier, "from the very beginning of the Great Controversy in heaven, it has been Satan's purpose to overthrow the law of God. ... To deceive men, and thus lead them to transgress God's law, is the object that he has steadfastly pursued. ... The last great conflict between truth and error is but the final struggle of the long-standing controversy concerning the law of God."[187]

Some ask, why? Why wasn't the Great Controversy over when Jesus died on the Cross? And why isn't the controversy over for persons who believe that Jesus indeed died on the cross for them? Why do we make such a big deal about the Ten Commandments, for example, if we believe that Jesus has already "paid the price" for our salvation? What is so fundamental about one's relation to the law of God that it will determine one's destiny? Doesn't that sound like legalism? Why do we say that a person's character determines our destiny,[188] if Jesus is our Substitute and that it's His character that God looks at, not mine? Or is there something wrong with the way these questions are asked?

Remember, Satan charged that God's law was unfair, too severe and arbitrary and restricted the freedom of intelligent beings.[189] After Adam and Eve sinned, Satan added more venom to his charge that God's law could not be obeyed and that it would be unfair for God to judge His creation by laws that could not be kept. How could God best answer these charges?

JESUS ANSWERED ALL SATAN'S CHARGES

We noted earlier that one of the reasons Jesus came to earth was to show Satan's accusations to be false and self-serving. Jesus said that He had "not come to destroy, but to fulfill" the law (Matthew 5:17); that is, "to fill up the measure of the law's requirements, to give an example of perfect conformity to the will of God. ... He was to show the spiritual nature of the law, to present its far-reaching principles, and to make plain its eternal obligation. ... By his own obedience to the law, Christ testified to its immutable character and proved that through His grace it could be perfectly obeyed by every son and daughter of Adam."[190]

In His Sermon on the Mount (Matthew 5–7),

---

[187] *The Great Controversy,* 582.
[188] "Character decides destiny." —*Christ's Object Lessons,* 74; see also 84, 123, 260, 269, 270, 271, 310, 356, 365, 378, 388.
[189] See 38-40
[190] *Thoughts From the Mount of Blessing,* 48, 49.

"Christ showed how far-reaching are the principles of the law spoken from Sinai. He made a living application of that law whose principles remain forever the great standard of righteousness—the standard by which all shall be judged in that great day when the judgment shall sit, and the books shall be opened. He came to fulfill all
righteousness, and, as the head of humanity, to show man that he
can do the same work, meeting every specification of the requirements of God. Through the measure of His grace furnished to the
human agent, not one need miss heaven. Perfection of character is
attainable by every one who strives for it. This is the very foundation
of the new covenant of the gospel. The law of Jehovah is the tree; the
gospel is the fragrant blossoms and fruit which it bears."[191]

Instead of the law being an arbitrary standard that called for mere external behavior, Christ's life on earth swept "away the exactions which had
encumbered the law of God, He showed that the law is a law of love." In living color, "He showed that in obedience to its principles is involved the happiness of mankind, and with it the stability, the very foundation and framework, of human society." In fact, instead of "arbitrary requirements," He
made clear that "God's law is given to men as a hedge, a shield." Instead of
static commands, "Christ came to demonstrate the value of the divine principles by revealing their power for the regeneration of humanity. He came
to teach how these principles are to be developed and applied."[192]

One of Satan's chief charges was that God's law of love was "a law of selfishness" and that "it is impossible for us to obey its precepts." He pointed to "the
fall of our first parents, with all the woe that has resulted" and charged all this
suffering on "God's" bungled universe, "leading men to look upon God as the
author of sin, and suffering, and death." Jesus came "to unveil this deception.
As one of us He was to give an example of obedience. … As the Son of man,
He gave us an example of obedience; as the Son of God, He gives us power to
obey."[193] Do those words make you melt as you think about that sentence?

After the fall of Adam and Eve, Satan had great hopes that he could make
his accusations against God stick. No doubt he thought he could; perhaps Satan
thought that a sobered and compliant Adam could negotiate a new arrangement
with an infinitely gracious God regarding the broken law! But "had the law of
God been changed in one precept since the expulsion of Satan from heaven,
[Satan] would have gained on earth after his fall that which he could not gain

[191] *Review and Herald,* April 5, 1898. "In no case did He come to lessen the obligation of men to be
perfectly obedient. He did not destroy the validity of the Old Testament Scriptures. He fulfilled
that which was predicted by God Himself. He came, not to set men free from the law, but to
open a way whereby they might obey that law and teach others to do the same."
—*Ibid.,* November 15, 1898.
[192] *Education,* 76, 77.
[193] *The Desire of Ages,* 24.

in heaven before his fall."[194] It was left for Jesus to step in and demonstrate that men and women, even in fallen, sinful flesh, can withstand every temptation from whatever the source, *even as He did* (Romans 8:3, 4; Revelation 3:21).

HOW JESUS GOT OUR ATTENTION AND OUR TRUST

In so many ways, it is obvious that "Christ's favorite theme was the paternal tenderness and abundant grace of God." He wrapped all other subjects, such as "the holiness of His character and His law," around this theme."[195] His parables of the Waiting Father, the Determined Housewife, the Persevering Shepherd (Luke 15), highlighted how God always reaches out to wayward men and women, even as He did toward the troubled angels before one-third fell for Satan's deceptions. God has always been reaching out in "paternal tenderness" to every human being, no matter how close or far from "home" he or she might be.

Paul never tired of singing God's praises as the Great Reconciler: "God was in Christ reconciling the world to Himself" (2 Corinthians 5:19). He did not wait for men and women to seek Him out; He has been seeking lost men and women even as He sought Adam and Eve when they hid in guilt among the beautiful Edenic shrubs.

In many ways, Bible writers emphasize that God's front door has never closed—He has kept it open for everyone: "He restored the whole race of men to favor with God."[196] He always has the light on and the way back home is not far—no further away than a whisper of "Please, Lord, hear me. I am a sinner who needs Your forgiveness and Your help." No sinner has to do something to make God a Forgiver—the Cosmic Lover by definition is a Forgiver. That is the good news that everyone has to hear, understand, and never forget.

GOD ALWAYS TAKES THE INITIATIVE

This simple fact about God taking the initiative has been very difficult for men and women to appreciate. Every pagan philosophy and religion builds on a god that must be appeased before "god" will look kindly on the anxious, fearful suppliant. Think of those religions that suggest that trips to various holy sites (such as Mecca, a Buddhist temple, or special steps in Rome) will make them right with God. Or if we say the right words in our prayers. Or, from another direction, philosophers and theologians have proposed a "god" that rules the universe, in some way, but does not get involved directly, personally, with human beings. Aristotle's "Unmoved Mover"[197] is just one example among many who have imagined gods who were the Original Idea or the Causal Source of the world, but none of these "gods" personally related to men and women.

---

[194] *Mind, Character, and Personality*, vol. 1, 248.

[195] *Christ's Object Lessons*, 40.

[196] *Selected Messages*, bk. 1, 343.

[197] Richard McKeon, editor, "Physics, bk. VIII, ch. 5, 6, *The Basic Works of Aristotle* (New York: Random House, 1941), 368–394.

However, our Creator God, with Jesus making all this clear, has loved sinners before they had a kind or grateful thought toward Him. Listen to Paul sing his favorite song: "But God demonstrates His own love toward us, in that while we were still sinners, Christ died for us. Much more than that, having now been justified by His blood, we shall be saved from wrath through Him. For if when we were enemies we were reconciled to God through the death of His Son, much more, having been reconciled, we shall be saved by His life. And not only that, but we also rejoice in God through our Lord Jesus Christ, through whom we have now received the reconciliation" (Romans 5:8–11). Some song!

LINCOLN'S EMANCIPATION PROCLAMATION

Ellen White makes a fascinating connection between President Lincoln's "Emancipation Proclamation" covering the Southern slaves and how Jesus "with His own blood ... has signed the emancipation papers of the [human] race."[198] Issued on September 22, 1862, the Proclamation became effective on January 1, 1863. The Southern slaves were free, all of them, without any action on their part. For many slaves, it was too much to be believed! They did not have to pay for freedom, they did not have to work for freedom—they only had to accept it, freely bestowed.

This kind of news—that our Lord's blood paid the price of everyone's freedom and gave "the world" (John 3:16) a peek into how much He loves all of us before we asked for His acceptance—most of this world still does not understand! Somehow, even faithful Christians have difficulty understanding that God reconciled the world [each one of us] unto Himself through Jesus— before any one of us made a move toward Him. Even as a genuine earthly parent never thinks about not forgiving wayward children, and never closes the front door, so God wants it known everywhere, in all lands, in every home, that He does not wait for His wayward children to "come" to Him before He opens heaven's front door! As the Waiting Father, He stands there, looking down the road, with the light of love beaming with forgiveness—that is the great Reality that can truly melt the hearts of wayward children. Paul said it well: "The goodness of God leads you to repentance" (Romans 2:4; 1 John 4:9).

Of course, we must not misunderstand what Paul and Ellen White are saying. They are not talking about universal salvation whereby everyone who has ever lived will someday, somehow, be redeemed. Nor are they saying that just because our Heavenly Father has the front door always open and has paid the "price" of justice in our behalf, that everyone is automatically a Christian. Even though our Lord signed our "emancipation papers" on the cross, even though Jesus "justifies [sets right] the ungodly" (Romans 4:5), there is something that "justified" sinners must yet do. They must respond with heart-felt appreciation, that wonderful New Testament

---

[198] *The Ministry of Healing*, 90.

response called "faith."[199] That marvelous response to the Father's embrace ushers the repentant sinner into the experience of "justification by faith" (Romans 3:22, 27, 28, 31; 4:5, 13, 16; 10: 9, 10; Galatians 3:7, 9, 22).

The emancipated slaves were legally free, but few knew about it on January 1, 1863. Somebody had to tell them the good news—and that took time for everyone to grasp the good news.

God's Emancipation Proclamation

To know that God truly loves me despite of the kind of person I am, that He reached out to me with His reconciling Hand before I reached up to Him—that is tremendous good news—the gospel! Paul wrote Timothy that Jesus "is the Savior of all men, especially of those who believe" (1 Timothy 4:10). What is Paul saying here? Just what He had been saying in his letter to the Romans—God has given to all men and women their emancipation papers—the good news that His front door is always open.

We need to be reminded—daily—that "while we were still sinners, Christ died for us [every man and woman]" (Romans 5:8), "reconciling the world to Himself, not imputing their trespasses to them" (2 Corinthians 5:19). The terrible fact here is that not everybody has heard this good news! Most men and women have never heard that God really has loved them this much! Most Christians have not yet understood just how glorious this good news is! Knowing Jesus as we do, we don't need to beg for forgiveness. Just accept it like any child would who really knows his or her loving father! Love and forgiveness are two sides of the same coin. That kind of knowledge about God draws us back to Him as we stumble through life, ever learning how to be a better son or daughter.

Your sins are not imputed to you. Believe it! You are a child of God whom He has never stopped loving, no matter where you are or what you have become! Believe me, when sinners, old and young, hear this good news instead of the cloudy message usually heard (that somehow God does not have a forgiving face unless sinners first make their pleas) a light is turned on in their head!

All this good news helps us to understand better our Lord's message in John 3 that seems as fresh today as it did to the ears of Nicodemus. In the Judgment, we are not condemned because we are sinners. That was cared for on the cross! We will be condemned because we did not believe and accept this good news! We will be condemned because "light has come into the world" and we "loved darkness rather than light, because [our] deeds were evil" (John 3:17–20). God can give us light but He cannot make us love it!

Not Condemned Because We Are Sinners

What more could Jesus have said to convey the way that God thinks about us! Accept the good news! The only way that anyone will be lost is to

---

[199] See "Appendix K: Faith, The One Word That Decides Everything"

"love darkness rather than light." The only way that I will be lost is to "resist this love … refuse to be drawn to Christ." But "if [I do not] resist, [I] will be drawn to Jesus … [and I will be led] to the foot of the cross in repentance."[200] Sinners will one day acknowledge: "We have destroyed ourselves by our determined rejection of His love."[201]

God has made it clear in so many ways that "He will accomplish this [salvation] for all who do not interpose a perverse will and thus frustrate His grace."[202] In fact, "God's love has made it hard for the heedless and head-strong to destroy themselves."[203] That is amazing! Even though it too often appears that self-indulgence is the easy way to go, that going with the flow is more profitable, Satan's temptations are always dead-ends, the price is too much. To put God's program into perspective: it is easier to be saved than to be lost, in spite of the warfare with the Evil One. How can that be? Simple: The grace of the Holy Spirit is far stronger than the wily temptations of the Evil One (Romans 8:31–39; Ephesians 4:17–5:10; Philippians 4:13).

Think of Christ's promise: "Take My yoke upon you and learn from Me … For My yoke is easy and My burden is light" (Matthew 11:29, 30). Think of Christ's warning to Paul on the Damascus Road: "I am Jesus, whom you are persecuting. It is hard for you to kick against the goads [a pointed rod to urge on an animal]" (Acts 9:5). Paul, it is harder to kick against the Holy Spirit goading your conscience than it is to cease resisting His power to help us in our temptations.

Paul wanted the Galatians to understand this good news: "I say then: Walk in the Spirit, and you shall not fulfill the lust of the flesh. For the flesh lusts against the Spirit, and the Spirit against the flesh; and these are contrary to one another, so that you do not do the things that you wish [that you lust for]" (5:16, 17). That's the promise: Walk with the Spirit and you will not do what would otherwise come naturally![204] In other words, with our consent the Holy Spirit is stronger than the promptings of our sinful thoughts and habits. That's good news!

---

[200] *Steps to Christ*, 27.

[201] *Ibid.*, 34.

[202] "Yet do not therefore conclude that the upward path is the hard and the downward road the easy way. All along the road that leads to death there are pains and penalties, there are sorrows and disappointments, there are warnings not to go on. God's love has made it hard for the heedless and headstrong to destroy themselves. It is true that Satan's path is made to appear attractive, but it is all a deception; in the way of evil there are bitter remorse and cankering care." —*Thoughts From the Mount of Blessing*, 76.

[203] *Ibid.*, 139.

[204] "'Walk in the Spirit, and ye shall not fulfil the lust' [or desire] 'of the flesh.' (verse 16). To prove, namely, that those who 'walk by the Spirit,' do not 'fulfil the lusts of the flesh,' he immediately adds, 'For the flesh listeth against the Spirit; and the Spirit listeth against the flesh, (for these are contrary to each other,) so that ye may not do the things which ye would.' So the words are literally translated: … not, 'So that ye cannot do the things that ye would;' as if the flesh overcame the Spirit; a translation which hath not only nothing to do with the original text of the Apostle, but likewise makes his whole argument nothing worth; yea, asserts just the reverse of what he is proving." —John Wesley, *The Works of John Wesley*, Third Edition (Kansas City, MO: Beacon Hill Press, 1978), vol. V, 88.

CHAPTER ELEVEN:
JESUS REVEALED THE CONSEQUENCES OF SIN

A nother central fact in God's salvation plan was that Jesus would also prove Satan to be a liar when he told Eve that "you shall not surely die" (Genesis 3:4). One of the ways that Satan gets around the obvious fact that death has been with us since Cain slew Abel is to promise that "death" as we know it is not the end—that is, "death is not the end, just the beginning, just a transition!"

Satan's lie to Eve "was the first sermon ever preached upon the immortality of the soul."[205] And this lie regarding the "immortal" soul has echoed throughout history, from the earliest pagan civilizations to weekly sermons on television or in thousands of pulpits the world over.[206]

But Jesus proved that God was telling the truth to Adam when He said that disobedience (sin) leads to death (Genesis 2:17). Paul reiterated that sober fact when he said that the "wages of sin is death" (Romans 6:23).

Now, how did Jesus go about proving God right and Satan a liar? In our Lord's conversation with Nicodemus, Jesus nailed down the broad outline of the good news: "For God so loved the world that He gave [not lent] His only begotten Son, that whoever believes [Lit: "has faith"] in Him should not perish [Lit: "commit spiritual suicide"] but have everlasting life" (John 3:16).

JESUS SATISFIED DIVINE JUSTICE
In becoming a human being, our Lord's life and death fully satisfied justice (which Satan had made a core issue in the Great Controversy when God offered "the gift of ... eternal life in Christ Jesus" (Romans 6:23). Christ's life proved that God was fair and just in the face of Satan's charges that God had made laws that were unfair and could not be kept.[207]

---

[205] *The Great Controversy,* 533.

[206] Think of the long list of ways that Satan has maneuvered men and women to believe that life flows on after what appears to be death. Ancient civilizations had their own ways of providing this false assurance, such as Egyptian embalming the dead, with nearby food to aid the departed on their way; or Norse boats in which the dead sailed into their future. Think of Catholicism's elaborate scheme of Limbo and Purgatory on the way to heaven. Add, of course, the many forms of spiritualism, which teach the close communication between the living and the dead. The typical Protestant funeral places the honored dead in heaven, watching over loved ones left behind. And on it goes.

[207] "By His life and His death, Christ proved that God's justice did not destroy His mercy, but that sin could be forgiven, and that the law is righteous, and can be perfectly obeyed. Satan's charges were refuted. God had given man unmistakable evidence of His love." —*The Desire of Ages,* 762. Here is made plain what it meant for Jesus to satisfy "justice."

How did Jesus do it? He became "sin for us" (2 Corinthians 5:21); that is, He took our place, that place where our sins would have led us if those sins could not be forgiven and overcome. That place, called the second death, is the only real death (Revelation 20:13–15). In other words, Jesus went to "that place" where all sinners would go in reaping the inevitable consequence of self-destructive sins. In other words, Jesus is the only Person in the universe *who has really died!* (Those now in their graves are, in biblical language, only sleeping (John 11:11–14; 1 Thessalonians 4:13–17).

Paul in more theological terms spelled out the eternal implications of the death of Jesus: "God offered him, so that by his sacrificial death he should become the means by which people's sins are forgiven through their faith in him. God did this in order to demonstrate that he is righteous. In the past he was patient and overlooked people's sins; but in the present time he deals with their sins, in order to demonstrate his righteousness. In this way God shows that he himself is righteous and that he puts right everyone who believes [has faith] in Jesus" (Romans 3:25–26, TEV). This is probably the Mt. Everest of Holy Scripture!

In Gethsemane and on the Cross, we may reverently observe what it means to die the sinner's death. In the Garden, Jesus felt what it means to be "separated from His Father. The gulf was so broad, so black, so deep, that His spirit shuddered before it. This agony He must not exert His divine power to escape. As man He must suffer the consequences of sin."[208]

On Calvary, our only hope was that He could endure "all the taunts and abuse that men could heap upon Him. The only hope of humanity was in this submission of Christ by all that He could endure from the hands and hearts of men."[209]

More, Satan's "fierce temptations wrung the heart of Jesus."[210]

And still more,

> "It was not the dread of death that weighed upon Him. It was not the pain and ignominy of the cross that caused His inexpressible agony. ... His suffering was from a sense of the malignity of sin, a knowledge that through familiarity with evil, man had become blinded to its enormity."[211]

But more yet,

> Now with the terrible weight of guilt He bears, He cannot see the Father's reconciling face. The withdrawal of the divine countenance ... pierced His heart with a sorrow that can never be fully understood

---

[208] *The Desire of Ages,* 686.
[209] *Ibid.,* 703.
[210] *Ibid.,* 753.
[211] *Ibid.,* 752, 753.

by man. ... Christ felt the anguish which the sinner will feel when mercy shall no longer plead for the guilty race."[212]

If one wants to get a picture of the agony of spirit that everyone will feel dying the second death, the final death, watch Jesus die! If one wants to measure the wages of sin, watch Jesus die! If one wants to measure the depth of love God has for His rebel children on Planet Earth, watch Jesus die![213]

WHAT MORE DID JESUS GIVE TO PLANET EARTH?

How long did Jesus remain a human being? Whatever else God "gave" to Planet Earth, it was the simple truth that Jesus became part of the human family forever. Forever, and forevermore, He would retain His human nature!

Jesus came to this world and took our human nature not for 33 years, "but to retain his nature in the heavenly courts, an everlasting pledge of the faithfulness of God."[214] Jesus truly "gave" Himself to Planet Earth.

God adopted human nature *forever!* That's why Paul could rejoice that Jesus has gone back to heaven to "become High Priest forever" (Hebrews 6:20). Forever He will be at the heart of the universe, visibly connecting the whole universe to this struggling rebel Planet Earth. He is vitally connected with the Great Controversy struggle going on in each of our lives today. He has been here and He knows exactly what we need to "overcome ... as [He] also overcame" (Revelation 3:21).

Jesus, forever at the heart of the universe, now and evermore, will be an eternal reminder of how much freedom costs, how much God was willing to risk in order to have a safe, secure universe. No one will ever question God's motives again. No one will ever wonder if God Himself practices self-denial or if He can be trusted. Just look at His hands! Those hands will tell us without further words how much He denied Himself, how much His love embraces, how far He went to rescue any one of the redeemed!

All this and more will remind us forever why:

> "The Saviour has bound Himself to humanity by a tie that is never to be broken. ... To assure us of His immutable counsel of peace, God gave His only-begotten Son to become one of the human family, forever to retain His human nature. ... God has adopted human

---

[212] *Ibid.*, 753.

[213] "Jesus, by the law of sympathetic love, bore our sins, took our punishment, and drank the cup of the wrath of God apportioned to the transgressor. ... He bore the cross of self-denial and self-sacrifice for us, that we might have life, eternal life. Will we bear the cross for Jesus?" —*Mind, Character, and Personality,* vol. 1, 248.

[214] *Selected Messages,* bk. 1, 258.

nature in the person of His Son, and has carried the same into the highest heaven."[215]

IMPRISONED WITH HIS OWN CREATION

Contemplate the thought. It staggers the mind. We can understand somewhat the marvel of our Lord's birth in Bethlehem when He imprisoned Himself within His own creation. But for the Lord of Creation, who walked among the stars and whirled new galaxies into their orbits, to be *forever* cabined within time and space—this stretches our minds across unlimited oceans of love. Something like a Great Inventor who created a machine that would solve all the energy and environmental problems of earth, but it would not work unless He got within it and never again would get out! Jesus locked Himself within human nature forever—just to save you and me!

This thought alone will hold us virtually speechless as long as bluebirds fly in the celestial skies of the New Earth.

I remember the first time, many years ago, when I saw that magnificent lady in New York Harbor. The reality surpasses the pictures I had seen. Since 1886, the Statue of Liberty, one of the most colossal sculptures in the history of the world, has greeted many millions of the oppressed and the venturesome that hopefully sought freedom and opportunity. Her torch, 305 feet (92.99 m) above the water, was the first glimpse of freedom that millions had seen; that light has stirred the battle-scarred hearts of millions of soldiers, sailors, marines, and coast guards as they returned from horrific wars.

Emma Lazarus captured the essence of what that Grand Lady has meant to all these millions; her words are now etched above the Statue of Liberty's main entrance. The last five lines have been etched also into the minds of most school children ever since:

"Give me your tired, your poor,
Your huddled masses yearning to breathe free,
The wretched refuse of your teeming shore,
Send these, the homeless, tempest-tost to me,
I lift my lamp beside the golden door!"

---

[215] *The Desire of Ages*, 25. "Christ thought it not robbery to be equal with God, and yet He pleased not Himself. He took upon Himself human nature for no other purpose than to place man on vantage ground before the world and the whole heavenly universe. He carries sanctified humanity to heaven, there always to retain humanity as it would have been if man had never violated God's law. The overcomers, who upon the earth were partakers of the divine nature, He makes kings and priests unto God."—Manuscript 156, Oct. 26, 1903, cited in *Upward Look*, 313; "As the Son of God He gives security to God in our behalf, and as the eternal Word, as one equal with the Father, He assures us of the Father's love to usward who believe His pledged word. When God would assure us of His immutable counsel of peace, He gives His only begotten Son to become one of the human family, forever to retain His human nature as a pledge that God will fulfill His word." —*Review and Herald*, April 3, 1894.

Every time I say these words, at the end of a sermon or quietly to myself, I think of Jesus as the forever Lamp welcoming each of us to walk through His golden door to forever. The same Jesus on Calvary's cross, who stretched out his arms long years ago, pleading for the "tired, your poor, your huddled masses yearning to breathe free," stands before us every day of our lives with the same message: "Send these, the homeless, tempest-tost to me."

Not only today and tomorrow, but every day throughout forever, we will see His Lamp reminding us of the cost of freedom as well as its blessings. Talk about a forever gift! But why did Jesus come to earth?

CHAPTER TWELVE:
WHY JESUS CAME TO EARTH
—A REVIEW

To adequately unfold all the reasons and blessings for which Jesus came to this earth would require another book. We are only highlighting a few of the reasons in these pages.[216]

- *To Tell the Truth About God.* Telling the truth about God is the highest purpose for Christ becoming a human being. Everything else in the Great Controversy, every other purpose for Jesus to become human, depends on how well Jesus fulfilled this job description. If men and women did not get a correct picture of God as revealed through Jesus, all attempts at explaining the gospel and the atonement would miss the truth by a million light years!

"The Father was revealed in Christ as altogether a different being from that which Satan had represented him to be. ... [T]he whole purpose of his own mission on earth,—to set men right through the revelation of God. In Christ was arrayed before men the paternal grace and the matchless perfections of the Father. ... When the object of his mission was attained—the revelation of God to the world—the Son of God announced that his work was accomplished, and that the character of the Father was made manifest to men."[217]

- *To Bear the Penalty for Our Sins.* Probably the first and most eloquent reason for which we thank Jesus for coming is that He died for you and me:

"Jesus came to bear the penalty of man's transgression, to uphold and vindicate the immutability of the law of God, and the rectitude of His government. He came to make an end of sin, and to bring in everlasting righteousness. He can lift sinners from their low estate, and in so doing magnify the law of Jehovah. These thoughts make me almost forget my pain."[218]

---

[216] See "Appendix I: Why Jesus Came."
[217] *Signs of the Times,* January 20, 1890.
[218] *Manuscript Releases,* vol. 8, 45.

- *To Show What Men and Women May Become.* One of the chief reasons Jesus "came to this world" was:

> "To show what every human being might become; what, through the indwelling of humanity by divinity, all who receive Him would become."[219] This is another way of saying that the purpose of the gospel is more than forgiving sinners—the gospel *restores* men and women to the original purpose for their creation.[220]

We have only a limited gospel, an inadequate understanding of why Jesus came to earth if we think that:

> "The forgiveness of sins is … the sole result of the death of Jesus. He made the infinite sacrifice, not only that sin might be removed, but that human nature might be restored, rebeautified, reconstructed from its ruins, and made fit for the presence of God."[221]

THE PITY OF A LIMITED GOSPEL

It seems a pity that most of the Christian world has bought into this limited gospel wherein grace is limited primarily to forgiveness—thus failing to see the full dimension of the New Testament gospel. Wherever we turn, from Matthew through the Revelation, we hear this emphasis:

> "The religion of Christ means more than the forgiveness of sin; it means taking away our sins, and filling the vacuum with the graces of the Holy Spirit. It means divine illumination, rejoicing in God. It means a heart emptied of self, and blessed with the abiding presence of Christ. When Christ reigns in the soul, there is purity, freedom from sin. The glory, the fullness, the completeness of the gospel plan is fulfilled in the life."[222]

When has language described "the completeness of the gospel plan" better than that? In simple words, Jesus is not only the Great Forgiver, He is our Great Restorer.[223]

---

[219] *Education*, 74.

[220] "He is the Restorer, and as you work under His supervision, you will see great results." —*Christ's Object Lessons*, 388. John 10:10; Ephesians 4:13; Philippians 1:9–11; Revelation 3:21.

[221] *Testimonies*, vol. 5, 537. "No human being has ever possessed so sensitive a nature as did the sinless, Holy One of God, who stood as head and representative of what humanity may become through the imparting of the divine nature." —*Mind, Character, and Personality*, vol. 1, 249.

[222] *Christ's Object Lessons*, 419, 420.

[223] "The central theme of the Bible, the theme about which every other in the whole book clusters, is the redemption plan, the restoration in the human soul of the image of God." —*Education*, 125.

- *To Become the Example for Every Man and Woman.* Peter said it well: "For to this you were called, because Christ also suffered for us, leaving us an example, that you should follow His steps: 'who committed no sin, nor was guile found in His mouth'" (1 Peter 2:21–22).

We are discussing one of the elliptical treasures of the plan of salvation. Jesus came not only to be our Substitute and Savior on one hand, but also to be our Healer and Example. In the ellipse of truth the two foci are needed to get the whole truth about a subject, even as hydrogen and oxygen are both needed to give us a glass of water.[224] That is why it would be impossible to imagine completely what this world would have deteriorated into

"If Jesus had not come down to our world to be man's Savior and Example. In the midst of a world's moral degradation, He stands a beautiful and spotless character, the one model for man's imitation. We must study, and copy, and follow the Lord Jesus Christ."[225]

Becoming man's Example not only shut Satan's accusing mouth regarding whether God's laws were fair or not, Christ's Example also shut the mouths of men and women who relentlessly look for ways to serve Him without obeying Him. His Example leaves us without excuse. Ellen White said it scores of times:

"The great teacher came into our world not only to atone for sin, but to be a teacher both by precept and example. He came to show man how to keep the law in humanity, so that man might have no excuse for following his own defective judgment. … His life was without sin. His lifelong obedience is a reproach to disobedient humanity."[226]

On one of the most significant pages of theological literature anywhere, we read "Jesus accepted humanity when the race had been weakened by four thousand years of sin. Like every child of Adam, He accepted the results of the working of the great law of heredity. What these results were is shown in the history of His earthly ancestors. He came with such a heredity to share our sorrows and temptations, and to give us the example of a sinless life."[227]

I have never read another theological writer who emphasized more clearly or more often the importance of accepting the biblical instruction

---

[224] See the "Appendix L: The Ellipse of Truth."
[225] *Signs of the Times*, December 22, 1887.
[226] *Selected Messages*, bk. 3, 135.
[227] *The Desire of Ages*, 49.

that Jesus came as all babies come into this world—carrying the genetic stream, the DNA, of His earthly ancestors.

This is why Ellen White could say, "The humanity of the Son of God is everything to us. It is the golden chain that binds our souls to Christ, and through Christ to God. This is to be our study. Christ was a real man."[228]

HIS HUMANITY IS EVERYTHING TO US

In fact, she said, "This subject demands far more contemplation than it receives." Why? Because "Christians strike too low. They are content with a superficial spiritual experience, and therefore they have only the glimmerings of light, when they might have far greater knowledge, when they might discern more clearly the wonderful perfection of Christ's humanity. ... Christ's life is a revelation of what fallen human beings may become through union and fellowship with the divine nature. The more deeply we study the life and character of our Redeemer, the more clearly shall we see the Father as He is, full of goodness and mercy, love and truth."[229] Can any words anywhere be clearer or more motivating?

From another direction, the importance of getting "the humanity of the Son" right was drilled into me some years ago when I read a study sponsored by the Lutheran Church, highlighting the direct relationship between a person's understanding of Jesus' humanity and that person's character profile. The research, costing $425,000 (in the middle 1970s) and covering more than two and one-half years of study, concluded that belief or misbelief is more than a mental exercise and that what a person believes theologically will affect his social attitudes. In other words, misbelief generates poor personalities and more.

The authors of the study declared that for Lutherans in the United States, "the divinity of Jesus is strongly emphasized while Jesus' human nature is underemphasized. ... Lutherans as a group ... reflect the ancient heresy of separating the two natures of Jesus Christ."

By comparing the respondents' answers to other questions with their concept of Jesus, it became clear that "those who most emphatically deemphasized the humanity of Jesus were the ones most resistant to change, more authoritarian, and more prejudiced in their attitude toward others. ... Those who recognize Christ's humanity, or view his two natures in balance, are generally more ready to take the initiative on church and public issues and to be more forgiving in their relationships with others."[230]

---

[228] *Ibid.,* bk. 1, 244.

[229] *Manuscript Releases,* vol. 18, 332.

[230] Merton P. Strommen, *et al, A Study of Generations* (Minneapolis: Augsburg Publishing House, 1972), 117, 289.

This conclusion should not surprise us. What is new is the voluminous research that supports their conclusions. It does make a difference as to what and how a person thinks about God in the person of Jesus Christ. The difference is not merely an academic argument. It affects character development and ultimately that person's fitness for heaven. No wonder Ellen White exclaimed that "the humanity of the Son of God is everything to us." Further, that His Example "left us a plain pattern which we are to copy. By His words He has educated us to obey God, and by His own practice He has shown us how we can obey God. This is the very work He wants every man to do, to obey God intelligently."[231]

Bible writers and Ellen White are clear, direct, and unambiguous about how seriously we should respond to the fact that Christ's Example is not some poetic ideal, nice to look at but unachievable, inspiring but an unrealistic goal. We could amass biblical counsel such as Paul's appeal to the Corinthians: "Come to your right mind, and sin no more" (1 Corinthians 15:34, RSV)! Or John's, "And everyone who has this hope [to be like Jesus] purifies himself, just as He is pure" (1 John 3:3). Or Peter's, "For to this you were called, because Christ also suffered for us, leaving us an example, that you should follow His steps: 'Who committed no sin, nor was guile found in His mouth.'" (1 Peter 2:21).

Ellen White emphasized hundreds of times that:

> "Christ came to bring divine power to unite with human effort, so that although we have been debased by perverted appetite, we may take courage, for we are prisoners of hope. ... Everyone that is in harmony with Christ will bear the Christ-like mold. ... He came to our world to show us how to live a pure, holy life, and I have purposed in my heart that He shall not have lived and died in vain for me."[232]

In plain language, she encouraged everyone to remember that "no one need be enslaved by Satan. Christ stands before us as our divine example, our all-powerful Helper."[233]

In a very interesting letter to Dr. J. H. Kellogg, Ellen White connected, as usual, our Lord's role as our Example with His own human-level face-off with Satan from His earliest years:

---

[231] Manuscript 1, 1892, reprinted in *Review and Herald*, June 17, 1976.

[232] *Signs of the Times*, August 4, 1890; "Christ came to teach us how to live. He has invited us to come to Him, to learn of Him to be meek and lowly of heart that we may find rest unto our souls. Because Jesus has lived our example, we have no excuse for not imitating His life and works. Those who profess His name and do not practice His precepts are weighed in the balances of heaven and found wanting." —*Ibid.*, July 18, 1892.

[233] Manuscript 76, 1903 in *SDABC*, vol. 6, 1074.

"Christ Jesus our Lord was a faultless character, a perfect example of heavenly grace and loveliness. From His birth to His death He gave us an example of what men and women must be, if they are accepted as His disciples, and hold the beginning of their confidence firm unto the end. In the first period of His human existence, He did not deviate from what every child should be educated to be. He preserved His honesty, truthfulness, and integrity. He was a specimen of heaven here on the earth—an example of what every child, every youth, may be in the family home, in the manifestation of tenderness. Through His experience, during the thirty-three years He spent on this earth, Christ was beset with all the temptations wherewith the human family are tempted; yet He was without a stain of sin."[234]

I know, that may sound too much, especially for teenagers. But let's examine what is really going on here. Teenagers should understand the truth about Jesus! He was totally involved in being a teenager. Teenagers should know that Jesus did not come to this earth as a "reverse astronaut." He did not come as a superhuman being from out of the blue merely to tell us that God is alive and well and that He loves His creation very much. Ah, much more!

We can send individuals to the moon, but they remain "earthmen." They must live with space suits that keep them untouched by the real world of the moon on which they land. They live and eat, perform normal acts common to earthmen, yet they are insulated from their new environment.

NOT A REVERSE ASTRONAUT

Jesus was no reverse astronaut. No protective space suit—either visible or invisible—separated Him from our world and His contemporaries. As we noted earlier,[235] Bible writers emphasize as clearly as language can that Jesus became man "in every respect" (Hebrews 1:17, RSV). If the human hereditary stream was broken between Mary and Jesus, the Bible fails to suggest it. And Ellen White emphatically denies it.[236]

Perhaps the primary reason for our many academic excursions that attempt to keep Jesus from coming too close to earth, from becoming too much like us, is that we think we need an excuse to save us from noonday clarity and responsibility: Jesus has shown us that Satan can be resisted,

---

[234] Letter 303, August 29, 1903.

[235] See 66–70.

[236] *The Desire of Ages*, 49. At the same time we must always remember that Jesus was not "exactly" like us in some respects. He never sinned. He never had to ask for forgiveness. Never dallied with sin except to resist it. And He also chose His own mother! But He was not "exempt" from inherited weaknesses, whether they were physical, mental, emotional or moral (See *Selected Messages*, bk. 1, 267, 268).

that sin is not a necessity! He has taken away our excuses! In fact, Jesus said bluntly: "If I had not come and spoken to them, they would have no sin, but now they have no excuse for their sin" (John 15:22).

The Bible and Ellen White could not be clearer in pointing out the goal of the gospel: not only forgiveness but also restorative power to resist and remove the guilt and power of sin: "Freely will He pardon all who come to Him for forgiveness and restoration."[237]

What does all this mean to us today? Is all this only poetic liberty, just a North Star to guide but never to be reached? How realistic are all these beautifully sounding words?

---

[237] *Ibid.*, 568. "The plan of redemption contemplates our complete recovery from the power of Satan." —*The Desire of Ages*, 311; "It was His [Christ's] mission to bring men complete restoration. He came to give them health and peace and perfection of character." —*The Ministry of Healing*, 17; "This sacrifice [Christ] was offered for the purpose of restoring man to his original perfection; yea, more. It was offered to give him an entire transformation of character, making him more than a conqueror. Those who in the strength of Christ overcome the great enemy of God and man will occupy a position in the heavenly courts above angels who have never fallen." —*General Conference Bulletin*, April 1, 1899; "The work of restoration can never be thorough unless the roots of evil are reached. Again and again the shoots have been clipped, while the root of bitterness has been left to spring up and defile many; but the very depth of the hidden evil must be reached, the moral senses must be judged, and judged again, in the light of the divine presence. The daily life will testify whether or not the work is genuine." —*The Youth's Instructor*, December 22, 1898.

CHAPTER THIRTEEN:
DID JESUS ASK TOO MUCH FROM HUMAN BEINGS?

How could God make it any clearer, from Genesis to Revelation, that He had the power available for men and women of faith to live joyfully obedient lives? That was implicit in the first gospel sermon in Eden (Genesis 3:15) and very clear in Revelation (2:11, 17, 26; 3:5, 12, 21; 14:12, 21:7; 22:14).

Paul was explicit: "Awake to righteousness, and do not sin; for some do not have the knowledge of God. I speak this to your shame" (1 Corinthians 15:34); "Let us come boldly to the throne of grace, that we may obtain mercy and find grace to help in time of need" (Hebrews 4:16). And Jude could sing: "Now to him who is able to keep you from stumbling and to present you faultless before the presence of His glory with exceeding joy, To God our Savior" (June 24, 25).

And Ellen White often echoed this biblical refrain: "As the Son of man, He gave us an example of obedience; as the Son of God, He gives us the power to obey."[238]

DIVINE POWER CONNECTS WITH NEEDY MEN AND WOMEN

John devoted three chapters (14–16) to God's special agent, the Holy Spirit, whereby men and woman can receive "power to help in time of need" (Hebrews 4:16). Different English versions call him Helper (John 14:26, NKJV, TEV), Counselor (RSV), and Comforter (KJV).

Ellen White has expressed some of the most powerful comments regarding the role of the Holy Spirit in the lives of men and women of faith. The connection between the job description of the Holy Spirit and that of Jesus in the plan of salvation is truly awesome. It is, however, perhaps the least understood aspect of the gospel! It is at the core of many denominational differences.

Note Ellen White's clarity:

> "The Spirit was to be given as a regenerating agent, and without this the sacrifice of Christ would have been of no avail. The power of evil had been strengthening for centuries, and the submission of men to this satanic captivity was amazing. Sin could be resisted and overcome only through the mighty agency of the Third Person of the Godhead, who would come with no modified energy, but in the fullness of divine power. It is the Spirit that makes effectual what has

---

[238] *The Desire of Ages*, 24.

been wrought out by the world's Redeemer. It is by the Spirit that the heart is made pure. Through the Spirit the believer becomes a partaker of the divine nature. Christ has given His Spirit as a divine power to overcome all hereditary and cultivated tendencies to evil, and to impress His own character upon His church."[239]

That was an amazing paragraph! It turns much conventional theology on its head!

The gift of the Holy Spirit provides for us everything we need. He is "another Helper" [another, just like Jesus] (John 14:16), the "Spirit of Truth" (John 14:17), our "Teacher" (14:26), our Sin Detector (16:9), and Glorifier of Jesus (16:14).

Paul echoes our Lord's job description of the Holy Spirit when he wrote Titus: "According to His mercy He saved us, through the washing of regeneration and renewing of the Holy Spirit" (3:5). The Cross and the Holy Spirit are inseparable in the ellipse of salvation.

OUR REGENERATING AGENT

The Spirit's role as our "regenerating agent" needs to be emphasized, not only in our theological discussions, but also in our own lives, hour by hour. Note these powerful words:

> "The Holy Spirit was promised to be with those who were wrestling for victory … endowing the human agent with supernatural powers, and instructing the ignorant in the mysteries of the kingdom of God. That the Holy Spirit is to be the grand helper is a wonderful promise. Of what avail would it have been to us that the only begotten Son of God had humbled Himself, endured the temptations of the wily foe, and wrestled with him during His entire life on earth, and died the Just for the unjust, that humanity might not perish, if the Spirit had not been given as a constant, working, regenerating agent to make effectual in our cases what had been wrought out by the world's Redeemer?"[240]

The more we learn about God's plan to "save His people from their sins" (Matthew 1:21), the more we are overwhelmed with His thoughtfulness! What is there that God overlooked? Everything that we need to be "overcomers" and to avoid embarrassing His Name is laid out before us; so simple that a child can grasp it (and they do) and so profound that the most advanced theologian is awed and humbled.

It seems the Lord is never finished with giving us whatever is necessary so that we can live with Him forever! He keeps giving, giving, giving …

---

[239] *Ibid.*, 671.
[240] *Selected Messages*, bk. 3, 137.

CHAPTER FOURTEEN:
HOW JESUS AS HIGH PRIEST RELATES TO THE GREAT CONTROVERSY

I s it not strange that our Lord's current work as High Priest, so often referred to in the Book of Hebrews, is one of the least discussed topics in systematic theologies today, never mind in Christian pulpits? Nothing pleases Satan more!

The last time men and women saw Jesus on earth was on Mount Olivet when they watched, speechless, as "He was lifted up, and a cloud took Him out of their sight" (Acts 1:9). Was He gone forever? Where did He go?

Jesus, the Carpenter of Nazareth, the Friend of the multitudes, the gracious Healer, *is now in heaven,* not as a disembodied spirit, not with the "form of God" that was His before He came to this earth (Philippians 2:6), but as a man, retaining His human nature forever.

As such Stephen recognized Him in heaven. God graciously parted the veil between heaven and earth moments before Stephen was killed under the stones hurled by men who couldn't stand the truth. "But he, being full of the Holy Spirit, gazed into heaven and saw the glory of God, and Jesus standing at the right hand of God, and said, 'Look! I see the heavens opened, and the Son of Man standing at the right hand of God'" (Acts 7:55, 56)!

Paul heard His voice that fateful day on the Damascus road. In the midst of Paul's spiritual banditry, Jesus stepped into his life with the breathtaking question: "'Saul, Saul, why are you persecuting Me?' And he said, 'Who are You, Lord?' And the Lord said, 'I am Jesus, whom you are persecuting'" (Acts 9:4, 5).

John was given an awesome glimpse of his Master while he was exiled on rocky Patmos. Wasn't that a gracious gesture on our Lord's part—to give His old friend, who had witnessed gloriously to His cause, the final assurance that all was not in vain! "When I saw Him, I fell at His feet as dead. But He laid His right hand on me, saying to me, 'Do not be afraid; I am the First and the Last. I am He who lives, and was dead, and behold, I am alive forevermore. Amen. And I have the keys of Hades and of Death'" (Revelation 1:17).

LOSING SIGHT OF WHERE JESUS IS NOW

But as time went on something very curious and sad happened to the Christian church. They lost sight of where Jesus is *now* and what He is *now* doing on our behalf. Over the centuries, many in the church fixed their attention on Him dying on the cross—the personification of human tragedy. Many exalted Jesus as the greatest teacher this planet has ever seen, honored Him for untainted integrity in full blossom, and revered Him for the moral impulse He injected into human history. They are moved by the utter abandonment to His ideals that drove Him to the cross rather than flinch or concede to evil. But that is where they last see Him—on the cross.

Other Christians went further; they fixed their attention on Jesus as the resurrected Savior. They saw Him mingle with His followers for 40 days and then marvelously ascend to heaven. But somehow they lost Him in the vagueness of light-years and theological jargon regarding the atonement. Although they know that He is in heaven "at the right hand of God" they have no clear-cut understanding of Christ's continuing role in working out the plan of salvation.

Even those who believe Jesus is their resurrected Lord often believe that His role as our Savior is limited to the Cross; they see Jesus only in part. Of course, the Cross is awesomely appealing and winsome as a beautiful demonstration of love unlimited—God paying the price for a fallen race, and rising triumphantly from the grave—a dual manifestation of love and power.

Still, it remains only a partial picture of our Lord's ministry. A partial picture of Jesus leads to important misunderstandings that have split the Christian church, such as (1) believing that His love is irresistible and that someday in God's good time all men and women (wherever they are in their departed state) will be won back to a reunited kingdom of grace and love. Or (2) that simple gratefulness in believing that Jesus died for everyone's sin is in itself the test of a person's fitness to be saved.

BEING HIGH PRIEST DOES NOT DEPRECIATE THE CROSS.

Seventh-day Adventists believe that there is more to our Lord's role in the plan of salvation than to see Him only on the Cross. Or even as our resurrected Lord. They follow Jesus into the heavenly sanctuary; they fix their eyes on Him, the Great High Priest of the human family, the living hope of everyone who seeks pardon and victory over the forces of sin.

Throughout the Book of Hebrews, Paul sings the glorious song of our Lord's continuing ministry for fallen men and women. For example: "Seeing then that we have a great High Priest who has passed through the heavens, Jesus, the Son of God, let us hold fast our confession" (Hebrews 4:14).

Paul declares that a clear understanding of Jesus as our High Priest is "an anchor of the soul, both sure and steadfast, and which enters the Presence behind the veil, where the forerunner has entered for us, even Jesus, having become High Priest forever" (Hebrews 6:19, 20). He proclaimed that

Christians can boldly "enter the Holiest [Lit: 'holy places'] by the blood of Jesus, by a new and living way which He consecrated for us, through the veil, that is, His flesh, and having a High Priest over the house of God, let us draw near with a true heart in full assurance of faith, … Let us hold fast the confession of our hope without wavering, for He who promised is faithful" (Hebrews 10:19–23).

Something very significant to the plan of salvation is going on in heaven today because Jesus is our High Priest. Something very significant and special should be going on in the lives of His followers on earth because of Jesus' role as our High Priest.

Following Jesus into the heavenly sanctuary does not depreciate the cross. Hardly! Without the cross there would have been no High Priest in the heavenly sanctuary today. But what Jesus is now doing is probably the most important subject to be understood by those on Planet Earth.

Ellen White focuses on the importance of Jesus as our High Priest: "The intercession of Christ in man's behalf in the sanctuary above is as essential to the plan of salvation as was His death upon the cross. By His death He began that work which after His resurrection He ascended to complete in heaven."[241] That is an unambiguous statement: *What Jesus is doing now is as essential to the plan of salvation as was His death on the Cross!*

To help us get the point, Mrs. White further wrote: "God's people are now to have their eyes fixed on the heavenly sanctuary, where the final ministration of our great High Priest in the work of the judgment is going forward—where He is interceding for His people."[242]

Easily we can understand why Paul urged his readers:

> "Seeing then that we have a great High Priest who has passed through the heavens, Jesus the Son of God, let us hold fast our confession. For we do not have a High Priest who cannot sympathize with our weaknesses, but was in all points tempted as we are, yet without sin. Let us therefore come boldly to the throne of grace, that we may obtain mercy and find grace to help in time of need" (Hebrews 4:14–16).

So what is so distinctive about the sanctuary doctrine, our understanding of what Jesus is now doing in heaven today? Why is this understanding unique in the theological world? Especially when Ellen White wrote: "The correct understanding of the ministration in the heavenly sanctuary is the foundation of our faith."[243]

---

[241] *The Great Controversy,* 489.
[242] *Evangelism,* 223.
[243] *Ibid.,* 221.

THE CENTER OF GRAVITY OF THE PLAN OF SALVATION

From the standpoint of the Great Controversy Theme, the sanctuary doctrine is the center of gravity for the plan of salvation, the hub of the theological wheel, which explains and connects all the biblical truths that Christians hold dear, especially those truths that have been overlooked for centuries. Ellen White pointed out that the sanctuary doctrine "opened to view a complete system of truth, connected and harmonious, showing that God's hand had directed the great Advent Movement, and revealing present duty as it brought to light the position and work of His people."[244]

But we are interested in more than an academic understanding of what Jesus is now doing. It has much to do with the quality of our own relationship with Him. Listen to this heads-up:

> "The subject of the sanctuary and the Investigative Judgment should be clearly understood by the people of God. All need a knowledge for themselves of the position and work of their great High Priest. Otherwise, it will be impossible for them to exercise the faith which is essential at this time, or to occupy the position which God designs them to fill."[245]

This is another paragraph that should be read more than once!

Why is understanding the sanctuary doctrine so important? "The sanctuary in heaven is the very center of Christ's work in behalf of men. It concerns every soul living upon the earth. It opens to view the plan of redemption, bringing us down to the very close of time, and revealing the triumphant issue of the contest between righteousness and sin."[246]

How does Satan do his best to confuse the minds of people about the sanctuary doctrine? All Christians should have their guard up: "The work in the heavenly sanctuary becomes obscure to the minds of those who are controlled by the temptations of the evil one, and they engage in side issues to gratify their own selfish purposes, and their true moral standing is determined by their works. ... It is Satan's studied effort to

---

[244] *The Great Controversy,* 423.

[245] *Ibid.,* 488. "The intercession of Christ in man's behalf in the sanctuary above is as essential to the plan of salvation as was His death upon the cross. By His death He began that work which after His resurrection He ascended to complete in heaven." *Ibid.,* 489.

[246] *Ibid.* "We are in the day of atonement, and we are to work in harmony with Christ's work of cleansing the sanctuary from the sins of the people. Let no man who desires to be found with the wedding garment on, resist our Lord in His office work. As He is, so will His followers be in this world. We must now set forth before the people the work, which by faith we see our great High Priest accomplishing in the heavenly sanctuary. Those who do not sympathize with Jesus in His work in the heavenly courts, who do not cleanse the soul temple of every defilement, but who engage in some enterprise not in harmony with this work, are joining with the enemy of God and man in leading minds away from the truth and work for this time." —*Review and Herald,* January 21, 1890.

make of none effect saving, testing truth through the lives of those who preach the truth to others and who in their daily practices deny what they preach."[247]

When we are told that "the subject of the sanctuary and the Investigative Judgment should be clearly understood," this knowledge is to be more than a textbook understanding. It could involve the destiny of our souls.[248]

"So," we ask, "why is Ellen White so emphatic? What is there about the sanctuary doctrine that is so fundamental to a correct understanding of the message and mission of the Seventh-day Adventist Church? Furthermore, why is there such silence in the Christian church generally, and Adventist pulpits in particular, regarding the sanctuary truths? Why a strange boredom among so many regarding what Jesus is now doing if these sanctuary truths are so vital to the spiritual health of each church member, especially since 1844?"

The answer is simple: Satan does not want the towering truths about Jesus, which are embodied in the sanctuary doctrine, to be understood. He doesn't mind if church members pay their tithe, recognize the Sabbath as God's holy day, and build larger schools and hospitals. He is not too troubled if church members pray daily for Jesus to forgive their sins and for Him to return soon to this earth. After all, people who did similarly once crucified Jesus!

SATAN HATES TWO GREAT TRUTHS ABOUT JESUS

But Satan knows what matters most. He hates "the great truths that bring to view an atoning sacrifice and an all-atoning sacrifice and an all-powerful mediator. He knows that with him everything depends on his diverting minds from Jesus and His truth."[249]

So where does he direct his attack? "Satan invents unnumbered schemes to occupy our minds, that they may not dwell upon the very work with which we ought to be best acquainted."[250] In other words, if Satan can cause confusion or boredom with two central truths in the Great Controversy Theme, he cares not how much else we may know or do. These central truths are (1) Christ's "atoning sacrifice" and (2) Christ as our "all-powerful Mediator."

POWER OF THE ELLIPSE OF TRUTH

Here we see again the power of the ellipse of truth.[251] When we separate each focus in the ellipse (making two circles instead of one ellipse), each

---

[247] Ibid.
[248] Ibid.
[249] Ibid.
[250] Ibid.
[251] See "Appendix L: The Ellipse of Truth."

truth slips into mere theology that can be argued over as to which circle is more important. In this separation, we lose the power that God intended in the sanctuary service. Together (even as hydrogen and oxygen *together* produce water and *separately*, nothing close to water) "atoning Sacrifice" and "all-powerful Mediator" link indissolubly what Jesus has done *for us* and what He wants to do *in us*.

What I want to note here is that our Lord's twofold job description as our High Priest is aimed at Satan's loudest charges. The sanctuary service was the Israelite's desert sandbox in which God depicted His counterattack against the Great Deceiver. Let's now review how the sandbox story still reveals God's masterstrokes for us today.

A major and perennial problem of Christianity through the centuries is that men and women tend to focus on what Jesus (Savior) has done for us and rarely on what He wants to do in and through us as our High Priest through His Holy Spirit. When His atoning sacrifice (what Jesus has done *for us* on the Cross) is primarily featured, too often the record shows that the work of the Holy Spirit is muted, leading often to a cold, rigid, doctrine-oriented religion. For many prominent churches, faith thus becomes more of a list of doctrines to be believed, and the motivation to be doctrinally correct usually transcends or mutes the call for character transformation.

The historical record also shows that a reaction to this one-sided overemphasis (one side of the ellipse of truth) inevitably develops. Realizing Christianity should be relevant and reasonable, with a sense that it should be personally meaningful, we have Pietists, Quakers, and charismatic movements offering personal meaning and feeling that their truth is "for them." The history of the Christian church can be viewed as a seesaw of these contrasting religious movements.[252]

And we surely see this standoff today. It is easy to recognize the churches that represent either side of our Lord's role (either Sacrifice or High Priest connecting with the Holy Spirit). Many churches through the years have reacted against the over-intellectualized religion of those who focus primarily on what Jesus did for *us* on the cross. This primary emphasis does not fill the void in those who sense that faith should have personal meaning, that Jesus should make a difference in their lives. They reach out for religion either with confidence in their reason or in their feelings. Those who

---

[252] Historical theologians generally discuss this historical oscillation in terms of transcendence and immanence. See Emil Brunner, *Truth as Encounter* (Philadelphia: The Westminster Press, 1943, 1964); John Macquarrie, *Twentieth-Century Religious Thought* (New York: Harper & Row, Publishers, 1963); Stanley J. Grenz & Roger E. Olson, *20th Century Theology* (Downers Grove, IL: InterVarsity Press, 1992); David L. Smith, *A Handbook of Contemporary Theology* (Wheaton, IL: Victor Books, 1992).

emphasize "feeling" often focus on their understanding of the gifts of the Holy Spirit.

But—when one focuses primarily on what Christ does *in us,* the governing authority of the Bible is often muted. Faith now becomes more a matter of feeling and a reflection of a person's religious experience rather than an obedient response to God and His expressed will. We note the excesses of what some understand to be the evidence of truth—manifestations of what they claim are the "gifts" of the Spirit.

THE ELLIPSE OF TRUTH UNITES AGE-OLD DIVISIONS

How is this historic, age-old standoff solved? By putting back together what Satan has often divided. Instead of two fighting circles of partial truths, the sanctuary doctrine unites the core values of each: It joins what Jesus has done *for us* as our "atoning Sacrifice" with what He wants to do *in us* and *through us* as our "all-powerful Mediator."[253] Only the ellipse of truth can make clear what Jesus is now doing as our High Priest.[254] The sanctuary doctrine when properly understood brings together the twin truths why Jesus became man and serves as our High Priest.

What Satan fears most is that some generation will take God seriously and listen to Him tell us why Jesus is our High Priest! Satan fears that some generation will take God at His word and cooperate with Him in working out His will *in us* and *for us.* Satan fears that some generation will join their concern for commandment keeping with the "faith of Jesus" (Revelation 14:12). Satan fears that those who sincerely desire the "faith of Jesus" will also develop the character of Jesus. Satan fears that those who develop the character of Jesus through faith in God's abiding power will prove him wrong before the observing universe. And prove God right in the Great Controversy!

Satan fears that these glorious possibilities will be uncovered when men and women study the sanctuary doctrine. Therefore, he will try all kinds of distractions to divert our minds from that ellipse of truth: as Sacrifice He provided the basis for our salvation and made pardon possible; as High Priest He supplies the power to meet the conditions of salvation. Pardon and power—"the double cure."[255]

As we have seen, the Christian church has more generally understood our Lord's sacrificial atonement rather than His High Priestly role. In fact, the fuller understanding of our Lord's work as mediator (1 Timothy 2:5) is

---

[253] *The Great Controversy,* 488.

[254] "Our only ground of hope is in the righteousness of Christ imputed to us, and in that wrought by His Spirit working in and through us." —*Steps to Christ,* 63.

[255] *Education,* 36. See first stanza, "Rock of Ages," Augustus M. Toplady.

a unique theological position of the Seventh-day Adventist church (not that we created it—we only recovered it in its biblical beauty), especially in view of our emphasis on the pre-Advent judgment as the closing phase of His High Priestly ministry.[256]

HIGH PRIEST ROLE AS ESSENTIAL AS SACRIFICE ON THE CROSS

Clearly, we must keep in mind that "the intercession of Christ in man's behalf in the sanctuary above is as essential to the plan of salvation as was His death upon the cross."[257] Thus, we must consider further His role as our High Priest, the most misunderstood part of His role as the One whose primary task is to tell the truth about God and about how He plans to restore rebels into men and women "safe to save."[258]

His intercessory role as our High Priest is divided into two time segments: the first, extending from His ascension to 1844; the second, from 1844 until His return. Throughout both segments He continues to apply "the benefits of His mediation."[259] In His second segment, He is finishing the "last acts of His ministration in behalf of man—to perform the work of Investigative Judgment and to make an atonement for all who are shown to be entitled to its benefits."[260]

So two questions: What are the benefits that He has been applying since His ascension by virtue of His sacrificial atonement? And what are Christ's "last acts of His ministration" involving the work of pre-advent judgment?

FIRST ROLE AS OUR HIGH PRIEST

Since His ascension, Jesus has been fulfilling two specific roles as High Priest. In His first role, He silences the accusations of Satan "with arguments founded not upon our merits, but on His own."[261] His perfect life of

---

[256] "At-one-ment is an expression of the divine intention to destroy sin that ruptured the universe. Restoration to oneness was not consummated at the cross. The sin problem has not yet been finally resolved. The cross is the supreme act of God for man's redemption. But that is only one aspect of Christ's work toward the final at-one-ment. Reconciliation is effected by the living Christ. It is not something that happened two thousand years ago. At-one-ment is experienced only as men daily live a life of trust and dependence on Him. ... It may be that the failure to grasp the whole work of our Lord, both on the cross and from the heavenly sanctuary, leaves man with less than a complete knowledge of all the truth the Bible reveals as to the full meaning of the atonement. ... Both the triumph at the cross and the work of Christ as priest in heaven are the hope and pledge of final renewal and at-one-ment." —Edward Heppenstall, *Our High Priest* (Washington, DC: Review and Herald Publishing Association, 1972), 29, 31.

[257] *The Great Controversy,* 489.

[258] "Those who refuse to cooperate with God on earth, would not cooperate with Him in heaven. It would not be safe to take them to heaven." —*Christ's Object Lessons,* 280. "Then the Lord can trust them to be of the number who shall compose the family of heaven." —*Ibid.,* 15.

[259] *The Great Controversy,* 430.

[260] *Ibid.,* 480.

[261] *Testimonies,* vol. 5, 472.

obedience (in the same human situation that every person has been born with since Adam and Eve[262]), sealed by a death that wrung the heart of God exposed the awfulness and the terrible consequence, of sin.[263] This public expression of the unlimited love and grace of God became the basis of reconciliation and atonement between God and man. He not only *earned* the right to forgive sinners,[264] He had shut Satan's mouth regarding the fairness, justice, and utter self-denying love of God. Our Lord's life and death satisfied any question in anyone's mind, among angels or unfallen worlds, as to whether God was fair and just in dealing with sin.

In His first role as our High Priest, His perfect life and death are constantly "interceding" for us as our "atoning Sacrifice." In sanctuary language, His shed blood cares for "every offense and every shortcoming of the sinner."[265] His shed blood is God's own answer to the charge that God was not just. Every man or woman or child should know that Christ's blood intercedes when anyone anywhere would charge that it is not fair that sinners should be so completely pardoned. Somebody else, not the sinner, has paid the cost of proving God right, that sin does bring forth death and complete separation from God. And that Somebody also paid the cost of proving that God was fair in asking for obedience and love as the only way to secure the future of the universe. That is so much intercession, one cannot properly put it into words.[266] All I can say is that He did it for me. And for you.

Seen in the light of the Great Controversy, the entire sanctuary service of the Old Testament previews how Jesus would be the Ultimate Sacrifice and Ultimate High Priest.[267] In Old Testament sanctuary language, Jesus, the Lamb of God, is represented by the slain lamb (Exodus 29; John 1:29; 1 Peter 1:19; Revelation 14:4, 17:14, etc). He is also represented by Aaron and other High Priests. The daily sacrifice and the Day of Atonement sacrifice typified the two phases of Christ's double role as Sacrifice and High Priest.

---

[262] See 66–70.

[263] See 77–81.

[264] *Ibid.*

[265] *Selected Messages*, bk. 1, 344.

[266] C .S. Lewis responds to those who have difficulty "understanding" various theories as to why Jesus had to die: "You may ask what good it will be to us if we do not understand it. But that is easily answered. A man can eat his dinner without understanding exactly how food nourishes him. A man can accept what Christ has done without knowing how it works; indeed, he certainly would not know how it works until he has accepted it." —*Mere Christianity,* 55.

[267] Heppenstall, *op. cit.,* 19—"In the heavenly sanctuary all is vital, dynamic, genuine, and concerned with eternal issues. The sanctuary truth treats Satan as the real enemy, the forces of evil as real, in conflict with Christ in a war that affects every creature in the universe. Here alone the destinies of men are decided for weal or for woe. Here the realities of God's truth and purpose can be clearly seen."

When Satan says that sinful men and women do not deserve forgiveness, that they are not entitled to eternal life anymore than he is, that God has asked too much from His created beings and is therefore unreasonable—in the Old Testament, the faithful Israelites looked to the Sanctuary in the midst of the camp and got the message. Since the Ascension, we can look at Jesus standing up in full view of watching worlds and angels—good and bad—the eternal answer to all these questions.

SECOND ROLE AS OUR HIGH PRIEST

What do angels and others see? They see a man, a Jewish carpenter, who had once faced Satan on his home court, who "had to be like his brethren in every respect, so that he might become a merciful and faithful high priest" (Hebrews 2:17, RSV). They see a man who conquered every temptation to serve Himself, proving that all men and women, with the same power available to them that He had, can live a victorious life in the face of evil. Our Lord's 33 years of perfect obedience to God's will, fighting "the battle as every child of humanity must fight it,"[268] silences every one of Satan's accusations. He stands up at the center of the universe as Man's Advocate (1 John 2:1) and as God's Express Image (Hebrews 1:3). And Satan knows that the Seed is bruising his head (Genesis 3:15)—that he has not much time left to do whatever he must do to save the world for himself (Revelation 12:12)

But now in His second role as my Intercessor, He is our "all-powerful Mediator."[269] Because He had earned the right to be our High Priest,[270] He now could freely provide the "grace to help in time of need" (Hebrews 4:16) to all who choose to live overcoming lives.

Ellen White said it succinctly: "He is the High Priest of the church, and He has a work to do which no other can perform. By His grace He is able to keep every man from transgression."[271] What more could anyone ask for—pardon and power, exactly what we all need, day after day!

As our "all-powerful Mediator," His powerful arm of grace reaches out to everyone who has committed the keeping of his or her soul to Him. He has won the right to intercede in the lives of His followers. He breaks through the power with which Satan has held them captive, developing within His faithful followers a strengthened will to resist sinful habits and tendencies. It is the same defense system by which He Himself conquered sin.[272]

---

[268] *The Desire of Ages*, 49.
[269] *The Great Controversy*, 488.
[270] *The Desire of Ages*, 745.
[271] *Signs of the Times*, Feb. 14, 1900.
[272] See 69.

Kept By His Daily Intercession

This kind of intercession men and women need daily, hourly, until Jesus returns. Note this powerful promise:

> "Everyone who will break from the slavery and service of Satan, and will stand under the blood-stained banner of Prince Immanuel will be kept by Christ's intercessions. Christ, as our Mediator, at the right hand of the Father, ever keeps us in view, for it is as necessary that He should keep us by His intercessions as that He should redeem us with His blood. If He lets go His hold of us for one moment, Satan stands ready to destroy. Those purchased by His blood, He now keeps by His intercession."[273]

What could be more graphic? If I saw an intruder coming into a room with a club to hurt someone unaware of his presence, and I "interceded" between that attacker and his victim, I would be demonstrating what Jesus is doing through the Holy Spirit every time we breathe a prayer for help, for power to keep our minds single and pure. That's why Jesus promised the Holy Spirit to be our Helper—to "intercede" between us and the "fiery darts of the wicked one" (Ephesians 6:16).

What could give us more assurance? Here, in the second role of the Mediator (that of providing sustaining grace to keep from sinning), rests the hope of every Christian.[274] Through what He has done *for us,* Jesus will do His part in silencing the accusations of the accuser. But He cannot keep silencing satanic accusations if we do not give Jesus permission to do His work *in us.*[275]

Our Lord's double role as our all-powerful Mediator focuses on the heart of the plan of salvation—to restore in men and women the image of God and to eradicate sin from the universe. This is *not done by declaring* it eradicated, or by *declaring* the image of God restored. Sponging clean everyone's life record with a mighty sweep of mercy will not do it. If this were

---

[273] *Manuscript Releases,* vol. 15, 104.

[274] "The scenes connected with the sanctuary above should make such an impression upon the minds and hearts of all that they may be able to impress others. All need to become more intelligent in regard to the work of the atonement, which is going on in the sanctuary above. When this grand truth is seen and understood, those who hold it will work in harmony with Christ to prepare a people to stand in the great day of God, and their efforts will be successful. By study, contemplation, and prayer God's people will be elevated above common, earthly thoughts and feelings, and will be brought into harmony with Christ and His great work of cleansing the sanctuary above from the sins of the people. Their faith will go with Him into the sanctuary, and the worshipers on earth will be carefully reviewing their lives and comparing their characters with the great standard of righteousness. They will see their own defects; they will also see that they must have the aid of the Spirit of God if they would become qualified for the great and solemn work for this time which is laid upon God's ambassadors." —*Testimonies,* vol. 5, 575.

[275] "Our only ground of hope is in the righteousness of Christ imparted to us, and in that wrought by His Spirit working in and through us." —*Steps to Christ,* 63.

possible, the wisdom and justice of God Himself would be forever suspect; nothing would have been settled in the Great Controversy as to whether God was fair in setting up laws that no one could keep and whether He was just in irrevocably casting from heaven Satan and one third of the angels (see Revelation 12:7, 8).

The only way for sin to be destroyed while preserving both the sinner and God's justice is for the rebel to become a loyal son or daughter, willingly and habitually. Sin is a clenched fist in the face of his crucified Lord; sin is the creature distrusting God's love and wisdom, deposing Him as the Lord of his or her life. The consequences of such rebellion are deadly, as the history of this dreary world reveals. And as Gethsemane and Calvary prove.

Only the sinner who confesses his sins *and* forsakes them "will have mercy" (Proverbs 28:13; 1 John 1:9). God is not interested in destroying men and women; His first goal is to save them, to rescue them from their self-centeredness, to appeal to their better judgment, and to restore them to a happy, willing relationship of trust.

But one thing God cannot overlook is sham. Nothing is settled if church members claim the name of Christ, but not His power; or claim His power, but not His character.[276] For this reason Ellen White emphasized a fundamental biblical doctrine when she wrote: "The religion of Christ means more than the forgiveness of sin; it means taking away our sins, and filling the vacuum with the graces of the Holy Spirit."[277]

IN SUMMARY

The intercessory work of Jesus as our "all-powerful Mediator" not only supplies to repenting sinners the pardon made possible by His atoning sacrifice, it also supplies the power through the Holy Spirit by which those sins are truly eradicated from the character of trusting, willing Christians.[278] This astounding good news can never be repeated enough; yet it is rarely heard throughout the pages of church history. It is the truth that Satan fears most.[279]

---

[276] "Lucifer desired God's power, but not His character." —*The Desire of Ages*, 435.

[277] *Christ's Object Lessons*, 419, 420. "To be pardoned in the way that Christ pardons, is not only to be forgiven, but to be renewed in the spirit of our mind." —*Review and Herald*, August 19, 1890. "The grace of Christ purifies while it pardons, and fits men for a holy heaven." —*That I May Know Him*, 336.

[278] "Through the perfect obedience of the Son of God, through the merits of his blood, and the power of his intercession, man may become a partaker of the divine nature." —*Signs of the Time*, July 6, 1888.

[279] *The Great Controversy*, 488. "If those who hide and excuse their faults could see how Satan exults over them, how he taunts Christ and holy angels with their course, they would make haste to confess their sins and to put them away. Through defects in their character, Satan works to gain control of the whole mind, and he knows that if these defects are cherished, he will succeed. Therefore he is constantly seeking to deceive the followers of Christ with his fatal sophistry that

The Old Testament Day of Atonement was the most solemn day of the Israelite year (Leviticus 16). It prefigured earth's "day of atonement period" that began in 1844. From 1844 on, Christians have added urgency to respond to the mediatorial work of Christ wrought through the Holy Spirit. It truly is judgment time and will close when a given generation of people worldwide makes up their mind regarding God's last-day messages.[280]

---

it is impossible for them to overcome. But Jesus pleads in their behalf His wounded hands, His bruised body; and He declares to all who would follow Him, 'My grace is sufficient for thee.' ... Let none, then, regard their defects as incurable. God will give faith and grace to overcome them." —*Ibid.*, 489.

[280] *Ibid.*, 479–491. See also Roy Gane, *Altar Call* (Berrien Springs, MI: Diadem, 1999), 298–324.

The cost of freedom is being paid every day on Planet Earth—as people have paid the cost for thousands of years!

Think of Mohammed el-Rehaief, that Muslim Iraqi lawyer who risked his life and that of his wife's, a nurse at the hospital outside of Nasiriyah, Iraq. Early April 2003, he stopped by the hospital to see his wife and noticed the ominous presence of security agents. A physician pointed through a window to a wounded young woman covered with a white blanket. He watched while a black-clad Iraqi slapped Pfc. Jessica Lynch repeatedly, no doubt seeking information. As soon as he could, the lawyer sneaked into the room to tell her, "Don't worry, don't worry!"

Quietly, Mohammed worked his way out of the city, walking six miles, down a road, which Americans had already called "Ambush Alley," looking for the Marines. He took the chance of being killed by Saddam's Fedayeen or skeptical Marines. After convincing the Marine patrol that he was believable, the Marine command told the lawyer to return to the hospital for more information. Back he went through the rain of air strikes. At the hospital again, he had to be sure that no one would recognize him. He silently counted the 41 Fedayeen at the hospital, noted the four guards in civilian clothes who stood watch with their Kalashnikov assault rifles and radios, and traced the routes that commandos could use in case of a rescue mission. *He made two more trips back and forth to get the exact information needed.* Fedayeen discovered the nurse missing and guessed her involvement with her husband meant something ominous. Just hours before Lynch's rescue, the Fedayeen raided their home.

However, Mohammed, with his wife and 6-year-old daughter, had already walked again those six treacherous miles. They drew five maps and the Special Ops team of Navy SEALS, Army Rangers, Marines, and Air Force Special units organized their daring rescue—one of the few times an American prisoner of war has been successfully rescued.

Marine Col. Bill Durrett said, "The information was dead-on." And Lt. Col. Rich Long noted, "He is an extremely courageous man who should serve as an inspiration to all of us to do the right thing."

Doing "the right thing" is the price of freedom; the price of overturning evil's coercion, threats, intimidations, and torture as well as freeing those caught in life's unknown terrors such as fire, hurricanes and earthquakes.

Men and women risk their lives every day, not only in military combat, but also in law enforcement and fire response teams. Some pay the ultimate cost; others live to serve another day. The cost of freedom is incalculable!

Peter Baker, *Washington Post Foreign Service*, Friday, April 4, 2003; *Sacramento Bee*, April 4, 2003.

SECTION FOUR

God created human intelligences on this planet to be His laboratory in which the principles of His government and those of Satan could be fully displayed. How should men and women of faith respond to God's plan for them and how do they help to vindicate God's character and government? Why did God risk all in putting His case before the universe in the hands of men and women who professed to be followers of Jesus?

CHAPTER FIFTEEN:
WHAT KIND OF JOB DESCRIPTION DID JESUS GIVE TO THE CHURCH?

Before Jesus ascended, He laid out the job description for the Christian Church. John records part of our Lord's incredibly moving prayer to His Heavenly Father wherein He said: "As you have sent me into the world, I also have sent them into the world" (John 17:18; see also 20:21).

Obviously, this requires a second reading on our knees. Could He possibly mean what He said? What Jesus was sent into this world to do, so He sends us to do! Could it then be that, in some important aspects, the plan of salvation depends on His disciples' doing faithfully what He did so faithfully! And if they do not, they would be His followers in name only! And some day such followers will hear those dreadful words, "I never knew you [for what you said you were]" (Matthew 7:23).

When I read this job description, I see God as our Heavenly Franchiser. He has something special to offer everyone who would "buy" from Him. He offers these franchises freely to all who will commit themselves to represent what He stands for—faithfully, clearly, day in and day out.

His market plan is to set up franchises with everyone who is convinced that what He is selling is the most important enterprise in which anyone could invest.

Franchises in the normal business world are often taken back because local franchises did not live up to the name and expectations of the head office. They did not faithfully reproduce the Master Pattern or the Master Recipe.

Jesus is the Divine Franchiser who offers local franchises to men and women in every generation. He has had many takers. Some wanted His name but not His quality control. Some wanted His power but not His Spirit. Some wanted to capitalize on His advertising but not His character.

But Jesus has always found some, in every generation and in all lands, who get the point. They discovered that working for the Heavenly Franchise became their life! Nothing was more exciting! These local franchises know that they are not as perfect as their Head Office. But they also know that if they will keep listening to Headquarters, and stay close to company representatives (who are always on their side to help them reach all expectations), their local franchise would increasingly reflect the original Pattern of the Divine Franchiser.[281]

At this point we must take a deep breath. We have come almost full circle since pages 45–49 when we observed that God made created intelligences on Planet Earth for a significant role in telling His side of the story in the controversy with Satan and his fallen angels.

Why did He make "human beings ... a new and distinct order"? Because the human family would become one of His best laboratories for the working out of His "side" of the conflict as well as an open display of how Satan's principles would work out.

As we said earlier, this "new and distinct order" of created intelligences was the "talk" of the universe: "All heaven took a deep and joyful interest in the creation of the world and of man. ... They were made 'in the image of God' and it was the Creator's design that they should populate the earth."[282]

Further, the longer that men and women (this "new and distinct order" of creation) would live:

> "The more fully [they] should reveal this image [Genesis 1:27], — the more fully reflect the glory of the Creator. ... Throughout eternal ages he would have continued to gain new treasures of knowledge, to discover fresh springs of happiness, and to obtain clearer and yet

---

[281] "When Christ left the world, He committed His work to His followers. He came to represent the character of God to the world, and we are left to represent Christ to the world." —*Signs of the Times*, April 15, 1889. "God designs that every one of us shall be perfect in Him, so that we may represent to the world the perfection of His character. He wants us to be set free from sin, that we shall not disappoint the heavenly intelligences, that we may not grieve our divine Redeemer. He does not desire us to profess Christianity and yet not avail ourselves of that grace which is able to make us perfect, that we may be found wanting in nothing, but unblamable before Him in love and holiness." —*Ibid.*, February 8, 1892. "In the exercise of His sovereign prerogative He imparted to His disciples the knowledge of the character of God, in order that they might communicate it to the world." —*Ibid.*, June 27, 1892.

[282] *Review and Herald*, February 11, 1902.

clearer conceptions of the wisdom, the power, and the love of God. More and more fully would he have fulfilled the object of his creation, more and more fully have reflected the Creator's glory."[283]

GOD HAD GREAT PLANS FOR THE HUMAN RACE

Even further, God had planned that in the development of the human race He would "put it in our power, through co-operation with Him, to bring this scene of misery to an end."[284] That sounds like a lot of responsibility—the capacity to hasten the advent (or delay it)!

Now, hours before Calvary and only a few weeks before His ascension, Jesus was putting Plan C into action. Plan A failed when Adam and Eve walked out of the Garden. Plan B failed when Israel missed its opportunity to be God's faithful franchise. Israel's privilege and mission, as God's "chosen people," was:

> "To reveal the principles of His kingdom.... to represent the character of God. ... He designed that the principles revealed through His people should be the means of restoring the moral image of God in man. ... God withheld from them nothing favorable to the formation of character that would make them representatives of Himself. ... God furnished them with every facility for becoming the greatest nation on the earth. ... To all the world the gospel invitation was to be given. Through the teaching of the sacrificial service, Christ was to be uplifted before the nations. ... As the numbers of Israel increased, they were to enlarge their borders, until their kingdom should embrace the world."[285]

Even after the Babylonian captivity, Plan B was still workable, even in Christ's day! This is truly one more example of God's infinite patience: "If the leaders and teachers at Jerusalem had received the truth Christ brought, what a missionary center their city would have been! Backslidden Israel would have been converted. ... How rapidly they could have carried the gospel to all parts of the world."[286] If Jerusalem's leaders "had heeded the light which Heaven had sent her, she might have stood forth in the pride of prosperity, the queen of kingdoms. ... the mighty metropolis of the earth. ... the world's diadem of glory."[287] God never gave up; Israel did![288]

---

[283] *Education*, 15.

[284] *Ibid.*, 264.

[285] *Christ's Object Lessons*, 285–290. See Isaiah 43:10, 12; 44:8.

[286] *Ibid.*, 232.

[287] *The Desire of Ages*, 576.

[288] "This promise of blessing should have met fulfillment in large measure during the centuries following the return of the Israelites from the lands of their captivity. It was God's design that the whole earth be prepared for the first advent of Christ, even as today the way is preparing for His second coming."—*Prophets and Kings*, 703, 704. "Jerusalem would have stood forever, the elect of God." —*The Great Controversy*, 19.

And then Plan C—the Christian church! Men and women of faith would become His divine franchises throughout the world, building the case that God can be trusted, that He is fair with His laws, that He is merciful beyond words, and that His grace melts our hearts and empowers weak wills so that His will can be done on earth even as it is done by joyful, enthusiastic, compliant angels in heaven (Luke 11:2). "That which God purposed to do for the world through Israel, the chosen nation, He will finally accomplish through His church on earth today."[289]

CHRISTIANS SHOULD LEARN FROM ISRAEL

Surely the Christian church would get the point! "Don't make Israel's mistakes!" "Don't create a gap between belief and life!" "Learn the lessons of Israel!" So what happened?

In Plan C we have the same mission and purpose for the church that God had for Adam and Eve and for the Jewish nation: "Through His people Christ is to manifest His character and the principles of His kingdom. ... He desires through His people to answer Satan's charges by showing the results of obedience to right principles."[290]

Plan C is a task not only for the corporate church. These "right principles" in contrast to satanic principles "are to be manifest in the individual Christian. ... All are to be symbols of what can be done for the world. They are to be types of the saving power of the truths of the gospel. All are agencies in the fulfillment of God's great purpose for the human race."[291]

What specifically are these "right principles"? Christians, by definition, are to "possess the principles of the character of Christ."[292] Their appeal to the world will not be primarily in terms of denunciating "their idols, but by beholding something better. God's goodness is to be made known. 'Ye are My witnesses, saith the Lord, that I am God'" (Isaiah 43:12).[293]

This connection between God's commission to the church—that the Christian's reflection of His character and principles would be His "witness" to the world, and that the return of Jesus depends on when this "witness" has been faithfully done—is neatly summarized in these words:

> "It is the darkness of misapprehension of God that is enshrouding the world. Men are losing their knowledge of His character. It has been misunderstood and misinterpreted. At this time a message from God is to be proclaimed, a message illuminating in its influence and saving in its power. His character is to be made known.

---

[289] *Prophets and Kings,* 713, 714.
[290] *Christ's Object Lessons,* 296.
[291] *Ibid.,* 296, 297.
[292] *Ibid.,* 298.
[293] *Ibid.,* 299.

Into the darkness of the world is to be shed the light of His glory, the light of His goodness, mercy, and truth. … Those who wait for the Bridegroom's coming are to say to the people, 'Behold your God.' The last rays of merciful light, the last message of mercy to be given to the world, is a revelation of His character of love. The children of God are to manifest His glory. In their own life and character they are to reveal what the grace of God has done for them. The light of the Sun of Righteousness is to shine forth in good works—in words of truth and deeds of holiness."[294]

This is an amazing statement. Frankly, very unambiguous! It simply amplifies our Lord's prediction: "This gospel of the kingdom will be preached in all the world as a *witness* to all the nations, and then shall the end come" (Matthew 24:14).

Witnesses in any court do not repeat hearsay! They can speak only of what they personally know. God's faithful in the endtime will be personal witnesses to what the gospel has done for them and what it will surely do for all those who also "come and see."

Could it be said any clearer?

"All who receive Christ as a personal Saviour are to demonstrate the truth of the gospel and its saving power upon the life. God makes no requirement without making provision for its fulfillment. Through the grace of Christ we may accomplish everything that God requires. All the riches of heaven are to be revealed through God's people. 'Herein is My Father glorified,' Christ says, 'that ye bear much fruit; so shall ye be My disciples'" (John 15:8).[295]

---

[294] *Ibid.*, 415, 416.
[295] *Ibid.*, 301.

CHAPTER SIXTEEN:
HOW DOES THE CHRISTIAN'S WITNESS RELATE TO THE GREAT CONTROVERSY?

First, we should ask several questions: If Jesus beat Satan at every turn, if all heaven and unfallen worlds saw Satan unmasked when Jesus died,[296] why isn't the war over? If Jesus vindicated the character and government of God, what more is needed in order to end the Great Controversy? If Jesus settled everything in His life and death, why does God stand by and permit the horrors and sadnesses of the past 2,000 years? Was there something still unfinished after the cross?

Answers to these questions bring us back to why God created men and women as His "new and distinct order" in the universe.[297] The human race was created to play an important role in the Great Controversy. They were not created to merely make Planet Earth more interesting. In some special way, men and women were to be the laboratory test of whose principles work best, God's or Satan's.[298]

In becoming a man "in every respect" (Hebrews 2:14, 17), Jesus led the way in shutting down Satan's accusations. But He also made it clear that more was yet to be done by those following His example. He set up local franchises to continue doing throughout the world what He did for 33 years in a very limited area, east of the Mediterranean Sea.

What does this mean within the big picture? Ellen White sharpens our focus: "Satan was not then destroyed [at the cross]. The angels did not even then understand all that was involved in the Great Controversy. The principles at stake were to be more fully revealed. And for the sake of man, Satan's existence must be continued. Man as well as angels must see the contrast between the Prince of light and the prince of darkness. He must choose whom he will serve."[299]

FOOT SOLDIERS WITH COSMIC SIGNIFICANCE

Philip Yancey captures the mystique of the Book of Job. Although He once wrote about Job's experience as "the Bible's most comprehensive look at the problem of pain and suffering," he later came to see the bigger picture:

> "The contest posed between Satan and God is no trivial exercise. Satan's accusation that Job loves God only because 'you have put a hedge around him' stands as an attack on God's character. It implies that God is not

---

[296] When Jesus died on the cross, "Satan saw that his disguise was torn away." —*The Desire of Ages*, 761.

[297] See 46.

[298] "Our little world is the lesson book of the universe." —*The Desire of Ages*, 19.

[299] *The Desire of Ages*, 761.

worthy of love, in himself, that people follow God only because they get something out of it or are 'bribed' to do so. ... The book hinges on the issue of integrity. Job acts as if God's integrity is on trial.

"The opening chapters of Job, however, reveal that God staked a lot on one man's wickedness or righteousness. Somehow, in a way the book only suggests and does not explain, one person's faith does make a difference. ... Job reminds us that the small history of mankind on this earth—and, in fact, my own small history of faith—takes place within the larger drama of the history of the universe. We are foot soldiers in a spiritual battle with cosmic significance. ... God's plan to reverse the Fall depends on the faith of those who follow him."[300]

Our Lord's divine franchises, representing the quality and spirit of Home Office, became the arena where "the principles at stake were to be more fully revealed." In God's infinite wisdom, He put Himself at risk again when He gave to Christians the mission of completing the controversy between Him and Satan. The Christian church is God's Plan C "in the fulfillment of God's great purpose for the human race."[301]

Again, looking at the big picture, the Great Controversy Theme explains why no one on earth would know what really happened on the cross *unless* "disciples" made it known. Would these "disciples" be believed if the "good news" they talked about did not make a difference in their lives, when compared with others who also had strong religious beliefs in their "gods"? Would anyone really have given Paul any attention if he had not been convinced that the crucified Jesus had indeed came from heaven with God's good news—and that it made a difference?

Paul was not "ashamed of the gospel of Christ"! Why? Because everywhere the gospel was proclaimed, Paul and many others saw "the power [Lit: 'dynamite'] of God" at work (Romans 1:16)!

IRREFUTABLE EVIDENCE

What kind of power? He commended the Corinthians for choosing to make Jesus their Lord, Corinthians who once were "fornicators, idolaters, adulterers, homosexuals, sodomites, thieves, covetous, drunkards, revilers, and extortioners" (1 Corinthians 6:11). These early Christians began the long, glorious line of men and women who would present irrefutable evidence before Satan and all other doubters as to whether God can provide all that is needed to thwart evil whenever and however it shows itself.

Those early Christians were indeed "foot soldiers in a spiritual battle with cosmic significance."

---

[300] Philip Yancey, *The Bible Jesus Read* (Grand Rapids, MI: Zondervan Publishing House, 1999), 46–67.

[301] *Christ's Object Lessons*, 297.

If Satan with his accusations had put God on trial before the universe, then this evidence proving God trustworthy must drive him furious—which is exactly what is happening (Revelation 12:17).

Paul looked forward to the day when Christians the world over and before the entire universe would make God look good and Satan exceedingly furious:

> "I am less than the least of all God's people; yet God gave me this privilege of taking to the Gentiles the Good News about the infinite riches of Christ, and of making all people see how God's secret plan is to be put into effect. God, who is the Creator of all things, kept his secret hidden through all the past ages, in order that at the present time, by means of the church, the angelic rulers and powers in the heavenly world might learn of his wisdom in all its different forms" (Ephesians 3:8-10, TEV; see also 1:4–12).[302]

GOD AND THE CHURCH BOTH ON TRIAL FOR THE SAME REASONS

We have noted throughout this book that God has allowed Himself to be put on trial before the universe.[303] God and the church are both on trial for the same reasons: to prove Satan wrong in all the charges and accusations that he has brought against the character and government of God. It could be argued that God needs you as much as you need Him to get the Great Controversy settled!

No wonder Ellen White was concerned enough to ask:

> "In this crisis, where is the church to be found? Are its members meeting the claims of God? Are they fulfilling His commission, and representing His character to the world? Are they urging upon the attention of their fellowmen the last merciful message of warning?"[304]

---

[302] "The point seems to be that the Lord is using us earthly benefactors of his cosmic victory (the church) to display to the angelic society of the heavenly realms, including the now defeated powers, the greatness of the Creator's wisdom in defeating his foes. We who used to be captives of the Satanic kingdom are now the very ones who proclaim its demise. The church is, as it were, God's eternal 'trophy case' of grace—we eternally exist 'to the praise of his glorious grace' (Ephesians 1:6, 12). —Gregory A. Boyd, *God At War* (Downers Grove, Ill: InterVarsity Press, 1997), 252.

[303] In Plan C, "the professed followers of Christ are on trial before the heavenly universe." —*Christ's Object Lessons*, 303.

[304] *Ibid.*, 302. "It is God's purpose to manifest through His people the principles of His kingdom. That in life and character they may reveal these principles, He desires to separate them from the customs, habits, and practices of the world. ... A great work is to be accomplished in setting before men the saving truths of the gospel. ... To present these truths is the work of the third angel's message. The Lord designs that the presentation of this message shall be the highest, greatest work carried on in the world at this time. ... The Lord designs through His people to answer Satan's charges by showing the result of obedience to right principles. ...The purpose that God seeks to accomplish through His people today is the same that He desired to accomplish through Israel when He brought them forth out of Egypt. By beholding the goodness, the mercy, the justice, and the love of God revealed in the church, the world is to have a representation of His character. And when the law of God is thus exemplified in the life, even the world will recognize the superiority of those who love and fear and serve God above every other people on the earth." —*Testimonies*, vol. 5, 9–12.

Now the question: Is it possible that professed followers of Jesus Christ could ever be expected to help vindicate God in the Great Controversy? Everything we have said so far goes a long way toward answering that question. But let's linger at the implications that the question brings up.

Ezekiel in his day was concerned with this question and its answer. He was a captive with many other Israelites in Babylon; for hundreds of years, they had truly become an embarrassment to their Lord and He could no longer defend them.

In referring to Plan B, God told Ezekiel how Israel had brought dishonor on His name and failed to fulfill their mission:

> "But when they came to the nations, wherever they came, they profaned my holy name, in that men said of them, 'These are the people of the Lord, and yet they had to go out of his land.' But I had concern for my holy name, which the house of Israel caused to be profaned among the nations to which they came. Therefore … It is not for your sake, O house of Israel, that I am about to act, but for the sake of my holy name, which you have profaned among the nations. … And I will vindicate the holiness of my great name, which has been profaned among the nations. … and the nations will know that I am the Lord … when through you I vindicate my holiness before their eyes" (36:20–23 RSV).

How did God give Israel their last chance? He had been very patient with Israel, as He had with Lucifer in heaven.[305] Even though the Israelite people were in captivity, they had not yet crossed the line; they had still time to learn from the mistakes of their fathers. So God beamed the light of hope on those exiles in Babylon; He would resurrect Plan B, one more time.

Those exiles heard the promise that God would "gather you from all the countries, and bring you into your own land." And now the conditions—it was a question of whether they wanted hearts of stone or of flesh: "A new heart I will give you, and a new spirit I will put within you; and I will take out of your flesh the heart of stone and give you a heart of flesh. And I will put my spirit within you, and cause you to walk in my statutes and be careful to observe my ordinances" (36:25–27, RSV).

TWO PHASES IN VINDICATING THE CHARACTER OF GOD

As we have seen, Plan B failed.[306] God then initiated Plan C, His last plan, when He established the Christian church.

Our Lord's life and death were one phase of the vindication of God that lies at the heart of the Great Controversy. The second phase of vindicating the Name—the character—of God would be lived out through the work of grace in the lives of loyal Christians: "The Savior came to glorify the Father

---

[305] See 34–36.
[306] See 107.

by the demonstration of His love; so the Spirit was to glorify Christ by revealing His grace to the world. The very image of God is to be reproduced in humanity. The honor of God, the honor of Christ, is involved in the perfection of the character of His people."[307]

The character of endtime Christians who "keep the commandments of God and the faith of Jesus" reflects the same quality exhibited in the lives of Enoch, Daniel and all the others in times past who have let God give them new hearts and new spirits, hearts of flesh instead of hearts of stone.[308]

Job's experience has been the template for faithful men and women: "According to his faith, so was it unto Job. 'When He hath tried me,' he said, 'I shall come forth as gold' (Job 23:10). So it came to pass. By his patient endurance he vindicated his own character, and thus the character of Him whose representative he was."[309]

CHRISTIAN'S HIGHEST PRIVILEGE

When we understand that the Christian's highest privilege is to join with Jesus in vindicating the character of God throughout the universe, our whole religious direction is turned upside down. Or is it right side up? Instead of focusing on self-centered reward and need for constant approval, the deepest impulse becomes one of making the vindication of God, defending the goodness of God, supreme. Such is the gratitude of agape love in response to His magnificent love toward us.

J. B. Phillips said it well: "The responsibilities which faced Christ as a human being would be, if we stop to think, enough to drive the most balanced man out of his mind. But He maintained His poise, His joy and His peace. He did the Father's will; and that is both the most and the highest that we can do."[310]

When the clear outline of the issues in the Great Controversy are seen and brought home to the heart, the Pharisee's heart is transformed. He suddenly realizes that in truly doing God's will, he could never find the joy of salvation in external religious behavior only. The elder brother is brought face to face with his father's love, perhaps understanding agape (love) for

---

[307] *The Desire of Ages*, 761.

[308] "The honor of Christ must stand complete in the perfection of the character of His chosen people." —*Signs of the Times*, November 25, 1890. "Enoch was a representative of those who will be upon the earth when Christ shall come, who will be translated to heaven without seeing death." —*Last Day Events*, 761.

[309] *Education*, 156. "It is God's purpose that His people shall be a sanctified, purified, holy people, communicating light to all around them. It is His purpose that, by exemplifying the truth in their lives, they shall be a praise in the earth. The grace of Christ is sufficient to bring this about. But let God's people remember that only as they believe and work out the principles of the gospel, can He make them a praise in the earth. ... Not with tame, lifeless utterance is the message to be given, but with clear, decided, stirring utterances. ... The world needs to see in Christians an evidence of the power of Christianity." —*Testimonies*, vol. 8, 14–16.

[310] *Making Men Whole* (London: Fontana Books, 1952), 79.

the first time. When legalists are suddenly aware of what sin has cost God and how much they need His daily pardon and power, they are smothered in appreciation. Why? Before understanding the issues in the Great Controversy, the Pharisee, the elder brother, the legalist had been "working, not from love, but from hope of reward."[311] They each were doing their "duty" not to honor God or their father, but to impress Him!

Plan C embraces all aspects of the Christian's life. Everything takes on a new color; a new kind of breeze is blowing. A new reason for everything we do becomes clear and motivating. Ellen White's plea echoes throughout her writings:

> "If there was ever a people in need of constantly increasing light from heaven, it is the people that, in this time of peril, God has called to be the depositaries of His holy law, and to vindicate His character before the world. Those to whom has been committed a trust so sacred must be spiritualized, elevated, vitalized, by the truths they profess to believe."[312]

Further, "It becomes every child of God to vindicate His character. You can magnify the Lord; you can show the power of sustaining grace."[313] Would any Christian who understands what Jesus did in the Garden and on the Cross want to do any less? Those who understand how much God needs their witness are on the way to fulfilling God's Plan C.

Yancey finds enormous significance in the cosmic wager between God and Satan as revealed in the Book of Job. He sees the same "wager" being played out "in other believers as well. We are God's Exhibit A, his demonstration piece to the powers in the unseen world. ... The New Testament insists that what happens among us here will, in fact, help determine the future of that universe. Paul is emphatic: 'The whole creation is on tiptoe to see the wonderful sight of the sons of God coming into their own.' [Romans 8:19, Phillips]. ... God has granted to ordinary men and women the dignity of participating in the Great Reversal which will restore the cosmos to its pristine state."[314]

---

[311] *Christ's Object Lessons*, 209. Even the disciples had difficulty getting all this straight. "While they had been attracted by the love of Jesus, the disciples were not wholly free from Pharisaism. They still worked with the thought of meriting a reward in proportion to their labor. They cherished a spirit of self-exaltation and self-complacency, and made comparisons among themselves ... He would not have us eager for rewards, nor feel that for every duty we must receive compensation. We should not be so anxious to gain the reward as to do what is right, irrespective of all gain. Love to God and to our fellowmen should be our motive." —*Christ's Object Lessons*, 396–399.

[312] *Testimonies*, vol. 5, 746.

[313] *Ibid.*, 317. "Like our Savior, we are in this world to do service for God. We are here to become like God in character, and by a life of service to reveal Him to the world. In order to be coworkers with God, in order to become like Him, and to reveal His character, we must know Him aright." —*The Ministry of Healing*, 409.

[314] Philip Yancey, *Disappointment With God* (Grand Rapids, MI: Zondervan Publishing House, 1988), 170–173.

HONORING GOD RATHER THAN IMPRESSING HIM

Vindicating the character of God cannot be done with a religious posture that aims at *impressing* God with good deeds, even with faithful tithing and Sabbath observance. Vindicating and reflecting the character of God involves *honoring* God in tithing and Sabbath hours—the difference between "the yoke of bondage" (Galatians 5:1) and the joy of commitment.

For centuries, the armies of earth have had their flags that became their center, their inspiration to do what seemed impossible. "It's striking how often flags are mentioned in the [Congressional] Medal of Honor citations for the Civil War. Out of 1,520 Medal of Honor actions during the Civil War, 467 were given to men who either defended the flag of their side or captured a flag of the Confederate."[315]

The flag-bearer was at the center of the storm of battle, the most vulnerable. Although he carried no weapons, he was always at the head of the charge. Soldiers always kept one eye on his flag because it told him if his group was advancing or retreating. And, of course, the enemy kept their eye on that flag. They knew that bringing down the flag-bearer was the quickest way to disrupt the attack. The command, "rally 'round the flag" was not merely a romantic phrase; it meant the difference between success and failure for the regiment.

Very few held the flag throughout the war; too many fell. But one, Leopold Karpeles of the 46th Massachusetts Volunteer Regiment (later the 57th), volunteered to be the color-bearer in 1862 and was invalided on July 30, 1864—too wounded to continue. Leaving Prague when he was eleven, he was forever grateful for his newfound freedom in America. This gratitude gave him the motivation to pay back what he owed to his new homeland. His exploits in the various battles, beginning with the Goldsboro Expedition and through the Battle of the Wilderness, Spotsylvania and the Battle of the Crater—became legendary. His commanders were in awe with his courage, always exposing himself to the blizzard of lead in order to make the flag more visible.

His CMH citation included these words: "While color bearer, rallied the retreating troops and induced them to check the enemy's advance ..."[316]

Throughout human history, God has had His color bearers, His flag-bearers. Many known, many more unknown. When we think of Joseph, Moses, Joshua, Elijah, Daniel and Paul, our hearts skip a beat. Somewhere in God's universe, something even more meaningful than the CMH will be given to their kind—even today we are rallying "round the flag" because of their courage and desire to do nothing that would bring dishonor to the flag of truth and the Name of God.

---

[315] Allen Mikaelian, *Medal of Honor* (New York: Hyperion, 2002), 19.
[316] *Ibid.*, 19-40.

In the endtime, God's last-day loyalists will raise the flag in the face of its enemies. Honest men and women the world over will eventually rally "round the flag" represented by the seventh-day Sabbath. It will take all the perseverance, courage, and quiet loyalty of Leopold Karpela for God's loyalists to face latter-day blizzards, not of soft lead but of ridicule, disdain, or material hardship.

The Sabbath Flag

This Sabbath flag represents the honor of God in the Great Controversy. It is surely under attack wherever one looks these days. But God has given His flag to men and women who claim His name. They will be the color bearers in the last scene in the great drama when the curtain is about to come down. They will have a message so compelling that honest man and women around the world will "step out from the rebel flag" and stand under freedom's flag—" the blood-stained banner of Prince Emmanuel."[317]

Sounds like a lot of responsibility to be dumped on frail men and women, even though they call themselves Christians. So we ask, how can weak human beings ever be expected to "vindicate" the character of God? To carry His flag so that He will not be embarrassed?

How will they become safe to give the flag to? They do it by "faith." But how much faith will they need to have?

---

[317] *Review and Herald,* July 7, 1904.

Chapter Seventeen:
Church Members Become Men And Women Of Faith

L et's pause for a moment and recall the purpose of the gospel and why this purpose has much to do with helping God settle the Great Controversy.

In *Education*, Ellen White highlighted the "central theme" of the plan of salvation—"the theme about which every other in the whole book clusters … the restoration in the human soul of the image of God. … The burden of every book and every passage of the Bible is the unfolding of this wondrous theme—man's uplifting—the power of God, 'which giveth us the victory through our Lord Jesus Christ'" (1 Corinthians 15:57).[318]

"Restoration in the human soul of the image of God"—*the purpose of the gospel.* Not only forgiveness but also the eradication of all that sin has damaged so that the "restored soul" will be safe to save in a universe eternally secure from all rebellion.[319] The Greek word for "Savior" can just as easily be translated "Healer."[320] Whatever has been damaged by sin—physically, mentally, emotionally, socially, or spiritually—will be restored to wholeness and health in those who permit the Great Physician to do His work.[321]

As Ellen White emphasized in so many ways:

> "The religion of Christ means more than the forgiveness of sin; it means taking away our sins, and filling the vacuum with the graces of the Holy Spirit. … When Christ reigns in the soul, there is purity, freedom from sin. The glory, the fulness, the completeness of the gospel plan is fulfilled in the life [restoration]."[322]

---

[318] Page 125. "Freely will He pardon all who come to Him for forgiveness and restoration" —*The Desire of Ages,* 568.

[319] See 26, 177, 396, 462.

[320] The Greek σωζώ, either "to save," or "to heal." See Matthew 8:25; 9:22; 16:25; Mark 5:24; 13:20; Luke 8:36, 48, 50; 23:35; John 12:27; Romans 8:24; Titus 3:5; Hebrews 5:7; Jude 5, etc.

[321] Dick Winn's *God's Way to a New You* (Nampa, ID: PPPA, 1979) may be the clearest book published that explains the Great Controversy in terms of restoration: "Why will Jesus be so special to all the universe? Will it be only that He has restored this errant human race? Surely that is a part. But remember that the controversy began *before* this little planet rebelled! Jesus will be special to all the universe, because, through His work in the restoration of man (in cooperation with His Father) He will have restored in the eyes of the universe the image and reputation of the Godhead. And so it can be truly said that, through His work in the restoring of man, God the Restorer will have Himself been restored. Not an intellect anywhere in doubt! Trust and freedom everywhere. The restoration is complete!" 171.

[322] *Christ's Object Lessons,* 419, 420. "The forgiveness of sins is not the sole result of the death of Jesus. He made the infinite sacrifice, not only that sin might be removed, but that human nature might be restored, rebeautified, reconstructed from its ruins, and made fit for the presence of God." —*Testimonies,* vol. 5, 537.

Let's look at all this through the word "atonement"—a word that has been terribly mutilated through the centuries:

> "The atonement of Christ is not a mere skillful way to have our sins pardoned; it is a divine remedy for the cure of transgression and the restoration of spiritual health. It is the Heaven-ordained means by which the righteousness of Christ may be not only upon us but in our hearts and characters."[323]

Here again Ellen White focuses on both Jesus as humanity's Healer and on the purpose of the gospel.

CONVENTIONAL WORDS BECOME FRESH IN THE BIG PICTURE

Ellen White puts all elements of traditional theology into the big picture of the Great Controversy. In doing so, most of the conventional theological words, such as atonement, grace, faith, covenants, obedience, and overcoming, take on new and fresh meaning. This larger picture of the Great Controversy becomes the clearest restoration of the New Testament gospel that I know of.[324]

For example, Jesus not only "saves" us by what He has done *for us*, He heals us by what He does *in us*.[325] God desires to heal us, to set us free from the clutches and consequences of sin. But this healing "requires an entire transformation, a renewing of our whole nature. We must yield ourselves wholly to Him."[326]

Note how Ellen White links "salvation" with "harmony with God," "obedience," and "redemption": "The plan of salvation made it possible for man again to be brought into harmony with God, and to render obedience to His law, and for both man and the earth to be finally redeemed from the power of the wicked one."[327]

So back to the question: How does all this work out in the Christian's life? The Bible answers, "By faith—righteousness by faith."

Wars have been fought over this powerful phrase—"righteousness by faith." Why should this be? If you were Satan, would you not do your best to confuse Christians over something so fundamental in the Great Controversy? He surely doesn't care how much we talk or sing about "righteousness" or "faith" as long as we are confused about what Bible writers meant by these words!

---

[323] Letter 406, 1906, cited in *SDABC*, vol. 6, 1074.
[324] See "Appendix M: Recovering Truth Hidden for Ages."
[325] "Our only ground of hope is in the righteousness of Christ imputed to us, and in that wrought by His Spirit working in and through us." —*Steps to Christ*, 63.
[326] *Ibid.*, 43.
[327] *Patriarchs and Prophets*, 331.

If restoring in men and women the image of God (that is, reflecting the character of Jesus, which is Paul's song in all of his epistles), then "righteousness by faith" must be the description of that wonderful relationship! The confusion in the Christian church has been over the New Testament meaning of "righteousness" and "faith"—two words that have divided Christianity for 2,000 years. And if we misunderstand either one of those words, Satan could not be happier. Further, our misunderstanding today will be as far off the mark as most Christian churches have been for centuries![328]

Let's take a quick look at "righteousness."[329] One of the difficulties that readers of English New Testaments have had for centuries is that translators have not made clear that the same Greek word (Δικαιοσύνη) translated "righteousness" is the same Greek word often translated "justification." This has led many down the road to confusion in either equating "righteousness by faith" with their limited understanding of "justification by faith" or in making a sharp distinction between the concepts of "justification" and "sanctification."[330]

All churches, through the years, have generated more heat than light in their tensions over these basic New Testament teachings. Let's see if we can make all this as simple as God intended the Bible to be in our next chapter.

---

[328] I am making a distinction here between "righteousness by faith" and "justification by faith," phrases that have been unfortunately interchanged because many have limited "righteousness by faith" to their limited understanding of "justification by faith."

[329] Gr. Δικαιοσύνη —"righteousness, "uprightness." Arndt & Gingrich, *A Greek-English Lexicon of the New Testament* (Chicago: The University of Chicago Press, 1957), 195, 196: "uprightness ... as a characteristic of a judge; ... righteousness in the sense of fulfilling the divine statutes; ... righteousness, uprightness as the compelling motive for the conduct of one's whole life; ... in specific Pauline thought . ... the righteousness bestowed by God ... to be apprehended by faith. ... Since δικαιοσύνη constitutes the specific virtue of Christians, the word becomes almost equivalent to Christianity." G. Abbot-Smith, *A Manual Greek Lexicon of the New Testament* (Edinburgh: T. & T. Clark, 1954), 116: "In broad sense, *righteousness,* conformity to the Divine will in purpose, thought and action."

[330] "Many commit the error of trying to define minutely the fine points of distinction between justification and sanctification. Into the definitions of these two terms they often bring their own ideas and speculations. Why try to be more minute than is Inspiration on the vital question of righteousness by faith? Why try to work out every minute point, as if the salvation of the soul depended upon all having exactly your understanding of this matter? All cannot see in the same line of vision." —Manuscript 21, 1891, cited in *SDABC*, vol. 6, 72.

CHAPTER EIGHTEEN:
THE NEW TESTAMENT MEANING OF "RIGHTEOUSNESS BY FAITH"

*V*incent's *Word Studies in the New Testament*,[331] a standard reference for many decades, is refreshingly clear, even though Vincent frequently interchanges the English words, "righteousness" and "justification." But you will see why he can do that interchanging—he rightly understands the biblical definitions.[332]

Vincent commented on "righteousness" in Romans 1:17: "Δικαιοσύνη, *righteousness,* is therefore that which fulfills the claims to δίκη *right.* 'It is the state commanded by God and standing the test of His judgment; the character and acts of a man approved of Him, in virtue of which the man corresponds with Him and His will as His ideal and standard' (Cremer).

"The medium of this righteousness is *faith.* Faith is said to be *counted* or *reckoned* for righteousness; *i.e.,* righteousness is ascribed to it or recognized in it (Romans 4:3, 6, 9, 22; Galatians 3:6; James 2:23).

"In this verse the righteousness revealed in the Gospel is described as a righteousness *of God.* This does not mean righteousness *as an attribute of God,* as in iii 5; but *righteousness as bestowed on man by God.* The state of the justified man is due to God. The righteousness which becomes his is that which God declares to be righteousness and ascribes to him. Righteousness thus expresses *the relation of being right into which God puts the man who believes.* …

"We may rightly say that the revealed righteousness of God is *unto* faith, in the sense of *with a view to produce faith;* but we may also say that faith is a *progressive* principle; that the aim of God's justifying righteousness is *life,* and that the just lives by his faith (Galatians 2:20), and enters into 'more abundant life' with the development of his faith."

MORE THAN A LEGAL TRANSACTION

In his comments on Romans 3:20:

"The word δικαιοσύνη is not, however, to be construed as indicating a mere legal transaction or adjustment between God and man, though it preserves the idea of relativity, in that God is the absolute standard by which the new condition is estimated, whether we regard God's view of the justified man, or the man's moral condition when justified. The element of character must not only not be eliminated from it; it must be foremost in it.

---

[331] (Peabody MA: Hendrickson Publishers, n.d.), 13, 14.
[332] I quote Vincent at length because this Greek scholar has said in a few words what many others would try to say in a whole book, and still not get it right!)

"Justification is more than pardon. Pardon is an act which frees the offender from the penalty of the law, adjusts his outward relation to the law, but does not necessarily effect any change in him personally. It is *necessary* to justification but not *identical* with it.

"Justification aims directly at *character*. It contemplates making *the man himself right*; that the new and right relation to God in which faith places him shall have its natural and legitimate issue in *personal rightness*. The phrase *faith is counted for righteousness*, does not mean that faith is *a substitute* for righteousness, but that faith *is* righteousness; righteousness *in the germ* indeed but still *bonâ fide* righteousness. The act of faith inaugurates a righteous life and a righteous character. The man is not made inherently holy in himself, because his righteousness is derived from God; neither is he merely *declared* righteous by a legal fiction without reference to his personal character; but the justifying decree, the declaration of God which pronounces him righteous, is literally true to the fact in that he is in real, sympathetic relation with the eternal source and norm of holiness, and with the divine personal inspiration of character.

"Faith contains all the possibilities of personal holiness. It unites man to the holy God, and through this union he becomes a partaker of the divine nature, and escapes the corruption that is in the world through lust (2 Peter 1:4).

"The intent of justification is expressly declared by Paul to be conformity to Christ's image (Romans 8:29, 30). Justification, which does not *actually remove* the wrong condition in man that is at the root of his enmity to God, is not justification. In the absence of this, a legal declaration that the man is right is a fiction. The declaration of righteousness must have its real and substantial basis in the man's actual moral condition.

"Hence justification is called justification *of life* (Romans 5:18); it is linked with the saving operation of the life of the risen Christ (Romans 4:25; 5:10); those who are in Christ Jesus 'walk not after the flesh, but after the Spirit' (Romans 8:1); they exhibit patience, approval, hope, love (Romans 5:4, 5). Justification means the presentation of the self to God as a living sacrifice; non-conformity to the world; spiritual renewal; right self-estimate—all the range of right practice and feeling which is portrayed in the twelfth chapter of this Epistle."[333]

I would suggest that you pause and reread Vincent's summary of how Paul used the word δικαιοσύνη, "righteousness." This lucid understanding of

---

[333] *Ibid.*, 39, 40.

righteousness will be the framework for our comments on such topics as faith, grace, and the "robe of Christ's righteousness." Further, we will see that Ellen White's many comments on these precious words thoroughly embrace the linguistic position of Vincent as well as other New Testament scholars.

COMPARISON OF VINCENT'S LINGUISTIC ANALYSIS WITH ELLEN WHITE'S TEACHINGS

Let's compare Vincent's understanding of "righteousness" and "justification" with Ellen White's grasp of these essential New Testament words:

- Righteousness is not only an attribute of God; it is also bestowed on men and women.

"Righteousness is holiness, likeness to God, and 'God is love' (1 John 4:16). It is conformity to the law of God, for all Thy commandments are righteousness' (Psalm 119:172), and 'love is the fulfilling of the law' (Romans 13:10). Righteousness is love, and love is the light and the life of God. The righteousness of God is embodied in Christ. We receive righteousness by receiving Him. Not by painful struggles or wearisome toil, not by gift or sacrifice, is righteousness obtained; but it is freely given to every soul who hungers and thirsts to receive it."[334]

- Righteousness defines the person who is in the right relationship to God.

"Let us place ourselves in right relation to Him who has loved us with amazing love. Let us avail ourselves of the means provided for us that we may be transformed into His likeness. ... How shall a man be just with God? How shall the sinner be made righteous? It is only through Christ that we can be brought in harmony with God, with holiness."[335]

- Righteousness is another way of describing the maturing life of faith.

"The righteousness which Christ taught is conformity of heart and life to the revealed will of God. Sinful men can become righteous only as they have faith in God and maintain a vital connection with Him. Then true godliness will elevate the thoughts and ennoble the life. Then the external forms of religion accord with the Christian's internal purity. Then the ceremonies required in the service of God are not meaningless rites, like those of the hypocritical Pharisees."[336]

---

[334] *Thoughts From the Mount of Blessing*, 18.
[335] *Steps to Christ*, 22, 23.
[336] *The Desire of Ages*, 310.

"In order for man to be justified by faith, faith must reach a point where it will control the affections and impulses of the heart; and it is by obedience that faith itself is made perfect."[337]

• Righteousness is more than a legal transaction or legal adjustment between God and men and women. "Justification" that does not actually remove the offending, wrong condition of the sinner is not genuine justification. Without a change of attitude and wholehearted desire to conform to God's righteousness, any use of the term "justification" would then be a legal fiction.

"Many have a nominal faith in Christ, but they know nothing of that vital dependence upon Him which appropriates the merits of a crucified and risen Saviour. Of this nominal faith James says: 'Thou believest [have faith] that there is one God; thou doest well: the devils also believe, and tremble. But wilt thou know, O vain man, that faith without works is dead?' (James 2:19, 20). Many concede that Jesus Christ is the Saviour of the world, but at the same time they hold themselves away from Him, and fail to repent of their sins, fail to accept of Jesus as their personal Saviour. Their faith is simply the assent of the mind and judgment to the truth; but the truth is not brought into the heart, that it might sanctify the soul and transform the character."[338]

MORE THAN "ONLY BELIEVE"

"From the pulpits of today the words are uttered: 'Believe, only believe. Have faith in Christ; you have nothing to do with the old law, only trust in Christ.' How different is this from the words of the apostle who declares that faith without works is dead. He says, 'But be ye doers of the word, and not hearers only, deceiving your own selves' (James 1:22). We must have that faith that works by love and purifies the soul. Many seek to substitute a superficial faith for uprightness of life and think through this to obtain salvation."[339]

"No one can believe with the heart unto righteousness, and obtain justification by faith, while continuing the practice of those things which the Word of God forbids, or while neglecting any known duty."[340]

---

[337] *Faith and Works,* 100.

[338] *Selected Messages,* bk. 1, 389.

[339] *Faith and Works,* 89. "This goody goody religion that makes light of sin and that is forever dwelling upon the love of God to the sinner, encourages the sinner to believe that God will save him while he continues in sin and he knows it to be sin. This is the way that many are doing who profess to believe present truth. The truth is kept apart from their life, and that is the reason it has no more power to convict and convert the soul. There must be a straining of every nerve and spirit and muscle to leave the world, its customs, its practices, and its fashions." —*Manuscript Releases,* vol. 6, 12.

[340] *Selected Messages,* bk. 1, 39.

- Righteousness maintains God as the absolute standard for the new relationship.

"There are great principles of righteousness to control the life of all intelligent beings, and upon conformity to these principles the well-being of the universe depends. Before this earth was called into being, God's law existed. Angels are governed by its principles, and in order for earth to be in harmony with heaven, man also must obey the divine statutes."[341]

- Justification is *more than pardon* (though pardon, as commonly understood, is included) because justification aims directly at character.

"By the manifestation of His love, by the entreating of His Spirit, He woos men to repentance; for repentance is the gift of God, and whom He pardons He first makes penitent."[342]

"In order to obtain the righteousness of Christ, it is necessary for the sinner to know what that repentance is which works a radical change of mind and spirit and action. The work of transformation must begin in the heart, and manifest its power through every faculty of the being; but man is not capable of originating such a repentance as this, and can experience it alone through Christ."[343]

"The disciples of Christ must obtain righteousness of a different character from that of the Pharisees, if they would enter the kingdom of heaven. God offered them, in His Son, the perfect righteousness of the law. If they would open their hearts fully to receive Christ, then the very life of God, His love, would dwell in them, transforming them into His own likeness; and thus through God's free gift they would possess the righteousness which the law requires."[344]

"The Jews had been wearily toiling to reach perfection by their own efforts, and they had failed. Christ had already told them that their righteousness could never enter the kingdom of heaven. Now He points out to them the character of the righteousness that all who enter heaven will possess [as unfolded in the Sermon on Mount]."[345]

---

[341] *Thoughts From the Mount of Blessing,* 48.
[342] *Selected Messages,* bk. 1, 324.
[343] *Ibid.,* 393.
[344] *Thoughts From the Mount of Blessing,* 54.
[345] *Ibid.,* 77.

- Righteousness (justification) aims at making men and women right because faith naturally issues in a new and personal rightness with God.

"Jesus knew that of yourself you could not obey God's law; for you were sold under sin; therefore He came to our world to bring to you moral power, that through faith in His name you might live. He brings his divine power to combine with your human efforts, that through His righteousness appropriated to yourself, you can keep His law."[346]

"In order for man to be justified by faith, faith must reach a point where it will control the affections and impulses of the heart; and it is by obedience that faith itself is made perfect."[347]

- Men and women of faith are not inherently righteous and neither are they merely declared righteous (which would be a legal fiction when separated from character change).

"None of the apostles or prophets ever claimed to be without sin. Men who have lived nearest to God, men who would sacrifice life itself rather than knowingly commit a wrong act, men whom God had honored with divine light and power, have confessed the sinfulness of their own nature. They have put no confidence in the flesh, have claimed no righteousness of their own, but have trusted wholly in the righteousness of Christ. So will it be with all who behold Christ."[348]

"But while God can be just, and yet justify the sinner through the merits of Christ, no man can cover his soul with the garments of Christ's righteousness while practicing known sins, or neglecting known duties. God requires the entire surrender of the heart, before justification can take place; and in order for man to retain justification, there must be continual obedience, through active, living faith that works by love and purifies the soul."[349]

- God's declaration of righteousness is literally true when a person of faith is in a right relationship with God.

"As the sinner, drawn by the power of Christ, approaches the uplifted cross, and prostrates himself before it, there is a new creation. A new heart is given him. He becomes a new creature in Christ Jesus.

---

[346] *Review and Herald,* July 29, 1890.
[347] *Selected Messages,* bk. 1, 366.
[348] *Christ's Object Lessons,* 160.
[349] *Selected Messages,* bk. 1, 366.

Holiness finds that it has nothing more to require. God Himself is 'the justifier of him which believeth in Jesus'" (Romans 3:26).[350]

GENUINE FAITH COMBINES WITH CHRIST'S POWER

"Genuine faith appropriates the righteousness of Christ, and the sinner is made an overcomer with Christ; for he is made a partaker of the divine nature, and thus divinity and humanity are combined."[351]

- Faith contains all the possibilities of personal holiness (righteousness).

"Genuine faith appropriates the righteousness of Christ, and the sinner is made an overcomer with Christ; for he is made a Partaker of the divine nature, and thus divinity and humanity are combined. … All that man can do without Christ is polluted with selfishness and sin; but that which is wrought through faith is acceptable to God. When we seek to gain heaven through the merits of Christ, the soul makes progress. 'Looking unto Jesus, the author and finisher of our faith,' we may go on from strength to strength, from victory to victory; for through Christ the grace of God has worked out our complete salvation.'"[352]

- The intent of justification is conformity to Christ's image (Romans 8:29, 30).

"And 'whom He justified, them He also glorified' (Romans 8:30). Great as is the shame and degradation through sin, even greater will be the honor and exaltation through redeeming love. To human beings striving for conformity to the divine image there is imparted an outlay of heaven's treasure, an excellency of power, that will place them higher than even the angels who have never fallen."[353]

"All these [professed Christians only] expect to be saved by Christ's death, while they refuse to live His self-sacrificing life. They extol the riches of free grace, and attempt to cover themselves with an appearance of righteousness, hoping to screen their defects of character; but their efforts will be of no avail in the day of God. …The righteousness of Christ will not cover one cherished sin. A man may be a law-breaker in heart; yet if he commits no outward act of transgression, he may be regarded by the world as possessing great integrity. But God's law looks into the secrets of the heart. Every act is judged

---

[350] *Christ's Object Lessons*, 163.
[351] *Faith and Works*, 93.
[352] *Ibid.*, 94.
[353] *Christ's Object Lessons*, 162.

by the motives that prompt it. Only that which is in accord with the principles of God's law will stand in the judgment. ... Those who reject the gift of Christ's righteousness are rejecting the attributes of character which would constitute them the sons and daughters of God."[354]

- Genuine justification or righteousness must be rooted in an actual change of moral condition.

"The essence of all righteousness is loyalty to our Redeemer. This will lead us to do right because it is right—because right-doing is pleasing to God."[355]

"The condition of eternal life is now just what it always has been—just what it was in Paradise before the fall of our first parents—perfect obedience to the law of God, perfect righteousness. If eternal life were granted on any condition short of this, then the happiness of the whole universe would be imperiled. The way would be open for sin, with all its train of woe and misery, to be immortalized. ...

"Christ has made a way of escape for us. He lived on earth amid trials and temptations such as we have to meet. He lived a sinless life. He died for us, and now He offers to take our sins and give us His righteousness. If you give yourself to Him, and accept Him as your Saviour, then, sinful as your life may have been, for His sake you are accounted righteous. ...

MORE THAN THIS

"More than this, Christ changes the heart. He abides in your heart by faith. You are to maintain this connection with Christ by faith and the continual surrender of your will to Him; and so long as you do this, He will work in you to will and to do according to His good pleasure. So you may say, 'The life which I now live in the flesh I live by the faith of the Son of God, who loved me, and gave Himself for me' (Galatians 2:20). ... Then with Christ working in you, you will manifest the same spirit and do the same good works—works of righteousness, obedience."[356]

- Justification or righteousness (same Greek word) describes the person who chooses to be a "living sacrifice," in non-conformity with the world—all the range of right practice and feeling portrayed in Romans 12.

---

[354] *Ibid.*, 316, 317.
[355] *Ibid.*, 98.
[356] *Steps to Christ*, 62.

"Righteousness is right doing, and it is by their deeds that all will be judged. Our characters are revealed by what we do. The works show whether the faith is genuine."[357]

"By the wedding garment in the parable is represented the pure, spotless character which Christ's true followers will possess. ... The fine linen, says the Scripture, 'is the righteousness of saints' (Revelation 19:8). It is the righteousness of Christ, His own unblemished character, that through faith is imparted to all who receive Him as their personal Saviour."[358]

"When we submit ourselves to Christ, the heart is united with His heart, the will is merged in His will, the mind becomes one with His mind, the thoughts are brought into captivity to Him; we live His life. This is what it means to be clothed with the garment of His righteousness."[359]

"It is in this life that we are to put on the robe of Christ's righteousness. This is our only opportunity to form characters for the home which Christ has made ready for those who obey His commandments."[360]

SUMMARY OF VINCENT'S AND WHITE'S UNDERSTANDING OF RIGHTEOUSNESS BY FAITH

It is gratifying to see how clearly Ellen White understood the larger meaning of "righteousness" and "justification." She recognized, with Vincent and others, that these terms have the same basic meaning. Unfortunately, many through the years have often used these two English words in two distinctly different ways.

In summary, "righteousness" for both Vincent and White describes a person who, by the grace of God, has been set right (by what Jesus has done *for us*) and is kept right (by what Jesus is doing *in* and *through* us).[361] It depicts a person in harmony with God, beginning with repentance, contrition, and a desire to grow in grace in maturing this right relationship with God. Righteousness, the goal of all interaction between God's grace and man's faith, is precisely the purpose of the gospel—the restoration in men and women of the image of God.[362]

---

[357] *Christ's Object Lessons*, 312.
[358] *Ibid.*, 310.
[359] *Ibid.*, 312.
[360] *Ibid.*, 319.
[361] "So we have nothing in ourselves of which to boast. We have no ground for self-exaltation. Our only ground of hope is in the righteousness of Christ imputed to us, and in that wrought by His Spirit working in and through us." —*Steps to Christ*, 63.
[362] See "Appendix K: Faith, The One Word That Settles Everything."

I find it more than interesting how Ellen White connected "righteousness by faith" with the core issues in the Great Controversy, at times without always using the precise phrase. For example:

> "The law of Jehovah was burdened with needless exactions and tra-
> ditions, and God was represented as severe, exacting, revengeful,
> and arbitrary. He was pictured as one who could take pleasure in
> the sufferings of his creatures. The very attributes that belonged to
> the character of Satan, the evil one represented as belonging to the
> character of God. Jesus came to teach men of the Father, to correctly
> represent Him before the fallen children of earth. Angels could not
> fully portray the character of God, but Christ, who was a living
> impersonation of God, could not fail to accomplish the work. The
> only way in which *He could set and keep men right* [note the ellipse of
> truth] was to make Himself visible and familiar to their eyes."[363]

To put all this in another way, think of what Jesus said to Nicodemus: "You must be born again" (John 3:7). Every birth is an event and a process. Stillborns (an event without a process) are truly sad for all concerned—parents, medical team and friends. Something indeed happened, but the baby did not continue to live; it did not grow. Spiritually, to be born again (conversion) implies that growth has begun. Between the event (birth) and the growth (process) God and the baby (soon to become what he/she was born to be) work together. In both the event and process God provides the energy and wisdom to meet all of life's challenges.

Faith is that interface between God and the baby at birth and between God and the growth of the child. God and faith interfacing is the simple picture of how God is needed for what theologians call justification (event) and sanctification (process). And how the constant decision of men and women of faith is also needed for both event and process.[364]

Freedom is best understood by those who have a clear picture of their own weaknesses and a picture of an all-powerful God who will move heaven and earth to help men and women to be free from the shackles of sin's consequences. Free, indeed!

Remarkable co-op plan God set up to get us to live forever! How does it really work?

---

[363] *Signs of the Times,* January 20, 1890, italics supplied.
[364] "The writers of the New Testament Epistles never regarded the Christian religion as an 'ethic,' still less a performance. To them it was an invasion of their own lives by the living Spirit of God; their response in repentance and faith provided the means by which the divine could penetrate the merely human. They lived lives of super-human quality because they believe quite simply that Christ Himself was alive within them." —Phillips, *op. cit.,* 10, 11.

CHAPTER NINETEEN:
HOW GRACE RELATES TO FAITH AND RIGHTEOUSNESS

A t first glance, this chapter may seem like heavy theology. But not really! Conventional words like "grace" and "faith" either bore people or cause arguments? Why? Because for centuries these two words have been fogged over by theological debate, often with deadly results. Why? Because these simple biblical words have not been understood within the Great Controversy! Freedom happens when grace and faith are fully understood.

The word "grace" is as woefully misunderstood as "faith" has been for 2,000 years. Grace is a powerful word! Grace,[365] a facet of God's love (agape) and as generally used in the New Testament, describes whatever God has done, is doing, and will do to help conform men and women "to the image of His Son" (Romans 8:29). Our human minds cannot fathom what all this means. Grace is whatever men and women need in order to be saved. It is exactly what men and women do not have, nor ever will have, of themselves.

In the God-man relationship, grace has two sides: grace that forgives (Romans 3:24; 5:15) and grace that empowers (2 Corinthians 12:9). For example, in Hebrews 4:16, Paul focused on the empowerment of grace: "Let us therefore come boldly to the throne of grace, that we may obtain mercy and find grace to help in time of need."

One of the indications of a limited gospel is an over-emphasis on the mercies of grace with a muted glance at the empowerment of grace—whereby men and women find all the help they need to resist the Evil One. A limited understanding of grace leads to a false gospel.

But in God's plan, grace cannot by itself save men and women. Paul has given us the classic formula of salvation: "For by grace you have been saved through faith, and that not of yourselves; it is the gift of God, not of works, lest anyone should boast. For we are His workmanship, created in Christ Jesus for good works, which God prepared beforehand that we should walk in them" (Ephesians 2:8–10).

---

[365] Gr. Χαρις—a word with wide meaning in both secular and biblical writings: "attractiveness" — Luke 4:22; "favor" —Acts 15:26; "found favor" —Luke 1:30; "grace to you" (Christian greeting) —Galatians 1:3; "God of all grace," —1 Peter 5:10; "Spirit of grace,"—Hebrews 10:29; "grace given to me," —Romans 12:3; "grace by which we may serve," — Hebrews 12:28; "find grace to help in time of need," Hebrews 4:16. Perhaps the one English word that best translates Χαρις would be "generosity." The stupendous generosity of God exceeds our ability to describe His graciousness and shared power whereby we turn from self-centered ways and join Him in self-denial and self-sacrifice for the good of others.

God will do all that an infinitely gracious and patient Lover can do to woo His bride, hoping one day to get her to the altar (Revelation 19:7–9). But even God cannot force His "bride" to love Him back or to find a wedding dress! Love cannot be forced!

All that a gracious God can do in wooing men and women is to appeal for fair and undivided attention—long enough to hear Him speak to their inmost thoughts, to listen to reason (Isaiah 1:18). And the favorable response He seeks is called, in the New Testament, "faith."[366]

Faith is the human response to grace. Faith is that appreciation, appropriation and acceptance of grace that opens the door for grace to continue its work in the life of the sinner. In short, faith permits grace to do its work.[367] Here is another example of the ellipse of truth—grace and faith are the two foci that make salvation happen.[368]

Faith is the condition that makes salvation possible. Although faith does not possess merit in itself, the absence of faith frustrates grace. Though grace is the source of salvation, we have no salvation without faith—even as we have no salvation without grace.

PAUL'S ANATOMY OF SALVATION

Paul's classic definition (Ephesians 2:8–10) of the anatomy of salvation should have served as a barrier against two monstrous perversions that have divided Christian churches for centuries. On one hand, we have a large body of Christians who believe that grace covers men and women of faith in such a way that they are no longer "under the law" (Romans 6:15). On the other hand, we have Christians who believe worthy acts (so-called "acts of faith") in some way earn and/or satisfy God's love, and thus in some way help to secure their salvation.

---

[366] Edward W. H. Vick has an exceedingly lucid chapter on the meaning of New Testament faith in *Is Salvation Really Free?* (Hagerstown, MD: RHPA, 1983), 60–69.

[367] "Genuine faith appropriates the righteousness of Christ, and the sinner is made an overcomer with Christ; for he is made a partaker of the divine nature, and thus divinity and humanity are combined. ... In order to meet the requirements of the law, our faith must grasp the righteousness of Christ, accepting it as our righteousness. Through union with Christ, through acceptance of His righteousness by faith, we may be qualified to work the works of God, to be colaborers with Christ. If you are willing to drift along with the current of evil, and do not cooperate with the heavenly agencies in restraining transgression in your family, and in the church, in order that everlasting righteousness may be brought in, you do not have faith. Faith works by love and purifies the soul. Through faith the Holy Spirit [grace] works in the heart to create holiness therein; but this cannot be done unless the human agent will work with Christ. We can be fitted for heaven only through the work of the Holy Spirit [grace] upon the heart; for we must have Christ's righteousness as our credentials if we would find access to the Father. In order that we may have the righteousness of Christ, we need daily to be transformed by the influence of the Spirit [grace], to be a partaker of the divine nature. It is the work of the Holy Spirit [grace] to elevate the taste, to sanctify the heart, to ennoble the whole man." —*Selected Messages*, bk. 1, 363, 374.

[368] See "Appendix L: The Ellipse of Truth."

The first group is called "antinomians," that is, they believe that grace "stands instead of the law." The second are often labeled as "legalists," those in bondage to "righteousness by works."

How does Paul's ellipse of salvation, rightly understood, prevent these two errors? When grace is misunderstood, we immediately misunderstand faith. When we misunderstand faith, God's sovereignty and fairness, and thus grace, is misunderstood.

One of the major factors that helps us to understand Paul's focus on grace and faith is to remember the kind of human being God created in the Garden of Eden. And why!

What was the point in creating human beings as a "new and distinct order"?[369] Men and women were created to be part of God's answer to Satan's accusations that created intelligences—angels, inhabitants of other worlds, and human beings—with a free will could not and would not obey God's will because His commandments were unfair and suffocating.[370] So in God's grand plan to secure the universe, the human family would be the laboratory test as to whether men and women could and would choose to be cheerfully obedient. The evidence would be in the kind of people they turned out to be!

We learned earlier (on page 48) that God would risk the future of His universe (1) on this "new and distinct order" and (2) on that one word we have been looking at throughout this book—that word is "freedom." As you would expect, that same word lies at the bottom of the 2,000-year-old controversy over the meaning of both grace and faith.

Was Adam given freedom to choose or not? Was Adam responsible for his actions or was He predestined to sin? Did Adam have freedom to respond to God's counsel, that is, was he "responsible" (that is, able-to respond)? Did God risk the future of the universe on the knife-edge of human freedom? The answers are all "yes!"

FAITH DESCRIBES THE PROPER RESPONSE TO GOD'S GRACE

Faith is the New Testament word that describes a responsible person's free response to God's free grace.[371] But the meaning of "faith" depends on the kind of God we are relating to and how we understand human responsibility.

If one thinks of God as Sovereign in such a way that no man or devil can thwart His will, that whatever God wants He gets or does, then human beings can be no more responsible than a dog.[372] In such thinking, faith tends to become only passive acceptance of what God has done. Human accountability is limited to an intellectual acceptance of His marvelous gift. This "knowledge" is expressed in the joy of knowing that Jesus paid the price

---

[369] See 46.
[370] See 40.
[371] See "Appendix K: Faith, The Word That Settles Everything."
[372] See 24, 28.

for one's salvation—and that nothing more can be, or needs to be, done to "add" to Christ's death on the cross. Logically and ethically (history so sadly reveals), such thinking leads to a lessened regard for disciplined, obedient concern for growth in character. A cognitive disconnect exists between the sinner's awareness of his/her to overcome sin and the empowering Role of the Holy Spirit who is always ready to help.

But faith can be misunderstood from another direction. An overemphasis on the human side of the divine-human equation in Paul's anatomy of salvation leads to an overemphasis on the reliability of reason or on emotional experiences. This overemphasis, though called "faith", fails to grasp the magnitude and depth of sin. Such optimism believes, in some way, that a divine spark of goodness lodges within everyone, merely waiting for the touch of God to fan it. Many have gone down this road, assuming that humanity needs a Teacher more than a merciful Savior.

Here again the ellipse of truth[373] (a right definition of grace and faith) will save us from these two errors: from the over-emphasis on Jesus as our Savior that mutes His role as our Teacher/Example, on one hand, or, on the other hand, from an over-emphasis of His role as our Teacher and Example while muting His role as our Savior.

Dietrich Bonhoeffer, that heroic German pastor who showed all Christians how they should have responded to Nazi terror, spoke out plainly against these two perennial theological errors. "The truth is that so long as we hold both sides of the proposition together they contain nothing inconsistent with right belief, but as soon as one is divorced from the other, it is bound to prove a stumbling-block. 'Only those who believe [have faith] obey' ... and 'only those who obey believe [have faith]' . ... If the first half of the proposition stands alone, the believer is exposed to the danger of cheap grace, which is another word for damnation. If the second half stands alone, the believer is exposed to the danger of salvation through works, which is also another word for damnation."[374]

CHEAP GRACE

Bonhoeffer saw the damage clearly: "Cheap grace is the deadly enemy of our Church. We are fighting today for costly grace. ... In such a Church, the world finds a cheap covering for its sins; no contrition is required, still less any real desire to be delivered from sin. ... Cheap grace means the justification of sin without the justification of the sinner. ... Cheap grace is the grace we bestow on ourselves. ... It is a fatal misunderstanding of Luther's action to suppose his rediscovery of the gospel of pure grace offered a general dispensation from obedience to the command of Jesus, or that it was the great discovery of

---

[373] See 458 ff.
[374] *The Cost of Discipleship* (New York: The Macmillan Company, 1959, hardback), 58. See "Appendix O: Bonhoeffer's Exposé of Cheap Grace."

the Reformation that God's forgiving grace automatically conferred upon the world both righteousness and holiness. ... The word of cheap grace has been the ruin of more Christians than any commandment of works."[375]

Bonhoeffer's statement is similar to one by Ellen White as she commented on those who "expect to be saved by Christ's death, while they refuse to live His self-sacrificing life. They extol the riches of free grace, and attempt to cover themselves with an appearance of righteousness, hoping to screen their defects of character; but their efforts will be of no avail in the day of God."[376]

When faith is confused with mere belief, we have Christians who emphasize doctrine and orthodoxy of belief as the test of faith.[377] Often their main refrain is "only believe."[378] Grace is then misunderstood as God's all-encompassing gift of salvation "finished" on the Cross without any human responsibility involved in character transformation.

When we confuse faith primarily with cool reason or warm feelings, we have another large group that emphasizes good fellowship, warm harmony, tolerance of belief, because (some say) "all roads lead to heaven."[379] Grace

---

[375] *Ibid.,* 45–59. See Vick, *op. cit.,* 78–79.

[376] *Christ's Object Lessons,* 316.

[377] Yesterday I received a small pamphlet from a stranger entitled, "Who's Right?" It appealed to the reader "to believe in our hearts that Jesus died and rose again, then we can be saved from our sin. He goes on to say that if we will call upon His name we will be saved." This was helpful—but it does not go as far as Jesus would go. Think of His many parables regarding heart transformation and the connection between believing and doing (Matt. 7:21–29).

[378] "It is not enough for us to believe that Jesus is not an impostor, and that the religion of the Bible is no cunningly devised fable. We may believe that the name of Jesus is the only name under heaven whereby man may be saved, and yet we may not through faith make Him our personal Saviour. It is not enough to believe the theory of truth. It is not enough to make a profession of faith in Christ and have our names registered on the church roll. ... 'Hereby we do know that we know Him if we keep His commandments' 1 John 3:24; 2:3. This is the genuine evidence of conversion. Whatever our profession, it amounts to nothing unless Christ is revealed in works of righteousness." — *Christ's Object Lessons,* 312, 313. "Many concede that Jesus Christ is the Saviour of the world, but at the same time they hold themselves away from Him, and fail to repent of their sins, fail to accept of Jesus as their personal Saviour. Their faith is simply the assent of the mind and judgment to the truth; but the truth is not brought into the heart, that it might sanctify the soul and transform the character." —*Selected Messages,* bk. 1, 389, 390.

[379] "Do you want a special feeling or emotion to prove that Christ is yours? Is this more reliable than pure faith in God's promises? Would it not be better to take the blessed promises of God and apply them to yourself, bearing your whole weight upon them? This is faith." —*Review and Herald,* July 29, 1890. "We can see the importance, then, of having true faith, for it is the motive power of the Christian's life and action; but feeling is not faith; emotion is not faith. We must bring our very work and thought and emotions to the test of the word, and true faith will be profoundly impressed by the voice of God, and will act accordingly. If people would only search the Scriptures more diligently, false doctrines and heresies would be fewer." —*Signs of the Times,* November 24, 1887. "Genuine faith is founded on the Scriptures; but Satan uses so many devices to wrest the Scriptures and bring in error, that great care is needed if one would know what they really do teach. It is one of the great delusions of this time to dwell much upon feeling, and to claim honesty while ignoring the plain utterances of the word of God because that word does not coincide with feeling. Many have no foundation for their faith but emotion. Their religion consists in excitement; when that ceases, their faith is gone. Feeling may be chaff, but the word of God is the wheat. And 'what,' says the prophet, 'is the chaff to the wheat'?" —*Review and Herald,* November 25, 1884.

then becomes a matter of believing in a very generous God who has many different mansions for the various religious groups of the world, all traveling up the mountain but along different paths.[380]

This confusion of faith with "common values" will be the driving force behind the prevailing threat and countervailing resistance in the endtimes to a church emphasizing the "commandments of God" and the "faith of Jesus" (Revelation 14:12).[381] Whenever we emphasize "common values," the concern for doctrinal purity fades. Many will vote with their feet for a church that provides an exciting "experience," with hugging, lively praise songs often devoid of content but captivating with beat and repetition, and a friendly "coffee hour."

No one can be against a friendly church and relevant music. Too often there can be a disconnect between "faith" and an interest in clear biblical doctrine. Why? Because in our post-modern culture of politically correct speech, the emphasis on doctrine is considered divisive—thus unacceptable for a "loving" fellowship. In fact, to raise doctrinal issues would violate the rights of others to believe what they want to. Tolerance becomes the key word, not what is truth! Whenever feelings replace facts, we have a rapidly swirling sinkhole that will increase in speed as the end of the endtime draws nearer. More later![382]

But now, back to the relationship between grace and faith—a clarity that is needed more and more wherever we look.

MARY IS A CAMEO PICTURE

Mary Magdalene's experience is a cameo picture of how grace and faith work. We are told that she was converted and fell away big time—seven times (Luke 8:2)! I suspect that most of us can relate in some way to Mary's struggles. It may not be lust and forbidden sexual pleasures. But every one of us has some weakness that guardian angels would consider big-time, even though we may not! And we can identify with Mary's determination to overcome these weaknesses!

Remember when Jesus stepped into Mary's life, saving her from being stoned to death (John 8:3–12). Frightful scene, hypocrites getting their kicks out of putting Mary down, for sins they themselves participated in!

But for some time, Jesus had been working with weak Mary. He knew her heart; He "saw the better traits of her character." She "had heard His

---

[380] Here is a sample of what we can read in any newspaper or newsmagazine, several times a week: "The key to finding the balance of truth found in all spiritual paths and that accommodates varying religious beliefs is the recognition that each religion contains elements of truth. By accepting this principle, we are then free to view each religion as a spiritual path to the infinite, eternal, and omnipotent divine source of all things. We can each follow our own path; share our faith with others without hatred, scorn, or violence; and accept others' paths as equally valid to our own." —Letter to the Editor, *U.S. News & World Report*, June 24, 2002.

[381] See 69, 97, 145, 163, 186.

[382] See 288–290.

strong cries to the Father in her behalf."[383] She knew she had failed Him again and again and that she did not deserve another chance.

But Jesus saw the picture differently. You know the story well. After writing incriminating information in the sand, He asked Mary where her accusers were. Then Jesus showered grace on Mary, "Neither do I condemn you; go and sin no more." Grace met human need and Mary's responsibility. Grace does not and would not keep Mary from sinning again without Mary's cooperation. Mary's part was to respond to grace with faith.

Remember the occasion, later in Simon's house, at a gathering of the "spiritually elite." Mary slipped in and indeed put Jesus in an awkward position—washing His feet with her tears and hair! Even kissing His feet! Awkward situation for everyone present!

But for Mary, it seemed that only Jesus mattered. She knew how weak and sordid she had been—so did Jesus. But she also knew that the only person in the world who seemed to really care about her was this Teacher from Nazareth. He was the only one who had treated her as if she might be worth something. And she was grateful!

Jesus must have astonished the assembled guests by saying to Mary: "Your sins are forgiven" (Luke 7:48). But He was not finished: "Your faith has saved you. Go in peace" (Luke 7:50). Can we find a better example of grace and faith at work!

After that earlier temple experience when she had faced death, Mary clung to Jesus' confidence in her. Day after day, she responded to His confidence with everything that we have been saying about faith. And now, in Simon's home, Jesus was recognizing her growth, her victory over lust—and He commended her "faith." "Mary, your faith has saved you!"

That interchange with Mary may be the template for my life and yours. How many times has Jesus said to you: "Your faith has saved you!" Not that you overcame all by yourself! Hardly! But Jesus could not have "saved you" if you, like Mary, had not responded in faith to His confidence in you. Faith is very, very important in our salvation. Without faith, grace is not only frustrated, it is shut down as far as you and I are concerned—we cannot "be saved"!

Is there anything about your experience that is worse than Mary's? I doubt it. You too will find the sweetness of victory if you keep coming back to grace with your maturing faith, just as Mary did!

In other words, the God of grace initiates, men and women of faith respond. A gracious God explains, men and women of faith cooperate. The Lord of grace offers pardon and power and He waits for men and women of faith to freely grasp both.[384] On His side, it is all grace, while on our side, it is all faith—faith

---

[383] *The Desire of Ages*, 568.
[384] See *Education*, 36.

that permits God's full authority to have His will done. Paul's anatomy of salvation could not have been said more clearly to the Ephesians (2:8–10).

GRACE NEEDED FROM START TO FINISH

From the first whisper of grace wooing sinners to seek their Savior, through the period of growth, until transformed sinners "reflect the image of Jesus fully,"[385] it is the same grace operating. It is God at work pursuing His original objective of changing sinners into "a new creation, ... so that in Him we might become the righteousness of God in Him" (2 Corinthians 5:17, 21).[386] The purpose of the gospel is reached—the "restoration" of the lost image of God in men and women of faith.

When we understand that the same grace and the same faith are functioning, from the beginning of the Christian's commitment to his or her eventual "fitness" for heaven,[387] every theological problem dividing Christian groups today would vanish.

When faith claims God's gracious pardon, when faith claims God's gracious power in resisting evil—it is the same quality of grace and faith operating. Bible writers make no distinction in grace or in faith between their functions in justification and sanctification. Ellen White frequently described this twin function of grace and faith without using conventional theological terms: "Freely will He pardon all who come to Him for forgiveness and restoration."[388] For Ellen White, the purpose of the gospel is always "restoration"[389]—the wonderful product of grace and faith.

What may seem to be a difference (faith receiving grace in either pardon or power) arises because one may be looking at faith as one would a windowpane. A person may see one side of the pane from the inside of the room; later, that same person my go outside and see the same window but through the other side of the pane. But it's the same windowpane! Men and women of faith, from one point of view, see faith as a passive response to God's grace—faith with its empty hands pleading for God's grace, for His mercies and pardon. But they also see faith as an active response—faith with its weak hands pleading for God's grace, for His power to overcome all hereditary and cultivated tendencies to sin.

---

[385] *Early Writings*, 71.
[386] "God was to be manifest in Christ, 'reconciling the world unto Himself.' 2 Corinthians 5:19. Man had become so degraded by sin that it was impossible for him, in himself, to come into harmony with Him whose nature is purity and goodness. But Christ, after having redeemed man from the condemnation of the law, could impart divine power to unite with human effort. Thus by repentance toward God and faith in Christ the fallen children of Adam might once more become 'sons of God' (1 John 3:2)." —*Patriarchs and Prophets*, 64.
[387] "Fitness," see *Christ's Object Lessons*, 96, 221, 288, 307, 309, 310, 312, 355, 356, 360, 384, 408, 412.
[388] *The Desire of Ages*, 568.
[389] *Education*, 15, 16.

We are not describing two kinds of faith any more than we are describing two separate pieces of glass, as if we can separate the windowpane into two separate pieces. Men and women of faith need and accept pardon and power because such gifts are exactly what men and women of faith know they need.

JOHN WESLEY, A BRIGHT BEACON

John Wesley, having seen all this clearly, became a bright beacon in his day amidst Calvinism in the Reformed denominations, on his right hand, and Arminianism, on his left. Note how he sorted all this out:

> "By justification we are saved from the guilt of sin, and restored to the favor of God; by sanctification we are saved from the power and root of sin, and restored to the image of God. All experience, as well as Scripture, show this salvation to be both instantaneous and gradual. It begins the moment we are justified, in the holy, humble, gentle, patient love of God and man."[390]

The Reformed denominations (Calvinistic) taught that the elect only were given saving faith; that they would be justified by irresistible grace and would be saved unconditionally. Most Arminians, in their emphasis on free grace and the free response of faith, erred in teaching that faith was unconditional. That is, they taught (in Wesley's words) that "Christ abolished the moral law. ... that Christian liberty is liberty from obeying the commandments of God, that it is a bondage to do a thing because it is commanded. ... that a Preacher ought not to exhort to good works; not unbelievers, because it is hurtful; not believers, because it is needless."[391]

These two theological errors still divide every Christian denomination in the 21st century! All because of confusion regarding that one word, "faith." Out of that confusion, we continue to have misunderstandings of grace, justification, sanctification, works, law or righteousness by faith.

On one hand, Wesley had to contend with those who thought he did not value justification highly enough because of his emphasis on sanctification. On the other, he had to resist those who thought he did not understand justification because he insisted on the growth of the moral life, the whole-hearted obedience to the will of God.

In responding to both errors over a number of years, Wesley emphasized, with Paul, that "faith is imputed for righteousness to every believer; namely, faith in the righteousness of Christ."

But Wesley always hastened to clarify what he and Paul meant when someone would ask, "Must not we put off the filthy rags of our own righteousness, before we can put on the spotless righteousness of Christ?" Wesley replied:

---

[390] Wesley, John, *The Works of John Wesley,* Third Ed. (Kansas City, Mo: Beacon Hill Press, 1978), vol. VII, 509.
[391] Wesley, *op. cit.,* vol. VIII, 278.

"Certainly we must; that is, in plain terms, we must repent, before we can believe the gospel. We must be cut off from dependence upon ourselves, before we can truly depend on Christ. ... But do not you believe inherent righteousness? Yes, in its proper place; not as the ground of our acceptance with God, but as the fruit of it; not in the place of imputed righteousness, but as consequent upon it. That is, I believe God implants righteousness in every one to whom he has imputed it. ...

"In the meantime, what we are afraid of is this—lest any should use the phrase, 'The righteousness of Christ,' or, 'The righteousness of Christ is imputed to me,' as a cover for his unrighteousness. We have known this done a thousand times. A man has been reproved, suppose for drunkenness: 'O,' said he, 'I pretend to no righteousness *of my own;* Christ is *my righteousness.*' Another has been told, that 'the extortioner, the unjust, shall not inherit the kingdom of God;' He replies, with all assurance, 'I am unjust in myself, but I have a spotless righteousness in Christ.' And thus, though a man be as far from the practice as from the tempers of a Christian; though he neither has the mind which was in Christ, nor in any respect walks as He walked; yet, he has armour of proof against all conviction, in what he calls 'the righteousness of Christ.'

"It is the seeing of so many deplorable instances of this kind, which makes us sparing in the use of these expressions."[392]

FAITH NOT GOD'S WORK BUT OURS

In reviewing all this, we must be crystal clear: even though faith is prompted and awakened by God in every one (Romans 12:3; John 1:9 reminds us that Jesus is the "Light which gives light to every man"), faith is not God's work but ours—the human response to God's call for men and women to represent Him in proving Satan wrong. For men and women to respond to God's wooing, God must wait. He cannot, by the nature of His character, force faith. He can appeal to faith, win it, but never coerce it. He does not even give "grace to help in time of need" (Hebrews 4:16) if it is not asked for! Even as He does not give the peace of forgiveness unless it is asked for by the sincerely repentant, those who confess and forsake their sins (Proverbs 28:13; 1 John 1:9)![393]

---

[392] Wesley, *op. cit.,* vol. V, 241, 244.

[393] We must not confuse "repentance" with "coming to Jesus." The precious word, "Come," especially when the sinner sees God's love through Jesus on the Cross, is the pulling power that breaks the sinner's heart. In other words, the remorseful sinner "must go to Christ in order that he may be enabled to repent." —*Review and Herald,* September 3, 1901. "Just here is a point on which many may err, and hence they fail of receiving the help that Christ desires to give them. They think that they cannot come to Christ unless they first repent, and that repentance prepares for the forgiveness of their sins. It is true that repentance does precede the forgiveness of sins;

In other words, faith is an attitude of saying "yes" to grace—to whatever God wants us to say or do. For that reason we speak of the experience of faith as God's way of reestablishing the reign of love (Galatians 5:6). Faith is not genuine, is not complete, unless it produces a truly loving person and that remarkable development is a result of grace at work.[394]

Grace And Faith Produce Love

John Wesley could easily be called the Preacher of Love.[395] Of all the major Protestant reformers, Wesley understood most clearly the plan of salvation. He saw the correct connection between grace, faith and love:

> "Faith, then, was originally designed of God to re-establish the law of love. Therefore, in speaking thus, we are not undervaluing it, or robbing it of its due praise; but, on the contrary, showing its real worth, exalting it in its just proportion, and giving it that very place which the wisdom of God assigned it from the beginning. It is the grand means of restoring that holy love wherein man was originally created. It follows, that although faith is of no value in itself, (as neither is any other means whatsoever,) yet as it leads to that end, the establishing anew the law of love in our hearts; and as, in the present state of things, it is the only means under heaven for effecting it; it is on that account an unspeakable blessing to man, and of unspeakable value before God."[396]

Both Wesley and Ellen White, at the core of their theologies, are motivated by Paul's message to the Galatians: "For we through the Spirit eagerly wait for the hope of righteousness by faith. For in Christ Jesus neither circumcision nor uncircumcision avails anything, but faith working through love" (5:5, 6).

---

for it is only the broken and contrite heart that will feel the need of a Saviour. But must the sinner wait till he has repented before he can come to Jesus? Is repentance to be made an obstacle between the sinner and the Saviour? The Bible does not teach that the sinner must repent before he can heed the invitation of Christ, 'Come unto Me, all ye that labor and are heavy-laden, and I will give you rest' (Matthew 11:28). It is the virtue that goes forth from Christ, that leads to genuine repentance." —*Steps to Christ*, 26.

[394] "Genuine faith always works by love. When you look to Calvary it is not to quiet your soul in the non-performance of duty, not to compose yourself to sleep, but to create faith in Jesus, faith that will work, purifying the soul from the slime of selfishness. When we lay hold of Christ by faith, our work has just begun. Every man has corrupt and sinful habits that must be overcome by vigorous warfare. Every soul is required to fight the fight of faith. If one is a follower of Christ, he cannot be sharp in deal, he cannot be hardhearted, devoid of sympathy. He cannot be coarse in his speech. He cannot be full of pomposity and self-esteem. He cannot be overbearing, nor can he use harsh words, and censure and condemn. The labor of love springs from the work of faith." —Ellen White Comments, *Seventh-day Adventist Bible Commentary (SDABC)*, vol. 6, 1111.

[395] One of the most compelling reviews of John Wesley's theology was written by Mildred Bangs Wynkoop, *A Theology of Love: The Dynamic of Wesleyanism* (Kansas City, Mo: Beacon Hill Press, 1972.

[396] Wesley, *op. cit.*, vol. V, 464.

Thus through men and women of faith, the universe sees the intrinsic reality of the plan of salvation manifested, validated, and vindicated. When God goes about providing grace to men and women of faith, it is an ethical matter and not merely a judicial act leading to legal fiction. The gospel is concerned about redemption, not legal transactions. Grace liberates men and women of faith from their sins by helping them to overcome them, not cover them by some kind of theological magic or legal fiction—and then call all this "righteousness by faith."[397]

Paul urges us all "not to receive the grace of God in vain. ... Since we have these promises, beloved, let us cleanse ourselves from all filthiness of the flesh and spirit, perfecting holiness in the fear of God" (2 Corinthians 6:1; 7:1).

In this matter, John E. MacArthur Jr., is very constructive in his clear distinction between grace, as he understands it, and the general understanding of most Evangelicals today where grace slips into a new kind of antinomianism. In *The Vanishing Conscience,* as with his other books, he makes a strong case that "grace is to free us from sin. ... is much more than forgiveness for our sins, or a free ride to heaven. ... Grace is no sanction for sin. On the contrary, it grants the believer freedom *from* sin. ... it frees us to obey God."[398]

Mildred Wynkoop said it well: "Men [and women] are always trying to find some way to escape personal responsibility for being what they are, and to avoid having to confess it and do something about it. ... They (or we) are seeking an escape from inner evil in some magical way that evades the mature demand of meeting moral demands head on."[399]

The persistent problem even to our day is that too many feel that one must choose between Paul's faith and James's faith—that is, the notion that Paul's faith is some kind of "only believe" and James's faith is some kind of good works. Paul's confused followers end up trusting their knowledge of salvation. James's confused followers end up trusting in their faithfulness to commandment keeping. Both groups are missing the joy of salvation. Whether we trust in our brain or in our muscles—in the end we are building our sense of salvation on sand and not on the Rock. Until we learn how to trust the promises of God and His promised energy through His Holy Spirit, our Christian walk

---

[397] "The religion of Christ means more than the forgiveness of sin; it means taking away our sins, and filling the vacuum with the graces of the Holy Spirit. It means divine illumination, rejoicing in God. It means a heart emptied of self, and blessed with the abiding presence of Christ. When Christ reigns in the soul, there is purity, freedom from sin. The glory, the fullness, the completeness of the gospel plan is fulfilled in the life. The acceptance of the Savior brings a glow of perfect peace, perfect love, perfect assurance. The beauty and fragrance of the character of Christ revealed in the life testifies that God has indeed sent His Son into the world to be its Savior." —*Christ's Object Lessons,* 419, 420.

[398] (Dallas, TX: Word Publishing, 1994), 222. MacArhur's *Faith Works* (Dallas, TX: Word Publishing, 1993) is probably the clearest explanation of how Evangelicals are divided between "Lordship" and "No-Lordship" advocates, a distinction that every Christian church must settle.

[399] Wynkoop, *op. cit.,* 164.

will be more drudgery, whether we are mentally trying to have enough faith or whether we are physically trying to prove our faithfulness.

But before we move on, some may be wondering—how does a person actually get this kind of faith that builds on the Rock. Obviously, it is more than simply "believe." And it is also more than simply "obeying" even the Ten Commandments and staying out of jail.

DISCIPLES HAD TO LEARN FAITH

We discover faith as the disciples learned to have faith. We follow their path as they became acquainted with Jesus and learned to trust Him. Those disciples went through some tough times with Jesus. They studied Him and how He lived above ridicule. They watched Him react to those who spent their best brains trying to entrap Him. They not only trusted His teachings, they admired His courage and commitment to His Father's will. They watched Him die with forgiveness on His lips. And then resurrection Sunday! Everything He kept telling them about His mission before Calvary now suddenly appeared as clear as the noonday sun. They had seen and heard the Truth and their lives were forever changed. No one could shake their new confidence, their new ring of faith, because they now saw for themselves, not merely their Lord's teachings but His Lordship of their own lives. Faith became unshakeable because head and heart joined in total submission to a Person, not merely to theology.

We today must become first-century believers. We must not only be impressed with sound theological thinking, we must be overwhelmed by a Person. This is the purpose of the Holy Spirit's ministry—to make us experience what the disciples experienced. When that happens, Jesus today can give us the same authentic connection with Him that the disciples discovered. This connection, this experience, is what changed Saul the persecutor into Paul the messenger of love. And this same path is open to each of us. To find Jesus as first-century disciples did is to discover freedom that will change our lives.[400] You become a contemporary disciple with Peter, John, James and the rest of the 11 who told the world where faith would lead.[401]

No wonder God is always working on giving us reasons to have faith in Him. His purpose is to change us from self-oriented men and women—to free us from sinful weaknesses. To keep us thinking straight He keeps pointing us to our responsibilities. Why?

---

[400] "Faith involves a rediscovery and indeed a re-enactment of this original encounter. Recovery of authentic faith involves a dialogue between the claim of the present and the model encounter in the past." —Jack Boozer & William A. Beardslee, *Faith to Act* (Nashville, TN: Abingdon Press, 1967), 55, 56.

[401] Perhaps the clearest presentation of how to become a "contemporary disciple" is found in Soren Kierkegaard, transl. David F. Swenson, *Philosophical Fragments* (Princeton, NJ: Princeton University Press, 1969), 68–88.

CHAPTER TWENTY:
HOW WORKS RELATE
TO GRACE AND FAITH

Obviously, we can have no discussion about faith and grace without discussing "works"—that New Testament word that helped to focus the hostility between Jews and early Christians. Disagreement over what Paul or James meant by "works," or "righteousness by works," has continued to divide Christians to this day. Is it a matter of definitions only, or does it involve different ways of looking at the gospel? Getting a clear picture of what Paul and James meant has much to do with understanding how the Great Controversy plays out in our individual lives.

Paul would say: "A man is not justified by the works of the law but by faith in Jesus Christ" (Galatians 2:16); further, "We conclude that a man is justified by faith apart from the deeds of the law" (Romans 3:28).

But James said: "You see then that a man is justified by works, and not by faith only. ... for as the body without the spirit is dead, so faith without works is dead also" (2:24, 26).

What shall we make of this apparent contradiction?

THE PURPOSE OF THE GOSPEL

The first step in resolving what appears to be a contradiction is to remember the purpose of the gospel and how God plans to make the universe eternally secure.[402] Because the purpose of the gospel is to "restore in man the image of His Maker" and because only habitually loyal, obedient men and women of faith can guarantee an eternally secure universe, any discussion of faith and works must focus on the end product—the transformed rebel who can be safe to save.[403]

The well being of any country depends on loyal citizens, especially in times of national crisis. When immigrants request citizenship, they must answer many questions regarding their desire for citizenship papers. Witnesses are required who will vouch for the applicant's sincerity. All loyal citizens feel safer when their borders are properly guarded. The same sense for security that citizens of any country demand prevails throughout the unfallen worlds and heavenly angels—they don't want to jeopardize the security of the universe with "redeemed" people who can't be trusted with eternal life, people who are not safe to save.

---

[402] See 26, 27, 79, 99, 118, 133, 166, 178, 185, 218, 222, 287, 312, 391, 392, 440.
[403] See 98, 118, 181, 185, 210, 214, 339, 371, 388, 391, 398, 400, 402, 424, 438, 440.

Our second step is to understand what the context was for Paul and for James when they made their apparently contradictory statements. We know what they said, now what did they mean?

James was primarily concerned with the misunderstanding of faith. That same misunderstanding has troubled the Christian church from the first century to ours. John Wesley faced the same problem—that is, unconditional faith that viewed the law of God to be no longer binding on those who were "under grace" (Romans 6:15).[404] James is exceedingly clear regarding the authority of God's law, especially the Ten Commandments (see 2:8–12).[405]

James understood the gospel; he was a lucid teacher. He not only clarified the binding authority of the Ten Commandments, he drilled home the clearest statement regarding sin in the Bible: "Therefore, to him who knows to do good and does not do it, to him it is sin" (4:17). He gave no comfort to those who believed that genuine faith no longer was subject to the Ten Commandments, or to any other expression of the will of God.

The Book of James has been a profound source of strength for serious Christians through the years. He wrote during tough times. He saw his colleagues killed for the truth and he knew he was on Caesar's short list. But listen to him sing: "Count it all joy when you fall into various trials, knowing that the testing of your faith produces patience [Lit: "endurance;" compare Revelation 14:12], but let patience ["endurance"] have its perfect work, that you may be perfect and complete lacking nothing" (1:2–4).

James's message is full of counsel as to how to endure and to receive the "crown of life" (1:12): "Therefore lay aside all filthiness and overflow of wickedness, and receive with meekness the implanted word, which is able to save your souls. But be doers of the word, and not hearers only, deceiving yourselves" (1:21, 22).

JAMES ECHOES JESUS

I think James is echoing his Lord's searing warning that ended the Sermon on the Mount: "Not everyone who says to Me, 'Lord, Lord,' shall enter the kingdom of heaven, but he who does the will of My Father in heaven" (Matthew 7:21).

---

[404] See 139, 140.

[405] "The apostle James saw that dangers would arise in presenting the subject of justification by faith, and he labored to show that genuine faith cannot exist without corresponding works. The experience of Abraham is presented. 'Seest thou,' he says, 'how faith wrought with his works, and by works was faith made perfect?' Thus genuine faith does a genuine work in the believer. Faith and obedience bring a solid, valuable experience. There is a belief that is not a saving faith. The word declares that the devils believe and tremble. The so-called faith that does not work by love and purify the soul will not justify any man." —*Signs of the Times*, May 19, 1898.

The Book of James is worth a reread every year at least. He warns against "cheap grace" and against the bewitching slogan "Only believe!" Faith for James was the wholehearted response to God's grace—the heart appreciation that is grateful for forgiveness and for God's power to help in overcoming the sins that needed to be forgiven.

Now back to Paul. How could Paul be against James's sturdy appeal? Of course, Paul is not contradicting James. Paul was talking about a different issue when he targets "works" as the wrong way to find harmony with God and His righteousness. Paul was answering the same question that James addressed: How do we become righteous and holy, "without which no one will see the Lord" (Hebrews 12:14)? But he was looking at the question from another direction.

Paul emphatically agreed with James that it was an error for "Christians" to consider themselves righteous and holy by "believing" that Jesus did all that was necessary for their salvation on the Cross, that His grace now covers their unholy lives because Jesus had kept the law for them (Romans 6–8; 1 Corinthians 15:34; 2 Corinthians 7:1).

THE FIRST ERROR AT WHICH PAUL AIMED

Paul was aiming at another fundamental problem that has plagued men and women since Cain slew Abel—especially those who believe that they are God's chosen people! The problem is this: Those who sincerely try to make themselves righteous and holy by strenuous religious effort.

Paul saw it in the Jewish rituals of his earlier religious experience; no matter how hard one tries, no matter how many holy places one visits, no matter how much "self-imposed religion, false humility, and neglect of the body" (Colossians 2:23), a person can never restore himself in the image of our Maker; never convince the angels, or beings on other worlds, or God that he should be trusted with eternal life based on his actions.

Religious people obviously do religious things, such as following strict dietary habits, being careful in Sabbath observance (especially about what we *don't* do), tithing scrupulously and withdrawal from "worldly" pleasures. In other words, many sincere religious people can say with Paul, as he looked back on his former, exemplary life as a Jewish leader, "concerning the righteousness which is in the law, [I was] blameless" (Philippians. 3:6)!

Because Paul knew all this firsthand, he took dead aim on a particular kind of "righteousness, which is in the law." This is what he calls "the works of the law" (Galatians 3:5) or his "own righteousness, which is from the law" (Philippians 3:9). It should be obvious that Paul's context is light years away from what James was concerned with.

In Galatians especially, Paul is highlighting the confusion that some Jewish Christians were dumping on new believers in Galatia. In a way they had some logic and appeal—or they wouldn't have had anybody listening to them! The main issue was circumcision, a God-given command given to the father of the Faithful, Abraham himself. And who wouldn't want to be a "child" of Abraham! For the Jewish male, circumcision was the gold standard of "assurance" that he was right with God! But it was a presumptuous assurance!

The problem was that the significance of this rite had been lost through the centuries; it had become a loyalty test much as some today view saluting the flag. No salute—you must be unpatriotic; no circumcision—you must be an unbeliever!

Paul's argument was that after Jesus came, believers no longer needed circumcision to identify them as believers; Christian baptism replaced circumcision as the outward sign of loyalty to God: "In Him you were also circumcised with the circumcision made without hands, by putting off the body of the sins of the flesh, by the circumcision of Christ, buried with Him in baptism, in which you also were raised with Him through faith in the working of God, who raised Him from the dead" (Colossians 2:11, 12; see also Ephesians 2:11–15).

But baptism for Christians can become as meaningless as circumcision had become to the Jews. Baptism without continuing heart commitment is as unrelated to holiness as circumcision was to the "faithful" Jew.

Paul's use of the phrase "works of the law" referred to those in the church who were insisting that Christians should also "observe days and months and seasons and years" (Galatians 4:10) and that Gentiles should be circumcised: "Indeed I, Paul, say to you that if you become circumcised, Christ will profit you nothing. And I testify again to every man who becomes circumcised that he is a debtor to keep the whole law. You have become estranged from Christ, you who attempt to be justified by law; you have fallen from grace. ... For in Christ Jesus neither circumcision nor uncircumcision avails anything but faith working through love" (Galatians 5:2–6).

This question of circumcision kept the early church in turmoil (for example, Acts 15). Paul called it and any other insistence on Jewish law given as types of Christ, "a yoke of bondage" (Galatians 5:1; see Acts 15:10).

THE SECOND ERROR AT WHICH PAUL AIMED

Why was Paul and other Christian leaders so adamant regarding "the works of the law," calling them "a yoke of bondage" that "neither our fathers nor we were able to bear" (Acts 15:10)?

This leads us into the deeper meaning behind "works of the law." Paul was not limiting this phrase to circumcision only, though it became the lightning rod of contention. What really stunned the Galatians (and Christians ever since who want to grasp Paul's dramatic Matterhorn view of faith) was that he was including *all law*, even the Ten Commandments, in his phrase, "works of the law."[406] This must have been the theological hydrogen bomb that echoed throughout the early Christian church; it still has a blockbuster impact in many Christian churches today. No wonder the Jewish party was scandalized!

Without a correct understanding of the meaning of Paul's entire argument in his letter to the Galatians, noble Christians even today remain confused. They are reluctant to include the Ten Commandments within "works of the law" (as Paul used the phrase in the Galatian letter).

Why is this so? This leads us into the second error Paul was concerned about when he wrote against "the works of the law." He could see that both Jews and some early Christians were *misunderstanding the difference between the old and new covenants*.[407] However, Paul does not finish his Galatian letter containing this startling concept that "keeping" the Ten Commandments should be included in his condemnation of the "works of the law" without explaining just what he meant. He certainly was not an antinomian (belief that grace and faith substitutes for our obedience)!

Clearly, Paul was not downgrading the authority of the Ten Commandments. Hardly! Not Paul who would write: "The law is holy, and the commandment holy and just and good" (Romans 7:12). Or "Awake to righteousness, and do not sin; for some do not have the knowledge of God" (1 Corinthians 15:34). Or "For we must all appear before the judgment seat of Christ; that each one may receive the things done in the body, according to what he has done, whether good or bad" (2 Corinthians 5:10).

Paul, in Romans and Galatians, was clarifying the role of *law,* even the Ten Commandments that he said "gives birth to bondage" (Galatians 4:24). To the Romans he wrote that one of the purposes of the law is to provide "the knowledge of sin" (3:20).

As the result, *law,* even the Ten Commandment law, can only provide the honest worshipper "wretchedness" and the sense of living with "the body of death" (Romans 7:24). Paul knew by experience that "keeping the law" provided the security of "righteousness that is from the law" (Philippians 3:9). But when he heard the gospel and called Jesus his Lord, all

---

[406] "Paul here refers not so much to the ritual observances of the ceremonial law alone as to the Jewish concept that a man could save himself by meticulously keeping 'the law,' which consisted of moral, ceremonial, and civil precepts. ... Paul is concerned [in Galatians] only with the moral and ceremonial codes. The civil code apparently did not enter directly into the problem under discussion. The Jews erred in (1) considering that salvation could be attained to by one's own efforts, through compliance with the requirements of 'the law,' and by virtue of a meritorious life in which a surplus of good deeds would cancel out evil deeds; (2) adding to the law, as given by God, a mass of man-made requirements commonly called 'tradition'; and (3) extending, and attempting to enforce, certain features of the ritual and ceremonial provisions of 'the law' beyond the cross, when they expired by limitation. ... The word 'law' as used by Paul in the Book of Galatians, includes both the moral law, or Decalogue, and the ceremonial law. But Paul is not concerned so much with either of these, as such, as he is with the Jewish legal system of righteousness by works, which was based upon them." —*SDABC*, vol. 6, 949.

[407] See "Appendix N: The Difference Between the Old and New Covenants."

the good works of the law he "counted loss for Christ … and count them as rubbish" (Philippians 3:7, 8).

That new experience of finding grace, grace in freely given pardon and power, lifted Paul from the burden of works-righteousness to the joy of "the righteousness which is from God by faith" (Philippians 3:9). No longer did sin have to reign. Paul could sing to the Romans: "For you are not under law (the yoke that reveals sin) but under grace (the grace of pardon and power)" (Romans 6:14).[408]

Then Paul uses an interesting metaphor: Before the gospel, they were sinners and could do nothing about it—they were *slaves* to their desires. After the gospel when they were "obey[ing] from the heart that form of doctrine to which you were delivered. And having been set free from sin, you became *slaves* of righteousness for holiness. … But now having been set free from sin, and having become *slaves* of God, you have your fruit to holiness, and the end, everlasting life" (Romans 6:17–22).[409]

DIFFERENCE BETWEEN OLD AND NEW COVENANTS

Now let's pick up our earlier reference to the old and new covenants. The old covenant does not describe a time period, from Sinai to the Cross, but an attitude that reflects reliance on external obedience to law without the heart's transformation that produces "the fruits of the Spirit."[410]

Thus, the experiences of the *new* and the *old* covenants are like parallel tracks running from Abel and Cain to the Second Advent. The two covenants are heart-experience related, not time related. The difference between an honest person within the "yoke of bondage" of the old covenant and an honest person within the joy of the new covenant is the experience of faith. Paul was honest while burdened with the bondage of external commandment keeping—the old covenant experience. Paul was also honest, but relieved and at peace, with the joy of knowing that God both freely forgives and empowers his honest commitment to doing God's will—the new covenant experience.

---

[408] "'The law was our schoolmaster to bring us unto Christ, that we might be justified by faith.' In this scripture, the Holy Spirit through the apostle is speaking especially of the moral law. The law reveals sin to us, and causes us to feel our need of Christ, and to flee unto Him for pardon and peace by exercising repentance toward God and faith toward our Lord Jesus Christ. … "The law of ten commandments is not to be looked upon as much from the prohibitory side as from the mercy side. … To the obedient it is a wall of protection. We behold in it the goodness of God, who by revealing to men the immutable principles of righteousness seeks to shield them from the evils that result from transgression." —Manuscript 23a, 1896, cited in *SDABC*, vol. 6, 1110.

[409] "Obedience to God is liberty from the thralldom of sin, deliverance from human passion and impulse. Man may stand conqueror of himself, conqueror of his own inclinations, conqueror of principalities and powers, and of 'the rulers of the darkness of this world,' and of 'spiritual wickedness in high places'" (Ephesians 6:12). —*The Ministry of Healing*, 131.

[410] *Patriarchs and Prophets*, 372. Indebted to Paul Penno for "two parallel tracks" metaphor.

What makes the difference between the two covenants? Genuine faith makes the difference. Only a correct understanding of faith can bring real peace and real victory in a Christian's life (Romans 5:1, 2).

GOD'S GOOD PLEASURE

All this may sound too abstract, too theological. How does this all work so that average, non-theological men or women can easily understand how to get right and stay right with His Lord so that they can "work … His good pleasure"?[411]

Peter spoke to the average person: "So then, have your minds ready for action. Keep alert and set your hope completely on the blessing that will be given you when Jesus Christ is revealed. Be obedient to God, and do not allow your lives to be shaped by those desires you had when you were still ignorant. Instead, be holy in all that you do, just as God who called you is holy. The scripture says, 'Be holy because I am holy'" (1 Peter 1:13, 14, TEV).

To the Thessalonians, Paul wrote: "Finally, our brothers, you learnt from us how you should live in order to please God. This is, of course, how you have been living. And now we beg and urge you in the name of the Lord Jesus to do even more" (1 Thessalonians 4:1, 2 TEV).

To the Philippians, Paul emphasized his interest in pleasing God: "Therefore [in view of Christ's example and ministry] … work out your own salvation with fear and trembling; for it is God who works in you both to will and to do for His good pleasure. Do all things without murmuring and disputing, that you may become blameless and harmless, children of God without fault in the midst of a crooked and perverse generation, among whom you shine as lights in the world" (Philippians 2:12–15).

God's "good pleasure" is our salvation! Restoring His universe in such a way that no angel or human being would ever again want to think a rebellious thought—that would be God's good pleasure! Enjoying the eternal security of all His creation—that would be God's good pleasure!

But are Peter and Paul's admonitions being made clear these days? It doesn't seem so! Many voices in all churches insist that to focus on the Christian life (that is, on sanctification) is to emphasize behaviorism, even legalism! They say that to include sanctification within "righteousness by faith" is to retreat to Rome and papal doctrine; to ask for holy lives, as part of the gospel message, is to lay a crushing burden on "saved" Christians. They insist that this burden leads to frustration, perhaps even to despair. After all, their favorite argument is, "Who is holy?" Or "Show me a perfect person!"

---

[411] "It is not so essential to understand the precise particulars in regard to the relation of the two laws. It is of far greater consequence that we know whether we are transgressing the law of God, whether we stand in obedience or disobedience before the holy precepts." —Letter 165, 1901, cited in *SDABC*, vol. 6, 1110.

"THE RELENTLESS PURSUIT OF PERFECTION"

So we ask the question: Are the apostles (and God) asking the impossible when they call us to "work out" our salvation—to "be holy"? Is this so-called impossible goal really God's will? Perhaps the marketers of the Lexus automobile may understand all this better than some Christians when they emblazon their motto the world over: "The relentless pursuit of perfection!"

Isn't it interesting? To suggest that God is asking the impossible is to repeat exactly what Satan has been saying from the beginning—and what he has artfully confused the minds of many professed Christians to believe! Truly, Satan is the Grand Deceiver and Master Liar (Revelation 12:7; John 8:44)!

Consider Ellen White's observation:

> "Through defects in the character, Satan works to gain control of the whole mind, and he knows that if these defects are cherished, he will succeed. Therefore he is constantly seeking to deceive the followers of Christ with his fatal sophistry that it is impossible for them to overcome."[412]

Further:

> "Satan has asserted that men could not keep the commandments of God. To prove that they could, Christ became a man, and lived a life of perfect obedience, an evidence to sinful human beings, to the worlds unfallen, and to the heavenly angels, that man could keep God's law through the divine power that is abundantly provided for all that believe. In order to reveal God to the world, to demonstrate as true that which Satan has denied, Christ volunteered to take humanity, and in His power, humanity can obey God."[413]

THEOLOGICAL EXCUSES

Many Christians have found psychological relief in Satan's lies; too often we believe what our desires want us to believe. Their theological excuses go in several directions: 1) the cross of Christ canceled the demands of the law, placing all believers under grace (we have seen this argument before); 2) trying to keep the law is unnecessary because Jesus, as our Substitute, kept the law for us; 3) trying to keep the law is a foolish attempt because overcoming sin completely is not possible while we still live in sinful flesh; 4) trying to keep the law leads either to frustration, despair, or legalism; 5) this emphasis on Jesus being our Example goes too far because He was "exempt" from His mother's DNA and genetic code —thus, asking humans to "perfectly reflect His character" is asking for the impossible.

---

[412] *The Great Controversy,* 488.
[413] *Signs of the Times,* May 10, 1899.

However, these theological excuses arising from psychological desires are attempts to evade the clear call of Jesus: "Therefore whoever hears these sayings of Mine, and does them, I will liken him to a wise man who built his house on the rock" (Matthew 7:24).

We have already looked at two of the reasons why Jesus came to earth, not only to be our Loving, Forgiving Savior, but also to give humanity His Example and the indwelling power to beat Satan down—just as He did in human flesh.[414] Bible writers were unified and clear that Christians have the same resources available that Jesus had so that all Christians may overcome, "as I [Jesus] also overcame" (Revelation 3:21). Jesus came to demolish our excuses!

Let the Bible speak to us. Let's hear what Paul heard and passed on to fellow Christians (for example, Hebrews 2:17, 4:15, for starters). Let's remove the filters of theological debate and the blinding limitations of many Bible commentaries. Let the simple words speak directly, personally, quietly to our souls. Let's review the scores of unambiguous counsel in the writings of Ellen White.

Ponder what Jesus meant when He said, "strive to enter through the narrow gate" (Luke 13:24). Selfish, rebellious people cannot inherit the kingdom of God because they carry too many excuses with them—they look for a wider gate! The clearest, most consistent bottom line of Scripture, hammered home from Genesis to Revelation, is that God has supplied whatever we need to get through the "narrow gate."

All that is enough to thank God again, right now!

---

[414] See 84–88 "The Lord Jesus came to our world, not to reveal what a God could do, but what a man could do, through faith in God's power to help in every emergency. Man is, through faith, to be a partaker in the divine nature, and to overcome every temptation wherewith he is beset. The Lord now demands that every son and daughter of Adam through faith in Jesus Christ, serve Him in human nature which we now have." —Manuscript 1, 1892, printed in The *Review and Herald*, June 17, 1976. See "Appendix I: Why Jesus Came."

CHAPTER TWENTY-ONE:
GOD LEAVES US IN THE DRIVER'S SEAT

B
ut we must be clear as to how all this works! We all know how persistently weak we are. Is it a matter of developing our willpower—of simply striving harder? No! Never! God has given us a better plan—a plan that works whenever we buy into it!

That is why the Holy Spirit led Peter to write: "His divine power has given to us all things that pertain to life and godliness, through the knowledge of Him who called us by glory and virtue, by which have been given to us exceedingly great and precious promises, that through these you may be partakers of the divine nature, having escaped the corruption that is in the world through lust" (2 Peter 1:3, 4).

Note that God does not push us out of the driver's seat. He does not do the driving for us, as the Greyhound bus ad reads! God's terrific goal for us is to help us be responsible, predictable, trustworthy drivers of our own destinies—persons made safe to drive the highways of the hereafter, made worthy by His infinite grace.[415] That's plenty of reason to live joyfully today in the "assurance of faith" (Hebrews 10:22)!

Now back to Philippians 2:12, 13. Here Paul is telling us how God will make us safe drivers, today and forever—how we "may be partakers of the divine nature, having escaped the corruption that is in the world through lust." In other words, Paul is explaining how the Holy Spirit empowers our "works" in making us overcomers (good and safe drivers)!

PAUL'S FORMULA

This is Paul's formula for overcoming our self-centered habit patterns, inherited or acquired: *Our will + God's grace = overcomers who fulfill God's "good pleasure"!* In this life? Absolutely, it's the only one we have. There is no second chance after death—we are having our second chances every day we wake up. In this life, we seal our destiny. In fact, every day we are becoming more mature wheat or tares.[416]

It's the relentless appeal of Revelation: "To him who overcomes I will give to eat from the tree of life" (2:7); "He who overcomes shall not be hurt by the second death" (2:11); "To him who overcomes I will give some of the hidden manna to eat" (2:17); "He who overcomes, and keeps My works until the end, to him I will give power over the nations" (2:26); "He who

---

[415] Paul emphasized this empowerment in his Ephesian letter: "He would grant you, according to the riches of His glory, to be strengthened with might through His Spirit in the inner man" (3:16).

[416] See 202, 209, 468.

overcomes shall be clothed in white garments" (3:5); "He who overcomes I will make him a pillar in the temple of My God" (3:12); "To him who overcomes I will grant to sit with Me on My throne" (3:21). All that should take our breath away!

To make this business of overcoming even more relevant to each of us today, especially to those who live in the end of the endtimes, let's consider carefully these blazing paragraphs:

> "When He comes He is not to cleanse us of our sins, to remove from us the defects in our characters, or to cure us of the infirmities of our tempers and dispositions. If wrought for us at all, this work will all be accomplished before that time. When the Lord comes, those who are holy will be holy still. Those who have preserved their bodies and spirits in holiness, in sanctification and honor, will then receive the finishing touch of immortality. But those who are unjust, unsanctified, and filthy will remain so forever. No work will then be done for them to remove their defects and give them holy characters. The Refiner does not then sit to pursue His refining process and remove their sins and their corruption. This is all to be done in these hours of probation. It is now that this work is to be accomplished for us. …

> "As we come under the influence of that truth, it will accomplish the work for us which is necessary to give us a moral fitness for the kingdom of glory and for the society of the heavenly angels. We are now in God's workshop. Many of us are rough stones from the quarry. But as we lay hold upon the truth of God, its influence affects us. It elevates us and removes from us every imperfection and sin, of whatever nature. Thus we are prepared to see the King in His beauty and finally to unite with the pure and heavenly angels in the kingdom of glory. It is here that this work is to be accomplished for us, here that our bodies and spirits are to be fitted for immortality."[417]

We have just read a very sobering description of reality. When our probation closes, no replays! No mulligans! No second editions! That paragraph deserves a rereading. It reflects Paul's formula: *Our will + God's grace = overcomers, who fulfill God's "good pleasure."*

Our part of the formula is spelled out in many ways in the New Testament: "strive" (Luke 13:2); "put off the old man" (Colossians 3:9); "be diligent" (Hebrews 4:11); "lay aside every weight and the sin which so easily ensnares us, and let us run with endurance" (Hebrews 12:1); "resist the devil" (James 4:7). These are only samples!

Now for God's part: He will provide "grace to help in time of need" (Hebrews 4:16) so that we should "be strengthened with might through

---

[417] *Testimonies*, vol. 2; 355, 356.

His Spirit in the inner man. ... according to the power that works in us" (Ephesians 3:16, 20). He "is able to keep you from stumbling and to present you faultless before the presence of His glory" (Jude 24).

NOONDAY DESCRIPTION

A noonday sun description of how Paul's formula works in our lives is found in that helpful book *Messages to Young People*:

> "While these youth [Hebrew young men] were working out their own salvation, God was working in them to will and to do of His good pleasure. Here are revealed the conditions of success. To make God's grace our own, we must act our part. The Lord does not propose to perform for us either the willing or the doing. His grace is given to work in us to will and to do, but never as a substitute for our effort. Our souls are to be aroused to co-operate. The Holy Spirit works in us, that we may work out our own salvation. This is the practical lesson the Holy Spirit is striving to teach us. 'It is God which worketh in you both to will and to do of His good pleasure'"[418]

To highlight the biblical view of God's divine-human co-op plan, Ellen White could not be clearer:

> "The work of gaining salvation is one of copartnership, a joint operation. There is to be co-operation between God and the repentant sinner. This is necessary for the formation of right principles in the character. Man is to make earnest efforts to overcome that which hinders him from attaining to perfection. But he is wholly dependent upon God for success. Human effort of itself is not sufficient. Without the aid of divine power it avails nothing. God works and man works. Resistance of temptation must come from man, who must draw his power from God. ...

> "God wishes us to have the mastery over ourselves. But He cannot help us without our consent and co-operation. The divine Spirit works through the powers and faculties given to man. Of ourselves, we are not able to bring the purposes and desires and inclinations into harmony with the will of God; but if we are 'willing to be made willing,' the Saviour will accomplish this for us. ... Day by day God works with him, perfecting the character that is to stand in the time of final test. And day by day the believer is working out before men and angels a sublime experiment, showing what the gospel can do for fallen human beings."[419]

---

[418] Page 147. "God does not dispense with man's aid. He strengthens him, cooperating with him as he uses the powers and capabilities given him." —*The Desire of Ages*, 535.

[419] *The Acts of the Apostles*, 83, 484.

Paul also uses an interesting phrase in his classic formula for the overcomer: "work … with fear and trembling" (verse 12). What could he possibly mean? For one thing, Paul is not throwing a dark cloud over the striving Christian. Nor is he placing the Christian in the impossible position of Sisyphus—always rolling the huge rock almost to the top of the hill only to have it to roll back again. And again. Forever!

When God cooperates with our best efforts, no one needs to fear failure. God always lives up to His promises. He will never grow weary of picking us up, any more than parents grow impatient with their child learning to walk.

FEAR HAS ITS PLACE

However, in a special sense, fear has its place in working out our salvation. Remember how Solomon put it: "In the fear of the Lord there is strong confidence. … The fear of the Lord is a fountain of life" (Proverbs 14:26, 27).[420]

Don't we all fear embarrassing our closest friends or anyone who trusts us. I know that I fear ever embarrassing my wife or my children. I fear misusing the trust that people have built up in me over the years. I fear that I could mislead somebody with hasty words in a sermon. Above all, I fear that I will say or do something that will not "hallow" our Lord's name. Because I fear embarrassment! Maybe, but that is not the greatest fear. *The greatest fear is to look into faces that I have "let down."*

Perhaps the following counsel will help us:

> "God does not bid you fear that He will fail to fulfill His promises, that His patience will weary, or His compassion be found wanting. Fear lest your will shall not be held in subjection to Christ's will, lest your hereditary and cultivated traits of character shall control your life. 'It is God which worketh in you both to will and to do of His good pleasure.' Fear lest self shall interpose between your soul and the great Master Worker. Fear lest self-will shall mar the high purpose that through you God desires to accomplish. Fear to trust to your own strength, fear to withdraw your hand from the hand of Christ and attempt to walk life's pathway without His abiding presence."[421]

This life of cooperation with the mind and power of God, this working out of God's "good pleasure," this life of abiding in Christ, is what Paul calls "the righteousness from God that depends on faith" (Philippians 3:9).

---

[420] "The fear of the Lord prolongs days" (Proverbs 10:28); "The fear of the Lord is to hate evil" (Proverbs 8:13); "The fear of the Lord is the beginning of wisdom" (Proverbs 9:10).

[421] *Christ's Object Lessons*, 161. One of the most meaningful promises, words that I have murmured night and day for decades, is Proverbs 3:5–8. In the middle of this passage we find "Fear the Lord and depart from evil. It will be health to your flesh, and strength to your bones." Note the powerful ellipse of truth.

But we still have that lingering question: How does God's power work His will within us? The key thought, the open secret, to Paul's salvation formula regarding our part and God's part in working out our salvation is the work of the Holy Spirit, the indwelling Energizer.

PRIMARY FUNCTION OF THE HOLY SPIRIT

Strange to say, but the primary function of the Holy Spirit has been rarely described throughout the Christian era! Along with His work as the Convincer of sin, as the helpful Tutor as we read the Bible, His highest purpose, toward which all other functions focus, is to reproduce in us the character of Jesus. This is the only way the Holy Spirit (or anyone else) can truly witness to Jesus: "The Spirit of truth, who proceeds from the Father, he will bear witness to me" (John 15:26). We witness to Jesus by letting the Holy Spirit do His work in us!

Perhaps this has never been stated more clearly:

> "The Holy Spirit is the breath of spiritual life in the soul. The impartation of the Spirit is the impartation of the life of Christ. It imbues the receiver with the attributes of Christ. Only those who are thus taught of God, those who possess the inward working of the Spirit, and in whose life the Christ-life is manifested, are to stand as representative men, to minister in behalf of the church."[422]

Never will the time come when we will no longer need the friendly energy of the Holy Spirit. Until the Christian dies, or until even after probation closes in the endtime, every genuine, faithful Christian will feel the appeal of sin, the tug of Satan, even as Jesus did—even to the end of His earthly life in Gethsemane and on Calvary.

Now let's get practical—where does the Holy Spirit "get into" our lives? At what point does He intersect with you and me? Surely not through our fingernails or liver!

This fact is one of the most essential truths we could ever know: Our "brain nerves ... are the medium through which heaven communicates with man." And this connection "affects the inmost life." Now the obvious:

---

[422] *The Desire of Ages*, 805. "In describing to His disciples the office work of the Holy Spirit, Jesus sought to inspire them with the joy and hope that inspired His own heart. He rejoiced because of the abundant help He had provided for His church. The Holy Spirit was the highest of all gifts that He could solicit from His Father for the exaltation of His people. The Spirit was to be given as a regenerating agent, and without this the sacrifice of Christ would have been of no avail. The power of evil had been strengthening for centuries, and the submission of men to this satanic captivity was amazing. Sin could be resisted and overcome only through the mighty agency of the Third Person of the Godhead, who would come with no modified energy, but in the fullness of divine power. It is the Spirit that makes effectual what has been wrought out by the world's Redeemer. It is by the Spirit that the heart is made pure. Through the Spirit the believer becomes a partaker of the divine nature. Christ has given His Spirit as a divine power to overcome all hereditary and cultivated tendencies to evil, and to impress His own character upon His church." —*Ibid*, 671.

"Whatever hinders the circulation of the electric current in the nervous system, thus weakening the vital powers and lessening mental susceptibility, makes it more difficult to arouse the moral nature."[423]

BRAIN'S FRONTAL LOBE

The brain's frontal lobe (where all our decisions are made) is a kind of computer where thought and emotions "happen."[424] At this point, about an inch behind our forehead, the Holy Spirit accesses human beings. This surely is an advertisement for the purpose of the distinctiveness of the Adventist emphasis on health principles! More about this later.[425]

This interaction, this intersecting of the Holy Spirit and the mind of responsible men and women, has been vastly unappreciated. It was this interaction with the Spirit that helped Jesus to increase "in wisdom and stature, and in favor with God and men" (Luke 2:52). And now the promise, "And the grace that He received is for us."[426]

Our task is to keep our frontal lobes fresh with pure blood, flooded with oxygen (daily exercise) and nutrition (a careful diet). Further, our thought processes should guard the avenues to the brain, the avenues of sight, feeling, and touch. Why? So much of what we think and do can overload the frontal lobe so that the quiet voice of the Holy Spirit cannot be heard. For without His voice and His energy, we can never expect to be overcomers!

---

[423] *Education*, 209.

[424] "In recent years the artificial division between thoughts and emotion has begun to give way. Anatomical studies reveal extensive connections between those parts of the brain traditionally associated with our emotions, the limbic system in particular, and the frontal lobes. When the frontal lobes are damaged or destroyed, a person's ability to synthesize signals from the environment, assign priorities, or make balanced decisions is impaired. Once the frontal lobes disconnect from the rest of the brain, the limbic system is free to fire its messages of emotion. The control made possible by the frontal-limbic connections is weakened, and behavior becomes erratic and unpredictable. ... What does become clear is that even tiny changes in the physical, chemical, and electrical state of the brain can lead to significant shifts in behavior." —Richard M. Restak, M.D., *The Brain* (New York: Bantam Books, 1984), 152. "The frontal lobe ... the most forward portion, the prefrontal fibers, exert an inhibitory control over our actions, bring them into line with social expectations. Injuries to this area may cause offensive, socially unacceptable behaviors. ... Anatomists as far back as da Vinci noted that the frontal lobes in human beings were dramatically 'overdeveloped' in comparison to the same region in animals, occupying about one third of the cerebral hemispheres. They are crucial to the functioning of mind in a wide variety of ways, and damage or injury can have many consequences. ... Patricia Goldmen-Rakic, who is an authority on the prefrontal cortex, notes, 'If thinking is the process of using information to make decisions, then the frontal lobe is crucial for thinking. Without the frontal lobes, we're at the mercy of environment. We respond to events without reflection. We are unable to plan for the future. And it is this capacity to plan for the future that distinguishes us from all other species.'" —Richard M. Restak, M. D., *The Mind* (New York: Bantam Books, 1988), 18, 266, 267).

[425] "The brain is the capital of the body, the seat of all the nervous forces and of mental action. The nerves proceeding from the brain control the body. By the brain nerves, mental impressions are conveyed to all the nerves of the body as by telegraph wires; and they control the vital action of every part of the system. All the organs of motion are governed by the communications they receive from the brain." —*Testimonies*, vol. 3, 69.

[426] *The Desire of Ages*, 73.

AFTER THE CLOSE OF PROBATION

Before moving on, let's clear up some confusion regarding the Christian's relationship to Jesus and the Holy Spirit after the close of probation and during the seven last plagues. Some opine that when Jesus leaves the sanctuary as our Mediator, God's people will have to "go it alone" during the plagues. This notion has been a special concern for many, leaving them with a frightful lack of assurance that they could "ever make it on their own."

This confusion arises from a misunderstanding of the role of the Holy Spirit—*He never leaves those who ask for His guidance and empowerment.* In other words, there is no connection between Jesus ceasing His work as High Priest and the continuing, abiding presence of the Holy Spirit. God never intends for believers to ever feel that sometime in the future they must "go it alone" just to prove how perfect they are! This notion does not flow from either the Bible or the writings of Ellen White. Those thoughts grow out of a profound misunderstanding of the character of our Heavenly Father, as well as a hasty, even careless, reading of sacred materials.

Between now and the return of Jesus, our task is to continue cooperating with the Holy Spirit, "work[ing] out [our] salvation with fear and trembling" letting God [Holy Spirit] work in us "both to will and to do for His good pleasure" (Philippians 2:12, 13). Nothing changes. This is how Jesus lived His life and as many God-fearing, God-loving people have done in every generation since Creation.

Take courage from these thoughts:

> "Some few in every generation from Adam resisted his every artifice and stood forth as noble representatives of what it was in the power of man to do and to be—Christ working with human efforts, helping man in overcoming the power of Satan. Enoch and Elijah are the correct representatives of what the race might be through faith in Jesus Christ if they chose to be. Satan was greatly disturbed because these noble, holy men stood untainted amid the moral pollution surrounding them, perfected righteous characters, and were accounted worthy for translation to Heaven."[427]

But I hear the question, what about "legalism"? Whenever we emphasize "grow in grace" (2 Peter 3:18), "overcoming," and "commandment keeping," most will nod in agreement. But back in their heads, they hear the charge of "legalism" from some of their friends. How does legalism fit into all this emphasis on character transformation so that we can be trusted with eternal life? We'll tackle "legalism" in the next chapter.

---

[427] *Review and Herald,* March 3, 1874.

CHAPTER TWENTY-TWO:
WHAT DOES A LEGALIST LOOK LIKE?

S eventh-day Adventists have defined themselves as Sabbath keepers and heralds of the Advent. We are distinguished by our high regard for the commandments of God. We take Revelation 14:12 and other Scripture very seriously. The question is not *should* we be faithful commandment-keepers, but *how*.

We have been observing how Bible writers and others use the ellipse of truth when describing the purpose of the gospel.[428] That is, the gospel comes to us with two hands and we receive it with two hands; we need the grace of pardon and the grace of power (two foci of the ellipse). Both are gifts. Both are exactly what men and women of faith need daily.[429]

Even as we need both hydrogen and oxygen in order to drink water, so men and women of faith need both pardon and power in a saving relationship with Jesus. Without both, they soon lapse either into legalism or license.[430]

Why, then, the confusion regarding grace, faith, and assurance that permeates the Christian world? Because men and women in all ages, in all places, have devised ways to calm their hearts into thinking that what they "think" or "do" or "feel" would somehow get God's attention and satisfy the requirements for salvation. They seek assurance and security on their own terms! Of course, many have sincerely done all this ignorantly, and God has His own gracious way of dealing mercifully and appropriately with honest seekers, whether early Vikings, Babylonians, and Egyptians, or Pharisees in Christ's day, contemporary New Agers, or those who have "only believe" as their mantra.

LEGALISM OR LICENSE

It's hard to know what is more self-defeating—legalism or license. Both are surely contemporary problems in all churches. But at the moment, let's follow Paul's concern for legalism.

On one hand, Paul was troubled (as all Christians should be) by those who "insist on being saved in some way by which they may perform some important work. When they see that there is no way of weaving self into the work, they reject the salvation provided."[431] It seems he described this group

---

[428] See "Appendix L: The Ellipse of Truth."
[429] "Another lesson the tabernacle, through its service of sacrifice, was to teach,—the lesson of pardon of sin, and power through the Saviour for obedience unto life." —*Education*, 36.
[430] See 163.
[431] *The Desire of Ages*, 280.

in Colossians 2:16 with those who focused on their external behavior—with exacting concern for what they ate and drank, for special religious days, false humility, and physical self-denial.

On the other hand, he spoke unambiguously to those who did not practice what they preached—to those who found theological excuses whereby they would be comfortable to be saved in their sins. For example, he wrote to the Colossian church members as "elect of God" but his strong words and dire warnings could not be misunderstood. They may have turned their backs on "fornication, uncleanness, passion, evil desires, and covetousness," but "now you must also put off all these: anger, wrath, malice, blasphemy, filthy language, … lying, etc" (3:5–9). They were "good and regular members" from the standpoint of external behavior; but they still had much to do in areas even more important in the eyes of God—their interpersonal (more hidden) behavior and attitudes.

Ellen White clearly delineated these two kinds of church members who had not yet grasped the healing power of the gospel: "those who would be saved by their merits, and those who would be saved in their sins."[432] In a way, they are both legalists. They both want salvation without character transformation!

What does legalism mean? So many definitions afflict us. For example, many in the Christian world think that a legalist is one who does not understand the liberation of grace; thus, any attempt to keep God's laws is wrongheaded and simply an example of "righteousness by works."[433] For them, any effort to pattern our lives after our Lord's example is hopelessly impossible and results in legalism.

Another faction, with a slightly different twist, believes that sanctification is not an integral or necessary part of the gospel equation (pardon and power). In doing so, they think that Paul's overcoming formula is being misunderstood, at least misleading. For them, faith is essentially mental appreciation, without necessary character transformation because in their limited understanding of the purpose of the gospel, they say that we can do nothing to add to what Jesus "did" on the Cross.[434] For this group, anything

---

[432] *The Great Controversy*, 572.

[433] See 133, 144, 365, 457.

[434] See 96, 97, 135. Interesting, but this very confusion is dividing Evangelicalism today (of whom most are Calvinists; it is called the "Lordship/no-Lordship salvation" controversy. After noting that both groups are predestinarians, the debate is virtually identical to what has tended to divide the Seventh-day Adventist church for the past 50 years. Reading and listening to what John F. MacArthur, Jr. (as the leading representative of Lordship salvation) teaches and to what Zane Hodges and Charles Ryrie (as leading spokesmen for no-Lordship salvation) are saying, one hears strange echoes of the same issues that Paul faced, and every other church leader from his day to ours. See John F. MacArthur, Jr., *Faith Works, the Gospel According to the Apostles* Dallas: Word Publishing, 1993), especially chapter 2, "A Primer on the 'Lordship Salvation' Controversy." However, MacArthur and I differ fundamentally on the definition of "faith" which colors his defense, even though he is vastly more correct than his opponents.

that we think we should "do" is thus legalism at work. "Perfection," for them, should be dropped from the Christian's vocabulary![435]

PERFECTION OR PERFECTIONISM

The bottom line problem is that too often "perfection" is confused with "perfectionism." "Perfectionism" leads to two false doctrines: 1) Our sinful "nature" can be eradicated before Jesus returns by some kind of "garden experience" (spiritual lobotomy) and to its equally fatal teaching that 2) In retaining sinful "nature" until the resurrection, it is impossible for anyone to overcome sin.

"Perfection" embraces the biblical concept of maturity wherein Christians are destined to reach "the measure of the stature of the fullness of Christ" (Ephesians 4:13; Matthew 5:48; 1 Corinthians 15:34). We measure this "stature by the fruit of the Spirit" (Galatians 5:22–25).[436]

The Adventist Church has always emphasized that men and women of faith joyfully comply with the Ten Commandments (and anything else that comes to them as "light") as their part in the divine-human co-op program—without which salvation would not happen! And some have accused this emphasis to be either perfectionism or legalism! Because of this withering charge, the sense of assurance, for some, becomes unsettled. Let's define our terms!

LEGALISM DEFINED

Ellen White has described various forms of legalism in contrast to commandment keepers who, in genuine faith, rely fully on God to "will and do for His good pleasure" in their lives:

> "All legalism … [does not] have a proper estimate of sin."[437]

> Legalists, like the priests and rulers in Christ's day, were "fixed in a rut of ceremonialism … satisfied with a legal religion … made up of ceremonies and the injunctions of men."[438]

> A legalist who "is trying to reach heaven by his own works in keeping the law is attempting an impossibility. There is no safety for one who has merely a legal religion, a form of godliness."[439]

---

[435] Following this logic, one would repudiate the binding authority of the fourth commandment as well as all the others. The only moral restraints would then be the ever-changing laws of one's community.

[436] "God will accept only those who are determined to aim high. He places every human agent under obligation to do his best. Moral perfection is required of all. … We need to understand that imperfection of character is sin." —*Christ's Object Lessons*, 330.

[437] *Signs of the Times*, April 9, 1894.

[438] *Acts of the Apostles*, 15.

[439] *The Desire of Ages*, 172.

"A legal religion can never lead souls to Christ; for it is a loveless, Christless religion. ...The round of religious ceremonies, the external humiliation, the imposing sacrifice, proclaim that the doer of these things regards himself as righteous, and as entitled to heaven; but it is all a deception."[440]

"Icy hearts have[ing] only a legal religion."[441]

Legalists "go crippling along, dwarfed in religious growth, because they have in their ministry a legal religion. The power of the grace of God is not felt to be a living, effectual necessity, an abiding principle."[442]

"The spirit of bondage is engendered by seeking to live in accordance with legal religion, through striving to fulfill the claims of the law in our own strength."[443]

"A legal religion is insufficient to bring the soul into harmony with God. The hard, rigid orthodoxy of the Pharisees, destitute of contrition, tenderness, or love, was only a stumbling block to sinners."[444]

"Legal religion will not answer for this age. We may perform all the outward acts of service, and yet be as destitute of the quickening influence of the Holy Spirit as the hills of Gilboa were destitute of dew and rain."[445]

But those trapped in "legalism" affect more than their own spiritual growth. They can cast a dark shadow over their family, their church, and their workplace. Long the list could get of families or church congregations that have been lashed with harsh, judgmental members. They not only misrepresent their Lord whom they profess with destructive criticism, they act out their legalistic sense of rightness in their power over others (whether administratively or with overbearing personalities) in their votes on committee, their mishandling of children or parents, and in their abrasive evangelistic outreaches. Legalism, like child abuse, often creates a continuum of coldness and judgmentalism from one generation to another generation.

WORDS BUT NOT THE MUSIC!

In summary, a legalist has the words but not the music! He sees the importance of obedience; he flees from license, from pushing the envelope to the extremes. In a way, legalists get satisfaction out of punishing themselves

---

[440] *Ibid.*, 280.
[441] *Selected Messages*, bk. 3, 377.
[442] *Ibid.*, 189.
[443] *The Youth's Instructor*, September 22, 1892, cited in *SDABC* vol. 6, 1077.
[444] *Thoughts From The Mount of Blessings*, 53.
[445] *Testimonies*, vol. 6, 417.

into "being good," precisely what Paul calls the "yoke of bondage" that he applies to all commandment keepers who are trying their best to be good without the "power of the grace of God." They enjoy only a crippled, dwarfed Christian experience. They need to hear the fullness of the gospel!

As C. S. Lewis put it, some think "that God wanted simply obedience to a set or rules; whereas He really wants people of a particular sort."[446]

This whole subject of legalism, the relation between grace and faith, between gospel and law, between Christ as Savior and as Lord, was on display at the General Conference in Minneapolis in 1888. I have never seen it better put than in the following words—words written to help clarify the 1888 issues:

> "Let this point be fully settled in every mind: If we accept Christ as a Redeemer, we must accept Him as a Ruler. We cannot have the assurance and perfect confiding trust in Christ as our Saviour until we acknowledge Him as our King and are obedient to His commandments. Thus we evidence our allegiance to God. We have then the genuine ring in our faith, for it is a working faith. It works by love."[447]

We must understand the issues of that 1888 Conference. Clarity on these issues will greatly simplify and strengthen our personal response to God's call for a special people with a special message for a special time. The speakers at the Minneapolis Conference nailed legalism to the wall (as they did enthusiastically in following years), and it should never have been a problem ever again—but it keeps getting down off the wall![448]

Speakers at the 1888 Conference went further back than the Protestant Reformation in opening up the purpose of the gospel more completely. The Adventist Church, as well as the rest of the world, needed to hear what was said at that conference.

ISSUES AT MINNEAPOLIS IN 1888

What was happening within the Seventh-day Adventist Church during the 1880s that brought these core issues to a head? Many references describe Adventism during the 1880s in bleak terms. Admittedly, they were adamant regarding the immutability of the Ten Commandments; they could debate down anybody regarding the continuing authority of the Sabbath commandment.

---

[446] Lewis, *Mere Christianity,* 80.

[447] *Faith and Works,* 16.

[448] In 1888, the essence of the messages brought by Elders A. T. Jones and E. J. Waggoner and Ellen White recovered lost or compromised biblical truths. It was not merely a recovery of Protestant Reformation theology. Hardly! No Reformer could be used as a reference. As their contribution, the Reformers did agree on the Protestant principle that rejected the papal principle of church authority over biblical authority, opening up the world to a different way of listening to truth. For their courage and clear thinking, we will always be in their debt. See also "Appendix M: Rediscovering Truths Hidden for Ages."

But many were blind to Ellen White's charge that they were Laodiceans, virtually legalists. This lukewarm "Laodicean" condition was partly due to early preaching that focused on the Sabbath truth and the soon return of Jesus, while *assuming* that justification by faith was a given and well-understood. Unconsciously, "keeping the commandments" eventually became the same as "the faith of Jesus" and "loving God." This silent shift eroded Christian experience, beclouded an intimate personal relationship with Jesus and set the stage for Ellen White's charge that their religion was as dry as the "hills of Gilboa."[449]

In the early 1880s, Ellen White spoke to Adventist ministers: "Too often this truth is presented in cold theory. ... A theory of the truth without vital godliness cannot remove the moral darkness which envelops the soul."[450]

Many had drifted into a legalistic experience while holding fast to the their commandment keeping. But a rich, Spirit-filled life—a heart religion—that moves people from one victory over sin to another, from self-centeredness to a generous, loving spirit, was often lacking.

Consequently, the world had not been given a fair picture of what the messages of the three angels (Revelation 14) were meant to be. Therefore, the great need for a re-emphasis of the "everlasting gospel" within the setting in 1888:

> "The message [brought by A. T. Jones and E. J. Waggoner] of the gospel of His grace was to be given to the church in clear and distinct lines, that the world should no longer say that Seventh-day Adventists talk the law, but do not teach or believe Christ."[451]

What follows may be the most informed description of the 1888 focus on the Adventist message (it may not have been so explicitly set forth since the days of Paul):

> "The Lord in His great mercy sent a most precious message to His people through Elders Waggoner and Jones. This message was to bring more prominently before the world the uplifted Saviour, the sacrifice for the sins of the whole world. It presented through faith in the Surety; it invited the people to receive the righteousness of Christ, which is made manifest in obedience to all the commandments of God. Many had lost sight of Jesus. They needed to have their eyes directed to His divine person, His merits, and His changeless love for the human

---

[449] *Testimonies*, vol. 6, 417. "As a people, we have preached the law until we are as dry as the hills of Gilboa that had neither dew nor rain. We must preach Christ in the law, and there will be sap and nourishment in the preaching that will be as food to the famishing flock of God. We must not trust in our own merits at all, but in the merits of Jesus of Nazareth. Our eyes must be anointed with eye-salve." —*Review and Herald*, March 11, 1890.

[450] *Ibid.*, vol. 4, 313, 314.

[451] *Testimonies to Ministers*, 92.

family. All power is given into His hands, that He may dispense rich gifts unto men, imparting the priceless gift of His own righteousness to the helpless human agent. This is the message that God commanded to be given to the world. It is the third angel's message, which is to be proclaimed with a loud voice, and attended with the outpouring of His Spirit in a large measure."[452]

That is a remarkable paragraph! In it we have the distinctive message of the Seventh-day Adventist Church regarding righteousness by faith; here also we see why the emphasis of 1888 was light years ahead of our illustrious Protestant Reformers.

That paragraph summarizes in different words the purpose of the gospel and God's plan for placing the universe on a secure basis.[453] It sets forth the relationship of justification (setting right) and sanctification (keeping right) within the "righteousness of Christ, which is made manifest in obedience to all the commandments of God." These "priceless gifts" were pardon and power to "the helpless human agent." Is there any other church with this clear mission statement? Apparently, it is the core of the "loud cry" that will be "attended with the outpouring of the His Spirit."

NAILED LEGALISM TO THE WALL

The 1888 messages not only nailed legalism to the wall, they opened up the floodgates of joy for those who received them.

The point I am making here is that the coldness of nineteenth-century orthodoxy (primarily concern for doctrinal correctness) that prevailed generally in Protestantism eventually overcame zealous Adventists. The result: "too many Christless sermons preached." Legalism prevailed! Assurance of salvation rested on external conformity to the law (which, of course, can be measured and ticked off like a checklist, providing a presumptuous assurance of salvation).

When legalism prevails, either self-righteousness and pride or discouragement and spiritual depression soon follow. Intent on being Christians, legalists (most often unknowingly) see only rigor, demand, and checklists. Jesus as their personal Savior, their personal Enabler, their closest Friend, their faithful High Priest, becomes obscured under the weight of one demand after another. Duty is not a delight—just one more step to climb. Though such church members desire to please God, they feel the stress and see only the cloud.

Those who do keep up their courage believe they must try harder, thinking that that's the way to find peace and assurance. (Here again is a good example of not understanding the full meaning of "faith" and how to "trust

---

[452] *Ibid.*, 91.
[453] See 144.

in God's faithfulness."[454] Unconsciously, they become more focused on law keeping than on the Christ of the law. How would they do that? By becoming even more circumspect in their business dealings, in their Sabbath-keeping, in being even more careful about their dress, in their television watching, and whatever else. Burdened with that misunderstanding of faith and assurance, no wonder people never feel that they have done "enough."

All this loyalty to the law is most commendable in the unbridled license of the 21st century when moral standards seem to have evaporated. But there is no joy in simply trying harder—no matter how much approval they may be getting from others! However, more rigor—more devotion even to Bible study and prayer—is not the answer to the joyless though satisfied heart of a legalist!

The answer to cold legalism was clearly presented in the "precious message" that Elders Jones and Waggoner and Ellen White brought to the 1888 General Conference and in their various books and sermons after that momentous gathering. That message was not a "get-ready-or-else" threat, but tremendous good news as to "how" to live the Christian life and prepare to live forever. That message restored Jesus as one who was very "near" to His people, near even before sinners realized the Godhead's love for them. He was seen as one who, in His human nature, completely identified with fallen men and women.[455] And as One who showed us how we may become conquerors over sin. His role as our High Priest was given a clear focus in the 1888 messages as a vital element in helping us to overcome our sins as we help to close the Great Controversy.[456]

The golden thread of this "good news" (to which Ellen White, in response, said, "Every fiber of my hearts said, 'Amen.'"[457]) links these thoughts: Our standing with God does not depend upon our rigor or even our initiative in claiming His promises, but on our willingness to receive what He has already provided—and that He will continue to provide salvation for us, if we do not frustrate His will.[458] That thought stands legalism on its head!

---

[454] See 142.

[455] See 84–88.

[456] See 100–102. "There is a difference between the forgiveness of sins and the blotting out of sins. There is a difference between the gospel being preached for the forgiveness of sins and the gospel being preached for the blotting out of sins. Always, and today, there is abundant provision for the forgiveness of sins. In our generation comes the provision for the blotting out of sin. And the blotting out of sin is what will prepared for the coming of the Lord; and the blotting out of sin is the ministry of our High Priest in the most holy place of the heavenly sanctuary; and it makes a difference to the people of God today in their ministry, in their message, and in their experience, whether they recognize … or experience the fact of the change. … That should be distinctly brought out in the third angel's message; and with that, of course, will come the clearest revelation of the gospel ministry for this time, … thus preparing the way of the Lord." —W. W. Prescott, *General Conference Bulletin*, 1903, 53, 54.

[457] *The Ellen G. White 1888 Materials,* vol. 1, 349.

[458] See 76, 132, 137, 428.

A haunting warning hangs over all of us today as we relate to this "precious message" that remains perennially relevant:

> "I have no smooth message to bear to those who have been so long as false guideposts, pointing the wrong way. If you reject Christ's delegated messengers, you reject Christ. Neglect this great salvation, kept before you for years, despise this glorious offer of justification through the blood of Christ and sanctification through the cleansing power of the Holy Spirit, and there remaineth no more sacrifice for sins, but a certain fearful looking for of judgment and fiery indignation."[459]

I ask, after reading that paragraph, could our understanding regarding the elements of righteousness by faith be made any clearer?

VIRUS OF LEGALISM ALWAYS PRESENT

Some say, with plenty of reasons, that our problem in the Adventist Church today is not legalism but rampant license. Perhaps! But the sly, subtle, ever-present inclination toward legalism resides as a virus in every religious body—corporately and individually—ready to multiply into open disease unless the immune system is kept healthy. Especially is this virus alive within those who try to *impress* God with their "commandment keeping"![460]

The virus of legalism (self-dependence) saps the enthusiasm and vitality of a dedicated Christian, even when performing the noble virtues of Christianity. The virus provides the words but not the music; somehow "doing" religion overshadows "being" religious! The following counsel is most helpful to all of us:

> "Some who come to God by repentance and confession, and even believe that their sins are forgiven, still fail of claiming, as they should, the promises of God. They do not see that Jesus is an ever-present Saviour; and they are not ready to commit the keeping of their souls to Him, relying upon Him to perfect the work of grace begun in their hearts. While they think they are committing themselves to God, there is a great deal of self-dependence. There are conscientious souls that trust partly to God and partly to themselves. They do not look to God, to be kept by His power, but depend upon watchfulness against temptation and the performance of certain duties for acceptance with Him. There are no victories in this kind of faith. Such persons toil to no purpose; their souls are in continual

---

[459] *Testimonies to Ministers,* 97, 98.
[460] Legalism is the absurdity of thinking that man takes credit for something that only God can do. When the believer hears the command, "Obey and live," he knows that God alone can give him power to obey—but the decision to obey is his. Legalism is misunderstood when it is ascribed to man's role and responsibility in the salvation process.

bondage, and they find no rest until their burdens are laid at the feet of Jesus.

"There is need of constant watchfulness and of earnest, loving devotion, but these will come naturally when the soul is kept by the power of God through faith. We can do nothing, absolutely nothing, to commend ourselves to divine favor. We must not trust at all to ourselves or to our good works; but when as erring, sinful beings we come to Christ, we may find rest in His love. God will accept every one that comes to Him trusting wholly in the merits of a crucified Saviour. Love springs up in the heart. There may be no ecstasy of feeling, but there is an abiding, peaceful trust. Every burden is light; for the yoke that Christ imposes is easy. Duty becomes a delight, and sacrifice a pleasure. The path that before seemed shrouded in darkness becomes bright with beams from the Sun of Righteousness. This is walking in the light as Christ is in the light."[461]

So let's get practical. For example: Adventists with their special emphasis on health principles especially should ask themselves: Why am I a vegetarian? Why do I avoid tobacco and alcoholic beverages, even caffeine products? Is it primarily a sense of demand—"I must be a faithful health reformer to gain God's approval?"

The answer is "yes" and "no."

No in the sense that God already has reconciled Himself to you (2 Corinthians 5:18, 19)—all the good and all the bad you do will not change His love for you.

No in the sense that the purpose of health reform is not primarily to please God; He gave us the health message as all parents give their children counsel. Parents give counsel because they love their children and want to see them avoid terrible mistakes. When children take advice readily, obviously their parents are happy and approve what they are doing.

Yes, God does love us unconditionally. No, God does not approve what we do unconditionally. God is not happy nor can He approve of us when He sees us destroying ourselves, or diminishing our potential!

The one question that may help all of us to think carefully about the cloud of legalism is this: Am I keeping the Sabbath carefully, paying tithe faithfully, and giving Bible studies diligently *to impress God or to honor Him*? The answer may take some thought. The question needs to be asked every day. It is so easy to slip into legalism!

Remember our Lord's warning regarding the Pharisees? "Unless your righteousness exceeds the righteousness of the scribes and Pharisees, you will by no means enter the kingdom of heaven" (Matthew 5:20).

---

[461] *Faith and Works*, 38.

What was wrong with these commandment-keeping, health-reforming, tithe-paying church members (who eventually murdered Jesus)? They had a "legal religion." To put it bluntly:

> "All their pretensions of piety, their human inventions and ceremonies, and even their boasted performance of the outward requirements of the law, could not avail to make them holy. They were not pure in heart or noble and Christlike in character.

> "A legal religion is insufficient to bring the soul into harmony with God. The hard, rigid orthodoxy of the Pharisees, destitute of contrition, tenderness, or love, was only a stumbling block to sinners. They were like the salt that had lost its savor; for their influence had no power to preserve the world from corruption."[462]

LEGALISM IS LETHAL!

Another unintended consequence of legalism is the judgmental Christian who believes in keeping the church "pure" by rigorously measuring everyone else with external checklists. They do so with Pharisaical precision, but without our Lord's weeping heart. They do not often read Matthew 23. They do not often see themselves as those who humble themselves as servants, in spirit and word.

Their harshness "shut[s] up the kingdom of heaven against men" (verse 13). Legalism can even turn church leaders on all levels into those "say and do not do" (verse 3). Sometimes we all have shot at a principle and down comes a person! Legalism is lethal!

But there is another angle—we should not accuse all legalists of being too proud to seek forgiveness, too proud to be repentant. Many thrive on repeated moments of repentance (which may be only confession), on rising and falling, sinning and seeking forgiveness, as if that were all they could expect this side of heaven.[463]

The danger is that legalists (unless they finally see the fullness of the gospel) do not go on in their Christian growth, reaching out constantly for "moral renovation and the necessity of divine enlightenment. ... Christ presented their [Pharisees] religion as devoid of saving faith. There are many who will be lost, because they depend on legal religion, or mere repentance for sin. But repentance for sin alone cannot work the salvation of any soul.

---

[462] *Thoughts From the Mount of Blessing*, 53.

[463] "Are there those here who have been sinning and repenting, sinning and repenting, and will they continue to do so till Christ shall come? May God help us that we may be truly united to Christ, the living vine, and bear fruit to the glory of God!"—*Review and Herald*, April 21, 1891. An article in *Christianity Today* nailed the problem: "Whatever Happened to Repentance?" The author pointed out that "we've come to think our faith is about comfort. It's not. ... We live in a time when it's hard to talk about Christian faith at all, much less about awkward topics like repentance." February 4, 2002.

Man cannot be saved by his own works. Without Christ it is impossible for him to render perfect obedience to the law of God; and heaven can never be gained by an imperfect obedience; for this would place all heaven in jeopardy, and make possible a second rebellion."[464]

We all should beware of pointing the finger at legalists. Why? Because "the spirit of Pharisaism is the spirit of human nature."[465] How many are guilt-free from doing religious things, hoping to have others notice our good works, our wonderful intentions!

The problem is that "careful" commandment keeping, on one hand, and "good works" for the sick, the homeless, or the handicapped, on the other, may not spring from the purest motive. Both groups may operate from self-centered motives, often unknowingly.

WHAT HONEST LEGALISTS ARE MISSING

But there is still another group—the struggling Christian with the right motive, who may be living in legalistic gloom. Sad! They need to hear *all* the good news! Obviously, they shouldn't relax their commandment keeping; but they do need to take the hand of Him who provides the inner strength to be joyfully obedient to His Father's will. They need to see God as their Friend, not as their severe Taskmaster. They need to hang their helpless souls on their great Friend who never lets go! They need to fall often into their Lord's everlasting arms (where forgiveness is His nature) whenever we don't measure up to His gracious, loving Example. He does not condemn us for our sins but for our reluctance to keep walking into the Light we all have (John 3:17–21). He is always there to help us get up and to keep walking

Over the years, these "faithful" church members have given their best to the church—but not with much joy! Think of it, for more than a century a good percentage of Adventist tithes and offerings have come from the pockets of those whom others have called legalists! In contrast were church members who wanted the "blessing" of Christianity without the responsibility of genuine faith-obedience.[466]

Both groups need to hear the fullness of the gospel! Both groups need to hear the Lord say, *today*: "I know you for what you are and for what you want to be!" Both groups need to have genuine assurance *today!* Both groups will melt under the radiant sunshine of joy and peace when they understand how eager Jesus wants to give them assurance *today* that He will walk them all the way into the kingdom.

---

[464] *Signs of the Times,* December 30, 1889.

[465] *Thoughts From the Mount of Blessing,* 79.

[466] "They extol the riches of free grace, and attempt to cover themselves with an appearance of righteousness, hoping to screen their defects of character; but their efforts will be of no avail in the day of God." —*Christ's Object Lessons,* 316.

Both groups need to hear *daily* that their "hope is not in [themselves]; it is in Christ. Your weakness is united to His strength, your ignorance to His wisdom, your frailty to His enduring might."[467]

FULLNESS OF THE GOSPEL

It is possible that all professed Christians regardless of their church affiliation need to hear the fullness of the gospel! For example, and not suggesting in the slightest any derogation to Mormons in Utah, recent research finds Utah leading the United States in antidepressant prescriptions. Such drugs are prescribed in Utah (70 percent of the state's population belongs to the Church of Jesus Christ of Latter Day Saints) "more often than in any other state, at a rate nearly twice the national average."

Dr. Curtis Canning, president of the Utah Psychiatric Association, said that "few here question the veracity of the study, which was a tabulation of prescription orders."

Canning continued: "In Mormondom, there is a social expectation—particularly among the females—to put on a mask, say 'yes' to everything that comes at her and hide the misery and pain. I call it the 'Mother of Zion' syndrome. You are supposed to be perfect because Mrs. Smith across the street can do it and she had three more kids than you and her hair is always in place. I think the cultural issue is very real. There is the expectation that you should be happy, and if you're not happy, you're failing."[468]

The gospel is not all demand; the gospel is also grace—the double gift of pardon and power. Legalism sees and feels the demand but it also must look higher and see that God is our Helper to provide for every circumstance wherein our sense of responsibility places us. He doesn't expect us to be good as if it were a human achievement. He does expect us to trust Him to do His special work, which is helping us to be good for His sake and honor.

We will examine how God does this!

---

[467] *Steps to Christ*, 70.
[468] Julie Cart, *L.A. Times* Staff Writer, *latimes.com*, February 20, 2002.

CHAPTER TWENTY-THREE:
WHEN DO WE GET
THE ROBE?

O bviously, all that we have been saying about legalism, "working out our salvation," or the gospel, requires a look at another divisive question: Why do some say that the "robe" and the "wedding garment" is God's gift without any contribution of any kind from men and women of faith, that it "has in it not one thread of human devising?"[469]

The Bible talks about a "wedding garment" that the redeemed will wear (Matthew 22:1–14; Ephesians 5:26, 27). In fact, John the Revelator wrote that our Lord's bride (the redeemed) would wear this garment—"in fine linen, clean and bright, for the fine linen is the righteous acts of the saints" (Revelation 19:8).

Those who are troubled about "works righteousness" have difficulty with this text. The usual explanation is that this garment is really the robe of Christ's righteousness that is imputed to all believers. They go on to say that any attempt to make this "robe" into anything that a Christian must "do" is pure legalism and not the message of grace. Further, they say, if one focuses on the "righteous deeds of the saints," how could he have any "assurance" of salvation *now*?

What shall we make of these two stark differences, both looking at the same biblical texts? How do these texts relate to the Great Controversy over the loyalty of men and women and their eternal trustworthiness?

TRUSTED WITH ETERNAL LIFE

Let's remember that the ultimate purpose of the gospel is to prepare a people who can be trusted with eternal life.[470] When we recognize that the Good News provides both pardon and power in God's plan to restore in us His "image," it should seem easier to figure out how the "robe" and wedding garment are acquired. But let's review how everything we have learned so far helps us to answer those who may be confused regarding certain biblical statements.

In Matthew 22:1–14 Jesus gave the parable of the wedding feast. The high point of the parable focuses on the king greeting the wedding guests. But the king discovers "a man who did not have on a wedding garment" (verse 11). Bad news—he was punished irrevocably!

---

[469] *Christ's Object Lessons*, 311.
[470] See 144.

Now, what shall we make of this parable? Jesus did not elaborate. However, there are insights in Ellen White's exposition of this parable that parallel the New Testament teaching of the full gospel.

We are told that "the parable … opens before us a lesson of the highest consequence" and that "the wedding garment represents the character which all must possess who shall be accounted fit guests for the wedding."[471]

How do men and women acquire this wedding garment?

> "The fine linen, says the Scripture (Revelation 19:8) is 'the righ-
> teousness of the saints.' It is the righteousness of Christ, His own
> unblemished character, that through faith is imparted to all who
> receive Him as their personal Saviour. … Christ in His human-
> ity wrought out a perfect character, and this character He offers to
> impart to us."[472]

Here we have in parable form the outline of "righteousness by faith" (how righteousness is acquired by faith) that we reviewed earlier. Men and women of faith, from their first repenting moment, through many repenting moments thereafter, have cooperated with the Holy Spirit as He reproduces the character of Christ in them.[473] Their part in character development is to cooperate with God who is willing to do His good pleasure in men and women of faith.

The developing character that is reflecting Jesus more and more is not a product of "human devising." Any man or woman of faith knows that all too well. The most we can do is to keep our eye single, not double-minded (James 1:8), trusting in His promises that He will "complete" the good work that He began (Philippians 1:6). The new covenant experience reflects a character development void of "human devising" because it grows out of the Lord's promise to "put My laws into their hearts, and in their minds I will write them" (Hebrews 10:16).

THE NEW COVENANT EXPERIENCE

Jesus often described how others can tell if one is living in the New Covenant experience. The Beatitudes (Matthew 5) gives us a cameo of lives that are letting the Holy Spirit write God's "laws into their hearts." In His galvanizing parable of the judgment (Matthew 25) when the sheep and the goats are separated, He described the sheep as those who cared for the hungry, the thirsty, and the stranger; they clothed the forsaken, helped

---

[471] *Christ's Object Lessons*, 307.

[472] *Ibid.*, 310,311.

[473] See 89, 90. Victorious Christian living is not spiritual surgery whereby our sinful human nature is removed. Overcomers are receiving the Holy Spirit to subdue the impulses of the sinful flesh, not eliminate it, which would be impossible. The Holy Spirit transforms our mind (Romans 12:2) so that in the resurrection our bodies will be translated because our minds have already been transformed.

the sick, and visited those in prison. Not especially front-page stories. But the sheep were reflecting His character, permitting the Holy Spirit to make them fit to live forever!

This kind of character transformation was not a mere poetic ideal. Early Christians caught on quickly! James wrote that "pure and undefiled religion" could be recognized when Christians "visit orphans and widows in their trouble, and to keep oneself unspotted from the world" (1:27).

To put it another way, the kind of people that God is making ready to live forever are those who permit the Holy Spirit to live out the "fruit of the Spirit" ... "love, joy, peace, longsuffering, kindness, goodness, faithfulness, gentleness, self-control" (Galatians 5:22, 23).

This character transformation is another way of describing, "what it means to be clothed with the garment of His righteousness."[474] Here again Ellen White puts light on the meaning of "righteousness":

> "Righteousness is right-doing, and it is by their deeds that all will be judged. Our characters are revealed by what we do. The works show whether the faith is genuine. ... Whatever our profession, it amounts to nothing unless Christ is revealed in works of righteousness."[475]

We are dealing with metaphors when we talk about "garments" and "robes." What we are really talking about is character transformation that is surely a gift, but a gift that is imparted, not only imputed.[476]

> "Those who reject the gift of Christ's righteousness are rejecting the attributes of character which would constitute them the sons and daughters of God. They are rejecting that which alone could give

---

[474] "When we submit ourselves to Christ, the heart is united with His heart, the will is merged in His will, the mind becomes one with His mind, the thoughts are brought into captivity to Him; we live His life. This is what it means to be clothed with the garment of His righteousness." —*Christ's Object Lessons*, 312.

[475] *Ibid.*, 312, 313.

[476] *Ibid.*, 316, 317, 319. Some may say that Zechariah 3 tells us something much different regarding the believer's "robe." Not really. The wonderful good news is that Jesus can outshine Satan's accusations with the bright light of the Cross—no person who repents needs to carry the burden of guilt. Christ imputes His righteousness not to cover the believer's "filthy garments" but to "take away the filthy garments." Genuine faith is penitent when it asks for pardon and that is why "the Angel of the Lord" admonished forgiven Joshua as to how to walk in his new freedom: "If you will walk in My ways, And if you will keep My command, Then you shall also judge My house, And likewise have charge of My court; I will give you places to walk among these who stand here" (Zechariah 3:1-7). "As Joshua pleaded before the Angel, so the remnant church, with brokenness of heart and unfaltering faith, will plead for pardon and deliverance through Jesus, their Advocate. ... The assaults of Satan are strong, his delusions are subtle; but the Lord's eye is upon His people. Their affliction is great, the flames of the furnace seem about to consume them; but Jesus will bring them forth as gold tried in the fire. Their earthliness will be removed, that through them the image of Christ may be perfectly revealed. ... He does not leave His people to be overcome by Satan's temptations. ... To those who call upon Him for strength for the development of Christian character, He will give all needed help." —*Prophets and Kings*, 588–590. See *SDABC*, vol. 5, 480.

them a fitness for a place at the marriage feast. … It is in this life that we are to put on the robe of Christ's righteousness. This is our only opportunity to form characters for the home, which Christ has made ready for those who obey His commandments.[477]

LIGHT YEARS AWAY FROM PERFECTIONISM

Powerful parable that embraces all aspects of the everlasting gospel! The Bible's emphasis on "righteous behavior" is light-years away from an abstract perfectionism—anymore than Jesus was an abstract perfectionistic example!

Closely linked to this wedding parable is the dramatic, full-color, preview of the real wedding for which the whole universe is waiting—the marriage of the Lamb!

When men and women of faith walk into the "marriage of the Lamb" they walk in as His bride! But notice how John carefully chose his words: the bride, the Lamb's wife "has *made herself* ready" (Revelation 19:7).

How did she make herself "ready"? (After all, no bridegroom makes his bride ready for her wedding! The bride has preparation to do that no bridegroom can do for her.)

What was her preparation that no one else could do for her? John tells us that the bride finally comes to the altar, at last, after keeping the Bridegroom waiting at the altar for a long, long time. She comes "arrayed in fine linen, clean and bright, for the fine linen is the righteous acts[478] of the saints" (Revelation 19:8). This picture is enough to take our breath away.

Men and women of faith, symbolized by the bride, are at the wedding because the Bridegroom "can trust them."[479] The bride has demonstrated her wholehearted appreciation for His gift of love and all that comes with it. She can offer the Bridegroom only her purity and her improving track record (her "righteous acts") for the Bridegroom to trust.

GOD HAS BEEN WAITING A LONG TIME AT THE ALTAR

This wedding has been on God's heart for a long, long time. This is His reward for taking the risk of making men and women a part of His plan to settle the Great Controversy. They have settled the question as to whether sinful men and women could ever freely reverse themselves by the grace of God and be restored to a life that truly reflects their Maker.

---

[477] "The people of God must cleave to God, else they will lose their bearings. If they cherish hereditary and cultivated traits of character that misrepresent Christ, while professedly His disciples, they are represented by the man coming to the gospel feast without having on the wedding garment, and by the foolish virgins which had no oil in their vessels with their lamps. We must cleave to that which God pronounces to be truth, though the whole world may be arrayed against it." —Manuscript 140, 1901 cited in *SDABC* vol. 4, 189.

[478] Δικαιώματα, "righteous deeds." Here the focus is on the outward behavior of "righteous" character, the sanctified deeds of Christians empowered by the Holy Spirit.

[479] *Christ's Object Lessons*, 315.

We have discovered through these pages that "Satan had claimed that it was impossible for man to obey God's commandments; and in our own strength it is true that we cannot obey them. ... [But] when a soul receives Christ, he receives power to live the life of Christ."[480] And when that restored life becomes a forever habit pattern, "they have a right to join the blood-washed throng."[481]

Men and women of faith will one day have the "right" (by the grace of God) to live forever! Potent words! Why? God can "trust" them! Why? "Character ... decides destiny"[482] and that has been the whole purpose of the gospel, of why Christ came to earth and died. Such men and women of faith help to place the universe "on an eternal basis of security."[483]

John Greenleaf Whittier grasped this concept well:

"The tissue of the Life to be
We weave with colors all our own,
And in the field of Destiny
We reap as we have sown."[484]

And what will the universe say about God's risk and His judgment regarding the redeemed? Listen to the chorus echoing from world to world: "Alleluia! Salvation and glory and honor and power to the Lord our God! For true and righteous are His judgments" (Revelation 19:1, 2; also Revelation 15:3)

All this reality on the horizon today should give men and women of faith plenty of hope. But more—knowing that the Lord at the end of the road is the One who is walking beside them today should give us *present assurance* of salvation.

No mystery about who wears the robe of Christ's righteousness! Wearing the robe today means that we are "abiding in Him" *today!* Wearing the robe means that we are choosing to walk *today* "just as He walked" (1 John 2:6). Wearing the robe means that we are saying "yes" to whatever Light the Holy Spirit is shining on our paths *today.*

But there remains that lingering worry: This sounds almost too good to be true! It sounds too much like "perfectionism"—and that's scary![485] How can we understand the difference between "perfectionism" and possessing the right to join the blood-washed throng? In the next chapter we will look more carefully at what the Bible means by "perfection"?

---

[480] *Ibid.*, 314.

[481] *Ibid.*, 315. "Regeneration is the only path by which we can enter the city of God. ... The old, hereditary traits of character must be overcome. The natural desires of the soul must be changed. All deception, all falsifying, all evil speaking, must be put away. The new life, which makes men and women Christlike, is to be lived" —*Testimonies*, vol. 9, 23.

[482] See *Christ's Object Lessons*, 74, 84, 123, 260, 264, 270, 310, 356, 365, 378, 388.

[483] *The Desire of Ages*, 759.

[484] "Raphael," Stanza 16.

[485] See 162, 176.

Chapter Twenty-Four:
Perfection
—The Endless Journey

I remember those many weeks in 1993 when I thought I would never walk again without a cane, or perhaps a walker. After two surgeries for herniated discs (surgeon said, "exploded") I needed much time with Phil Stoddard, an expert, empathetic physical therapist in Auburn, California. We inched along, reducing pain and stretching for lost strength in my strangely numb but painful right leg.

On Phil's wall is a poster, a Nike ad: "There is no finish line." Three times a week, for months, I contemplated that message. It fit exactly a chapter in a book I was completing at that time, on the Books of Philippians and Colossians.[486]

That motto became Paul's message from the day he met Jesus face-to-face on the road to Damascus until he was beheaded in Rome, action-packed years later. It became his memorable counsel in Philippians:

> "Not that I have already attained, or am already perfected; but I press on, that I may lay hold of that for which Christ Jesus has also laid hold of me. Brethren, I do not count myself to have apprehended; but one thing I do, forgetting those things which are behind and reaching forward to those things which are ahead, I press toward the goal for the prize of the upward call of God in Christ Jesus" (3:12–14).

Before Damascus, he thought he had it all—wrapped up in prestige and power. In a way, he had the future wrapped up—totally secure with 1) the approval of the highest religious leaders and with 2) his spiritual assurance that he was a member of the spiritual elite.

Presumptuous Assurance

After Damascus Paul realized that he had been resting for years in presumptuous assurance. Even his friends had considered him "blameless" (Philippians 3:6)! But after meeting Jesus as his new Friend, his spiritual world turned upside down. He shifted from the security of righteousness gained by conforming to legal requirements to the "surpassing worth of knowing Christ Jesus my Lord" (3:8).

I read somewhere that driving at a speed of 30 miles an hour one can absorb only seven words from a billboard. People pay big money to catch my attention—with only a few words.

---

[486] *Rediscovering Joy* (Hagerstown, MD: RHPA, 1994), 160.

The same goes for bumper stickers. Some make sense; some you wish you had not read! Sometimes we have to get very close to get the point, such as the one that read: "The main thing is to keep the main thing the main thing."

Paul's "main thing" after Damascus was to do "one thing ... forgetting what lies behind and straining forward to what lies ahead, I press on toward the goal for the prize of the upward call of God in Christ Jesus" (verses 13, 14). What did Paul mean? So much misunderstanding has occurred through the centuries as to what Paul meant—*and those misunderstandings directly affect one's understanding of Christian assurance and that troubling word, "perfection."*

- Paul is reemphasizing our Lord's harvest principle (Mark 4; Revelation 14:14–16), which interlaces his many letters.[487] We plant hard, dry corn seeds and then we nurture them to "press on" toward the goal for which they were planted. Perfect corn seeds are expected to mature, to produce a harvest—if they do not keep growing, they cease to be "perfect." Plants that stop growing do not reach "the goal, the prize." They may have started well, but they missed the point of how to remain perfect in the eyes of their planters.[488]

- Paul is passing out an open secret of happy Christians: forget the past! But that may be easier said than done.

STOP LOOKING OVER YOUR SHOULDER

The Greek word we translate as "forgetting" is an ancient athletic term that describes a runner who surpasses another. The athlete knows that he must not be distracted by looking back over his shoulder—he must keep his eyes on the prize ahead. The Greek term is intensive—*don't keep looking over your shoulder!*

Growing Christians believe their Forever Friend—when He emphasizes that the burden of past failures has been lifted, if it has been confessed and forsaken (Proverbs 28:13, 1 John 1:9). The load is gone; they can face the future with new joy. Further, they know that their Forever Friend is helping them to redirect those neural paths that led them into those moral quagmires.[489]

---

[487] See 223, 372.

[488] "The germination of the seed represents the beginning of spiritual life, and the development of the plant is a beautiful figure of Christian growth. As in nature, so in grace; there can be no life without growth. The plant must either grow or die. As its growth is silent and imperceptible, but continuous, so is the development of the Christian life. At every stage of development our life may be perfect; yet if God's purpose for us is fulfilled, there will be continual advancement. Sanctification is the work of a lifetime. As our opportunities multiply, our experience will enlarge, and our knowledge increases. We shall become strong to bear responsibility, and our maturity will be in proportion to our privileges." —*Christ's Object Lessons*, 65, 66.

[489] See Chapter 25, "What Do Habits Have To Do With Assurance?"

Paul is also asking us to forget those spiritual crutches that we once used to impress God. Forget the notion that we are good because we are not really bad! Forget the idea that we can be Christians without knowing, in a trusting, experiential way, Jesus as our personal Savior from sin!

- Paul reminds us that this focus on pressing on "toward the goal for the prize of the upward call" is not a once-a-week affair—say, when only in church.

The Greek word translated "press" depicts a runner or a chariot racer who leans into the race, stretching every muscle, never giving up, and keeping his eyes on his prize. The word is similar in meaning to other words we have used in previous chapters, such as "strive" and "abide." Paul made a life habit after meeting Jesus, of leaning into the future, with his eyes zoomed in on his goal—honoring God, doing His service. For Paul there was "no finish line."

DIRECTION, NOT PERFECTION

Paul's emphasis is on direction, not perfection. Perfection is a word that must be used carefully because of its rampant abuse. We could present the gospel and the whole intent of the Bible without using this English word, but we wouldn't be using the whole Bible!

When Jesus and others used the Greek word we translate as "perfect," and "perfection," they are not referring to a state or level in which a person is beyond temptation or beyond the possibility of sin—any more than Jesus (a perfect person) was beyond temptation. Neither does the Bible mean that perfection demands a level of physical and mental accomplishments in which no illnesses arise or no mental mistakes (such as in mathematics) are made.

Jesus and the apostles did not speak with ambiguity; when some point out so-called contradictory statements, we ask that they read the context of those alleged contradictions and all that Jesus and the apostles have said about the subject. Jesus did not contradict Himself when He challenged us on one hand to "be perfect" (Matthew 5:48) and to "go and sin no more" (John 8:11) and, on the other, "No one is good but One, that is, God" (Mark 10:18). Neither did Paul contradict his admonishings to "sin not," (1 Corinthians 15:34; Titus 2: 11,12, NIV) when he quoted the Psalmist in Romans 3:10, that "there is none righteous, no, not one." Embracing all that Jesus said, or that of any gospel writer, will quickly resolve apparent contradictions.

The template that is needed in these topics such as "perfection," "righteousness," etc., is the overarching theme of the Great Controversy and the purpose of the gospel. God's promise to us all is that the gospel brings forgiveness and empowerment, reconciliation and restoration. The goal of the gospel is to prepare people to live forever, to be safe to save—men and women who can be entrusted with eternal life. When one places this template over the Bible, a clearer, consistent coherent picture of God's plan unfolds.

Now, let's look at that Greek word often translated "perfection." Many English translations interchange such terms as "maturity" or "completeness." But what does biblical perfection or maturity or completeness mean? Those words sound ominous, even scary.

EMOTIONS TAKE OVER

When some people see that word *perfection,* something tends to freeze up. Emotions take over. God's promises and Christ's support system seem to get blurred. Why? For two reasons: 1) Most of us are well aware of our deficiencies, and 2) we don't see very many "perfect" people.

Consequently, we try to slide over those biblical texts that clearly hold up the Christian's goal of perfection.[490] And we often discount Ellen White's emphasis on perfection.

But what are the Bible and Ellen White really saying about "perfection"? First of all, they are not working from Greek philosophical definitions, such as absolute perfection, beyond which there is no need to grow mentally, physically, and emotionally. Hardly! Their concern is "moral perfection."

Before and after Ellen White's statement that "moral perfection is required of all," she provides her context that few read. Ellen White explains this subject as well as anyone I have ever read:

> "The Lord chooses His own agents, and each day under different circumstances He gives them a trial in His plan of operation. In each true-hearted endeavor to work out His plan, He chooses His agents not because they are perfect but because, through a connection with Him, they may gain perfection.

> "God will accept only those who are determined to aim high. He places every human agent under obligation to do his best. *Moral perfection is required of all.* Never should we lower the standard of righteousness in order to accommodate inherited or cultivated tendencies to wrong-doing."[491]

In other words, God is in charge of "perfecting" His people. He is looking for people who want to cooperate with Him and who will let the purpose of the gospel be worked out in their lives. All He wants from us is our 1) willingness to stay connected with Him, 2) our determination to aim high in all aspects of our lives, and 3) our integrity in honoring His high standards.

---

[490] Such as Matthew 5:48; 19:11; Romans 12:2; Ephesians 4:13; Philippians 3:12, 15; Colossians 1:28; 4:12; Hebrews 2:10; 5:10; 7:19; 9:9; 10:1; 14, 11:40; 12:23; James 1:4, 17, 25; 2:22; 3:2; 1 John 4:17, 18.
[491] *Christ's Object Lessons,* 330.

As I said earlier, maybe the makers of the Lexus automobile have discovered the truth about the big picture that most theologians have missed. Lexus manufacturers are committed to "the relentless pursuit of perfection." Like the Apostle Paul, they never think that they have "arrived" (Philippians 3:12). They are relentlessly pursuing the "perfect car." They will continue to aim high, never lowering their standards.

Those who understand Paul's "relentless pursuit" don't spin his counsel such as: "Awake to righteousness, and do not sin; for some do not have the knowledge" (1 Corinthians 15:34); or, "For the grace of God that brings salvation, has appeared to all men. It teaches us to say "no" to ungodliness and worldly passions, and to live self-controlled, upright and godly lives in this present age" (Titus 2: 11, 12 NIV).

Nor do they put their spin on Peter's admonition: "Therefore, since all these things will be dissolved, what manner of persons ought you to be in holy conduct and godliness. ... Therefore, beloved, looking forward to these things [return of Jesus], be diligent to be found of Him in peace, without spot and blameless" (2 Peter 3:14).

Doesn't all this sound like the program we all will be on in the new earth? Always pursuing the goal of Christlikeness! Forever learning how to be more gracious, more considerate, more capable of explaining the plan of salvation to others on worlds afar!

STANDING BIBLE WRITERS ON THEIR HEADS

One thought that should seem obvious: In our "relentless pursuit" of "moral perfection," we should always be aware that it is impossible to say, "We have reached our goal!" Such a thought stands Bible writers and Ellen White on their heads!

In fact, Ellen White could not be clearer:

> "So long as Satan reigns, we shall have self to subdue, besetting sins to overcome; so long as life shall last, there will be no stopping place, no point which we can reach and say, I have fully attained. Sanctification is the result of lifelong obedience.

> "None of the apostles and prophets ever claimed to be without sin. Men who have lived the nearest to God, men who would sacrifice life itself rather than knowingly commit a wrong act, men whom God has honored with divine light and power, have confessed the sinfulness of their nature. They have put no confidence in the flesh, have claimed no righteousness of their own, but have trusted wholly in the righteousness of Christ.

> "So will it be with all who behold Christ. The nearer we come to Jesus, and the more clearly we discern the purity of His character,

the more clearly shall we see the exceeding sinfulness of sin, and the less shall we feel like exalting ourselves. There will be a continual reaching out of the soul after God, a continual, earnest, heartbreaking confession of sin and humbling of the heart before Him. At every advance step in our Christian experience our repentance will deepen. We shall know that our sufficiency is in Christ alone and shall make the apostle's confession our own: 'I know that in me (that is, in my flesh,) dwelleth no good thing.' 'God forbid that I should glory, save in the cross of our Lord Jesus Christ, by whom the world is crucified unto me, and I unto the world.'" (Romans 7:18; Galatians 6:14).[492]

How does this all work? On one hand, God is working on willing Christians, building "up a strong, symmetrical character . ... Daily [helping them to] learn the meaning of self-surrender. ... Day by day God works ... perfecting the character that is to stand in the time of final test. And day by day the believer is working out before men and angels a sublime experiment, showing what the gospel can do for fallen human beings."[493]

On the other hand, the maturing Christian is facing Satan's fiery darts (Ephesians 6:16), trusting completely on Jesus for coping power, daily deepening their spirit of repentance, knowing that without the strong Arm of their Heavenly Intercessor, they surely would fail the daily test of self-surrender.[494] Maturing Christians know that without the "all powerful Mediator,"[495] they would be "rising and falling" at best,[496] and truly miserable in their religious life—if they even remain in the church.

To say it differently, the Christian, nourished by the vine, builds branches of strength to carry the growing fruit. That is how perfect plants grow perfectly. The sun beats down, the storm weather tosses the branches, sometimes violently. But the vine and the branches and the budding fruit grow stronger, becoming ready, cultivated by the Heavenly Gardener.

DESCRIPTION OF THE "PERFECT" CHRISTIAN

Paul's Philippian letter, from start to finish, amplifies the biblical description of what "perfect" people are like: They keep facing the future

---

[492] *Acts of the Apostles*, 560, 561.

[493] *Ibid.*, 483.

[494] "Everyone who will break from the slavery and service of Satan, and will stand under the blood-stained banner of Prince Immanuel will be kept by Christ's intercessions. Christ, as our Mediator, at the right hand of the Father, ever keeps us in view, for it is as necessary that He should keep us by His intercessions as that He should redeem us with His blood. If He lets go His hold of us for one moment, Satan stands ready to destroy. Those purchased by His blood, He now keeps by His intercession." —*MS* 73, 1893, cited in SDABC, vol. 6, 1078.

[495] *The Great Controversy*, 488.

[496] "Are there those here who have been sinning and repenting, sinning and repenting, and will they continue to do so till Christ shall come? May God help us that we may be truly united to Christ, the living vine, and bear fruits to the glory of God." —*Review and Herald*, April 21, 1891.

trusting their Lord. They keep growing. They make it a habit to let God work out His good pleasure in their lives. They never give up! They endure, regardless of earthly circumstances.

Then Paul says something very wistful, perhaps springing from what he had noticed in the early Christian church: Some did not keep pressing on; some felt that they had already attained; some put their religious experience into neutral. And they began to lose what they had.

SLIPPERY SLOPE OF UNINTENDED CONSEQUENCES

Perhaps every reader has experienced "losing what we had." We have read many biblical descriptions of what happens when we drift first into a spiritual holiday, then, soon, onto that slippery slope of unintended consequences. We can lose in an hour what had taken months, perhaps years, to gain. Not a fair trade—but such is the nature of growth.

Some plants are that way—they receive months of careful attention, but after careless neglect for a few days they are barely recoverable. However, the good news is, no matter how much neglect we allow to settle in, God has marvelous ways to "restore to you the years that the locust hath eaten" (Joel 2:25 KJV). Our friendly Lord has not turned down one request, and won't!

This chapter ends where we began: "No finish line!" Further, God is in the business, not only Lexus manufacturers, of moving His grand experiment onward in the "relentless pursuit of perfection." Two million years from now, His redeemed will be still "reaching forward to those things which are ahead" (Philippians 3:13).[497]

And when the question is asked, "Have you ever seen a perfect person?" the only answer is, "That's God's department, not mine. All I can see is my deficiencies and the road ahead—and I know that He has not given up on me. All He asks from me is to keep abiding in Him, to continue walking with Him on the road to forever."[498]

That's the rub! This sounds almost too good to be true! Some say that they have a track record of failure—not always big-time, but enough to know that they are off the wagon as much as they are on.

They know that they must have more consistency in their lives. That leads us into the next chapter. How do we develop habit patterns so that "abiding in Him" becomes second nature? And that is exactly what Jesus promised Nicodemus—a new birth, a second nature (John 3).

---

[497] During the late 1930s, Seabiscuit became an American legend—no other racehorse rivaled his fame or his sway over the nation's imagination. After one of his earlier victories, his owner, Charles Howard, announced to the surrounding reporters and radio announcers, "This isn't the finish line. The future is the finish line. Seabiscuit is the horse to get us there!" In other words, for Seabiscuit, there would be no stopping place as long as life would last.

[498] For a clear, compelling, presentation on the subject of Christian perfection, see J. R. Zurcher, *What Inspiration Has to Say About Christian Perfection,* translated by Edward F. White (Hagerstown, MD: RHPA, 2002).

CHAPTER TWENTY-FIVE:
WHAT DO HABITS HAVE TO DO WITH THE GREAT CONTROVERSY?

W e have been focusing on the kind of people whom God makes ready to live forever. They are the pay-off of God's risk in creating them! They have faced up to the cost of freedom on God's part and the freedom they gained when they turned from the path of self-gratification.

Jesus said in His famous Sermon on the Mount that people safe to save have built their lives on the Rock instead of sand. Prepared people build on the rock of Christ's words, the basis of the "assurance of faith" (Hebrews 10:22).

Those who thought they were saved, living with presumptuous assurance, will discover that Jesus must say, though reluctantly: "I never knew you for what you said you were" (Matthew 7:23). Their lives were based on principles that were primarily self-centered. They did their good works to impress others, either their friends or God Himself. Their lives amounted to only sandcastles to be washed away by the restless sea.

Those who built on principles and truth that were rock-secured, not only endured the troubles of this life—they are safe to save![499] In practical terms, what was the difference in the lives of those with presumptuous assurance (sand castles) and those with genuine assurance (rock-assurance)?[500] What was going on in their neural patterns that made them think and act the way they did?

Let's first ask a question that we have looked at before. What does it mean to build on the Rock?

Building on the Rock is the same as "abiding in Christ."[501] Ellen White is very insightful regarding how we are to build on the Rock (after discussing Christ's analogy of rock and sand):

---

[499] See 144.

[500] Presumptuous assurance is provided by fashion shops in Beijing using "magic mirrors," devices that have dramatically increased sales. To fool overweight women into thinking they look stunning and slimmer in their clothes, fitting rooms have specially-made mirrors with a curved surface to make people look more slender. The ruse was finally discovered when one customer who bought a dress after it seemed to make her look thinner only to find back at home the garment actually accentuated her ample proportions. —Hong Kong (dpa), *Drudge Report*, August 6, 2003.

[501] See 156, 221.

"We build on Christ by obeying His word. It is not he who merely enjoys righteousness, that is righteous, but he who does righteousness. Holiness is not rapture; it is the result of surrendering all to God; it is doing the will of our heavenly Father.

"Religion consists in doing the words of Christ; not doing to earn God's favor, but because, all undeserving, we have received the gift of His love. Christ places the salvation of man, not upon profession merely, but upon faith that is made manifest in works of righteousness. Doing, not saying merely, is expected of the followers of Christ. It is through action that character is built. ... As you receive the word in faith, it will give you power to obey. As you give heed to the light you have, greater light will come. You are building on God's word, and your character will be builded after the similitude of the character of Christ."[502]

It would be hard to misunderstand these two paragraphs! Our question is: How is this done? How does it happen so that "through action ... character is built"? That is a powerful concept. Not through words only, not even through Bible study and prayer only—but through "action ... character is built"! How do actions affect character?

The word is "habit." Those who are eventually redeemed will be habitually "keep[ing] the commandments of God and the faith of Jesus" (Revelation 14:12, Lit: "making a life-habit of keeping"). So let's talk about habits!

LET'S TALK ABOUT HABITS

Habits cannot be measured like muscles or observed on a electro-cardiogram. *Habit* is a word that describes what happens when thoughts or acts are repeated. Habits are truly good friends! Think of the time we save (without taking time to think it out as we once did) when we tie our shoes, drive cars, or use the typewriter or computer! Remember the hours and weeks it took to develop these skills that we no longer have to *consciously* repeat, over and over, just to get it right! I like the way Ellen White put it:

"The power of self-restraint strengthens by exercise. That which at first seems difficult, by constant repetition grows easy and right thoughts and actions become habitual."[503]

Habits are our built-in, anti-stress kits. To the extent wholesome habits control our lives, to that extent we enjoy life. I don't mean that we can be

---

[502] *Thoughts From the Mount of Blessing*, 149, 150.
[503] *The Ministry of Healing*, 491.

happy all the time, but we can live with a deep sense of joy about the bigger issues of life—all the time! If we are not enjoying life, we may be plugged into the wrong socket. Some other power may be giving us energy!

Habits have lasting consequences: "Actions repeated form habits, habits form character, and by the character our destiny for time and for eternity is decided."[504]

When we remember that God will not and cannot save rebels, the issue of "character" becomes profoundly important—especially when we remember that when Jesus comes "He is not to cleanse us of our sins, to remove from us the defects in our characters, or to cure us of the infirmities of our tempers and dispositions."[505]

How are habits made or unmade? Wise Solomon said that as a man thinks, "so is he" (Proverbs 23:7). We think with brain cells that lie about an inch behind our forehead. These brain cells are the capital of the body, the power center for all that happens to every nerve and muscle. The brain's messages are sent "electrically" at astonishing speeds that scientists have not yet been able to replicate on the most advanced computer. And we have some computers making billions of decisions every second![506]

Most of the illnesses that physicians see in their offices are mentally or emotionally induced (psychosomatic). We have all experienced the truth of this fact. When our willpower is at low ebb; when the mind or emotions wrestle with bad news, we have difficulty resisting cold symptoms, or an upset stomach. But this same principle can reverse physical problems. With habits of positive attitudes and trust in God, our bodies respond to our thoughts and we resist disease and overcome illnesses.[507]

Surpasses World's Largest Computers

So how does the brain do this work? The entire brain operates on 10 watts of electricity and performs math calculations that far outrun the world's largest computers. Each brain cell has many fibers called dendrites that receive all kinds of information constantly. One long fiber called the axon transmits messages between cells.[508]

---

[504] *Christ's Object Lessons*, 356.

[505] *Testimonies*, vol. 2, 355; See also 154.

[506] See 298.

[507] "Right and correct habits, intelligently and perseveringly practiced, will be removing the cause of disease and the strong drugs will not be resorted to." —*Medical Ministry*, 222. See also *Testimonies*, vol. 3, 157.

[508] "The brain is the capital of the body, the seat of all the nervous forces and of mental action. The nerves proceeding from the brain control the body. By the brain nerves, mental impressions are conveyed to all the nerves of the body as by telegraph wires; and they control the vital action of every part of the system. All the organs of motion are governed by the communications they receive from the brain." —*Testimonies*, vol. 3, 69. See also *Education*, 197.

The microscope shows us that on the end of the axon are tiny enlargements called boutons (French for "buttons"). These boutons secrete chemicals (ACH and GABA) that stimulate the next cell to send a message down the nerve path to whatever muscle or organ is to be activated. But there is no direct connection between the axon and the next cell's dendrites, only a tiny space, called the synapse. How does the message get across this synapse? Through the chemicals of the boutons.

Here is where it gets interesting. Some axons have more boutons than others. Why? Because that axon has been stimulated more than others. More stimulation, more boutons. With more boutons, the easier it is the next time for similar messages to flow along that particular pathway. Habits are forming!

How are boutons formed? Any thought or act forms a bouton. Thoughts and acts often repeated build more boutons on the end of that particular axon so that it becomes easier to repeat that same thought or act when the same situation is again faced. Just like cutting across the lawn eventually wears a worn path, so repeated thoughts actually produce physical and chemical changes in our nerve pathways. Thoughts don't vanish into thin air, they are etched into a biochemical pattern that we call habits.

BOUTONS NEVER DISAPPEAR

The good news and the bad news is that boutons never disappear. Right! Frightening, as well as assuring! For example, recovered alcoholics tell each other that they "are always" alcoholics. So they avoid friends who drink and places where alcohol beverages are likely to be served Chocoholics and those involved in "fatal attractions" never lose those boutons that make it easier for them to "cave in, again."[509]

But the good news is that the bad-habit boutons can be "overpowered" by good-habit boutons. Those who find it easy to be angry, to be lazy or self-centered, can believe that with the right set of the mind and the power of God, new habits of self-control, industriousness, and caring can be established firmly. *We are what we think.*

Sounds too easy? Here is how we build more yes or no boutons, whichever is appropriate for the occasion. For example, when we are used to saying "yes" to bad choices, we must build "no" boutons.

---

[509] "Let none flatter themselves that sins cherished for a time can easily be given up by and by. This is not so. Every sin cherished weakens the character and strengthens habit; and physical, mental, and moral depravity is the result. You may repent of the wrong you have done, and set your feet in right paths; but the mold of your mind and your familiarity with evil will make it difficult for you to distinguish between right and wrong. Through the wrong habits formed, Satan will assail you again and again." —*Christ's Object Lessons*, 281.

Research indicates that we can change most any habit in a matter of weeks—some say 21 days! When we choose to resist temptation (that is, whatever obscures "abiding in Christ"), when we say, "no!" the GABA secretion is secreted at the synapse. GABA puts the brakes on and keeps that cell from firing. With repeated resistance (repeatedly saying, "no," when before the choices were repeatedly saying, "yes"), more "no" boutons are formed. With more "no" boutons on the end of that axon that had formerly led to inappropriate sexual behavior or quick anger, GABA (the brakes) is even more powerful, making it virtually impossible to do wrong in that particular situation again.

Sound too simple? There is a warning. The GABA secretion does not function well, most often not at all, when we lose sleep or get fatigued for whatever reason, good or bad. GABA (the brake on our decision making) is affected by fatigue much sooner than ACH (the accelerator on our decision making). That is, when we are tired, we find it easier to do and say what we please, long after we have lost our braking power. That is why committee meetings in the evenings, Saturday night flings, and nighttime confrontations with others (children, spouses, etc.) most often turn into regrettable experiences. When we are tired, the go-for-it, tell-it-like-it-is, have-fun attitude has no GABA to say, "no!"

To get even more practical, most of life is a matter of conflicting choices— shall I, or shall I not? One brain cell says, "Why not? Go for it!" The other says, "No, you'd better not!" Which one wins? The one with the most boutons built up by habit! One brain cell sees the extra piece of scrumptious pecan pie or the banana sundae; or the possibility of getting a better grade by cheating because everyone is doing it; or eating between meals and skipping breakfast; or undue familiarity with the opposite sex. However, another brain cell now becomes activated; it sees the same opportunities and says, "No, there's a better way. I choose to abide in Christ and all those negative choices will keep me from my full potential. I want to honor my parents (or my spouse, or my God). I want to be trusted."

All this choosing (mental activity) takes electrical energy. When negative temptation of any kind says "Go for it! Looks good, take a piece;" or "Go for it, no one will ever know"—30 millivolts, shall we say, of ACH energy surges into your action cell. But your better self says (if you are not in fatigue), "Hold it, there are consequences down the road I don't want to live with. Don't fire! [That is, 'Don't cheat,' 'Don't take that extra piece of pie!']." If the better brain cell has more boutons, GABA jumps into action with 40 millivolts, shall we say, of electrical power, saying, "no!" Because it takes only 10 millivolts for a cell to fire, the brain cell with the most boutons wins![510]

---

[510] Elden M. and Esther L. Chalmers, *Making the Most of Family Living* (Nampa, ID: PPPA, 1979), 61–67.

The scenario, of course, can be reversed. If the brain cell saying, "Go for it!" has the most boutons, ACH wins. Especially if the brain cells are tired and GABA is not functioning.

Let's consider this again! All it takes to say "no" *when you should* is a difference of 10 millivolts of electrical power. The brain cell is making a fast algebraic decision in a matter of a thousandth of a second—and the 10 millivolts will win.

HOW HABITS ARE FORMED

This is how habits are formed: More boutons (because of the same thoughts and actions repeated often) equal more electric current to say "no" or "yes" at the proper times. The more boutons producing a certain habit pattern, the more spontaneous, habitual, and natural will be the ability to make right decisions in the future. That is how right decisions form right habits that form right characters.[511]

The eminent Harvard psychologist, William James, observed:

> "Could the young but realize how soon they will become mere walking bundles of habits, they would give more heed to their conduct while in the plastic state. We are spinning our fates, good or evil, and never to be undone. Every smallest stroke of virtue or vice leaves its never-so-little scar. ... The drunken Rip Van Winkle, in Jefferson's play, excuses himself for every fresh dereliction by saying, 'I won't count this time!' Well! He may not count it, and a kind Heaven may not count it; but it is being counted nonetheless. Down among his nerve cells and fibers the molecules are counting it, registering and storing it up to be used against him when the next temptation comes. Nothing we ever do, in strict scientific literalness is wiped out.

> "Of course, this has its good sides as well as its bad one. As we become permanent drunkards by so many separate drinks, so we become saints in the moral, and authorities and experts in the practical and scientific spheres, by so many separate acts and hours of work."[512]

---

[511] "The power of self-restraint strengthens by exercise. That which at first seems difficult, by constant repetition grows easy, until right thoughts and actions become habitual. If we will we may turn away from all that is cheap and inferior, and rise to a high standard; we may be respected by men and beloved of God." —*The Ministry of Healing*, 491.

[512] Chalmers, *op. cit.*, 66, 67.

Christians, of all people, should be realists—negative habits are always there in the shadows, because all boutons remain in place.[513] We may repent and set our feet in right paths but the familiarity with the former temptations is a crease in the paper that cannot be completely unfolded.[514] That is why wise Paul could say, "Let him who thinks he stands take heed lest he fall" (1 Corinthians 10:12).

WILL POWER NOT ENOUGH

At this point, at this crucial knife edge of each person's future on which all else balances, we must be very clear and honest unto ourselves: Willpower, no matter how strong a person is, will never be sufficient to build enough boutons so that we will be above temptation. We live in a very dynamic universe and forces beyond the human are impressing us constantly (Ephesians 6:12, 13).

Only by the empowering of the personal intervention of the Holy Spirit, the Eternal Energy of the universe, can any of us be prompted even to begin wanting to make the right boutons along the right axons. Even God chooses not to make the right boutons for us—if we do not *choose* His way. This choosing, this response to the prompting of the Spirit, is the first step in making new boutons. *God does not choose for us any more than He does our breathing for us!*[515]

The good news is that He has wired us to succeed with a neural system that defies human imagination or duplication. All He wants from us is our choice. Each right choice becomes another bouton, until the "weight" of boutons forms a strong and good habit.

Our brain cells make all this happen. You would think that caring for our brain cells would be our highest priority. How can we make healthy brain cells every day? First, make sure that we are feeding them with rich, pure blood. How do we do that? By eating food that is healthful, such as fruit, nuts, vegetables, and grains. By avoiding animal products that send

---

[513] "We should not be slow in breaking up a sinful habit. Unless evil habits are conquered, they will conquer us, and destroy our happiness." —*Testimonies*, vol. 4, 654.

[514] "What the child sees and hears is drawing deep lines upon the tender mind, which no after circumstances in life can entirely efface. The intellect is now taking shape, and the affections receiving direction and strength. Repeated acts in a given course become habits. These may be modified by severe training, in afterlife, but are seldom changed." —*Child Guidance*, 99, 200.

[515] "While these youth [four Hebrew youth in Babylon] were working out their own salvation, God was working in them to will and to do of His good pleasure. Here are revealed the conditions of success. To make God's grace our own, we must act our part. The Lord does not propose to perform for us either the willing or the doing. His grace is given to work in us to will and to do, but never as a substitute for our effort. Our souls are to be aroused to cooperate. The Holy Spirit works in us, that we may work out our own salvation. This is the practical lesson the Holy Spirit is striving to teach us." —Ellen White Comments, *SDA Bible Commentary*, vol. 4, 1167.

cholesterol and other undesirable elements zinging through our blood stream. By drinking plenty of water daily. By breathing deeply in fresh air. By exercising daily so that all that water, good nutrients, and fresh oxygen is hurried through the blood stream, feeding those brain cells minute by minute!

When brain cells are not fed properly, we doze at the wheel of our car as well as in class lectures, or in church; we make poor decisions; we become lazy, grouchy, and miserable.

But brain cells are even more important than helping us to think clearly and quickly. They are not only where habits are formed. *Brain cells must be kept healthy because the brain is the only place in our bodies where the Holy Spirit connects with us.*

Let the following quotation sink in:

> "The brain nerves that connect with the whole system are the medium through which heaven communicates with man and affects the inmost life. Whatever hinders the circulation of the electric current in the nervous system, thus weakening the vital powers and lessening mental susceptibility, makes it more difficult to arouse the moral nature."[516]

Think about it! Anything we do to improve our general health makes it easier to hear the Holy Spirit! When I discovered that principle some years ago, I surely paid more attention to what I ate, how I exercised, and when I rested. The thought also occurred to me that when I violated simple health rules, I was tuning down the Holy Spirit and thus not getting the confirming Voice of assurance, which I want to live with day by day (1 John 3:24).

Imagine that! How I treat my physical body directly affects my mental and moral sensibilities and thus my character development. And without question, my daily sense of a saving relationship with Jesus! That sounds very much like "doing" the will of God (Philippians 2:13) and building on the rock that Jesus talked about (Matthew 7:21, 24).

JUMP-STARTING OUR ELECTRICAL SYSTEM

Through it all, God holds before us, day and night, the reasons why we should choose His way of making sense out of our lives. He never wearies. He is always ready to provide the electrical energy that jump-starts our electrical system whenever we choose to plug into His power. And He never gives up on us, even if we fail again and again in the self-correcting

---

[516] *Education*, 209.

process of reaching our goals. He is already there to jump-start us again with more energy to make more boutons of the right kind. That is what Paul meant when he said, "God is at work in you, both to will and to do His good pleasure."[517]

Paul understood all this. As we have said in many ways in these pages, Paul saw the principles of the Great Controversy working out daily in the lives of church members as well as the general public. Note his counsel to the Galatians: "You, my friends, were called to be free men only: only do not turn your freedom into license for your lower nature, but be servants to one another in love. … I mean this: if you are guided by the Spirit you will not fulfill the desires of your lower nature" (5:13, 16 NEB).

The good news is that the more we get into the practice of permitting the Holy Spirit to help us say "yes" to His plans for us, the easier it becomes to keep adding boutons on the right axons. That is why we must make a daily habit of focusing on those things that are true, honest, just, pure, lovely, and of a good report, as Paul put it so eloquently (see Philippians 4:8). Each act of focusing becomes a new bouton until what one focuses on becomes a fixed habit and is reflected in the Christian's character.

One added thought. Some very nice people still honestly believe that it is impossible for sinful human beings to overcome sinful attitudes, actions, or feelings. Contrary to the golden thread throughout the Bible that "overcomers" will occupy the new earth,[518] they hope that in some way all their sinful habits for which they keep asking forgiveness will be erased from their frontal lobes in the resurrection. Perilous close to thinking like the presumptuous "believers" who want to know why the Lord does not "know" them (Matthew 7:22).

The gold standard, the rock of truth, is that the Holy Spirit's awesome task is to redirect our neural patterns so that it becomes a habit to think right-wisely (righteously). Whether we want to believe it or not, the day is coming when those prepared for the Lord to come will have settled "into the truth, both intellectually and spiritually, so they cannot be moved."[519] Or, more settled into self-centered, envious, hateful persons, so they too cannot be moved!

---

[517] Philippians 2:13. See 150–156.

[518] See 144.

[519] In fact, God is waiting for such people who will permit the Holy Spirit to complete His work in them (Philippians 1:6). See *Christ's Object Lessons*, 9.

HABIT PATTERNS THAT NEVER CHANGE

How does this happen in my life and in yours? By the development of a habit pattern in thinking and doing that will never change.[520] In many ways, Ellen White is consistent and clear:

> "If our hearts are softened and subdued by the grace of Christ, and glowing with a sense of God's goodness and love, there will be a *natural* outflow of love, sympathy, and tenderness to others."[521]

> "The grace of Christ must mold the entire being, and its triumph will not be complete until the heavenly universe shall witness *habitual* tenderness of feeling, Christlike love, and holy deeds in the deportment of the children of God."[522]

> "That which at first seems difficult, by constant repetition grows easy, until right thoughts and actions become *habitual*. If we will we may turn away from all that is cheap and inferior, and rise to a high standard; we may be respected by men and beloved of God."[523]

> "When self is merged in Christ, love springs forth *spontaneously*. The completeness of Christian character is attained when the impulse to help and bless others *springs constantly* from within—when the sunshine of heaven fills the heart and is revealed in the countenance."[524]

> "The principles of God's law will dwell in the heart, and control the actions. It will then be as *natural* for us to seek purity and holiness, to shun the spirit and example of the world, and to seek to benefit all around us, as it is for the angels of glory to execute the mission of love assigned them. None will enter the city of God but those who have been doers of the word."[525]

This is powerful, good news! We don't have to be grouchy, stingy, self-centered or angry forever. Not when the Holy Spirit gets to work! The Spirit restores freedom lost through sin! Freedom from the tyranny of self; mastery

---

[520] Of course, this equally applies to maturing wheat as well as to maturing tares, to those becoming more like Jesus or those becoming more like Satan.

[521] *Testimonies*, vol. 5, 606 (italics supplied).

[522] *Amazing Grace*, 235 (italics supplied).

[523] *The Ministry of Healing*, 491 (italics supplied).

[524] *Christ's Object Lessons*, 384 (italics supplied).

[525] *Review and Herald*, October 23, 1888 (italics supplied).

over self-destructive habits! This kind of freedom sings with David: "I will walk at liberty, For I seek Your precepts" (Psalm 119:45).[526]

Perhaps you have some anxious thoughts regarding how all this fits into some scary feelings regarding the Investigative Judgment. You think, how can anybody have solid assurance today when nothing is settled until our names "come up" in the pre-advent judgment?

But there is no need for anyone to worry about the Investigative Judgment. The Investigative Judgment, the pre-advent judgment before the return of Jesus, is a time for good news.

---

[526] Robert J. Wieland, *Dial Daily Bread*, September 10, 2001.

T he cost of freedom is incalculable. Ask those 102 (some say 103) Pilgrims and others in the autumn of 1620 who departed from Southampton, England, in their little, 180-ton ship named the Mayflower. Back in 17th-century England, religious freedom did not exist. King James, speaking about religious dissenters, said: "I will make them conform themselves, or else I will harry them out of the land."

In 1618, they applied for approval to settle in Virginia, securing an investor to finance their way. (By means of beaver skins, they repaid this debt, though it took 40 years due to exorbitant interest rates.) In the summer of 1620 they joined the crew of 58, expecting a journey of the usual 30 days. It lasted 66! They left behind their material assets, their families, their country, and for many, their lives. William Bradford, 35 years their governor, wrote: "We are in such a strait at present, as we are forced to sell away 60 worth [sic] of our provisions ... [that put them into] 'great extremities.'"

The Mayflower left at the beginning of the worst time of the year to cross the Atlantic. Bradford later wrote that "many fierce storms with which the ship was shrewdly shaken." They were all chilled to the bone. Waves of icy water splashed over the ill and frightened passengers. No oilskins or rubber clothing protected them. Foul smells reeked the ship. The Mayflower became a floating slum. The crowded conditions, the meager diet and never being able to bathe, they wore the same clothes without any change for two months! Rats and cockroaches everywhere, flour and biscuits were either moldy or full of weevils and maggots. No bathroom, only buckets.

Yet, in the face of fierce winds and rain, the devout Pilgrims sang songs for hours at a time. With tears coursing down their cheeks, they prayed, terrified but never looking back. Church services were held daily. In the middle of all this terror, a baby was born to Elizabeth Hopkins, little Oceanus, named after the Atlantic Ocean.

In the middle of November they arrived off the coast of Cape Cod in Massachusetts. Blown off their course, unprepared for a New England winter, the first thing they did was to fall on their knees and praise God. Little did they then know that only 51 would survive the first winter.

Even before they finally landed at Plymouth, Massachusetts, harsh voices veered toward mutiny. Some of those not Pilgrims feared the type of government that the religious leaders wanted, hoping for a land where they could do as they pleased, knowing little about the yearn for freedom that kept their ocean journey together. So they thought through what we today call "The Mayflower Compact." It rested on the basic principle that the settlers agreed to form a government and be bound by its rules, that for a government to be legitimate, it must derive from the consent of the governed. Its throbbing pulse rested in their words that they had "undertaken [this new government] for the Glory of God, and Advancement of the Christian Faith." Forty-one men signed the document, many of whom never lived to see springtime. They all paid the price of freedom. For them, freedom was incalculable.

www.geocities.com/divine_principle/2_1620/part6a.html; www.pbs.org/wnet/historyofus/web03/ ; www.rootsweb.com/~mosmd/ -

God will have a people who will rightly represent Him and help present to the world His final appeal before the forces of Good and Evil come to their final clash and before Jesus returns. Is it possible that God would risk all in placing the future of the universe on the last generation who will be the targets of Satan's fiercest attacks?

CHAPTER TWENTY-SIX:
THE BIBLE OVERVIEW OF
THE "LAST DAYS"

We now turn to our responsibilities today. We live in the endtime, perhaps more specifically, "in the end of the endtime." The endtime brings all the issues in the Great Controversy that we have been discussing into sharp focus.[527] Satan truly knows that "he has a short time" (Revelation 12:12). What does the Bible tell us about what to expect in these last days?

Daniel 11 keeps our eyes on a dominant religious power, its development, temporary decline, and eventual world leadership in the last days. Throughout this remarkable preview, we are pointed to the counter forces of atheism, non-Christian powers, as well as Christian parties.[528]

Daniel traces the high-water mark of the Persian Empire, the remarkable rise of young Alexander, the split of the Grecian empire after Alexander's untimely death, and the rise and interactions of the kings of the North and the South (representing the Seleucid and Ptolemaic kingdoms, respectively).

---

[527] "Eschatology [last-day events] is the keystone of the edifice of theological thinking, holding the whole building together. ... Belief in the faithfulness of God is the ground of eschatological hope. Equally, eschatological experience will provide the ultimate vindication of belief in that God," —John Polkinhorne, *The God of Hope and the End of the World* (New Haven: Yale University Press, 2002), 140, 148.

[528] See C. Mervyn Maxwell, *God Cares*, vol. 1 (Nampa, ID: PPPA, 1981), 283–298.

These powers segued into pagan Rome and Egypt, followed by papal Rome and the Muslim powers. In all these political developments, the people of God were being affected; for example, "the wise" are felled "by the sword and flame, by captivity and plunder" (verse 33).

Verses 40–45 seem best interpreted as an outline of the coalition power of the papacy and its military arm—the United States with its vast resources.[529] The parallels between Daniel 7 and Revelation 17, 18, are instructive: "He shall come to his end, and no one will help him" (verse 45); "For in one hour she is made desolate" (Revelation 18:19). In reviewing an overview of Revelation, we will find more details.[530]

Second Thessalonians 2:1–11 points to a religious power that "sits as God in the temple of God, showing himself that he is God" (verse 4). His vast influence will be "according to the working of Satan, with all power, signs, and lying wonders, and with all unrighteous deception among those who perish, because they did not receive the love of the truth, that they might be saved" (verses 9, 10). The importance of Paul's preview is that he is specifically discussing the days immediately preceding the return of Jesus (verses 1–3).

Second Timothy 3:1–5 focuses predominantly on Paul's preview of prevailing lifestyles in the endtime. Although there is nothing new under the sun, it seems that Paul is beaming prophecy's searchlight on an unprecedented surge of self-centered living in the "last days [when] perilous times will come" (verse 1). His description boldly describes the departure of the restraining power of the Holy Spirit, leading to the day when even

---

[529] Any reference to the papacy is just that and not a condemnation of our Roman Catholic friends. Ellen White's counsel is clear: "Notwithstanding the spiritual darkness and alienation from God that exist in the churches which constitute Babylon, the great body of Christ's true followers are still to be found in their communion. ... There are now true Christians in every church, not excepting the Roman Catholic communion, who honestly believe that Sunday is the Sabbath of divine appointment. God accepts their sincerity of purpose and their integrity before Him." —*The Great Controversy,* 390, 449. "Let not those who write for our papers make unkind thrusts and allusions that will certainly do harm and that will hedge up the way and hinder us from doing the work that we should do in order to reach all classes, the Catholics included. It is our work to speak the truth in love and not to mix in with the truth the unsanctified elements of the natural heart and speak things that savor of the same spirit possessed by our enemies. ... We are not to use harsh and cutting words. Keep them out of every article written; drop them out of every address given. Let the Word of God do the cutting, the rebuking; let finite men hide and abide in Jesus Christ." —*Testimonies,* vol. 9, 240, 241, 244. "We should weed out each expression in our writings, our utterances, that, if taken by itself, could be misinterpreted so as to make it seem antagonistic to law and order. Everything should be carefully considered lest we place ourselves on record as uttering things that will make us appear disloyal to our country and its law." —Letter 36, 1895, cited in *Last-Day Events,* 90. "Christianity is not manifested in pugilistic accusations and condemnations." —*Testimonies,* vol. 6. 397. "Those who have had great privileges ... but who have lived to please ... are in greater danger and in greater condemnation before God than those who are in error upon doctrinal points, yet who seek to live to do good to others. Do not censure others; do not condemn them." —*Testimonies,* vol. 9, 243. Think of Mother Teresa!

[530] See C. Mervyn Maxwell, *God Cares,* vol. 2 —*The Message of Revelation for You and Your Family* (Nampa. ID: PPPA, 1981).

the restraints of government no longer apply—when most people feel unfettered in their pursuit of pleasure and gain at the expense of anybody in their way.

SPOTLIGHTING SATAN'S FURY

Revelation 12:17 spotlights Satan's fury as he sees that God's plan for proving him wrong is picking up power and credibility. If anyone thinks that Satan has been furious before in his attacks on God's people, whether during Old and New Testament times or during the Dark Ages—we haven't seen anything approaching his rage in the last days.

Revelation 13 outlines in three-dimensional color and drama how the dominant religious power that Daniel 11 pointed to establishes world prominence. Note: "All the world marveled and followed the beast. So they worshiped the dragon who gave authority to the beast; and they worshiped the beast, saying, 'Who is like the beast? Who is able to make war with him'?" (verses 3, 4). The stage is the world, not merely a particular nation.

But there is more. Another world power emerges out of virgin territory and eventually "exercises all the authority of the first beast ... and causes the earth and those who dwell in it to worship the first beast, whose deadly wound was healed" (verse 12).

This second beast will become a surrogate to the first beast, "perform[ing] great signs, so that he even makes fire come down from heaven. ... He deceives those who dwell on the earth by those signs which he was granted to do in the sight of the best, telling those who dwell on the earth to make an image to the beast" (verses 13, 14).

This second world power, this political government, will emerge as a religion-empowering force, "grant[ing] power to give breath to the image to the beast, that the image of the beast should both speak and cause as many as would not worship the image of the beast to be killed ... and that no one may buy or sell except one who has the mark or the name of the beast" (verses 15-17).

This is an astonishing preview of last-day events. Later we will examine in more detail what we have been looking at through the broad sweep of prophetical language.

MESSAGES OF THREE ANGELS HITS SATAN HEAD-ON

In *Revelation 14,* God reveals His last-day strategy as to how He will get the truth of His side in the Great Controversy to the world *through His people.* This gospel witness will be presented more clearly and more forcibly than at any time in this world's history. Three angels represent three phases in God's endtime, earth-enveloping movement beginning in the early 1800s. The messages of the second and third angels build and enlarge on the scope of the first angel's message.

In these three messages, God dramatically confronts Satan's world (John 12:31; 16:11) that has been deluded as to what kind of a God created this planet and its inhabitants.

The first angel emphasizes that God's good news is the same today as it was in the Garden of Eden—the "everlasting gospel" is God's answer to Satan's lies. And this heavenly response to Satan's lies will be heard all over the earth—an event never fully imagined by John the Revelator. But today with the Internet and radio, with television antennas and satellite dishes popping up on most every home on all continents, the messages of the three angels indeed are going "to every nation, tribe, tongue, and people" (verse 6).

The thrust of the first angel is that God is our Creator and worthy of our worship, that He is not the kind of God that Satan has made Him out to be. And then—earth-shaking news—that *now* is the time for bringing the curtain down on Satan's laboratory experiment with this earth: "The hour of His judgment has come" (verse 7)! God is now calling the universe, including those on Planet Earth, to judge whether He has been fair and worthy of their worship

We are living within the time of the three angels! Now is the time to think through all the issues we have been discussing in this book. Now is decision time for every man and woman and child. Now is the time when the final barrage of lies and deceit from the arch-deceiver will be exposed by all this "good news" about God, "that old serpent of old, called the Devil and Satan" (Revelation 12:9).[531]

The second angel's message focuses on developing events in this confrontation between God's loyalists and Satan's deluded followers. In some potent, dramatic way, the message goes out: "Babylon is fallen ... because she has made all nations drink of the wine of the wrath of her fornication" (verse 8). Babylon[532]—that collective word used often in the Bible to describe the confusion of lies and false religions energized by Satan—flowers in the last days in worldwide religious communities that promise salvation to its devoted worshippers without the necessity of character transformation. Here we see the Great Controversy Theme in 3-D Technicolor: God's loyalists head to head with those deluded by Satan, not necessarily lost, but deluded until they respond to the Three Angels.

---

[531] The attack on the reliability of the Bible and the relevancy of Christianity erupted in the middle of the 19th century. The message of the first angel could not have been more timely.

[532] "Protestants since Luther's day had correctly seen Babylon as a symbol of the Roman church, a Christian body whose leaders at worst rejected elements of Bible truth and persecuted Christians who chose to believe them." Further, Advent leaders noticed that "Babylon herself a 'harlot,' is the 'mother of harlots.' Daughter harlots carry their mother's name. [They] felt compelled to draw the conclusion that Babylon's daughters are Protestant churches, which, like the Roman church, reject Bible truth and harass those who accept it. ... When we come to Revelation 18:4 we'll hear Jesus make His final appeal to His dear followers who are still members of the 'Babylon' churches. 'Come out of her'—that is, Come out of Babylon—He says, 'lest you take part in her sins, lest you share in her plagues.'" —Maxwell, *God Cares*, vol. 2, 367, 368.

The general Advent movement in the 1840s first understood this message of the second angel. The response of most Christian churches reflected a general disdain for any emphasis on the soon return of Jesus. Rather, most Christian churches believed that the world would first enjoy a 1,000-year period of peace and prosperity before the Second Coming—a belief that has no biblical support. The second angel's appeal becomes increasingly timely as the end draws near (Revelation 18:4).

Then that third angel! Graphic language, clear as the brightest searchlight! On one hand, the dire warning against staying in Babylon and, on the other, the comforting good news that God will indeed have a people who cooperate with Him by faith and keep His commandments (Revelation 14:12).

Those loyalists here described believe, among other salient biblical truths, that the first angel's message announced the beginning of the pre-advent judgment in 1844.[533] Because of this prophetic date nailing down the 2,300-year prophecy of Daniel 8:14, they also knew, just as emphatically, that the Lord's return should be near.

JESUS IN FINAL PHASE OF HIS MINISTRY

Further, because of their understanding that the pre-advent judgment was the antitype of the Old Testament Day of Atonement, they now saw Jesus in His final phase of His High Priestly work. Verse 12 took on new significance within this fresh framework. In this last phase of His mediatorial work, Jesus was preparing a people to be His final witness to "the everlasting gospel." They would not only witness to the world that the end was near, they would reflect the purpose of the gospel and one of Christ's reasons for coming to earth: "You shall call His name Jesus, for He will save His people from their sins" (Matthew 1:21).[534]

The message and work of the endtime loyalists are exactly what the world needs. The good news of God's side of the controversy bears good fruit. Listening carefully to God's wisdom, letting Him work out His will in their lives, the loyalists will reflect God's better plan in distinctive systems of education[535] and health practice.[536] And they invite people all over the world to join them and to enjoy the benefits of God's wisdom.

The stark contrast between receiving the mark of the beast and receiving the seal of God highlights the importance of understanding the messages of the three angels. Implications of the mark and the seal will be discussed on page 338ff.

---

[533] See 207–221.
[534] God's people in the endtime will expose Satan's lies regarding God's laws such as "You *need not* keep them," "For your own good you *shouldn't try* to keep them, or you would be a legalist," and "You *cannot* keep them." See Maxwell, *God Cares,* vol. 2, 376.
[535] See 233–236.
[536] See 229–232.

Revelation 15 and 16 begin the last half of the last book of the Bible. Chapters 1–14 unfold the Great Controversy Theme from the first century to our day. Chapters 15–22 focus on events yet to transpire—events in the end of the endtime.[537] Anyone reading these pages may see these earthshaking events on cable news within the next few years. We should be prepared. Survivalists prepare for all eventualities!

Wonderful is the song John was privileged to hear, the song of Moses and the Lamb, sung by those who had wrestled in the arena with the Prince of Darkness: "Great and marvelous are Your works, Lord God Almighty! Just and true are Your ways, O King of the saints!" (Revelation 15:3). The echo and refrain will be heard throughout the universe of intelligent beings.

And then those plagues in chapter 16. Note that the plagues fall only on those who refused the messages of the three angels of Revelation 14—that is, on those who "had the mark of the beast and those who worshiped his image" (Revelation 16:2). The plagues with their global footprint commence after final decisions are made, after habits have become forever grooved into neural paths, after the wheat and tares are fully revealed. We call this moment the close of probation.[538]

The sequence is clear:

> "When the third angel's message closes ... the final test has been brought upon the world. ... Every case has been decided for life or death. ... The restraint which has been upon the wicked is removed and Satan has entire control of the finally impenitent. ... Satan will then plunge the inhabitants of the earth into one great, final trouble. ... The whole world will be involved in ruin more terrible than that that came upon Jerusalem of old. ... The plagues upon Egypt when God was about to deliver Israel, were similar in character to those more terrible and extensive judgments which are to fall upon the world just before the final deliverance of God's people."[539]

---

[537] "Like each of the four divisions in the first half of Revelation, the seven-plague division also begins with an introductory sanctuary scene. ... The seven churches start with Jesus as High Priest among the lampstands; the seven seals open with Jesus as the Lamb close beside the throne; the seven trumpets begin with an angel offering incense at the golden altar; and the great-controversy scenes commence with a view of the ark containing the Ten Commandments in the inner part of the heavenly temple. ... As we enter ... Revelation's second half, the introductory sanctuary scene differs from the others. ... in it the temple opens to release the seven plague angels and then *closes up*; and the scene is *accompanied* by a view of the redeemed singing on the sea of glass." —Maxwell, *Ibid.*, 422.

[538] See *Last-day Events,* 227–237.

[539] *The Great Controversy,* 613, 614, 627, 628.

SEALING OUR OWN DESTINIES

The burning truth about the close of probation is *just that*—no more time to procrastinate or to change one's mind. Of course, we are sealing our individual probations while we live and before we die, either maturing wheat or maturing tares. Death settles the matter—our characters have determined our eternal destiny.[540]

When probation closes for the world (after the proclamation of the third angel's message has gone to every nation), there will be no replays, no mulligans, no second chance (or for that matter, no 100,456,000 more chances)—a warning that John gives in Revelation 18:4 that we will look at shortly. This is a fact that does not seem to be clear for many now alive.[541] The words of Jeremiah will sink like lead on those who put off for another day their reckoning with truth: "The harvest is past, The summer is ended, And we are not saved" (8:20)!

Whenever I think of the close of probation and how so many keep ignoring its reality, I think of Harry Truman, who owned Mount St. Helens Lodge in southwestern Washington State.

In May 1980, I saw and heard Harry talking to a television news team that had come to interview the great master of the mountain. "No, I'm not gonna leave," he said, "I'm gonna stay… Take a look at that mountain. I'm completely north and completely east of that there mountain. There's no way that mountain will come my way." His face glowed with emotion.

For several months, Mount St. Helens had been spewing steam and rumbling ominously. State officials had ordered out those living near the mountain. But Harry Truman stayed on. He said that he had been there too long and that he and the mountain were friends.

---

[540] "No one will be carried into the kingdom of heaven against their will by an overpowering act of divine power." —John Polkinghorne, *The God of Hope and the End of the World* (New Haven: Yale University Press, 2002), 136.

[541] "When He comes He is not to cleanse us of our sins, to remove from us the defects in our characters, or to cure us of the infirmities of our tempers and dispositions. If wrought for us at all, this work will all be accomplished before that time. When the Lord comes, those who are holy will be holy still. Those who have preserved their bodies and spirits in holiness, in sanctification and honor, will then receive the finishing touch of immortality. But those who are unjust, unsanctified, and filthy will remain so forever. No work will then be done for them to remove their defects and give them holy characters. The Refiner does not then sit to pursue His refining process and remove their sins and their corruption. This is all to be done in these hours of probation. It is now that this work is to be accomplished for us. We embrace the truth of God with our different faculties, and as we come under the influence of that truth, it will accomplish the work for us which is necessary to give us a moral fitness for the kingdom of glory and for the society of the heavenly angels. We are now in God's workshop. Many of us are rough stones from the quarry. But as we lay hold upon the truth of God, its influence affects us. It elevates us and removes from us every imperfection and sin, of whatever nature. Thus we are prepared to see the King in His beauty and finally to unite with the pure and heavenly angels in the kingdom of glory. It is here that this work is to be accomplished for us, here that our bodies and spirits are to be fitted for immortality." —*Testimonies*, vol. 2, 355, 356. See also *The Great Controversy*, 623.

In fact, Harry said, he had a little talk with Jesus about it and he was sure that he was on safe ground. All across America, people were talking about Harry Truman. They cheered and cheered. He became a folk hero and songs were written about him. Until May 18, 1980. Then the cheering stopped.

It began at 8:32 A.M. with a strong 5.1 earthquake. Within seconds the whole north face of the mountain came flying Harry's way. Mud, heated to near boiling by hot air from deep within the earth, buried Harry and his lodge under 30 feet of boiling mud.

Harry believed that he knew more than the authorities on earthquakes and volcanoes. But a storm came, unrelenting in its fury. More than one cubic mile of rock, or 12 percent of the once beautiful mountain, was blasted away. The height of the mountain dropped 1270 feet—just gone. For many miles north and east, once beautiful Washington looked like the moon— 200,000 acres of prime forest seared and flattened.

ANOTHER STORM COMING RELENTLESS IN ITS FURY
Another storm is coming following the close of probation. It will be devastating in its fury.[542] It follows our Lord's judgment: "He who is unjust, let him be unjust still; ... he who is righteous, let him be righteous still" (Revelation 22:11). No reruns, no replays, no extra innings, no overtimes.

Revelation 15 and 16 give in detail what Daniel had forecast: "At that time Michael shall stand up, The great prince who stands watch over ... your people; And there shall be a time of trouble, Such as never was since there was a nation, Even to that time. And at that time your people shall be delivered, everyone who is found written in the book" (12:1).

What needs to be remembered is that God is not meting out vengeful punishment on those who resisted His love and wooing. That would be precisely how Satan would want God perceived. In the Great Controversy, the same Jesus who wept over unresponsive Jerusalem (Matthew 23:37, 38) weeps over last-day rejecters of His mercies—as the plagues fall!

EVIL UNRESTRAINED
As the Jewish leaders spurned Jesus, many in the endtime will spurn the restraining power of the Holy Spirit (that Voice speaking to their conscience). Those resisting that Voice will become fully controlled by Satan. Unrestrained men and women driven by Satanic fury once crucified Jesus; the same unrestraint will drive men and women in the endtime to join with Satan as he tries to finally obliterate God's loyalists and the voice of truth.

---

[542] "A storm is coming, relentless in its fury. Are we prepared to meet it? We need not say: The perils of the last days are soon to come upon us. Already they have come." —*Testimonies*, vol. 8, 315.

Ellen White gives us further insights:

> "The judgments of God would not come directly out from the Lord upon them, but in this way: They place themselves beyond His protection. … He does not commission His angels to prevent Satan's decided attacks upon them. It is Satan's power that is at work at sea and on land, bringing calamity and distress, and sweeping off multitudes to make sure of his prey. And storm and tempest both by sea and land will be, for Satan has come down in great wrath. … He knows his time is short and, if he is not restrained, we shall see more terrible manifestations of his power than we have ever dreamed of."[543]

Revelation 17 and 18 brings the events of the seven last plagues into sharper focus. We see the predictions of Revelation 13 in clearer detail. The world confederation of "the kings of the earth" (17:2), inspired by a dominant religious power, symbolized by the woman on the scarlet beast "drunk with the blood of the saints" (verse 6), will "be of one mind … to give their kingdom to the beast" (on whom the woman sits, verse 17).

But this world confederation that eventually aims to destroy God's loyalists and silence truth comes to its frightful end. The plagues fall—"death, and mourning and famine. And she [the dominant religious power that controls the nations] will be utterly burned with fire, for strong is the Lord God who judges her" (18:8).

Now the good news! Up to the end of time, before probation closes, many of God's people are still in Babylon. For most of their lives, they have been deluded by the confusion of religious bodies that have been proclaiming 1) the wrong picture of God, 2) the wrong picture of how sinners are to be saved, and 3) the wrong picture of who will live forever. But now, in the endtime, their picture is suddenly in focus. Because God's loyalists will have witnessed well for their Lord, many Hindus, Buddhists, New Agers, skeptics, atheists, and long-time members of Christian churches—all see clearly the difference between clear-cut gospel principles and the irrationality of error.

LOUD CRY

The "loud cry" of God's loyalists will be heard powerfully throughout all classes of society, in every land: "'Babylon the great is fallen, is fallen, and has become a habitation of demons.' … And I heard another voice from heaven saying, 'Come out of her, my people, lest you share in her sins, and lest you receive of her plagues'" (Revelation 18:2, 4).

---

[543] *Manuscript Releases*, vol. 14, 3. "The same destructive power exercised by holy angels whom God commands, will be exercised by evil angels when He permits. There are forces now ready, and only waiting the divine permission, to spread desolation everywhere." —*The Great Controversy*, 614.

This is the last act! The curtain is about to come down! The Great Controversy is in the last half of the last inning. John the Revelator is exceedingly graphic!

Revelation 19–22, in startling contrast to the dreary scenes of the plagues, portrays a victory parade down the streets of gold, something far more grand than the marching heroes who have cheered the innumerable multitudes along Fifth Avenue, New York City, or Champs Élysées, Paris, or Piccadilly Square, London after World War I and II.

Again we hear the swelling chorus of the universe sing out: "Alleluia! Salvation and glory and honor and power to the Lord our God! For true and righteous are His judgments" (Revelation 19:1, 2). God at risk, yes! But His patience and wisdom have paid off!

God's bride (His loyal followers of all the ages) has finally made herself ready (Revelation 19:7).[544] Her righteous character is the forever validation of God's plan to rid the universe of the rebel mind (Revelation 19:8).

And God's rebels discover the truth about Satan's big lie (Genesis 3:4): Rebels do die, the wages of sin is death, character does count regarding who can be trusted with eternal life (Revelation 20:12, 15; 21:8; 22:11, 14, 15).

We now turn to various aspects and events of the endtime and why understanding the importance of 1844 has much to do with our preparation to meet our returning Lord.

---

[544] See 176, 288.

CHAPTER TWENTY-SEVEN:
THE ROLE OF THE INVESTIGATIVE JUDGMENT IN THE GREAT CONTROVERSY

I remember the afternoon well. The sun was streaming through my office window at Pacific Union College. I was busily correcting examination papers. And the door burst open. A former student, now graduated, flung himself into the chair beside my desk. I had not seen him for several years. His face was wrinkled with despair. Out poured his anguish. He had been in jail for a few months. Over and over he repeated that probation had closed for him! He was certain now that his name had "come up" in the Investigative Judgment and that he was a lost man!

He was always a very likable young man—full of courtesies and smiles. But somehow, after graduation, an intense battle had been fought over his soul. In reflecting on all this, his new agony was caused by a wrong understanding of what Jesus had wanted to do for him as his High Priest in the Heavenly Sanctuary. This led to a scary understanding of the pre-advent Investigative Judgment.

What notion had muddled his thinking? Unfortunately, the thinking goes like this: Since 1844, angels have been turning pages in the books of heaven, each page representing the record of each person's life, beginning with Adam and Eve. Pages turning, day and night! Each person's future—eternal life or damnation—is settled after each page is examined. Never tiring, the angels move through the years until the present. When the pages of the living come up—it's judgment time, ready or not! In some way, the whole universe looks at all our sins. If one is judged to be unfit for eternal life on the day one's name "comes up," probation is over. The Holy Spirit no longer speaks to that person—their probation is closed. The unsaved now live out their desires and passions, unrestrained by the Holy Spirit speaking to the conscience. And so the scary notion goes.

I think I have heard the echo of my young friend's agony in certain sermons through the years. Perhaps a camp meeting sermon: "Get right with God today, at this camp meeting! Who knows when your name will come up in the judgment? It may be tonight! You may never have another camp meeting!"

OBVIOUS MISUNDERSTANDINGS

What is wrong here? It is hard to know where to begin! Let me list some obvious misunderstandings, most of which we have already discussed in this book:

- God doesn't close our individual probation—we do. Grace will keep pressing its appeal, night and day, never holding back its promises of pardon and power—unless men and women tune out the Spirit's pleading. God's gracious promises are always on the table, His front door is always open, His light is always on: "The one who comes to Me I will by no means cast out" (John 6:37).[545]

To be perfectly clear, men and women who are making a habit of saying "no" to the Spirit, who stubbornly resist whatever light of Truth they have, *they are closing their own probation. Not God!*

- Therefore, as far as the living are concerned, the Investigative Judgment is not focused on angels, or even God, turning pages but on the maturing of a person's life. The one question is: Is that person maturing into one who can be trusted with eternal life?[546]

- God the Father is not the Judge "for the Father judges no one, but has committed all judgment to the Son" (John 5:22, 27–30). But the kind of "judgment" given to Jesus is not like an earthly court (as we shall see): "For God did not send His Son into the world to condemn the world, but that the world through Him might be saved" (John 3:17).[547]

- If Jesus is not the frowning Judge so often seen in medieval art, how then does He do His job of saving the world (which is His way of "judging" the world)? By bringing light "to every man who comes into the world" (John 1:9), by revealing truth in some way to everyone on which moral decisions are made. Thus, *those who reject this light are condemning (judging) themselves* (John 3:18–21).

- Contrary to some allegations of the past few years, Christ's record does not stand in place of our records when our names come up in the Investigative Judgment.[548] Truly, as we have seen in earlier

---

[545] See 138.

[546] See 144. "The grace of God must be received by the sinner before he can be fitted for the kingdom of God. ... As the leaven when mingled with the meal, works from within outward, so it is by the renewing of the heart that the grace of God works to transform the life." —*Christ's Object Lessons*, 97.

[547] The biblical court system is not like ours with a defense attorney and prosecuting attorney and an impartial judge. In the Bible we see the accused, the accuser and the judge, i.e., Solomon and the two women. The judge is not impartial; he is on the side of the accused until its proved otherwise (Deuteronomy 19:16–19); the judge is thus the defense attorney as well. Jesus is our judge and our defense attorney. How could we lose when we choose to follow the Light on our path.

[548] "Christ on the Mount of Olives pictured to His disciples the scene of the great judgment day. And He represented its decision as turning upon one point. When the nations are gathered before Him, there will be but two classes, and their eternal destiny will be determined by what they have done or have neglected to do for Him in the person of the poor and the suffering. *In that day Christ does not present before men the great work He has done for them in giving His life for their redemption. He presents the faithful work they have done for Him.*" —*The Desire of Ages*, 637, (italics supplied).

chapters, we are not to be saved by our works, but our works surely will judge us: "They were judged each one according to his works" (Revelation 20:13). "For we must all appear before the judgment seat of Christ, that each one may receive the things done in the body, according to what he has done, whether good or bad" (2 Corinthians 5:10). "For the Son of man will come in the glory of his Father with his angels; and then He will reward each according to his works" (Matthew 16:27). The redeemed will be more than admirers of Jesus; they will be His followers who are determined to overcome evil even as He had overcome (Revelation 3:21).

The whole point of the gospel is to restore men and women to the place where they can be trusted to say "yes" to God's will as forever examples of divine-human cooperation.[549]

Title and Fitness

This does not mean that we "deserve" salvation or that we have in any way "earned" eternal life. Hardly! The righteousness of Christ alone provides our "title" to heaven and our "fitness" for heaven is made possible by His grace that supplies the power to overcome; otherwise, none of us could be trusted with eternal life. The Investigative Judgment separates those who have claimed the Lord's name but not His character (Matthew 7:21–23) from those who have seriously and genuinely accepted the way of the Cross, and like Paul, "die daily" (1 Corinthians 15:31) to all self-centered, self-glorifying desires. The issue is not who has absolute perfection but who has, with the time lived, given the angels, the unfallen worlds, and God Himself, a trajectory of what his or her life would be if time were to be continued. This kind of genuine faith describes the thief on the Cross as well as that of Enoch. That spread of experience will include every one of us!

In contrast to these misunderstandings, here are some basic thoughts that we must understand before we get too far into our description of what has been going on in heaven since 1844:

- The judgment books (Revelation 20:12) record our choices, whether we are becoming more like Jesus or more like His adversary, the devil. The Bible uses various analogies, such as sheep and goats (Matthew 25:32, 33), wheat and tares (Matthew 13:24–30) and the seal of God and the mark of the beast (Revelation 7:3; 13:16, 17; 14:9). How these records are kept are beyond our imagination. However, with modern computer memory systems, with trillions of computations performed virtually simultaneously, we get a faint idea of how

---

[549] "Those who refuse to cooperate with God on earth would not cooperate with Him in heaven. It would not be safe to take them to heaven." —*Christ's Object Lessons*, 280.

the mind of God "records" the DNA, including the character configuration of every one who has ever lived. Then when we think of the marvels of modern CD or video recordings and storage, we get further glimpses of how any episode since creation can be replayed instantly. Nothing will be subject to guesswork. As Jesus said, "For by your words you will be justified, and by your words you will be condemned" (Matthew 13:37).[550]

- Jesus does not arbitrarily balance out one's good deeds and bad deeds in determining one's eternal future. One's future is determined by whether a person's character is becoming safe to save or not, whether his or her life trajectory shows a person who, if time were given, could be trusted with eternal life.[551]

> "The character is revealed, not by occasional good deeds and occasional misdeeds, but by the tendency of the habitual words and acts."[552]

> "When those who claim to be children of God become Christlike in character, they will be obedient to God's commandments. Then the Lord can trust them to be of the number who shall compose the family of heaven. ... They have a right to join the blood-washed throng. ... He expects us to overcome in His name. Those who reject the gift of Christ's righteousness are rejecting the attributes of character which would constitute them the sons and daughters of God. They are rejecting that which alone could give them a fitness for a place at the marriage feast. ...There will be no future probation in which to prepare for eternity. It is in this life that we are to put on the robe of Christ's righteousness. This is our only opportunity to form characters for the home which Christ has made ready for those who obey His commandments."[553]

---

[550] "In the book of God's remembrance every deed of righteousness is immortalized. There every temptation resisted, every evil overcome, every word of tender pity expressed, is faithfully chronicled. And every act of sacrifice, every suffering and sorrow endured for Christ's sake, is recorded. ... There is a record also of the sins of men. ... The secret purposes and motives appear in the unerring register; for God 'will bring to light the hidden things of darkness, and will make manifest the counsels of the hearts.' (1 Corinthians 4:5). ... Every man's work passes in review before God and is registered for faithfulness or unfaithfulness. Opposite each name in the books of heaven is entered with terrible exactness every wrong word, every selfish act, every unfulfilled duty, and every secret sin, with every artful dissembling. Heaven-sent warnings or reproofs neglected, wasted moments, unimproved opportunities, the influence exerted for good or for evil, with its far-reaching results, all are chronicled by the recording angel." —*The Great Controversy,* 481, 482.

[551] See 144.

[552] *Steps to Christ,* 57, 58.

[553] *Christ's Object Lessons,* 315, 317, 319.

- Adventists do believe that sins are forgiven when they are confessed and forsaken. Adventists don't wait until the Investigative Judgment to know with certainty that their sins are covered by the mercies of Jesus. Further, they rejoice with New Testament writers who describe Christ's atoning (or, reconciling) work as twofold: not only for Christ's forgiveness but also for His "cleansing," (Proverbs 28:13; 1 John 1:9) "Cleansing" is John's word for "grace to help in time of need" (Hebrews 4:16).

- Jesus has done this wonderful ministry of forgiveness and cleansing (empowering) since He ascended to heaven. But since 1844, He has added a new phase to His work as our Mediator. In addition to His twofold ministry since the Cross,[554] the Investigative Judgment is now concerned with the judgment of character and the preparation of a people to meet Him at the second advent

Satan Muddles Our Thinking

It is absolutely essential that we understand why Satan is doing his fiercest to muddle our thinking regarding the Investigative Judgment. The college graduate I mentioned at the beginning of this chapter is a classic example of what happens when wrong notions are believed. How does Satan go about this nefarious work?

- He "invents unnumbered schemes to occupy our minds that they may not dwell upon the very work with which we ought to be best acquainted."[555] Can you think of dozens of peripheral topics that we so easily would rather discuss then what Jesus is doing now in the heavenly sanctuary?

- He "hates the great truths that bring to view an atoning sacrifice and an all-powerful Mediator."[556] Can you see the importance of the ellipse of truth wherein two great truths must be kept in equal focus—Sacrifice and Mediator?

- He will divert our minds from the fact that "the subject of the sanctuary and the Investigative Judgment should be clearly understood by the people of God."[557]

- Why is Satan doing his utmost to fog our minds regarding the Investigative Judgment? Because he knows that if he succeeds, "it will be impossible for [us] to exercise the faith which is essential at this time, or to occupy the position which God designs [us] to fill."[558]

[554] See 98–102.
[555] *The Great Controversy,* 488.
[556] *Ibid.*
[557] *Ibid.*
[558] *Ibid.*

- He doesn't mind if we sing praise choruses—or even hymns—about the Cross and focus on Jesus as our Savior, as long as we don't join His work as "atoning Sacrifice" with His role as our "all-powerful Mediator." Why? Because he knows that gazing at Jesus on His Cross ("atoning sacrifice") without following Him to heaven as our High Priest ("all-powerful Mediator") will divert us from understanding the power of the gospel and the primary work of the Holy Spirit. Satan will do anything and everything to keep us from recognizing that "the intercession of Christ in man's behalf in the sanctuary above is as essential to the plan of salvation as was His death upon the Cross. By His death He began the work which after His resurrection he ascended to complete in heaven."[559]

- *Let that thought sink in. Keep your eyes on where Jesus now is and what He is now doing on our behalf!*

WHY SOME REJECT THE INVESTIGATIVE JUDGMENT CONCEPT

Before we go further, it is essential that we understand why some biblical scholars have *rejected* the concept of the Investigative Judgment. The late Donald Grey Barnhouse, former editor of *Eternity* magazine, described this doctrine as "the most colossal, psychological, face-saving phenomenon in religious history."[560] In this book we have already reflected on certain presuppositions that Barnhouse and others have had that keep them from seeing the biblical need for the Investigative Judgment. Their problem is threefold:

- True, the Scriptures do not mention the term, "the Investigative Judgment," but the need for the pre-Advent judgment is called for throughout the Bible. In addition to various biblical texts we have already noted, consider Christ's words to the Sadducees calling for an Investigative Judgment prior to endtime events regarding those who are "counted worthy to … the resurrection from the dead" (Luke 20:35; see also 21:36; Acts 5:41). When are people "counted worthy" prior to the resurrection?

- Because Barnhouse and others believe that Christ made a final atonement on the Cross, they seem to be blinded to our Lord's ministry in the heavenly sanctuary as set forth in the Book of Hebrews. As we have seen already, and will see later, the work of Christ in the heavenly sanctuary is as essential as His work on the Cross.[561] Limited gospels lead to incomplete pictures of what Jesus is doing now.

---

[559] *The Great Controversy*, 489.

[560] *Eternity*, September, 1955.

[561] "The intercession of Christ in man's behalf in the sanctuary above is as essential to the plan of salvation as was His death upon the cross. By His death He began that work which after His resurrection He ascended to complete in heaven." —*The Great Controversy*, 489.

- The Investigative Judgment concept is built into the core Adventist belief that, before Jesus returns, a worldwide movement will reflect the messages of the three angels in Revelation 14. Those messages, as well as the rest of the Bible, emphasize how important God's loyal followers are to Him as well as to the world as they proclaim God's last-day appeal before the crash and horror of the seven last plagues. God will have a prepared people. The Investigative Judgment reflects this preparation on earth and the whole unfallen universe endorses God's judgments regarding their fitness to live forever.

What Happened In 1844?

So what really has been happening since 1844? Many good books have been written on the significance of 1844 as the terminal date for the majestic time prophecy of Daniel 8:14.[562] Our concern here is to focus on what has been going on in heaven since 1844.

- *From the standpoint of angels,* some kind of Investigative Judgment must occur before Jesus comes. Once Jesus resurrects the sleeping saints, the angels will obviously know how to link up families and which ones to gather for the trip to heaven.[563]

- *From the standpoint of people on earth,* some kind of examination should be going on in their lives. If ever we take Paul's advice, it should be now: "Examine yourselves as to whether you are in the faith. Prove yourselves" (2 Corinthians 13:5). And Peter's counsel: "Therefore brethren, be even more diligent to make your calling and election sure, for if you do these things you will never stumble" (2 Peter 1:10). And Ellen White's encouragement: "Through the grace of God and their own diligent effort they must be conquerors in the battle with evil. While the Investigative Judgment is going forward in heaven. … there is to be a special work of purification, of putting away of sin, among God's people upon earth. When this work shall have been accomplished, the followers of Christ will be ready for His appearing." [564]

- *From the standpoint of God in heaven,* another kind of Investigative Judgment must occur before Jesus comes. The first angel of

---

[562] See Roy Gane, *Altar Call* (Berrien Springs, MI: Diadem, 1999); Frank Holbrook, *The Atoning Priesthood of Jesus Christ* (Berrien Springs, MI: Adventist Theological Society Publications, 1996); Arnold V. Wallenkampf, Richard Lesher, Frank B. Holbrook, editors, *The Sanctuary and the Atonement* (Silver Spring, MD: Biblical Research Institute, 1989).

[563] See 1 Thessalonians 4:14–17. Might there be a connection between the investigative judgment and Paul's insight in 1 Corinthians 4:9—"For we have been made a spectacle to the world, both to angels and to men?"

[564] *The Great Controversy,* 425.

Revelation 14 announced "the hour of *His judgment* has come" (verse 7, italics supplied).

What could the angel mean? Yes, the time would come, prior to the Advent, when God permits Himself to be placed on trial! Can we imagine greater love or humility than this—that the Creator of the universe should put Himself in the dock and have all the universe judge whether He has been fair, just, and merciful in His dealings with sinners?

John tells us how this "trial" turns out. The judgment of the universe is: "Great and marvelous are Your works, Lord God Almighty! Just and true are Your ways, O King of the saints" (Revelation 15:3); "Alleluia! Salvation and glory and honor and power to the Lord our God! For true and righteous are His judgments" (Revelation 19:1, 2). But what kind of trial did God go through before He was accorded this magnificent acquittal?

KEEP EYES ON THE BIG PICTURE

We must keep our eyes on the big picture. Whatever else we may learn about the pre-advent Investigative Judgment, the primary focus is on how this remarkable event vindicates God's side of His controversy with Satan. This is done with a double emphasis:

- The eyes of the universe are on God's judgment as to whom He says are safe to save. Our Lord's evidence will be endorsed by on-looking angels and beings on other inhabited worlds;

- The eyes of the universe will see the consequences of rebellion in final display, ending with the din and crash of the seven last plagues. Satan's argument from the beginning has been that God intimidates, that He asks for the impossible from created beings, and thus He is unfair in the way He runs the universe. And now it is showdown time![565]

C. S. Lewis noted that "ancient man approached God (or even the gods) as the accused person approaches his judge. For the modern man the roles are reversed. He is the judge: God is in the dock. ... Man is on the Bench and God in the Dock."[566] If Lewis could have seen the bigger picture, he would

---

[565] 1 Corinthians 4:9—"spectacle [Lit. "theater"] to the world, both to angels and to men." That this planet is a stage for the universe to observe the interplay of good and evil and how every person since Adam has had his or her part to play in the drama— is an awesome thought. Imagine: "The Monarch of the universe and the myriads of heavenly angels are spectators ... they are anxiously watching to see who will be successful overcomers, and win the crown of glory that fadeth not away." —*Testimonies*, vol. 4, 34. "The whole universe is looking with inexpressible interest to see the closing work of the Great Controversy between Christ and Satan. At such a time as this, just as the great work of judging the living is to begin, shall we allow unsanctified ambition to take possession of the heart." —*Testimonies*, vol. 5, 526.

[566] *God in the Dock* (Grand Rapids, MI: William B. Eerdmans Publishing Company, 1970), 244.

see how his insights would have taken on universal proportions. In a very real sense, during the Investigative Judgment, God indeed is in the dock, as we shall now see.

This emphasis on the big picture—final vindication of God's justice, patience, and loving wisdom—is foretold in Daniel and Ezekiel, and amplified in Revelation.

In Daniel 7: 9–27, we trace the prophet's grand vision of the court session in heaven prior to the end of the last days. This overview of a court session wherein the Son of man, symbolically depicted, enters a new phase of our Lord's mediatorial work is not describing Christ's second advent.[567] (No reference is made to the symbolic "stone" of Daniel 2:44, 45, or to any other indication that Daniel is referring to the first resurrection or to the end of this world as we now know it.) This court scene is describing the events begun on October 22, 1844.[568]

The Investigative Judgment is not necessary to inform an all-wise God who are eligible to live forever. He certainly knows what has been written in "the books." But He wants every angel and every inhabitant of unfallen worlds to see the evidence, to make up their own mind as to whether Jesus is fair when He makes up His kingdom.

Whose names are in "the books [that] were opened" (Daniel 7:10) leading to the "judgment … made in favor of the saints" (Daniel 7:22)? These books called the Book of Life (Revelation 20:12) contain the names of "all those who have ever entered the service of God."[569] (The names of sinners who have never responded to God's entreaties, who have never asked for His pardon and power, are not recorded in the Book of Life.)

WHY ARE "BOOKS" OPENED

Again, "the books" are opened in the pre-advent judgment for two special reasons:

- To give angels and created beings in unfallen worlds an opportunity to review God's judgments "made in favor of the saints of the Most High" (after all, they are really interested in who their eternal neighbors will be);

- To prepare the angels for those who will be raised in the first resurrection (Matthew 24:31).

---

[567] "The coming of Christ here described is not His second coming to the earth. He comes to the Ancient of days in heaven to receive dominion, and glory, and a kingdom, which will be given Him at the close of His work as a mediator." —*The Great Controversy,* 480.

[568] For the validity of October 22, 1844, see Siegfried Horn and Lynn Wood, *The Chronology of Ezra 7,* 2nd Edition (Washington, DC: Review and Herald, 1970); William H. Shea, *Selected Studies on Prophetic Interpretation* (Washington, DC: Review and Herald, 1982), 132, 137; William H. Shea, "When Did the Seventy Weeks of Daniel 9:24 Begin? *Journal of the Adventist Theological Society,* vol. 2, no. 1, 1991.

[569] *The Great Controversy,* 480.

Throughout the Bible, God has made it clear that He is interested in character, not mere words or even acts that are only a pretense of full commitment. On different occasions, Jesus spoke of those who profess loyalty but who did not practice their profession. He likened them to the foolish that built on sand (Matthew 7:26), to tares who at first looked like wheat but more fully revealed in the harvest (Matthew 13:30), to the five foolish bridesmaids (Matthew 25:10), to the lazy servant entrusted with talent (Matthew 25:30), and to "goats" (Matthew 25:46).

All these representations of those who had once professed loyalty to God had their names in "the books" (probably considered "members in good and regular standing" in their local churches!) but their characters did not reflect what they "believed."[570] During the Investigative Judgment, their life records are reviewed and found wanting. Their names are "blotted out … from the Book of Life" (Revelation 3:5).[571]

Daniel wrote about other matters that will be accomplished during the time of the Investigative Judgment. In some magnificent way, the universe will be cleansed from all the lies and misrepresentations that Satan has heaped upon God, on one hand, and on God's people, on the other. God's final witness to the power of the Gospel (Matthew 24:14; Romans 1:16) will be manifested through those whose neural patterns are cleansed of desires and habits that once were in contradiction to God's will.[572]

THREE ENGLISH NUANCES

The word used for "cleansed" in Daniel 8:14 has "such a breadth of meaning that it cannot be captured by a single English word." The Hebrew *nitsdaq* conveys at least three English "nuances" such as "(1) to 'set right/restore' (as emphasized in Isaiah 46:13), (2) to 'cleanse' (as emphasized in Job 15:14; 4:17; and 17:9), and (3) to 'vindicate' (as in Isaiah 50:8)."[573]

In view of the Great Controversy, all three "nuances" together convey what transpires during Christ's role as our High Priest during the Investigative Judgment.

- "To set right or to be restored."[574] Since 1844, the first angel of Revelation 14 proclaims that once again the world will hear the full-orbed "everlasting gospel." For centuries this world has heard a

---

[570] See 133–135, 142, 146, 160.

[571] I think of John Greenleaf Whittier's lines in "Maud Muller"—"For of all sad words of tongue or pen, The saddest are these: 'It might have been!'"

[572] See previous chapter on "What Do Habits Have To Do With the Great Controversy?"

[573] Richard M. Davidson, "In Confirmation of the Sanctuary Message," *Journal of the Adventist Theological Society*, vol. 2, no. 1, 1991; "The Meaning of Nitsdaq in Daniel 8:14," *Ibid.*, vol. 7, no. 1, 1996.

[574] RSV (1952) reflects this understanding: "… then the sanctuary shall be restored to its rightful state"; TEV: " … will be restored."

limited gospel, one that focuses primarily on forgiveness while muting the empowering grace that God has promised to overcomers.[575] But the "everlasting gospel" truly "restores" the truth about God's salvation plan—more than "cheap grace,"[576] more than rigorous pilgrimages, more than good fellowship and warm spiritual feelings.[577]

- "To cleanse."[578] In this text, so much of the Old Testament typology looms depicting how the "sins" of the people, transferred to the sanctuary during the year, are finally "cleansed" on the annual Day of Atonement.[579] When we look at the larger picture that God intended the sanctuary service to teach us, we learn that "the tabernacle, through its service of sacrifice, was to teach—the lesson of pardon of sin, and power through the Saviour for obedience unto life."[580]

The earthly sanctuary revealed many aspects of Christ's role as our Sacrifice and Mediator for one transcending purpose: "In all [earthly sanctuary services], God desired His people to read His purpose for the human soul." It was the same purpose Paul had emphasized: "Do you not know that you are the temple of God and that the Spirit of God dwells in you?" (1 Corinthians 3:16).[581]

Ellen White connects the earthly sanctuary with its divine purpose even more directly when she notes that the "Jewish tabernacle was a type of the Christian church," that those "faithful and loyal to God" form the "true tabernacle," and "Christ is the … high priest of all who believe in Him as a personal Saviour."[582]

A Review Of Those Who Can Be Trusted With Eternal Life

During the pre-advent judgment, unfallen worlds and the angels are reviewing (investigating) the characters of those who have died and the maturing characters now living to see who have been truly serious about joining them in a sin-free universe.

---

[575] See 136–139.

[576] Dietrich Bonhoeffer's famous phrase. *See* "Appendix O: Summary of Bonhoeffer Exposé of 'Cheap Grace.'"

[577] See 136.

[578] KJV, ASV, Moulton's.

[579] "In the ancient sanctuary the solemn services of the annual Day of Atonement brought the yearly ritual cycle to a close (Leviticus 16). The work of atonement, or reconciliation, performed on that day brought to completion all that the sanctuary and the priests could do for repentant sinners, and cleansed the sanctuary and the people." —Don F. Neufeld, editor, *The Seventh-day Adventist Encyclopedia*, Revised Edition (Washington, DC: Review and Herald, 1976), 95.

[580] *Education*, 36.

[581] *Ibid.*

[582] *Signs of the Times*, February 14, 1900.

Especially will this be true of those whom Christ is preparing to represent Him during the endtime when His loyal witnesses will indeed proclaim the "everlasting gospel" to all the world (Matthew 24:14). In fact, the successful completion of the gospel commission depends on "cleansed" Christians who want God's character as well as His power. Only then will their witnessing be believable.[583]

In a special sense, in view of the larger, antitypical meaning of the sanctuary symbolism, the Investigative Judgment since 1844 is a matter of "cleansing" the human temple from the defilement of sin.

In a sermon delivered at the Minneapolis General Conference in 1888, Ellen White emphasized this point:

> "Now Christ is in the heavenly sanctuary. And what is He doing? Making atonement for us, cleansing the sanctuary from the sins of the people. Then we must enter by faith into the sanctuary with Him, we must commence the work in the sanctuary of our souls. We are to cleanse ourselves from all defilement. We must 'cleanse ourselves from all filthiness of the flesh and spirit, perfecting holiness in the fear of God.'"[584]

Many last-day events are held in suspension until this "cleansing" reaches that point where God will not be embarrassed to give His endtime people the promised "latter rain."[585] The eyes of the unfallen universe are not on this world's dreary parade of wars, famines, and natural disasters as they try to figure out when Jesus will return. They have been patiently waiting for God's professed people to cooperate with Him in "hastening the advent" (2 Peter 3:12).[586]

- Now, our third "nuance" reflected in Daniel 8:14: "to vindicate."[587] God's loyalists in the endtime eventually vindicate His patience, wisdom, and "grace to help in time of need" (Hebrews 4:16). In

---

[583] "By revealing in our own life the character of Christ we co-operate with Him in the work of saving souls. It is only by revealing in our life His character that we can co-operate with Him. And the wider the sphere of our influence, the more good we may do. When those who profess to serve God follow Christ's example, practicing the principles of the law in their daily life; when every act bears witness that they love God supremely and their neighbor as themselves, then will the church have power to move the world." —*Christ's Object Lessons*, 340.

[584] Cited in A. V. Olson, *Thirteen Crisis Years*, (Washington, DC: RHPA, 1981), 276.

[585] *Testimonies*, vol. 5, 214.

[586] See Herbert E. Douglass, *The End* (Brushton, NY: TEACH Services, Inc., 2001; PPPA, 1979) for 31 references in the writings of Ellen G. White which support Peter's admonition in 2 Peter 3:12.

[587] See NASB, margin. See *The International Critical Commentary* New York: Scribner's, 1927), 342. "A significant feature of the final judgment is the vindication of God's character before all the intelligences of the universe. The false charges that Satan has lodged against the government of God must be demonstrated as utterly groundless. God must be shown to have been entirely fair in the selection of certain individuals to make up His future kingdom, and in the barring of others from entrance there. ... Thus the Hebrew *sadaq* [cleansed, restore, vindicate] may convey the additional thought that God's character will be fully vindicated as the climax to "the hour of his judgment" (Revelation 14:7), which began in 1844." —*SDABC*, vol. 4, 845.

> Ezekiel 36, we can see God's big picture as to how essential to God's plan is the faithful response of His faithful.[588]

Running down parallel tracks in the endtime, the truth about Satan's wicked plans will be dramatically revealed as well as the truth about God's character and His promises to His faithful. In both cases, God is vindicated.[589]

Here is how Frank Holbrook describes it:

> "We must keep our reasoning straight here. The controversy that began with God does not merely end with the judgment of *man*. If it began with God, it must end with God. That is, if the great moral controversy, which has troubled our universe for millennia, began with false accusations against the Deity, it can only terminate— with a secure universe—if the Deity is cleared or vindicated of these charges. In actuality, God 'cannot' reaffirm the justification of His genuine, repentant people unless He Himself and His plan of salvation are acknowledged by the loyal universe as true and just, and the same loyal intelligences agree with God that Satan is a wicked rebel and his accusations against God are false. The ultimate purpose of final judgment is not simply to vindicate an omniscient Deity, but also to draw all created intelligences both loyal and redeemed—and the lost—into a willing agreement with God and His view of matters."[590]

Hour Of Rejoicing, Not Fear

After outlining all this good news about the Investigative Judgment which God and His loyalists have looked forward to for thousands of years, one more thought needs to be said: For those living during this time of judgment, it should be their hour of rejoicing, not fear. Fear, yes, for those who have a wrong picture of God that Satan has painted so effectively since his rebellion in heaven. Fear, yes, for the shame they will feel when, after spending their lives in self-seeking, they at last look into the eyes of Jesus whom they had resisted for so long. But for those who see God through Jesus, judgment time is good news—His coming is near!

---

[588] See 113.

[589] "In the antitype also, against Satan's false claim that God cannot fulfill His new covenant promises, God gathers an entire generation to Himself at the consummation of history who demonstrate the ultimate effectiveness of the gospel. ... Not only do the *saints* serve to vindicate God's character. Ezekiel uses the same language to describe the final judgment upon the *wicked*, and in particular their leader (Ezekiel 38:16, 22, 23, RSV). The final judgment reveals not only the ultimate effectiveness of the gospel but also the full ripening of iniquity." —Richard M. Davidson, "The Good News of Yom Kippur," *Journal of the Adventist Theological Society*, vol. 2, no. 2, 1991.

[590] Frank B. Holbrook, *The Atoning Priesthood of Jesus Christ* (Berrien Springs, MI: Adventist Theological Society Publications, 1996), 174.

Loyalists today rejoice in Daniel's categorical declaration that the Investigative Judgment is "made in favor of the saints of the Most High" (Daniel 7:22). Loyalists rest in our Lord's assurance that "he who hears My word and believes in Him who sent Me has everlasting life, and shall not come into judgment, but has passed from death into life" (John 5:24).

Loyalists sing with Job, even during tough times: "For I know that my Redeemer lives, And He shall stand at last on the earth; And after my skin is destroyed, this I know, That in my flesh I shall see God" (Job 19:25, 26).

Loyalists daily thank the Lord for the assurance that they are "accepted in the Beloved" (Ephesians 1:6), that if they keep "walk[ing] in the light as He is in the light … the blood of Jesus Christ … cleanses us from all sin" (1 John 1:9), that all who make Jesus the Savior and Lord of their lives can claim His promise, "I give them eternal life and they shall never perish; neither shall anyone snatch them out of My hand. My Father who has given them to Me, is greater than all; and no one is able to snatch them out of My Father's hand" (John 10:28, 29).

Loyalists have discovered that "the faith of Jesus" (Revelation 14:12) helps them to endure life's troubles, that "perfect love casts out fear" (1 John 4:18).

Men and women of faith are not afraid of the Investigative Judgment. They know that Jesus as their Intercessor, their Mediator, met Satan face-to-face on this earth. With the same human equipment we all have, without any special advantages, He proved that men and women this side of Eden can overcome any temptation hurled by Satan.[591] He gave us courage and took away our excuses. He not only led the way through a world of "fiery darts of the wicked one" (Ephesians 6:16) to show it could be done, He comes back through His Holy Spirit to give us the same power He had.[592] That is why John could pass on to us our Lord's promise that we too "may overcome" even as He "overcame" (Revelation 3:21).

---

[591] *The Desire of Ages,* 24, 762.

[592] "The Spirit was to be given as a regenerating agent, and without this the sacrifice of Christ would have been of no avail. The power of evil had been strengthening for centuries, and the submission of men to this satanic captivity was amazing. Sin could be resisted and overcome only through the mighty agency of the Third Person of the Godhead, who would come with no modified energy, but in the fullness of divine power. It is the Spirit that makes effectual what has been wrought out by the world's Redeemer. It is by the Spirit that the heart is made pure. Through the Spirit the believer becomes a partaker of the divine nature. Christ has given His Spirit as a divine power to overcome all hereditary and cultivated tendencies to evil, and to impress His own character upon His church." *Ibid.,* 671. "The Holy Spirit was promised to be with those who were wrestling for victory, in demonstration of all mightiness, endowing the human agent with supernatural powers, and instructing the ignorant in the mysteries of the kingdom of God. That the Holy Spirit is to be the grand helper, is a wonderful promise. Of what avail would it have been to us that the only begotten Son of God had humbled Himself, endured the temptations of the wily foe, and wrestled with him during His entire life on earth, and died the Just for the unjust, that humanity might not perish, if the Spirit had not been given as a constant, working, regenerating agent to make effectual in our cases what had been wrought out by the world's Redeemer." —*Manuscript Releases,* vol. 2, 14.

Our All-Powerful Mediator

In the Investigative Judgment, as our "all-powerful Mediator"[593] Jesus can face down all of Satan's charges against His people. When Satan objects to God's rulings in favor of those men and women of faith who have honored Him with their loyalty, Jesus points first to His own unsullied record in His dueling with Satan; then He points to the records of His loyal followers, to their "diligent" faithfulness and their maturing faith trajectory.[594]

Further, His loyalists know that Jesus stands in the courts above as their High Priest today, not only as their Example showing the way to overcome sin, but also as their Enabler to help them prove Satan wrong, even as He did. This insight sparkles with heavenly dynamics:

> "Everyone who will break from the slavery and service of Satan, and will stand under the blood-stained banner of Prince Immanuel will be kept by Christ's intercessions. Christ, as our Mediator, at the right hand of the Father, ever keeps us in view, for it is as necessary that He should keep us by His intercessions as that He should redeem us with His blood. If He lets go His hold of us for one moment, Satan stands ready to destroy. Those purchased by His blood, He now keeps by His intercession."[595]

A Powerful Intercessor

If I should see a man with a baseball bat entering the room behind your back, my instincts would be to intercede and do all I could to keep him from hurting you. I would be your "intercessor" at that point in your life. Jesus is doing just that every hour of the day and night for you and me through angels and the Holy Spirit.[596] We can count on His powerful intercessions in our lives today, even as we have been counting on the fact that He died for us on that horrible Cross!

All that adds up to sky-high assurance for loyalists during the Investigative Judgment! One day soon, if we keep abiding in Christ, walking into the Light He gives us daily, we will be part of that great multitude that declares God's judgments to be "true and righteous" (Revelation 19:2). We will be part of

---

[593] *The Great Controversy*, 488.

[594] *Ibid.*, 425.

[595] Ellen White Comments on Romans 8:34, *SDABC*, vol. 6, 1078.

[596] "The intercession of Christ in man's behalf in the sanctuary above is as essential to the plan of salvation as was His death upon the cross. By His death He began that work which after His resurrection He ascended to complete in heaven. We must by faith enter within the veil, 'whither the forerunner is for us entered.' Hebrews 6:20. There the light from the cross of Calvary is reflected. There we may gain a clearer insight into the mysteries of redemption. The salvation of man is accomplished at an infinite expense to heaven; the sacrifice made is equal to the broadest demands of the broken law of God. Jesus has opened the way to the Father's throne, and through His mediation the sincere desire of all who come to Him in faith may be presented before God."
—*The Great Controversy*, 489.

the eternal answer to Satan's lies. We will be part of the reason that guarantees to the unfallen worlds and unfallen angels that the whole universe will finally and eternally be secure from all rebellion.[597] We will be telling the universe that God did not risk His universe on human beings in vain!

The faithful today know that their loyalty to God is not based on their efforts to seek His favor, but in the sense of privilege that they can honor God in "the hour of His judgment." The question always is: Do I enjoy known duty and am I responding as one who wants to honor God in every aspect of my life? If so, God is winning and Satan is losing!

Those who live daily with the "assurance of faith" (Hebrews 10:22) know, with a quiet humility, void of pride, that the Investigative Judgment is nothing more than an ongoing record that reflects one's daily walk with the Spirit. This heavenly review mirrors those in the endtime who have taken Peter's counsel seriously: "Therefore, since all these things will be dissolved, what manner of persons ought you to be in holy conduct and godliness, looking for and hastening the coming of the day of God, because of which the heavens will be dissolved being on fire, and the elements will melt with fervent heat" (2 Peter 3:11, 12).

There is no despair in all this "good news!" But there is more!

---

[597] *The Desire of Ages*, 759.

CHAPTER TWENTY-EIGHT:
THE HARVEST PARABLE PREVIEWS THE END OF THE WORLD

Among Christ's parables that teach something specific about the kingdom of God,[598] the harvest parable is exceedingly instructive regarding an important aspect of the Great Controversy—it gives us a clear clue as to *when* Christ will return to earth:

> "He said, 'The kingdom of God is as if a man should scatter seed on the ground. … For the earth yields crops by itself, first the blade, then the head, after that the full grain in the head. But when the grain ripens, immediately he puts in the sickle, because the harvest has come" (Mark 4:26–29).

> "Then I looked, and lo, a white cloud, and seated on the cloud one like a son of man, with a golden crown on his head, and a sharp sickle in his hand. And another angel came out of the temple, calling with a loud voice to him who sat upon the cloud. 'Put in your sickle, and reap, for the hour to reap has come, for the harvest of the earth is fully ripe'" (Revelation 14:14–16, RSV).

First, this harvest analogy is a straightforward description of how gospel truth transforms our lives step-by-step—ever moving toward the purpose of why the gospel seed is planted. Character transformation fulfills the intent of the gospel sower. Good seed, if permitted to grow properly, will reproduce the plant or tree it came from; bad seed (not sown by the sower) becomes weeds, and weeds do not fulfill the purpose of the farmer.

But the parable and its extension in Revelation 14 are telling us something else: Jesus is describing the timing of the Second Advent. He wants us today to be clear about why His return has been delayed: *He will wait for the harvest to become "fully ripe."*

Our Master Teacher is telling us that the goals of the kingdom of God and of the field of grain are the same—each is ready to be harvested when the seed has matured.

When I plant my garden[599] I do so with the reasonable hope that I will have a harvest. I enjoy the garden, but I don't plant corn only to have fun pulling weeds! I look toward the day when the ear of the corn is fully developed—that's why I planted corn in the first place!

---

[598] See "Appendix P: The Great Controversy in the Parables of Jesus."
[599] I have had a garden every year since I was 10 years old—some too big for the family to enjoy!

After the corn (or any other plant or seed) is safely in the ground, I check off the days on my kitchen calendar as to when I should expect ripe corn, according to the seed packet or seed catalog. Early corn, the seed catalog says, can be ready in 68 days, some in 77 days, or late corn in 88 days.

Fine, but does my wife put the kettle on to boil when the 68th day comes? Hardly! Why? The catalog tells us when the harvest *should* be mature, when it *could* be picked—*if all growing conditions were favorable.* But if the summer is too hot or too cold, too dry or too wet, or if the ground is undernourished, the time of the harvest will be directly affected. We wait until the corn is ripe, sometimes at a much later period than we first hoped, because some of the growing conditions were beyond our control.

OUR GARDENS HELP US TO UNDERSTAND WHEN JESUS WILL RETURN

All that we understand about our gardens will help us when we try to understand why Jesus chooses to wait—when His return seems delayed. Jesus deliberately gave this harvest parable because He knew that men and women everywhere on this planet understand, to some degree, why rice or wheat, tomatoes or corn, do not ripen as soon as they had hoped.

What does the Lord want us to learn from His harvest parable? Even as wise backyard gardeners or big farm operators wait for their seed to mature, so Jesus chooses to wait until the gospel seed has produced a people prepared for His return, a people who have matured to that point where He dares to give them "latter-rain" power to complete the gospel commission. This significant group of people have been identified as those who have the "patience [endurance] of the saints ... those who keep the commandments of God and the faith of Jesus" (Revelation 14:12).[600]

But there are other interesting parallels between the harvest of the gospel and that of literal seed. For instance, farmers and prophets engage in conditional prophecy. Farmers know that they must keep their eyes on their corn rather than on the seed catalog and the calendar. No one wants to harvest a premature crop! A premature crop is a waste; the wise farmer waits for a ripe crop, for that is what being a farmer is all about.

---

[600] Ellen White develops the implications of the harvest principle in numerous places, but probably never clearer than in *Christ's Object Lessons:* "The object of the husbandman in the sowing of the seed and the culture of the growing plant is the production of grain. He desires bread for the hungry, and seed for future harvests. So the divine Husbandman looks for a harvest as the reward of His labor and sacrifice. Christ is seeking to reproduce Himself in the hearts of men; and He does this through those who believe in Him. The object of the Christian life is fruit bearing—the reproduction of Christ's character in the believer, that it may be reproduced in others. ... 'When the fruit is brought forth, immediately he putteth in the sickle, because the harvest is come.' Christ is waiting with longing desire for the manifestation of Himself in His church. When the character of Christ shall be perfectly reproduced in His people, then He will come to claim them as His own. It is the privilege of every Christian not only to look for but to hasten the coming of our Lord Jesus Christ, (2 Peter 3:12, margin). Were all who profess His name bearing fruit to His glory, how quickly the whole world would be sown with the seed of the gospel. Quickly the last great harvest would be ripened, and Christ would come to gather the precious grain." —67, 69.

Jesus is not returning for a "premature" church. He could have returned for an unprepared church and world many years ago. The divine catalog said, "Anytime within the generation living after 1844!" That may sound like a new thought to some. But it has been standard Adventist thinking for more than a century. We are now living in the time of the delayed advent. Why? Because the Christian witness that the gospel seed was meant to produce has not yet matured.

In 1883 Ellen White pleaded with fellow church members to understand why Jesus was delaying His return:

> "It is true that time has continued longer than we expected in the early days of this message. Our Saviour did not appear as soon as we hoped. But has the word of the Lord failed? Never! It should be remembered that the promises and threatenings of God are alike conditional . ... Had Adventists, after the great disappointment in 1844, held fast their faith, and followed on unitedly in the opening providence of God, receiving the message of the third angel and in the power of the Holy Spirit proclaiming it to the world, they would have seen the salvation of God, the Lord would have wrought mightily with their efforts, the work would have been completed, and Christ would have come ere this to receive His people to their reward."[601]

DELAY NOT THE WILL OF GOD

Then she went a step further:

> "It was not the will of God that the coming of Christ should be thus delayed. God did not design that His people, Israel, should wander forty years in the wilderness. He promised to lead them directly to the land of Canaan, and establish them there a holy, healthy, happy people. But those to whom it was first preached, went not in 'because of unbelief' (Hebrews 3:19). Their hearts were filled with murmuring, rebellion, and hatred, and He could not fulfill His covenant with them. ... For forty years did unbelief, murmuring, and rebellion shut out ancient Israel from the land of Canaan. The same sins have delayed the entrance of modern Israel into the heavenly Canaan. In neither case were the promises of God at fault. It is the unbelief, the worldliness, unconsecration, and strife among the Lord's professed people that have kept us in this world of sin and sorrow so many years."[602]

---

[601] *Selected Messages*, bk. 1, 68.

[602] *Ibid.*, 69. In 1901, Ellen White counseled, referring to the delayed advent, that "we may have to remain here in this world because of insubordination many more years, as did the children of Israel; but for Christ's sake, His people should not add sin to sin by charging God with the consequence of their own wrong course of action." —Letter 184, 1901, cited in *Evangelism*. 696.

A delay, yes! But there will be a harvest. Scripture explains why there is a delay—the harvest is not yet "fully ripe." I like the ring in Mrs. White's look into the future: "The great, grand work of bringing out a people who will have Christlike characters, and who will be able to stand in the day of the Lord, is to be accomplished."[603]

Ellen White's clarion challenge still rings in our ears:

> "By giving the gospel to the world it is in our power to hasten our Lord's return. We are not only to look for but to hasten the coming of the day of God. (2 Peter 3:12, margin). Had the church of Christ done her appointed work as the Lord ordained, the whole world would before this have been warned, and the Lord Jesus would have come to our earth in power and great glory."[604]

Our task is to keep our eyes on the big picture—that God will have a people who will restore the truth about God's plan of salvation. They permit His Holy Spirit to complete His cleansing work in the sanctuary of their soul and vindicate His character and government before a world on the brink of eternity.[605]

Vindicating His character and His government is more than a private affair. In His sermon on the mountain (Matthew 5–7), Jesus described how His followers would be recognized the world over as producers, not consumers; their deeds would be seen as "the salt of the earth" and "the light of the world." Their contributions, whether in the professional or academic world, or in the vast world of entrepreneurs, with its support system of office or factory employees—God's loyalists would be distinguished for their honesty, integrity, graciousness, and trustworthiness with the happy result that their "good works" will "glorify your Father in heaven" (Matthew 5:16).

Such "good works" include participating in and contributing to local communities, as well as to state and federal issues. God's loyalists will be known for their appreciation for all the hard-fought contributions of those who have gone before—men and women who paid the price for such "luxuries" we enjoy today, such as "due process," the Bill of Rights, and the rule of law rather than the whims of a dictator or even the fads of the majority.

---

[603] *Testimonies*, vol. 6, 129.

[604] *The Desire of Ages*, 633.

[605] Beatrice S. Neall said it well: "It ought not to be a matter of theological concern if God should lift a whole generation to a height of holiness rarely achieved before in order to give to the world the last revelation of God's love. The 144,000 standing on Mount Zion with the seal of God illuminating their faces are the final witness to a world called to choose between the worship of God and the worship of the beast (Revelation 14:1–12). Instead of a pitiful remnant—Noah's eight, Elijah's 7,000—God will have a full complement of saints to call the world out of Babylon." —"Sealed Saints and the Tribulation," *Symposium on Revelation*, (Silver Spring, MD: Biblical Research Institute, 1992), 277.

Such "good works" are always contested by forces of evil. Satan will do his best to misrepresent and cast aspersion on any effort to glorify God. Every day is an arena for the Great Controversy to be played out in every individual's life. These individual contests between good and evil will increase in intensity in the endtime, as we will soon discover personally.

The Bible's big picture describes the Great Controversy as growing in global dimensions, leading to the final Battle of Armageddon (Revelation 12:17; 16:14–16). *The issue in Christ's day* focused on Calvary; as far as heaven and the unfallen worlds, Christ won the war, exposing Satan as a liar (Revelation 12:9, 10).

THE ISSUES IN THE ENDTIME

The issue in the endtime focuses on the loyalty of Christ's followers and whether "created" intelligences can really fulfill Christ's expectations—that "created" intelligences, especially rebels, can "overcome" all the "fiery darts of the wicked one," even as Christ "also overcame" (Revelation 3:21).

Roland Hegstad wrote:

> "Let me put it to you straight: if one sinner in all the universe—rebel, thief, murderer, liar, adulterer, homosexual, hypocrite, whatever— can stand up in the judgment and with all the records opened, show that God did not live up to His promises, that all power was not put at our command, that we could not conquer in the name of Christ, then, I say, the Great Controversy over whether God is worthy to rule must be decided in favor of the Rebel Leader."

> "But such shall not be: God will have a people who proves the goodness of His great name. And the universe unanimously will confirm the verdict: "As I live, saith the Lord, every knee shall bow to me, and every tongue shall confess to God" (Romans 14:11).[606]

For those living since Calvary and before the plagues fall, the Great Controversy continues until the last person on earth has decided to say "no" to Rebel Leader's seductive charm and "yes" to God's clear call for loyalty. John describes God's loyalists from the first century to the end of the endtime: "They overcame him [Satan] by the blood of the Lamb and by the word of their testimony, and they did not love their lives to the death" (Revelation 12:11).

NOT AN INSURANCE POLICY

This is not an impersonal relationship with the Lamb (Jesus). His blood does not cover us as an insurance policy would (that is, you pay the premium— "I accept Jesus"—and you worry no more!). Overcoming by the "blood of

---

[606] Hegstad, *op. cit.*, 20, 21.

the Lamb and by the word of their testimony" involves a very close relationship with Jesus. Paul described that relationship: "I have been crucified with Christ; it is no longer I who live, but Christ lives in me, and the life which I now live in the flesh I live by faith in the Son of God" (Galatians 2:20)

Helping us to "overcome" is Christ's work as our powerful High Priest through His Holy Spirit. The whole point of the antitypical Day of Atonement is that God will have a prepared people, a cleansed people, before probation closes. His bride will "have made herself ready" (Revelation 19:7).

The real question that all the universe is asking (and so should we) is not "How long, O Lord?" but "How long, O professed followers of Christ, will it take to become a prepared people?"[607] When we ask, How long will it take the High Priest, Jesus Himself, to cleanse the sanctuary from the sins of His people—the answer is, "Not long, if His people will let Him do it." The cleansing of human hearts determines when the heavenly sanctuary will be cleansed!

Have we been given any specific instruction as to how to become prepared people? Is it instruction that everyone can easily understand? Yes! Indeed, God has given us *very specific* suggestions.

---

[607] "While the angels hold the four winds, we are to work with all our capabilities. ... We must give evidence to the heavenly universe, and to men in this degenerate age, that our religion is a faith and a power of which Christ is the Author and His word the divine oracle. Human souls are hanging in the balance. They will either be subjects for the kingdom of God or slaves to the despotism of Satan. All are to have the privilege of laying hold of the hope set before them in the gospel, and how can they hear without a preacher? The human family is in need of a moral renovation, a preparation of character, that they may stand in God's presence. There are souls ready to perish because of the theoretical errors which are prevailing, and which are calculated to counterwork the gospel message. Who will now fully consecrate themselves to become laborers together with God?" —*Testimonies*, vol. 6, 21.

Chapter Twenty-Nine:
The Health Message Connects With The Great Controversy

We will now focus on several specific aspects affecting those living since 1844 that are directly connected to the Great Controversy. Those who are developing the characteristics that God and His angels can endorse as worthy of eternal life look carefully at their health—physically, mentally, socially, emotionally, and spiritually. All that depends on how well we respect the laws of health.

- They are living during the time of "His judgment"—the time that God has arranged for Himself to be put in the "dock," as C. S. Lewis described it.[608] In the big picture, the plan of salvation is primarily God-centered, not man-centered.[609]

- Since 1844 they have been living in the antitypical Day of Atonement. On the Israelite Day of Atonement (in type) the High Priest "cleansed" the people, that they "may be clean from all [their] sins" (Leviticus 16:30). Since 1844, (in antitype) our High Priest's primary goal is to "cleanse" His people from their sins—for the many reasons we have been noting in previous pages. At the close of our Lord's High Priestly ministry, the words will be heard: "He who is unjust, let him be unjust still; he who is filthy, let him be filthy still; he who is righteous, let him be righteous still; he who is holy, let him be holy still" (Revelation 22:11). Our High Priest today has a special goal—not only to prepare His people to die but to prepare them to be translated at His return.

Before the Cross, the whole sanctuary service was an illustration of how God was dealing with sin. Day by day, innocent animals representing the Lamb of God were slain, signifying the cost of sin and how an innocent party would bridge the horrible gap between rebellious people and a holy God. But in the process, God intended that men and women would grasp the symbolism, open their sinful souls to a gracious God, accept His hand of forgiveness and power, and commit themselves to follow Him wherever

---

[608] See 214.
[609] See 34–36.

He would lead. Men and women of faith did just that and we have their life stories throughout the Old Testament. But many did not believe, that is, they did not have the faith to keep saying "yes" to God.[610]

However, the annual typical Day of Atonement was a very special time. While the High Priest was doing his appointed work on that day, the people were to "afflict [their] souls" (Leviticus 16:29). They were to examine themselves, even as Christians solemnly examine themselves prior to partaking of the Lord's Supper (1 Corinthians 11:28), and even more frequently to "examine [themselves] as to whether [they] are in the faith" (2 Corinthians 13:5).

The earthly Day of Atonement taught that the sanctuary itself could not be cleansed until each Israelite was cleansed. When the stream of sins forgiven is stopped, then the sanctuary ceremonies taught that the sanctuary itself would be cleansed. Herein is the heart of the everlasting gospel. Forgiveness always, but cleansing from sin is the end purpose of the gospel!

ANTITYPICAL DAY OF ATONEMENT VERY PERSONAL

During the antitypical Day of Atonement, since 1844, Christians who are looking at the big picture of the Great Controversy will also truly "afflict their souls" and "examine themselves." Why? To see if they are honoring God or embarrassing Him! In other words, are they truly reflecting God's description of those who truly honor Him: "Here are those who keep the commandments of God and the faith of Jesus" (Revelation 14:12)?[611]

It would be difficult to misunderstand Ellen White's counsel:

> "We are in the day of atonement, and we are to work in harmony with Christ's work of cleansing the sanctuary from the sins of the people. Let no man who desires to be found with the wedding garment on, resist our Lord in His office work. As He is, so will His followers be in this world. We must now set before the people the work which by faith we see our great High Priest accomplishing in the heavenly sanctuary. Those who do not sympathize with Jesus in His work in the heavenly courts, who do not cleanse the soul

---

[610] See "Appendix K: Faith, the One Word That Decides Everything."

[611] "God's judgment boils down to a test of loyalty. Will people pledge allegiance to Him, His law of love, and salvation through faith in Christ, or will they rebel against Him and the life He freely offers? By the end of the judgment, as on the Israelite Day of Atonement, two groups will be clearly apparent: Those who are loyal to God and those who are not." —Roy Gane, *Altar Call* (Berrien Springs, MI: Diadem, 1999), 314–324.

temple of every defilement, but who engage in some enterprise not in harmony with this work, are joining with the enemy of God and man in leading minds away from the truth and work for this time."[612]

The point is this: The "hour" has come—the whole universe is now reviewing the evidence to see if God's message through the sanctuary service works. Or is Satan right—that created beings either could not or should not try to obey God! Again, the Great Controversy on full display! If God's plan did not save people from their sins, then the plan fails and God is embarrassed. *A solemn time to be living during the antitypical Day of Atonement!*[613]

- Because of these astounding, even wonderful, expectations that God wants His loyalists to fulfill during the antitypical Day of Atonement, loyalists need to take seriously how well they care of themselves physically. Why? Because "anything that lessens physical strength enfeebles the mind, and makes it less capable of discriminating between right and wrong. We become less capable of choosing the good, and have less strength of will to do that which we know to be right."[614]

ADVANCED HEALTH PRINCIPLES

For this reason Adventists have been given advanced health principles that are often called the "health message." In addition to our emphasis on the humanitarian principle (focus on lessening suffering through home remedies, hospitals and clinics[615]), and on the evangelical principle (health message being the bridge over which the gospel can meet people where they are[616]), we have the even higher purpose reflected in the salvation principle.

---

[612] *Review and Herald,* January 21, 1890; also, February 13, 18, 1890; March 11, 1890; April 8, 1890.

[613] For a penetrating analysis of how Christians should relate to this Day of Atonement since 1844, see Gane, *Altar Call,* 314–324.

[614] *Christ's Object Lessons,* 146. The connection between a healthy brain and the ability to "listen" to the Holy Spirit should be self-evident in view of modern research. But a century ago Ellen White wrote: "The brain nerves that connect with the whole system are the medium through which heaven communicates with man and affects the inmost life. Whatever hinders the circulation of the electric current in the nervous system, thus weakening the vital powers and lessening mental susceptibility, makes it more difficult to arouse the moral nature." —*Education,* 209. See also *Testimonies,* vol. 2, 347.

[615] *Testimonies,* vol. 9, 112.

[616] *Evangelism,* 513, 514.

The health message reflected in the salvation principle is a distinctive Adventist way of looking at health— "to fit a people for the coming of the Lord."[617] Further, "He who cherishes the light which God has given him upon health reform has an important aid in the work of becoming sanctified through the truth, and fitted for immortality."[618]

THREEFOLD LINKAGE

This threefold linkage has not always been understood. Some made the health message an end in itself in developing a worldwide network of hospitals and clinics; others made the health message into a compelling public relations stratagem whereby non-Adventists would become interested enough to sit through an evangelistic sermon. Both were worthy uses of Adventist health principles—but short of the primary purpose that made Ellen White's health emphasis distinctive. The primary purpose was to join the spiritual with the physical on the practical daily level of the average person.[619]

In many ways, Ellen White instructed her audiences: "There is so close a relation between the mind and the body that it is not possible to secure the health of the one without giving special care to the other."[620]

Here again we see reflected the purpose of the gospel within the Great Controversy Theme—"the restoration in the human soul of the image of God."[621] Whatever sin has damaged, God will work to restore. The Adventist health message is not meant primarily to add 10 years to one's life, or even to add quality to life. The health message is designed to eliminate (as much as possible in this life) any physical, mental, social, or moral habit that clouds the brain or damages the body.

Why? So that people will think more clearly and more consistently between right and wrong (see Hebrews 5:14). Further, that people will have more energy, more dynamic ability to share good news with others. Even further, when they do share good news, their witness will be validated by their cheerful, clear mind and by their enthusiastic energy to do others good. Bottom line: The "health message" should be just what most of us need to add cheeriness, energy, and clear thinking to our Christian responsibilities.

---

[617] *Testimonies,* vol. 3, 161.

[618] *Christian Temperance and Bible Hygiene,* 10.

[619] See Herbert E. Douglass, *Messenger of the Lord* (Nampa, ID: PPPA, 1998), 278–342 for a review of the emergence of the health message, the relationship of health to a spiritual mission, the subsequent quality improvement in the health of Seventh-day Adventists, the principles and policies of the health message, and a review of scientific corroboration for these distinctive health principles.

[620] *Manuscript Releases,* vol. 11, 197.

[621] *Education,* 125.

But the health message needs an educational program that will make health principles clear and winsome to young parents, to children in elementary schools, to teenagers in high schools and academies, and to students in higher education. That is why our next chapter focuses on the distinctive educational principles given to the Adventist church.

CHAPTER THIRTY:
DISTINCTIVE EDUCATIONAL PRINCIPLES CONNECT WITH THE GREAT CONTROVERSY

Everything we have been saying so far calls for a distinctive educational system with special priorities. How else would young people understand their roles in the Great Controversy? What makes the Adventist educational system distinctive? Its clearly defined purpose!

The Adventist educational system's mission statement is exactly the same as that of the "everlasting gospel":

> "To restore in man the image of his Maker, to bring him back to the perfection in which he was created, to promote the development of body, mind, and soul, that the divine purpose in his creation might be realized—this was to be the work of redemption. This is the object of education, the great object of life."[622]

When we understand the purpose of the "everlasting gospel" and the Great Controversy to be "restoration" as well as "forgiveness," we are ready to grasp the distinctive principles of the Seventh-day Adventist educational philosophy![623]

EVERY CLASS UNFOLDS SOME ASPECT OF THE GREAT CONTROVERSY

In what practical way does this connection between the Adventist's educational philosophy and the Great Controversy theme affect Adventist classrooms on all levels?

Ellen White was very clear:

> "The student should learn to view the [Scriptures] as a whole, and to see the relation of its parts. He should gain a knowledge of its grand central theme, of God's original purpose for the world, of the rise of the Great Controversy, and of the work of redemption. He should understand the nature of the two principles that are contending for supremacy, and should learn to trace their working through the records of history and prophecy, to the great consummation. He should see how this controversy enters into

---

[622] *Ibid.*, 15.
[623] "Through Christ, restoration as well as reconciliation is provided for man." —*Selected Messages*, bk. 1, 363.

every phase of human experience; how in every act of life he himself reveals the one or the other of the two antagonistic motives; and how ... he is even now deciding upon which side of the controversy he will be found."[624]

Even further, Ellen White outlined the core curriculum:

"In order to understand what is comprehended in the work of education, we need to consider both the nature of man and the purpose of God in creating him. We need to consider also the change in man's condition through ... a knowledge of evil, and God's plan for still fulfilling His glorious purpose in the education of the human race."[625]

Like a laser beam, Mrs. White kept the big picture always in view because the Great Controversy Theme was her defining principle in all that she wrote. By keeping in mind why God created men and women,[626] the nature of sin,[627] and God's plan to restore sinners, enabling them to be fitted to live forever,[628] Jesus would be clearly seen as our Savior as well as our Example. Such a Great Controversy focus releases us from being self-centered about our own salvation and riveted on how we can honor the name of God.

One of the central principles in the Great Controversy is that men and women are responsible beings, free to say "yes" or "no" to God's entreaties. They are not to be unresponsive such as a tree or a cow.[629] That is why understanding the Great Controversy Theme is so vital to the Adventist educational philosophy, in theory and in practice.

Again, Ellen White spoke to this point:

"Every human being, created in the image of God, is endowed with a power akin to that of the Creator—individuality, power to think and to do. The men in whom this power is developed are the men who bear responsibilities, who are leaders in enterprise, and who influence character. It is the work of true education to develop this power, to train the youth to be thinkers, and not mere reflectors

---

[624] *Ibid.*, 190. "The central theme of the Bible, the theme about which every other in the whole book clusters, is the redemption plan, the restoration in the human soul of the image of God. From the first intimation of hope in the sentence pronounced in Eden to that last glorious promise of the Revelation, 'They shall see His face; and His name shall be in their foreheads,' the burden of every book and every passage of the Bible is the unfolding of this wondrous theme—man's uplifting—the power of God, 'which giveth us the victory through our Lord Jesus Christ.'" —*Education*, 125, 126.

[625] *Ibid.*, 14, 15.

[626] See 48.

[627] See 37–40.

[628] See 144.

[629] See 49.

of other men's thought. ... Instead of [producing] educated weaklings, institutions of learning may send forth men strong to think and to act, men who are masters and not slaves of circumstances, men who possess breadth of mind, clearness of thought, and the courage of their convictions."[630]

Throughout her educational philosophy, Ellen White kept the end-view ever before teachers and students:

"Let the youth and the little children be taught to choose for themselves that royal robe woven in heaven's loom—the 'fine linen, clean and white' (Revelation 19:8), which all the holy ones of earth will wear. This robe, Christ's own spotless character, is freely offered to every human being. But all who receive it will receive and wear it here ... They are clothing themselves with His beautiful garment of character. This ... will make them beautiful and beloved here, and will hereafter be their title of admission to the palace of the King. His promise is: 'They shall walk with Me in white: for they are worthy.'" (Revelation 3:4).[631]

KNOWLEDGE ALONE DOES NOT MAKE ONE FREE

Armed with this clearly focused educational philosophy, the student will not be misled into thinking that "*knowledge* shall make you free," rather than *truth* making us free (John 8:32). They will be aware of Satan's sly gospel counterfeit that Christians should think of "restoration" as a concept to be put off until the resurrection. They will not be deluded into thinking that this educational philosophy is only for grade-school teachers, but not applicable for historians or theologians. They will rise above the avalanche of many motivational speakers and others that focus on competition as the strongest motivator for success; they will resist all the subtle appeals to being "first," to being Number One—from the first grade through graduate school, and throughout one's adult life.[632]

Above mastering mathematics and the study of the rise and fall of nations, above speaking and writing skills, above all requirements for diplomas and certifications—Christian teachers should keep the highest goals before their students:

"To aid the student in comprehending these principles [that the work of education and the work of redemption are one], and in entering into that relation with Christ which will make them a

---

[630] *Education*, 17, 18.
[631] *Ibid.*, 249.
[632] See Herbert E. Douglass, "Spirit of Prophecy Perspectives: Education's Grand Theme." —*Journal of Research on Christian Education*, vol. 10, Summer 2001, Special Edition; also see Douglass, *Messenger of the Lord*, 344–353.

controlling power in the life, should be the teacher's first effort and his constant aim. The teacher who accepts this aim is in truth a co-worker with Christ, a laborer together with God."[633]

Yet keen teachers and administrators balance the "oughtness." When they focus on the "ought" more than reality, regardless of honest intentions, an intolerable judgmental atmosphere prevails. Young students are bewildered enough by simply "growing up." They are rough and unpolished and when they live under a condemning atmosphere, either resistance or depression overtakes them.

Teachers and administrators who understand their "first effort" is the preparation of their students (regardless of their career choices) for Christian service and an eternity of joy and research will become revered mentors. Students will recognize quickly those who have the patience and compassion of Jesus. As days pass, such students will be the first to understand the character of God more clearly. Such an educational atmosphere is validating the principles of God's government in the Great Controversy

But as we will discover, Satan plans to torpedo the plans that God has for His people in the last days!

---

[633] *Education*, 30.

GUADALCANAL—1942

The cost of freedom is incalculable. Ask those 11,000 19-year-old teenagers (the average age of the First U.S. Marine Division) who landed August 7, 1942, on the north shore of Guadalcanal, a small tropic island not far from Australia. Guadalcanal became the first time that American forces stopped the Japanese sweep in the South Pacific.

But at what cost? Guadalcanal was expected to be secured in five or six days— two weeks at most. Instead, it dragged on for six grueling months, inch by bloody inch. Because of fear that the Japanese navy (with their superior, much longer range, torpedoes) was rolling in, the U.S. naval forces pulled away from the landing beach, leaving the young marines without proper air support, without most of their heavy weapons, tanks, and other necessary supplies (such as food). Despite horrendous odds, those teenagers hung on in that rain-soaked, malaria-ridden land, fighting off the snakes, leeches, jungle rot, and a well-entrenched enemy. They were alone, no turning back.

Many were the moments of extraordinary courage— young men paying the cost of freedom. For instance, the Battle of Bloody Ridge (Edson's Ridge) that began on September 12, 1942. More than 3,000 Japanese surged toward Henderson Field, guarded by 700 of Lt. Col. Merritt Edson's Raiders. Edson knew that Henderson Field was America's last hope of keeping a toehold in the South Pacific. "If they lost the ridge, then Henderson Field would fall. If Henderson was lost, then the war in the Pacific might well be lost too. Edson's men knew the stakes were high and vowed to fight to the death." Over the next two days, after some of the most violent hand-to-hand fighting imaginable, after wave after wave of fanatic assaults, those sleepless, half-starved Marines still clung to the ridge with bloodstained hands. The Japanese had lost half of their force. It was the turning of the tide in the South Pacific

For the next six months (many months when the battle was much in doubt), Guadalcanal became hell for both the young marines and the defenders. When, in early 1943, the Japanese pulled out, only 12,000 were left of their original 40,000. In all, Americans had 6000 casualties, of which 1600 were killed. Another 700 suffered from a wide range of jungle diseases. The dog-tired, emaciated First Marines required a full year of rehabilitation before they could be called a fighting unit again, having lost many thousands, dead and wounded.

Ask those young Marines if their payment on the cost of freedom was worth it! They never considered retreat. The cost of freedom is incalculable. They look at their dead comrades, at their amputated legs, and cry! But they also look at the alternative—what the world would have looked like if they had not faced death, day after day, until the enemy staggered in retreat. The cost of freedom is incalculable.

Joseph N. Mueller, *The Marines Strike Back* (Oxford, England: Osprey Publishing Co. 1992).

What will be Satan's last-day deceptions and assaults as he furiously challenges God's plan to have a special people with a special message for the endtime? How will God's people thwart Satan's final attempt to wrest this planet from God's control?

CHAPTER THIRTY-ONE:
SATAN ORCHESTRATES HIS BATTLE PLAN FOR THE ENDTIME

Others have focused on the usual endtime events such as what appears to be an increase in natural disasters, wars, and environmental concerns. Our interest here is on those areas where Satan has directly impacted this world morally, intellectually, religiously, and politically. He is the master of confusion, deception, and distraction. Men and women in the endtime will be smoke-screened by Satan, as were Noah's contemporaries when Noah preached "righteousness" to them prior to the Flood (2 Peter 2:5).

In fact, when that solemn moment comes (the "close of probation") and before the seven last plagues, the parallel between Noah's day (when God finally closed the door of the ark) and the closing of probation will be profoundly similar:

> "Christ declares that ... as the people of Noah's day 'knew not until the Flood came, and took them all away; so shall also the coming of the Son of man be' (Matthew 24–39). When the professed people of God are uniting with the world, living as they live, and joining with them in forbidden pleasures; when the luxury of the world becomes the luxury of the church; when the marriage bells are chiming, and all are looking forward to many years of worldly prosperity—then, suddenly as the lightning flashes from

the heavens, will come the end of their bright visions and delusive hopes."[634]

Earlier, Ellen White added a significant description to those years just preceding the seven last plagues—that "when religious leaders are magnifying the world's progress and enlightenment, and the people are lulled in a false security ... then ... shall sudden destruction come."[635]

What are we to make of these explicit descriptions of that awesome moment? Whatever else we can say, we can at least say that when probation closes (from one point of view), this world will never have had it so good— "all are looking forward to many years of worldly prosperity." No doubt, we will be dazzled by the astounding success of medical research wherein cancer and Parkinson's disease (and all those other dreaded words) will be history, even as polio and smallpox is as I write. Most probably, we will have fuel cells (non-fossil, not polluting, energy devices) running our vehicles and airplanes; heating and cooling units will perform at minimal costs and without environmental concerns.[636]

From all that most observers will see and hear just before the close of probation and the seven last plagues, this world should last a long, long time! Of course, there will be profound crises in the natural world and international tensions. But haven't men and women bumbled through all these crises before? Now, in the endtime, the world will be finally confronted with a peace plan engineered by the world's most highly respected religious leader—*and everyone signs on*—Jews, Muslims, Hindus, Buddhists, Shintoists, including all Christian groups! No wonder religious leaders the world over will think the millennium has come!

Satan is "slick," with plenty of practice! He knows how to distract the modern mind with pursuits that in themselves are "lawful" and "good." After all, what's wrong with marriages, and business plans, and being optimistic?

Now, let's look at some of the ways Satan will do his distracting. Remember—he is an expert on turning minds from the truth, from listening to the voice of God in the soul, anything to keep people from listening to the "everlasting gospel."

---

[634] *The Great Controversy,* 338.

[635] *Ibid.,* 38; see also, " Silently, unnoticed as the midnight thief, will come the decisive hour which marks the fixing of every man's destiny, the final withdrawal of mercy's offer to guilty men. ... Perilous is the condition of those who, growing weary of their watch, turn to the attractions of the world. While the man of business is absorbed in the pursuit of gain, while the pleasure lover is seeking indulgence, while the daughter of fashion is arranging her adornments—it may be in that hour the Judge of all the earth will pronounce the sentence: 'Thou art weighed in the balances, and art found wanting' (Daniel 5:27)." —*Ibid.,* 491.

[636] See "Appendix P: Comparing the End of the World with Noah's Flood."

TOLERANCE—ONE OF THE KEY WORDS IN THE ENDTIME

"Tolerance" is an interesting word. Its first meaning is the "capacity to endure pain or hardship"; its second meaning is to "show sympathy or indulgence for beliefs or practices differing from or conflicting with one's own."[637] In recent years this second meaning has segued into an atmosphere that forbids open discussion of one's personal views; if those views differ from a *militant minority*, then those views are considered automatically intolerant! Censorship, in a backhanded way, soon trails the skirts of "tolerance." The expression of opposing views, for many, becomes "hate speech";[638] thus, the expression of different opinions (no matter what the evidence is) reveals intolerance!

All this leads to a society so "tolerant" that a legitimate discussion regarding biblical morality would quickly move beyond free discussion to political incorrectness, to coercion and oppression.[639] In the context of the Great Controversy, such a strategy by Satan is exactly what may be expected in the endtime, even in a land that probably has the strictest "free speech" laws in the world![640] How would one have the freedom to discuss historical accuracy and biblical interpretation regarding the Sabbath-Sunday issue in a society that forbids any negative remarks about anybody else's religion?

However, another side of tolerance is the post-modern flood that sweeps away critical thinking: everyone has the "right" to choose the "truth" that appeals to him or her BECAUSE moral absolutes don't exist! One's personal opinion is as good or as valuable as anyone else's. In that climate, tolerance is expected in religious matters and discussions of moral values, for there is no such thing as "absolute truth"! All this with the

---

[637] *Webster's Ninth New Collegiate Dictionary* (Springfield, MA: Merriam-Webster, Inc., Publishers, 1988).

[638] Of course, anybody in his or her right mind is against "hate speech" that is abusive, insulting, or intimidating—often leading to violence. Some talk shows are plain shock shows, calculated to vilify and demean others. Words are like bullets and can be turned into bullets. No Christian should defend this kind of "hate speech." No Christian should ostracize gays or lesbians because their belief system contradicts what many feel is a biblical issue. Not only should Christians defend them from "hate speech," they should be defended against "hate discrimination" of any kind. Christians like their Master should value the person, getting beyond a person's clothing or social choices.

[639] A student at Boalt Hall, the law school of the University of California-Berkeley, thinks that a long-term trend is developing in that any dissent from the gay agenda constitutes a form of illegitimate speech: "An opinion contrary to the majority opinion at Boalt in favor of gay rights might be treated as the equivalent of racist hate speech." Or open debate on the subject "would be treated as creating a hostile work environment." Cited in John Leo, "Coercion on Campus," *U.S. News & World Report*, May 15, 2000.

[640] "The USA, as the least censored society in the world, has held firmly to the First Amendment and to Article 19 of the Universal Declaration of Human Rights, which has meant that attempts to make provision against hate speech have almost all been disallowed by the Supreme Court." —Ursula Owen, "The Speech That Kills," Iain Walker Memorial Lecture, Oxford University, 1999.

perfume of "political correctness."[641] Not only is tolerance expected, it will be enforced by legal means.

Ellen White could not be more relevant:

> "The position that it is of no consequence what men believe is one of Satan's most successful deceptions. He knows that the truth, received in the love of it, sanctifies the soul of the receiver; therefore he is constantly seeking to substitute false theories, fables, another gospel."[642]

George Barna, founder and president of Barna Research Group, has written 31 books, mostly based on research related to church dynamics and spiritual growth. In his book *The Second Coming of the Church,* he reports that "Americans align themselves with values that give them control. ... To the average American, truth is relative to one's values and circumstances. Only one out of four adults—and even fewer teenagers—believe that there is such a thing as absolute moral truth. Human reason and emotion become the paramount determinant to all that is desirable and appropriate."

He continued: "Without absolute truth, there can be no right and wrong. Without right and wrong, there is no such thing as judgment and no such thing as condemnation. If there is no condemnation, there is no need for a Savior."

Barna quoted a 24-year-old: "It's a pretty cool thing because there is no right or wrong when it comes to faith. You believe what you believe, for whatever reasons seem right to you, and nobody can take that away from you. And then, if you change your mind, that's not an admission of failure or being wrong, but just a change of heart or maybe a sign that you've learned or grown. It's not like math. In spiritual matters the playing field is wide open."[643]

---

[641] The "intellectual's" ideal has been traditionally associated with a commitment to universal truths but history shows that "they" have had difficulty living up to their ideal. Note Heidegger's Nazism in German, Lukács' Fascism in Hungry, and D'Annunzio's Communism in Italy, for starters. But since post-modernism has swept the world, including intellectuals, "the greatest cost of the demise of the intellectuals might be a lack of confidence in those universal principles. ' Now,' says McClay, 'even the public senses that there is no bearer of disinterested truth.'" —Jay Tolson, "All Thought Out?" *U. S. News & World Report,* March 11, 2002.

[642] *The Great Controversy,* 520. "By the cry, Liberality [or, tolerance, open-mindedness], men are blinded to the devices of their adversary, while he [Satan] is all the time working steadily for the accomplishment of his object. As he succeeds in supplanting the Bible by human speculations, the law of God is set aside, and the churches are under the bondage of sin while they claim to be free." —*The Great Controversy,* 522.

[643] *The Second Coming of the Church* (Nashville, TN: Word Publishing, 1998), 61, 62, 75. *Newsweek,* May 8, 2000, in its cover story, "What Teens Believe," noted: "Rather than seeking absolute truths in doctrine, they cross denominational boundaries. ... In place of strict adherence to doctrine, many teens embrace a spirit of eclecticism and a suspicion of absolute truths."

For Many, Truth Is What The Majority Thinks

In other words, for a growing number, truth is whatever the majority thinks it is—or whatever some aggressive minority group may champion regardless of its merits. Allan Bloom noted in 1987 that "there is one thing a professor can be absolutely certain: almost every student entering the university believes, or says he believes, that truth is relative. … The relativity of truth is not a theoretical insight but a moral postulate, the condition of a free society, or so they see it. … That it is a moral issue for students is revealed by the character of their response when challenged—a combination of disbelief and indignation. … The danger they have been taught to fear from absolutism is not error but intolerance. … The students, of course, cannot defend their opinion. It is something with which they have been indoctrinated. The best they can do is point out all opinions and cultures there are and have been. What right, they ask, do I or anyone else have to say one is better than the others?"[644]

Satan obviously has done his work well! And his pitch for tolerance gathers momentum: "In 2001, more than 29.4 million Americans said they had no religion—more than double the number in 1990—according to the American Religious Identification Survey 2001 (AIRS). People with no religion now account for 14 percent of the nation, up from 8 percent … in 1990. … For them, Sundays are just another Saturday."[645]

In a nutshell, "tolerance" and "love" become interchangeable; "diversity" means everyone can express themselves except Christians, especially Christians who are faithful to the teachings of Jesus. Code words such as "sensitivity training" and "multiculturalism" reflect the lowest common denominator on which "diversity" will unite the majority.

William J. Bennett wrote, "It is, therefore, past time for what novelist Tom Wolfe has called the 'great relearning.' We have engaged in a frivolous dalliance with dangerous theories—relativism, historicism, and values clarification. Now, when faced with evil on such a grand scale [September 11, 2001], we should see these theories for what they are: empty. We must begin to have the courage of our convictions, to believe that some actions are good and some evil and to act on those beliefs to prevent evil."[646]

---

[644] Allan Bloom, *The Closing of the American Mind* (New York: Simon & Schuster, Inc., 1988), 25, 26.

[645] *USA TODAY*, Thursday, March 7, 2002. "According to the World Values Survey, conducted by sociologists in 65 nations since 1981, 'We see it (a religious attitude) when we ask how often people spend time thinking about the meaning and purpose of life. We see it in people's attitude toward the environment and in the growth of a worldview that sees all life as sacred and invests nature with dignity and sacred quality. … 'Thou shalt not pollute' is a new commandment that has snuck into the canon, even in public schools where old-fashioned moral instruction is supposedly taboo. The environmental and peace and gender-equality movements are clearly inculcating values without being specifically religious. … Contrary to the well-known secularization theory that God is dead and will soon drop off the consciousness map, the USA is a holdout. Spirituality is actually growing in USA." —*USA TODAY*, March 7, 2002.

[646] "Count one blessing out of 9/ll tragedy: moral clarity," *Houston Chronicle*, October 7, 2001.

This most brief overview of this remarkable and rapid drift from moral absolutes to a spirituality that is measured by feeling and opinion is chiefly due to dismay with the doctrinal confusion that abounds in Christian churches generally.

DOCTRINAL CONFUSION

But the confusion reaches beyond Christianity when leading non-ortho-dox, but "conservative" rabbis representing the majority of Jews in the United States are telling their congregations that "the story of Noah was probably borrowed from the Mesopotamian epic Gilgamesh," "that the way the Bible describes the Exodus is not the way it happened, if it happened at all," that archeologists digging in the Sinai have "found no trace of the tribes of Israel—not one shard of pottery," "that the 'tales' of Genesis… were a mix of myth legend, distant memory and search for origins, bound together by the strands of a central theological concept." Liberal Protestants have been talking like that for more than a century—but now "conservative" Jewish leaders?[647]

Ellen White foresaw this religious crisis and nailed its cause: "The vague and fanciful interpretations of Scripture, and the many conflicting theories concerning religious faith, that are found in the Christian world, are the work of our great adversary, to confuse minds so that they shall not discern the truth. And the discord and division which exist among the churches of Christendom are in a great measure due to the prevailing custom of wrest-ing the Scriptures to support a favorite theory."[648]

After years of looking at church squabbles over petty doctrinal argu-ments, after observing that loyal church goers are not much better people than non-goers, after hearing the limited gospel preached every weekend, whether in pulpits, on television or radio, where the most they hear is a gos-pel of free forgiveness but not the gospel that includes responsibility and divine power to transform the life—is it any wonder that the restless youth, as well as their jaded parents, are voting with their feet?[649]

---

[647] Michael Massing, "As Rabbis Face Facts, Bible Tales Are Wilting," www.nytimes.com. 2000/03/09.

[648] *The Great Controversy,* 520.

[649] Barna, *op. cit.* After his extended research, Barna concedes "we [Christians] think and behave no differently from anyone else." Then, on page 6, he proceeded to give examples of similarities of behavior between Christians and non-Christians: Have been divorced (among those who have been married)—Christians: 27%; non-Christians, 23%. Gave money to a homeless person or poor person in past year—Christians: 24%; non-Christians: 34%. Took drugs or medication prescribed by physician in past year—Christians: 7%; non-Christians: 8%. Watched an X-rated movie in the past 3 months—Christians: 9%; non-Christians: 16%; Donated any money to a nonprofit organization in past month—Christians: 47%; non-Christians: 48%. Bought a lottery ticket in the past week—Christians: 23%; non-Christians: 27%. Feel completely or very successful in life—Christians: 58%; non-Christians: 49%. It is impossible to get ahead because of your financial debt—Christians: 33%; non-Christians: 39%. You are still trying to figure out the purpose of your life—Christians: 36%; non-Christians: 47%. Satisfied with your life these days —Christians: 69%; non-Christians: 68%. Your personal financial situation is getting better —Christians: 27%; non-Christians: 28%.

On October 21, 2003, George Barna announced his latest update of "Americans Describe Their Views About Life After Death." After reporting divergent views, Barna pointed out "Americans' willingness to embrace beliefs that are logically contradictory and their preference for blending different faith views together create unorthodox religious viewpoints. ... Millions of Americans have redefined grace to mean that God is so eager to save people from Hell that He will change His nature and universal principles for their individual benefit. It is astounding how many people develop their faith according to their feelings or cultural assumptions rather than biblical teachings."[650]

In some special way, God's loyalists in the endtime will present the truth about God in such a way that it will come to the world-weary, the confused, the turned-off, as something far more appealing, more believable, than any of the conventional, limited gospels that no longer are credible. The Great Controversy Theme will recast the Bible story in a framework of believability; its freshness will answer the core questions for which all spiritually open people are.

PHENOMENA OF SPIRITUALISM

Another last-day phenomenon that Satan uses to distract people from the truth about "life after death," heaven and hell, is "the delusive teachings and lying wonders of Spiritualism."[651]

Begun in Eden with Satan's first lie, "You will not surely die" (Genesis 3:4), "the doctrine of man's consciousness in death ... has prepared the way for modern Spiritualism."[652] This immortality of the soul notion is reflected in such activities as séances, Ouija boards, psychic powers, channeling, Wicca, "out-of-body" experiences, demonology, witchcraft, or astral projection.

I remember in 1993 through 1994 when *Embraced by the Light* spent many weeks on the *New York Times* best-seller list. Why did Americans gobble it up? Because most people want assurance of life beyond the grave. Saturated with New Age notions, it is the author's account of her "out of body experience" or as some others call it, "near death experience."

Why are these many tools of Spiritism so appealing, so alluring? They appeal to the sophisticated as well as the less educated. Voodoo and its assorted witchcraft may captivate the uneducated, but channeling, out-of-body experiences, astral projection, even the Ouija board, fascinate the most educated. Paganism, including witchcraft and sorcery, is rising rap-

---

[650] www.barna.org/cgi-bin//PagePressRelease.asp? (October 24, 2003).
[651] *The Great Controversy*, 524. See L. E. Froom, *The Conditionalist Faith of Our Fathers*, vol. II (Washington, DC: Review and Herald, 1965), 1051–1197, for an exhaustive historical review of Spiritualism and its basic conflict with Christianity.
[652] *Ibid.*, 551.

idly in Britain reports Ronald Hutton at Bristol University: "[Paganism] is a religion that meets modern needs. Traditional religious have so many prohibitions. ... But Paganism has a message of liberation combines with good citizenship."[653]

At the Naval Medical Center in Portsmouth, Virginia, a registered nurse is also the "pagan resource" person—the man who is called upon "to offer spiritual aid to patients who describe themselves as witches, Wiccans, Odinists or followers of other Earth-centered belief systems. ... On behalf of pagan servicemen and servicewoman, Harris has handcrafted and consecrated healing talismans, cleansed hospital rooms of negative energy and helped arrange healing rituals by covens."[654]

In a very instructive article in *Christianity Today*, Marvin Olasky, professor at the University of Texas (Austin), quotes historian Frank Podmore in listing four major reasons for Spiritism's appeal:

1) "The ranks of the Spiritualists were naturally recruited, largely from those who had freed themselves entirely from the Christian tradition, and had therewith lost all definite hope or belief in a future life.

2) "Some flocked to spiritism because within it there was no real good or evil, and no sin. People could follow their 'naturally benevolent instincts.'

3) "Spiritist showmanship was appealing.

4) "Spiritism certainly appealed to those who had lost a spouse or child and hoped beyond hope to converse with the dead."

Olasky ends his article by saying that "those who try to syncretize New Age and Christian doctrines, either by proclaiming humanity's essential goodness or recommending 'visualization' techniques that place us at the center of things, should not be allowed to be church leaders."[655] It seems to me that he would have made his case stronger if he, himself, did not believe in an "immortal soul"! In the endtime, we can expect Satan's brilliance to dazzle the senses of all, the sophisticated and the less educated, in a way that has never yet been seen on this planet. "So closely will the counterfeit resemble the true that it will be impossible to distinguish between them except by the Holy Scriptures. By their testimony every statement and every miracle must be tested."[656] Why? Because impersonations of departed loved ones, astounding healings and shocking miracles of all kinds will overwhelm everyone who is not grounded in biblical truth.

---

[653] June 19, 2003 Reuters in MSN International News.

[654] Associated Press, March 18, 2002.

[655] *Christianity Today*, December 14, 1992. Between 1990 and 2001, Wiccans have jumped 1,572 percent, from 8,000 to 134,000 self-proclaimed witches. —*USA TODAY*, December 24, 2001.

[656] *The Great Controversy*, 593.

The Melding Element

In the endtime, Spiritism will be the melding element that unites Protestants and Catholics. Again, why? Because both groups, with few exceptions, have bought Satan's lie regarding the immortal soul. Because of this common bond, it will be easier for these two groups to join together on an international Sunday law.

Mrs. White is unambiguous:

> "Through the two great errors, the immortality of the soul and Sunday sacredness, Satan will bring the people under his deceptions. While the former lays the foundation of spiritualism, the latter creates a bond of sympathy with Rome. The Protestants of the United States will be foremost in stretching their hands across the gulf to grasp the hand of spiritualism; they will reach over the abyss to clasp hands with the Roman power; and under the influence of this threefold union, this country will follow in the steps of Rome in trampling on the rights of conscience."[657]

But more than astounding miracles (which only become window-dressing), the real point of Satan's deceptions is the doctrinal delusions that come with the package. After "seeing" one's departed parents or children, doctrinal clarity gets fuzzy. For too many, it will be only a half step to rejecting "cold doctrine" for the "real" thing—talking with a departed parent or child.[658]

We are even asked to believe in death as a "graduation." In her latest book, her autobiography, Elisabeth Kübler-Ross writes: "When we have passed the tests we were sent to Earth to learn, we are allowed to graduate. We are allowed to shed our body, which imprisons our soul the way a cocoon enclosed the future butterfly, and when the time is right, we can let go of it. Then we will be free of pain, free of fears and free of worries … free as a beautiful butterfly returning home to God."[659] This from a best seller today written by one who captured the minds of many in 1969 with her first book, *On Death and Dying.*

This romance with death coupled with the suggestions that "each mind" should judge for itself, that "sins are really innocent mistakes," or God is too loving "to condemn those who try," sets Satan up to further entice the slipping mind until feelings become the test of truth, even for those who have been known to be loyal commandment keepers.[660]

---

[657] *Ibid.,* 588.

[658] "The forms of the dead will appear, through the cunning device of Satan, and many will link up with the one who loveth and maketh a lie. I warn our people that right among us some will turn away from the faith and give heed to seducing spirits and doctrines of devils, and by them the truth will be evil spoken of. A marvelous work shall take place. Ministers, lawyers, doctors, who have permitted these falsehoods to overmaster their spirit of discernment, will be themselves deceivers, united with the deceived. A spiritual drunkenness will take possession of them." —Letter 311, October 30, 1905, cited in *The Upward Look,* 17.

[659] *The Wheel of Life* (New York: Scribner, 2001), 284.

[660] See *Education,* 227, 228; *The Great Controversy,* 558; *Patriarchs and Prophets,* 588.

Everyone in the endtime will repeat Eve's test of looking at "forbidden fruit."[661] Today the "forbidden fruit" comes in many flavors and shapes, such as Zen yoga, visualization, mind-altering drugs, séances, certain aspects of New Age movements, or channeling. No one is immune to this enticement because Satan knows exactly where one's weakest avenue to the soul may be. Only the prepared survive![662]

SATAN, A MYTH OR A METAPHOR FOR EVIL

De-personalizing himself has to be one of Satan's ultimate deceptions. Nothing would give Satan more glee than to have Christians so mystified that they no longer see Satan as a personal being! And he must be laughing night and day![663]

Many years before this erosion in Christian thought, Ellen White foretold "that another subtle and mischievous error is the fast-spreading belief that Satan has no existence as a personal being; that the name is used in Scripture merely to represent men's evil thoughts and desires."[664] How could people believe in the Great Controversy if there is no real contest going on? That is, if all allusions to Satan in the Bible are pure psychological projections, why even speculate about a cosmic conflict!

Even though the de-personalizing of Satan is full-blown today, Christian thinkers have long blurred the personality of Satan. Augustine, one of the champion thinkers for the Roman Catholic Church, ruled out a personal Satan on the basis of his doctrine of predestination. For Augustine, evil, as a person or substance, did not exist except in the wrong use of the human will. If God were all-powerful, He would make a world into which nothing could break in and destroy what God had made! Evil was man's fault in conflicting with the will of God.[665]

---

[661] See "Appendix F: The Wife of Bath Principle."

[662] Think of films such as *Casper,* the friendly ghost; or the Harry Potter series in books and film; or Tolkien's *Lord of the Rings* trilogy. Children may be told that all this is only make-believe but impressions are left such as 1) demon possession is no big deal; 2) ghosts and witches can be good, they have feelings, just like any human; 3) it's OK to befriend ghosts, witches, demons, etc.; 4) ghosts, witches, demons can be very loving; 5) ghosts, witches, demons have power over life and death; 6) the spirit world is not so bad and they have no need for Jesus. I am indebted to Berit Kjos, *The Front Page,* Tulsa, OK, August, 1995, for these six "impressions."

[663] "There are two equal and opposite errors into which our race can fall about the devils. One is to disbelieve in their existence. The other is to believe, and to feel an excessive and unhealthy interest in them. They themselves are equally pleased by both errors and hail a materialist or a magician with the same delight … Readers are advised to remember that the devil is a liar. Not everything that Screwtape says should be assumed to be true even from his own angle." —C. S. Lewis, *The Screwtape Letters* (HarperSanFrancisco, Collins edition, 2001), ix.

[664] *The Great Controversy,* 524.

[665] *The Confessions of Saint Augustine,* translated by Edward B. Pusey (New York: Random House—*The Modern Library,* 1949), 134–137.

Moreover, any suffering or disaster that inflicts anyone contrary to his or her will, Augustus opines, is ultimately the will of God![666] Satan and evil as personal forces do not seem to exist for Augustine.

In fact, Augustine said that God would never create anybody whose wickedness He could foreknow, unless God could also see the good that could flow from that wickedness—so that the future would be that much better off![667] Amazing, but it shows what one theological premise will do to all further thinking; that is, when predestination becomes the primary theme, then everything else is bent to conform to the major theme.

Since Augustine, it has been rare, including with the Reformers, to find anyone thinking of Satan as being relevant to the origin of evil. As Gregory Boyd wrote: "It is remarkable that the one who in Scripture and in the earliest post-apostolic fathers is depicted as the ultimate originator of evil and the one ultimately behind all the world's horrors has been thoroughly ignored in discussions on the problem of evil."[668]

In modern times the situation is even more complex. Many modern theologians, following Rudolf Bultmann, have thought that much of the Bible needs to be demythologized; that is, so-called supernatural events have to be recast in naturalistic terms, which includes angels, miracles, etc.[669] For many, the demonic should be understood in psychological terms only.

Of course, we have always had Satan in cartoon form, the red devil with his pitchfork. Or in medieval and modern literature as Mephistopheles, the devil in the legend about Faust, a magician who sold his soul to the devil in return for 24 years of the devil's services, after which the devil dragged Faust down to hell. Yet all that, cartoon or legend, is only one more way to depersonalize the real Satan.[670]

THE HEALING SERPENT

I think Satan's most fascinating *coup de maître* has been his mystical insinuation that at the "heart" of the healing arts is the healing serpent symbolized in the caduceus, which has two snakes entwined on a staff

---

[666] Augustine, *The City of God,* 5.10—"Therefore, whatsoever a man suffers contrary to his own will, he ought not to attribute to the will of men, or of angels, or of any created spirit, but rather to His will who gives power to wills." See The Christian Classics Ethereal Library of Calvin College, NPNF (Internet).

[667] Augustine, *The City of God,* 11.18—"For God would never have created any, I do not say angel, but even man, whose future wickedness He foreknew, unless He had equally known to what uses in behalf of the good He could turn him, thus embellishing, the course of the ages, as it were an exquisite poem set off with antitheses." See The Christian Classics Ethereal Library of Calvin College, (Internet).

[668] Boyd, *God At War* (Downers Grove, IL: InterVarsity Press, 1997), 55.

[669] *Jesus Christ and Mythology* (New York: Charles Scribner's Sons, 1958); *Theology of the New Testament,* vols. I and II, tr. by Kendrick Grove (New York: Charles Scribner's Sons, 1951–1955).

[670] In the television show *Brimstone,* John Glover plays the devil "as a green-eyed guy with a wicked sense of humor and a drive-time-radio DJ voice. ... He materializes . ... as a college guidance counselor encouraging a nubile student to work her way through school as a stripper. He wears ordinary duds and needs no pitchfork to prod people." —*USA TODAY,* October 29, 1998.

surmounted by two wings. Aesculapius, in Greek mythology the son of Apollo and the first physician, is represented in art as a strong youth bearing a serpent-entwined staff. Even today, the caduceus, in some form, is stylized as the symbol of the medical corps of most modern armies.[671]

All churches today have members who scorn the literal use of the Bible, finding no place for a personal Devil in their speculations regarding the age of the earth or as the cause of evil horror. It is little wonder that Ellen White used those discerning words—"mischievous error"—when she included the depersonalization of Satan as one of the snares of the endtimes.

One of the most ominous phenomena in recent years has been the development of a "favorable climate for the occurrence of demonic possession." Part of this development coincides with a growing consensus within both Catholicism and Protestantism that a personal Satan does not exist resulting in a diminished "opposition to Satanism, including ritualistic Satanism." Satan wins on both accounts: "It is the ultimate camouflage. Not to believe in evil is not to be armed against it. To disbelieve is to be disarmed. If your will does not accept the existence of evil, you are rendered incapable of resisting evil. Those with no capacity of resistance become prime targets for Possession."[672]

MISUNDERSTANDING THE NATURE OF CHRIST, EITHER HIS DIVINITY OR HIS HUMANITY

Obviously confusion over who Jesus is would be one of the foremost strategies of our Lord's archenemy—around this truth lies one of the core issues in the Great Controversy. Those who deny "the deity of Christ, claiming that He had no existence before His advent to this world ... can [not] have a true conception of the mission of Christ, or of the great plan of God for man's redemption."[673]

Much has been written in the last century debunking the pre-existence of Jesus. We note at least three distinct periods when the "quest for the historical Jesus" permeated biblical scholars: the first ending with Albert Schweitzer's

---

[671] "It appears evident that at all times and among all peoples, it was believed that the snake had a close connection with the mystery of life and death and a mysterious power of healing. In the Temple of Aesculapius, as in the Hindu Stupas, in the shrines of Jerusalem, and in the sanctuaries of the Acropolis, in the temple of the Mexican gods as in the huts of the Polynesian tribes, the serpent was for thousands of years the object of the worshipping of all sufferers, from which recovery was expected. ... In this as in many other ancient myths, recent studies have proved that there was a pre-logical explanation of a mystery that is now solved. The principle of immunity, and the co-existence of antagonistic elements in the same substance which belong to the triumphant conquest of modern medicine are first asserted form time immemorial in the myth of the serpent and its healing powers." —Arturo Castiglioni, M.D., "The Serpent As Symbol," *Ciba Symposia*, vol. 2, (March 1942), 1186.

[672] Malachi Martin, *Hostage to the Devil* (San Francisco: HarperCollins*Publishers*, 1976, 1992), xi.–xv.

[673] *The Great Controversy*, 524.

devastating *The Quest of the Historical Jesus* which seemed to stand liberal-ism on its head in that Jesus was not their beloved ethical teacher but only an apocalyptic preacher who was doomed to be rejected.[674]

The second "quest" reached its zenith under Rudolf Bultmann (and his avid students) who simply dug Schweitzer's hole even deeper by "demythol-ogizing" the historicity of the Bible—not scrapping it, but looking at it exis-tentially, subjectively, to see what can be "interpreted" from the "events" which really did not happen as reported.[675]

The third "quest" erupted in the late 1980s and hit major media expo-sure in the 1990s.[676] The Jesus Seminar eventually published their provoca-tive best seller *The Five Gospels* (which included the Gospel of Thomas). A "seminar" composed of, at times, 200 members of well-known seminaries and universities, assumed that the gospel narratives were loyal memories by those who embellished the story of Jesus with plausible fictions. All this based on so-called historical objectivism! Jesus, for some, seemed more like a wandering cynic; for others, Mark's gospel was fiction.

If there will be a fourth "quest" we can expect a further downward spiral away from New Testament historicity.[677] The point here is that Satan would

---

[674] "The Jesus of Nazareth who came forward publicly as the Messiah, who preached the ethic of the Kingdom of God, who founded the Kingdom of Heaven upon earth, and died to give His work its final consecration, never had any existence. He is a figure designed by rationalism, endowed with life by liberalism, and clothed by modern theology in an historical garb. ... Jesus means something to our world because a mighty spiritual force streams forth from him and flows through our time also. ... It is the solid foundation of Christianity. ... But the truth is, it is not Jesus as historically known, but Jesus as spiritually arisen within men, who is significant for our time and can help it . ... The names in which men expressed their recognition of Him as such, Messiah, Son of Man, Son of God, have become for us historical parables . ... He comes to us as One unknown, without a name, as of old, by the lake-side, He came to those men who knew Him not, He speaks to us the same word: 'Follow thou me!'" —(New York: The Macmillan Company, 1961), 398–403.

[675] "New Testament and Mythology," in H. W. Bartsch (ed.), *Kerygma and Myth* (London: SPCK, 1952), 1–44. John Knox, a reputable New Testament scholar stated the question (or contradiction) that modern scholars struggle with: "We can have the humanity without the pre-existence and we can have the pre-existence without the humanity. There is absolutely no way of having both." —cited in, John A. T. Robinson, *The Human Face of God* (Philadelphia: The Westminster Press, 1973), 144.

[676] On Easter weekend, April 9, 1996, the editions of *Time, Newsweek,* and *U. S. News & World Report* were side by side with cover pictures of the risen Jesus. But the cover stories focused on the so-called impact of The Jesus Seminar, which believes, as the articles bore out, that the resurrection of Jesus as an historical event did not happen. The *Newsweek* article commented: "According to this elaborate academic protocol, the Resurrection is ruled a priori out of court because it transcends time and space" (65).

[677] From another viewpoint, the modern shift away from the theology of redemption to a theology of creation exposes again the problem that many "Christian" theologians have with Jesus. "The final word of the new theology is not what God can do and wills to do in the gospel, but what God has done in creation. ... The new theology often assumes that what *is* is essentially good, The paradigm shift changes the theological proclamation of the church from a call to *transformation according to the image of Jesus* to one of *affirmation* of who I am as I am. The proclamation of the saving grace of the gospel has usually been expressed in transitive verbs of change—believe, turn, repent, follow. The new theology is couched in intransitive verbs of affirmation—being and becoming." —James R. Edwards, "The Jesus Scandal," *Christianity Today,* February 4, 2002.

have it no other way! Anything that appeals to the modern cynic, skeptic, or burned-over church member, will be part of Satan's last-day assault on the credibility of the Bible and the perennial lie that Jesus of history is not the person that the Bible has made Him out to be![678]

The fundamental question for all Christians is that we cannot fully understand both the deity of Jesus and the full humanity of Jesus unless we understand *why* He came and *why* He died. We must break out of the conventional theological straitjackets that don't answer these questions in light of the Great Controversy.[679]

WILD, EXTRA-BIBLICAL DOCTRINES, SUCH AS ETERNAL HELL-FIRE, MAKE SKEPTICS

Satan had this all figured out long ago, literally since the Garden of Eden. When he slyly promised Eve that she would "not surely die" (Genesis 3:4), he set up all manner of mischief with the notion of the immortal soul.[680]

The whole concept of people suffering forever in hell-fire has to be the wildest belief anyone could believe with a straight face. After all, how could flesh and bones last very long in any kind of fire, never mind one that lasts forever? Where did such notions begin?

Everyone today seems to have some fixed idea about "hell"—the scoffer dismisses it as a scare tactic; the sophisticated uses the term to represent "turmoil, despair, or alienation"; the literal hell has many defenders;[681] and those who reject the concept of an immortal soul view hell as the Day of Judgment when all of Christ's comments about the future of the wicked are focused on their merciful annihilation.

In a poll taken in 1997, asking the question "Is there a hell?"—52 percent were certain, and 27 percent think there might be; 48 percent said it is a place where people suffer eternal fiery punishment, 46 percent said it was an anguished state of existence rather than an actual place; 6 percent did not know.[682]

Satan's promise to Eve lived on throughout the ancient civilizations of Egypt, Mesopotamia, Greece, and Rome. They all exhibit "a tension

---

[678] For an excellent review and response to The Jesus Seminar notions, see Gregory A Boyd, *Cynic, Sage or Son of God? Recovering the Real Jesus in an Age of Revisionist Replies* (Wheaton, IL: Bridgepoint, 1995).

[679] See "Appendix I: Why Jesus Came" and "Appendix J: Why Jesus Died."

[680] "It is beyond the power of the human mind to estimate the evil which has been wrought by the heresy of eternal torment. The religion of the Bible, full of love and goodness, and abounding in compassion, is darkened by superstition and clothed with terror. When we consider in what false colors Satan has painted the character of God, can we wonder that our merciful Creator is feared, dreaded, and even hated? The appalling views of God which have spread over the world from the teachings of the pulpit have made thousands, yes, millions, of skeptics and infidels." —*The Great Controversy*, 536.

[681] Alan E. Bernstein, *The Formation of Hell* (Ithaca, NY: Cornell University Press, 1993), ix.

[682] *USA TODAY*, October 31, 1997.

between two fundamentally different views: neutral death and moral death. In the first, all the dead live on without any distinction between the good and the wicked. In the second, the good are rewarded and the wicked are punished."[683]

PREDESTINATION AND IMMORTAL SOUL

In Christian thought, Augustine again functions as the high-water source for the awful notions that flow through the twin concepts of predestination and the immortal soul (one needs the other). He forcefully taught the eternal torture of the wicked and that the ability of the wicked to withstand eternal burning was another example of "a miracle of the most omnipotent Creator, to whom no one can deny that this is possible, if he be not ignorant by whom has been made all that is wonderful in all nature."[684]

In the middle 1800s, objection to eternal hell-fire was being raised by Christian pastors but it drew a fierce response by Charles Spurgeon, one of the most successful evangelists of his day: "I fear that at the bottom of all this there is a rebellion against the dread sovereignty of God. There is a suspicion that sin is not, after all, so bad a thing as we have dreamed. ... I am afraid it is the old nature in us putting on the specious garb of charity."[685]

Although Billy Graham believes in the immortal soul, his view of hell has a different twist. Recognizing that the wicked are not heaven-bound yet live somewhere forever, he defines "hell" as "a burning thirst for God that is never quenched. What a terrible fire that would be never to find satisfaction, joy, or fulfillment!"[686]

What I have found most interesting and encouraging is that a significant number of biblical scholars have emerged in the last few decades defending the merciful annihilation of the wicked. Many of them had for years defended the Augustinian-Calvinistic notion of the immortal soul never dying in hell-fire—but no more! This list would include Clark Pinnock, Edward Fudge, F. F. Bruce, Kenneth Kantzer and John R. W. Stott (though some still believe in the immortal soul notion).

---

[683] Ibid. See "Appendix R: The Difference Between the Neutral and Moral Concepts of Hell."

[684] Augustine, *The City of God*, 21.9—The Christian Classics Ethereal Library of Calvin College (Internet). "But that hell, which also is called a lake of fire and brimstone, will be material fire, and will torment the bodies of the damned, whether men or devils,—the solid bodies of the one, aerial bodies of the others; or if only men have bodies as well as souls, yet the evil spirits, though without bodies, shall be so connected with the bodily fires as to receive pain without imparting life. One fire certainly shall be the lot of both, for thus the truth has declared." *Ibid.*, 21.10.

[685] Iain Murray, *The Forgotten Spurgeon* (Edinburgh: The Banner of Truth Trust, 1978), 13.

[686] "A Biblical Standard for Evangelists"—a commentary on the 14 Affirmations made by participants at the International Conference for Itinerant Evangelists in Amsterdam, The Netherlands, July 1983, 45–47. See also similar comments Graham made to Richard Ostling, *Time*, November 15, 1993. J. I. Packer, a senior editor of *Christianity Today*, also holds this position. See also Lewis, *The Great Divorce*, 65.

I want to believe that the angels of Revelation 14 are whispering to keen biblical scholars and New Agers alike, as well as to everyone else, the truth about God, that He is not the God Satan has made Him out to be—a God who would be pleased to exact vengeance on those who rejected His love, a vengeance that would burn forever on those who could never look forward to relief!

When the Great Controversy is understood, they will then appreciate one of the purposes that beckoned Jesus to this world. In Gethsemane and on the Cross, Jesus experienced the last drop of hell. He is the only person who has ever died—truly. Everyone else is now "sleeping" (John 11:11–15). Jesus, however, endured the real hell of separation from the Father: "My, God, My God, why have You forsaken Me" (Matthew 27:46)? That terror, which every sinner will one day face, forced our Lord's God-forsaken loneliness. This was more painful than a fiery furnace.[687]

The New Ager's relationship to hell is also interesting. Again we see how closely the age-old thread of the immortal soul notion links New Agers and Spiritists. Though they all believe in the immortal soul, the New Ager, for example, sees "no evil, no sin, no devil," says Matthew Gilbert, editor of NAPRA ReView, a trade magazine for alternative products. Further, "Darkness is not generally acknowledged except as a psychological concept, as shadows inside ourselves, secret or unconscious parts of ourselves that might sabotage our lives."[688]

SECOND COMING TRIVIALIZED BY "RAPTURE" CONFUSION

I find it fascinating that Satan takes every truth about God and His salvation plan and turns it either slightly or upside down—spinning them so artfully that people would rather believe the lie than the truth![689]

For example, let's take a quick look at modern interest in "end of the world" talk. Satan knows that he can't eliminate the subject. But he can surely warp it with fanciful topics such as the "secret rapture" and other defining elements of dispensationalism. We don't have the space here to review the history of, or the lack of biblical support, for this modern phenomenon but others have.[690]

---

[687] See "Appendix J: Why Jesus Died."

[688] *USA TODAY,* October 29, 1998. For a keen overview of what is generally meant by New Age, see Tex Sample, *U.S. Lifestyles and Mainline Churches* (Louisville, KY: Westminister/John Knox Press, 1990), 30.

[689] "It is one of Satan's devices to combine with falsehood just enough truth to give it plausibility."— *The Great Controversy,* 587.

[690] See Samuel Bacchiocchi, *Hal Lindsey's Prophetic Jigsaw* (Berrien Springs, MI: Biblical Perspectives, 1987); Howard Peth, *Vanishing Saint: Is the Rapture Real?* (Sacramento: Amazing Facts, 1987); Steve Wohlberg, *Exploding the Israel Deception* (Fort Worth, TX: Amazing Discoveries, 1998); Wohlberg, *Truth Left Behind,* PPPA, 2001.

My concern here is to merely note that the overwhelming barrage of public attention given to the Second Advent for the past 50 years has come predominantly from secret-rapture spokespersons. If one were to ask anyone in the street what comes to his or her mind regarding Jesus and the end of the world, by far most people would think of the *Left Behind* series of films and books written by Tim LaHaye and Jerry B. Jenkins.[691] Or they would have seen films such as *The Rapture, A Thief in the Night, The Road to Armageddon,* or *Image of the Beast.* In the 1970s and 1980s, they would have instantly thought of Hal Lindsey's *The Late Great Planet Earth,* the best-selling nonfiction book of the 70s. In this one book, Lindsey seemed to lurch the religious world into a fresh focus on the prophetical significance of Israel and the coming "rapture."

Nearly all of the big-time electronic church preachers have been solidly "rapture" preachers—Jerry Falwell, Jimmy Swaggart, Pat Robertson, Oral Roberts, Kenneth Copeland, Paul Crouch and Rex Humbard. "Network and cable stations carried Christian programs which analyzed current events from a dispensational [rapture] perspective: Paul Crouch's Trinity Broadcasting Network, *Jack Van Impe Presents,* Pat Robertson's *700 Club, Charles* Taylor's *Today in Bible Prophecy,* and Ray Brubaker's *God's News Behind the News.*"[692]

Some of the "reasons" why the rapture aspect of premillennialism took off in the last half of the last century was because several world events seemed to fit their prophetic map and time table. With the skill of the best in media coverage, they focused on the emergence of the State of Israel in 1948 and then the 1967 Six-Day War wherein Israel captured the Sinai Peninsula, the Gaza Strip, the Golan Heights, the West Bank, and especially Jerusalem. For them, what greater proof for their prophetic map and the soon-to-be rapture?

The development of the atomic and hydrogen bombs, for "rapture watchers," seemed to be exactly what certain biblical passages predicted would be signs of the last days. The Persian Gulf War in 1991 was another hot moment to sell books and crank out more films.[693] Wrap all this up with certain scientists who predicted the end of the world in a few short years, or at least impending ecological disasters, either ending in a freeze or an overheated planet—and you have the apocalyptic excitement that sells Tim La Haye's books and fuels Sunday morning television sermons. But all this is pure satanic slickness—clever decoys, more of Satan's sly distractions in the endtime to smother the voice of the three angels (Revelation 14).

---

[691] At the time of writing, the volumes one to ten include: *Left Behind, Tribulation Force, Nicolae, Soul Harvest, Apollyon, Assassins, The Indwelling, The Mark,* and *Desecration.*

[692] Richard Kyle, *The Last Days Are Here Again* (Grand Rapids, MI: Baker Books, 1998), 115, 116.

[693] John V. Walvoord, *Armageddon, Oil and the Middle East Crisis* (Grand Rapids, MI: Zondervan, 1990).

The "art" of those who are afflicted with the "end-of-the-world" fever (but without the big picture of the Great Controversy Theme) is reflected in their constant adjustments to suit current events. Obviously, this recycling of "Bible prophecies" should be self-defeating, but it doesn't seem to work that way. Pat Robertson predicted that by 1982, the Soviet Union would invade Israel, the Middle East would explode, and 2 billion people would be killed at Armageddon. Hal Lindsey, in his *The Late Great Planet Earth* (1970), predicted that the rebirth of Israel in 1948 signaled that "within 40 years or so of 1948, all these things could take place."

We could list others, including Grant R. Jeffrey (*Armageddon: Appointment with Destiny*, 1988) "around the year 2000"; Chuck Smith (*Future Survival*, 1978) "the Lord is coming for His church before the end of 1981; Jack Van Impe (in *Jack Van Impe Presents*, 1992) that the rapture, World War III, and Armageddon should be expected in about eight years (2000); Edgar Whisenant (*88 Reasons Why the Rapture Will Be in 1988*) dated the beginning of World War III on October 3, 1988. Each of these men was forced either to push their "last days" into the future a few years or pull back and deal more with generalities.[694]

Think of the *USA TODAY* advertisement (June 21, 1991) that headlined: "IN AUTUMN 1992, JESUS IS COMING AGAIN." In the body, "In 1991, human history will end," followed by an earthly millennium. Think of the rash predictions that the year 2000 would see a host of problems hitting the planet and the return of Jesus!

THOUGHTFUL PEOPLE TURNED OFF

Is it any wonder why so many thoughtful people are turned off by the ranting and absurdities of those in recent times who have been pitching "the rapture" or some other reason for the end of the world? Satan has done his job well!

To top all this off, note *Time* magazine's cover story for July 1, 2002: "The Bible & The Apocalypse—Why more Americans are reading and talking about THE END OF THE WORLD." And whose voice and books did it feature? Tim LaHaye and Jerry B. Jenkins and their *Left Behind* series. By 2002, this series of books had already sold 36,000,000 copies! And I can't even imagine how many more after this fantastic coverage in *Time*.

Of course, the "supermarket tabloids" have for years beat the "last-days" drum. On July 23, 2002, the *Sun* featured, "End Times Have Begun." This is the terrifying warning from Monsignor Stuart Lorimar, a "renowned scholar" who made a shattering discovery while pursuing his studies in the Vatican archives. Lorimar concludes his article: "When things seem their bleakest, a figure of hope will emerge from the East—possibly China or

---

[694] See Kyle, 118–129.

Japan. This gentle hero will spread a message of peace, and back it up with a concrete plan for rebuilding our past prosperity by building a moneyless society.

"Once he performs three miraculous events—feeding the poor, healing the sick, and making poisoned fields grow fresh grain—he will be acknowledged by the faithful survivors as none other than the Second Coming of Christ."

Nevertheless, in spite of this distracting phenomenal media blitz in magazines, newspapers, radio and television focusing on "the end of the world," in some equally phenomenal way, the truth symbolized in Revelation's three angels will be heard before the "end" really comes. And it will slice through the flood of "last-day" books, films, and television programs that have hitherto dominated the front pages for at least 50 years.

But perhaps the most important development in world events, as well as the least expected, has been the re-emergence of the Roman Catholic Church as a world power.

CHAPTER THIRTY-TWO:
RE-EMERGENCE OF THE PAPACY AS WORLD POWER

How does the phenomenal rise of the Papacy to world influence since the late 1920s fit into the Great Controversy Theme?

Before anything else, we should consider how we (who are cooperating with the four angels of Revelation 14 and 18) should personally relate to the Papacy, as well as to members in its churches in these endtimes.

First, we must remember that the four angels of Revelation are calling seekers of truth "out of Babylon"! God's people everywhere—in all churches and in all religions—in the last days will be moving toward the center of truth, toward those who "keep the commandments of God and the faith of Jesus" (Revelation 14:12).[695] Commandment keepers, by definition, have the faith and spirit of Jesus. They do not condemn; they say, with their Lord, "Come." (Matthew 11:28; Revelation 22:17).

Second, we must remember that "no one has yet received the mark of the beast," that "there are true Christians in every church, not excepting the Roman Catholic communion," and that "none are condemned until they have had the light and have seen the obligation of the fourth commandment."[696]

Third, unfortunately, there is always the "danger that our ministers will say too much against the Catholics;"[697] though "decided proclamations are to be made. ... be guarded. ... make no personal thrusts at other churches, not even the Roman Catholic Church. Angels of God see in the different denominations many who can be reached only by the greatest caution."[698] However, "plain statements must be made. Unvarnished truth must be spoken."[699]

---

[695] "Keep," [Greek, literally, "guard, preserve, pay attention to"]. More than an intellectual awareness, "keep" emphasizes a positive stance—"to observe and defend" against an enemy, against detractors, against spiritual laziness or compromises.

[696] *Evangelism*, 234. "There are now true Christians in every church, not excepting the Roman Catholic communion, who honestly believe that Sunday is the Sabbath of divine appointment. God accepts their sincerity of purpose and their integrity before Him. But when Sunday observance shall be enforced by law, and the world shall be enlightened concerning the obligation of the true Sabbath, then whoever shall transgress the command of God, to obey a precept which has no higher authority than that of Rome, will thereby honor popery above God. He is paying homage to Rome and to the power which enforces the institution ordained by Rome." —*The Great Controversy*, 49. See also *Prophets and Kings*, 188, 189; *Selected Messages*, bk. 3, 386.

[697] *Ibid.*, 574.

[698] *Manuscript Releases*, vol. 20, 127.

[699] *Ibid.*, vol. 19, 383.

As we profile the contributions and goals of the Roman Catholic Church, we must recognize and put proper weight on the amazing earthquake of the 1960s that shook the Catholic Church in what they called *aggiornamento*—their renewal.[700] The seismic tremors are still shaking the Catholic world. The document on religious liberty was a stunner for many. It declared that everyone should be free from any coercion in religious matters, that everyone should be free to choose his religion and practice. Lying on this basic foundation was the new definition of "ecumenism." Heretofore, it meant the possible reunification of all Christian churches. Now "ecumenical gatherings" included, not only Roman Catholics and Protestants, but also Jews, Muslims, Buddhists, Shintoists and a host of other non-Christian groups. The shift of church focus was away from the transcendent to the immanent, less on the afterlife to helping build man's home on earth. All this led to the enormous wave of Liberation Theology where the poorer nations especially espoused socialist and communist principles. For many, especially younger members of the church, traditional respect for Catholic tradition and the Sacraments of the Church was replaced by appeals to human solidarity, lay leadership, and the rejection of the authority of Rome.[701]

MODERN CATHOLICISM SINCE THE 1960S

In other words, many thoughtful Roman Catholics today live with a "new perspective" regarding the role of their church in world affairs. Forty years after the *aggiornamento* of the 1960s, centuries of Catholic thought and tradition are now generally considered irrelevant having been superseded by Modern Catholicism; the word "Roman" is frequently dropped and they "have ceased to be Catholic in any sense that would have been recognized by Pope John XXIII as he summoned his Second Vatican Council to "open the windows" of this church to the world."[702]

In any references to the Catholic Church in the pages to follow you should keep in mind the way that Catholics look at themselves this side of the 1960s. Further, we should understand and accept any who may feel that the following pages are both irrelevant and superfluous because of their new perspective, especially those who have grown up since the 1960s. My attempt in the pages to follow is to link various events of the last few decades to the big picture of the Great Controversy, not to merely get drunk on amassing too many "irrelevant" details. The prescient view of the Catholic Church in the endtime, written in the closing years of the nineteenth century, obviously was written before the Church's *aggiornamento* of the 1960s; yet the underlying insights are probably more distinct today than when they were written.

---

[700] Vatican II, called by Pope John XXIII, consisted of four sessions, from the autumn of 1962 until December 1965.

[701] See Malachi Martin, *The Keys of This Blood* (New York: Simon & Schuster, 1990), 258–265.

[702] *Ibid.*, 264.

Some of the reasons for the increased admiration and high regard by Protestants for Roman Catholics, as well as by secular world leaders, in the endtimes would include:

1) "An increasing indifference concerning the doctrines that separate the reformed churches from the papal hierarchy."[703]

2) "Defenders of the papacy declare that the church has been maligned; and the Protestant world are inclined to accept the statement."[704]

3) "Protestants have tampered with and patronized [Catholicism]; they have made compromises and concessions which [Catholics] themselves are surprised to see and fail to understand."[705]

4) "The religious service of the Roman Church is a most impressive ceremonial. Its gorgeous display and solemn rites fascinate the senses of the people, and silence the voice of reason and of conscience."[706]

5) "The church's claim to the right to pardon, leads [Catholics] to feel at liberty to sin; and the ordinance of confession, without which her pardon is not granted, tends also to give license to evil."[707]

6) "The Roman Church now presents a fair front to the world, covering with apologies her record of horrible cruelties."[708]

7) "As the Protestant churches have been seeking the favor of the world, false charity has blinded their eyes. They do not see but that it is right to believe good of all evil; as the inevitable result, they will finally believe evil of all good."[709]

8) "The Papacy is well adapted to meet the wants of all these. It is prepared for two classes of mankind, embracing nearly the whole world—those who would be saved by their merits, and those who would be saved in their sins. Here is the secret of its power."[710]

---

[703] *The Great Controversy,* 363.
[704] *Ibid.*
[705] *Ibid.,* 566.
[706] *Ibid.*
[707] *Ibid.,* 567.
[708] *Ibid.,* 571.
[709] *Ibid.,* 572.
[710] *Ibid.*

PROTESTANTS WILL OPEN THE DOOR

In view of these eight characteristics of the Catholic Church predicted for the endtime, what developments should we be expecting, ever keeping in mind Revelation 13–18?[711]

- First, strange as it may seem, the Catholic Church will have the door opened for them by Protestants in the United States, regaining "in Protestant America the supremacy which she has lost in the Old World."[712] How can this be? "Through the timeserving concessions of the so-called Protestant world."[713]

- Second, in some remarkable manner, the scenes of the past that "clearly reveal the enmity of Rome toward the true Sabbath and its defenders … are to be repeated as Roman Catholics and Protestants shall unite for the exaltation of the Sunday."[714] In fact, "in both the Old and the New World, the papacy will receive homage in the honor paid to the Sunday institution, that rests solely upon the authority of the Roman Church."[715]

- Third, in a prediction that carries with it ominous conflicts of interest, "the Roman Catholic Church, with all its ramifications throughout the world, forms one vast organization under the control, and designed to serve the interests, of the papal see. Its millions of communicants … are instructed to hold themselves as bound in allegiance to the pope. Whatever their nationality or their government, they are to regard the authority of the church as above all other. Though they may take the oath pledging their loyalty to the state, yet back of this lies the vow of obedience to Rome, absolving them from every pledge inimical to her interests."[716] Consider the plight of the legislator or judge in matters of religious concern: *who has his or her higher allegiance*—a nation's constitution or the church's dogma?

- Fourth, with this conflict of interest in place, it is not difficult to imagine how, even in the United States, "that the church may employ or control the power of the state; that religious observances may be enforced by secular laws; in short, that the authority of church and state is to dominate the conscience, and the triumph of Rome in this

---

[711] For papal influence on the development of the Sunday Law in the United States, see the next chapter.
[712] *The Great Controversy,* 573.
[713] *Ellen White Comments, SDABC,* vol. 7, 975.
[714] *The Great Controversy,* 578.
[715] *Ibid.,* 578.
[716] *Ibid.,* 580.

country is assured."[717] Even now, by noting the rise of Catholic legislators and judges in the United States, we can see that "she is silently growing into power. Her doctrines are exerting their influence in legislative halls, in the churches, and in the hearts of men."[718]

POPE JOHN PAUL II SINCE 1976

Pause, for a moment. What has been the astonishing record since 1976?

- September 1976. An obscure Polish archbishop from Krakow stood before an audience in New York City and made "one of the most prophetic speeches ever given: 'We are standing in the face of the greatest historical confrontation humanity has gone through ... a test of two thousands years of culture and Christian civilization, and with all of its consequences for human dignity, individual rights and the rights of nations. ... wide circles of American society and wide circles of the Christian community do not realize this fully.'" In two years, that Polish archbishop would become Pope John Paul II.[719]

- September 28, 1978. After being pope for 33 days, Albino Luciani, now known as Pope John Paul, died. During this short time he had initiated various courses of action that would have changed the direction of one-fifth of the world's population, especially in such areas as the role of Masonry among Catholics, artificial forms of birth control, and irregularities at the Vatican bank. It seemed he was a targeted man.[720]

- October 30, 1978. Pope John Paul II said: "We are now facing the final confrontation between the church and the antichurch, of the Gospel vs. the anti-Gospel."[721]

- May 13, 1981. After two-and-one-half years into his pontificate, Pope John Paul II was shot by a professional "hit man" in St. Peter's Square in the presence of some 78,000 people and before 11 million watching on television. Not an isolated moment, it was "entirely predictable,

---

[717] *Ibid.*, 581.

[718] In January 2001, of the 535 members of the 107th Congress, 150 are Roman Catholic; Baptists, 72; Methodists, 65; Presbyterians, 49; Episcopalians, 41; Jewish, 37; Lutherans, 20; Mormons, 15; plus others. —PCUSA.NEWS@ecunet.org January 9, 2001.

[719] Malachi Martin, *The Keys of This Blood* (New York: Simon & Schuster, 1990), 16.

[720] See David A. Yallop, *In God's Name, an Investigation into the Murder of Pope John Paul I* (New York: Bantam Books, 1984.

[721] *U. S. News & World Report*, October 30, 1978.

indeed inevitable" in the wake of his fast-growing geopolitical presence."[722] Already, John Paul could not be ignored.

• June 7, 1982. President Ronald Reagan and Pope John Paul II talked for 50 minutes in the Vatican Library, later called "one of the great secret alliances of all time;" its purpose—the collapse of the Soviet Union and the encouragement of reform movements in Hungary, Czechoslovakia, and the Pope's beloved Poland.[723]

• 1984. On September 22, 1983, Dan Quayle appealed to the United States Senate: "Under the courageous leadership of Pope John Paul II, the Vatican State has assumed its rightful place in the world as an international voice. It is only right that this country show its respect for the Vatican by diplomatically recognizing it as a world state."[724] In the following year, President Reagan appointed the first ambassador to the Vatican (not a personal representative) thereby recognizing for the first time the political significance of the central government of the Roman Catholic Church.[725]

• December 1, 1989. Vatican Summit—President Gorbachev and the Pope represented two contrasting visions of a "new world order." When Gorbachev addressed John Paul II as "the world's highest moral authority," he recognized that he was not dealing with a "straw man"[726] Gorbachev, several years later, said: "I have carried on an intensive correspondence with Pope John Paul II since we met at the Vatican in December 1989. And I think ours will be an ongoing dialogue. … I am certain that the actions undertaken by John Paul II will play an enormous political role now that profound changes have occurred in European history."[727]

---

[722] "No attempt would have been made to cut him down so early in his pontificate if indeed as spiritual leader he represented no political threat into those who ordered his assassination. The present Dalai Lama, the Archbishop of Canterbury, or Billy Graham are not likely to undergo a like fate. They don't matter, as John Paul matters." —Malachi Martin, *The Decline and Fall of the Roman Church* (New York: G. P. Putnam's Sons, 1981), 294. See also Martin's *The Keys of this Blood* (New York: Simon & Schuster, 1990), 46.

[723] *Time,* February 24, 1992, 28.

[724] Pope John Paul II "insists that men have no reliable hope of creating a viable geopolitical system unless it is on the basis of Roman Catholic Christianity." —Malachi Martin, *The Keys of This Blood* (New York: Simon & Schuster, 1990), 492.

[725] Thomas P. Melady, *The Ambassador's Story—The United States and the Vatican in World Affairs* (Huntington, IN: Our Sunday Visitor, Inc., 1994), 50.

[726] *Ibid.,* 491.

[727] *South Bend Tribune,* March 9, 1992, cited in Dwight K. Nelson, *Countdown to the Showdown* (Fallbrook, CA: Hart Research Center, 1992), 40, 41.

- 1989. Collapse of the Soviet Union was due primarily to the "great secret alliance"; and "the rush to freedom in Eastern Europe is a sweet victory for John Paul II."[728] "While Gorbachev's hands-off policies were the immediate cause of the chain reaction of liberty that has swept over Eastern Europe in the past few months, John Paul deserves much of the longer-range credit."[729]

- 1990. The publishing of Malachi Martin's *The Keys of This Blood*[730] has to be considered one of the most astounding events of the century dealing with the aspirations and strategies of a pope. His phenomenal focus on Pope John Paul II staggers the mind as he outlines the Pope's strategy for world domination that (at the time of this printing) is being worked out with astounding rapidity.

- May 1, 1991. Pope John Paul II's *Centesimus Annus* (The Hundredth Year: On the Hundredth Anniversary of *Rerum Novarum*). A remarkable *restatement* of Pope Leo XIII's overview of the rights of workers worldwide and how various government forms deny these rights. Ironically, both popes argue for religious liberty for all and yet call for government recognition of Sunday as the workers' day of rest and worship.[731]

- February 24, 1992. Cover story of *Time* magazine: "Holy Alliance— How Reagan and the Pope conspired to assist Poland's Solidarity movement and hasten the demise of Communism: An Investigative Report." Carl Bernstein reported: "Step by reluctant step, the Soviets and the communist government of Poland bowed to the moral, economic, and political presence imposed by the Pope and the President."[732]

- Summer, 1993, Colorado Youth Festival. After the Pope's visit to Colorado, the Vatican sensed a new opportunity to forge with the United States a plan to exert a "moral authority in world affairs."[733]

- January 9, 1994. Israel and Vatican sign a "fundamental agreement" after 45 years of troubled relationships. Israeli diplomats say that "the agreement acknowledges the inherent stake of the Catholic Church

---

[728] *Life,* December 1989.
[729] *Time,* December 4, 1989.
[730] New York: Simon & Schuster, 1990, 1–735.
[731] www.ewtn.com/library/ENCYC/JP2HUNDR.HTM
[732] *Time,* February 24, 1992, 24–35.
[733] Alan Cowell in *New York Times,* August 18, 1993.

in the Holy Land; the church is not a guest ... but part and parcel of the reality of Israel."[734]

- March 29, 1994. "Evangelicals and Catholics Together: The Christian Mission in the 3rd Millennium"—a meeting and document that many say reversed 500 years of church history. To imply that both sides preach the same Christ, understand authority and the "church" the same way, or hold the same understanding of "justification by grace through faith," is the test of credulity, but no matter: both sides "contend together" to uphold "sanctity of life, family values, parental choice in education, moral standards in society, and democratic institutions worldwide." Further, "We affirm that a common set of core values is found in the teachings of religions, and that these form the basis of a global ethic ... and which are the conditions for a sustainable world order." New phrases such as the church being responsible "for the right ordering of civil society" are more than interesting. Further, they agree that "it is neither theologically legitimate nor a prudent use of resources" to proselytize among active members of another Christian community.[735] As many say, "an historic moment."[736] Indeed!

- September 5–13, 1994. The International Conference on Population and Development in Cairo demonstrated to the world the political clout of Pope John Paul II. Surprisingly, the Papacy joined with Muslim leaders in protesting pro-abortion phrases and funding that included abortion as a method for family planning. This coalition and their combined clout awakened the world to many liaisons through the decade where Muslims and Catholics have been working together on common concerns.

- October 16, 1994. Israel's first ambassador to the Vatican said his meeting with the Pope opened a "new epoch of cooperation." The Pope expressed his long-standing request for "international guarantees" to protect the "sacred character of Jerusalem," a city sacred to Christians, Muslims and Jews.[737]

---

[734] *National Catholic Register,* January 9, 16, 1994.
[735] Full text of the document in Clifford Goldstein *One Nation Under God?* (Boise, ID: PPPA, 1996), 143–160. See "Catholics and Evangelicals in the Trenches," *Christianity Today,* May 16, 1994; J. I. Packer, "Why I Signed It," *Ibid.,* December 12, 1994.
[736] John White, former president of the National Association of Evangelicals, *USA TODAY,* March 30, 1994. On March 29, 1994, *The Oregonian* summarized an Associated Press story with subtitle: "Catholic and evangelical leaders vow to join in a common bond to work toward shared values."
[737] *National Catholic Register,* October 16, 1994.

• November 10, 1994. In his apostolic letter, *Tertio Millennio Adventiente* (The Coming Third Millennium), the Pope built on the new era opened up by Vatican II—the "profound renewal" that opened up the Catholic church to other Christians, the focus of each year from 1995 to the Grand Jubilee year of 2000, symbolic journeys to Bethlehem, Jerusalem and Mount Sinai "as a means of furthering dialogue with Jews and the followers of Islam, and to arranging similar meetings elsewhere with the leaders of the great world religions." The time between 1994 and 2000 were busy indeed as the Pope fulfilled the plans laid out in this letter.[738]

• November 13, 1994. In his column, "Why Catholics Are Our Allies," Charles Colson wrote (carrying through the agenda developing for decades): "Believers on the front lines, battling issues such as abortion, pornography, and threats to religious liberty, find themselves sharing foxholes with conservatives across denominational lines—forging what theologian Timothy George calls 'an ecumenism of the trenches.'... The great divides within Christendom no longer fall along denominational lines but between conservatives and liberals *within* denominations. ... Let's be certain that we are firing our polemical rifles against the enemy, not against those fighting in the trenches alongside us in defense of the Truth."[739]

• January 2, 1995. *Time* –"John Paul II, Man of the Year." "People who see him—and countless millions have—do not forget him. His appearances generate electricity unmatched by anyone else on earth. ... When he talks, it is not only to his flock of nearly a billion; he expects the world to listen. ... In a year when so many people lamented the decline in moral values or made excuses for bad behavior, Pope John Paul II forcefully set forth his vision of the good life and urged the world to follow it. ... John Paul's impact on the world has already been enormous, ranging from the global to the personal. ... With increased urgency ... John Paul presented himself, the defender of Roman Catholic doctrine, as a moral

---

[738] *National Catholic Register,* December 11, 1994.

[739] *Christianity Today,* November 14, 1994. One of the books I read in my early ministry was Paul Blanchard's *American Freedom and Catholic Power* (Boston: The Beacon Press, 1949). A breathtaking book, he revealed the strategy of how the Catholic church would eventually dominate the politics of the United States, long before others were writing with such precision. How would they do this? The Church would turn the eyes of conservative Protestant America toward common values such as birth control, abortion, family values, and control of education In that same year, America saw a very effective advertising campaign sponsored by the Knights of Columbus to remove misconceptions about Rome. —*EndTime Issues,* September 1999.

compass for believers and nonbelievers alike. ... Billy Graham said, 'He's been the strong conscience of the whole Christian world.'"[740]

• January 21,1995. In Colombo, Sri Lanka, "Pope John Paul II ended an exhausting Asian tour with a call for the world's great religions to unite on behalf of shared moral values."[741]

• May 30, 1995. Papal encyclical, *Ut Unum Sin* (That They May be One), laid out, unambiguously, a powerful strategy for church unity, on one front to develop a nonconfrontational relationship with Islam, on the other, throughout the Christian world. This document committed the Roman Catholic Church to full communion with the Eastern Orthodox Church, that unity is more important than jurisdiction. And to the Protestant churches he reminded them that the "Petrine ministry" belongs to all Christians, whether they recognize it or not.[742]

• October 7, 1995. When Pope John Paul II presided at a mass in New York's Central Park, an estimated 125,000 people turned out to see, not only the leader of the world's largest Christian church, but also an ecumenical procession of Protestant, Orthodox and other non-Catholic religious leaders, including "political power broker Pat Robertson at the head of the line." After the mass and an intimate visit with the Pope, Robertson "insisted that a new day is dawning in the relationship between conservative Protestants and traditional Roman Catholics."[743]

• July 7, 1998. *Dies Domini* (Lord's Day). From the first sentence, the Pope focused on "the Lord's Day—as Sunday was called from Apostolic times." The entire document is amazing in subtle malexegesis, but very persuasive to the surface reader. Outlined in 87 sections, note the following: "62. It is the duty of Christians therefore to remember that, although the practices of the Jewish Sabbath are gone, surpassed as they are by the 'fulfillment' which Sunday brings, the underlying reasons for keeping 'the Lord's Day' holy—inscribed solemnly in the Ten Commandments—remain valid, though they need to be reinterpreted in the light of the theology and spirituality

---

[740] December 26, 1994, January 2, 1995, 53, 54.
[741] *The Orlando Sentinel,* January 22, 1995.
[742] www.vatican.va/holy_father/John_Paul_II/encyclicals/document. Richard John Neuhaus, *The Wall Street Journal,* July 6, 1995.
[743] Joseph L. Conn, "Papal Blessing?" *Church and State,* November, 1995.

of Sunday. ... 66. ... My predecessor Pope Leo XIII in his Encyclical *Rerum Novarum* spoke of Sunday rest as a worker's right which the State must guarantee. ... 67. ... Therefore, also in the particular circumstances of our own time, Christians will naturally strive to ensure that civil legislations respects their duty to keep Sunday holy."[744]

- October 27–28, 1998. Archbishop Lean-Louis Tauran said that Jerusalem "has long been at the center of the Holy See's concerns and one of its top priorities for international action. ... The Holy See believes in the importance of extending representation at the negotiating table in order to be sure that no aspect of the problem is overlooked."[745]

- October 30, 1998. A nine-page document signed by Cardinal Ratzinger emphasized that popes alone can determine the limits of those at the negotiating table (above). Publicly, Ratzinger said that "it is clear that only the pope ... as successor of Peter, has the authority and the competence to speak the last word on the means of exercising the pastoral ministry of the universal truth." "The papacy," he said, "is not an office of the presidency ... and cannot be conceived of as a type of political monarchy."[746]

- May 12, 1999. Anglican-Roman Catholic International Commission (18 Anglican and Roman Catholic members), continuing a dialogue that began in 1981, published an agreed statement with amazing convergences such as: "62. An experience of universal primacy of this kind would confirm two particular conclusions we have reached: 1) that Anglicans be open to and desire a recovery and re-reception under certain clear conditions of the exercise of universal primacy by the Bishop or Rome; and 2) that Roman Catholics be open to and desire a re-reception of the exercise of primacy by the Bishop of Rome and the offering of such a ministry to the whole Church of God."[747]

---

[744] www.vatican.va/holly_father/john_paul_IIapostolic_letters/enframe28_en.htm

[745] www.vatican.va

[746] Associated Press, 10/30/98 1:12, P.M.

[747] www.ewtn.corn/liberty/theology/arcicgh1 John Wilkins, editor of *The Tablet*, commented: "This 'Gift of Authority' now joins the other documents developed by this conference as an agenda in waiting. The commission's work is like a deposit in a bank. Its value will be evident when the time comes for it to be withdrawn for us." www.natcath.com/NCR_Online archives. Dr. George Carey, Archbishop of Canterbury said: "In a world torn apart by violence and division, Christians need urgently to be able to speak with a common voice, confident of the authority of the gospel of peace."—Oliver Poole, "Churches Agree Pope Has Overall Authority," BBCNews, May 13. www.antipas.org/magazine/articles, churches_agree_people

- September 1, 1999. March 8, 12, 23, 2000. Pope apologizes for "its past mistakes, … and to ask pardon for the historical offenses of its sons [sic]. … The wounds of the past, for which both sides share the guilt, continue to be a scandal for the world." Auxiliary Archbishop Rino Fisichella of Rome said of the March 12 meeting in St. Peter's: "Pope John Paul II wanted to give a complete global vision, making references to circumstances of the past, but without focusing on details out of respect for history . … The Church is not the one who has sinned, the sinners are Christians, and they have done so against the Church, the bride of Christ."[748]

- October 31, 1999. In the spring of 2000, my wife and I visited Augsburg, Germany, with one purpose—to visit the Reformation Church in which the Confession of the Princes was presented to Charles V in 1530. D'Aubigné wrote that "this was destined to be the greatest day of the Reformation, and one of the most glorious in the history of Christianity and of mankind. … The Confession of Augsburg will ever remain one of the masterpieces of the human mind enlightened by the Spirit of God."[749] But on October 31, 1999, in that very church, 482 years to the day after Martin Luther had nailed those 95 theses to the door of the village church in Wittenberg, the Lutheran World Federation (not including all branches of the Lutheran Church, such as the Missouri Synod) signed with the Roman Catholics the Joint Declaration on the Doctrine of Justification, after 30 years of consultation.

What is so amazing is that 400 years ago, Protestants and Catholics were in profound disagreement over the doctrine of justification, leading to vicious, deadly consequences. Just one more example of how diminished clarity of truth is today and how much "relationship" and "unity" have emerged as the most important issue for so many leading voices in modern Christianity.[750] All these thoughts blew through my mind as I sat solemnly in those same pews, where stalwart princes once

---

[748] *Zenit,—Rome,* March 12, 13, 2000. "John Paul has one foot in the dimension of history (where mess, error, violence, fanaticism and stupidity flourish merrily) and the other in the dimension of eternity (where he must insist, the holiness and infallibility of the church as the mystical body of Christ remain intact). It is awkward: How does infallibility own up to its fallibilities and yet remain infallible? The Pope's solution: by being vague about the actual sins and by attributing them, in any case, to men and women who are Catholics and not to the Catholic Church itself." —Lance Morrow, "Is it Enough to Be Sorry?" *Times,* March 27, 2000.

[749] J. H. Merle D'Aubigné, *History of the Reformation of the Sixteenth Century* (New York: Robert Carter and Brothers, 1875), bk. 14, ch. 7, 563, 566.

[750] *Christianity Today,* October 25, 1999; www.tcsn.net/fbchurch/fb/cdecia.htm

put their lives on the line and where, 482 years later, "princes of the church" voted in the fog of their lost precision of thought.

- November 7, 1999. In New Delhi, India, Pope John Paul II, recognizing Catholicism's minority status in India, said that "no state, no group has the right to control either directly or indirectly a person's religious convictions ... or the respectful appeal of a particular religion to people's free conscience."[751]

- January 27, 2000. Congressional Gold Medal (USA): "To authorize a gold medal to be awarded on behalf of the Congress to Pope John II in recognition of his many and enduring contributions to peace and religious understanding, and for other purposes. ... The Congress finds that Pope John Paul II ... is recognized in the United States and abroad as a preeminent moral authority; has dedicated his Pontificate to the freedom and dignity of every individual human being and tirelessly traveled to the far reaches of the globe as an exemplar of faith; has brought hope to millions of people all over the world oppressed by poverty, hunger, illness, and despair; transcending temporal politics, has used his moral authority to hasten the fall of godless totalitarian regimes, symbolized in the collapse of the Berlin wall; has promoted the inner peace of man as well as peace among mankind through his faith-inspired defense of justice; and has thrown open the doors of the Catholic Church, reconciling differences within Christendom as well as reaching out to the world's great religions."[752]

- June 5, 2000. President Putin asks Pope John Paul II for "help in gaining Russia's political and military integration in Europe." Putin called his stop "a very significant visit."[753]

- September 5, 2000. *Dominus Jesus*: A 36-page update from the Congregation for the Doctrine of the Faith, it rejects in unambiguous terms the notion that "one religion is as good as another," that the Catholic Church is "complementary" to other religions, and that Protestants, for example, are "Churches in the proper sense."[754]

- October 2000. Queen Elizabeth II, head of the church and state of England, visited Pope John Paul II, and was "pleased to note the important progress that has been made in overcoming historic

---

[751] Associated Press, November 8, 1999.

[752] Internet: www.feds.com/basic_svc/public_law/106-175.htm

[753] *CNN.com.* June 5, 2000.

[754] Catholic World News—Vatican Updates—09/05/2000; *Christianity Today,* September 11, 2000.

differences between Anglicans and Roman Catholics—as exemplified in particular by the meeting of Anglicans and Roman Catholics in Canada this year. I trust that we shall continue to advance along the path which leads to Christian unity."[755]

- January 6, 2001. The Pope's Apostolic Letter, "At the Beginning of the New Millennium," among other directives, emphasized the importance of Sunday as "a special day of faith, the day of the Risen Lord and of the gift of the Spirit, the true weekly Easter. ... We do not know what the new millennium has in store for us, but we are certain that it is safe in the hands of Christ, the 'King of kings and Lord of lords' (Revelation 19:16); and precisely by celebrating his Passover not just once a year but every Sunday, the Church will continue to show to every generation 'the true fulcrum of history, to which the mystery of the world's origin and its final destiny leads."[756]

- January 31, 2001. President Bush told 25 Catholic leaders that his interest was to "draw on Catholic wisdom and experience. ... I think you are seeing a historic and ground-breaking moment in the participation of Catholics in public life." Archbishop Caput, present for the dialogue, said Catholic social teaching is based on two pillars: dignity of the individual and commitment to the common good. Bush has often referred to the "common good" as an important administrative goal.[757]

- March 22, 2001. Washington, D.C.'s Pope John Paul II Cultural Center opened; first proposed for Krakow, Warsaw, or Rome, but the Pope chose Washington, D.C., which he described as "the crossroads of the world."[758] "Cardinal Maida said there was no illusion that putting the center in Washington would precipitate an immediate change in the thinking of presidents, Supreme Court Justices, Members of Congress or other officials. ... But as we tell the story better, people will be affected by osmosis."[759]

- May 2001, the Pope, the first Catholic leader to enter the Umayyad Mosque in the Syrian capital of Damascus, participated in an organized prayer service. For Muslims it is the oldest stone mosque in

[755] www.britain.it/royalvisit/3e.html

[756] www.vatican.va/holy_father/John_Paul_it/apost_letters/documents/

[757] "Bush Meets With Catholics on Faith-based Initiatives," *National Catholic Register*, February 11–17, 2001.

[758] Pat McCloskey, "Washington's New Pope John Paul II Cultural Center," *St. Anthony Messenger*, April 2001.

[759] *The National Catholic Register*, October 26–November 1, 1997.

the world, while for Christians it is the alleged place where John the Baptist was buried. The Pope led in Christian prayers, while his Moslem counterpart, Sheikh Ahmed Kataro, led in Moslem prayers. By this dramatic act of worshiping in a mosque, the Pope underlined his commitment to work toward a rapprochement with the Muslims.

• September 2001, in Almaty, Kazakhstan, 12 days after the horrors of September 11, 2001, the Pope renewed his commitment to work toward a new partnership with Moslems in his message to the predominantly Muslim nation of Kazakhstan. The Pope declared: "'There is one God'. The Apostle proclaims before all else the absolute oneness of God. This is a truth which Christians inherited from the children of Israel and which they share with Muslims: it is faith in the one God, 'Lord of heaven and earth' (Luke 10:21), almighty and merciful. In the name of this one God, I turn to the people of deep and ancient religious traditions, the people of Kazakhstan."[760]

The Pope then appealed to both Muslims and Christians to work together to build a "civilization of love": "This 'logic of love' is what he [Jesus] holds out to us, asking us to live it above all through generosity to those in need. It is a logic that can bring together Christians and Muslims, and commit them to work together for the 'civilization of love'. It is a logic which overcomes all the cunning of this world and allows us to make true friends who will welcome us 'into the eternal dwelling-places' (Luke 16:9), into the 'homeland' of heaven."

• January 24, 2002. In Assisi, Italy, the Pope and more than 100 religious leaders from around the world, including Orthodox patriarchs, Jewish rabbis, grand muftis, sheikhs and other Muslim representatives, Buddhists and Shinto monks, Hindu leaders, Zoroastrians whose adherents are mostly in India and Iran, leaders of traditional African religions, Protestant leaders and 25 Roman Catholic cardinals and approximately 30 bishops shared in a day pursuing "authentic peace." Ending the day, the Pope lit a symbolic lamp of peace with the words: "Violence never again! War never again! Terrorism never again! In God's name, may all religions bring upon earth justice and peace, forgiveness, life and love!"[761]

---

[760] http://www.vatican.va/holy_father/john_paul_ii/homilies/2001/documents/hf_jpii_hom_20010923_kazakhstan_astana_en.html

[761] *Christian Science Monitor,* January 24, 2002; "Pope hosts ecumenical assembly for peace at Assisi," *Inq7.net,* January 24, 2002.

- October 16, 2003. In celebrating Pope John Paul II's 25 years as leader of the Roman Catholic Church, Tracy Wilkinson of the *Lost Angeles Times* wrote: "This planet now is a very different place [compared to October 16, 1978], and John Paul II … has had a hand in shaping events to a degree unrivaled by any other religious figure in modern history. His election on Oct. 16, 1978 'was itself a breaker of precedents,' the Jesuit magazine *America* said in an editorial this month, 'and ever since his election John Paul II's pontificate has been setting records that none of his predecessors could have imagined.'"[762]

Where is all this leading? Let's find out!

---

[762] *The Sacramento Bee*, October 16, 2003.

The cost of freedom is incalculable. Ask those 189 men who died on March 6, 1836, at the old Spanish mission called the Alamo, "the cradle of Texas Liberty." Although Texas had been Mexican territory for many decades, many Americans were allowed to settle as part of Mexican land development under the Mexican Constitution. But in 1824, the dictator Santa Anna overturned the constitution supported by American settlers; they were angry that their liberties and freedom were no longer guaranteed. The Mexicans, in turn, were determined to stop more Americans from settling in Texas.

Mexican central government heavy-handedly tried to enforce their new regulations. Settlers were split; some favored peace, others believed it was time for independence from a government that no longer recognized their own constitution. In the autumn of 1835, William Barret Travis, lawyer and military officer joined up with Stephen Austin, the founder of Austin, Texas, at the siege of Bejar (San Antonio), eventually capturing the Mexican-held city under the control of General Cos, brother-in-law of Santa Anna on December 10. The Mexican leadership went south only to return with a larger army and revenge.

The Texans now knew there was no turning back. The stories of brutal mutilations of even surrendering Texans steeled their determination. They established a garrison in the old mission named the Alamo (now in downtown San Antonio) and sent messages to the rest of Texas to rally with them in the battle for freedom. Some 145 Texans in the area took refuge in the old mission under the joint command of William B. Travis (for the regulars) and Jim Bowie (for the volunteers).

For two weeks following February 23, 1836, Santa Anna and his brother-in-law added to their troops until he had more than 2,000 regulars, pressing the Texans constantly. During that time, a few reinforcements came in response to Travis' famous "Appeal for Aid," managing to penetrate enemy lines, bringing the total strength of the defenders to about 189 men. On March 5, reports say, Travis drew a line in the sand and gave every man the choice to cross the line and join him in a fight to the death to defend the Alamo, thereby giving Sam Houston time to get a larger army mobilized. All but one crossed. Scouts were sent to Houston to hurry, but it was a forlorn hope.

After nearly two weeks of constant attack, on March 6, 1836, the Mexicans attacked in wave after wave under the bugle call of "No quarter!" The 189 Alamo defenders died to the last man, among them such famous names as William Travis, Davy Crockett, and Jim Bowie. After the battle, some 1,600 Mexicans soldiers lay dead and another 500 were wounded. Susanna Dickinson and her baby were spared with some servants. Santa Anna wanted their story to reinforce his goal to terrorize all Texas against further fights.

A few days later, on April 21, San Houston's Texans routed the Mexican Army under Santa Anna at the Battle of Jacinto near Houston while the Texans shouted, "Remember the Alamo! Remember the Alamo!" The cost of freedom is incalculable.

How will Satan use the United States, the beacon of freedom for more than two centuries, as his laboratory and launching pad for world domination, not militarily but through religious legislation? What will be his decoy thrusts that will obscure his primary goals in bringing on the Sunday laws and ultimately their enforcement?

CHAPTER THIRTY-THREE:
CHARACTERISTICS OF ULTIMATE EVIL

A t Calvary, all angels (loyal and evil) and inhabitants of unfallen worlds saw all history from the beginning of time focus on that awful moment when Satan faced Christ nose to nose. Very soon now, as I write, these same angels and other worlds, *plus all nations on earth*, will see history *since the Cross* converge on the United States in the endtime—even as all previous chapters in this book converge on these closing chapters.

In this endtime, again the fury of Evil will face not Christ only, but also His followers in another life-and-death struggle. Knowing that his days are numbered and with the madness of super-heated hate, Satan will spew his serpentine venom on those who hold their heads high, "keep[ing] the commandments of God ... hav[ing] the testimony of Jesus Christ" to guide them through unparalleled troubles during this earth's last days (Revelation 12:17).

All this will play out in the United States—the prophetically fateful arena that eventually involves all other nations on earth—with no holds barred and no replays.

Throughout this book, we have been talking about ultimate Evil—the full-blown personification of self-centeredness, void of any concept of what love is. Lucifer-turned-Satan, the proto-type of Evil, has demonstrated what happens when freedom is betrayed by narcissistic pride that would not submit, the will that would not bow, the desire to be willful rather than willing.[763]

SATAN'S AGENDA

To further his agenda, Satan became skilled in

- *Pretense*—the use of consistent, destructive lies under the cloak of loyalty;

- *Scapegoating*—blaming others for the damage he was doing;

- *Word obfuscation*—redefining the meaning of words, including the substitution of personal opinion for absolute truths; and

- *Coercion*—the use of power to control or destroy others.[764]

Those who have been infected with Satan's self-centeredness develop intolerance to criticism, a bottomless hate for the reprover (whether God or man), an intellectual deviousness that glorifies the means rather than the end, and a ghastly use of power to coerce others. All the while, those on the pathway of evil learn ways to pretend they are respectable, trustworthy, deeply concerned about the feelings of others, and, yes, the champions of individual rights and "freedom."

The end of all this evil (and all that Satan represents) is "to kill life."[765] That is exactly the framework in which the United States provides the last act of the Great Controversy—"He was granted power to give breath to the image of the beast, that the image of the beast should both speak and cause as many as would not worship the image of the beast to be killed" (Revelation 13:15).[766]

---

[763] M. Scott Peck, M.D., *People of the Lie* (New York: Simon & Schuster, Inc., 1983), 43. Peck highlights the words, "pretense" and "scapegoating" as common characteristics of evil—those who consistently lie.

[764] George Orwell (Eric Hugh Blair) wrote one of the most remarkable books of the twentieth century, *1984*, published first in 1949 (hardback), later in paperback (Hammondsworth, England: Penguin Books, 1954, reprinted at least 26 times. This prescient book describes the totalitarian state where Doublespeak reverses language, obliterates or revises history to suit the state, where freedom of thought is allowed to the masses because they don't think! Three chapters are entitled "War is Peace", "Ignorance is Strength", and "Freedom is Slavery." Freedom is the "freedom to say two plus two equals five." Ministry of Peace is actually the Ministry of War; joycamp is really the labor camp—examples that words mean the exact opposite of what they appear to mean. Orwell got some of his inspiration from Nazi German and Communist Russia that had employed some of the methods of *1984*. Yet much of the book can be thought of as an overview of the endtime when the world generally will believe the Big Lie and falsified history, leading to the attempted extinction of those guilty of "Thoughtcrimes."

[765] *Ibid.* 79. Interesting, evil is only "live" spelled backwards.

[766] Evil has been written across the pages of history, but probably no more awful than in the twentieth century during the horror of Stalinism, the terror of Nazism, the atrocities of Pol Pot in Cambodia and the Japanese in China. One of the most starkly illuminating records of daily life for a Jew in Dresden during Hitler's reign is Victor Klemperer's *I Will Bear Witness* (New York: Modern Library Paperback Edition, 1999).

CHARACTERISTICS OF THE "OTHER BEAST" OF REVELATION 13

In earlier thoughts on Revelation 13 (see page 260), we noted that John saw:

- "Another beast coming up out of the earth [appearing first] like a lamb [but eventually speaking] like a dragon" (verse 11);

- That this second beast "exercises all the authority of the first beast [the blaspheming religio-political power which had great earthly authority and coercive power]" (verse 12);

- That this second beast "causes the earth and those who dwell in it to worship the first beast, whose deadly wound was healed" (verse 12);

- That this second beast "performs great signs, so that he even makes fire come down from heaven … in the sight of men" (verse 13);

- That this second beast "deceives those who dwell on the earth by those signs" (verse 14);

- That the second beast tells "those who dwell on the earth to make an image to the beast who was wounded by the sword and lived" (verse 14);

- That the second beast will "give breath to the image of the beast, that the image of the beast should both speak and cause as many as would not worship the image of the beast to be killed" (verse 15); and

- That the second beast will "cause all … to receive a mark on their right hand or on their foreheads and that no one may buy or sell except one who has the mark or the name of the beast, or the number of his name" (verses 16, 17).

Surely this is an astonishing preview of last-day events; events that center in "another beast" that arises in, relatively speaking, unpopulated territory—but in a short while becomes an unrivalled world power with enormous influence.[767] Its influence is so compelling and global that the entire world will follow its lead in developing religiously designed legislation that will appear worthy of universal support. Further, it will take the lead in convincing the world that certain politically sensitive legislation is so timely and necessary that all offenders should be killed!

---

[767] Nineteenth century historians believed that the rise of the United States "demonstrated as did no other episode in history the benignness of the Creator. The origin of the United States had been glorious, indeed little short of miraculous (some thought that it was positive proof of God's intervention in history and thus not *short* of a miracle at all. … the history of the United States constituted the greatest success story since man had emerge from prehistory." —Page Smith, *The Shaping of America*, vol. 3 (New York: McGraw-Hill Book Company, 1980), xii.

What could John be describing? Or to ask the question in another way, what world power in modern times could possibly fit John's prophetic drama? The only answer is the United States of America, a truly difficult statement for a blue-blooded American to make![768] I know that such a thought of coercive persecution of a minority in the United States may have seemed far-fetched a few years ago. But perhaps less so since September 11, 2001!

A nation that can cause "all" the world to unite under its plan for world peace and religious harmony (religion being the cause of most world conflicts) must be a very powerful, most persuasive world voice.

THE ONLY WORLD SUPER POWER

Incredible as it may sound today, the United States, in a few short years has been vaulted by circumstances into the position of being the only Super Power on Planet Earth. No other world power in history—not the Persian nor Roman nor Spanish nor British empires—has ever been the "sole" Super Power. Today the United States has no close competitors. America, for example, outspends the next 20 countries combined on its military that the rest of the world expects us to employ as the world's first response to troubles anywhere. But far beyond its military might is America's leadership in technology, economic strength, and humanitarian relief.[769]

Since September 11, 2001, in Afghanistan and Iraq, the world has seen an unfolding of astonishing military capabilities. For instance, with a relatively few special operations men, utilizing GPS systems and pilotless planes, they changed the course of history in a few days in Afghanistan; with the combined capabilities of especially trained men and women, they changed the course of history in Iraq in a few short weeks. Terrorists are being caught, killed or pursued all over the planet by the most sophisticated gear imaginable.

With the world slipping into common talk of the New World Order (or whatever we may yet call it in the near future), the thought that only America could make it happen is the world's no-brainer.[770]

---

[768] For helpful expansion of this designation of the United States in prophecy, see Maxwell, *op. cit.,* 340–349; Clifford Goldstein, *Day of the Dragon* (Boise, ID: PPPA, 1993), 127. For an historical overview of the concept that the two-horned beast in Revelation 13 and the reasoning of John N. Andrews represented the United States, see Leroy Froom, *"The Prophetic Faith of Our Fathers,* vol. IV (Washington: RHPA, 1954), 1098–1103.

[769] Charles Krauthammer, *Imprimis,* January 2003.

[770] Poll taken in December 2002 reported that in the United States, 59 percent said religion is "very important" in their lives, well above other industrialized nations including Britain (33 percent), Canada (30 percent), Italy (27 percent), South Korea (25 percent), Germany (21 percent), Japan (12 percent), and France (11 percent. —*Sacramento Bee,* December 12, 2002.

But what is so incongruous, so difficult to put together, is that the United States, though admittedly the most powerful political nation on earth, is also the foremost example of a nation established on the principles of freedom, both political and religious! The world had never before seen a nation that so resolutely wrapped itself within a phenomenal Declaration of Independence and unparalleled Constitution, such as the first 13 colonies did in 1776 and 1787-9, with 1791 being the year when the Bill of Rights, after ratification by the states, became effect as the first Ten Amendments.

SIMPLE PRINCIPLES

Both of these unique documents rested on simple principles that were nobly set forth in the Declaration of Independence—"truths to be self-evident, that all men are created equal, and that they are endowed by their Creator with certain unalienable [incapable of being surrendered] rights, among which are life, liberty, and the pursuit of happiness." The document was signed by 56 heroic men under their own personal commitment: "With a firm reliance on the Protection of Divine Providence, we mutually pledge to each other our Lives, our Fortunes and our sacred Honor."[771]

The first amendment of the Constitution of the United States reads "Congress shall make no law respecting an establishment of religion, or prohibiting the free exercise thereof; or abridging the freedom of speech, or of the press; or the right of the people peaceable to assembly, and to petition the Government for a redress of grievance."[772]

Just reciting and keying these excerpts onto this page brings tears to my eyes. These conceptual giants and valiant signers of these documents indeed pledged, and many sacrificed, their personal "fortunes" for this new experiment with "freedom." And none besmirched their "sacred honor!" They opened up a new world of political and religious freedom, providing an atmosphere for the development of the most influential, most powerful nation on earth. Freedom's soil is very fertile. Always![773]

---

[771] The Declaration of Independence (1776) cited in *Harvard Classics,* vol. 43, 160.

[772] Cited in *Harvard Classics,* vol. 43, 207.

[773] "No other government in history had launched itself without the help of officially recognized gods and their state-connected ministers. It is no wonder that, in so novel an undertaking, it should have taken a while to sift the dangers and the blessings of the new arrangement, to learn how best to live with, to complete the logic of its workings. ... But, at the least, its meaning has been one of freedom—the free exercise of the churches, free not only from official obstruction but from compromising favors. A burden was lifted from religion when it ceased to depend on the breath of princes, when it had nothing by way of political office with which to lure or tempt people into the fold or into the ministry. Thrown back on themselves the churches were encouraged to search for their own essence, make their moral case on truly religious grounds, reward people in the proper spiritual currency," —Garry Wills, *Under God* (New York: Simon and Schuster, 1990), 383, 384.

These signers turned their backs on nations that were either taxing its citizens to support a state church or imprisoning those who did not conform to the religion of the majority. They bravely declared the young colonies to be a fresh, brazenly new kind of government.[774] Freedom was its flag.

But, as John foresaw, all that freedom would one day evaporate under the hot sun of crisis in the endtime. However, this loss will not be so perceived in the eyes of the majority of Americans at that time. Freedom would still be their password but it would be reset in another context—something like: "To maintain America's freedom, and in the interest of the 'general welfare,' certain individual rights must necessarily be submerged under the greater good of the majority—in times of crisis, survival of a free nation is more important than individual rights."

You say, "Impossible! Not in America!" Recall what happened in the early 1940s for one example among many, to the "relocation" of 70,000 Japanese Americans into hastily built quarantine camps. The Supreme Court ruled that in the name of "common defense" that Japanese-Americans were traitors and that "war is an aggregation of hardships."[775] (We did not relocate German-Americans or Italian Americans!)

Commenting on this "relocation," two Constitutional authorities warned: "In future wars, no person belonging to a racial, religious, cultural, or political minority can be assured that community prejudice and bigotry will not express itself in a program of suppression justified as 'military necessity,' with resulting destruction of his basic rights as a member of a free society."[776]

The upshot seems obvious, it seems to me—when civil rights are limited, generally the environment to limit religious "rights" and freedom is closing in.

Another reality check: Charlton Heston commented on the astonishing percentage of Americans after September 11, 2001, who, along with Tom Brokaw (NBC commentator) said: "We need to re-examine our freedoms because of this attack." Former Secretary of Defense William Cohen said Americans will need to make "choices between security and civil liberties."

Heston responded: "What I'm talking about is the headlong rush to sacrifice liberty on the altar of safety. ... And all too often [we] lose both liberty and safety."[777]

Heston was referring to the numerous polls that were taken in the United States soon after September 11. For instance, the *Reader's Digest*/Yahoo poll (September 24, 2001) revealed that of 35,000 respondents: 70 percent favor

---

[774] Katharine Lee Bates captured this stellar look into the future in her beloved song, "O Beautiful for Spacious Skies": "O beautiful for patriot dream that sees beyond the years ..."

[775] *Korematsu v. United States* (1944). Cited in Maxwell, *op. cit.*, 345.

[776] Alfred H. Kelly & Winfred A. Harbison, *The American Constitution: Its Origins and Development*, rev. ed. (New York: W. W. Norton & Company, Inc., 1948, 1955), 861. Cited in Maxwell, *op. cit.*, 345.

[777] *America 1st Freedom*, December 2001.

the use of wiretaps by intelligence agencies; 78 percent find it acceptable to videotape public places; 71 percent want a new national ID system based on both fingerprinting and retinal scans.[778]

THE PRETENSE OF EVIL

What happens to individuals, legislatures, even Supreme Courts, when arguments used are mere "lies" in respect to what they are supposed to be upholding? Why the pretense of honor, or love, or justice when someone's freedom is limited because of his or her color or religion?

In the family we often see a spouse pretending love, all the while destroying the mate or child with suffocating control or searing blame. In the military we are told that we must "waste" a village to save a country. Even the Supreme Court of the United States had approved, in the name of a free America, imprisoning Jehovah Witnesses who choose not to salute the American flag (for religious reasons).[779] How many decades did the highest Court in the United States classify American blacks as only two-thirds of a citizen and protected a slave-holder's ownership of slaves as personal property—in a country that told the world that "all men are created equal"?[780]

This is not the place to argue the past. We do, however, have a responsibility to discern the signs of the times, not only as citizens of the "land of the free and the home of the brave," but as students of prophecy. John the Revelator tells us that, in the endtime, Satan and his followers, angels and humans, will exercise all their skill in making evil so deceptive that most of the world "marveled and followed the beast" as they beheld his amazing power and authority—and most of the world will join Satan, finally, in attempting to kill those who resist their lies.

SETTING UP THE UNITED STATES

So how will Satan's lies set up the United States to be the world leader in uniting all nations under a religious authority that has universal clout and enough muscle to enforce economic hardship and persecution on those they hate? How will satanic lies become so believable that "the world worshiped the beast" (Revelation 13:4)?

---

[778] *USA TODAY*, September 24, 2001

[779] *Minersville School District v. Gobitis*, 310 US 586 (1940). The Court portrayed the case as balancing conflicting claims of liberty and authority. The school's interest in creating national unity was more important than the rights of the students to refuse to salute the flag. However, the Supreme Court overruled their previous decision in *West Virginia Board of Education v. Barnette*, 319 U.S. 624 (1943), recognizing the fundamental right to religious liberty when it held that Jehovah's Witness schoolchildren could not be penalized when they refused to salute the American flag for religious reasons. In an opinion noted for its eloquence, Justice Robert H. Jackson wrote, "If there is one fixed star in our constitutional constellation, it is that no official, high or petty, can prescribe what shall be orthodox in politics, nationalism, religion, or other matters of opinion or force citizens to confess by word or act their faith therein."

[780] *Ibid.*, 384–391.

- By pretense, consistent lies, though appearing to serve a noble purpose;

- By blaming those they hate for causing the national crises;

- By causing confusion in substituting policy for principle (the end justifies the means), substituting opinion for absolute truths, redefining the meaning of words;

- By employing various forms of coercion—and all to one end, the eradication of dissent and individual freedom.

While writing these pages, I have noted how masters of evil will always find an audience who will believe them, despite of what seems to others as clear reality. In 2003, during the spring war in Iraq, Information Minister Mohamed Saeed al-Sahaf had been denying reports that U.S. Army and Marine forces were moving freely in the center of Baghdad, even when his audience could hear the coalition tanks nearby. He was assuring the Iraqi people that the Republican Guard was in control of the airport. Then he offered to take reporters to the airport to prove it! Of course, most of them had already been to the airport and had seen the coalition forces for themselves.

Day after day in early April 2003, the world awaited al-Safaf's latest daily virtuoso performance. Some of his comedic propaganda included: "They say they brought 65 tanks into the center of the city. I say to you it is not true. This is part of their sick mind. There is no presence of infidels in the city of Baghdad at all." (All the while he had to speak loudly because of the gunfire in the streets below his hotel.) Further, daily ritual included, "U.S. troops were poisoned yesterday" and "U.S. troops are committing suicide."

Ted Simons commented, "We are entering an era in which the news media and the general public's adeptness at detecting and dissection spin in public discourse is matched only by the messengers' confusion. Put simply, it's hard, and getting harder, to know whom to believe."[781]

BLIZZARD CLAIMS AND BIAS

This is just one analysis of what is behind and under the blizzard of false advertising claims, media bias, outrageous political accusations and cheating scandals. In other words, it has become fashionable to deny truth, to scoff at any information that is contrary to personal opinion, to revise history, and to blame others for whatever happens. It clearly is a time when political correctness is legislating a new society of victims and tolerance for what once was unacceptable conduct.

---

[781] Editor-in-Chief, *Presentations Magazine*, March 2003.

One example of this moral confusion, pretense, scapegoating and mental/moral coercion is to observe how skeptical younger men and women are whenever they look at a corporation's balance sheet, listen to many stock brokers, and hear the tongue-gymnastics of politicians and religious leaders who parse phrases so that they sound believable. The operative words are, "What are they holding back!"

What I am getting at (in a time of moral confusion and financial crisis) is it would be a perfect time for certain leaders (who have beguiled others by appealing to their feelings, not their heads with truth) to promise, in a fresh, captivating way, that they have the solution for peace, unity, and brotherhood of all mankind (where everyone's opinion and lifestyle is equally as good as anyone else's).

Especially in a time of complex social and economic forces that are unsettling young and old, rich and poor; everywhere, people are hungry for a simple response. Hitler knew it in the early 1930s in Germany. Scapegoats are always available—just find those who may look different or worship differently. If the majority doesn't respond immediately, the minority tyranny will always gain power and lead the way.

In 1972, Rene Girard, a French literary critic, focused on the question of the *violent* root of culture through literature, anthropology, psychology, and biblical criticism. Through a succession of books and articles, he has pursued what he calls his *idée fixe:* the way in which scapegoats found, preserve and unify culture. Girard found societies resort to acts of violence to restore order: "By organizing retributive violence into a united front against an enemy common to all the rivals, either an external enemy or a member of the community symbolically designated as an enemy, violence itself is transformed into a socially constructive force."[782]

Girard went on to say, "Where only shortly before a thousand individual conflicts had raged unchecked between a thousand enemy brothers, there now reappears a true community, united in its hatred for one alone of its members. All the rancors scattered at random among the divergent individuals, all the differing antagonisms, now converge on an isolated and unique figure, the surrogate [scapegoat] victim."[783]

In the Great Controversy, scapegoating has been Satan's method par excellence. Think of Caiaphus and Christ and Calvary. That same sinister mind will duplicate his Calvary madness in the endtime when "a 'true' community, united in its hatred for one alone of its members," declares that member expendable to save the larger community from pending chaos. Scapegoating of the ages becomes fully blossomed in the end.

Let's see how we will know when that scapegoating time is near.

---

[782] James l. Fredericks, The Cross and the Begging Bowl: Deconstructing the Cosmology of Violence." *Buddhist-Christian Studies* 18 (1998), 155.

[783] Rene Girard, *Violence and the Sacred* (Baltimore: The Johns Hopkins University Press, 1977), 79.

CHAPTER THIRTY-FOUR:
CIRCUMSTANCES CONTRIBUTING TO THE COMING CRISIS—PART 1

We have been warned that "the final movements will be rapid ones,"[784] that "perplexities ... scarcely dreamed of are before us,"[785] that "events of the future ... will soon come upon [us] with blinding force,"[786] that "a storm is coming, relentless in its fury,"[787] that "no one [should] feel that he is secure from the danger of being surprised,"[788] that we should be preparing for what is about "to break upon the world as an overwhelming surprise,"[789] and that we should be able to "catch the steady tread of the events."[790]

In previous pages, we have been reviewing "the steady tread of the events" predicted for the endtime.[791] Let's look more closely at what we should expect as the cosmic conflict heats up. *If you were Satan,* knowing that time was short—time to pull out all the stops (Revelation 12:12)—*what would you do as the "ruler of this world,"*[792] the head of the "rulers of the darkness of this world"?[793]

If you were Satan, you would do all you could to:

- Create panic, through "natural" disasters and environmental stress

- Manipulate and unsettle the economic systems of the world

- Confuse further by offsetting the growing stress, fears, and anxieties with optimistic scientific and medical promises for a world without food or energy shortages and without dreaded illnesses

- Create moral insensitivity to horror, iniquity, and lust so that each new level of evil and thrills will be entered unconsciously

- Promote the efficiency and desirability of universal peace through religious cooperation among all world religious leaders

- Employ all the tricks available to create legislation that would restrict freedom in the name of security

---

[784] *Testimonies,* vol. 9, 11.
[785] *Ibid.,* 43.
[786] *Manuscript Releases,* vol. 4, 74.
[787] *Testimonies,* vol. 8, 315.
[788] *Last-Day Events,* 16.
[789] *Testimonies,* vol. 8, 28.
[790] *Testimonies,* vol. 7, 14.
[791] See 319, 324, 325.
[792] John 12:31; 14:30; 16:11.
[793] Ephesians 6:12.

- Cover your tracks with "pretense"

- "Scapegoat" (blame) on the very ones you are trying to destroy all your evil happenings

- Manage all these lines of stress so that they converge simultaneously, forcing an unprecedented world crisis.

All this strategy reminds us of how Satan managed his rebellion in heaven![794] Let's see how these nine areas of crisis building will eventually affect "the remnant" (Revelation 12:17) that is directly in the cross hairs of Satan's hate.

"NATURAL" DISASTERS AND ENVIRONMENTAL STRESS

Obviously, this planet has always had earthquakes, tornadoes, floods, hurricanes, typhoons and volcanoes. Some of the worst, considering human casualties, occurred centuries ago.[795] For that reason, Jesus Himself warned us of placing too much emphasis on these "natural" disasters as special signs of the end.[796] Nevertheless, in the endtime we should expect a dramatic increase in such "natural" disasters. Why? Satan wants to keep minds around the world on current distress and not on eternal matters: "Famines will increase. Pestilences will sweep away thousands. Dangers are all around us from the powers without and satanic workings within, but the restraining power of God is now being exercised."[797]

---

[794] See 29–36.

[795] For example, Krakatoa off the coast of Java (August 27, 1883), reckoned to be only the fifth most explosive volcano in history, was heard 2000 miles away, killing 40,000 people, causing huge tidal waves worldwide—the most devastating volcanic event in modern recorded history. —Simon Winchester, *Krakatoa* (New York: HarperCollins*Publishers*, 2003).

[796] "And there will be famines, pestilences, and earthquakes in various places. All these are the beginning of sorrows" —Matthew 24:7, 8. In other words, there would be *far more convincing evidence* that the end is near, such as comparing the endtime with Noah's day (verses 37-39) and the completion of the gospel commission (verse 14).

[797] *Manuscript Releases,* vol. 19, 382. "Satan is working in the atmosphere; he is poisoning the atmosphere, and here we are dependent upon God for our lives—our present and eternal lives. And being in the position that we are, we need to be wide-awake, wholly devoted, wholly converted, wholly consecrated to God. But we seem to sit as though we were paralyzed. God of heaven, wake us up!"—*Selected Messages,* bk. 2, 52. "Satan works through the elements also to garner his harvest of unprepared souls. He has studied the secrets of the laboratories of nature, and he uses all his power to control the elements as far as God allows. ... Satan has control of all whom God does not especially guard. He will favor and prosper some in order to further his own designs, and he will bring trouble upon others and lead men to believe that it is God who is afflicting them. While appearing to the children of men as a great physician who can heal all their maladies, he will bring disease and disaster, until populous cities are reduced to ruin and desolation. Even now he is at work. In accidents and calamities by sea and by land, in great conflagrations, in fierce tornadoes and terrific hailstorms, in tempests, floods, cyclones, tidal waves, and earthquakes, in every place and in a thousand forms, Satan is exercising his power. He sweeps away the ripening harvest, and famine and distress follow. He imparts to the air a deadly taint, and thousands perish by the pestilence. These visitations are to become more and more frequent and disastrous. Destruction will be upon both man and beast." —*The Great Controversy,* 589.

For example, something so universal, so precious, as water has become an international problem. *U. S. News & World Report* devoted a cover and a major article on "The Future of Water: Costly, Dirty, Scarce." Within the article, we read that "drought breeds anger: The CIA predicts that by 2015, drinking-water access could be a major source of world conflict."[798]

However, our eyes should not focus on these "signs," even though they seem to be greatly accelerated, as if they were central features of last-day events. They are simply setting the stage for the big crisis by promoting general unease and worldwide anxiety.[799] They are preparing the way for "leaders on white horses" who promise new ways to control "natural" disasters—such as "prophets" or religious leaders who can demonstrate their mystical powers by "performing great signs" (Revelation 13:13).

But the main event is elsewhere. The main event is still freedom and how it will eventually be restricted and then overridden as the world powers of Revelation 13 "deceive the whole world" into thinking that security is the sister of freedom, that the "general welfare" of the majority is the highest priority.

UNSETTLED ECONOMIC SYSTEMS WORLDWIDE

Every magazine, every business section of the newspaper, and most every financial journal seem to be singing the same tune (as I write) concerning the fragility of the world's economy. Among the developed countries, Japan, Argentina and now Germany are reeling in their financial troubles. And if Japan gets worse, the pullout of Japanese money from United States stocks and bonds would quickly drain an already frail system.

The largest accounting firms in the world, as well as gigantic world corporations, are either teetering on bankruptcy, are bankrupt, or subject to enormous fines—many of their top executives are already in prison. These are unheard of times. Difficulties in once-trusted accounting audits are causing a shudder throughout corporate America and diminishing the former trust of investors, large and small. All this adds up to unprecedented anxiety regarding the future of pensions, jobs, and the ability to pay off unparalleled mountains of debt. The Pension Benefit Guaranty Corporation, the Federal agency charged with insuring the pensions of an estimated 44 million American workers, has announced that its $8 billion surplus in 2001 had disappeared, replaced by a $3.6 billion deficit and rising.[800] In 2002 Americans set a new record for bankruptcies.[801] And few can see when the "good old days" will return.

---

[798] *U. S. News & World Report,* August 12, 2002.
[799] "Recognize that disasters in our era are not unique. ... As we have observed earlier, ... no scientific evidence exists that calamities like earthquakes, floods, plagues, and famines are more frequent now, in the final decades of this century, than the were as a whole in earlier times." —Russell Chandler, *Doomsday* (Ann Arbor, MI: Servant Publications), 296.
[800] Martin Weiss' *Safe Money Bulletin,* Mid-February, 2003.
[801] "The Dobbs Report," *U. S. News & World Report,* July 21, 2003.

One word, "uncertainty," is called a greater challenge than any other problem that the United States has waded through since the collapse of the stock market. Alan M. Webber listed four of the most telling uncertainties: criminal uncertainty in the business world; technological uncertainty without imaginative leadership to take advantage of known breakthroughs; political uncertainty as to how government and politicians can help each other; and policy uncertainties where the federal government does not speak with one voice.[802]

We are not totally blind as to what may be ahead. In Germany during the 1920s, we have a miniature preview of the last days. When an economy depends more and more on credit, its thirst will never stop, fueling an inflation that wipes out the middle class, provoking serious revolution in all social classes. In 1921, a dollar would buy 276 marks. By August 1923, it would buy 5 million! Unemployment in the millions became a constant torment; the spirit of speculation raised fruitless hopes; incalculable moral and intellectual values followed. Those nightmare years prepared Germany for the rise of a dictatorship that promised a new Germany with a new economic and social order.

Déjà vu! By August 2003, Germany's jobless rate rose to 10.4 percent (18.5 percent in eastern Germany). Germany is in its third year of stagflation with no relief in sight.[803]

All this reminds me of a laser-like insight into the economic world in the endtime:

> "There are not many, even among educators and statesmen, who comprehend the causes that underlie the present state of society. Those who hold the reigns of government are not able to solve the problem of moral corruption, poverty, pauperism, and increasing crime. They are struggling in vain to place business operations on a more secure basis."[804]

---

[802] *USA TODAY,* June 11, 2002.

[803] *Washington Post,* August 6, 2003. "The U.S. economy is out of control. The Fed is out of control. The world's biggest credit bubble is out of control. In fact, America's entire financial system is out of control and is headed for a crack-up." —Donald S. McAlvany, editor, *The McAlvany Intelligence Advisor,* January 2003.

[804] *Testimonies,* vol. 9, 13. "Many who have followed their own unsanctified will seek to end their unprofitable lives by suicide. Iniquity and crime of every order are found in the high places of the earth, and those who assent to these wrongs are seeking to shield the guilty ones from punishment. Not one-hundredth part of the corruptions that exist is being made plain to the world. Little of the cruelty that is carried on is known. The wickedness of men has almost reached its limit. In many ways Satan is revealing that he rules the world. He is influencing the hearts of men and corrupting their minds. Men in high places are giving evidence that their thoughts are evil continually. Many are seeking after riches and scruple not to add to their wealth through fraudulent transactions. The Lord is permitting these men to expose one another in their evil deeds. Some of their iniquitous practices are being laid open before the world, that thinking men who still have a desire in their hearts to be honest and just with their fellowmen may understand why God is beginning to send

Nothing would play into Satan's plans more than unrelenting economic unrest around the world, but especially so in the United States. Why? Because if the United States sneezes, the rest of the world gets pneumonia! Further, the United States runs on a river of credit and on something close to unbridled optimism. But when 401K plans dry up and one's home's value is less than its mortgage, politicians will feel the heat of the voting public.[805] Americans are quick to seek scapegoats even when the causes are purely market factors at work, or their own greed.[806] An economic crash, far exceeding the meltdown of 1929, 1987 or 2001–2, will profoundly provide the climate for Revelation 13 to heat up![807]

WHEN EVERYONE'S OPINION IS OF EQUAL VALUE—
WHEN TOLERANCE TRUMPS LOVE

The notion that there is no absolute truth is as old as human history, but it was heard only in offbeat classrooms or ranting soapbox speakers. However, probably at no time in human history is this notion more generally accepted than it is today. Gone are the days when the Bible was the common authority for all Christians and biblical principles formed the framework for the American mind. Today, especially since the 1960s, in what is called post-modernism, even rational appeals for goodness, virtue, and the right versus the wrong, are scoffed at.

His judgments on the earth." —*Testimonies to Ministers,* 457. I never was able to understand fully the observation regarding the impact of last-day "fraudulent transactions" until the Enron/Arthur Anderson Accounting debacle (and others) wherein the worst of deceit and collusion was practiced at the expense of tens of thousands of jobs, of hundreds of millions of stockholder dollars, and of hundreds of thousands of pensions that were wiped out virtually overnight. And then watch, as weeks went by, those who were not directly injured and how easily the prediction fit: "Iniquity is becoming so common a thing that it no longer shocks the senses as it once did." —Letter 258, 1907, cited in *Last Day Events,* 27.

[805] Michael J. Mandel's column in *Business Week* (February 25, 2002) highlights the "moral outrage" of those hurt by not only the Enron collapse (2001) but the general burst of the stock market bubble (2000–2001): "Basically, investors and workers are incensed at being snookered into taking risks they didn't understand and wouldn't have willingly accepted. Enron lied to stockholders and workers about the risks they faced. Venture capitalists brought high-risk startups public without clearly informing investors of the dangers. And more broadly, greedy executives and financiers have been shifting risk to other people without their informed consent, undermining their security." 114.

[806] Alan Greenspan observed that "an infectious greed seemed to grip much of our business community. It is not that humans have become any more greedy than in generations past. It is that the avenues to express greed had grown so enormously." —*New York Times,* July 17, 2002. How true it is: Even the rosiest dawn of greed sooner or later gives way to a cold midnight of fear.

[807] In the French election in May, 2002, Jean-Marie Le Pen, although defeated, used an appeal that attracted many: "When people hungry for a simply response in complex social and economic forces unsettling their lives, they offered a scapegoat: people who look different and represent change. If the majority parties don't respond, the demagogues gain power. ... Europe today is in the throes of dramatic change brought on by economic globalization and declining birth rates. —*USA TODAY,* May 6, 2002.

This approach to right and wrong surely sets the world up to believe in anything, if it satisfies the need of the moment. For instance, why let old ideas about which day is the Sabbath of the Fourth Commandment get in the way of a united America? Why should old enmities between Protestants and Catholics divide people in the twenty-first century when we have more reasons to unite than to stay divided?

John Stott, pastor of All Souls Langham Place in London since 1950 (his only pastorship), has been called "the most influential clergyman in the Church of England during the twentieth century."[808] Stott recently addressed the question of why so many moderns do not listen to the Christian gospel—"critics accuse us of intolerance and proselytism."

Then he defined the semantic problem with the word "tolerance": "First, there is *legal* tolerance, fighting for the equal rights before the law. ... Second, there is *social* tolerance, going out of our way to make friends with adherents of other faiths. ... Third, there is *intellectual* tolerance. This is to cultivate a mind so broad and open as to accommodate all views and reject none. ... To open the mind so wide as to keep nothing in it or out of it is not a virtue; it is the vice of the feebleminded."

But, or Stott, his "main concern for the church everywhere is that we often do not look like what we are talking about. We make great claims for Christ, but there is often a credibility gap between our words and our actions."[809]

All this tolerance in religious matters especially soon develops into unintended consequences. Suddenly college campuses are in uproar when "the politically correct left now relies more on coercion than on persuasion or moral appeal. The long-term trend is to depict dissent from the gay agenda as a form of illegitimate and punishable expression. ... Will the leaders of the gay-rights movement please speak a little more clearly about freedom of speech and freedom of religion?"[810]

NO GLOSSING OVER

In a very insightful letter written to her nephew, Frank Belden, in 1878, Ellen White reflected clearly how upside-down moral values will be viewed in the judgment:

> "Every man's work will stand for just what it is. There will be no glossing over of wrongs and sins. Right will stand out, clear and prominently, as right; fidelity and true integrity will not be called narrowness or meanness. Lawlessness and unfaithfulness will not be

---

[808] *Christianity Today* September 16, 1996.
[809] *Christianity Today,* September, 2003.
[810] John Leo, "Coercion on Campus," —*U. S. News & World Report,* May 15, 2000.

termed liberality, toleration, and benevolence. Neglect and unfaith-fulness will be neglect and unfaithfulness."[811]

The path to the end of the endtime becomes cloudy with slippery phrases such as political correctness and greased with word-reversals: love becomes tolerance and responsibilities become rights. For instance, on one hand, political correctness spawns diversity of behavior and ideas but it usually does not include diversity of ideas with which they do not agree.[812] Words like multiculturalism, diversity, values-clarification, and sensitivity training have become code words for the amazingly successful attack on fundamental Judeo-Christian principles.

When *The Day American Told the Truth* was published in the early 1990s the results were astounding—not because they were unexpected but because of the phenomenal differences between the 1950s and the early 1990s. Using state-of-the-art research techniques, it was the largest survey of private morals ever undertaken. Among the comparisons, Americans now are making up their own rules: in the '50s, a moral consensus existed when "all our institutions commanded more respect." Lying has become "an integral part of the American culture, a trait of the American character. ... And the people we lie to most are those closest to us."[813]

HURRICANE FORCE SINCE THE 1960S

Most observers agree that the great divide in social/moral areas has blown with hurricane force, beginning in the middle 1960s. Daniel Yankelovich, one of America's most respected analysts of social trends and public attitudes, devoted a book to detailing the tectonic shift in America from generations of responsibility, self-denial for the sake of family and others, and deferred gratification to that of self-fulfillment and rejection of consensus in what is right and wrong.[814]

Yankelovich wrote: "The ethics of the search for self-fulfillment discard many of the traditional rule of personal conduct. They permit more sexual

---

[811] *Manuscript Releases*, vol. 20, 70.

[812] Think of the left's assault on free speech when they organized the enormous boycott of television stations and willing sponsors in their successful attempt to drive Dr. Laura Schlessinger off television in 2001. Dr. Schlessinger's daily radio program is one of the most listened to programs in the United States, constantly upholding the Ten Commandments and fidelity in all areas of life.

[813] James Patterson and Peter Kim, *The Day America Told The Truth* (New York: Prentice Hall, 1991), 3–8.

[814] Daniel Yankelovich, *New Rules* (New York: Random House, 1981). The cover story of *Time*, October 5, 1992, was "Lying, Everybody's Doing It (Honest)." One of the letters to the editor, October 26, 1992, said, "I can think of no better way to encourage lying than to tell people that 'everybody's doin' it." Another letter remembered a cartoon that showed a vending machine where for 25 cents you could get the "truth"; for 50 cents, you could get the "whole truth"; and for 75 cents you could get" the truth, the whole truth, and nothing but the truth."

freedom, for example, and they put less emphasis on sacrifice 'for its own sake.' In their extreme form, the new rules simply turn the old ones on their head, and in place of the old self-denial ethic we find people who refuse to deny *anything* to themselves—not out of bottomless appetite, but on the strange moral principle that 'I have a duty to myself.'"[815]

One of the interesting features of the self-fulfillment era is that freedom is indeed "exhilarating," holding a "theory of freedom that seems to presuppose that you are free only when you do not commit yourself irrevocably."[816] Spell that "living together with the significant other," "religion matters when it feels right" or "all paths to heaven lead to the top."

Yankelovich shows in many areas how these "new rules" have probably changed the American landscape forever: "Virtually all the recent normative changes in America have moved toward great tolerance, openness, choice and a wider range of acceptable behavior." But to where does all this choice lead: "The error of replacing self-denial with a duty-to-self ethic has proven nearly fatal, for nothing has subverted self-fulfillment more thoroughly than self-indulgence."[817]

Summing up, Yankelovich reports:

> "The self-denial ethic was itself a response to signals that to gain the 'getting' part of the giving/getting compact, Americans needed to surrender important aspects of self. For generations, life experience reinforced this response: self-denial did pay off. Once the signals shifted, the self-denial ethic began to lose its appeal. ... It responded to false economic signals that said affluence comes automatically, entitlements are guaranteed by government, more of everything is a realistic goal and the problems of supply are solved forever. It also responded to misleading psychological signals that inner feelings are sacred objects and that undivided dedication to them will satisfy one's cravings for transcendence."[818]

I am not primarily concerned at this point with analyzing in detail the social/moral landscape of the early twenty-first century. Although tempted, I don't have the space to examine the "victimhood" phenomena since the 1960s. Too often, it has become another form of rights substituting for responsibilities. Nor am I especially concerned here with the cult of the disadvantaged, wherein too many overreach their situation as they focus on

---

[815] *Ibid.*, xvii.
[816] *Ibid.*, 61.
[817] *Ibid.*, 87, 146.
[818] *Ibid.*, 260. See also Tex Sample, *U.S. Lifestyles and Mainline Churches* (Louisville, KY: Westminister/ John Knox, 1990, 9–21.

the "duty-to-self" ethic; nor with the mushrooming of "grievance groups" that expect to be "greeted with compassionate acceptance."[819]

Obviously, many in these groups have legitimate concerns and need whatever help is available. But too often this emphasis on entitlement rights and the muting of personal responsibility, this knee-jerk support for any group that defends its own diversity (or deviation) with legal coercion against those who think and act differently is setting the stage for the end of the endtime. The social landscape becomes used to legal coercion by any group that seems "different."

Judge Learned Hand, 1872–1961, arguably "the greatest judge never appointed judge of the Supreme Court," feared the emotional and political climate (diverse groups promoting ample laws to protect their interests, laws that give them speedy access to the court system to sue those who disagree with them) developing in his day: "[This] much I do know—that a society so riven that the spirit of moderation is gone, no court *can* save; that a society where that spirit flourishes, no court *need* save; that in a society which evades its responsibility by thrusting upon the courts the nurture of that spirit, that spirit in the end will perish."[820]

SUPREME COURT REVERSES

One of the more interesting examples of how the Supreme Court has reversed itself in recent years is *Agostini v. Felton*, a 1997 establishment clause case. Twelve years earlier, the Court had ruled against New York City's plan to pay the salaries of public employees who offered remedial courses in parochial schools in *Aguilar v. Felton*, 473 U.S. 402 (1985). However, in *Agostini v. Felton*, 521 U.S. 203, 117 (1997), disregarding their own precedent, the Court ruled that public school money could pay for instruction in parochial schools.

Referring to the Supreme Court's recent overturning of anti-sodomy laws in the United States in June 2003, Justice Ruth Bader Ginsberg said

---

[819] For example, the rage among some deaf people against cochlear implants because it is an "example of intolerance and aggression that removes deaf children from their culture. ... Though obesity is rarely thought of as a disability, the size-acceptance movement uses the same logic as the disabilities movement. Trying to reduce a child's weight is positioned as an illegitimate attack on the differently sized. Words such as 'overweight' and 'fit' are often put in quotation marks to isolate their own standards and the idea that stoutness is a problem."—John Leo, "Deaf to good sense," *U.S. News & World Report*, March 25, 2002.

[820] Cited in Robert H. Bork, "No Court Can Save Us," *Wall Street Journal*, December 5, 2000. I am reminded of Charlton Heston's speech at the Harvard Law School Forum, February 16, 1999, wherein he said that "a cultural war is raging across our land, in which, with Orwellian fervor, certain acceptable thoughts and speech are mandated. ... If Americans believed in political correctness, we'd still be King George's boys—subjects bound to the British Crown. ... Underneath, the nation is roiling. Americans know something without a name, is undermining the nation, turning the mind mushy when it comes to separating truth from falsehood and right from wrong."

that the Court "is looking beyond America's borders for guidance in handling cases on issues like the death penalty and gay rights." She said that the justices referred to the findings of foreign courts in their own ruling, which led some in the minority to wonder what would come next with that kind of reasoning.[821] Justices Breyer and Kennedy have also considered the emerging world consensus on cases under their view.[822] *The mood of the changing majority overrules.*

Gerald C. Grimaud, former Pennsylvania assistant attorney general, wrote recently, "The courts are the final guardians of our individual and minority rights. When the majority of the U.S. Supreme Court fails to follow its own precedents, fails to consider the great history and utility of the establishment clause, we're in trouble."[823]

Grimaud is prescient. His warning applies to many areas of concern that work their way through the courts. What once was considered right or wrong is now up for grabs. We all know the problem of confronting this mental "mush." No one enjoys being labeled intolerant.[824] How often has a thought leader called hate-filled, obscene lyrics in best-selling CDs (celebrated as expressions of youth culture!) exactly what they are—evil? Not often, for they would be "mean-spirited" and "intolerant." What happens when brave parents and a few national leaders speak up for Christian principles? They are labeled "intolerant." The world is fast becoming a place in which people embrace lies and run from the truth. It is difficult for truth to survive when we lose the language of truth. Even more difficult, when free-swinging zealots for free expression flee from debate while attacking and excoriating ad hominem (attack the person, not his arguments).

Talk shows, columnists, those on the right and left, observe this late phenomenon: everyone except religious folks seem to have the right to express an opinion. When the topic is alternative lifestyles or values-free sex education, those who object are ridiculed. But even when prayer is voluntary, students are suddenly labeled a "captive audience." Religious freedom stops when somebody claims to be offended. "The courts have granted First Amendment protection to behaviors that offend all but a very few. How can they deny protection to prayers that offend only a few?"[825]

Sidney Hook, political scientist, starkly observed: "I believe any people in the world, when roused to a fury of nationalistic resentment, and convinced that some individual or group is responsible for their continued and extreme misfortunes, can be led to do or countenance the same things the Germans

---

[821] "Ginsburg: Int'l Law Shaped Court Rulings," Gina Holland, Associated Press Writer, Yahoo! News, August 2, 2003.

[822] "Creeping transnationalism," John Leo, *U.S News & World Report,* July 21, 2003.

[823] "Collateral Attack on the Establishment Clause," *Liberty,* September/October, 2003, 14.

[824] See 288.

[825] Rep. Ernest Istook, RS-Okla., *The Sacramento Bee,* August 18, 1997.

did. I believe that if conditions in the United States were ever to become as bad psychologically and economically as they were in Germany in the 1920s and 1930s, systematic racial persecution might break out. It could happen to the Blacks, but it could happen to the Jews too, or any targeted group."[826]

Only a few living today can measure how far most Christian churches have come in half a century, at least in the United States. For example, some call it distressing as they see Adventists increasingly choosing a church to "visit" on Sabbath mornings. Few of their reasons are inherently "bad," but all too often people are choosing their church services without regard for doctrinal purity or reliable teaching. Convenience, comfort, and emotion tend to be the values that drive too many—with the result that many Adventists are indistinguishable from the general public.[827]

We are talking about our responsibilities in these cloudy times. How do Sabbath-keepers respond to the lies, contrived logic and even self-serving laws that have been drawn up in the past few years *that suddenly will be aimed at them?* We can't merely call all this mental "mush." That would only infuriate those who already are mentally shaped by the prevailing mood of these last days. It is a time for great prudence and common sense, a time when it has never been more relevant to proclaim the Sabbath more fully.[828]

FREEDOM, THE CORE ISSUE

The issues are freedom of choice, of whom to worship, and a timely, re-emphasis on America's richest heritage built into its historic fabric.[829] No longer will the issues center on a particular denomination grasping for its rights. God's loyalists will simply be America's spokesmen, flying the flag that its illustrious founders first unfurled at the risk of their fortunes and their lives.[830]

---

[826] Ursula Owen, "Hate Speech, The Speech that Kills," Iain Walker Memorial Lecture, Oxford University, 1999.

[827] Compare Charles Colson, "Breakpoint," *Commentary* #0110719, 7/19/2001.

[828] "I saw that God had children who do not see and keep the Sabbath. They have not rejected the light upon it. And at the commencement of the time of trouble, we were filled with the Holy Ghost as we went forth and proclaimed the Sabbath more fully. This enraged the churches and nominal Adventists, as they could not refute the Sabbath truth. And at this time God's chosen all saw clearly that we had the truth, and they came out and endured the persecution with us. I saw the sword, famine, pestilence, and great confusion in the land. The wicked thought that we had brought the judgments upon them, and they rose up and took counsel to rid the earth of us, thinking that then the evil would be stayed." —*Early Writings*, 33.

[829] One test of our clear understanding of freedom of choice is to consider the implications of "flag-burning." Other than the emotional resentment, especially by members of the armed forces or their grieving families, the larger issue according to Justice Brennan in his Opinion of the Court is: "We do not consecrate the flag by punishing its desecration, for in doing so we dilute the freedom that this cherished emblem represents." —*Texas v. Johnson*, 491 U.S. 397, 420 (1989). "Forced allegiance detracts from free-will allegiance big time." —Gerald Grimaud, attorney in Tunkhannock, PA, in a personal letter, February 16, 2002.

[830] U.S. Declaration of Independence.

Supreme Court Justice Clarence Thomas said recently that "by yielding to a false form of civility, we sometimes allow our critics to intimidate us. Active citizens are often subjected to truly vile attacks, they are branded as mean-spirited, racist, Uncle Tom, homophobic, sexist, etc." As a result, he added that sometimes "we censor ourselves. This is not civility; it is cowardice, a well-intentioned self-deception at best." Further, "we are required to wade into those things that matter to our country and our culture, no matter what the disincentives are or the personal cost."[831]

Of course, for different reasons, "self-censorship" is a biblical principle (Matthew 5:37; 7:1–6; 12:36, 37; 1 Corinthians 9: 19–23; Titus 3:2, etc.). Jesus counseled His disciples that they should be "wise as serpents and harmless as doves" (Matthew 10:16). Christians should be examples of those who are most careful and civil in "attacking" other religions. They withhold "truth," that is, biblical teachings that may appear offensive if not approached wisely, awaiting the occasion when "truth" will be best understood. That is not cowardice, but simply kindness and gentleness in loving others.

Interesting times ahead! Like storm clouds on the near horizon!

---

[831] February 13, 2001, Associated Press Writer, Laurie Asseo, *Yahoo News.*

CHAPTER THIRTY-FIVE:
CIRCUMSTANCES CONTRIBUTING TO THE COMING CRISIS—PART 2

Think of those two friends on the corner of Fifth and Broadway, New York City, watching two others carrying sandwich signs. One sign said, "The world is about to end." The other, "The world will never end." Then one bystander said to other, "One of those men is an optimist and the other is a pessimist. But I can't tell which is which!"

This interesting choice is not merely academic or humorous. I remember when 1984 came and went. The world relaxed because George Orwell's *1984* failed to appear in the dark world of Big Brotherhood. But we seem to be numb to another dark world also predicted—Aldous Huxley's *Brave New World.* Orwell foresaw an externally imposed oppression; Huxley predicted that people, still with their history intact, would come to love their oppression, to adore their blessed technologies that would undo their ability to think. Orwell feared those who would ban books; Huxley feared the time when happy people would not sense the necessity to read. Orwell dreaded those who would hide truth; Huxley dreaded the day when truth "would be drowned in irrelevance."

Huxley noted that Orwell in *1984* saw people controlled by others who inflicted pain, but in his *Brave New World,* inflicting pleasure controls them. "In short, Orwell feared that what we hate will ruin us. Huxley feared that what we love will ruin us."[832]

EASY TO BE PESSIMISTIC

Pessimism is easy to come by in a world that seems to be schooled in the sciences, wherein reality alone can be true if it is measured and weighed. Any idea that there is "a better day" coming for this planet of limited resources "has been disrupted by natural sciences. ... We have to learn that there is no scientific justification of hope. All long-term predictions seem to be clearly contradictory to hope. ... Recent theories of cosmology agree that the world will come to an end either by slowly, yet certainly, going cold—or just the other way: by progressive warming up and burning. The result seems to be the same: extermination."[833]

On May 5, 2002, investment guru, the Sage of Omaha, Warren Buffet warned more than 10,000 of his Berkshire Hathaway shareholders that

---

[832] Postman, Neil, *Amusing Ourselves to Death* (New York: Penguin Books, 1985), vii, viii.

[833] Polkinghorne, John, and Michael Welker, eds., *The End of the World and the Ends of God* (Harrisburg, PA: Trinity Press International, 2000), 218, 219.

another terrorist attack on American soil is "virtually a certainty" and that Washington and New York would be the top two targets because terrorists want to traumatize the country and kill as many people as possible.[834]

Pessimism can overwhelm those who focus on "avoiding Armageddon," the title of a disturbing four-part, eight-hour documentary series on PBS that began on March 4, 2003. Intoned by Walter Cronkite, the episodes focused on "poisons and plagues," nuclear nightmares, "young terrorists," and "turning the tide of AIDS and world instability." *The New York Times* opined, "These nightly editions create an almost unbearable tension that may send many viewers fleeing from their televisions in anxiety. ... This well-intentioned series does little more than fan flames of fear."[835]

Such will be some of the murky choices in the crescendo of last-day events, especially in the United States. And this is exactly how Satan will keep the issues confused. We have been looking at pessimistic events in the endtime, such as increasing "natural" disasters, astounding "fraudulent transactions" that shatter confidence and cause huge personal distress, over-whelming concessions to immorality wherein nothing is right or wrong but merely a matter of opinion.

But Satan is not dumb! He knows that pessimism often leads many to seek help from a Higher Power; church attendance goes up in times of crisis (if only temporarily). He is only interested in confusion, either playing up what seems to be to some horrendous predictions of world disasters because some revel in the dark side,[836] or for others, playing the optimism card.

OPTIMISM IS APPEALING

So let's follow the other side of Satan's endtime strategy—the appeal of better days ahead! When probation closes, for most people, this world would never have looked so good! Even as Noah could not pierce the fog of lies that preachers, teachers, and politicians had spread in his day, so last-day heralds of Christ's soon return will meet the same optimistic fog.

Note the clarity of this statement:

> "Come when it may, the day of God will come unawares to the ungodly. When life is going on in its unvarying round; when men are absorbed in pleasure, in business, in traffic, in money-making; when religious leaders are magnifying the world's progress and enlightenment, and the people are lulled in a false security—then, as the midnight thief steals within the unguarded dwelling, so shall sudden destruction

---

[834] Associated Press, Sunday, May 5, 2002.

[835] Ron Wertheimer, "Cronkite on Famine, Pestilence and Death," *The New York Times*, March 4, 2003.

[836] *The Futurist* (Jan/Feb 1995) exposed the fallacies of bogus doomsday predictions such as global famine, exhaustion of nonrenewable resources, rise of air pollution, coming ice age, Antarctic ozone hole, and global warming.

come upon the careless and ungodly, 'and they shall not escape'"
(1 Thessalonians 5:3).[837]

For a little perspective, think about the past 50 years. Think about what
transistors and microelectronics have done for almost every industry, every
home. Think about computers that can make trillions of computations
per second![838] Think about Sun Microsystems that has discovered a way to
transmit data inside a computer 60 to 100 times faster as the present fastest
computer, eliminating the traditional circuit board.[839] Think of nanotech-
nology (one nanometer is one-billionth of a meter, roughly four atoms, with
75,000 nanometers to equal a human hair) that will make transistors 100-
times smaller and 1,000-times faster than the present smallest transistor.
One benefit—they will possess the heat therapy capable of targeting only
cancer cells. Think about MRI and CAT body scanners, Teflon, lasers, organ
transplants, polymers, discovering the DNA double helix, screen stents for
blocked arteries, and plastic splices for aneurysms—just for starters! Or the
Salk vaccine (when was the last time we visited a polio victim in the hospital).[840] Problems that seemed formidable only 50 years ago are now forgotten as if they had never existed—or, if remembered, only as relics of what
seem to be medieval times! Now, multiply these successes by a factor of 100
and you will begin to realize what we can expect in the next few years!

According to medical research, soon we can expect vaccines to inocu-
late against most forms of cancer even as we have virtually freed the world
of smallpox, whooping cough, and polio in the last few years. For example,
treatment of pancreatic cancer, probably one of the most vicious of all cancers, has shown remarkable results with a new vaccine that eliminates the
need for conventional treatments such as chemotherapy and radiotherapy.
Similar cancers have also shown gratifying results. Though only on limited
numbers, research continues on larger testing groups.[841]

The amazing speed in deciphering the entire human DNA (genome)
with its 60,000 or so genes has been far faster and cheaper than first estimated. Genetic engineering will pinpoint the faulty genes that cause many

---

[837] *The Great Controversy,* 38; see also 338.

[838] IBM's ASCI Purple and Blue Gene/L are the fastest and most powerful computers ever built. Purple
will "complete 100 thousand billion calculations per second (a speed known as 100 teraflops)."
Blue, with a broader range of functions will have" a maximum speed of 360 teraflops." —Mark
Henderson, TIMESONLINE, November 19, 2002.

[839] *New York Times,* September 19, 2003.

[840] I remember vividly my days in the Hinsdale Sanitarium and Hospital (1952), diagnosed with
polio. All around me were iron lungs, helping other patients to breathe. Parents were not allowing
children to go to swimming pools or grocery stores. It was a very stressful time for many parents. I
thank the Lord for one miraculous night when the fever left suddenly and polio germs died in the
spinal column.

[841] www.thisislondon.co.uk/news/articles/68192027?version=1 ©2003 Associated New Media.

of our diseases, inherited and acquired. These findings not only help physicians diagnose problems even in the womb, they provide ways by which the mutated gene can be manipulated to offset the potential damage. It has been estimated that half of our drugs in the next few years could result from gene therapy.[842]

In other words, DNA vaccines will soon be as common as tetanus shots. As I write, researchers are finishing their successful experiments with monkeys that promise a DNA vaccine to prevent rabies, which kills 40,000 people annually. DNA vaccines are inexpensive to make and require no refrigeration—a great benefit to developing nations.

Molecular biologists are predicting that living to the age of 600 is now believable. In fact, an editorial titled, "Where is Thy Sting?" (referring to 1 Corinthians 15:55; Hosea 13:14) said that "genetic medicine is making enormous strides, and it may hold the promise—or maybe its peril—of eventually making us something closer to immortal. 'Our life expectancy will be in the region of 500 years' in rich countries in the year 2100 predicts Aubrey de Grey, a scholar at Cambridge University."[843]

Soon, most anybody will be able to put a navigational device (global positioning system) in the palm of one's hands. Already being used by the military and available for approximately $2,000 in some automobiles, this gadget will give holders their exact position on earth, how far to any other spot on earth, providing the precise road directions to get there at selected speeds, the total distance, and time of sunrise and sunset. Bouncing off satellites, this navigation device will make it impossible for anyone to be lost, either for the holders or for those desiring to know their location! As I write, hand-held units with limited but amazing capabilities are available with built-in software for around $200. That seems astonishing! But we haven't seen anything yet!

Wherever we look, pessimistic doomsayers are continually being proven wrong. This world will soon find sources for renewable energy other than oil and gas. The so-called population explosion, the scarcity of food and world famine, the environmental hysteria including Carl Sagan's "nuclear winter" frenzy, the "greenhouse effect" and atmospheric pollution that some opined

---

[842] A largely unanticipated bonus provided by DNA research has been its exposure of system flaws in the criminal justice system. Its certainty in identifying people far surpasses the accuracy of fingerprints. "The odds against DNA mismatches are said to be in the realm of a quadrillion to one. ... Police and prosecutorial misconduct are among the most frequent facts in wrongful convictions, according to the Innocence Project, which has championed the use of DNA evidence." As of August 2002, "108 wrongfully convicted individuals served a total of 1,119 years in prison"—truly a microcosm of the Great Controversy wherein justice and misrepresentation are in combat. See William DiMascio, "DNA evidence exposes system flaws," —*The Philadelphia Inquirer*, August 7, 2002.

[843] Nicholas D. Kristof, "Where is Thy Sting?" —*New York Times*, August 12, 2003. See *Ananova*, "Humans could live for hundreds of years," www.ananova.com/news/story 10/24/2003.

would create a clutch of worldwide disorders—all these dreary forecasts are being eclipsed by modern discoveries and everyday wonders.[844] According to the experts, we can look forward to an increased cadence of startling and wonderful breakthroughs in the near future.

Really, who wouldn't say that the world is getting better and better? Especially when a new cruise liner, *The World*, with its 110 apartments, is sailing the oceans. Costs range from $2 million to $6.8 million for the biggest 300 square meters, three-bedroom apartment. Extra charges per apartment range from $100,000 to $340,000 a year to pay for the 320 crew and other expenses.

Included are Jacuzzis on private terraces, a casino, a sauna, a real grass putting green and a tennis court. Before the inaugural voyage on February 20, 2002, 80 of the 110 apartments had been sold with the rest expected to be sold within the year. The average owner's age is about 55. Forty percent are from the United States with the rest from Europe and elsewhere. *The World* is only one of many other places on earth where money is never an issue and an opulent lifestyle is as common as the nearest Denny's restaurant.[845]

OPTIMISTS ARE BOTH RIGHT AND WRONG

No, optimists are right—the world will not end in either a whimper or a bang. World nuclear powers will not incinerate the earth; we will not drown or be suffocated in our own garbage, nor shrivel up in mass starvation.

But optimists are also wrong—the future is not in the hands of ingenious men and women who, up to now, have always come up with the necessary solutions to "whatever" problems. Technology will not cure, for example, the self-interest of relatives or neighbors, or nations, as they grab for what they have not earned, trampling others in their pursuit. Technology may recycle used glass and metals, but not the rising tide of moral garbage that mocks the rising standard of living everywhere on this planet.

Technology will not eliminate deceit and spinmeisters who make a career out of repackaging morally deficient leaders. Technology, in itself, will not be able to produce trust and fairness—regardless of Hollywood's ability to substitute style for substance.

What indeed could be more suffocating than a disease-cured world, filled with computerized homes with the latest labor-saving devices for all, guaranteeing adequate food for every man, woman, and child (all very probable expectations)—if that world wallows in its comforts and sensual excesses, valuing security above freedom, while scorning the time-honored values of

---

[844] Sallie Baliunas, Astrophysicist, Harvard-Smithsonian Center for Astrophysics, reviewed the Kyoto Protocol. After analyzing all the arguments, she summarized that "on scientific, economic and political grounds, the Kyoto Protocol as an attempt to control this risk while improving the human condition is flawed." —*Imprimis*, March, 2002.

[845] Reuters, Trondheim, Norway, February 20, 2002.

honesty, fidelity in marriage and concern for constitutional freedoms. In this new era of genetic medicine, life tends to be commodity rather than a creation. When we lose our ethical compass, the question becomes, "What is possible?" rather than "What is right?"

So, with this unprecedented "wonderful" world full of more promises than we can keep up with, Satan will try hard to keep comfortable, disease-free, over-stimulated men and women occupied and unconcerned regarding real events in these endtimes. Even as Noah's contemporaries choked on the fog of optimism, so will those unprepared for the return of Jesus.

CREATE MORAL INSENSITIVITY

Jesus compared the endtime with the frightful days Noah lived in prior to the Flood: "But as the days of Noah were, so also will the coming of the Son of Man be" (Matthew 24:37). What could Jesus have meant? What do we know about the "days of Noah"?

Very early in the history of humanity, men and women must have been magnificent physical specimens and incredibly knowledgeable in all things mechanical, medical, and philosophical—compared to us! But we read the dark side of this morning of world history in Genesis 6: "Then the Lord saw that the wickedness of man was great in the earth, and that every intent of the thoughts of his heart was only evil continually. ... The earth is filled with violence through them" (Genesis 6:5, 13).

Why aren't the front pages of newspapers and prime-time television and radio filled with outrage at the hundreds of Christian martyrs killed monthly on Planet Earth! Most persecution and death occur in Saudi Arabia, Myanmar, Sudan, Somalia, China, Iran, Morocco, Libya, Egypt and Algeria. And every death is a story of how that person was "faithful unto death" (Revelation 2:10). Every year the U. S. State Department prepares a major document on global religious persecution—and it is promptly filed away. Why? International relations and trade is more important than the worth of an individual: the end justifies the means if it is for the "common good."[846]

But Christians are not the only ones killed for their religious beliefs. Note the horror in India for decades between Hindus and Moslems. While writing these lines, close to one hundred Shiites and their leading cleric were killed outside their mosque in Najaf, Iraq (August 2003). Whatever the religious beliefs, martyrs for their religious convictions keep adding to the blood spilled in this world ruled by the Evil Empire.

---

[846] World Refugee Survey 2002, World Refugee Statistics, U. S. Committee for Refugees, U.S. Government; www.houstonperspectives.com/mission

And we must never forget that Christians have often been the "killers"—even in modern times—let's not forget Nazi Germany's Christians who knew about and participated in the Jewish Holocaust!

What happens to any of us when long exposed to horror or lust or deceit? We all know the experience of reading or seeing on television the stories of Bosnian or Cambodian massacres, or years of Iraqi suppression by a ruthless leader, of rampaging hurricanes and floods, of Sudanese famine, of Colombian executions of civic and church leaders. It may be on the first page at first, maybe, but soon we flip the pages numbly—we have seen it all before. It takes a huge disaster, and it must be closer to home, before we realize the horror of such things and stop to read beyond the headline.

The same happens with pornography. It may begin with magazines flaunted at the super-market checkout stands. Perhaps an interesting book, true or fiction. For hundreds of thousands, a couple of pecks on the computer keyboard and the world of pornography blasts one's senses. I have heard about a pastor's wife who became so involved with her intriguing obsessions that she didn't feed her children with any pattern or continue to care for her home—nor did she contest the forthcoming divorce. But this pattern—the innocent moment, the flirting kiss, the hidden magazine or website, the exciting rendezvous—almost always leads downhill fast. Lust is always played out on a slippery slope and no one knows that better than Satan.

No one starts out knowing the end of that first slip into moral numbness. But is there anyone alive in any country of this world who is immune to the steady tug of lust, now tolerated in most schools everywhere, or in the most degraded slums or fanciest condos, or in office parties or college campuses, or wherever. Billboards, movie advertising trailers during innocent television programs, required reading in even religious schools—all function on a gutter level that would not have been permitted 40 years ago. The more we are immersed in lust or horror or deceit, the less evil it becomes, even for those who choose to avoid it![847]

Robert H. Bork, distinguished jurist and law professor, wrote:

> "So unrelenting is the assault on our sensibilities that many of us grow numb, finding resignation to be the rational, adaptive response to an environment that is increasingly polluted and apparently beyond our control. That is what Senator Daniel Patrick Moynihan calls 'defining deviancy down.' Moynihan cites the 'Durkheim constant.' Emile Durkheim, a founder of sociology, posited that there is a limit to the amount of deviant behavior any community can

---

[847] See 55 for Alexander Pope's remarkable insight into the slippery slope of evil.

'afford to recognize.' As behavior worsens, the community adjusts its standards so that conduct once thought reprehensible is no longer deemed so."[848]

In the late 1990s, the United States had a laboratory view of morality at work in public view. It was put forth that private character had nothing to do with public expectations, that lies about sex under oath don't matter, that we all should be less judgmental and more tolerant, more forgiving. If and when these arguments take root in American soil, whatever moral clarity has helped produce the American nation will be sadly missing.

Underneath these various examples of morality earthquakes is a strategy, not simply inevitable evolution. Note Berit Kjos' warning:

"Emotional shock therapy has become standard fare in public schools from coast to coast. It produces cognitive dissonance—mental and moral confusion—especially in students trained to follow God's guidelines. While classroom topics may range from homosexual or occult practices to euthanasia and suicide, they all challenge and stretch His moral boundaries. But why?

"'[Our objective] will require a change in the prevailing culture—the attitudes, values, norms and accepted ways of doing things,' says Mark Tucker, the mastermind behind the school-to-work and *workforce development* program now being implemented in every state. Working with Hillary Clinton and other globalist leaders, he called for a *paradigm shift*—a total transformation in the way people think, believe and perceive reality.

"This new paradigm rules out traditional values and biblical truth, which are now considered hateful and intolerant. ... All religions must be pressed into the mold of the new global spirituality. Since globalist leaders tout this world religion as a means of building public awareness of our supposed planetary oneness, biblical Christianity doesn't fit. It is simply 'too exclusive' and 'judgmental.'"[849]

---

[848] Robert H. Bork, *Slouching Towards Gomorrah* (New York: HarperCollins*Publishers*, 1996), 3. " The defining characteristics of modern liberalism are radical egalitarianism (the equality of outcomes rather than of opportunities) and radical individualism (the drastic reduction of limits to personal gratifications). These may see an odd pair, for individualism means liberty and liberty produces inequality, while equality of outcomes means coercion and coercions destroys liberty. ... Radical egalitarianism necessarily presses us towards collectivism because a powerful state is required to suppress the differences that freedom produces. That raises the sinister and seemingly paradoxical possibility that radical individualism is the handmaiden of collectivist tyranny. ... The upshot is that the democratic nation is helpless before an antidemocratic, indeed a despotic judiciary. The American people seem, at the moment, to be submissive and without the political will to reclaim the liberty that is rightfully theirs." 5, 6, 119.

[849] Berit Kjos, *Mind Control*, www.crossroad.to/text/articles/me 9/24/95.

Why do we need to say all this? Because the numbed mind with a cavalier attitude toward evil will find it virtually impossible to either grasp or appreciate the call to "worship Him who made heaven and earth" and to join those who "keep the commandments of God and the faith of Jesus" (Revelation 14:12). That's why Noah, "a preacher of righteousness" (2 Peter 2:5), found such resistance when the world was coming to its end in his day. And why Jesus sighed, "When the Son of Man comes, will He really find faith on the earth?" (Luke 18:8).

TERRORISM ADDS TO ENDTIME PERPLEXITIES

Every morning as I write these pages I check *The New York Times* for the latest headlines. I had been keeping count of those killed by suicide bombs or shot in the Palestine-Israeli conflict, but I gave up after 2,000 were killed! Think of Bali and the enormous truck bomb that hit the U.N. Headquarters in Iraq on August 19, 2003! Or the latest suicide bombings in Baghdad!

We can add the terror that lurks in the shadows daily in Ireland, Somalia, Sudan, Kosovo, Bosnia, Afghanistan, Iraq, Philippians, Sri Lanka, or throughout Indonesia. Most of these terror areas are generated by religious controversies!

But the oceans of the world barricaded the United States from these live-in terrorists—until September 11, 2001. When planes became missiles and icons of prosperity became targets, people died—blasted into eternity. No place on earth is safe from malevolent terrorists; no life is sacred, even in the "land of the free and the home of the brave."

Then add to this obvious threat of air terrorism the invisible touch of anthrax or similar deadly poison—and every home with a mailbox is a terrorist's target.

RASH OF CHILD ABDUCTIONS AND MURDERS

Another kind of terror has darkened American homes for years—the rash of child abductions and killings in recent months. Parents and children fear the night when abductors slip into their own bedrooms. Or snatch children on the way to school or in crowded malls. Fear of the unknown has become common talk, a phenomenon not known only a few years ago.

But think of teenagers, drenched in video horror games and armed to their teeth, killing off their fellow classmates and teachers. Columbine[850] has become a household word that puts a new level of dread into schools everywhere.

---

[850] On April 20, 1999, two students in black trench coats killed 12 schoolmates and a teacher at Columbine High School, most of them in the library. The gunmen, called the "Trenchcoat Mafia," killed themselves. Thirty explosive devices had been found in Columbine, in the killers' vehicles and at their homes.

I am not talking about "ordinary" terror such as neighborhood drive-by shootings, gang-related mayhem, or domestic violence. All this we have been willing to live with for years. But the terror of the past decade has put fear on an entirely new level of dread. When seasoned news commentators ask openly, "What kind of evil is loose today?"—then we get a sense of a ratcheted-up reign of terror not known a few years ago.

When mothers and fathers kill their young, when spouses conspire to kill their mates, when teenagers write their suicide notes and then march off to kill their teachers and classmates, when the young are trained to be suicide bombers—then we have a clue as to how far the Voice of God has been shut down and the empire of evil has overtaken the mind, young or old. The line is being crossed. The human mind is less and less restrained by the pleading of the Holy Spirit. Satan is chalking up points on the scoreboard of the universe.

Probably the most quoted poem of our time, with good reason, is William Butler Yeats's "The Second Coming" (1919):

> "Turning and turning in the widening gyre [circular or spiral motion]
> The falcon cannot hear the falconer;
> Things fall apart; the center cannot hold;
> Mere anarchy is loosed upon the world,
> The blood-dimmed tide is loosed, and everywhere
> The ceremony of innocence is drowned;
> The best lack all conviction, while the worst
> Are full of passionate intensity"[851]

All this adds up to enormous distractions at a time when God is trying to get the attention of the world to hear the messages of the Three Angels of Revelation 14. God through Jesus is the answer to the world's dreadful spin into terror on one hand, and into false hopes on the other.

But how will the world know about God's plan to bring peace and order to those who are trying to hang on to decency and civility in an increasingly out-of-control world? God has a people!

---

[851] www/online-literature.com/yeats/780

CHAPTER THIRTY-SIX:
UNIVERSAL PEACE THROUGH RELIGIOUS COOPERATION

We mentioned on page 265 how one of Pope John Paul II's primary goals was to unite the world's religions, especially in his 1994 apostolic letter, *Tertio Millennio Adventiente* (The Coming Third Millennium). This goal was more directly detailed in his 1995 encyclical *Ut Unum Sin* (That They May Be One). And then, among other events in 2000, the U.S. Congress authorized a Congressional Gold Medal to be presented to Pope John Paul II as a recognition of his "preeminent moral authority" and in "transcending temporal politics, has used his moral authority to hasten the fall of godless totalitarian regimes ... has promoted the inner peace of man as well as peace among mankind through his faith-inspired defense of justice, and has thrown open the doors of the Catholic Church, reconciling differences within Christendom as well as reaching out to the world's great religions."

Proceeding with his global peace plan, Pope John Paul II gathered more than 100 international religious leaders in Assisi, Italy, in 2002, pursuing "authentic peace."[852]

We also noted earlier how focused Pope John Paul II has been to woo Mecca to Rome. His emphasis that all Christians and Muslims worship the same God, that their mutual responsibility is to build a "civilization of love," that it is a "logic of love" that will bring all Christians and Muslims together in world peace.

All this is destined to bear fruit. The day is coming when something like the following *may* happen: Walking across the Hudson River and into the United Nations building, some religious figure (perhaps even a representation of the Virgin Mary[853]) will galvanize world leaders buried under the weight of dozens of world conflicts. From that powerful rostrum, world delegates will hear peace plans to solve Ireland's never-ending hostility between Irish Catholics and Protestants, proposals that will meld Israelis and Palestinians, and the same for racial divisions in all countries; Muslims and their neighbors the world over will suddenly see a workable plan for peace. The delegates stand in unison, recognizing that this dynamic religious leader has laid out the most sensible solutions for all their problems.

---

[852] See 272.

[853] For a remarkable overview of the "messages," apparitions, and signs purportedly given by Mary, the mother of Jesus, in the twentieth century, and how the Catholic world is waiting for her predictions of great global significance to be fulfilled, see Ted and Maureen Flynn, *The Thunder of Justice* (Sterling, VA: Maxhol Commitments, 1993).

They can only wonder why these solutions weren't thought of before! So reasonable, so believable!

The Papacy, working through these political and religious leaders, will soon have its way, breaking down all kinds of traditional international barriers as it receives the adulation of the whole world. Remember, "All the world marveled and followed the beast. So they worshipped the dragon [Satan]. ... who gave authority to the beast; and they [the world] worshipped the beast, saying, 'Who is like the beast?'" (Revelation 12:9; 13:3, 4)

RESPONDING TO DAZZLING PEACE PROPOSALS

The nations of the world, in response to these dazzling peace proposals, will act as "one mind, and they will give their power and authority to the beast" (Revelation 17:13).

How does all this relate to the United States? As we have noted, the United States "exercises all the authority of the first beast [Papacy] ... whose deadly wound was healed" (Revelation 13:11, 12).[854] Part of this "authority" is the making of the "image to the beast," which eventually leads to causing "as many as would not worship the image of the beast to be killed" (verses 14, 15).

The world federation that unites in a new, unprecedented era of peace is led by a spiritual power, a power that the United States, the most influential nation on earth, will actively support. To disagree with, or resist, the religious policies that unite all nations in this unparalleled peace movement, in the words of John the Revelator, sets one up to be economically boycotted and ultimately killed (see verses 17, 15).

---

[854] "One of the major documents issued by the Second Vatican Council, *Gaudian et Spes*, is typical: 'It is our clear duty, therefore, to strain every muscle in working for the time when all war can be completely outlawed by international consent. This goal undoubtedly requires the establishment of a universal public authority acknowledged as such by all the endowed with the power to safeguard on the behalf of all, security, regard for justice, and respect for rights.'... The Roman Church-State's grand design for world government rests on the fundamental theological assumption of the spiritual unity of the human race. ... The Roman Church-State sees itself as an unique institution that alone can accomplish this global unification. ... Few people understand the importance of the Roman Church-State in contemporary international affairs. When the United States appointed an ambassador to the Roman Church-State in 1984 during the Reagan administration, the Senate Committee on Foreign Affairs commented on the diplomatic significance of the Roman Church-State in its Report on the bill: 'The Vatican is an important player on the world stage. It maintains a diplomatic presence and has wide influence and access to important areas of great interest to the United States, such as Eastern Europe, Central American, Africa, and the Middle East. Vatican diplomats, widely regarded as among the most skilled in the world, play an active role in international political affairs.'... The Roman Church-State in the twentieth century, however, is an institution recovering from a mortal wound. If and when it regains its full power and authority, it will impose a regime more sinister than any the planet has yet seen." —John W. Robbins, *Ecclesiastical Megalomania, The Economic and Political Thought of the Roman Catholic Church* (The Trinity Foundation, U. S. A., 1999), 187–195. Emphasis supplied.

THE CATALYST THAT UNITES

We have been referring to the "image" and "mark of the beast" (Revelation 13:14–17) as central issues in Satan's attack on God's loyalists in the grand finale of the Great Controversy on Planet Earth. In some way, this "image" and "mark" will be the steel cord that unites all nations in their unprecedented peace movement. This "mark of the beast" is Sunday worship, one of the distinguishing characteristics of papal authority as they themselves admit:

In Peter Geiermann's *The Convert's Catechism of Catholic Doctrine*, he asks: Q. *Which is the Sabbath day?* A. Saturday is the Sabbath day. Q. *Why do we observe Sunday instead of Saturday?* A. We observe Saturday instead of Sunday, because the Catholic Church transferred the solemnity from Saturday to Sunday.[855]

How could this possibly be, that in traditionally Protestant America, the "land of the free and the home of the brave," that Sunday worship, the most distinctively visible mark of the Papacy, would become not only the choice of most Americans but the law of the land![856]

We have been watching, for more than a century, the Lord's Day Alliance and other Sunday movements as they focused on one goal: To make Sunday the official, legal, day of rest in the United States.[857] But those concerned with liberty of conscience and the free exercise of religion have far more to be concerned about than the influence of the Alliance!

True, we probably have fewer Sunday laws today in the United States than any other time in its history. Legalizing Sunday as a day of worship seems only a throwback to earlier centuries! A few try each year to introduce some kind of Sunday legislation in the U. S. Congress, but they die in committee. So what's the fuss about? *We must keep looking at the big picture, at the deep-water trends.*

It seems to many that nothing in America's history comes close to the rapid events of the past decade. In earlier pages, we reviewed the onward march of Pope John Paul II, one quick step after another in the past 20 years, as he unfolds his grand design for a world at peace and a common worship

---

[855] St. Louis: B. Herder Book Co., 1957, 50. This work in an earlier edition received the "apostolic blessing" of Pope Pius X, January 25, 1910.

[856] Jon Paulien, in his insightful book, *What the Bible Says About the Endtime,* makes a strong case for the relevance of the seventh-day Sabbath in the final crisis. (Hagerstown, MD: RHPA), 121–129.

[857] The Lord's Day Alliance, founded in 1888 by representatives of six major Protestant denominations, has as its stated mission: "to encourage Christians to reclaim the Sabbath—the Lord's Day—as a day of spiritual and personal renewal, enabling them to impact their communities with the Gospel. Supported by more than 20 Protestant denominations today, the Alliance has had significant impact on city and state legislation regarding Sunday-openings of expositions, movies, concerts, sporting events and general shopping in Canada and the United States. Many of their sponsored legislation was either repealed or overturned by court order. Although they supported punishment for violators of Sunday laws in the nineteenth century, I don't think that they are on record now as supporters of punishing violators today.

day for the world.[858] And we briefly highlighted the breathtaking union of "Evangelicals and Catholics Together; The Christian Mission in the Third Millennium."[859] Plus, we noted only one of many moments in the history of the United States when so-called constitutional safeguards have been overridden by "national emergencies."[860]

Most anyone watching all this convergence of attention on universal peace and on Sunday as the important avenue for achieving this universal accord must be wondering where all this is headed! *The facts are, we do know precisely each step ahead!*

CENTURY-OLD ROAD MAP NOW UNFOLDING

What we do know is that the road map drawn more than a century ago has been unfolding, and that pace can be measured. The next mileage marker looks like this:

> "When the leading churches of the United States, uniting upon such points of doctrine as are held by them in common, shall influence the state to enforce their decrees and to sustain their institutions, then Protestant America will have formed an image of the Roman hierarchy, and the infliction of civil penalties upon dissenters will inevitably result."[861]

Let's examine this remarkable prediction:

- Churches of the United States (Protestants and Catholics) "unite" on issues they hold in common. Among the best evidence for something that would not have been thought of 30 years ago is the 1994 document, "Evangelicals and Catholics Together," which acknowledges "a growing convergence and cooperation between Evangelicals and Catholics" on issues such as abortion, pornography, family values, educational choices, and other civil and political goals.[862] This joint pursuit of "common values" blends easily into the Papacy's emphasis on the "common good," a term that "appears scores of times in the papal encyclicals, in the *Catechism of the Catholic Church,* and in statements issued by the other bishops."[863]

- This broad-based coalition will "influence the state" regarding their common agenda. The political power of Evangelicals and Roman Catholics, evident in recent U.S. elections, is poised to exercise their

---

[858] See 265–272.
[859] See 264.
[860] See 280.
[861] *The Great Controversy,* 445.
[862] See 264, 265.
[863] Robbins, *op. cit.,* 155.

"contention" that "Christians individually and the church corporately also have a responsibility for the right ordering of civil society."[864]

- This "right ordering of civil society" fails to distinguish between legislating morality in the area of human freedom and laws that govern
how one worships the God of morality. It seems to me that "religious"
legislation in the endtime will come under the guise of laws that will
address social crises—a smooth way to segue into "rational" reasons
to unite for the "common good."[865]

- Further, as these two religious forces, Evangelicals and Roman
Catholics, unite in "common cause" pursuing the "common good,"
they will prod legislative assembles to "enforce their decrees and to
sustain their institutions" which, in essence, is a repeat of papal history who for centuries would use the state to sustain and enforce its
religious programs. This repeat of history is here called "an image of
the Roman hierarchy," a mirror reflection of centuries of church-state
union—and its appalling consequences.

- The result of this civil enforcement of religious decrees will be the
"infliction of civil penalties upon dissenters."

HARD TO BELIEVE
I know would shake their head in disbelief. Maybe in some other country without constitutional safeguards, they say, but *not in the United States*
with its safeguards that hundreds of thousands of brave, noble men and
women have died to preserve! But the same author we have been quoting
also wrote in the passage cited above that "In our land of boasted liberty,
religious liberty will come to an end."[866]

How could this happen? A long shadow may have been cast over the
"land of the free" in the Homeland Security Bill (November 2002) wherein
the Defense Department's Total Information Awareness program was tucked

---

[864] "For the religious right invisibility is no longer possible. From South Carolina to Oregon, state
parties are falling under its sway. … Across the nation, the flag and the cross are becoming one."
—Sidney Blumenthal, "Christian Soldiers," *The New Yorker*, July 18, 1994.

[865] By executive order on December 12, 2002, President Bush launched his Faith-Based Initiative, a
program that promotes federal funding of faith-based organizations. Although funding has been
available to religious social service agencies for many years, this executive order permits the giving
directly to churches. Gerald Grimaud, former Pennsylvania assistant Attorney General and currently
in private practice in Tunkhannock, PA, wrote: "With the breakdown of the wall of separation, both
church and state will pay a great price, as will the individual. Yes, church social programs and the
needy will benefit in the short run. However, with state funding comes government intrusion into
church programs, forms, applications, questions, monitoring, supervising, auditing, managing,
and even prosecutions. And over time, sadly, the mission of church programs will be neutered."
—*Liberty*, March/April 2003.

[866] *Evangelism*, 236.

in. Many have called this feature an unprecedented electronic dragnet and the most sweeping threat to civil liberties in U. S. history.[867]

William Safire, usually a conservative voice, wrote a blistering op-ed piece on November 14, 2002, in the *New York Times,* entitled, "You Are A Suspect." He compared this contemplated database to George Orwell's Big Brother government in his novel *1984*: "To this computerized dossier on your private life from commercial sources, add every piece of information that government has about you—passport application, driver's license and bridge toll records, judicial and divorce records, complaints from nosy neighbors to the FBI, your lifetime paper trail plus the latest hidden camera surveillance—and you have the supersnoop's dream, a 'Total Information Awareness' about every U. S. citizen."[868]

EMERGENCY POWERS

The point we have been making is that in times of crisis[869] the United States has a history of employing "emergency powers"[870] to respond to "urgent need." But, up to now, these "emergency powers" are not our final concern or focus. Why? Because the guardians of our Constitution are not the executive or legislative branches of the United States government—the Supreme Court is. *And therein lies our problem*: it is the flip-flopping of the Supreme Court on church-state issues that should give anyone pause regarding how unpredictable the Court may be in the future, especially in areas of national security and the common welfare of the majority.[871]

---

[867] However, the U.S. Congress called a halt on TIA because of its concern for privacy rights, *New York Times,* September 26, 1903.

[868] *New York Times,* November 14, 2002. Lance Morrow, in *Time,* March 17, 2003, wrote: "If Americans win a war (not just against Saddam Hussein, but the longer-term struggle) and lose the Constitution, they will have lost everything. ... The First Amendment may seem optional. ... A hard rain, in any case, is going to fall. Keep the Constitution dry and legible. The danger to America is that in trying to protect what it has, it will lose the very things worth having."

[869] See 312, 313.

[870] "The United States ... has on the books at least 470 significant emergency powers statutes without time limitations delegating to the Executive extensive discretionary powers, ordinarily exercised by the Legislature, which affect the lives of American citizens in a host of all-encompassing ways. This vast range of powers, taken together, confer enough authority to rule this country without reference to normal constitutional processes. These laws make no provision for congressional oversight nor do they reserve to Congress a means for terminating the 'temporary' emergencies which trigger them into use."—*A Brief History of Emergency Powers in the United States: Special Committee on National Emergencies and Delegated Emergency Powers, United States Senate* (Washington, D.C.: U. S. Government Printing Office, 1974), v., cited in Clifford Goldstein, *One Nation Under God?* (Boise, ID: PPPA, 1996), 116, 177. Editorial in *The New York Times,* December 2, 2001, entitled "Justice Deformed; War and the Constitution," deplored the Bush administration's infringement of civil liberties in pursuit and prosecution of terrorists, both for extreme nature of some measures—military tribunals, secret detentions or possible mistreatment of immigrants from Middle East—and for arbitrary way in which they were adopted, largely removed from ordinary oversight of Congress and courts; says American criminal justice system has shown itself fully able to try terrorists fairly and openly; says the U.S. must not treat non-citizens differently from Americans.

[871] For a review of Supreme Court equivocation on church-state matters, see Goldstein, *op. cit.,* 100–107.

Another frightening insight into Supreme Court thinking became obvious in the summer of 2003 when certain decisions were made on the premise that America "must bring itself into line with modern western thought, ... [that is] the U. S. Constitution may have to be adapted to foreign governing documents." John Leo summed up this "creeping transnationalism": "Here's a useful rule of thumb about international conventions, United Nations documents, and the findings of foreign courts: Anytime a judge cites one in an American court, something alarming is probably about to happen. The source of the alarm is usually that the judge has spotted some important 'emerging world consensus' that requires him to defy the plain meaning of American law."[872]

In other words, if Belgium and Germany declare Sunday to be a national day of rest, the Supreme Court of the United States would probably cite this as an "emerging world consensus" that trumps the traditional standards of the U. S. Constitution's First Amendment.[873]

Such thoughts are not my personal opinion. While I write, "Italian religious and political leaders have been caught up in a heated debate about the observance of the Sabbath. The European Union has set up the policy that every member-state must have one day of rest during the week. But the policy explicitly states that the designated day need not be Sunday, since for reasons of 'religious pluralism' a nation's government might choose another day.

"In Italy, the designation of Sunday as a 'day of rest' was first set in 1993. That policy was changed in 2000; however, when, in order to grant more flexibility for employers, that nation required only that every employer provide workers with a 24-hour rest period each week. But by August 2003, under the new European policy, Italy will again be required to fix a certain 'day of rest.'"[874]

POLITICAL CORRUPTION SKEWING JUSTICE

For the moment, let's observe another prediction that tracks events soon to transpire: "Political corruption is destroying love of justice and regard for truth, and even in free America rulers and legislators, in order to secure public favor, will yield to the popular demand for a law enforcing Sunday observance".[875] How could this possibly play out?

---

[872] John Leo, "Creeping transnationalism," *U. S. News & World Report,* July 21, 2003.

[873] Justice Ruth Ginsburg, before the first meeting of the American Constitution Society (August 2, 2003), said: "Our island or lone ranger mentality is beginning to change;" that the justices "are becoming more open to comparative and international law perspectives." —Associated Press, *Yahoo News,* August 6. 2003.

[874] CWNews.com (December 19, 2002).

[875] *The Great Controversy,* 592.

- Presidents and legislators hold office as long as they win elections. At the top of their daily agenda is their strategy to retain their elected office; that is not a pejorative statement, only realism.

- In times of crisis or national emergency, many are the examples of how swiftly public opinion polarizes and focuses on "doing something." Think of the response of the United States after the colossal terror attack on September 11, 2001. Think of the remarkable swiftness of Congress in responding to the President's requests for immediate emergency powers to find and contain potential terrorists in the United States and in other countries.

- Modern technology, including online, direct-dial, drive-by politics is changing the role of representative government. "The Capitol can be instantly inundated with unbridled emotions—and unlimited e-mail. Technology will soon make it possible to do away with representative government altogether. Just push a button on your television set and register your opinion on the budget, or Bosnia [or Iraq, homeland security, etc]. But direct democracy is inherently unstable. Government by plebiscite is too vulnerable to passing passions and devious demagogues."[876]

- After September 11, radio, television, magazines, and newspapers became a river of opinion regarding how much freedom one would give up for the promise of safety and security. The greater good, the general welfare of the majority, became the plumb line to test most any legislation, regardless whether some of the emergency legislation would be overriding the "constitutional rights" of the individuals concerned.

- Public debate swirls with concern for civil liberties. Some believe that the government's coined phrase, "war on terror," covers up the reality of many violations of "due process," and unlawful detentions, national ID cards and proposed electronic surveillance systems that will catalog every aspect of a person's life. Some see the United States counseling with their fears, rather than their values.

- Obviously a nation under attack must do all that is possible to forestall further calamities such as September 11, 2001. Protecting national borders historically is the first-line of defense. But before conceding any particular liberty for security, it seems wise to ask three questions: *which* liberty are we conceding, *whose* liberty are we conceding, and *how* will its suspension give more security to the country.[877]

---

[876] "Open arms for online democracy," *U.S. News & World Report*, January 16, 1995.
[877] Grimaud, *op. cit.*, a personal letter, January 18, 2002. See also William Safire, "Threat of National ID," *The New York Times*, December 24, 2001.

- Wondering if and when the day could come in the United States when "liberty of conscience … will no longer be respected," is today a no-brainer![878]

RESPONSE OF CHRISTIAN CHURCHES

What has been the response of Christian churches to these various events that surely impinge on the American sense of personal liberty to the minority as well as the majority?

Douglas Morgan, in his timely and provocative survey of the Seventh-day Adventist Church's historical positions on social and religious liberty issues, quoted Richard John Neuhaus, a well-known neoconservative analyst of religion in American public life. Neuhaus observed "the intriguing connection between the Seventh-day Adventists' apocalyptic beliefs and their involvement in the public order and warned that 'it would be a mistake to underestimate the influence of *Liberty* [Adventist journal] and the Seventh-day Adventist church in agitating church-state questions.'"[879]

Morgan also noted that the "editor of *Liberty* claimed in 1985 that the church's world headquarters had six officials assigned to matters of religious liberty while none of the nation's twelve leading Protestant bodies had even one full-time, trained specialist in that area. Moreover, the Adventist Church was the only one to publish a magazine devoted to religious liberty."[880]

Morgan's book clearly defines the essence of Adventism's mission and message as it grapples with both its specific views on apocalyptic prophecy and its humanitarian interest in vital concerns as slavery, temperance legislation, war, and public funds for religious purposes, and Sunday laws. Morgan pointed out that Adventism's "theology of history … has put much of the zeal into their efforts on behalf of oppressed minorities and outsides."[881]

Speaking directly to the present, Morgan observed that "for Adventists, America itself was always on the verge of becoming an apocalyptic villain, for the nation's experiment in freedom was being eviscerated from within by a spiritually bankrupt but imperialistic Christian coalition about to gain full dominance."[882]

So what will be the sudden catalyst that will bring all these last-day tensions into a roaring focus? The Bible gives the answer!

---

[878] Harold Bloom, distinguished Yale professor, wrote: "Authority, in the context of the American religion, is another form of gnosis, another knowing, and what it knows is that it must replace the purely secular authority brought about by the American Revolution. If the American Religion, as I surmised, began a generation after the Revolution, then it is a dangerous irony that, two centuries later, a belated version of our national faith is moving to abrogate our secular origins; so great a cloud of witnesses we yet may be to the triumphalism of our politicized shamans." —*The American Religion* (New York: Simon & Schuster, 1992), 271.

[879] Douglas Morgan, *Adventism and the American Republic* (Knoxville, TN: The University of Tennessee Press, 2001), 1, 2.

[880] *Ibid.*, 2.

[881] *Ibid.*, 209–212.

[882] *Ibid.*, 211.

CHAPTER THIRTY-SEVEN:
THE NEW TWIST—
GOD'S LAW SUDDENLY
BECOMES IMPORTANT

The cosmic Great Controversy has been playing out on Planet Earth. The driving passion for freedom has been constantly met by forces that thrive on coercion, subterfuge and deception. But history's greatest confrontation of these forces with the passion for freedom is just ahead.

Let's look at endtime United States from another angle. John the Revelator has described God's last-day loyalists: "Here are those who keep the commandments of God and the faith of Jesus" (Revelation 14:12). But Protestants who form an "image to the beast" are *suddenly*, for the most part, also motivated by high respect for the Ten Commandments, *including the fourth*—"Remember the Sabbath day to keep it holy" (Exodus 20:8). That startlingly fresh interest in the Fourth Commandment will greatly increase in the endtime.

STEADY DRUM BEAT

Pat Robertson, through his enormous public influence,[883] has drummed a steady beat for a decade that the issue today is moral clarity versus a moral abyss:

> "Through the history of what has been called Christian civilization, the Ten Commandments, given directly by the God of Jacob thirty-four hundred years ago to a great leader of the family of Jacob, named Moses, have been considered the heart of the universal moral law.

> "In one of the great tragedies of history, the Supreme Court of the supposedly Christian United States guaranteed the moral collapse of this nation when it forbade children in the public schools to pray to the God of Jacob, to learn of His moral law, or even to view in their classrooms the heart of the law, the Ten Commandments, which children must obey for their own good or disobey at their peril. ...

---

[883] Pat Robertson, LL.D., is (2002) founder and chairman of the Christian Broadcasting Network (CBN), president of United States Media Corporation, chairman of The Family Channel, and president of Operation Blessing. He is the host of the popular news-talk program, "The 700 Club," seen across North America and in 84 other countries. He is also founder and chancellor of Regent University.

"The Ten Commandments are for our own good. As Jesus Christ put it, 'The Sabbath was made for man.' How do these commandments relate to the world?

"The utopians have talked of world order. Without saying so explicitly, the Ten Commandments set the only order that will bring world peace—with devotion to and respect of God at the center, strong family bonds and respect next, and the sanctity of people, property, family, reputation, and peace of mind next."[884]

In respect to the Fourth Commandment, the Sabbath, Robertson wrote:

"The next obligation that a citizen of God's world order owes is to himself. 'Remember the Sabbath day, to keep it holy, is a command for the personal benefit of each citizen. Our minds, spirits, and bodies demand a regular time of rest. Perhaps God's greatest gift to mankind's earthly existence is the ability to be free from work one day a week."[885]

Pat Robertson is only one voice among many who are calling for the necessity of Sunday sacredness. From labor union leaders, official denominational resolutions, magazine columnists to the papacy, the crescendo is developing. Note Pope John Paul II's (July 7, 1998) apostolic letter *Dies Domini (The Lord's Day)*.[886]

---

[884] *The New World Order* (Dallas: Word Publishing, 1991), 233.

[885] *Ibid.*, 236.

[886] See 267. "62. It is the duty of Christians therefore to remember that, although the practices of the Jewish Sabbath are gone, surpassed as they are by the 'fulfillment' which Sunday brings, the underlying reasons for keeping 'the Lord's Day' holy—inscribed solemnly in the Ten Commandments—remain valid, though they need to be reinterpreted in the light of the theology and spirituality of Sunday. … 64. For several centuries, Christians observed Sunday simply as a day of worship, without being able to give it the specific meaning of Sabbath rest. Only in the fourth century did the civil law of the Roman Empire recognize the weekly recurrence, determining that on 'the day of the sun' the judges, the people of the cities and the various trade corporations would not work. … 65. By contrast, the link between the Lord's Day and the day of rest in civil society has a meaning and importance, which go beyond the distinctly Christian point of view. The alternation between work and rest, built into human nature, is willed be God himself, as appears in the creation story in the Book of Genesis. … In this matter, my predecessor Pope Leo XIII in his Encyclical *Rerum Nova.um* speaks of Sunday rest as a worker's right which the State must guarantee. In our own historical context there remains the obligations to ensure that everyone can enjoy the freedom, rest and relaxation which human dignity requires, together with the associated religious, family, cultural and interpersonal needs which are difficult to meet if there is no guarantee of at least one day of the week on which people can *both* rest and celebrate. … 67. … Therefore, also in the particular circumstances of our own time, Christians will naturally strive to ensure that civil legislation respects their duty to keep Sunday holy." —*Dies Domini*, July 7, 1998.

If anyone still wonders how Protestants will form an "image to the best" and how that may work out, consider the following:

- The connection between current Protestant concern for the Ten Commandments and Sunday sacredness, and the Pope's remarkable forthrightness regarding how Sunday has supplanted Saturday as the Christian's Sabbath;

- The mutual emphasis of both Protestants and Roman Catholics on the need for civil legislation to guard Sunday sacredness;

STRANGE AS IT MAY SEEM

In other words, strange as it may have seemed even 15 years ago, in the end-time we will have Protestant and Catholic stalwarts united in support of the Sabbath commandment, in fierce contention with "those who keep the commandments of God" (Revelation 14:12)! Protestants and Catholics will most likely clothe their appeal for civil laws guaranteeing Sunday sacredness with secular purposes such as "every worker deserves one day a week for rest," or "every home needs the support of the community in reserving Sunday for family time and recreation."

We are not dealing with future "maybes." In the Netherlands, on December 5, 2002, the *Nederlands Dagblads* reported that two opposing political parties voted to make Sunday a "Community Day" but "their ideas about such a day differ like night and day. The Christian Union asks for the closing of shops on Sundays and strives to make Sunday a day of rest for everyone. By contrast, the Labor Party allows people to do whatever they like on Sundays. …This law, however, will cut the weekend by 50 percent from the two days to only one day which will be Sunday, the only official day of rest."

I can assure you that more countries will soon follow—a coming Sunday law in the United States is as real as the sun shining tomorrow morning.

GROUNDWORK FOR NATIONAL SUNDAY LAW

We don't have to look far to see the groundwork already laid for a national Sunday law in the United States. In 1961, a majority ruling of the U. S. Supreme Court in *McGowan v. Maryland* upheld the constitutionality of Sunday laws even though they only happened "to coincide or harmonize" with a religion! Talk about legal fiction! The Court was telling Americans that if the majority were to enjoy the benefits of a uniform day of rest, that benefit would outweigh any burden that such a law would impose on a minority group. Of course, most anyone could see through that reasoning, *even as the dissenting judges did.* The case would not have come to the Supreme Court if religious underpinnings were not in place! *But the majority ruled.* This 1961 ruling has cast a dark shadow forward; soon thunderclouds will roll.

Pause, for a moment, and think how observers of the seventh-day Sabbath will be perceived by the new majority who will stoutly defend the need for adherence to the fourth commandment, *but now reinterpreted as Sunday sacredness?* We have this preview: "While Satan seeks to destroy those who honor God's law, he will cause them to be accused as lawbreakers, as men who are dishonoring God and bringing judgments upon the world."[887]

No one ever said that life would be fair! *Seventh-day Adventists, keeping the seventh-day holy "according to the commandment"* (Luke 23:56), *will one day be charged with law breaking!* Again, as it was in the beginning, the issue revolves around God's law and the cost of freedom—though now with a surprise twist!

All this reminds me of Catherine Crier's comment (youngest judge ever elected in Texas in 1984, currently one of Court TV's distinguished anchors) regarding the rule of law:

> "Our great cornerstone of democracy, the rule of law, has become a source of power and influence, not liberty and justice. I resent the insidious manipulations by those entrusted with such authority, but even more, I despise our deliberate ignorance and passive acceptance of these shackles on the American spirit. We have abdicated our freedom, literally our democracy, to the rule makers. Our institutions now serve these masters. They are the ones clearly winning the game. The rest of us are their timid and industrious sheep. It is time for a citizens' revolt. It is time to break the rules."[888]

What is also amazing is that events in the endtime have turned 180 degrees from what Adventists faced up to a few years ago. Since their early days Adventists have contended with other Christians who insisted that God's law had been done away with at the Cross, and that we now live under grace. Any appeal to the Law, they said, is either unnecessary because of the Cross or because it is a road that leads to legalism. But now, following the "Pied Piper" of Rome, Protestants have made the Sunday issue a "law" issue that firmly rests on their appeal to the Ten Commandments!

Again, the one who has been previewing our day with astonishing accuracy also wrote:

---

[887] *The Great Controversy,* 591. "In the warfare to be waged in the last days there will be united, in opposition to God's people, all the corrupt powers that have apostatized from allegiance to the law of Jehovah. In this warfare the Sabbath of the fourth commandment will be the great point at issue, for in the Sabbath commandment the great Lawgiver identifies Himself as the Creator of the heavens and the earth." —*Selected Messages,* vol. 3, 392, 393. "The corrupt powers that have apostatized" remain professed Christians, but in apostasy; they profess allegiance to the Lawgiver but obey Him on their own terms.

[888] Catherine Crier, *The Case Against Lawyers* (New York: Random House (Broadway Books), 2002), 5.

"The last great conflict between truth and error is but the final struggle of the long-standing controversy concerning the law of God.
Upon this battle we are now entering—a battle between the laws of
men and the precepts of Jehovah, between the religion of the Bible
and the religion of fable and tradition."[889]

STEADY TREAD OF EVENTS

What next? Let's keep watching the "steady tread of events."[890] As I see
it, the stage is set even as I write; in some way that next step may catch us by
surprise—not that it will happen, but how! Note the next "tread":

"To secure popularity and patronage, legislators will yield to the
demand for a Sunday law. … When Protestantism shall stretch
her hand across the gulf to grasp the hand of the Roman power,
when she shall reach over the abyss to clasp hands with spiritualism,
when, under the influence of this threefold union, our country
shall repudiate every principle of its Constitution as a Protestant
and republican government and shall make provision for the
propagation of papal falsehoods and delusions, then we may know

---

[889] *The Great Controversy,* 582. This core concept that the Great Controversy Theme exposes the "battle
between the laws of men and the precepts of Jehovah" does not begin and end with the Saturday-
Sunday controversy. Wherever we look, even in the daily practices of church organizations, we
are aware of these two principles in tension. One of the reasons why the U. S. Constitution is so
venerable and respected is that it recognizes certain realities of the human condition, including
humanity's selfishness and dishonest nature. That recognition led the framers to formulate our
nation's distinctive system of checks and balances. In other words, those men who worked so
diligently over a period of years to give Americans their unique Constitution recognized that what
"ought to be" must be balanced by "reality," that is, what "is." Church administrations function
best when they understand the principles that guided the framers of the Constitution. Though
"checks and balances" are in place by mandated audits, periodic constituent reviews, performance
evaluations, lay-worker governing committees, etc., the temptation to maneuver around these
"checks and balances," and to cover-up malfeasance, or any lack of "due process," or selective
enforcement of church discipline, or resisting the reality of good and bad leadership—all such
practices indicate that the principles of the Great Controversy remain vague to the detriment of
any organization, *especially* church organizations, I am reminded of John Adams' (U. S. second
president) clear warning in 1787: "If there is one central truth to be collected from the history
of all ages, it is this: that the people's rights and liberties, and the democratical mixture in a
constitution, can never be preserved without a strong executive, or, in other words, without
separating the executive from the legislative power. If the executive power, or any considerable
part of it, is left in the hands of an aristocratical or democratical assembly, it will corrupt the
legislature as necessarily as rust corrupts iron, or as arsenic poisons the human body; and when
the legislature is corrupted, the people are undone." —McCullough, *op. cit.,* 374, 375. See also
The Federalist, No. 47 (James Madison): "The accumulation of all powers, legislative, executive
and judiciary, in the same hands, whether of one, a few, or many, and whether hereditary, self-
appointed, or elective, may justly be pronounced the very definition of tyranny." Understanding
the issues in the Great Controversy would save us all from corrupting the legal wisdom in the
U. S. Constitution.

[890] *Testimonies,* vol. 7, 14.

that the time has come for the marvelous working of Satan and that the end is near."[891]

What shall we make of this phenomenal prediction? We have already surveyed the role spiritualism will play in the endtime.[892] Spiritualism for centuries has had an open door to both Protestants and Catholics because of their common belief in the immortal soul—the great lie of Satan (Genesis 3:4) that has become the belief of the masses worldwide, including most Christians as well as most heathen religions. Believe me, no one has seen anything yet like what lies ahead when this world will see "great signs … even fire come down from heaven" (Revelation 3:13).

"The rulers of the darkness of this age … [the] spiritual hosts of wickedness in the heavenly places" (Ephesians 6:12) will devise "signs and wonders" that will far outstrip the greatest magicians of all time. And they will do all this under the guise of establishing the credentials of that "threefold union" (Spiritualism-Catholics-Protestants) that will lead to the repudiation of "every principle of the Constitution as a Protestant and republican form of government"— truly "the marvelous working of Satan."

In the midst of astounding "great signs," and the repudiation of Constitutional guarantees, the United States will "establish"[893] a national Sunday law. What is the strategy? For whatever reasons (which we will suggest later) America will repudiate its Protestant and republican principles as it "makes provision for … propagation of papal falsehoods and delusions." (Protestantism symbolizes America's foundation as a country without higher allegiance to the pope, a people generally who place the Bible above Catholic tradition and councils. Republics derive their power from the people, not from kings; that is, leaders are elected by the people, thus not by rite of birth or military coups.)

---

[891] *Ibid.*, vol. 5, 451. *Webster's Ninth New Collegiate Dictionary* on "republic": "a government in which supreme power resides in a body of citizens entitled to vote and is exercised by elected officers and representatives responsible to them and governing according to law." Ellen White's description of the United States as a "Protestant" nation does not conflict with her conviction that the U. S. Constitution and the Bill of Rights forbids the "establishment" of a religion in the United States (See Article 14, Section 4 and the First Amendment). White used the term "Protestant" in the historical sense, in contrast to many countries in Europe from which most Americans emigrated where Catholicism was the prevailing religion and chief influence in those countries. The United States's Protestant heritage, for White, was reflected in the First Amendment's commitment to liberty of conscience. Early Americans sought a "Church without a bishop, a State without a King." —*The Puritans' Mistake*, published by Oliver Ditson, 1844. See also George Bancroft, *History of the United States*, vol. III, ch. VI.

[892] See 245, 246. For more detail in how spiritualism will probably enhance the appeal and power of both Catholicism and Protestantism, see G. Edward Reid, *Sunday's Coming!* (Fulton, MD: Omega Publications, 1996), 114–135.

[893] "Congress shall make no law respecting an establishment of religion, or prohibiting the free exercise thereof. …" —first two clauses of the First Amendment to the U.S. Constitution.

PERILS OF TOLERANCE AND PLURALISM

The time is coming in the United States when tolerance (everyone's opinion as valid as anyone else's) and pluralism (the majority accepting the prevailing notion of tolerance)[894] will prevail over traditional convictions that rest on the principles of Protestantism and a republican form of government—one opinion will be perceived as good as another and whatever the majority wants at any given time is the law of the people. We call that the tyranny of the majority.

On the Phil Donahue show, Norman Vincent Peale, probably the best known Protestant preacher in the middle of the twentieth century, announced: "It's not necessary to be born again. You have your own way to God; I have mine. I found eternal peace in a Shinto shrine. ... God is everywhere."

Phil Donahue was so shocked that he actually came to the defense of Christianity: "But you're a Christian minister and you're supposed to tell me that Christ is the way and the truth and the life, aren't you?"

Peale replied: "Christ is one of the ways. God is everywhere."[895]

Near our home a sign in front of a new church reads: "We Give You Fellowship, Not Religion." I am sure that "feel good" sermons and plenty of hugs will help the lonely. But where will worshippers go after church to find reasons for hope and for that Power that genuine religion alone can give them?

REVISING HISTORY

Another remarkable phenomenon of the last 40 years that contributes to misunderstood tolerance and the leveling effect of pluralism is the confusion over historical reality. We have witnessed the rewriting of history textbooks until we numbly reach "a level of comfort with dishonesty."[896] In Orwell's *1984,* the government deliberately shredded "old" history books, deleted names and events that were contrary to their present programs. The only history that young and old now knew was what was published as "real" history.[897] We all know that the former Soviet Union airbrushed officials out of old photos and thus remade history.[898] Doctoring the past, revising

---

[894] The danger of pluralism in religious matters is obvious. Many Christian leaders are blatantly announcing that there are many roads to heaven, Jesus being one Guide along with Buddha, etc. What may be truth for you, they say, may not be truth for somebody else—so we shouldn't be too hasty in condemning one another. What we used to think about doctrine is not meaningful today—just give us Jesus, not doctrine!. "If it tastes good, eat it; if it feels good, do it" seems to be the guiding light for so many. Tolerance trumps truth because loving one another (which means accepting one another's beliefs as equally valid), they say, is more relevant and necessary today than dividing families, neighborhoods, and nations over appeals to someone's opinion regarding absolute truths. See 288, 289.

[895] Dave Hunt, "Revival or Apostasy," *The Berean Call,* October 1997.

[896] John Leo, "Color me confounded," *U.S. News & World Report,* February 4, 2002.

[897] *Ibid.*

[898] *TV Guide* put Oprah Winfrey on a cover, then gave her Ann-Margaret's body. And on it goes. See *USA TODAY,* July, 11, 2002.

historical events, is a subtle device of the Evil One that will characterize the confusion of thought in the last days, especially when the Constitution of the United States will be conceptually revised until reality fuses with whatever the majority wants to believe.

In the early years of the twenty-first, century we have seen the general worldview that dominates American universities and the entertainment industry—"all religions deserve identical respect, or similar dismissal. Conventional wisdom holds that all faiths are comparably valid, beautiful paths to the same God. Or if the commentator feels ill-disposed toward religion, then all faiths manifest similar violent, anti-intellectual, intolerant tendencies."[899]

RELIGIOUS TOTALITARIANISM

Perhaps Thomas Friedman, three-time Pulitzer Prize winner and columnist for the *New York Times,* summed all this up in a direction that we see outlined in Revelation 12–18: "The real war … is not terrorism but religious totalitarianism … 'a view of the world that my faith must reign supreme, and can be affirmed and held passionately only if all others are negated.'" He looks for a "faith that embraces modernity [any truth and behavior is acceptable] without weakening religious passion, and in a way that affirms that God speaks multiple languages and is not exhausted by just one faith."[900] Where does that leave Jesus and New Testament faith?

Some say that they see nothing on the horizon like what we are describing. Impossible, they say, because we have too many groups such as the American Civil Liberties Union, People for the American Way, the American Jewish Congress, or Americans United for Separation of Church and State ready to make war against any attempt to favor a religious institution. Up to now, true! But the same one who has been hitting bull's-eyes regarding the endtime also wrote:

> "The Sunday movement is now making its way in darkness. The leaders are concealing the true issue, and many who unite in the movement do not themselves see whither the undercurrent is tending. … They are working in blindness. They do not see that if a Protestant government sacrifices the principles that have made them a free, independent nation, and through legislation brings into the Constitution principles that will propagate papal falsehood and papal delusion, they are plunging into the Roman horrors of the Dark Ages."[901]

---

[899] Michael Medved, "Admit terrorism's Islamic link," *USA TODAY,* June 24, 2002.

[900] November 27, 2001.

[901] *Review and Herald,* Extra, Dec. 11, 1888. "There are many, even of those engaged in this movement for Sunday enforcement, who are blinded to the results which will follow this action. They do not see that they are striking directly against religious liberty. There are many who have never understood the claims of the Bible Sabbath and the false foundation upon which the Sunday institution rests." —*Last Day Events,* 126.

FAITH-BASED INITIATIVE

I have found the recent tempest over President Bush's *Faith Based Initiative* most fascinating—and also filled with storm warnings. Unable to get immediate approval from Congress, the president pressed forward through Executive Orders 13, 270, 113, and 280. On the face of it, it is a partnership between the federal government and religious groups united in providing the social and motivational help disadvantaged people need, with clear policies against promoting individual religious teachings.

As President Bush said in his Philadelphia speech, December 12, 2002, "Government has no business endorsing a religious creed, or directly funding religious worship or religious teaching. That is not the business of the government. Yet government can and should support social services provided by religious people, as long as those services go to anyone in need, regardless of their faith. And when government gives that support, charities and faith-based programs should not be forced to change their character or compromise their mission."[902]

The issue, of course, is the meaning of the First Amendment of the U.S. Constitution's Bill of Rights. The rising chorus for support declares that the express language in the First Amendment does not forbid "cooperation" between church and state in matters that relate to the "common good."[903] The opposing chorus sees no positive good from this on-the-surface partnership. After all, who will make the decision in the future as to what "faith initiatives" should be included and approved by government support? It is *only a half step* to include a national rest day as a common good, and not many would see the cosmic implications. Unless they see the big picture!

HOW TO LIVE UNDER SUNDAY LAWS

But Sunday laws will be passed! That is not opinion but a fact to be soon realized. What then? Obviously it will create an unprecedented opportunity for great public discussion,[904] a time to speak out more fully regarding the significance of the Sabbath-Sunday issue,[905] a time when many judges and

---

[902] www.whitehouse.gov/news/releases/20021212.3

[903] It should be interesting that Ellen White, one of my principle references, never uses the phrase, "separation of church and state." Although in the 1890s church leaders such as A.T. Jones strenuously contended for this "separation," (a "separationist"), Adventist leaders ("accommodationists") for the last 50 years have accepted government aid in many countries of the world for social services as long as there were no strings attached that they would object to.

[904] "This time ... is the very opportunity to present to the world the true Sabbath in contrast to the false. The Lord in His providence is far ahead of us. He has permitted this Sunday question to be pressed to the front that the Sabbath of the fourth commandment may be presented before the legislative assemblies. Thus the leading men of the nation may have their attention called to the testimony of God's Word in favor of the true Sabbath." —*Manuscript Releases*, vol. 2, 197.

[905] *Early Writings*, 85.

lawyers now laboring to protect constitutional principles will suddenly see even deeper issues of freedom at stake.[906]

Let's keep our perspective! Sabbath-keepers will not be too inconvenienced after Sunday laws are in place, unless they own stores that normally would have been open on Sunday or want to do normal work around their home on Sunday. We have been given much counsel as to how best to relate to Sunday laws. None should show "defiance" or in any way do or say anything that "could be interpreted as maliciousness."[907] Some may feel "indignant" that their constitutional liberties are being eroded and may want to "fly into a passion over this matter," but no one should "boast unwisely of their [lost] liberty."[908] It will be a wonderful time to show "wisdom," giving no one an "occasion to call [Adventists] lawbreakers."[909]

No one needs to demonstrate their "civil rights" in defying the new Sunday laws by mowing lawns with power mowers on Sunday or in showing "independence" by selecting "Sunday as the day to exhibit their washing." In other words, it should be remembered that "refraining from work on Sunday is not receiving the mark of the beast."[910]

But wise Adventists will use the opportunity to explain why they keep Saturday as the Christian Sabbath. Cheerfully, they will expand their missionary work among their neighbors. Further, "whenever it is possible, let religious services be held on Sunday. Make these meetings intensely interesting."[911] After all, never before will so many be at home and not at work or at sporting events—if the Sunday laws are strictly enforced.

THE ENFORCEMENT OF SUNDAY LAWS

But the escalator of time, the "steady tread of events," moves forward inexorably. Various crises pile up on top of each other.[912] The time for open discussion will soon segue into the cry for *enforcement* of Sunday legislation. For those who know their history it seems like a repeat of the Dark Ages— the state legislating and enforcing religious laws.

Note how Ellen White predicts this tightening of government screws, the raising of the fist of majority tyranny empowered by the union of Protestants and Catholics:

---

[906] "While many of our rulers are active agents of Satan, God also has His agents among the leading men of the nation. ... Thus a few men will hold in check a powerful current of evil. The opposition of the enemies of truth will be restrained that the third angel's message may do its work. When the final warning shall be given, it will arrest the attention of these leading men through whom the Lord is now working, and some of them will accept it, and will stand with the people of God through the time of trouble." —*The Great Controversy,* 610, 611.

[907] *Last Day Events,* 138.

[908] *Ibid.*

[909] *Ibid.,* 139, 140.

[910] *Ibid.*

[911] *Ibid.*

[912] See 240, 282, 313.

"Let the principle once be established in the United States, that the church may employ or control the power of the state; that religious observances may be enforced by secular laws; in short, that the authority of church and state is to dominate the conscience, and the triumph of Rome in this country is assured."[913]

So now we have come to the *enforcement* of the national Sunday law. *Not yet have we come to the law that will be directly aimed at Sabbath-keepers.* Not yet, not in the national Sunday law will Revelation 13 be put in play when 1) the "mark of the beast" is "receive[d]" (verse 16); 2) when those who defy the authorities may not "buy or sell except everyone who has the mark of the beast" (verse 17); and 3) when those who do not "worship the image of the beast [are] to be killed" (verse 15).

Those will be the next steps in the "steady tread of events." But before we go there we need to step back, way back, as if we are on another planet watching all these almost unbelievable events, galloping full stride to a terrible climax. And ask two questions:

- *How could normally reasonable men and women from all walks of life, especially crack lawyers and jurists who are dedicated to fair play and the upholding of constitutional law, come to the place where they yield to the latest polls and the clamor of the crowds?*

The U.S. Patriot Act (October 31, 2001)[914] passed less than two months after the World Towers terrorism and approved by the majority of Americans in their hour of fear and uncertainty, ostensibly reaches out to protect the borders and interests of the United States. But in the light of the Great Controversy it seems that certain questions should be asked:

1. Could the word "terrorism" be so sanctified that it becomes an incantation that evaporates all existing limits on government power?

2. Could some of this rage against terrorists be directed against peaceful citizens whose religious beliefs my suddenly be judged "extremist," especially concerning a divisive issue as which day is the Sabbath of the Fourth Commandment?

---

[913] *The Great Controversy,* 581. "Soon the Sunday laws will be enforced, and men in positions of trust will be embittered against the little handful of God's commandment-keeping people." —*Manuscript Releases,* vol. 4, 278.

[914] Many are asking if the sudden decision for increasing the surveillance powers of the U. S. government after September 11, 2001, are only early warnings of powers to come. In the U.S. Patriot Act (October 31, 2001) passed overwhelmingly, (along with the TIPS program) a host of new powers became law, including secret searches, warrantless Internet surveillance, warrantless access to phone records, and a requirement that retailers report "suspicious" customer transactions to the Treasury.

3. Could literature that proclaims the everlasting gospel (Revelation 14) and identifies religious groups involved in last-day events (Revelation 13) be labeled as "hate literature?"

4. Is it possible because of fear and distrust of the unknown that the majority will revive the religious prejudices and persecution of the Middle Ages?[915]

- *How come legislators, lawyers, and jurists who for years have regarded freedom of conscience as the one shining beacon in this world of very limited liberties now capitulate to the hard fist or subtle bribe of other government and church leaders?*

Again Ellen White nails down the coming crisis:

"The dignitaries of church and state will unite to bribe, persuade, or compel all classes to honor the Sunday. The lack of divine authority will be supplied by oppressive enactments. Political corruption is destroying love of justice and regard for truth; and even in free America, rulers and legislators, in order to secure public favor, will yield to the popular demand for a law enforcing Sunday observance. Liberty of conscience, which has cost so great a sacrifice, will no longer be respected."[916]

SUDDEN DEMAND FOR ENFORCEMENT OF SUNDAY LAWS

But what is driving all this rather sudden interest in a "popular demand for a law enforcing Sunday observance"? What is Satan up to? What kind of national crisis is forcing men and women suddenly to turn religious and demand a "right-about-face" regarding the First Amendment of the U.S. Constitution that has guarded well for centuries the rights of Americans that guarantee "free exercise" of their religious convictions?

Let us review how Satan, in his fury against God's loyalists (Revelation 12:17), intends to create national panic (and universal panic as well) for the one purpose of "caus[ing] as many as would not worship the image of the beast to be killed" (Revelation 13:15).

Earlier, we noted specific areas of great stress, confusion, and distraction that forces of evil will cause in the endtime. All these areas of tension, bewilderment, and diversion are now converging as I write. Who could possibly deny that this is not so! *But how will all this create a perilous and stressful time for Seventh-day Sabbath-keepers?*

[915] Robert J. Wieland, *Dial Daily Bread*, February 4, 2003.
[916] *The Great Controversy*, 592.

Chapter Thirty-Eight:
National Troubles Blamed On "Seventh-Day" Sabbath-Keepers

Remember—one of the characteristics of ultimate Evil in the Great Controversy is the skill in blaming others for the distress Evil itself is causing.[917]

The author who has been dead right so far in predicting events in the endtime also wrote:

> "Satan puts his interpretation upon events, and they think, as he would have them, that the calamities which fill the land are a result of Sunday breaking. Thinking to appease the wrath of God these influential men make laws enforcing Sunday observance."[918]

Protestant and Catholics leaders will "put forth the claim that the fast-spreading corruption is largely attributable to the desecration of the so-called 'Christian Sabbath' and that the enforcement of Sunday observance would greatly improve the morals of society. This claim is especially urged in America, where the doctrine of the true Sabbath has been most widely preached."[919]

But there will be more. During the time when Sunday legislation is being debated and especially during the time after the Sunday law is passed, Sabbath-keepers, calmly, forthrightly, and wisely, will be proclaiming the big picture of why God's law has been a special target for many thousands of years. The history behind the attempted change to alter the Fourth Commandment, from Saturday to Sunday, will be prominently empha-sized in legislative halls, radio and television talk shows, and wherever else Sabbath-keepers can get a hearing.

Tightening Web Of National Troubles

All the while, the tightening web of national troubles will incite the emo-tions of many, especially those who are not dazzled by the optimistic scien-tists, philosophers, preachers, and politicians. Loss of paychecks, pensions, and the sense that terrible times are ahead, coupled with environmental disas-ters and world terror—all combine in creating fear and anxiety, especially in those who desire security above freedom. And that fear will create a national cry for God's help and the necessity for national unity. We already hear their rallying theme: "Righteousness exalts a nation" (Proverbs 14:34).

---

[917] See 42, 285, 354.
[918] *Last Day Events*, 129.
[919] *The Great Controversy*, 587.

The fervor that drove political and religious leaders to legislate Sunday laws is now ratcheted up against those who are "defying" this new demonstration of national unity. The polls will show that a huge percentage of Americans believe that God cannot bless America when Sabbath-keepers keep stirring the pot of unrest and division.

It may sound impossible and outrageous from any point of view today, but Sabbath-keepers will then be labeled unpatriotic and political troublemakers. Note this preview of things to come:

> [They will be] "denounced as enemies of law and order, as breaking down the moral restraints of society, causing anarchy and corruption, and calling down the judgments of God upon the earth. Their conscientious scruples will be pronounced obstinacy, stubbornness, and contempt of authority. They will be accused of disaffection toward the government. ... A false coloring will be given to their words; the worst construction will be put upon their motives."[920]

UNPATRIOTIC AND LAWBREAKERS

Unpatriotic and law-breakers! Hardly a fair description of Seventh-day Adventists, now or then! But such is the picture of the United States in the endtime. The freedom misused in heaven at the beginning of the Great Controversy is replicated in the one nation on earth that has been the beacon of freedom to this planet for more than 200 years! Hard to believe, but the same Satan who defied God in heaven will now attempt to crush His loyalists on earth, once and for all.

Of course, this crushing of the individual is not an endtime phenomenon. It has been the controlling philosophy of all dictators. But in the free air of American democracy, such thinking seems unbelievable. For instance, Senator Ted Kennedy, while extolling the "teamwork" of the New England Patriots as they celebrated their victory in Super Bowl XXXVI on January 31, 2002, said: "We must abolish the cult of the individual decisively, once and for all."[921] Soon such words in the air will become national axioms and beyond rational discussion.

NATIONAL APOSTASY

Pretense of righteousness, unfairness in blaming others for the troubles of the land, confusion caused by bribed legislators and jurists, and coercion as part of the standard response to silence truth—all reap bitter fruit. Although united, in a way, against a common enemy (Sabbath-keepers), evil principles do not bring forth love, kindness, or calm, rational thinking. Having a common enemy does not generate trust and confidence among themselves. It will be a time of great political and economic unrest!

---

[920] *Ibid.*, 592.
[921] Neal Boortz, "The war on individualism," October 1, 2002, ©2000 WorldNetDaily.com

What happens to America is almost too awful to contemplate! God does not cause the pending troubles. Evil is like self-consuming bacteria, it feeds on itself. And thus the prediction will be as certain as night follows day:

> "When our nation, in its legislative councils, shall enact laws to bind the consciences of men in regard to their religious privileges, enforcing Sunday observance, and bringing oppressive power to bear against those who keep the seventh-day Sabbath, the law of God will, to all intents and purposes, be made void in our land, and national apostasy will be followed by national ruin."[922]

What "national ruin" may be is not completely clear today. What we do know is that it surely includes harrowing circumstances for God's loyalists when they are forbidden to "buy or sell" (Revelation 13:17). For those connected with the "beast" power of Revelation 13, the one to whom the United States will "make an image" (Revelation 13:14), colossal economic disasters are ahead: "The merchants of the earth will weep and mourn over her, for no one buys their merchandise anymore. … All the things which are rich and splendid are gone from you, and you shall find them no more at all. The merchants of these things, who became rich by her, will stand at a distance for fear of her torment, weeping and wailing" (Revelation 18:11, 14, 15). What we do know is that appalling, frightful times are ahead for everyone!

SUNDAY LAWS FOCUS ON SABBATH-KEEPERS WORLDWIDE

Even more amazing will be the *worldwide* polarization against Sabbath-keeping Adventists. The universal authority of the "beast" power of Revelation 13 will, with great craft, use the panic being caused throughout the world by natural disasters, interlocking economic distress, and unsettled ethnic/religious conflicts to accomplish its long-sought goals. The prestige and power of the United States will become the model of how to unify the majority around the world in calling for God to calm the world's storms as surely as Jesus calmed the raging Sea of Galilee.

President George H.W. Bush, in his State of the Union Address, January 29, 1991, announced, "For two centuries we've done the hard work of

---

[922] *Last Day Events*, 133. "When the law of God has been made void and apostasy becomes a national sin, the Lord will work in behalf of His people." —*Selected Messages*, bk. 3, 388. "The people of the United States have been a favored people, but when they restrict religious liberty, surrender Protestantism, and give countenance to popery, the measure of their guilt will be full, and "national apostasy" will be registered in the books of heaven." —*Review and Herald*, May 2, 1893. "It is at the time of the national apostasy when, acting on the policy of Satan, the rulers of the land will rank themselves on the side of the man of sin. It is then the measure of guilt is full. The national apostasy is the signal for national ruin." —*Selected Messages*, bk. 2, 373 "When the state shall use its power to enforce the decrees and sustain the institutions of the church—then will Protestant America have formed an image to the papacy, and there will be a national apostasy which will end only in national ruin." —*Last Day Events*, 134.

freedom. And tonight we lead the world in facing down a threat to decency and humanity. What is at stake is more than one small country, it is a big idea—new world order, where diverse nations are drawn together in common cause to achieve the universal aspirations of mankind: peace and security, freedom, and the rule of law. Such is a world worthy of our struggle, and worthy of our children's future."[923]

"A new world order" based on a "common cause"! The drumbeat increases cadence. Such concepts foretold in Revelation 13 have become common currency throughout Europe and the United States!

I am reminded of a statement that Strobe Talbott, Deputy Secretary of State under President Clinton, made regarding his sense of globalism: "No matter how permanent or even sacred [all countries] may seem," they are in fact "artificial and temporary." Continuing, "Within the next hundred years, nationhood as we know it will be obsolete; all states will recognize a single global authority."[924]

It almost takes one's breath away, that when "America, the land of religious liberty, shall unite with the papacy in forcing the conscience and compelling men to honor the false sabbath, the people of every country on the globe will be led to follow her example."[925] "The Sabbath question is to be the issue in the great final conflict in which all the world will act a part."[926]

LAST ACT IN THE DRAMA

A significant time factor kicks in at this point—the enforcement of Sunday laws worldwide becomes "the last act in the drama. When this substitution becomes universal God will reveal Himself. When the laws of men are exalted above the laws of God, when the powers of this earth try to force men to keep the first day of the week, know that the time has come for God to work."[927]

One may wonder at this time how what seems to be an American issue could become so global so quickly. Reading Paul Jenkins' book, *The Next Christendom*, may help put all this in perspective. One of his basic themes is that Christianity in the "South" (that is, in the southern hemisphere throughout the earth) is far more vigorous than in the northern hemisphere. Its

---

[923] *Los Angeles Times,* January 30, 1991.

[924] Cited in Jesse Helms, "Emerging Threats to United States National Security," *Imprimis,* January 2002.

[925] *Last Day Events,* 135. "If ever the free institutions of America are destroyed, that event may be attributed to the consequence of the majority, which may at some future time urge the minorities to desperation and oblige them to have recourse to physical force. Anarchy will then be the result, but it will have been brought by despotism." —Alexis Tocqueville, *Democracy in America, Democracy in America* by Alexis de Tocqueville, edited and translated by Harvey C. Mansfield and Delba Winthrop, (Chicago: University of Chicago Press, 2000), bk. 1, ch. 15.

[926] *Ibid.*

[927] *Ibid.*

numbers will fast surpass by a huge margin the numbers of Christians in the North. But the South is not a mirror church of the North.

> "We have already seen that Southern churches [southern hemisphere] are quite at home with biblical notions of the supernatural, with ideas like dreams and prophecy. ... When we read the New Testament, so many of the basic assumptions seem just as alien in the global North as they do normal and familiar in the South."[928]

Whatever we may see in the religious context of Babylon as reflected in Revelation 13–18 will surely apply to the religious intensity now seen exploding in the southern hemisphere. The issues will not seem to them to be a "western" or "northern" church problem. The issues that we have been describing in these pages will seem even more relevant in the southern hemisphere than now appears in the northern. The Great Controversy is a worldwide conflict. No land is immune. For people everywhere, the issues will become increasingly relevant, personal, and urgent.

WORLDWIDE INFLUENCE AND POWER OF THE UNITED STATES

All of these suppositions regarding the impact of a politico-religio virus (such as the international enforcement of Sunday laws) that begins like a pimple in the United States but one day will spread rapidly through the blood stream of world communities is no longer a bad dream. Most dialogue on almost any television talk show or weekly magazine refers to the worldwide influence and power of the United States. When the United States selects the foreign countries that will receive billions of dollars annually on the basis of what's best for America, when terrible earthquakes and famines call forth massive U. S. humanitarian relief anywhere in the world, when the nations of the world expect the U. S. military to resolve civil wars overseas, no one any more doubts the clout of American opinion and action.

Since 9/11, the ability of U. S. might to remain a benign banker to the world morphed into the realization that something must be done to guarantee peace, prosperity, and the spread of human rights on every continent. Such goals in order to survive "will require the expenditure of American will and might." Condoleezza Rice, National Security Adviser to President George W. Bush when asked if the United States is "overly ambitious," replied: "Was it overly ambitious of the United States to believe that democracy could be fostered in Japan and that peace could finally be brought between Germany and France? It succeeded because it proceeded from values that Americans understand. Truman and his team understood that America could not afford to leave a vacuum in the world."[929]

---

[928] Philip Jenkins, *The Next Christendom* (Oxford: Oxford University Press, 2002), 217.
[929] Jay Tolson, "The New American Empire?" *U. S News & World Report,* January 13, 2003.

ENFORCEMENT OF SUNDAY LAWS LEADS TO DIRECT OPPRESSION

Obviously, this is almost too much to contemplate at this time. Adventists are known the world (in the Northern as well as Southern hemispheres) over as law-abiding, law-supporting people. In addition, they are also known for their unambiguous defense of America's liberties, even willing to die for them when their president calls for their services in time of war.

But because of world panic and the crafty manipulation of legislators and jurists, "the whole world is to be stirred with enmity against Seventh-day Adventists."[930] And the *pseudo-logic* will prevail:

> "The whole world keeps Sunday, they say, and why should not this people, who are so few in number, do according to the laws of the land?"[931] "The judges will refuse to listen to the reasons of those who are loyal to the commandments of God because they know the arguments in favor of the fourth commandment are unanswerable. They will say, 'We have a law, and by our law he ought to die.' God's law is nothing to them. 'Our law' with them is supreme. Those who respect this human law will be favored, but those who will not bow to the idol sabbath have no favors shown them."[932]

Adventists in many levels of government and in the academic and business world will discover that their friends of "wealth, genius, [and] education, will combine to cover them with contempt. Persecuting rulers, ministers, and church members will conspire against them. With voice and pen, by boasts, threats, and ridicule, they will seek to overthrow their faith. … [They] shall be treated as traitors, … denounced as enemies of law and order, as breaking down the moral restraints of society, causing anarchy and corruption. … Their conscientious scruples will be pronounced obstinacy, stubbornness, and contempt of authority."[933]

WORD GAMES

Of course, governments must balance liberty of the individual with security of the individual. The problem is that word games are often played, such as "anti-terrorism" or "child protection" and "common values." Such words can easily attack the constitutional rights of the proposed "enemy."

Well-intentioned prosecutors and courts can easily mask and override in the name of freedom fundamental rights such as preventive detention, denial of detainee's rights to counsel, the right to prepare a defense, to

---

[930] *Last Day Events*, 136.

[931] *Ibid.*

[932] *Ibid.*, 145. Note the counsel given to those who face court trials: "In cases where we are brought before the courts, we are to give up our rights, unless it brings us in collision with God. It is not our rights we are pleading for, but God's right to our service." —*Last Day Events*, 146.

[933] *Ibid.*, 146.

interview and call witnesses, the right to trial and due process before sentencing, etc.[934] These are basic rights that tens of thousands of American service men have fought and died for.

If ever there was a time for mental and moral clarity in the Adventist church, it is now! It is now time for Adventist lawyers and judges to speak out in defense of the God-given right of individual freedom when it comes to conscience and core beliefs. It is now time for church leadership, including pastors and administrators, to think boldly regarding their responsibility to lead their church into careful thinking—before the storm breaks! Emotional identification with euphemistic words snared Germany under Hitler.

A POWERFUL HEADS-UP

We are not talking in general terms nor in the complacency that it will not happen "in my day!" Nor should we think that the potential confusion and defections from the church will come from some other group than one's own! We should all contemplate in great seriousness the following prediction, a prediction just as certain as the coming of Jesus:

> "As the storm approaches, a large class who have professed faith in the third angel's message, but have not been sanctified through obedience to the truth, abandon their position and join the ranks of the opposition. By uniting with the world and partaking of its spirit, they have come to view matters in nearly the same light; and when the test is brought, they are prepared to choose the easy, popular side. Men of talent and pleasing address, who once rejoiced in the truth, employ their powers to deceive and mislead souls. They become the most bitter enemies of their former brethren. When Sabbath-keepers are brought before the courts to answer for their faith, these apostates are the most efficient agents of Satan to misrepresent and accuse them, and by false reports and insinuations to stir up the rulers against them."[935]

If this preview of things to come is not a powerful heads-up, then I don't know what can get our attention.

SOME NATIONAL LEADERS WILL OPPOSE SABBATH COERCION

Difficult as all this may be, it is not all bleak. While many leaders in government and church leaders will turn their blind eyes toward the Constitution, some national leaders will "oppose such propositions with

---

[934] These issues are now being played out, day after day, in the U.S. government's case against Zacarias Moussaoui, accused as a participant in the September 11, 2001, plane attack on the New York Trade Towers. The latest development in Moussaoui's trial in the Alexandria, VA, courtroom is recounted in "Moussaoui Defense Warns of 'Loophole,'" —*Washington Post*, November 22, 2003.

[935] *The Great Controversy*, 608.

unanswerable arguments. Thus a few men will hold in check a powerful current of evil." They will see the irrefutable logic and appeal of those proclaiming "the Sabbath more fully" and "some of them will accept it and will stand with the people of God through the time of trouble."[936]

Further, "the Lord will bring men of understanding from the various churches to combat the enforcement of a law, that the first day of the week shall be honored as a day when no business shall be transacted."[937]

Surely it will be a time when those "fearlessly serv[ing] God according to the dictates of conscience, will need courage, firmness, and a knowledge of God and His Word, for those who are true to God will be persecuted, their motives will be impugned, their best efforts misinterpreted, and their names cast out as evil."[938]

WHY ALL THIS MALIGNANT HATE?

The Great Controversy will end as it began. Satan's hatred toward God and His law, displayed in deceit, pretence, self-justification, confusion and coercion, will be duplicated in the endtime.[939] Even as God's character will be manifested in those who "keep His commandments and the faith of Jesus" (Revelation 14:12), so Satan's fury at God and His loyalists (Revelation 12:17) will be reflected in those who finally buy into his false worship called Babylon (Revelation 14:8; 18:2, 4).

Those who worship the beast and receive his "mark" (Revelation 13:16) will one day, unfortunately, manifest those same characteristics which Jesus identified when He described those who wanted to kill Him: "You are of your father the devil, and the desires of your father you want to do. He was a murderer from the beginning, and does not stand in the truth, because there is no truth in him. When he speaks a lie, he speaks from his own resources, for he is a liar and the father of it" (John 8:44).[940]

The skill and contrivances of Satan in the last days, hiding behind the mask of law and order, "will more than rival" all "previous persecutions of Protestants by Romans, by which the religion of Jesus Christ was almost

---

[936] *Ibid.,* 610, 611.

[937] Letter 163, 1909 to General Conference Officers.

[938] *Ibid.,* 147.

[939] Similar moments have happened when truth was in great peril and breathtaking courage was required by those representing the God of heaven. Think of Noah and his wild idea to build an Ark (Genesis 6); think of Shadrach, Meshach, and Abednego on the plain of Dura submitting to the fiery furnace and Nebuchadnezzar's fury (Daniel 3); or Esther's bold decision to save her countrymen, Jews in exile, from certain annihilation (Esther 5).

[940] "On the lips of a Jew of that period, the term 'murderer' did not have the legalistic meaning we have attached to it. The word had more the connotation of our 'blasphemy' or 'desecration.' The second aspect of Lucifer's rebellion, Jesus adds, was one of falsehood. Again, on the lips of Jesus, this word referred not so much to lying by words, to fibbing, as to what we call 'pretense,' 'deception,' 'false claims.'" —Malachi Martin, *Hostage to the Devil* (San Francisco: HarperCollins*Publishers,* 1976, 1992), 415.

annihilated."[941] In fact, we are warned that "we need not be surprised at any-thing that may take place now. We need not marvel at any developments of horror. Those who trample under their unholy feet the law of God have the same spirit as had the men who insulted and betrayed Jesus. Without any com-punctions of conscience they will do the deeds of their father the devil."[942]

THE "LITTLE" TIME OF TROUBLE

The prophet Daniel had much to say about last-day events. In the very end of the endtime he speaks of "Michael [Jesus] stand[ing] up, The great prince who stands watch over the sons of your people; And there shall be a time of trouble, such as never was since there was a nation, even to that time. And at that time your people shall be delivered, every one who is found writ-ten in the book" (12:1). This is a very sobering, yet cheery prediction! God and His people will have the last word! And it is deliverance and freedom!

But until then, before this final "time of trouble," the world will go through a "little" time of trouble—I don't know what else to call it.[943] The final time of trouble describes the "seven last plagues" (Revelation 15, 16)—a fearsome time for all those who chose to stay in Babylon, voting for secu-rity instead of freedom when the issues are clearly brought before them.

We have already reviewed how thoughtful Adventists will be treated with "contempt"[944] and their "motives … impugned, their best efforts misinter-preted."[945] But the escalator of troubles moves on.

ESCALATOR OF TROUBLES

Financial security, funds set aside for retirement, family bank accounts—all will soon "be worthless. When the decree shall go forth that none shall buy or sell except they have the mark of the beast, very much means will be of no avail."[946] "In the last great conflict in the controversy with Satan those who are loyal to God will see every earthly support cut off. Because they refuse to break His law in obedience to earthly powers they will be forbid-den to buy or sell."[947] In his hellish glee, Satan really believes that "for fear of wanting food and clothing they [God's loyalists] will join with the world in transgressing God's law. The earth will be wholly under my dominion."[948]

---

[941] *Last Day Events*, 147.

[942] *Ibid.*

[943] "The commencement of that time of trouble,' here mentioned, does not refer to the time when the plagues shall begin to be poured out, but to a short period just before they are poured out, while Christ is in the sanctuary. At that time, while the work of salvation is closing, trouble will be coming on the earth, and the nations will be angry, yet held in check so as not to prevent the work of the third angel" —*Early Writings*, 85, 86.

[944] *Last Day Events*, 146.

[945] *Ibid.*, 147. See *The Great Controversy*, 614.

[946] *Ibid.*, 148.

[947] *Ibid.*

[948] *Ibid.*, 149.

But the escalator moves on. "Many will be imprisoned, many will flee for their lives from cities and towns, and many will be martyrs for Christ's sake in standing in defense of the truth."[949] We are talking about serious times! God's loyalists, living on every continent, will know that they are "risk[ing] ... imprisonment, loss of property and even of life itself, to defend the law of God."[950] "They will even be betrayed both by parents, and brethren, and kinsfolks, and friends' [Luke 21:16], even unto death."[951]

What we are describing has no precedent. The only analogy would be the Nazi Gestapo relentlessly hunting down Jews, Allied pilots, and Resistance fighters, house by house across Europe from the wheat fields of the Ukraine to the shores of the Atlantic. But the Gestapo never had the tools now available to the United States' Pentagon program called CTS—"Combat Zones that See." This is not science fiction. According to Jim Lewis, who heads the Technology and Public Policy Program at the Center for Strategic and International Studies, "There's almost a 100 percent chance that it will work because it's just connecting things that already exist."[952]

CTS's stated purpose is to tighten the responsibilities of the Department of Homeland Security. But in a nutshell, it can track the movement of every individual, every vehicle, recording all the essential information that can be known about that individual or vehicle, day or night. The issue is not how we can stop all this. But how do we manage it? There will be no place to hide in the very near future and certainly nowhere to hide in the upcoming time of trouble.

What is God's comforting encouragement? "We are not to have the courage and fortitude of martyrs of old until brought into the position they were in. ... Should there be a return of persecution there would be grace given to arouse every energy of the soul to show a true heroism."[953]

ACTING PRUDENTLY

Obviously one would ask, what can be done to mitigate the persecution, how should I be prudent and protect my family? Much counsel has been given over the years to seek places in the country, away from the cities.[954] But not all have found such counsel to be possible. But now,

"As enmity is aroused in various places against those who observe the Sabbath of the Lord, it may become necessary for God's people

---

[949] *Ibid.,* 150.
[950] *Ibid.*
[951] *Ibid.*
[952] www.villagevoice.com/issues/shachtmann.php
[953] *Last Day Events.* "Friends will prove treacherous and will betray us. Relatives, deceived by the enemy, will think they do God service in opposing us and putting forth the utmost efforts to bring us into hard places, hoping we will deny our faith. But we may trust our hand in the hand of Christ amid darkness and peril." —*Ibid.*
[954] *Ibid.,* 95, 120.

to move from those places to places where they will not be so bitterly opposed. God does not require His children to remain where, by the course of wicked men, their influence is made of no effect and their lives endangered. When liberty and life are imperiled it is not merely our privilege, it is our positive duty to go to places where the people are willing to hear the Word of life and where the opportunities for preaching the Word will be more favorable."[955]

Those who have heeded Ellen White's counsel to get a well-rounded education, including some manual-labor skills, "will have the advantage where they are."[956]

God always waves the flag of courage and hope for His people, especially on this last battlefield of the Great Controversy. Take heart, father, mother, son, daughter, wife, husband—"When the storm of persecution really breaks upon us, the true sheep will hear the true Shepherd's voice. Self-denying efforts will be put forth to save the lost, and many who have strayed from the fold will come back to follow the great Shepherd."[957] Many people will remember Friday evening vespers, the songs and prayers at sunset, the tug of deep homesickness. Perhaps years away from home and the church, but world events are shaking the memories of Sabbath school classes and those college classes. Now with more mature and realistic mind, the quiet pleas of loved ones strike the deepest heart chord. And the voice of Jesus sounds like an old friend with arms wide open. What a promise!

But back to Satan's strategies. In this unprecedented crisis Satan is seemingly in charge of his plan to eradicate truth on the earth. Why does God permit him so much latitude? The answer is simple:

> "To the last, God permits Satan to reveal his character as a liar, an accuser, and a murderer. Thus the final triumph of His people is made more marked, more glorious, more full and complete"[958]

All this calls for decision-making. How do we make decisions today? Will this kind of thinking make it easier to make the big decisions in the unprecedented times ahead?

---

[955] *Ibid.,* 151, 211.

[956] *Ibid.,* 152.

[957] *Ibid., Testimonies,* vol. 6, 401.

[958] *Ibid.,* 153.

CHAPTER THIRTY-NINE:
THE SEAL AND THE MARK

One of God's principles in his confrontation with Evil, a principle observed throughout recorded history, is that God never permits His faithful to get into situations that are more than they can bear.

John's description of these endtime loyalists is graphic: "Here is the patience of the saints; here are those who keep the commandments of God and the faith of Jesus" (Revelation 14:12). The word "patience" is better-translated "endurance" (RSV). The Greek word, ὑπομονη [translated either as "patience" or "endurance"] is a combination word, "under-remaining." God's people have learned how to carry heavy loads—they remain under the loads without falling apart!

This endurance factor is what Satan hates with serpentine fury. He knows that God's grace is always sufficient, more than what is needed to "endure" all his temptations and persecution (2 Corinthians 12:9). God's loyalists "endure to the end" (Matthew 24:13) because they have these built-in promises:

> "[God] suffers no affliction to come upon the church but such as is essential for her purification, her present and eternal good. He will purify His church even as He purified the temple at the beginning and close of His ministry on earth. All that He brings upon the church in test and trial comes that His people may gain deeper piety and more strength to carry the triumphs of the cross to all parts of the world."[959]

Time out for a little reflection. Some misread the Bible and other writings that seem to suggest that God is the cause of our afflictions, temptations and adversities. In earlier chapters, we traced how Satan is the author of suffering and death although he has done a great job in convincing men and women that all this grief is ordered by God for our "purification." The only way we can connect God with our griefs is to remember two facts: 1) God does not tempt anyone to sin, but Satan does (James 1:13; 1 Peter 5:8, 9); 2) God will help us to endure Satan's attacks (Ephesians 6:10-18), supplying "all your need according to His riches" (Philippians 4:19, also 11-13), reminding us that our temptations and hardships are a replay of Christ's own life who was tempted and troubled with the same issues Satan throws at us today (Hebrews 2:18; 4:15, 16).

In other words, keep your eyes on Jesus and remember Satan was the cause of His troubles. His Heavenly Father was His strong Comforter as He battled life out with Satan. And He will do the same with us, all the way.

---

[959] *Ibid.*, 153, 154.

Further, we can be sure that God will intervene in ways that will surprise everyone. He will open doors, providing added resources, including people and other assets that no one could have predicted.[960]

THE SEAL OF GOD AND THE MARK OF THE BEAST

We have now come to the last act before the curtain falls. All previous decisive moments in the endtime scenario have pointed to this moment when the world, not only the United States, is divided into only two camps: "Each party is distinctly stamped, either with the seal of the living God, or with the mark of the beast or his image."[961]

At last, no place for so-called moderates, centrists and those who hide under the cloak of neutrality:

> "Some apparently may not engage in the conflict on either side. They may not appear to take sides against the truth, but they will not come out boldly for Christ through fear of losing property or suffering reproach. All such are numbered with the enemies of Christ."[962]

Will this "demarcation between the children of light and the children of darkness" be noticeable? "This difference is expressed in the words of Christ, 'born again'—created anew in Christ, dead to the world, and alive unto God."[963]

The Seal of God is more than something that a person can buy or do—it is God's way of signifying the kind of people who have helped Him shut Satan's mouth forever. The Seal is placed on those who are safe to save, those who have been the most faithful in sharing the everlasting gospel in the endtime.

The following description is worth memorizing:

> "Just as soon as the people of God are sealed in their foreheads—it is not any seal or mark that can be seen but a settling into the truth, both intellectually and spiritually, so they cannot be moved—just as

---

[960] "Let me tell you that the Lord will work in this last work in a manner very much out of the common order of things, and in a way that will be contrary to any human planning. There will be those among us who will always want to control the work of God, to dictate even what movements shall be made when the work goes forward under the direction of the angel who joins the third angel in the message to be given to the world. God will use ways and means by which it will be seen that He is taking the reins in His own hands. The workers will be surprised by the simple means that He will use to bring about and perfect His work of righteousness. ... He will raise up from among the common people men and women to do His work, even as of old He called fishermen to be His disciples. There will soon be an awakening that will surprise many. Those who do not realize the necessity of what is to be done will be passed by, and the heavenly messengers will work with those who are called the common people, fitting them to carry the truth to many places" —*Last Day Events*, 203, 204.

[961] *Review and Herald*, January 30, 1900.

[962] *Ibid.*, 215.

[963] *Ibid.*, 215, 216.

soon as God's people are sealed and prepared for the shaking, it will come. Indeed, it has begun already."[964]

God's loyalists have settled "into the truth." That means they know what the final issue is separating those who "keep the commandments of God and the faith of Jesus" (Revelation 14:12) from those who "marveled and followed the beast" (Revelation 13:3). The final issue will distinguish the biblical Sabbath from the papal Sabbath.[965]

Note that they have settled "into the truth, both intellectually and spiritually." This truly is the work of faith, the goal of faith—joining the head of certainty with the heart of certitude.[966] They have studied out the reasons for their commitment to God's call for loyal Christians and they have discovered the validating assurances of the Holy Spirit's presence.[967] The intellectual grasp of truth has reached its transforming purpose—men and women have developed characters that will vindicate God's wisdom as He waits for the purpose of the gospel to be full developed.

How is God's wisdom vindicated? By men and women who are so settled into the truth, "they cannot be moved." Whatever Satan may throw at them, they will never be moved! I can think of some who matured, intellectually and spiritually, until they could not be moved—Enoch, Daniel, John, and Paul.[968] The promise is that those who stand tall under God's flag in the endtime will have matured until they could not be moved, even during the toughest of times.

Jesus stood face-to-face with Satan and overcame him. On one occasion, Jesus declared, "The ruler of this world is coming, and he has nothing in Me" (John 14:30). That is exactly the position in which God's loyalists will be put—staring Satan down in those turbulent last days. And then, almost taking our breath away, is this comment: "This is the condition in which those must be found who shall stand in the time of trouble."[969]

How can this be done?

---

[964] *Ibid.,* 219, 220.

[965] "The seal of the living God is placed upon those who conscientiously keep the Sabbath of the Lord" —*Ibid.,* 220.

[966] See "Appendix K: Faith, The Word That Decides Everything."

[967] "It is the Spirit who bears witness, because the Spirit is truth." 1 John 5:6; 4:13; 3:24.

[968] "Enoch walked with God three hundred years previous to his translation to heaven, and the state of the world was not then more favorable for the perfection of Christian character than it is today. And how did Enoch walk with God? He educated his mind and heart to ever feel that he was in the presence of God, and when in perplexity his prayers would ascend to God to keep him. ... He was constantly shaping his way and course in accordance with God's commandments, and he had perfect confidence and trust in his heavenly Father, that He would help him. He had no thought or will of his own. It was all submerged in the will of his Father. Now Enoch was a representative of those who will be upon the earth when Christ shall come, who will be translated to heaven without seeing death." —*Last Day Events,* 71.

[969] *The Great Controversy,* 623.

"It is in this life that we are to separate sin from us, through faith in the atoning blood of Christ. ... The Lord is ever setting before us, not the way we would choose, which seems easier and pleasanter to us, but the true aims of life. It rests with us to cooperate with the agencies which Heaven employs in the work of conforming our characters to the divine model."[970]

The Seal of God is not a trivial or peripheral subject. For instance, many life-long Sabbath-keepers will receive the Mark of the Beast and not God's Seal! We are talking about something far greater than which day we worship on—we are talking about those who have settled into the truth so that no trial, no Satanic arrow, no threat of death can move them. That is why Ellen White wrote unambiguously that the Seal "will be placed upon those only who 'bear a likeness to Christ's character.'"[971]

If the Seal of God is placed on Christ-like men and women, then the Mark of the Beast distinguishes those who have allowed the characteristics of Satan to mature in their lives. Jesus referred to the wheat and the tares, representing the maturing of the harvest, both the looked-for wheat and the useless tares (Matthew 13:24–30). The principles that matured Satan and all his followers will be reflected in all those who think they are doing right by "caus[ing] as many as would not worship the image of the beast to be killed" (Revelation 13:15).[972]

---

[970] *Ibid.* These thoughts are reason to pause a moment and contemplate the amazing possibilities that God has planned for each of us. Let us not disappoint Him!

[971] *Last Day Events,* 221. Those who receive the seal of the living God and are protected in the time of trouble must reflect the image of Jesus fully." —*Early Writings,* 71. "The seal of God will never be placed upon the forehead of an impure man or woman. It will never be placed upon the forehead of the ambitious, world-loving man or woman. It will never be placed upon the forehead of men or women of false tongues or deceitful hearts. All who receive the seal must be without spot before God—candidates for heaven." —*Testimonies,* vol. 5, 216. "Love is expressed in obedience, and perfect love casteth out all fear. Those who love God, have the seal of God in their foreheads, and work the works of God." —*Last Day Events,* 221. "Those that overcome the world, the flesh, and the devil, will be the favored ones who shall receive the seal of the living God." —*Testimonies to Ministers,* 445."Are we striving with all our God-given powers to reach the measure of the stature of men and women in Christ? Are we seeking for His fullness, ever reaching higher and higher, trying to attain to the perfection of His character? When God's servants reach this point, they will be sealed in their foreheads. The recording angel will declare, "It is done." They will be complete in Him whose they are by creation and by redemption." —*Selected Messages,* bk. 3, 427.

[972] "Decisions we make in the course of our lives shape the context of our future decisions. ... Like every other process we see in nature, the ever-quickening current of life flows in only one direction. These past decisions not only condition our future choices about what we will *do* in life; they also condition the kind of person we will *be* and ever the amount of self-determination we have left to decide the matter. Decisions, however small, are not morally neutral activities. Certain decisions tend to create future possibilities, while other decisions tend to squelch them." —Gregory A. Boyd, *Satan and the Problem of Evil* (Downers Grove, IL: InterVarsity Press, 2001), 198, 199. See also 188, 189.

Just as the seventh-day Sabbath distinguishes those who have the Seal of God, so the papal Sunday will distinguish those who have the Mark of the Beast.[973]

WHEN DOES ONE RECEIVE THE MARK OF THE BEAST?

We can be sure of this: *No one has yet received the Mark of the Beast as understood in this endtime scenario.* Decision time is still open; many have never heard the truth about the seventh-day Sabbath or about the dire consequences of rejecting God's last call for honest seekers of the truth.

Furthermore, God does not close anybody's probation, no matter where they live on Planet Earth. Each of us closes our own probationary time. We either become so settled into the truth so that we will never be moved, or we become so settled into self-centered ways that we too will never be moved, never again have a gracious, forgiving, self-denying thought.

But decision time will come—generations will not roll on for hundreds of years to come! We have been studying how Satan is even now bringing the world of nature, of business, of politics, of religion, into frightful convergence. He indeed is forcing the last, stupendous crisis,

But God is also ratcheting-up His forces. His people will sense the urgency of the times and long-overdue, truth-sharing agencies will move out into the neighborhoods of the world, person-to-person, house-to-house, through radio and television. Truth will be told graciously, clearly, compellingly.

John saw how all this would develop: "After these things I saw another angel coming down from heaven, having great authority, and the earth was illuminated with his glory. And he cried mightily with a loud voice, saying, 'Babylon the great is fallen, is fallen, and has become a habitation of demons.'... And I heard another voice, from heaven saying, 'Come out of her, my people, lest you share in her sins, and lest you receive of her plagues" (Revelation 18:1–4).

At this late date in the endtime escalator, *most of God's people are still in Babylon,* still undecided, still open to truth. In fact, "the great body of Christ's true followers are still to be found in their communion."[974]

FALL OF BABYLON IS PROGRESSIVE

When we ask John when the fall of Babylon is complete, he says when "she made *all* nations drink of the wine of the wrath of her fornication" (Revelation 14:8). The day is still future, but not far away! The fall is

---

[973] "The mark of the beast is the papal sabbath. ... When the test comes, it will be clearly shown what the mark of the beast is. It is the keeping of Sunday. ... The sign, or seal, of God is revealed in the observance of the seventh-day Sabbath, the Lord's memorial of creation. ... The mark of the beast is the opposite of this—the observance of the first day of the week." —*Last Day Events*, 224.

[974] *The Great Controversy*, 390.

progressive and when "all nations" unite in legislating, then enforcing, Sunday laws, then the "fall" will be complete.

God does not expect His people to lose their perspective: Just because people are even in perfect darkness, they are not necessarily bad! God's people still in Babylon will be hearing facts and arguments for the first time about the darkening clouds of religious oppression and the sanctity of the seventh-day Sabbath. At that time, God's loyalists will be making a convincing case for the seventh-day Sabbath and a compelling rationale for freedom of conscience in the face of worldwide resistance.[975]

THE "LOUD CRY"

This profound prophetic witness is often called the "loud cry"[976]—"these announcements, uniting with the third angel's message, constitute the final warning to be given to the inhabitants of the earth."[977] No country of the world will be in the dark as to the implications of these universal Sunday laws—"the whole earth was illuminated" (Revelation 18:1).[978]

What I think is more than interesting is that Sabbath-keepers will no longer expect certain church leaders to represent them, such as the specialists in the Public Affairs and Religious Liberty Departments. The coming crisis in every country of the world will focus on individuals, and individuals will have to step up and explain why they should not be considered "lawbreakers"!

I am often reminded of what Martin Niemoller said after leaving the concentration camp at Dachau in 1945:

> "When Hitler attacked the Jews I was not a Jew, therefore I was not concerned. And when Hitler attacked the Catholics, I was not a Catholic, and therefore, I was not concerned. And when Hitler attacked the unions and the industrialists, I was not a member of the

---

[975] One of the Four Freedoms enunciated by President Roosevelt for which Americans would fight in World War II.

[976] As the third message swells to a loud cry and as great power and glory attend the closing work, "the faithful people of God will partake of that glory. It is the latter rain which revives and strengthens them to pass through the time of trouble." —*Last Day Events*, 201.

[977] *Ibid.*, 199. "The sins of Babylon will be laid open. The fearful results of enforcing the observances of the church by civil authority, the inroads of spiritualism, the stealthy but rapid progress of the papal power—all will be unmasked. By these solemn warnings the people will be stirred. Thousands upon thousands will listen who have never heard words like these." —*The Great Controversy*, 606.

[978] "The angel who unites in the proclamation of the third angel's message is to lighten the whole earth with his glory. A work of world-wide extent and unwonted power is here foretold. ... Servants of God, with their faces lighted up and shining with holy consecration, will hasten from place to place to proclaim the message from heaven. By thousands of voices, all over the earth, the warning will be given. ... The message of the angel following the third is now to be given to all parts of the world. It is to be the harvest message, and the whole earth will be lighted with the glory of God." —*Last Day Events*, 207, 208.

unions and I was not concerned. Then Hitler attacked me and the Protestant church—and there was nobody left to be concerned."[979]

We are living in the days of darkening clouds. Anyone who thinks that somebody, somewhere, will carry them through the tough times ahead better get real! Anyone who thinks that he or she has no responsibility to speak up for freedom now, whether a United States citizen or a citizen of China, Iran, or North Korea, is not only self-absorbed and myopic, he or she will some day soon discover that they blew past the time of preparation for themselves. Sad and scary!

Listen carefully:

> "It does not seem possible to us now that any should have to stand alone, but if God has ever spoken by me, the time will come when we shall be brought before councils and before thousands for His name's sake, and each one will have to give the reason of his faith. Then will come the severest criticism upon every position that has been taken for the truth. We need, then, to study the Word of God, that we may know why we believe the doctrines we advocate."[980]

What kind of response will this "loud cry" receive among most of the inhabitants of Planet Earth?

- They will be called "enthusiasts,"[981] as well as "law-breakers."[982]

- They will be rejected as Noah was by his contemporaries just before his world came to its end."[983]

- Sunday-keeping ministers will be "filled with anger as their authority is questioned, will denounce the message as of Satan, and stir up the sin-loving multitudes to revile and persecute those who proclaim it."[984]

- They "will be threatened with fines and imprisonment, and some will be offered positions of influence, and other rewards and advantages, as inducements to renounce their faith."[985]

---

[979] The exact text of what Martin Niemoller said appears in the Congressional Record, October 14, 1968, page 31636.

[980] *Ibid.*, 209. "Many will have to stand in the legislative courts; some will have to stand before kings and before the learned of the earth to answer for their faith. Those who have only a superficial understanding of truth will not be able clearly to expound the Scriptures and give definite reasons for their faith. They will become confused and will not be workmen that need not to be ashamed. Let no one imagine that he has no need to study because he is not to preach in the sacred desk. You know not what God may require of you." —*Ibid.*, 209.

[981] *Ibid.*, 210.

[982] *The Great Controversy,* 591.

[983] *Last Day Events,* 210.

[984] *The Great Controversy,* 607.

[985] *Ibid.*

But that is not all. Let's look at the cheery side.

- Many will respond to these last-day defenses of freedom and their "zeal will far exceed that of those who have stood in rank and file to proclaim the truth heretofore."[986]

- "Many who have strayed from the fold will come back to follow the great Shepherd."[987]

- "A good many do not see it now, to take their position, but these things [perplexing world events] are influencing their lives, and when the message goes with a loud voice they will be ready for it. They will not hesitate long; they will come out and take their position."[988]

- "Notwithstanding the agencies combined against the truth, a large number take their stand upon the Lord's side."[989]

However, that time will come when the last person will say either "yes" or "no" *finally* to the measure of light that each has. When is that time? "With the issue thus clearly brought him, whoever shall trample upon God's law to obey a human enactment, receives the mark of the beast; he accepts the sign of allegiance to the power which he chooses to obey instead of God."[990]

CROSSING THE LINE

When one crosses that line only God knows. What we do know is that no one will suffer the seven last plagues "until the truth has been brought home to his mind and conscience and has been rejected. ... Every one is to have sufficient light to make his decision intelligently."[991] God will never force

---

[986] *Last Day Events*, 211.

[987] *Ibid.*

[988] *Ibid.*, 212, 213. "Now the rays of light penetrate everywhere, the truth is seen in its clearness, and the honest children of God sever the bands which have held them. Family connections, church relations, are powerless to stay them now. Truth is more precious than all besides. Notwithstanding the agencies combined against the truth, a large number take their stand upon the Lord's side." —*The Great Controversy*, 612.

[989] *The Great Controversy*, 612.

[990] *Ibid.*, 604. "All must wait for the appointed time, until the warning shall have gone to all parts of the world, until sufficient light and evidence have been given to every soul. Some will have less light than others, but each one will be judged according to the light received" —*Last Day Events*, 217. "We have been given great light in regard to God's law. This law is the standard of character. To it man is now required to conform, and by it he will be judged in the last great day. In that day men will be dealt with according to the light they have received." —*Ibid.* "Those who have had great light and have disregarded it stand in a worse position than those who have not been given so many advantages. They exalt themselves but not the Lord. The punishment inflicted on human beings will in every case be proportionate to the dishonor they have brought on God." —*Ibid.* "Everyone is to have sufficient light to make his decision intelligently." —*The Great Controversy*, 605.

[991] *Ibid.*, 605. "Many who have not had the privileges that we have had will go into heaven before those who have had great light and who have not walked in it. Many have lived up to the best light they have had and will be judged accordingly." —*Last Day Events*, 216.

anyone to trust Him. He will give everyone time to decide without coercion of any kind—exactly the way He related to confused angels in heaven and to every man or woman on this earth.

The more I think of personal responsibility in helping to bring truth home to my loved ones, friends, neighbors and anyone who may listen, I think of Oskar Schindler. Wealthy manufacturer and entrepreneur, he personally rescued more than 1,200 Jews from certain death in concentration camps during the Nazi horror of the early 1940s. In the closing scene of the movie, *Schindler's List*, he is portrayed saying farewell to a group of Jews he had the privilege of saving at great personal sacrifice of both cash and risk. As he stands there next to his large, expensive automobile, he is suddenly gripped with the thought, "I could have done more. I should have sold this car. It would have been 10 more if I sold this car. This expensive pen in my pocket, it would have been five more. I could have gotten five more with this pen. This ring on my finger, with its gold I could have gotten two or at least one more." The camera then zooms in on the closing scene, showing Schindler weeping because he believed he could have done more.

Surviving "Schindlerjudens" and the Israeli government bestowed on him in 1962 a medal inscribed with the Talmudic verse in Hebrew and French: "He who saves one life, it is as if he saves the entire world." He is honored on the Avenue of the Righteous at Yad Vashem—"a righteous Gentile." He did what he could.

The question before me daily: "Am I doing what I can?" Some day we all cross that line in the sand. God can be trusted on that day. What about you and me?

CHAPTER FORTY:
THE SEVEN LAST PLAGUES

The Great Controversy between God and Satan will not go on forever! Reckoning day is just ahead! Ideas and decisions surely have consequences and it comes down to freedom versus coercion. The Bible previews time running out for Planet Earth.

The dreadful future awaiting those who "had the mark of the beast and those who worshipped His image" is described in Revelation 16. Contrary to what some may think, those fearful plagues are *not* the fiery vengeance of an offended God. The plagues are *not* evidence that God has been pushed too far and He now says, "I have had it!"

The seven last plagues are, however, the awful evidence of what satanic fever will do when unrestrained by the Holy Spirit and the good angels. The plagues are not God's character in full display but the unvarnished, horrific character of Satan, the master deceiver, who now unleashes his most dreadful hate on the people of God.[992]

We see part of the big picture in Revelation 7:1–3: "I saw four angels standing at the four corners of the earth, holding the four winds of the earth, that the wind should not blow on the earth, on the sea, or on any tree. Then I saw another angel ascending from the east, having the seal of the living God. And he cried with a loud voice to the four angels to whom it was granted to harm the earth and the sea, saying, 'Do not hurt the earth, the sea, or the trees till we have sealed the servants of our God on their foreheads.'"

The other side of the big picture is in Revelation 18:4: "And I heard another voice from heaven saying, 'Come out of her, my people, lest you share in her sins, and lest you receive of her plagues.'"

The plagues begin when God's loyalists are sealed and those who reject God's messages receive the Mark of the Beast and worship its image. Two groups are finally and clearly distinguished.

The important point, however, is that this is not a static situation. God's loyalists reflect the character of Jesus; Satan's loyalists reflect his character.

---

[992] "It is the restraining power of God that prevents mankind from passing fully under the control of Satan. The disobedient and unthankful have great reason for gratitude for God's mercy and long-suffering in holding in check the cruel, malignant power of the evil one. But when men pass the limits of divine forbearance, that restraint is removed. God does not stand toward the sinner as an executioner of the sentence against transgression; but He leaves the rejecters of His mercy to themselves, to reap that which they have sown. Every ray of light rejected, every warning despised or unheeded, every passion indulged, every transgression of the law of God, is a seed sown which yields its unfailing harvest. The Spirit of God, persistently resisted, is at last withdrawn from the sinner, and then there is left no power to control the evil passions of the soul, and no protection from the malice and enmity of Satan." —*The Great Controversy*, 36.

The last time we saw this clearly distinguished was at the Cross! Satan did his best to beat Jesus down, physically and emotionally—awful pressure. And he will do his best to beat down our Lord's faithful, in every way possible, when he has the greater majority of all worldly inhabitants primed to destroy those stubborn Sabbath-keepers.

Satan's hate is never calm. Ultimate selfishness lashes out unrestrained. And that is exactly what we see in the biblical overview of the seven last plagues—cartoon-like pictures of unrestrained evil, selfishness and rage. The wicked have been sheltered for years from the full venom of the Dragon (Satan) by the grace of God reaching for their hearts. But after probation has closed, after each person has chosen either to worship the God of the Fourth Commandment or the false gods represented by Babylon, the wicked, by their own choice, no longer are protected from evil forces in the universe.[993]

As the plagues begin to fall, those who are worshiping the image of the beast (Revelation 13:15) have further "reason" to hate God's loyalists. They have been "enraged" with the power that attended the "loud cry" and "their anger is kindled against all who have received the message." And now "those who honor the law of God have been accused of bringing judgments upon the world and they will be regarded as the cause of the fearful convulsions of nature and the strife and bloodshed among men that are filling the earth with woe."[994] They now blame all these terrible plagues on God's faithful as if they are responsible for what seems, to them, to be the anger of God!

This malignant rage aimed at those who fearlessly stand for freedom in a very troubled, angry world soon results in, not a stiffer Sunday law, but a new way to eliminate the Sabbath-keepers in their "semblance of zeal for God."[995] That new "way," unknown to the United States and so contrary to its historical principles, will be a Sabbath "decree," denouncing Sabbath-keepers "as deserving of the severest punishment, and giving the people [those worshipping the beast and its image] liberty, after a certain time, to put them to death."[996]

The entire universe will see the ultimate hatred of ultimate Evil once more. When the fiendish rage of Satan is focused on God's loyalists in this last hour of the endtime, the universe see again what happened at the Cross—Evil will again have its way, but only for a little while.

---

[993] "Unsheltered by divine grace, they have no protection from the wicked one. Satan will then plunge the inhabitants of the earth into one great, final trouble. As the angels of God cease to hold in check the fierce winds of human passion, all the elements of strife will be let loose. The whole world will be involved in ruin more terrible than that which came upon Jerusalem of old. ... The same destructive power exercised by holy angels when God commands, will be exercised by evil angels when He permits. There are forces now ready, and only waiting the divine permission, to spread desolation everywhere." —*The Great Controversy,* 614.

[994] *Ibid.,* 614, 615.

[995] *Ibid.,* 615.

[996] *Ibid.*

TIME OF JACOB'S TROUBLE

This death decree is often referred to as the "time of Jacob's trouble."[997] Reference is made to Jacob's "night of anguish, when he wrestled in prayer for deliverance from the hand of Esau"[998] and to Jeremiah's description of this most trying event: "Thus saith the Lord: We have heard a voice of trembling, of fear, and not of peace. ... All faces are turned into paleness. Alas! for that day is great, so that none is like it: it is even the time of Jacob's trouble; but he shall be saved out of it" (30:5–7).

Just as Satan had prompted Esau to "march against Jacob, so he will stir up the wicked to destroy God's people in the time of trouble ... but the little company who keep the commandments of God are resisting his supremacy. If he could blot them from the earth, his triumph would be complete."[999]

Again we have the showdown between God and Satan over God's fairness, similar to the conflict over Job. (See Job 1, 2.) And again God shows His confidence in the faith of His people. He permits Satan to throw his fiercest abuse at Sabbath-keepers—"to the uttermost." Their inner anxieties (they fear most to dishonor God in this horrific face-off with Satan) and their physical deprivations sap their physical and emotional reserve. Like Job, they are "severely tested."[1000]

God's faithful had done their best to "place themselves in a proper light before the people, to disarm prejudice, and to avert the danger which threatens liberty of conscience."[1001] But angry and confused men and women, unrestrained by the wooing pleas of the Holy Spirit, no longer are controlled by calm reason. Passion drives them to overlook the facts; they forget the record of decency they have observed in God's loyalists through the years—and all they want to do is to destroy their neighbors who will not bend to the tyranny of the majority regarding Sunday enforcement.

HOW DOES ONE PREPARE FOR THE TIME OF JACOB'S TROUBLE?

It seems to me that preparation involves whatever it takes in times of peace to listen carefully to God's advice regarding a healthy mind and body. Only the prepared survive. Serious Bible students know that our Lord's question to Jeremiah applies with devastating frankness: "If you have run with the footmen, and they have wearied you, then how can you contend with horses? And if in the land of peace, in which you trusted, they wearied you, then how will you do in the flooding of the Jordan" (12:5)?

Adventists know that some day soon the Jordan will swell, the easy paths will suddenly become treacherous with foes seen and unseen; the

---

[997] *Ibid.*, 616.
[998] *Ibid.*, 618.
[999] *Ibid.*
[1000] *Ibid.*, 618, 619.
[1001] *Ibid.*

wind will become brisk, even hurricane force. The past will not provide all the answers.

I think of a young man who worked for Lord Joseph Duveen. "Duveen, American head of the art firm that bore his name, planned in 1915 to send one of his experts to England to examine some ancient pottery. He booked passage on the *Lusitania.* Then the German Embassy issued a warning that the liner might be torpedoed. Duveen wanted to call off the trip: 'I can't take the risk of your being killed,' he said to his young expert.

"'Don't worry,' the young man replied. 'I'm a strong swimmer, and when I read what was happening in the Atlantic, I began hardening myself by spending time every day in a tub of ice water. At first I could stand it only a few minutes, but this morning I stayed in that tub nearly two hours.'

"'Naturally,' Duveen laughed. It sounded preposterous. But this expert sailed; the *Lusitania* was torpedoed. The young man was rescued after nearly five hours in the chilly ocean, still in excellent condition."[1002]

Obviously, preparation for the time of trouble involves more than physical training—but the point is made. Just as this young man prepared for the probable future, so must God's loyalists—for themselves as well as for others. In the quiet times, they must learn how to keep their eyes on Jesus in a daily companionship, conditioning themselves under the daily guidance of the Holy Spirit, finding easy victories in preparation for the tough times. Only the prepared survive![1003]

IN TIMES OF EASE

Survivors prepare in times of ease. They make a life habit of affirming—

- Daily Bible study, abiding in biblical principles;

- Gracious outreach to others for whatever their need may be;

- Clearheaded resistance to evil wherever found, empowered by the Spirit;

- All this must become a daily fact, embracing every decision, every commitment.

All this is not a "someday" option. Not a lifestyle to be suddenly pursued after one "sees events shaping up." When the *Lusitania* was sinking, it was too late for the young art collector to get ready for the freezing Atlantic Ocean!

Too often we slip into "playing church." But the future is not going to be more of the same. We have more to think about than a broad-brush hope that "God will take care of me!" We must remember what God has said about our own responsibilities in maintaining a secure relationship with Him.

[1002] Vernon Grounds, "Getting Into Shape Spiritually," *Christianity Today,* February 2, 1979.
[1003] Herbert E. Douglass, *How to Survive in the 21st Century* (RHPA, 2000), 1–139.

Ellen White could not be clearer:

> "Those who exercise but little faith now, are in the greatest danger of falling under the power of satanic delusions and the decree to compel the conscience. And even if they endure the test, they will be plunged into deeper distress and anguish in the time of trouble, because they have never made it a habit to trust in God. The lessons of faith which they have neglected, they will be forced to learn under a terrible pressure of discouragement. ...

> "The 'time of trouble such as never was,' is soon to open upon us; and we shall need an experience which we do not now possess, and which many are too indolent to obtain. It is often the case that trouble is greater in anticipation than in reality; but this is not true of the crisis before us. The most vivid presentation cannot reach the magnitude of the ordeal. In that time of trial, every soul must stand for himself before God."[1004]

LOVE FOR THE TRUTH

One of the surest ways to prepare for these most demanding times is to develop a love for truth. That means we should be walking into the Light, not only mentally but also spiritually. The advancing Light will help us make clearer decisions for whatever the future holds. Only those who have been "diligent students of the Scriptures, and who have received the love of the truth, will be shielded from the powerful delusion that takes the world captive. ... Are the people of God now so firmly established upon His word that they would not yield to the evidence of their senses?"[1005]

Could this appeal be any more compelling?

> "If the believers in the truth are not sustained by their faith in these comparatively peaceful days, what will uphold them when the grand test comes and the decree goes forth against all those who will not worship the image of the beast and receive his mark in their foreheads or in their hands? This solemn period is not far off. Instead of becoming weak and irresolute, the people of God should be gathering strength and courage for the time of trouble."[1006]

GENEVA'S WALL OF THE REFORMATION

I feel something special like goose bumps when we visit Geneva, Switzerland. In old Geneva, a remarkable monument in the shape of a wall

---

[1004] *The Great Controversy*, 622.

[1005] *Ibid.*, 625.

[1006] *Testimonies*, vol. 4, 251. "The season of distress and anguish before us will require a faith that can endure weariness, delay, and hunger—a faith that will not faint though severely tried. The period of probation is granted to all to prepare for that time. Jacob prevailed because he was persevering and determined." —*The Great Controversy*, 621.

100-meters long (328 feet) of Burgundian quartz and Mont Blanc granite remembers Reformation heroes. High above and easily read is the motto, *Post Tenebras Lux*—"Out of Darkness Light"! Ten large statues 6-meters high (19.68 feet) stretch across the length of the wall representing the foremost leaders in the Calvinistic phase of the Protestant Reformation. Every time I see this awesome statement of spiritual heroism, I think of those faithful who endured much persecution, even unto death.[1007] They all followed the Light as they knew it, throwing back the religious oppression of more than 1,000 years.

What they experienced in their time of troubles was only a slight fore-taste of what lies ahead for God's loyalists in the endtime. In the darkening clouds of global oppression when freedom is being choked by masterful Evil, this world will see again those who are worthy of Geneva's motto: *Out of Darkness Light.*

Only the prepared survive!

[1007] William Farel, John Calvin, Théodore de Bèze, John Knox, Gaspard de Coligny, William the Silent, Etienne Bocskay, Oliver Cromwell, Roger Williams, Frederick William.

CHAPTER FORTY-ONE:
HOW GOD PROTECTS

During this unparalleled time when evil is unrestrained and the whole world is in confusion and moved by fear, God's loyalists will "flee from cities and villages and associate together in companies, dwelling in the most desolate and solitary places."[1008]

What will be uppermost on their minds? They will remember Noah in the ark for seven days, door shut, no rain, and the sun still shining; Joseph in Potiphar's prison, falsely accused and no human hope for release; Elijah hunted by the king's secret service as Public Enemy Number One; Jeremiah up to his neck in the slime of a Jerusalem prison for his loyalty to God; the three worthies in their fiery furnace; Daniel in that fearsome lion's den—and on the list would grow.

Where will God be? Just where He was with Noah, Joseph, and the rest of our biblical heroes. But more than any other memory will be knowing where God was when Jesus sweat blood in Gethsemane and suffocated on the Cross. In all these stressful moments in the Great Controversy, God was energizing His own with His presence and His promises.

While God's loyalists are not free from suffering and in profound distress, "they will not be left to perish. ... While the wicked are dying from hunger and pestilence, angels will shield the righteous, and supply their wants." If they could see the "real" picture, "they would behold companies of angels that excel in strength stationed about those who have kept the word of Christ's patience."[1009]

One may ask, "Why is God permitting these awful troubles to get worse, month after month?" In the big picture of the Great Controversy, "they must wait a little longer." Why? "The very delay, so painful to them, is the best answer to their petitions. As they endeavor to wait trustingly for the Lord to work, they are led to exercise faith, hope, and patience [endurance], which have been too little exercised during their religious experience."[1010]

W. D. Frazee saw the issue clearly: "Then comes the period of demonstration, the great time of trouble. God's children reveal the power of His grace by loyally obeying even to the point of threatened death. The wicked exhibit their rebellion, finally attempting to murder every saint. Then the

---

[1008] *The Great Controversy,* 626.
[1009] *Ibid.,* 629, 630.
[1010] *Ibid.,* 630, 631.

whole universe will says, 'Enough!' Christ will come to destroy the impenitent and take His people home."[1011]

LIVING WITHOUT AN INTERCESSOR

What could this possibly mean—that after the close of probation God's people "must live in the sight of a holy God without an intercessor."[1012]

Living without a intercessor, that is, without Jesus as our High Priest, in no way means living without the enabling power of Christ through His Holy Spirit. The phrase only means living without the continuing need for forgiveness of ongoing sins.

Some may ask, how can that be? Earlier, we reviewed how God's loyalists, before probation closed, were settled "into the truth, both intellectually and spiritually, so they cannot be moved." They will be overcomers by the grace of God. Yet they will still be dependent on grace, its keeping power, to endure the awful trials of the seven last plagues.

In short, not needing an Intercessor/Mediator isn't the same as not needing Jesus or the Holy Spirit. An intercessor or mediator is needed only when differences arise. When our local teachers go on strike and the school board does not give them what they want, the teachers need a mediator. When all is OK, no mediator is needed. The disputes between God and man are called sins. When sins have been overcome by the grace of God, and the mind is settled into a habitual pattern of trusting obedience, Christ is no longer needed as a Mediator, though He is still needed to provide grace to help in time of need (Hebrews 4:16).[1013]

IN SUMMARY

We have only quickly reviewed how Satan will use the United States as his launching pad for world domination. We have noted his various strategies including pretense, scapegoating, confusion, and coercion to achieve his ends.

The core word that underlies God's relationship with Satan, as well as all other created beings, is *freedom*. To the end of the controversy, freedom is still God's greatest gift to His creation. In the world of rebellion against God's character and government, freedom costs. Freedom cost Jesus some very important eternal privileges but that gift to the universe as well as to this world set the tone for all those who are also willing the pay the cost of freedom.[1014]

[1011] W. D. Frazee, *Ransom and Reunion* (Nashville, TN: Southern Publishing Association, 1977), 87.
[1012] *The Great Controversy*, 614.
[1013] See *The Great Controversy*, 488, 489, 614, 620, 625, 633.
[1014] See 89.

In the endtime, God's loyalists will pay the cost of their freedom in ways that defy imagination at this time. But they too will learn that freedom not only costs, it also pays with eternal dividends.

Our next section focuses specifically on how God plans to prepare His people for the white-hot heat of the last days. And why God is willing to risk His role in the Great Controversy on His last-day loyalists.

Protestant theologian, Dietrich Bonhoeffer (1906–1945) was one of the very few church leaders of any church who stood in courageous opposition to Adolf Hitler. More then that, his views on the horror of Nazi policies, especially in its determination to kill all Jews, put him into profound conflict with his own German Evangelical Church, Germany's dominant church—with its compromises, complicities, and hypocrisies. Bonhoeffer was not a fiery agitator. His parents were both university graduates, his father a prominent professor of psychiatry and neurology. His parents emphasized strong moral and intellectual commitments. The Nazis executed two brothers and two brothers-in-law for their anti-government involvements.

At 21 Bonhoeffer completed his doctoral program and finished another degree in 1930 at Union Theological Seminary in New York. During these years, he was closely involved with the brightest theological minds in both Germany and America.

When Hitler rose to power in 1933, German Lutherans as well as most other churches faced their darkest hours. Shaped for centuries by nationalism and obedience to state authority, after the troubling chaos of the post-war years (World War I), Germany, including most all Protestants, welcomed a strong leader.

For German Protestants, the fact that the Nazis government asserted that the Jew was a non-Aryan and thus could not work in a civil service job did not greatly upset them. Soon a growing group within the church joined the state in proclaiming that no Jew could be a minister or religion teacher, then further, that no Jew could be even a member of the church through baptism. Bonhoeffer with a relatively small group (called the "Confessing Church,") bitterly opposed anti-Semitic laws, both in the state and in the church. When the Nazi dictatorship tightened its grip on all dissent, many even in the "Confessing Church" buckled, but not all. His April 1933 essay, "The Church and the Jewish Question," called for Christians to defend victims of state persecution. He now was in the cross hairs of both his tyrannical government and his own church! He was only 27 years old!

Under Gestapo observation, he was banned from Berlin in 1938. In June 1939, he left for New York to teach in the Union Theological Seminary. But soon after arriving he wrote to Reinhold Niebuhr: "I have come to the conclusion that I made a mistake in coming to America. … I shall have no right to take part in the restoration of Christian life in Germany after the war unless I share the trials of this time with my people." A month later, he returned to Germany. In October 1944, Bonhoeffer was placed in the dreaded Gestapo prison in Berlin; in February 1945 to Buchenwald and then to Flossenburg concentration camp where on April 9 he was hanged. The SS doctor who witnessed his death later recalled, "I have hardly ever seen a man die so entirely submissive to the will of God."

At 39 years, Bonhoeffer was on the edge of an extraordinary professional career, a preeminent author and speaker. But he heard freedom's call and paid the cost.

How will God's faithful respond to Satan's last-day deceptions and vindicate His judgment in their favor? What are the related events involving God's loyalists that will help determine the timing of the Second Advent? How will these events more fully vindicate God's wisdom and patience when He risked giving freedom to created intelligences?

CHAPTER FORTY-TWO:
JESUS DESCRIBED THE KIND OF PEOPLE READY FOR HIM TO RETURN

God doesn't ask His loyalists to "march to the sound of drums" without a clear battle plan. Freedom is not a foggy word! Whether one can spell out moving reasons for his or her desire for freedom, men and women know it when they see and feel it! But God did not leave His faithful in the last of the lastdays to stumble into the future. His battle plans are well known by both His loyalists and Satan's loyalists.

Jesus gave His church many clues describing the kind of people who will face Satan without flinching in the endtime—even as Jesus faced him during His 33 years on earth (Revelation 3:21).

In our Lord's answer to the disciples' question, "What will be the sign of Your coming?" (Matthew 24:3), we have the awesome overview of 1) what we should expect in the endtime and 2) what kind of people will be representing His side of the Great Controversy.

Among the identifying characteristics of God's loyalists is that "he who endures to the end shall be saved" (verse 13); that such people are "witnesses" to the clarity and power of the "gospel" (verse 14); and that they are "faithful and wise servants" who know how to give "food in due season" as their Master has directed (verse 45).

The question for all of us is, "Am I a faithful and wise servant"? In other words, for whom is Jesus waiting in the endtime? Jesus did not leave us to wonder. He proceeded to answer His own question (verse 45) by giving us four picture stories in Matthew 24 and 25—before He finished His answer to the disciples' questions regarding the end of the world.

The four picture stories (faithful and wise servant, ten bridesmaids, businessman distributing responsibilities to his employees, and sheep separated from goats) describe those who will be ready for probationary time to close; they are prepared for Jesus to come, and they are busy helping others be ready.

The common thread running through our Lord's answer to His question (verse 45) *and our personal answer* is that readiness for the advent is not a matter of crash preparation, as if one were preparing for an approaching hurricane. Although urgency is always a part of a committed Adventist's life, readiness for the advent is more a matter of a maturing character than emergency activity.

FAITHFUL AND WISE SERVANTS

These faithful and wise servants have what all men and women need—the truth about God and His plans for their future. They win the favorable attention of those who thirst for peace of mind during the turbulence of the endtime. Their words are compelling because their lifestyle is convincing. Such is one of the favorite themes of Ellen White:

> "A true, lovable Christian is the most powerful argument that can be advanced in favor of Bible truth. Such a man is Christ's representative. His life is the most convincing evidence that can be borne to the power of divine grace. When God's people bring the righteousness of Christ into the daily life, sinners will be converted, and victories over the enemy will be gained."[1015]

Towering responsibilities rest on those who claim to be God's loyalists—they exhibit a direct connection between their lives and the witness of the gospel! What kind of nourishment are they to give "in due season" to men and women the world over in the endtime? The "food" most needed is a clear picture of the gospel—what Jesus has said, done, and yet will do for men and women everywhere. Making this good news known is the wonderful task of the "faithful and wise servant."

Yet making this good news known is much more than reciting a list of biblical tests, repeated far and wide, in all languages. Men and women the world over have heard millions of sermons, read tons of written material, and been awarded hundreds of thousands of certificates for finishing Bible correspondence courses. And yet we have many millions who are "burned over," either living post-Christian lives or "turned off" by

---

[1015] *Review and Herald,* January 14, 1904.

professed Christians whose lives do not back up their "preaching." Whenever the truth of the gospel is heard without its transforming power, the net effect is rejection.

However, as we have said before, everyone living in the endtime will have a fair opportunity to know what he or she is accepting or rejecting when facing the truth about God, especially during the final clash between the Sabbath and the Sunday laws.[1016]

All will have the opportunity to decide 1) whether God can be trusted, and 2) whether Christianity is any different than any other religious philosophy. "Faithful and wise" servants will provide evidence that God has been abundantly fair and powerful. Note this counsel:

> "The world watches to see what fruit is borne by professed Christians. It has a right to look for self-denial and self-sacrifice from those who claim to believe advanced truth. … God has ordained that his work shall be presented to the world in distinct, holy lines. He desires his people to show by their lives the advantage of Christianity over worldliness. By his grace every provision has been made for us in all our transaction of business to demonstrate the superiority of heaven's principles over the principles of the world."[1017]

The focus of the universe is on God's loyalists in the endtime. Events such as the "latter rain," "the loud cry" and the "sealing work" will happen when God has a people who will not embarrass Him.

Peter looked forward to Christians in the endtime when he asked: "Therefore since all these things will be dissolved, what manner of persons ought you to be in holy conduct and godliness, looking for and hastening the coming of the day of God" (2 Peter 3:11, 12). On many occasions, Ellen White supported Peter:

> "Character is power. The silent witness of a true, unselfish, godly life carries an almost irresistible influence. By revealing in our own life the character of Christ we co-operate with Him in the work of saving souls. It is only by revealing in our life His character that we can co-operate with Him. … When those who profess to serve God follow Christ's example, practicing the principles of the law in their daily life; when

---

[1016] See 315ff.

[1017] *Ibid.*, July 27, 1905. "The world today is in crying need of a revelation of Christ Jesus in the person of his saints. God desires that his people shall stand before the world a holy people. Why? Because there is a world to be saved by the light of gospel truth; and as the message of truth that is to call men out of darkness into God's marvelous light, is given by the church, the lives of its members, sanctified by the Spirit of truth, are to bear witness to the verity of the messages proclaimed. … The world is in need of a demonstration of practical Christianity. In view of the fact that those who claim to be followers of Christ are a spectacle to an unbelieving world, it behooves them to make sure that they are in right relation with God." —*Review and Herald*, March 31, 1910.

every act bears witness that they love God supremely and their neighbor as themselves, then will the church have power to move the world."[1018]

This "power to move the world" is precisely how the Lord plans to foil Satan's plan to take over this world in the endtime.[1019]

"WICKED SERVANTS"

But before we move on to our Lord's second picture-story describing the faithful and wise servant who will have "power to move the world," we must pause and listen to what Jesus says about Adventists He calls, "wicked servants," who say, one way or another, "My master is delaying His coming" (Matthew 24:48).

What a frightful end for those once committed to the Lord of the advent! What happened? The "wicked servant" says, "I still have time to get ready. My master has not returned when we expected. I'll have my fling now, but when I see things shaping up, then I'll clean up my act. After all, the Sunday laws haven't been passed. Perhaps my master won't even come back in my lifetime!"

Either in spirit or word, the wicked servant, regardless of his good and regular standing as a church member, explains away the Lord's delay. Could it be that such Adventists will have lulled themselves into a false security? How would they do that? By thinking that the delay in the advent is caused by some yet unfulfilled prophecy in the political world, or not enough evil yet, or by some arbitrary time clock in the mind of God.

Ellen White spoke to this misguided thinking many times.[1020] For example, "We may have to remain here in this world because of insubordination many more years, as did the children of Israel; but for Christ's sake, His people should not add sin to sin by charging God with the consequence of their own wrong course of action."[1021]

The issue is not over whether there has been a delay. Christ's own words supported by many dozens of supporting statements by Ellen White confirm the delay in Christ's return. The real issue is the cause for the delay and how His return can be hastened.[1022]

The question is, "How much am I delaying the return of Jesus?"

[1018] *Christ's Object Lessons,* 340.

[1019] "The world can only be warned by seeing those who believe the truth sanctified through the truth, acting upon high and holy principles, showing in a high, elevated sense, the line of demarcation between those who keep the commandments of God and whose who trample them under their feet." —Ellen G. White Comments on Revelation 7, *SDABC,* vol. 7, 980.

[1020] See Herbert E. Douglass, *The End* (PPPA, 1979), 161–167.

[1021] *Evangelism,* 696.

[1022] See *The Desire of Ages,* 633, 634.

CHAPTER FORTY-THREE:
PORTRAIT OF THE BRIDEGROOM AND HIS TEN BRIDESMAIDS

The second snapshot of the "faithful and wise servant" describes two groups that have always existed in the Christian church—two groups bound together by common doctrines, both groups in "good and regular standing."

The element of "delay" is built into this snapshot also—"the bridegroom was delayed" (Matthew 25:5). According to Ellen White, the experience of the ten maids illustrates "the experience of the church that shall live just before His second coming."[1023]

Both groups, the wise and foolish bridesmaids, represent Adventists (anyone who believes in the soon-coming of Jesus) who "took their lamps and went out to meet the bridegroom" (verse 1). Both groups bear publicly their doctrinal lamps—all are recognized church members. The difference between them lies, not necessarily in the doctrine they believe about the return of Jesus, but in what the doctrine has done for them personally.

An oil lamp is not worth much on a dark night without oil, a flashlight[1024] is useless without batteries. The lamp is merely an instrument, and its only purpose is to make something happen—that is, to produce light!

THE LIGHT IN THE LAMP

In this parable, as in life, the light is neither the lamp nor the oil. In this parable, the light is not specifically biblical doctrine, no matter how pure or how much is known; nor is the Holy Spirit the light (in this parable). The light is the witness of the Christ-like life, transformed by the power of the Holy Spirit, molded by biblical principles. Note the clarity and precision of the following words:

> "Through the Holy Spirit, God's word is a light as it becomes a transforming power in the life of the receiver. By implanting in their hearts the principles of His word, the Holy Spirit develops in men the attributes of God. The light of His glory—His character—is to shine forth in His followers."[1025]

For Christians everywhere, the meaning is clear; Bible-quoting church members (and we need more Bible students) who have not been transformed

---

[1023] *Christ's Object Lessons*, 406.
[1024] Or "torch" for British English readers.
[1025] *Ibid.*, 414.

by the Holy Spirit into Christ-reflecting exhibits of the power of God are shutting themselves out of the kingdom of God as well as delaying the Advent! It would not be safe to give them latter-rain power—they would misrepresent God's kingdom. It would not be safe to allow them into heaven—they were not overcomers.[1026]

Sad—sadder than words can tell—to realize that those who know the way are eventually lost! Sad it is to be so busy selling peanuts that one misses the parade!

The foolish bridesmaids are not lost because they couldn't answer doctrinal questions or didn't know enough Bible texts. We are told that "all have a knowledge of the Scriptures. All have heard the message of Christ's near approach, and confidently expect His appearing."[1027]

DIFFERENCE BETWEEN OBJECT AND INSTRUMENT

Foolish bridesmaids are lost because they made biblical information an end, instead of a means to an end. The Bible did not become an instrument of faith but an object of faith. Faith became an intellectual exercise instead of a personal relationship of joyful, trusting obedience.[1028] They knew what the Bible said about God but did not know Him as their personal Friend.

The foolish bridesmaids can be compared to one who admires an expensive telescope and hastens to make that telescope his own. He knows just where he wants to put it to properly set if off—on his fireplace wall! He installs ceiling spotlights so that the silver filigree and the rich leather covering is properly appreciated. His neighbors and soon his whole town know about this wonderful telescope. Many are the nights his friends sit and admire that stunning telescope.

But hanging telescopes on fireplace walls misses the point of what a telescope is for. Telescopes are made to bring eternity into focus. Telescopes are made to see through—to catch the cadence of our Creator, to understand more clearly what God has on His mind for us to know. Telescopes are not made to look at or to embellish, *but to see through.*

The wise bridesmaids use the Bible to see what Isaiah saw, to hear what Paul heard—indeed, its intended purpose. The Bible becomes the instrument by which faith is awakened, by which men and women are introduced to a self-authenticating relationship with their Lord. The result of this living experience, this listening to eternity, is a determined commitment on the part of the wise to say "yes" to whatever God says, to make the principles set forth in the Bible the law of their lives by the power of the indwelling Spirit.

[1026] See 144.
[1027] *Christ's Object Lessons*, 408.
[1028] See "Appendix K: Faith, The Word That Decides Everything."

We have been warned:

> "It is not enough for us to believe that Jesus is not an impostor, and that the religion of the Bible is no cunningly devised fable. We may believe that the name of Jesus is the only name under heaven whereby man may be saved, and yet we may not through faith make Him our personal Saviour. It is not enough to believe the theory of truth. It is not enough to make a profession of faith in Christ and have our names registered on the church roll. 'He that keepeth His commandments dwelleth in Him, and He in him. And hereby we know that He abideth in us, the Spirit which He hath given us.' 'Hereby we do know that we know Him if we keep His commandments' (1 John 3:24; 2:3). This is the genuine evidence of conversion. Whatever our profession, it amounts to nothing unless Christ is revealed in works of righteousness."[1029]

In times of ease, the wise and foolish may have been difficult to distinguish. After all, both slept during the delay. But the wise awakened, they sensed the emptiness of their spiritual experience, and they determined to change by the grace of God. When emergencies came, they were better prepared.

SPIRITUAL ANEMIA

But when emergencies struck foolish church members, they behaved like anyone else who knew nothing about the Bible. Because they had been leaning on others to supply their spiritual strength for so long, they now were spiritually anemic without a chance for recovery. They were too far-gone for a blood transfusion. They discovered too late that courage, peace, trust, and strength of spirit could not be transferred.

Just as no one can breathe for another, so no one can trust for another. Nor can God give or credit His character to another in the judgment. "Character is not transferable."[1030] The Bible-quoting church member untransformed by the Holy Spirit into a Christ-reflecting man or woman will not be ready for probation to close. *Somewhere in the life, the foolish bridesmaids are still saying "no" to God; they are not acting on the truth that they know.* They remain rebels. How sad to observe that men and women "are shut out from heaven by their own unfitness for its companionship."[1031]

The wise bridesmaids, however, are exactly what the world needs. Ellen White etches deeply the challenge:

[1029] *Christ's Object Lessons*, 312, 313.
[1030] *Ibid.*, 412. "Christ Himself will decide who are worthy to dwell with the family of heaven. He will judge every man according to his words and his works. Profession is as nothing in the scale. It is character that decides destiny." —*Ibid.*, 74.
[1031] *Ibid.*, 413.

"So the followers of Christ [wise bridesmaids] are to shed light into the darkness of the world. Through the Holy Spirit, God's word is a light as it becomes a transforming power in the life of the receiver. By implanting in their hearts the principles of His word, the Holy Spirit develops in men the attributes of God. The light of His glory—His character—is to shine forth in His followers. Thus they are to glorify God, to lighten the path to the Bridegroom's home, to the city of God, to the marriage supper of the Lamb. ...

"It is the darkness of misapprehension of God that is enshrouding the world. Men are losing their knowledge of His character. It has been misunderstood and misinterpreted. At this time a message from God is to be proclaimed, a message illuminating in its influence and saving in its power. His character is to be made known. Into the darkness of the world is to be shed the light of His glory, the light of His goodness, mercy, and truth. ...

"Those who wait for the Bridegroom's comings are to say to the people, 'Behold your God.' The last rays of merciful light, the last message of mercy to be given to the world, is a revelation of His character of love. The children of God are to manifest His glory. In their own life and character, they are to reveal what the grace of God has done for them. ... The light of the Sun of Righteousness is to shine forth in good works—in words of truth and deeds of holiness."[1032]

What more did Jesus say about how we become wise members of the universe's grand wedding party?

[1032] *Ibid.,* 414–416.

CHAPTER FORTY-FOUR:
PROFITABLE AND
UNPROFITABLE EMPLOYEES

How does one become a "faithful and wise" servant and a wise bridesmaid? To answer that question, Jesus told the story of the businessman who distributed various responsibilities to his employees.

In fact, Jesus gave this parable to show "what it means to watch for His coming. The time is to be spent, not in idle waiting, but in diligent working."[1033]

Often we call this story the "parable of the talents." But how is Jesus using the word "talents"? In the parable, the "talent" is a specified amount of money. More talents (that is, more money) were given to those who had the experience and initiative to handle larger responsibilities for their employer. Those who had less experience and skills received less financial responsibility. All received as much as they could safely handle. As time went by, as each employee grew in ability to handle greater opportunities, the employer would gladly give each faithful employee more talents (more financial responsibility). Responsibility (talents) was keyed to each person's ability (natural and acquired) to handle it (Matthew 25:15).[1034]

Many talents given means much ability is recognized and—on that basis—heavy responsibilities are assigned. But some may ask, how does this work out in a practical way? What does this snapshot of endtime Christians have to do with Peter's call to "hasten the advent"? How does this parable add to what we know about the "faithful and wise servant," and to the kind of person who becomes a wise bridesmaid?

The parable of the profitable employees supplements the snapshots of the bridegroom and the bridesmaids—*it explains how men and women become light-producing, Christ-reflecting "faithful and wise servants."*

SELF-DEVELOPMENT

This leads us to the fundamental theme of the parable—that one principle that every Christian must face sooner or later: *Our first duty to God and man is self-development.*[1035] This is a very sobering thought, a crushing thought, for the self-indulgent—or for those who want Jesus to forgive their sins but not really to save them from their sins (Matthew 1:21).

[1033] *Christ's Object Lessons,* 325.
[1034] *Ibid.,* 328.
[1035] *Ibid.,* 329.

Ellen White's emphasis on self-development runs like a gold vein throughout her writings. She does not want us to measure ourselves against each other but "to become all that it is possible for us to be as workers for the Master." Further, "we should cultivate every faculty to the highest degree of perfection that we may do the greatest amount of good of which we are capable."[1036]

Whatever our natural abilities may be, each of us is given opportunities to improve what we have to give to someone else's need. That is why we should pay attention to developing our physical strength, our social skills, our economic know-how, and mental habits. Improving these personal areas reflects the intent of this parable.

For example, Ellen White counsels:

> "[God] designs that His servants shall possess more intelligence and clearer discernment than the worldling, and He is displeased with those who are too careless or too indolent to become efficient, well-informed workers. The Lord bids us love Him with all the heart, and with all the soul, and with all the strength, and with all the mind. This lays upon us the obligation of developing the intellect to its fullest capacity, that with all the mind we may know and love our Creator."[1037]

All this involves the right use of our time, speech habits, money and influence, the concern for accuracy, the willingness to take advice, and everything else that will improve us wherever we are, in whatever line of work we may engage.

But the question lingers, what does this have to do with God's endtime people? Much in every way. Self-development is the only way that a person can be ready for the call to service. No person is excluded. Everyone has some ability to love and serve—everyone has at least one talent of opportunity and matching ability. Our response to the daily call to serve others is the test of our fitness to live forever. *It reveals how much we know about love.*

SELF-DEVELOPMENT TAKES TIME

The parable's lesson is that no one learns how to be really useful over night. If parents are not preparing for the searching questions and self-asserting independence of their teenage son or daughter, they will have many difficult, bleak nights. Prepared parents are the truly loving parents; parents that their children can trust as well as respect. At the scene of an accident with severe injuries, who can best help? Those who wring their hands or those who clear air ways and stop the bleeding? It all depends on who took time to learn Red Cross First Aid!

[1036] *Ibid.*, 330.
[1037] *Ibid.*, 333.

Nurses or physicians, for example, who do not do their homework well, who memorize only to pass the next tests, who don't reach out for the latest research throughout their careers—will rarely be the cool, competent human solutions in desperate medical emergencies. Self-development is the route to genuine service. Self-development is the only habit pattern that truly loves.

Christians who understand this basic concept know that it takes more than sympathy when another hurts. What a pity that so many are sympathetic with another's need, whether it be physical distress, spiritual depression or moral weakness, and *yet are not able to do something substantial in relief?* "Faithful and wise servants" are not friends or parents who wring their hands in the face of another's needs; they are prepared servants who can shed light along the way, who can relieve human distress as God uses them to comfort the troubled.

The best part of our Lord's description of His maturing loyalists is that no man or woman is pegged forever at any level of ability. Those able to handle five talents worth of opportunity and responsibility will get more opportunities to serve others. Men and women who are equipped to handle one talent of opportunity and responsibility will develop into higher levels of responsibility—if they are faithful in what they are able to do.

Further, this parable makes clear that no one has ever reached his or her upper limits—and only God knows where that limit may be! It is part of the marvelous divine-human co-op plan: "The Lord desires us to use every gift we have; and if we do this, we shall have greater gifts to use. He does not supernaturally endow us with the qualifications we lack; but while we use that which we have, He will work with us to increase and strengthen every faculty."[1038]

DIRE CONSEQUENCES

Jesus added some further reality to His snapshot of endtime Christians. Dire consequences await those who refused to accept ever-increasing opportunities to grow, to serve, and to develop their moral, mental, physical, and social powers.

Charlie Brown and Lucy were taking a walk with Snoopy. Lucy speaks: "Sooner of later, Charlie Brown, there's one thing you're going to have to learn. … You reap what you sow! You get out of life exactly what you put into it! No more and no less!" They walk on in deep thought. Then Snoopy makes a comment—"I'd like to see a little more margin for error."

Snoopy's response reflects a moan that has arisen in every generation since our first parents left the Garden. It is heard throughout the pages of literature. Even God, because He chooses not to, will not alter the law

---

[1038] *Ibid.*, 353, 354.

of gravity or the law of seed sowing. He chooses a predictable universe, a kingdom of uncoerced sons and daughters who reap what they sow.

In stark reality, Jesus describes the fate of all who make themselves the center of their universe—they refused to take advantage of many opportunities to grow into usefulness and Christlikeness: "You wicked and lazy servant ... Take the talent from him. ... And cast the unprofitable servant into the outer darkness" (Matthew 25:26–30).

The "lazy servant" goes on record before the entire universe as one determined to do things his way. He proves to all that he would be unfit to save. He could not be trusted with eternal life.

The sad part of this parable is that the "lazy servant" who played it cool and just rocked along was an acceptable church member. He was not an open sinner. His sin was not some great evil. He great sin was what he had not done for himself and for others. He rebelled against he law of self-development. He closed up his own probation. No one drifts into the Kingdom—continual rebelling against the law of self-development merely hastens the day when those sad words are heard, "Take the talent from him."

Everyone of us needs to recognize reality: In our own lives as well as in the closing shadows of the endtime—none of knows exactly when the sun will finally set. But we hear the vesper bells, and they are ringing for you and me. Never too late to profit by this parable of the "talents"!

NOT ALL DEMAND AND WORK

However, the law of self-development is not all demand, and task, and work! If Jesus stopped here, He would be laying an impossible burden on our backs. He would be asking for more than we could deliver. It would be a depressing message to ask for continual improvement, even perfection, as if it were only a matter of self-development. The gospel is not only demand and obligation and requirements. Such would be legalism in new dress and just as futile as old Israel's attempt to reach righteousness by works—"a yoke on the neck ... which neither our fathers nor we were able to bear" (Acts 15:10).

An essential part of the gospel, that puts fresh air into our flat tires, is the news that God has never given a task without an assurance that "all His biddings are enablings."[1039] With the obligations come the gifts—all parts of the gospel treasure.[1040] God does not ask the impossible or the unreasonable.

That being the case, let's discover what the deepest motive is that compels men and women to become all that God designed them to be.

[1039] *Ibid.*, 333.
[1040] *Ibid.*, 112.

CHAPTER FORTY-FIVE:
THE PIVOTAL POINT ON WHICH OUR FUTURE DEPENDS

Jesus had one more snapshot to complete His portrait of His endtime loyalists. He knew He could not finish His famous reply to His disciples regarding the end of the world with the parable of the businessman and his employees. If He did, the thought could linger that the best Christian is the great achiever, the genius—the most brilliant, the most physically fit! The bronzed, muscular beach boys and the slim slenderellas would be closest to the Kingdom!

Self-development—no question. But there is more. Our Lord's last snapshot—that of the sheep and the goats—reminds us that fulfilling the goal of genuine Christianity (call it maturity, moral perfection, or righteousness produced by faith) is primarily in the world of being, far beyond the world of only knowing, or even doing "good" works. This the five foolish Adventist bridesmaids and the self-serving, talent-burying employees learned too late.

The conditions for belonging to the group on "his right hand" (Matthew 25:33), the group who are fit to live forever, are not beyond the reach of anyone. In this snapshot, we see that righteousness is not granted as a diploma after years of hard study or as a certificate for baptizing 100 persons annually, necessary and commendable as these achievements are. Entrance into the kingdom of God is not for those who merely kept the rules, maintained the standards, and answered all the questions with the right answers. But a wide and glorious welcome will be extended to those who know how to love freely and spontaneously.

THE KNIFE-EDGE

"Faithful and wise servants," wise bridesmaids, and responsible employees have directed their lives around one principle—the turning point in the judgment—the law of unselfish service. Not how much one knows, not how much applause we may get for our financial gifts, not how much respect for our unblemished reputation—the knife-edge on which destiny is decided—is explained in this last snapshot of God's last-day loyalists:

> "[Our Lord's decision] is turning upon one point. When the nations are gathered before Him, there will be but two classes. Their eternal destiny will be determined by what they have done or have neglected to do for Him in the person of the poor, the suffering. In that day Christ does not present before men the great work He has

done for them in giving His life for their redemption. He presents the faithful work they have done for Him."[1041]

ONLY LOVING PEOPLE ARE RIGHTEOUS

This last snapshot of "those who keep the commandments of God and the faith of Jesus" (Revelation 14:12) clears the air. Righteousness is not only accepting what Jesus has done for us; righteousness also includes what we permit Jesus, through the Holy Spirit, to do in and through us.[1042] Such Christians are not frightened into righteousness, because only the loving person is a righteous person. Only a loving person fulfills the law (Romans 13:10).

The fully committed Christian is a living demonstration of the fact that "when self is merged in Christ, love springs forth spontaneously. The completeness of Christian character is attained when the impulse to help and bless others springs constantly from within—when the sunshine of heaven fills the heart and is revealed in the countenance."[1043]

Spontaneous love—the habitual, predictable life pattern of mature Christians—is the only acceptable motivation for self-development, and the only proper motivation for Christian witnessing.

In the early twenty-first century (much different than even 50 years ago) secular people are driven by experience rather than knowledge (postmodernism has ambushed appeals to authority). But secular people have a "God-ache" as much as churchgoers. They just don't know how to deal with it. That is why we are especially urged in all of our Christian witnessing to recognize this basic truth: secular people will need to belong before he or she will believe.[1044] Outstretched, non-judgmental arms, welcoming others to a loving fellowship will be far more effective in "growing" a Christian commitment than premature appeals to join a Bible study. Love always trumps theory!

But loving people know that it is not always easy to love. Loving people guard their health so that they do not become ill and thus a burden on someone else. Loving people take time to do their homework—such as first-aid classes, Bible-study seminars, and discussion groups—so that they will be ready when opportunities arise. Loving people work at settling the deep questions and do not drift with every breeze, because they know that only those firmly convinced about truth can ever convince someone else.

[1041] *The Desire of Ages*, 637.

[1042] "Our only ground of hope is in the righteousness of Christ imputed to us, and in that wrought by His Spirit working in and through us." —*Steps to Christ*, 63.

[1043] *Christ's Object Lessons*, 384.

[1044] See Richard Rice's *Believing, Behaving, Belonging* (Roseville, CA: Association of Adventist Forums, 2002).

Nothing more can be expected from anyone than "the completeness of Christian character"—the outflow of spontaneous love. This kind of love depicted in the four snapshots of God's loyalists will settle many questions in the Great Controversy and will open the way for Jesus' return. This kind of people can be trusted to live forever because they have demonstrated not only a habit pattern that has become etched into their neural pathways by the Holy Spirit, but a posture toward God that will always say "yes" to whatever He wills. Rebellion is gone forever.

Consistent, mature Christians reflect the life and faith of Jesus. They will be safe to save. All other worlds could be safely exposed to them. Truth has settled so deeply into their brain cells that sin will never arise again.[1045]

Let's look even more closely at how God helps men and women to reflect the life and faith of Jesus.

[1045] "Just as soon as the people of God are sealed in their foreheads—it is not any seal or mark that can be seen, but a settling into the truth, both intellectually and spiritually, so they cannot be moved— just as soon as God's people are sealed and prepared for the shaking, it will come." —Ellen White Comments, SDABC, vol. 4, 1161.

CHAPTER FORTY-SIX:
CONDITIONS YET UNFULFILLED
—PART 1

In Section Seven, we reviewed last-day conditions (some would call them "signs") that would indicate that we are living in the endtime. I am reminded of some wise words that James White wrote in 1877: "In exposition of unfulfilled prophecy, where the history is not written, the student should put forth his propositions with not too much positiveness, lest he find himself straying in the field of fancy. There are those who think more of future truth than of present truth. They see but little light in the path in which they walk, but think they see great light ahead of them."[1046]

When we look into the future, we are reminded that if Jesus could have come before 1880 (any date during the generation that lived in 1844 would do) no specific Bible prophecy remains unfulfilled,[1047] except those which are consequences of certain unfulfilled conditions relating to the maturing of God's people.

The fact that these conditions regarding the state of God's people are unfulfilled has been kept before Seventh-day Adventists for over a century.[1048] These conditions are all elements in the harvest principle; they represent the contingencies that affect the time when Jesus decides that the "harvest is ripe" (Mark 4:29; Revelation 14:16).[1049]

FIRST CONDITION

We have already discussed this unavoidable condition in relation to the political-religious movements in the endtime. Here we will discuss the seal as it relates to the kind of people who "hasten the Advent" (2 Peter 3:12). We discovered that Christ's loyalists must have the "seal of God" (Revelation 7:1–4; 14:1–5) before the "latter rain,"[1050] before probation closes,[1051] before the seven last plagues.[1052]

[1046] *Review and Herald*, November 29, 1877.

[1047] "The signs which He Himself gave of His coming have been fulfilled, and by the teaching of God's word we may know that the Lord is at the door." —*Christ's Object Lessons*, 227.

[1048] P. Gerard Damsteegt, *Foundations of the Seventh-day Adventist Message* (Grand Rapids: William B. Eerdmans Publishing Company, 1977), 185, 211, 212, 216, 218, 226, 235, 245–247, 252, 253, 296.

[1049] See 223–227.

[1050] "Not one of us will ever receive the seal of God while our characters have one spot or stain upon them. It is left with us to remedy the defects in our characters, to cleanse the soul temple of every defilement. Then the latter rain will fall upon us as the early rain fell upon the disciples on the Day of Pentecost." —*Testimonies*, vol. 5, 214.

[1051] "An angel returning from the earth announces that his work is done; the final test has been brought upon the world, and all who have proved themselves loyal to the divine precepts have received 'the seal of the living God.' Then Jesus ceases His intercession in the sanctuary above. He lifts His hands and with a loud voice says, 'It is done.'" —*The Great Controversy*, 613.

[1052] *Ibid.*, 614.

The seal is not a mark that human eyes can see[1053] because it is recognition of character that has been transformed by the "power of [God's] grace." Such people are "distinguished from the world by the seal of the living God; their words and their works are to reveal that they are laborers together with God."[1054]

Sad, but those who are even teaching the truth to others may not themselves be sealed![1055] In fact, "the great mass of professing Christians will meet with bitter disappointment in the day of God. They have not upon their foreheads the seal of the living God. Lukewarm and halfhearted, they dishonor God far more than the avowed unbeliever."[1056]

NOT A MYSTERY

Receiving the "seal" is not a mystery. As with all biblical instruction, God can only invite us to accept His counsel and work His principles into our personal experience. Thus, "our own course of action will determine whether we shall receive the seal of the living God, or be cut down by the destroying weapons."[1057]

The message to all of us is that God's seal will not be placed on "an impure man or woman," on "an ambitious, world-loving man or woman" or on "men or women of false tongues or deceitful hearts."[1058] The seal will not be placed on those "who do not feel grieved over their own spiritual declension, nor mourn over the sins of others."[1059]

On the positive side, the seal will be placed on those "who bear a likeness to Christ in character," who "keep His commandments [and] bear the fruits of righteousness," and who "represent to the world the ineffaceable characteristics of the divine nature."[1060]

The issue of the seventh-day Sabbath, especially in the endtime, becomes the sign of those who have chosen to "keep His commandments" and "to bear the fruits of righteousness." In the Sabbath-Sunday crisis, the seventh-day Sabbath becomes "the mark of distinction between him that serveth God and him that serveth Him not."[1061] Truly honoring the

---

[1053] Ellen G. White Comments, *SDABC*, vol. 7, 968.

[1054] *Ibid.*, 969. "They have on the wedding garment, and are obedient and faithful to all God's commands." *Ibid.*, 968.

[1055] "There are many even among those who teach the truth to others who will not receive the seal of God in their foreheads. They had the light of truth, they knew their Master's will, they understood every point of our faith, but they had not corresponding works. These who were so familiar with prophecy and the treasures of divine wisdom should have acted their faith. ... By their lack of devotion and piety, and their failure to reach a high religious standard, they make other souls contented with their position." —*Testimonies*, vol. 5, 214.

[1056] Ellen G. White Comments, *SDABC*, vol. 7, 970.

[1057] *Testimonies*, vol. 5, 212.

[1058] *Ibid.*, 216.

[1059] *Ibid.*, 211.

[1060] Ellen G. White Comments, *SDABC*, vol. 7, 970, 269.

[1061] *Ibid.*, 270.

seventh-day Sabbath is the outward sign of God's seal of approval over that person who is choosing "to follow the Lamb wherever He goes" (Revelation 14:4).

After the plagues begin to trouble the earth, those who did their best to silence the advocates of the seventh-day Sabbath will see "too late ... that the Sabbath of the fourth commandment is the seal of the living God."[1062] That is, they see that the seventh-day Sabbath distinguishes those who are willing to suffer whatever it takes to remain loyal to all of God's commandments.

IMPORTANCE OF THE NAME

What can we learn today about our own possibilities of being among the "sealed"? In various texts in Revelation, we learn that God's seal is in fact His Name written on the foreheads of His loyalists (7:3; 14:1; 22:4). What could that mean?

In our kitchens, we find many appliances that bear the seal of the Underwriter's Lab. Electric appliances cannot be sold unless they have passed rigorous tests; only then do they get the seal and the approval of an important name.

Ask why people buy Tiger Wood or Arnold Palmer golf clubs, or Ralph Lauren shirts and Tommy Hilfiger sweaters. For most products, the name means everything. It means that the product carries the endorsement of someone who cares about quality, someone who can be trusted.

Remember those television ads for Hanes clothing? I can still see that determined female inspector with all her formidable charm, surveying the assembly line: *"The quality goes in before the name goes on."*

When God puts His signature on His loyalists, He is saying: "Here are people who have let my Holy Spirit do His work, people who indeed reflect my glory. I am not embarrassed by how they represent Me. They have my approval and my power. *'The quality goes in before the name goes on.'"*

But being ready for God's seal is not a sudden decision like raising a hand to be baptized. Like everything else, we have been saying in this book, character building takes time. Some can mature faster than others; some mature more quickly during tough trials. But developing habit patterns of saying "yes" to the light God gives us daily does take time! Note this counsel:

> "Courage, fortitude, faith, and implicit trust in God's power to save do not come in a moment. These heavenly graces are acquired by the experience of years. By a life of holy endeavor and firm adherence to the right the children of God were sealing their destiny."[1063]

[1062] *The Great Controversy*, 640.
[1063] *Testimonies*, vol. 5, 213.

All this is another way of re-emphasizing what we have been stressing on previous pages.[1064] The sealing work is a matter of deepening Christ-like habits into our neural pathways:

> "Just as soon as the people of God are sealed in their foreheads—it is not any seal or mark that can be seen, but a settling into the truth, both intellectually and spiritually, so they cannot be moved—just as soon as God's people are sealed and prepared for the shaking, it will come."[1065]

What is so helpful with this quotation is that Ellen White joins what we too often separate. Many are pleased to work on developing a devotional life without spending time working out the reasons for their religious commitments. Others have all the biblical reasons in order for what they believe, but, like the "foolish" bridesmaids, they have not let biblical principles transform their lives.

INTELLECTUALLY AND SPIRITUALLY

The "sealed" in the endtime have "intellectually and spiritually" joined their heart with their head and no devil or man will ever shake them—"they cannot be moved."

But we are not talking philosophically or dreamily looking into the future. In many ways Ellen White had said for years that our Lord's coming has been delayed, not because He wasn't ready, but because His followers had not kept their eyes on their main mission.[1066] For that reason, she said in 1897:

> "Because the people are disobedient, unthankful, unholy, as were ancient Israel, time is prolonged that all may hear the last message of mercy proclaimed with a loud voice. *The Lord's work has been hindered, the sealing time delayed.* Many have not heard the truth. But the Lord will give them a chance to hear and be converted, and the great work of God will go forward."[1067]

God is not finished with any of us yet!

[1064] See 338–342.

[1065] Ellen White Comments, *SDABC,* vol. 4, 1161.

[1066] See 225.

[1067] *Manuscript Releases,* vol. 15, 293. Emphasis supplied.

CHAPTER FORTY-SEVEN:
CONDITIONS YET UNFULFILLED
—PART 2

Because the sealing work has been delayed, the latter rain has been delayed! Could anything be more serious? Could there be any subject on the Adventist agenda more important than focusing on how we can cooperate with God so that the sealing work and the latter rain are delayed no longer?

THE LATTER RAIN DELAYED

Philip Yancey asks the same question:

"Why the delay? Why does God let evil and pain so flagrantly exist, even thrive, on this planet? Why does he let us do slowly and blunderingly what he could do in an eye blink?

"He holds back for our sakes. Creation involves us; we are, in fact, at the center of his plan. The Wager, the motive behind all human history, is to develop us, not God. Our very existence announces to the powers in the universe that restoration is under way. Every act of faith by every one of the people of God is like the tolling of a bell, and a faith like Job's reverberates throughout the universe."[1068]

The latter rain is delayed until God's loyalists can be trusted with it. God will send special power to energize the church's evangelistic outreach when He knows that His people will not embarrass the truth by their lives. Ellen White cautioned:

"I was shown that if God's people make no efforts on their part, but wait for the refreshing to come upon them and remove their wrongs and correct their errors; if they depend upon that to cleanse them from filthiness of the flesh and spirit, and fit them to engage in the loud cry of the third angel, they will be found wanting. The refreshing or power of God comes only on those who have prepared themselves for it by doing the work which God bids them, namely, cleansing themselves from all filthiness of the flesh and spirit, perfecting holiness in the fear of God."[1069]

[1068] Philip Yancey, *Disappointment With God* (Grand Rapids, MI: Zondervan Publishing House, 1988), 174.
[1069] *Testimonies*, vol. 1, 619.

Let's examine what we mean by the "latter rain."

- The spiritual "latter rain" is likened to the literal latter rain in Israel that falls at the end of the growing season; it ripens the grain, preparing it for the harvest.

- The spiritual "latter rain" prepares God's endtime church for His coming, earth's harvest.[1070]

- The spiritual "latter rain" "represents the completion of the work of God's grace in the soul. ... The moral image of God is to be perfected in the character."[1071]

- The spiritual "latter rain" follows the sealing work.[1072]

- The spiritual "latter rain" may "be falling on hearts all around us, but we shall not discern or receive it." Why? Because "unless we are daily advancing in the exemplification of the active Christians virtues, we shall not recognize the manifestations of the Holy Spirit in the latter rain."[1073]

- The spiritual "latter rain" cannot make up for what should have been done in the "early rain."[1074] The "early rain," the daily growth in character development, prepares us for the "latter rain"; those who hope to have their "lack ... supplied by the latter rain ... are making a terrible mistake."[1075]

- The "shaking time," directly related to the time of the "latter rain," is "caused by the straight testimony called forth by the counsel of the True Witness to the Laodiceans. ... Some will not bear the straight testimony. They will rise up against it, and this will cause a shaking among God's people. ... The solemn testimony upon which the destiny of the church hangs has been lightly esteemed, if not entirely disregarded." Those who accepted the "counsel" now spoke "the truth in great power. It had effect. ... 'What made this great change?' An angel answered, 'It is the latter rain, the refreshing from the presence of the Lord, the loud cry of the third angel.'"[1076]

[1070] *Testimonies to Ministers,* 506.

[1071] *Ibid.*

[1072] "Not one of us will ever receive the seal of God while our characters have one spot or stain upon them. It is left with us to remedy the defects in our characters, to cleanse the soul temple of every defilement. Then the latter rain will fall upon us as the early rain fell upon the disciples on the Day of Pentecost." —*Testimonies,* vol. 5, 214.

[1073] *Testimonies to Ministers,* 507.

[1074] *Ibid.,* 507, 509, 510, 511; *Selected Messages,* bk. 1, 191.

[1075] *Ibid.,* 507; *Testimonies,* vol. 1, 619.

[1076] *Testimonies,* vol. 1, 181–183.

- The church has been living in "the time of the latter rain" since the 19th century.[1077] L. E. Froom, secretary of the Ministerial Department, 1926 to 1950, and founder of *The Ministry* magazine, wrote, "We entered the '*time* of the Latter Rain and Loud Cry' in 1888. ... Though delayed, its fullness is destined to come ... He who denies that the Loud Cry began to sound in 1888 impugns the veracity of the Spirit of Prophecy [Ellen White]. He who asserts the Latter Rain did not then begin to fall challenges the integrity of God's message relayed to us."[1078]

- The "latter rain" will surpass the "former rain at the opening of the gospel." "Notwithstanding the agencies combined against the truth, a large number take their stand upon the Lord's side."[1079]

- The former rain and the "latter rain" is a perfect example of divine-human cooperation in fulfilling the purpose of the gospel.[1080]

- We are not to "trust in the ordinary working of providence" when God is ready to give His people the "latter rain."[1081]

- Those who receive the "latter rain" will be "fitted for the loud cry of the third angel."[1082]

- Many in 1865, though praying for the "latter rain" and a quick finish to the gospel commission, were not ready because they needed time "to develop character."[1083]

- Those who receive the "latter rain" will be "fitted for translation."[1084]

[1077] *Testimonies to Ministers* 510-512. "An unwillingness to yield up preconceived opinions, and to accept this truth, lay at the foundation of a large share of the opposition manifested at Minneapolis against the Lord's message through Brethren [E.J.] Waggoner and [A.T.] Jones. By exciting that opposition Satan succeeded in shutting away from our people, in a great measure, the special power of the Holy Spirit that God longed to impart to them. The enemy prevented them from obtaining that efficiency which might have been theirs in carrying the truth to the world, as the apostles proclaimed it after the day of Pentecost. The light that is to lighten the whole earth with its glory was resisted, and by the action of our own brethren has been in a great degree kept away from the world." —*Selected Messages*, bk. 1, 234. 235.

[1078] Froom, *Movement of Destiny* (RHPA, 1971), 667. See also 521.

[1079] *The Great Controversy*, 612.

[1080] "Divine grace is needed at the beginning, divine grace at every step of advance, and divine grace alone can complete the work. There is no place for us to rest in a careless attitude. ... If we do not progress, if we do not place ourselves in an attitude to receive both the former and the latter rain, we shall lose our souls, and the responsibility will lie at our own door." —*Testimonies to Ministers*, 507.

[1081] *Ibid.*, 509.

[1082] *Testimonies*, vol. 1, 186.

[1083] *Ibid.*, 187.

[1084] *Ibid.*, 188.

PRIMARY WORK OF THE HOLY SPIRIT

This brief overview of the "latter rain" reflects the purpose and primary work of the Holy Spirit. Those who are being sealed are working closely with the Holy Spirit, letting the Spirit do His most important work—reproducing in men and women the character of Jesus.[1085] The "latter rain" is the enormous intervention of God, providing "light and power"[1086] to His loyalists so that their public witness is tremendously more effective. They are now ready to be used, ready to be channels of God's awesome energy, ready to see wonders throughout the world, as difficult areas are suddenly open to hear the everlasting gospel.

Paul describes the kind of Adventists who sincerely long for Jesus to return as "peculiar people, zealous of good works" (Titus 2:14 KJV). The Greek word, here translated as "peculiar," joins two words, "being" and "beyond" (the same word we get the English "perimeter" or "border"). God's loyalists will be recognized as those who live "beyond" normally expected Christian behavior—in their "good works" as well as in their biblical clarity.

What happens when these "special" people, now prepared for the "latter rain," receive this unique infusion of God's amazing energy channeled through human beings?

[1085] "The impartation of the Spirit is the impartation of the life of Christ. It imbues the receiver with the attributes of Christ. Only those who are thus taught of God, those who possess the inward working of the Spirit, and in whose life the Christ-life is manifested, are to stand as representative men, to minister in behalf of the church." —*The Desire of Ages*, 805. See also 391.

[1086] *Testimonies to Ministers*, 510.

CHAPTER FORTY-EIGHT:
CONDITIONS YET UNFULFILLED
—PART 3

THE LOUD CRY

The "loud cry" is a term embedded in Revelation 18:1–4: "I saw another angel coming down from heaven having great authority, and the earth was illuminated with his glory. And he cried mightily with a loud voice, saying, 'Babylon the great is fallen.'" Joining this angel is another who says, "Come out of her, my people, lest you share in her sins, and lest you receive of her plagues."

This is showdown time. God's loyalists are face-to-face with Satan (the beast of Revelation). All Satan's malignant fury is now leveled at those who have not bent to his flatteries, trials, and abuse.

God's response through His people will even surprise Satan. In the darkening gloom of legislative, judicial and executive coercion in all lands, there will be an explosion of courage, clarity and cheerfulness as God's people proclaim truths in ways never before seen or heard.[1087]

In all lands, a "loud cry" will startle men and women in all walks of life. They will see and hear truths about God and the future of this planet for the first time by people whose personal witness backs up what they say.

- The "loud cry" is the clearest statement of the everlasting gospel since apostolic days, a statement that was called "a most precious message" in 1888.[1088]

- This clarification of the everlasting gospel in 1888 was the beginning of the loud cry of Revelation 18.[1089]

- Many who once heard the truth but strayed "will come back to follow the great Shepherd."[1090]

[1087] *Evangelism*, 694.

[1088] "This message was to bring more prominently before the world the uplifted Saviour, the Sacrifice for the sins of the whole world. It presented justification through faith in the Surety; it invited the people to receive the righteousness of Christ, which is made manifest in obedience to all the commandments of God. ... This is the message that God commanded to be given to the world. It is the third angel's message, which is to be proclaimed with a loud voice, and attended with the outpouring of His Spirit in a large measure." —*Testimonies to Ministers*, 92.

[1089] "The time of test is just upon us for the loud cry of the third angel has already begun in the revelation of the righteousness of Christ. ... This is the beginning of the light of the angel whose glory shall fill the whole earth." —*Review and Herald*, March 29, 1892.

[1090] *Evangelism*, 693. See *Testimonies*, vol. 6, 401.

- People "scattered all through the religious bodies answered to the call"; "mighty miracles were wrought, the sick were healed, and signs and wonders followed the believers."[1091]

- Satan also knows about God's plan to thwart him through the "loud cry" of truth in the endtime. In his strategy to pre-empt the impact of Revelation 18:1–4, Satan will promote "a spurious loud cry" in those churches who are losing ministers and parishioners to those who forcefully and clearly are proclaiming the everlasting gospel; those who reject these truths, seeing the false revivals in other churches, will "think that God is with them."[1092]

- Part of the Lord's strategy during the "loud cry" will be to work through "humble instruments ... laborers ... qualified rather by the unction of His Spirit than by the training of literary institutions."[1093]

- During the "loud cry" many long-standing Adventists will depart and join those forces against the everlasting gospel; but "the ranks will not be diminished. Those who are firm and true will close up the vacancies that are made by those who become offended and apostatize."[1094]

- Resistance to the clarity of the everlasting gospel in 1888 "is shutting away from our people, in a great measure, the special power of the Holy Spirit that God longed to impart to them. ... The light that is to lighten the whole earth with its glory was resisted, and by the action of our own brethren has been in a great degree kept away from the world."[1095]

DECISION TIME FOR ALL

In summary, the loud cry prophecy of Revelation 18 depicts decision time for the world and for the church. Church members who have procrastinated, who have been church-hopping without roots, or who have served both God and mammon, now make their irrevocable decision either to continue their rationalizing or to commit themselves unreservedly to God, demonstrating radically new life patterns. Faithful church members make new strides in Christian witnessing. Honest seekers of truth the world over will hear and see the truth about God that will give them courage to break with long-standing friends and loved ones and join those who "keep the commandments of God and the faith of Jesus" (Revelation 14:12).

[1091] *Early Writings*, 278, 279.
[1092] *Selected Messages*, bk. 3, 410; *Early Writings*, 261.
[1093] *The Great Controversy*, 606; see also, *Testimonies*, vol. 5, 80–82.
[1094] *Selected Messages*, bk. 3, 422; see *The Great Controversy*, 608.
[1095] *Ibid.*, bk. 1, 235.

The "sealing," the "latter rain" and the "loud cry" are closely connected events and occur in that order. Up to the close of probation, the group of sealed people continues to enlarge as the "latter rain" and "loud cry" are used by God to bring multitudes everywhere to final decisions.

God's last-day message will not be a squeaky plea from some dark corner of this planet. Hardly! When God opens doors that have been hitherto blocked, when God works through people who are sealed with His approval—people whose lives back up what they say about Him, all corners of the earth will be "illuminated with His glory" (Revelation 18:1).

Fulfilling God's predictions that the whole world will be "illuminated" with enough light to make personal, endtime decisions should not be scoffed at. The latest Nielsen/NetRatings that I have found (March 6, 2002) reported that a half-billion people worldwide now have home Internet access, with about one-third in the United States and Canada. Further, the rate of growth to Internet access worldwide is phenomenal, each quarter nearly doubling the previous quarter. But the number of homes owning televisions is far greater than a half-billion home computers! Yet still further, Internet speed hit a new record in March 2003, when scientists at the Stanford Linear Accelerator Center used fiber-optic cables to transfer 6.7 gigabytes of data (equivalent of two DVD movies) across 6,800 miles in less than a minute.[1096]

Don't worry—God knows what He is talking about! But He does want us to get serious and catch up!

GOD IS VINDICATED—AGAIN!

The time has come. All heaven has been waiting and waiting. The laboratory test that God set up when He created men and women[1097] is now validating the wisdom and patience of God. The formula to be tested has been written on the blackboard of the universe for thousands of years.

Even as Albert Einstein had written the famous formula ($E=MC^2$) many years before 1945, it was never tested until the atomic bomb ended World War II. Scientists had to take the formula off the blackboards of the classrooms and test its truthfulness. When the atomic bombs were dropped on Japan, Einstein was vindicated.

God challenged Satan in the Garden of Eden: "I will put enmity between you and the woman, and between your seed and her Seed; He shall bruise your head and you shall bruise His heel" (Genesis 3:15).

Earth's history has surely reflected the harm Satan has inflicted on humanity, especially on those who have called the Seed "Jesus." And often it was difficult to believe that the followers of the Seed would ever triumph and finally bruise Satan's head, once and for all time to come.

[1096] CNN.com./technology, March 7, 2003.
[1097] See 45–48.

But in the sealing of God's endtime loyalists, the gospel formula is finally being taken off the biblical blackboard. In this final showdown, it is being tested in the lives of people who have caught on to the purpose of the gospel. They are proving in their lives the wisdom that God had built into the plan of salvation. The laboratory test of God's formula is being worked out in the lives of young people and their older friends: God can be trusted; His formula ("the everlasting gospel") by which evil can be uprooted and the image of God restored is being demonstrated the world over. Satan is a defeated foe wherever God's loyalists join their wills to God's empowering Holy Spirit.

For more than a hundred years, God's formula has been outlined on the blackboard—waiting for His people to realize that He is not talking about information to be learned but a formula to be lived. Let us look again for the first time at the grand outline of the plan of salvation:

> "The very image of God is to be reproduced in humanity. The honor of God, the honor Christ, is involved in the perfection of the character of His people."[1098]

Just as Einstein was ultimately vindicated, so God will be vindicated in His endtime loyalists. No wonder Satan is "enraged" (Revelation 12:17), doing all that a malignant genius can do to prove that God's formula is wrong.

PROVING SATAN WRONG

God's decision to grant freedom of choice to created intelligences, beginning with Satan as the first to be created, was very risky. Satan's challenges rocked the universe. To prove Satan wrong, God populated Planet Earth with men and women who would be His laboratory in which His principles would be worked out.[1099]

Paul saw all this clearly. In the first chapter to the Ephesians, he framed the Great Controversy from beginning to end. Even before the creation of men and women, God had formulated His plan to create Laboratory Earth so that the entire universe could see His principles of running the universe in contrast to Satan's. Men and women would be, before the Controversy could be finished, "without blemish in his sight, to be full of love; and he destined us—such was his will and pleasure—to be accepted as his sons through Jesus Christ, that the glory of his gracious gift, so graciously bestowed on us in his beloved, might redound to his praise" (1:4–6 NEB).

Paul looked forward to the final scene in the Great Controversy: "He has made known to us his hidden purpose—such was his will and pleasure

---

[1098] *The Desire of Ages*, 671."The honor of His throne is staked for the fulfillment of His word unto us." See *Christ's Object Lessons*, 148.

[1099] See 46.

determined beforehand in Christ—to be put into effect when the time was ripe: namely, that the universe, all in heaven and on earth, might be brought into a unity in Christ" (1:9, 10 NEB; see Philippians 2:10, 11).

But all this planning involved great risk! Some say that God failed from the start in trying to get Lucifer to see the foolishness of his ways. And if we looked today at the numbers only, we could say that God has failed on earth to get people to trust Him.

But God's formula on the universe's laboratory chalkboard will eventually prove Him right and Satan wrong. We are all part of that experiment. We are all determining whose side is winning. The Great Controversy is being played out in each of our lives.[1100]

NOT A FLATTERING PICTURE

Let's be frank: Our Lord's description of His people in the endtime is not flattering. It describes a church who professes to know the formula on the chalkboard: "Because you say, 'I am rich, have become wealthy, and have need of nothing'—and do not know that you are wretched, miserable, poor, blind, and naked—I counsel you to buy from Me gold tried in the fire, that you may be rich, and white garments, that you may be clothed, that the shame of your nakedness may not be revealed, and anoint your eyes with eye salve, that you may see" (Revelation 3:17, 18).

At the same time, our Lord predicts He will have a people who will hear His rebuke, who will "open the door" so that He will "come in" with dynamic power and provide the capability to turn hearts of men and women toward endtime truths.

These "capabilities" will reverse the diminishing returns of conventional evangelism. People must see something to be converted to before they jump into a new spiritual framework. For too long the general public looks at Christians who are telling them to agree to their doctrines, say the enclosed prayer, and join their fellowship. But too many respond, "But you aren't any different from anybody else except for your particular doctrines. So what am I supposed to be converted to?"[1101]

In other words, intelligent people want to see changed lives before they change their theology. That is the essence of genuine church growth. When people see the difference, they want to be part of it, people who cannot be bought, people who tell the truth without embellishment, people who honor God rather than merely impressing Him. They take the formula off the blackboard and internalize it in their lives.

In summary, all of our decisions, in whatever aspect of our lives, are revealing whether God's formula is being worked out in our lives. God's

---

[1100] *Education,* 190.
[1101] Richard Foster in an interview, *Christianity Today,* October 5, 1992.

loyalists are proving that His gospel formula can be trusted, that eternal principles are safe to follow, that those principles are truly the happiest, healthiest and holiest way to live. Just like God said!

MORE THAN A DRAMATIC THEORY

We are not merely describing a dramatic theory. We have been unfolding what God has on His mind for His loyalists in the end of the endtime. We are not discussing one point of view among many. We are listening to the open secret of how God can show the universe that His plan for transforming rebels into His loyalists has been worth the wait!

Probation closes for this world when all men and women have decided to either listen and follow the Holy Spirit's directions or follow Satan's principles. This decision will be etched into the mental patterns of God's loyalists with God's seal of approval so that they will never be moved in their allegiance to Him. And the mental patterns of those who have lived self-gratifying lives, described as those who carry the mark of the beast, will have so lived that their character patterns also will be etched. No more time is necessary for loyalists or rebels to make up their minds—the issues are settled. Note how these final developments will settle everyone's destiny:

> "Those who are living upon the earth when the intercession of Christ shall cease in the sanctuary above, are to stand in the sight of a holy God without a mediator.[1102] Their robes must be spotless; their characters must be purified from sin by the blood of sprinkling. Through the grace of God and their own diligent effort, they must be conquerors in the battle with evil. While the Investigative Judgment is going forward in heaven, while the sins of penitent believers are being removed from the sanctuary, there is to be a special work of purification, of putting away of sin, among God's people upon earth. This work is more clearly presented in the messages of Revelation 14. When this work shall have been accomplished, the followers of Christ will be ready for His appearing. ... Then the church which our Lord at His coming is to receive to Himself will be 'a glorious church, not having spot, or wrinkle, or any such thing.'"[1103]

What a future just ahead for those serious about their loyalty to God. What is the eternal consequence for all these loyalists who have been cooperating with God in becoming all that they were made to be?

[1102] Living without a Mediator in no way means living without the need of the enabling power of Christ through His Holy Spirit. The saints after probation closes, whose minds are settled into the truth and will never be moved, will still be dependent on grace, its keeping power to endure the awful trials associated with the plagues and Satan's last assaults on those he hates most (Rev. 12:17). Jesus is no longer needed to provide the grace of pardon, but He surely will be needed to impart the grace of power to "help in time of need" (Hebrews 4:16).

[1103] *The Great Controversy*, 425.

DESMOND DOSS, THE UNLIKELIEST HOLDER OF THE CONGRESSIONAL MEDAL OF HONOR

The unlikeliest holder of the Congressional Medal of Honor is a soldier who never carried a gun. Instead of recognizing the courage and valor of those who made the difference in ghastly firefights where weapons were their only defense against great odds, Desmond Doss's commanders recognized the uncommon commitment of a company-aid man who faced death over and over again to help his fallen comrades under blizzards of enemy fire.

Desmond Doss (Private First Class, Medical Detachment, 307th Infantry, 77th Infantry Division) was drafted on April 1, 1942, and discharged November 25, 1945, a very long time to live during several invasions of hostile territory in the South Pacific. His story of breathtaking valor began long before his exceptional deeds on Okinawa. Members of his company during the Guam and Leyte invasions wanted him around when they went into battle.

But the Okinawa bloodbath was unspeakable. On Sabbath, May 5, the call came, "Doss, you are the only medic available. They need help on the ridge." He had been nursing his wounded leg but he sprang to his feet after praying, "Lord, help me." Company A climbed a heavily defended, 400-foot ridge, only to be bogged down on the escarpment. Doss's group was under the cliff ready to go up a rope ladder. Doss asked Lieutenant Gondo for a moment of prayer with his platoon comrades. After frightful moments climbing the ridge, battalion headquarters asked for a casualty count. Back went the reply, "Not a man!" His platoon knocked out eight pillboxes and joined up with the stalled Company A.

But the Japanese counterattacked in force, inflicting enormous casualties that forced the Americans off the ridge. Lieutenant Gondo called out for Doss, but he was still on the cliff. Soon his lonely voice was heard signaling that he would let some wounded men down by rope. According to his CMH citation, about 75 were safely removed under extreme enemy fire.

A little while later, Doss was wounded in both legs and litter bearers picked him up. Seeing another wounded in the head, he rolled off the litter, insisting that the soldier be carried first. Moments later a sniper's bullet shattered his arm. He was finally carried off the field and invalided home. This Seventh-day Adventist noncombatant has been hailed as the greatest hero of the Okinawa campaign.

His CMH citation tingles with respect for this courageous, single-minded man who was willing to help pay the cost of freedom. Words flowed such as "refused to seek cover," "advancing through a shower of grenades," "unhesitatingly braved enemy shelling and small-arms fire," "while continually exposed to enemy fire," "with magnificent fortitude." The citation closed: "Through his outstanding bravery and unflinching determination in the face of desperately dangerous conditions Pfc. Doss saved the lives of many soldiers. His name became a symbol through the 77th Infantry Division for outstanding gallantry far above and beyond the call of duty."

Desmond Doss knew before he was drafted that his Commander was God and that He wanted life, freedom and peace for all men and women. It was his time to contribute when freedom was attacked. Freedom was more than a slogan for Doss; it was a way of life to cherish and to defend. Freedom is never free!

Tom Caslini and Timothy Wallis, *Ordinary Heroes* (Zionsville, IN: Sweet Pea Press, 2000), 15, 50, 138, 139; A. W. Spalding, *Christ's Last Legion* (Washington, DC: RHPA, 1949), 642–647; *Newsweek*, May 21, 1945, October 22, 1945; *Time*, May 21, 1945, October 22, 1945.

The controversy will end after both God and Satan have had sufficient time to display the consequences of their plans for governing the universe. What is the core issue that will make the universe eternally secure? How will the evidence before the universe of 1) the consequences of evil and 2) the rewards of loyalty to God to provide this eternal security? How do the mental/physical habits of the redeemed, who have become so settled that sin will never arise again, add to this eternal security and demonstrate God's wisdom in granting freedom to created intelligences?

CHAPTER FORTY-NINE:
HOW WILL ANYONE KNOW THAT THE CONTROVERSY IS OVER?

In our opening pages, we recalled the dark days following the Japanese attack on Pearl Harbor, December 7, 1941. President Franklin D. Roosevelt gave what is known today as the "four freedoms speech" to the U.S. Congress and the world on January 6, 1942. His words spelled hope for millions around the world:

> "This nation has placed its destiny in the hands, heads, and hearts of its millions of free men and women, and its faith in freedom under the guidance of God. Freedom means the supremacy of human rights everywhere. Our support goes to those who struggle to gain those rights and keep them. Our strength is in our unity of purpose. *To that high concept there can be no end save victory.*"

From the earliest moment when the Godhead "planned" the creation of counterparts—intelligent, responsible, loving, faithful persons like themselves—the Godhead felt the stab of insincerity and rebellion: they were "slain from the foundation of the world" (Revelation 13:8).[1104]

The cost of freedom was first paid by the Father, Son and the Holy Spirit—and they have never stopped paying. Any time a man or woman shakes off their appeals, the Godhead is hurt beyond words. Even as any loving parent feels the heartbreak when their children stumble into their own troubles, sooner or later.

NO END SAVE VICTORY

But the Godhead never wavered. Although the universe was in jeopardy because of Satan's rebellion, the Godhead placed the universe and its destiny into the hands of truth and into the minds of faithful men and women who trusted that God who gave them freedom would guide them in overcoming the regime of evil. To each loyalist from Adam to our day, God has repeatedly said, "*Our strength is in our unity of purpose. To that high concept there can be no end save victory.*"

And victory will come. Those who stand on the sea of glass will sing: "Great and marvelous are Your works, Lord God Almighty! Just and true are Your ways, O King of the saints" (Revelation 15:3)! "Alleluia! Salvation and glory and honor and power to the Lord our God! For true and righteous are His judgments" (Revelation 19:1, 2).

But what about the losers? What about those who bought into the fog that God's business is to forgive and forget, that all roads lead to "heaven," that might makes right, that God knows we all were born sinners and can't help ourselves, that Jesus kept the law for us, with endless variations.

Condemnation, yes! But not from the Father (John 5:22) nor from Jesus (John 12:46). Sinners condemn themselves: "This is the condemnation, that the light has come into the world, and men loved darkness rather than light, because their deeds were evil" (John 3:19). When Jesus returns, the unsaved cry out in self-condemnation: "Hide us from the face of Him of sits on the throne and from wrath of the Lamb" (Revelation 7:16)!

In that final moment, the Great Controversy ends when the unsaved freely, voluntarily confess their stubbornness in spurning the many appeals of the Holy Spirit: "At the name of Jesus every knee should bow ... so that every tongue should confess that Jesus Christ is Lord, to the glory of God the Father" (Philippians 2:11). They too will say with the redeemed: "Just and true are His judgments."

ONE WILD TANTRUM

This pitiful confession does not mean that the unsaved are at last converted or safe to save. Far from it! Satan has one more, irresistible strategy.

[1104] See 23.

In one incredible, wild tantrum, he mobilizes the ocean of the damned in one mighty rush to capture the Holy City (Revelation 20:7–9). If ever there was a doubt anywhere in the universe, this last surge of stubbornness and hate proves to the watching universe that the lost are irrevocably unworthy of eternal life.

The war is over! The Great Controversy ends in such a way that it will never arise again!

But how will we know it is over and that sin and rebellion will never happen again?

God said early on, before the creation of this world, that He would play on Satan's turf, giving Satan every advantage to sell his side of the story. But that there would be *"no end save victory."*

God knew that time would be on His side. He gave Satan as much time as it would take to convince the world that he had a better way to run the universe than God did.[1105] But now the evidence was in, evidence that reached its fullness during the last few years of this earth's history. Century after century,

> "The aim of the great rebel has ever been to justify himself, and to prove the divine government responsible for the rebellion. To this end he has bent all the power of his giant intellect. He has worked deliberately and systematically, and with marvelous success, leading vast multitudes to accept his version of the Great Controversy which has been so long in progress. For thousands of years this chief of conspiracy has palmed off falsehood for truth. … In his last great effort to dethrone Christ, destroy His people, and take possession of the city of God, the arch-deceiver has been fully unmasked."[1106]

How was God's strategy validated? He let Satan expose himself to the universe, allowing enough time to remove all possible doubt that his lies were completely unsubstantiated. Does the Bible say anything about this grand review of the evidence, that God is vindicated and Satan has been exposed?

FINAL REVIEW

Paul was given some insights regarding this final review: "Do you not know that the saints will judge the world? And if the world is to be judged by you, are you unworthy to judge the smallest matters? Do you not know that we shall judge angels?" (1 Corinthians 6:2, 3).

[1105] "It was God's purpose to place things on an eternal basis of security, and in the councils of heaven it was decided that time must be given for Satan to develop the principles which were the foundation of his system of government. He had claimed that these were superior to God's principles. Time was given for the working of Satan's principles, that they might be seen by the heavenly universe." —*The Desire of Ages*, 759. Also 34, 36.

[1106] *The Great Controversy*, 670.

John the Revelator gives us an overview of this final review of the evidence: "Blessed and holy is he who has part in the first resurrection. Over such the second death has no power, but they shall be priests of God and of Christ, and shall reign with Him a thousand years. ... And the dead were judged according to their works, by the things which were written in the books" (Revelation 20:6, 12).

I like the way Gerald Winslow looks at that executive review: "The image of partnership with Christ in millennial judgment may have a further and more general implication for ethics now. This vision brings into sharp focus the character of a God who does not mind explaining at length the basis for proper judgment. If the saints are supposed to join in reigning and judging, they must understand the principles upon which the kingdom of God is founded. I like to think that the millennium symbolizes the willingness of God to take a very long time, from our present perspective, to make those principles clear."[1107]

Ellen White saw this clearly:

> "Every question of truth and error in the long-standing controversy has now been made plain. The results of rebellion, the fruits of setting aside the divine statutes, have been laid open to the view of all created intelligences. The working out of Satan's rule in contrast with the government of God, has been presented to the whole universe. Satan's own works have condemned him, God's wisdom, His justice, and His goodness stand fully vindicated. ...

> "With all the facts of the Great Controversy in view, the whole universe, both loyal and rebellious, with one accord declare, 'Just and true are Thy ways, Thou King of saints'" (Revelation 5:12).[1108]

Now the haunting question: How can we be sure that even after this "final" review of the Great Controversy that sin and rebellion will not arise sometime in the future? Let's think about it in our next chapter.

[1107] W. Teel, Jr., ed., *Remnant and Republic* (Loma Linda, CA: Loma Linda University Center for Christian Bioethics, 1995), 173.
[1108] *Ibid.*, 670, 671.

CHAPTER FIFTY:
THE UNIVERSE ETERNALLY
SECURE—NO MORE SIN!

Could it ever be possible that the redeemed in the New Earth, now basking in the light of God's presence and enjoying continual improvement of every skill and deepening love for all those around them—could it ever happen that someone would let a seed of jealousy arise or a wish to be the best in playing the violin? Yes, it could be possible! Satan lived in a similar, perfect environment, talking to God every day, practicing his singing skills and enjoying the respect that other angels showed him.

Why won't redeemed people, in the same kind of heavenly environment, slip into Satan's self-centered ways, or back into their own habits of self-gratification? *Because they have been there and done that!* And something more. Their lives of faith have brought them to the place where they have "settl[ed] into the truth, both intellectually and spiritually, so they cannot be moved."[1109] Their boutons have become so powerful in the development of habits that they will *never* choose to say "no" to God again![1110]

TRUSTED WITH ETERNAL LIFE

Choosing love and unselfishness will be as natural as finding "a" or "l" on your typewriter or computer keyboard blindfolded. Rebels, those who have made a practice of saying "no" to the light of truth, voted themselves out of forever! Why? Because they cannot be trusted with eternal life. No purgatory, no limbo, no second chances—it is in this life we are proving whether we can be safe to save.[1111]

No, God does not perform celestial surgery on the brains of the redeemed so that they can never again disagree with Him. *If He did that just to guarantee the security of the universe, He would lose everything He had gained in exposing Satan.*

But if God suddenly decided to redeem everyone who ever lived on Planet Earth, all the onlookers in worlds afar would not be able to smother the lurking suspicion that God has been playing a strange game with Satan and this earth. Yes, they would then think: God may have been very astute in outsmarting Satan and all those who followed him. But nothing really has been won—the reality remains: Just because God outsmarted Satan it doesn't mean that God can really be trusted. Even though He continues to claim that freedom is the safest way to secure the universe, there is something hidden in

---

[1109] *Last Day Events,* 219, 220; See 339–340.

[1110] See 187–194.

[1111] *Last Day Events,* 295; *Testimonies,* vol. 1, 705; *Ibid.,* vol. 2, 355; *Testimonies to Ministers,* 430.

His promise. The dark wonder about God's veracity would cloud their songs of happiness—watch it, God can't be trusted to abide by His own words.

But God thought that all through before He created intelligent beings. He knew the challenge and cost of freedom and the necessity of having His whole creation trusting Him implicitly. How did it happen? Not because they are overwhelmed with God's power and glory, but because by experience they have been melted by His love, patience, and fairness. Coercion by any means, including celestial lobotomies, has not been and will never be God's way of dealing with freedom and loyalty. That has never been God's way.

Throughout eternity, He will help us remember the cost of freedom. Every time we look at our Lord's hands and feet we will remember and He will remember. He will forever remember that there was nothing more He could have done for those who rejected Him, and we will remember that our choices and His response of Divine Energy created a mind that will never say "no" to Him again. Ever![1112]

GOD'S WILLINGNESS TO RISK

The universe is now secure because Laboratory Earth has vindicated God's willingness to risk the universe on the validity of the plan of salvation. God's loyalists have proven God right and Satan wrong. Satan's philosophy of pseudo-freedom, ersatz liberty, has been validated by thousands of years of heartbreak, wars, cruelty beyond words and deranged minds.

Laboratory Earth has proven that genuine freedom is never free. It must be paid for with vigilance, responsibility and ofttimes the sacrifice of personal comforts, even life itself.

The cost of freedom is always measured by what it pays for: How many have been protected from evil, how many have been given another chance to appreciate the foundation stones of freedom—politically, socially, economically and spiritually? All because Planet Earth has always had enough men and women who paid the cost of freedom so that others could enjoy what they died for.

Every lover of freedom singing under the tree of life will know that the cost has been worth it. But they know that they will never be able to repay the cost. That is why the heavenly chorus keeps finding new hymns to express their gratitude, on and on, through eternity. Forever they will be praising the Captain of their Salvation, who forever will be seen throughout the universe as the human Jesus, locked into time and space—like all the redeemed of earth.

I remember a speaking appointment in Corpus Christi, Texas, a few months ago. During some free time, my wife and I visited the *USS Lexington*, anchored in the harbor. It is the fifth ship in U.S. history to have that brave

---

[1112] Many see in Nahum 1:7–9 a forecast of the secure universe wherein sin will "not rise up a second time."

name. The fourth was lost in the Battle of the Coral Sea (May 1942) after a brilliant and heroic effort that stopped the advance of the Japanese toward Australia. As soon as this news hit America, the next aircraft carrier being built was named the *Lexington*, which also soon saw gallant action in the Pacific.

"THIS IS THE CAPTAIN SPEAKING"

On December 4, 1943, a Japanese bomber disabled this new *Lexington* on a moonlit night off Tarawa. The skipper, Captain Felix Stump, went to the ship speaker system so that all aboard could hear him: "This is the captain speaking. We have taken a torpedo hit in our stern and the rudder seems badly damaged. *Each man must do his job calmly and efficiently. Don't worry. That's my job. I got you here, and I'll get you out and home.*" Marvelous story of how they limped home!

But there's more to the story. More than 95 percent of those on board had never been in the open sea before. They were not seasoned sailors and pilots. Citizen sailors and pilots they were. Recently assembled, trained but unsure of themselves. On that moonlit night, they were an easy target, but the captain kept maneuvering the ship to face into the moonlight so that the *Lexington* would not give the bomber or submarine a broadside silhouette. He was all the time changing his speed and direction.

On the way back to Pearl Harbor with that disabled rudder, the Admiral of the fleet radioed to Captain Stump, "That was wonderful seamanship, Captain." The captain replied, "*Thank you, sir, my crew was magnificent!*"

Those words swept through the crew: They were magnificent in the eyes of their captain! The sailors wrote home about their captain. When they limped back to Pearl, they didn't need the serenade of the Navy Band to make them feel like they were heroes. They had already heard the commendation of their captain. Knowing their captain for what he was, kept them unafraid, kept them doing their duty. They could trust their captain, because he got them there and he would get them home.

One of these days, a wonderful group of people will, in a way, limp into the Harbor after the worst time of trouble ever to hit people on this earth. And they will hear their Captain say: "Well done, good and faithful servants … Enter into the joy of your lord" (Matthew 25:21).

And then He will turn to the unfallen worlds, to the unfallen angels, and wave His hand over the veterans from earth, and say, "My crew was magnificent!"

Here were the people upon whom God risked His integrity and government. In a very special way, the rest of the universe that had been watching Laboratory Earth will stand and salute these veterans of a very costly war! And then turn to their Captain of the universe and fall on their knees in a sob that will echo from galaxy to galaxy—a sob of relief and gratitude and love! The risk was worth it!

The Great Controversy embraces all aspects of the Christian's life. This includes his or her approach to the Bible, the study of all intellectual areas of interest, personal relationships with family and others, and to the way that his or her church reflects the Great Controversy Theme. This church reflection will be seen in such areas as humanitarian concern, educational institutions, health-related institutions, youth concerns, and methods to reach the unchurched.

CHAPTER FIFTY-ONE:
A SUMMARY—
THE GREAT CONTROVERSY THEME
SHOULD MAKE THE DIFFERENCE
IN HOW MEN AND WOMEN OF FAITH
THINK AND ACT IN THE ENDTIME

The Great Controversy Theme is God's way of explaining His side of the cosmic conflict with Satan, the master rebel. Its core principles should reflect the way that God's loyalists will think and act. Throughout these pages, we have seen how those principles have worked out, not only in the heavenly conflict between Lucifer and Jesus, but also in the living laboratory on Planet Earth. Let's review the core principles in the Great Controversy Theme.

THE BIBLE'S GRAND CENTRAL THOUGHT
"The grand central thought …the central theme of the Bible, the theme about which every other in the whole book clusters, is the redemption plan, the restoration in the human soul of the image of God."[1113]

[1113] *Education*, 125.

The goal of God's side of the Great Controversy is to undue sin's damages and to restore in men and women the image of God as reflected in the life and character of Jesus. *The goal of the gospel is our restoration, not only our forgiveness.*[1114] This theme should motivate and determine all aspects of the Christian's life, all aspects of church activities, including its educational and health principles, its evangelistic message and practice, its social responsibilities, its youth programs for all ages and its stewardship of God's blessings.

BUILT-IN PROMISE OF THIS CENTRAL THEME

"From the first intimation of hope in the sentence pronounced in Eden to that last glorious promise of the Revelation, 'They shall see His face; and His name shall be in their foreheads' (Revelation 22:4), the burden of every book and every passage of the Bible is the unfolding of this wondrous theme—man's uplifting—the power of God, "which giveth us the victory through our Lord Jesus Christ" (1 Corinthians 15:57).[1115]

This promise cannot be overemphasized—it is the everlasting gospel! God has put the integrity of His universe on the line when He promises His loyalists all that is necessary to overcome all habits of, and all tendencies to, sin. We call the "power of God" His "grace." Grace is whatever we need to fulfill this "wondrous theme" in the lives of loyal men and women; restoration of loyal men and women will guarantee the "eternal basis of security" for the universe.[1116]

THIS CENTRAL THEME BECOMES THE KEY THAT UNLOCKS
THE BIBLE AND LIFE'S GREATEST QUESTIONS

"He who grasps this thought has before him an infinite field for study. He has the key that will unlock to him the whole treasure house of God's word."[1117]

Without the cohering glue of the Great Controversy Theme, the Bible disintegrates into a book-by-book study, like pearls on a string. Without this inner coherence, much of the Bible is obscure no matter how much one understands its Hebrew or Greek, or its historical milieu. Understanding the everlasting gospel correctly, from Genesis to Revelation, helps the student to see the good news played out in each book. Knowing why sin exists and why suffering is so pervasive directs the student to understanding how sin and suffering will one day be eliminated from the universe. Without seeing the beginning and end of the Great Controversy, life itself loses its meaning and purpose.

[1114] See 83.

[1115] *Education,* 125.

[1116] *The Desire of Ages,* 759. See also 144.

[1117] *Education,* 126.

THIS CENTRAL THEME OUTLINES HOW TO READ THE BIBLE

"The Bible is its own expositor. Scripture is to be compared with scripture. The student should learn to view the word as a whole, and to see the relation of its parts. He should gain a knowledge of its grand central theme, of God's original purpose for the world, of the rise of the Great Controversy, and of the work of redemption. He should understand the nature of the two principles that are contending for supremacy, and should learn to trace their working through the records of history and prophecy, to the great consummation. He should see how this controversy enters into every phase of human experience; how in every act of life he himself reveals the one or the other of the two antagonistic motives; and how, whether he will or not, he is even now deciding upon which side of the controversy he will be found."[1118]

This unambiguous clarity of how we should let the Bible speak to us puts a higher purpose on all biblical studies. Many become experts on a particular biblical book but miss the larger issue for which that book is in the Bible. If in all our archeological research, linguistic insights, and chronological studies, we do not grasp the core concepts that unfold the Great Controversy Theme, all of our biblically oriented study is missing the point. Perhaps a lifetime of study could be irrelevant.

Urgency is breathed into genuine Bible study. Students are not passive spectators watching the parade of history. They are in the arena, whether they realize it or not. It would be a pity for students to earn all A's in their school work on all levels and yet flunk "Life 101"!

THE CENTRAL THEME SHAPES
THE LOYALISTS' EDUCATIONAL PHILOSOPHY

"In order to understand what is comprehended in the work of education, we need to consider both the nature of man and the purpose of God in creating him. We need to consider also the change in man's condition through the coming in of a knowledge of evil, and God's plan for still fulfilling His glorious purpose in the education of the human race."[1119]

When a school, from kindergarten to post-graduate work, frames its curriculum and lesson plans (whatever the subject) within this higher understanding of reality, the goal of the gospel will always be the "restoration" of Christ's character in all students—the end-plan of all educational pursuits. Further, the student will also see the "glorious purpose" of why men and women were created—to participate in the vindication of God's character and government. That God should be vindicated is a higher focus than focusing on one's own personal salvation.

[1118] *Education*, 190.
[1119] *Ibid.*, 14, 15.

EVERY FIELD OF STUDY WILL FIND GREATEST RELEVANCE WHEN REFLECTING THE CENTRAL THEME

"Immeasurably superior in value to the productions of any human author are the Bible writings, even when thus considered; but of infinitely wider scope, of infinitely greater value, are they when viewed in their relation to the grand central thought. Viewed in the light of this thought, every topic has a new significance. In the most simply stated truths are involved principles that are as high as heaven and that compass eternity."[1120]

I think often of those interesting observations that Ellen White made regarding the world's "great teachers, men of giant intellect and extensive research, men whose utterances have stimulated thought, and opened to view vast fields of knowledge." She saluted their contributions: "As far as their teaching is true ... the world's great thinkers reflect the rays of the Son of Righteousness. Every gleam of thought, every flash of the intellect, is from the Light of the world."[1121]

When we read the writings of these "giant intellects" within the larger view of the Great Controversy Theme, many of these flashes of intellect take on even greater meaning as they help unfold this central theme. That is what makes broad reading of these "great teachers" so interesting and ofttimes exceedingly helpful in fleshing out the purposes of God.

THEORY MERGED WITH PRACTICE

For decades Albert Einstein's famous formula, $E=MC^2$, remained in physics textbooks and on school blackboards around the world. Physicists knew how to explain the formula: Energy equals Mass times Speed of Light squared. Laboratory experiments seemed to affirm the formula but it wasn't really validated until the first atom bomb exploded over Los Alamos and then over Hiroshima in 1945. Theory merged with practice.

Gospel theory is no more powerful than Einstein's formula—both must merge into practice to be believable. The goal of the gospel is the vindication of God in the Great Controversy. But that was only theory until Jesus became a human being.

Jesus taught the theory of the Christian life, such as in His Sermon on the Mount. But His life merged theory and practice. His life became the Template for men and women, the benchmark of what it means to be truly human, unsullied by caving in to self-centered feelings and desires. He is called the "pattern man. ... His character is our model. ... As we look to Him and think of Him He will be formed within, the hope of glory."[1122]

Thus, His principles were God's way of helping us to understand what harmony with God truly is. Instead of asking, "What's wrong about this or

---

[1120] *Ibid.*, 125.
[1121] *Ibid.*, 13, 14.
[1122] *Maranatha*, 241.

that?" we should direct our thinking to "What's right about this or that?" If He is the pattern for every boy and girl, father and mother, questions about dress and personal grooming become easier to answer: the latest styles or peer pressure may not reflect Christ's pattern, Christ's principles. Biblical formulas should merge with practice for those concerned with making Jesus their "pattern."

The same reasoning applies to leisure-time activities, to hobbies, and to the choice of friends. When we think of the purpose of the gospel and the kind of people who will be safe to save, answers to these questions become amazingly simple.

We are not talking idealistically as if we were romanticizing what "might be." Jesus did not come into this world merely to be an Ideal which all of us should aim at, hoping that "aiming" at Him every day would be all that was expected. Jesus came into Satan's arena to show us how to cope and face down the Malicious Liar. We are talking about an Ideal that becomes our attainable goal!

"In Him [Jesus] was found the perfect ideal. To reveal this ideal as the only true standard for attainment; to show what every human being might become; what, through the indwelling of humanity by divinity, all who received Him would become—for this, Christ came to the world. He came to show how men are to be trained as befits the sons of God; how on earth they are to practice the principles and to live the life of heaven."[1123]

Job, among others, was a good example of merging these principles into practice. We all know, from earth's point of view, how God risked much in letting Satan plague Job. Without any Bible in his hand, without the example of Jesus to lean on, Job trusted what he had learned about God from experience and the enlightened testimony of faithful ancestors. Humanly speaking, he took what seems to have been Satan's full blast. "But according to his faith, so it came to pass. By his [Job's] patient endurance he vindicated his own character, and thus the character of Him whose representative he was."[1124]

But Job was only one example of what the Bible predicts will be what the universe looks for in earth's final hours. "If there was ever a people in need of constantly increasing light from heaven, it is the people that, in this time of peril, God has called to be the depositaries of His holy law, and to vindicate His character before the world. Those to whom has been committed a trust so sacred must be spiritualized, elevated, vitalized, by the truths they profess to believe."[1125]

[1123] *Education*, 73, 74
[1124] *Ibid.*
[1125] *Testimonies*, vol. 5, 746.

THE CENTRAL THEME SEPARATES THOSE WHO TRY
TO IMPRESS GOD AND THOSE WHO WANT TO HONOR HIM

One of the fundamental differences between God's principles and Satan's deceptions is portrayed in how Cain related to Abel. Men and women ever since have been divided between those who try to impress God and those who choose to honor Him. Earliest pagan nations had their priests and holy places. All paganism builds on securing their god's approval by "doing something." From their point of view, "doing something" gives them the security that they are approved in this life and in the hereafter.

Unfortunately, the Bible story also reflects this same pagan tendency to find God's approval and thus personal security and assurance in what men and women may "do." We call this "the old covenant" misunderstanding of how to gain God's approval. Some may call their god Baal and worship him on the "high places" with all the associated degradation that history records. Or some will call their God Elohim or Jehovah and seek to please Him with the "doing" of sanctuary rituals. They both end up in the same place—different forms of "righteousness by works." Trying to please God by *impressing* Him reveals a fundamental misunderstanding of the character of God and of the purpose of the Great Controversy Theme.

Satan's subtle deceptions have embraced nearly everyone since Cain: "those who would be saved by their merits, and those who would be saved in their sins."[1126]

But the God who made the universe and spun galaxies into space is not a Grecian or Egyptian deity. He does not need to be appeased. Nor does He require our "doing" before He gives us His attention. He is Love Personified. He breathes love, His arms are always outstretched with forgiveness—note Christ's words on the Cross, "Father, forgive them for they know not what they do." Seeing all the abuse in advance, He still thought the creation of intelligent beings worth the cost. Because we are His children, we are never far from His love. He is doing all that divine power and goodness can do to draw His children back home. He doesn't wait for us to confess something before He opens the front door. Realizing His love and forgiving heart is exactly what draws rebels back home (Romans 2:3). Think of the prodigal son!

Knowing that God is like the prodigal's waiting Father is the knife-edge that separates those who feel they must "do" something to gain God's favor from those who are drawn to God by who He really is! All that disobedient children can do to regain the sense of peace in their hearts is to honor their parents by considering their commands to be privileges. Honoring their parents is the highest way of showing their appreciation—and there is no way to "measure" how much honoring is enough! Just like a good marriage! No happy marriage is a 50-50 percent deal when spouses measure whether

[1126] *The Great Controversy*, 572.

they have done enough of their part of the bargain. Happy marriages are 100-100 percent deals when loving spouses never feel that they have done enough to honor their mate. Impressing one's spouse is short-range thinking; honoring them is a lifetime of mutual respect and endless love.

When one gets the character of God right nothing is mere obligation—that would be the mistake of the legalist who lives in the shadows of the old covenant. Living under the rainbow of God's promises, loyalists know that their best response to God is to trust His Word, powerful enough to create worlds and raise the dead. They live grateful lives because they know they are never out of the hands of God. Their highest duty is to follow "known duty," the light that the Holy Spirit beams into their minds daily. Such is the joy of the new covenant, the outworking of the gospel of grace, and the continuing vindication of God's way of running the universe. Impressing God is really self-centered motivation; honoring God is a forever relationship where His vindication is far more important than our salvation. His message is: "Trust God's promises and live."

THE GREAT CONTROVERSY THEME, THE "CENTRAL THEME OF THE BIBLE," BEGINS LIKE AN ACORN—THE GIANT OAK BECOMES GOD'S MIGHTY ANSWER TO SATAN'S LIES

This "central theme" embraces a cluster of interrelated doctrines that too often are considered separately, as one would view each pearl on a necklace, rather than as limbs integrated into a developing oak tree. For example, let's look at only one branch of this giant oak, the branch of *Adventist eschatology*.

Why is it that no other church looks at the Second Advent as Adventists do? We believe that we have captured the biblical picture of the endtimes as illuminated by the Great Controversy Theme. This picture is formed by a "mutually supportive cluster" of ideas, including conditional immortality, a premillennial historicist eschatology, health message, gift of prophecy, latter-rain and loud-cry symbolism, worldwide focus on seventh-day Sabbath and the closing of Christ's mediatorial work in the heavenly sanctuary.

Each of these subjects exists as relatively unconnected beliefs if they are not all seen as connected, integrated, inherent and subsumed in the Great Controversy Theme. When the purpose of the gospel and the "central theme" is kept clear and up front, each concept in the "cluster" is seen as inherently connected with each other concept.

For example: The gospel purpose is restoration, not only forgiveness; it prepares a people to meet the Lord and to be safe to save. Thus *character transformation* is a significant component of this last-day "cluster."

This concept of character transformation interacts with the *Adventist health emphasis*—not merely to live 10 years longer but to prepare the mind to think clearly, to detect right from wrong quickly and as a habit, so that truth can settle in (so deeply imbedded in neural pathways) that it will never again be moved to say "no" to God.

The concept of character transformation interacts with such concepts as *"latter rain" and "loud cry"*—that God waits until He has people He can trust with His power, people that won't embarrass Him with power without His character, people on whom He can write His name (Revelation 7, 14, 22).

The concept of character transformation interacts with the *worldwide gospel proclamation* (Matthew 24:14). Those described in Revelation 14:12 will be living "witnesses" to the power of the "everlasting gospel" that has been too long limited in its definition (that is, by those who skew the ellipse of salvation by making faith into either mental assent or emotional experience).

This dynamic cluster of eschatological concepts should be integrated as branches are to each other and to the trunk—or each concept becomes independently sterile. *The emphasis heard a century ago becomes a logical challenge: The SDA message is primarily concerned with preparing people to be translated, as well as preparing them to die.*

This principle of the gospel reflected in last-day Christians is pervasive throughout Ellen White's writings. For instance: "Character cannot be changed when Jesus comes, nor just as a man is about to die. Character building must be done in this life."[1127]

The Great Controversy Theme (GCT) not only saves us from the errors of the centuries, it provides the church and the world with a message that makes sense to those seeking mental certainty and emotional certitude. The GCT is not a notion that anyone thought up; it is old truth that became "present truth" entrusted by God to a humble, obedient woman, His messenger for these endtimes.

If one were to picture the GCT as a giant oak tree, we would begin before time in freedom's soil in which Satan's rebellion became the first casualty in the Great Controversy. God's response was to plant His acorn—His response to Satan's charges.

First in heaven, then on Planet Earth, the acorn becomes a sapling—the story of how God plans to rescue this rebellious planet with His *restoration* program. Promising His power to all those who trust His promises, God outlines the divine-human cooperation plan.

One major branch in this divine-human co-op is His *grace* that includes the great truths taught in the sanctuary service and then through Jesus, our Savior and Example.

The opposite branch is *responsibility* summed up in that fruitful response called *faith*: gratitude, appreciation, repentance, trust, willingness to follow

---

[1127] *Testimonies to Ministers*, 430.

"known duty," and the realization that only in this life can we demonstrate whether we can be trusted with eternal life.[1128]

As the oak develops, we have great branches called distinctive educational principles and interactive health principles—all fulfilling the purpose of the acorn. Restoration of men and women spiritually, mentally, physically focuses all these principles.

Other branches give strength to various church programs that proclaim to the world these distinctive principles and the unambiguous purpose of the gospel. Any church program that is not committed to the unfolding of the Great Controversy Theme (the maturation of the acorn) should be cut away as one would prune an adventitious branch.

In addition, the top branches embrace the eschatological concepts mentioned earlier—they all flow out of the purpose of the acorn—the restoration of the willing to life without end. In other words, what one believes about Righteousness by Faith, or the Atonement, or Christology, or Eschatology, is not self-contained. What one believes in one subject directly affects what one believes regarding the other subjects. Everything in truth is interconnected and flows out of one basic principle of the GCT: restoration of the willing into people safe to save.

If one plants an apple seed, it will not produce a giant oak. Further, one cannot graft an apple branch on to the oak tree and hope to be praised for tolerance. The Great Controversy oak is not a pluralistic collection of branches from palms or orange trees. Allowing the Great Controversy oak to grow becomes the only way that the Adventist church can find unity as well as its destiny.[1129]

[1128] "That religion which makes of sin a light matter, dwelling upon the love of God to the sinner regardless of his actions, only encourages the sinner to believe that God will receive him while he continues in that which he knows to be sin. This is what some are doing who profess to believe present truth. The truth is kept apart from the life, and that is the reason it has no power to convict and convert the soul." —*Testimonies*, vol. 5, 540.

[1129] "The servants of Christ are called to the same work [never purchase peace by compromise], and they should beware lest, in seeking to prevent discord, they surrender the truth. They are to 'follow after the things which make for peace' (Romans 14:19); but real peace can never be secured by compromising principle." —*The Desire of Ages*, 356.

POSTLUDE

On Wednesday evening, September 12, 2001, President George W. Bush spoke to the American people and the world. Heroic rescuers were still removing the injured from the blasted World Trade Center in New York City, the day after the horrific leveling of the Two Towers. He closed his address with these words: "The freedom-loving nations of the world stand by our side. This will be a monumental struggle of good versus evil."

On January 29, 2002, in his first State of the Union Address, President Bush spoke similar words: "We choose freedom and the dignity of every life. Steadfast in our purpose, we now press on. We have known freedom's price. We have shown freedom's power. And in this great conflict, my fellow Americans, we will see freedom's victory."

Such words sum up the compelling motivation behind the Father, Jesus and the Holy Spirit since the moment Satan decided to revolt. Such has been the promise that the Godhead has given to every man and woman of faith since the calamity in Eden—"we will see freedom's victory."

No declaring victory, no legal games that would try to substitute sham and double-talk for genuine victory! The evil empire will not be destroyed only to rise up again somewhere else in the universe. Sin will be seen for what it is—a revolt against all that is good, true, beautiful, and loving.

The consequences of sin will stand naked and revolting even to sinners. The consequences of loyalty and obedience are like bluebirds ever on the wing, the melodies of Beethoven echoing forever. The claims of God and the claims of Satan stand fully exposed, accentuated by Gethsemane and Calvary. The chorus of the redeemed sing "Great and marvelous are Your works, Lord God Almighty! Just and true are Your ways" (Revelation 15:3). Sung by informed wills freely exercised—truly God's reward and the redeemed's forever delight!

Responsibility will again be a treasured word—no longer considered a put-down for those who claimed their rights without making right choices or expected equal outcomes without personal discipline and without delaying gratifications. Self-fulfillment will not be seen as a higher goal than responsibility—they will mirror each other as long as the "pure river of water of life" flows, as long as the "tree of life" bears its fruit. Self-development will forever be seen as our first duty to God and to others as we discover new ways to serve both God and others.[1130]

T. S. Eliot may not have understood fully his own words that closed one of his "four quartets," but they surely sum up the thoughts of those

---

[1130] See *Christ's Object Lessons*,. 329. "The goal of self-determining freedom, I have argued, is to become a person who eternally receives and reflects God's love." —Boyd, *Satan, op. cit.*, 179.

who have observed the Great Controversy from beginning to end, "In my beginning is my end."[1131] The universe is again at peace, all questions settled. What God had given His universe "in His beginning," will be even more understood "in His end."

In his letter to faithful Abigail, John Adams wrote on July 3, 1776 (the day before the signing of the Declaration of Independence), "You will think I am transported by enthusiasm but I am not. I am well aware of the toil, and blood, and treasure that it will cost us to maintain this declaration and support and defend these states. Yet, through all the gloom, I can see the rays of ravishing light and glory. I can see that the end is more than worth all the means, and that posterity will triumph."[1132]

In a small way, but on the same key, Adams grasped the future as Jesus did on Calvary: "Yet through all the gloom, I can see the rays of ravishing light and glory. I can see the end is more than worth all the means, and that posterity will triumph!"

The End is more than worth all the Means! All the universe will sing that chorus with God leading the choir, for it means more to Him than to any other person in the universe. Every redeemed man and woman and child will look back on a very checkered, sometimes torturous path, and yet say, "The End is more than worth all the Means."

In President Bush's address to Congress and to the entire world on September 21, 2001, a few days after those planes crashed into the World Trade Center and the Pentagon, he concluded: "The course of this conflict is not known, yet its outcome is certain. Freedom and fear, justice and cruelty, have always been at war. And we know that God is not neutral between them."

Those who listen to the Bible story do know the "course of this conflict." God's loyalists will have lived out "its outcome." And the universe will forever know that God has not been "neutral" in this cosmic conflict!

Now and forever, with the consequences of evil only a memory, God's faithful will face the unending future with freedom to rise to the potential that God has given each one of us,[1133] to share throughout the vast universe of intelligent beings the experience that only the redeemed have learned—that freedom is easily lost without paying its costs. Such is our destiny that God has on His mind for you and me. What a life to live and a story to tell—forever!

And the Immortal Three—Father, Son, and Holy Spirit—will stand before the singing multitude on all the inhabited planets and say with a thundering echo: Freedom was worth the cost!

[1131] T. S. Eliot, *Four Quartet* (New York: Harcourt Brace & Company), "Burnt Norton."

[1132] McCullogh, *op. cit.,* 130.

[1133] "Higher than the highest human thought can reach is God's ideal for His children. Godliness— godlikeness—is the goal to be reached." —*Education*, 18.

APPENDIX A:
HOW WE DEFINE FREEDOM

The reason why I am here defining what I mean by freedom lies at the heart of the Great Controversy between God and Satan. Satan's main thrust and appeal to fellow angels was that he had a better plan to ensure their "freedom." So began the Great Controversy! Everything depends on what is meant by freedom![1134]

When we use words loosely, such as free will, choice, responsibility, causal determinants, freedom, independence, and liberty, we must state clearly what we mean by each word or we end up with confusion. Satan started the confusion and thereby caused the controversy in heaven. One of his chief weapons on Planet Earth as he continued his attack on God's government has been to muddle the mind of men and women regarding the meaning of freedom and liberty.

Abraham Lincoln said it well:

> "The world has never had a good definition of the word liberty, and the American people, just now, are much in want of one. We all declare for liberty; but in using the same word we do not all mean the same thing. With some the word liberty may mean for each man to do as he pleases with himself, and the product of his labor; while with others, the same word many mean for some men to do as they please with other men, and the product of other men's labor. Here are two, not only different, but incompatible things, called by the same name—liberty. And it follows that each of the things is, by the respective parties, called by two different and incompatible names— liberty and tyranny."[1135]

Most philosophers interchange the words "liberty" and "freedom."[1136] But these words do have shades of difference. Freedom focuses on the adjective "free"— freedom to act in accordance with desire. The word 'freedom' is more frequently employed in the discussion of free will.[1137] It sounds awkward to talk about "liberty of conscience" or "liberty from fear."

It seems to me that a free person is not shackled by ignorance, oppression or vice. As Robert P. George put it: "A free person is enslaved neither to the sheer will of another *nor to his own appetites and passions*. A free person lives uprightly, fulfilling his obligations to family, community, nation and God. By contrast, a

---

[1134] The Controversy can also be viewed as a contest of authority and independence, but underneath remains the freedom that God was willing to provide His created intelligences by which they made their choices.

[1135] *The Collected Works of Abraham Lincoln* edited by Roy P. Basler, vol. VII, "Address at Sanitary Fair, Baltimore, Maryland" (April 18, 1864), 301–302.

[1136] "The essence of liberty has always lain in the ability to choose as you wish to choose, because you wish so to choose, uncoerced, unbullied, not swallowed up in some vast system; and in the right to resist, to be unpopular, to stand up for your convictions merely because they are your convictions. That is true freedom and without it there is neither freedom of any kind, nor even the illusion of it. Isaiah Berlin, *Freedom and its Betrayal* (London, 2002), 103, 4. Berlin uses the words "freedom" and "liberty" interchangeably, as have others.

[1137] Mortimer Adler's *Syntopicon Essays* on "Liberty."

person given over to his appetites and passions, a person who scoffs at truth and chooses to live, whether openly of secretly, in defiance of the moral law is not free. He is simply a different kind of slave."[1138]

LIBERTY SEEMS TO BE MORE LIMITED THAN FREEDOM

Liberty seems to have a more limited range, emphasizing "freedom from," such as release from former restraints or compulsion. License implies freedom especially granted or even freedom misused.[1139]

Robert George sees the "license" implicit in the use of "liberty." He calls it "counterfeit freedom" when people embrace the notion that they are "free" from morality, responsibility, and truth. ... It is ironic, is it not, that people who celebrate slavery to appetite and passion call this bondage "freedom"?[1140]

And "independence" has a different emphasis, highlighting freedom from limitation, on one hand, and self-sufficiency and adequacy, on the other. (But only God can be truly "independent.")

I admit, so much that is written adds to the fuzziness of what freedom means. But let's look at freedom (and thus liberty) from a common sense point of view, informed by the Great Controversy between God and Satan.

Freedom can be understood negatively as well as positively. Negatively, it generally means not to be prevented from doing whatever one wishes. That is, freedom from coercion, from intimidation by a stronger person or power, freedom from restricting laws, freedom from frustration and obstacles that prevent one from realizing one's potential. In a nutshell, freedom to be left alone. Very self-defeating.

But freedom can be understood positively. That is, freedom to think, freedom to pursue self-development, freedom to worship without restraint, and freedom to be left alone. "Freedom is the ability to live and seek truth in an uninhibited fashion."[1141] Freedom becomes the lifeblood of the best that human beings are capable.

FREEDOM'S POSITIVE AND NEGATIVE ASPECTS

But the problem arises in trying to join both freedom's positive and negative aspects. At first glance, they seem to be irreconcilable.[1142] Just what Satan exploited in the beginning of the Great Controversy and in the Garden of Eden!

For instance, should democracy be promoted at the expense of individual freedom? Do laws, any law, encroach upon a person's desire to be left alone,[1143] or to

---

[1138] Robert P. George, McCormick Professor of Jurisprudence, Princeton University, "Freedom and Its Counterfeit," *Imprimis,* August 2003.

[1139] See Webster's *Ninth New Collegiate Dictionary,* comparison of freedom and liberty, 491.

[1140] George, *op. cit.*

[1141] Josh Siegel, "Concept of true freedom is found far beyond American ideal," *The State News,* MSU's independent voice, February 22, 2002.

[1142] Such as unrestrained capitalism versus unrestrained government control; social Darwinianism versus Christ's Sermon on the Mount. History is too clear: freedom for the foxes means death for the chickens.

[1143] George Bernard Shaw suggests that the only synonym for freedom is "leisure"—the absence of compulsion. Schopenhauer insists that only when a person is alone is he really free.

think and act differently from the majority? Does the minority have equal rights to freedom? What place is left for creativity and preference if the majority votes for equality of outcome or opportunity? Is independence really freedom if it mars or even destroys the tranquility of the majority? Should loyalty to authority forbid the pursuit of knowledge? Could too much freedom be self-destructive? When should mercy be hemmed in by justice? We could go on!

For centuries the central question has been, "Who shall govern us?" In the modern world, the question shifts to "How much government should there be?" Interesting shift from the objective to the subjective! How much frontier should there be between the individual and society? Let us listen to Satan's question: "Are we freest when we submit to a centrally administered code of laws or are we freest when centralized administration of law is absent?"

History is telling us that the rule of law founded on constitutions (such as United States') gives birth to individual rights—equality before the law. But when a country swerves to living under the rules of lawmakers who are intoxicated with clichés under the fog of social justice—we surely have the instability of a "rule of law" that shifts daily depending on what anyone says the law is. It is called a "living constitution." Social justice is spawned by the notion of group rights that obviously are the opposite of individual rights.[1144]

Forced Tolerance

All that I find interesting but in the modern view of freedom, especially of the past 40 years, social justice and the notion of self-development becomes mingled with the question, "Who decides what is best for the group as the society reaches higher and higher toward a more just and desirable world?" Suddenly, all separateness, all individualism, is unhealthy or bad. *Forced toleration becomes politically correct.* Everyone is like a river, all flowing together toward one big, undivided river. Government knows best as to how to bring everyone into an equal situation through definite educational structures, engineered economies so that equal outcome is guaranteed to all regardless of differences in input.[1145] This kind of freedom theory easily becomes the atmosphere for groupthink wherein society forbids disagreement for the sake of group harmony. We shall see how all this plays out in Satan's plan to control the world in the last days.

Let us now analyze how freedom is generally categorized into three basic points of view.[1146] Understanding these differences will help us grasp the kind of freedom God gave His created intelligences (angels, unfallen inhabitants of other worlds, and men and women on Planet Earth) and how Satan has prostituted this fundamental gift. Each category is different from the other:

[1144] Balint Vazsonyi, "Four Points of the Compass: Restoring America's Sense of Direction," *Imprimis*, November 1997.

[1145] Alexis de Tocqueville wrote: "There exists also in the human heart a depraved taste for equality, which impels the weak to attempt to lower the powerful to their own level, and reduces men to prefer equality in slavery to inequality in freedom." Cited in Robert J. Ringer, *How You Can Find Happiness During the Collapse of Western Civilization* (New York: QED/Harper & Row, 1983), 220.

[1146] I am indebted to Charles Van Doren's essay on the "Idea of Freedom," in Hutchins, Robert M., and Mortimer J. Adler, eds. *The Great Ideas Today, 1973* New York: Encyclopedia Britannica, Inc., 1973), 287–297.

1) Circumstantial freedom implies freedom to act—freedom to be able, under favorable circumstances, to act as one wishes for one's individual good as one sees it as long as others are not deprived of theirs.[1147] The emphasis is on freedom to act, not on the choice of the act. Thus, a person enslaved by passion or limited by heredity may be free to act as he wishes but he is not totally free, he is determined by habit or heredity. Some thus deny that we have a "free" will, that we are just another object of matter, that everything is caused by a previous act or force and any sense of freedom is purely an illusion. A person would be free only if nothing impedes what he wants to do. If this were all to "freedom," such words as "responsibility" or "punishment" would have to be redefined

2) Natural freedom implies self-determination—the freedom to choose, the power to choose one's course of action between alternatives.[1148] Different from "circumstantial freedom," we enjoy this capacity, not as a blessing of circumstance, but as an innate trait because we are human.[1149] Often espoused by social evolutionists, a common notion is that no one is really free until everyone is free. This notion of freedom dominates modern thought as observed in behaviorism, social engineering, Freudianism, or Marxism. But Milton had it right—when freedom appears to be prostituted or removed by force, something still remains untouched by the aggressor: "Who overcomes by force hath overcome but half his foe."[1150]

3) Acquired freedom implies the freedom to choose as one *ought*.[1151] Some call it self-perfection; that is, one is able, through acquired wisdom or virtue, to change one's character to live as one ought. The oughtness is determined by the moral law or by an ideal befitting human nature, a premise worked out best in modern times by Immanuel Kant's "practical" reason. Thus, we have freedom, not by circumstances, nor by some innate right, but, if at all, through personal development.[1152] To say, "I ought" implies thinking outside natural necessity (forced by motives or someone else's demand). Further, the oughtness must be possible; therefore, we must have the ability to satisfy this "moral imperative."

[1147] Leading advocates include Thomas Hobbes, Tolstoy, and John Stuart Mill.

[1148] Leading advocates include René Descartes, George Berkeley, and William James. Erich Fromm's *Escape From Freedom* (New York: Avon Books, 1941) emphasizes natural freedom: "Positive freedom on the other hand is identical with the full realization of the individual's potentialities, together with his ability to live actively and spontaneously." 297, and throughout the book.

[1149] The U. S. Declaration of Independence guarantees equal, unalienable rights, not equal opportunities (not everyone has the same heredity, intelligence, family money) or equal outcomes. Among these innate rights are "life, liberty (free to pursue one's potential), and the pursuit of happiness."

[1150] "Paradise Lost", bk. 1, *Harvard Classics* (edited by Charles W. Eliot), vol. 4, 106.

[1151] Leading advocates include Plato, Epictetus, and Immanuel Kant. Seneca (4 B.C.—A.D. 65) said: "Show me a man who isn't a slave. One is a slave to sex, another to money, another to ambition," indicating freedom as submission to a moral code. John Winthrop, governor of Massachusetts, in 1864, distinguished between "'natural liberty' which suggested 'a liberty to evil,' and 'moral liberty … a liberty to do only what is good.'"; cited in Eric Foner, *The Story of American Freedom* (New York: W. W. Norton & Company, 1998), 4.

[1152] See Adler's *Syntopicon Essays:* "Liberty."

Kant broke the freedom-necessity chain of his time by defining freedom as spontaneous originality—*the ability to begin a new causal series of events.* Here we have what other concepts of freedom have lacked, the sense of moral responsibility. He derived this conclusion from the existence of moral law, noting that we impose "practical" imperatives on ourselves giving evidence of the existence of freedom apart from the circumstantial or the acquired.

Thus for Kant, we have the ability to make a new start in life, to change old habits and correct our deficiencies.[1153] We thus are fundamentally responsible or irresponsible, but never un-responsible. That then suggests that we are either letting "truth … make us free" or we are adding to the long line who will eventually pay the consequences of their irresponsible ways. In other words, if we deny the existence and efficacy of moral law and the reality of the power of choice, if we believe that all choices are already determined by causes beyond are control, then the idea of responsibility is pure imagination. Further, no one then can be blamed or punished for his or her "badness"—it is all determined by forces beyond his or her control!

RELATION TO THE GREAT CONTROVERSY
The next level of our concern is how this description of freedom's three categories relates to the Great Controversy. And that leads to obvious questions:

What is the relationship between freedom and law, freedom and justice, freedom and equality? How free are we when our actions are regulated by law or coercion? Do considerations of justice draw the line between freedom and license? Does it make any difference to freedom whether the law is just or not? Does freedom increase as government control dwindles and reaches fullness with anarchy?

Can there be freedom apart from equality? If some are more gifted physically or mentally than others, how can law make up the difference and make sure that everyone becomes "equal?" Can freedom guarantee masterpieces in art, music, or inventiveness? It seems that where equality is given a higher priority than individual freedom, equality suffers; where freedom is pursued, equality improves.

Some well-meaning people, noting the obvious limitations and thus inequalities among individuals, seek to go beyond mere *equality under law* and try to enforce *equality by law.* This political solution always leads to unintended consequences and everyone loses.

The only equality in this kind of world beset with the controversy between God and Satan is that everyone is given the right to be free from any human coercion, to be free to realize one's potential within one's personal limitations. Jesus ably taught this concept in His parable of the business owner who distributes his responsibilities to his employees who had various levels of competency.

[1153] R. J. Rummel, "*Understanding Conflict and War*" (Beverly Hills, CA: Sage Publications, 1975), vol. 1, ch. 30, "Determinism and Free Will."

WHAT ABOUT SIN?

What about sin? How one answers that question depends on one's definition of freedom. For example, how much is anyone responsible for his or her actions when we take into consideration the vast differences in heredity, home life, or social limitations?

If theologians say that nothing happens unless God decrees it, then any perception of freedom of choice is merely the outworking of God's will. Or whatever happens may be beyond what God has foreseen, which brings up the question of a divine law, moral responsibility, and judgment.

Regarding law and freedom, if one believes that we are born free (that is, an innate quality) how much freedom do we lose in a civil society that interferes with our external actions?

When we observe that the law is good or just, then the freely chosen act may have the opposite quality of being bad or unjust; thus, freedom of the will is amoral—it can be exercised for good or evil. This the angels discovered after God exposed their rebellious thoughts. As we discover in this book, this creation of the free will in all created intelligences was an enormous risk on God's part.

But that brings up another question that God first tried to explain to the angels perplexed with Satan's deviousness and every parent on earth thereafter: Are we truly free when we are the slave of vices and inappropriate habits? In other words, freedom can be properly used and improperly used. Therefore, the difference between freedom and license lies in either choosing to do or not to do what the moral law commands. Only the criminal is coerced or restrained by good laws (1 Timothy 1:8–10).

Dinesh D'Souza, in his *USA TODAY* editorial (May 2, 2002) wrote, "Egyptian writer Sayyid Qutb, a leading theoretician of Islamic fundamentalism who has been called 'the brains behind Osama bin Laden,' argued in his books that the West is a society based on freedom, while the Islamic world is based on virtue. He argued: Look at how badly the West uses freedom—the materialism, triviality, vulgarity and promiscuity. Islamic societies may be poor, Qutb said, but they try to follow God's will. Islamic laws are based on divine law, higher than any human law. Virtue, Qutb insisted, is ultimately a higher principle than freedom."

DILEMMA OF FREEDOM

D'Souza went on to describe the dilemma of freedom that can be used badly as well as bring out the best in people. Then he added, "By contrast, the authoritarian society that Islamic fundamentalists advocate undermines the possibility of virtue. If the supply of virtue is insufficient in free societies, it is almost non-existent in Islamic societies, because coerced virtues are not virtues at all."

All history seems to write clearly that in the absence of law (the other side of freedom), tyranny flourishes. If law is justly applied, then its direction is what a free, moral person would choose. In fact, a free moral person would probably never think about law. If he did, it would only serve as a hedge to guard the path of life and thus a continuing aspect of a freely lived life. The purpose of life would not be to abolish law but to honor it because the essence of good law is to preserve freedom. In one sense, law is an obstacle to someone's freedom who is acting irresponsibly, but in another sense, law is a source of freedom (perhaps even a substantial part of what we call freedom). In other words, obedience to law is liberty or freedom.[1154]

The problem with the appeal for "self-government" and the "power of the people" is that these terms are deceptive. How does a group of self-governing individuals with individual concepts of self-government arrive at consensus? Who are the people who exercise the power? If the majority, how free is the minority? But what about a minority group that manipulates the governing process so that they can be accepted as the majority. This is one reason that Socrates deplores the spirit of democracy and why the U. S. Constitution describes a republican form of government.

DEMOCRACY AND ANARCHY

Socrates noted that real democracy approaches anarchy through relaxation of laws that some feel too restrictive, leading to lawlessness. Freedom, as we see in this book, flourishes in the atmosphere of justice and order. The opposite atmosphere leads to anarchy with each one doing one's own thing. We have only to scan the fallout from the Great Controversy from its inception to the present to validate this simple observation.[1155]

Joost Meerloo, who lived through the Nazi totalitarian occupation in the Netherlands, saw the mirror challenge of freedom in that we must fight against the dictatorship from without and destructiveness from within. Each person must battle against his inner will to power and the outer call to submit to other people. In other words, he is at his best when he "steps over into the world of self-chosen responsibility and limited freedom." The "choice in favor of freedom lies between self-chosen limitation—the liberation from chaos—and the pseudo-freedom of unconscious chaos."[1156]

Meerloo grasped the implications of the Great Controversy. In the light of freedom as acquisition and the release of the oughtness in human development, we observe in the Great Controversy how God's grace assists reason to conform to His moral law (Hebrews 4:16). Yet His grace does not abolish reason or free choice. Reason itself, contrary to many philosophers and theologians, cannot restrain us from not sinning. We will see that God intends through His grace of empowerment to lead us along to that place where we will choose habitually and spontaneously to do His will.

[1154] Above the pillars of the County Court House in Worcester, Massachusetts, are the words, "Obedience to law is liberty." God's law of the Ten Commandments, for example, is a description, not a prescription, of what the good life is. He appeals to humanity: "You want to be like me, don't you? So you don't want to lie, bear false witness, commit adultery but you do want to be honest and trustworthy, don't you?" Reminds me of a huge road-side sign in Arizona with only the following words against a deep black background: "What part of 'Thou Shalt Not...' didn't you understand?" —God.

[1155] In a private letter, Jack Blanco pointed out the result of destroying the ellipse of "unity and diversity": Unity—uniformity—conformity—coercion—destroys diversity; Diversity—individuality—freedom—license—destroys unity.

[1156] Meerloo, M.D., Joost A. M., *The Rape of the Mind* (New York: Grosset & Dunlap, 1956), 301.

FREEDOM AND RESPONSIBILITY

The final thought that the Great Controversy teaches us about freedom is that responsibility is its mirror image. All men and women are endowed with the sense of oughtness (Romans 2:18, 19). We are all responsible to the extent we are aware of what we ought to do. We are not responsible for the truth we are not yet clearly aware of (James 4:17).

Responsibility in response to God's grace is called faith in the New Testament. Not mere hope or a leap into the dark, but men and women choosing to say, "yes," to God and follow Him wherever He may lead. Law is God's promise that in saying, "yes," to Him we will be kept from dire mistakes, like ignoring the law of gravity. Freedom is the word we use in this book to embrace all these concepts so that we live in harmony with the God of truth, beauty and order who wishes the best in behalf of His creation.

Here follows a very relevant article that appeared in a Romanian newspaper, *Evenimentul zilei* (News of the Day), on September 24, 2002, written by Cornel Nisstorescu:

"An Ode to America"

Why are Americans so united? They would not resemble one another even if you painted them all one color! They speak all the languages of the world and form an astonishing mixture of civilizations and religious beliefs.

Still, the American tragedy turned three hundred million people into a hand put on the heart. Nobody rushed to accuse the White House, the army, and the secret services that they are only a bunch of losers. Nobody rushed to empty his or her bank accounts. Nobody rushed out onto the streets nearby to gape about. The Americans volunteered to donate blood and to give a helping hand.

After the first moments of panic, they raised their flag over the smoking ruins, putting on T-shirts, caps and ties in the colors of the national flag. They placed flags on buildings and cars as if in every place and on every car a government official or the president was passing. On every occasion, they started singing their traditional song: 'God Bless America!'

I watched the live broadcast and rerun after rerun for hours listening to the story of the guy who went down one hundred floors with a woman in a wheelchair without knowing who she was, or of the Californian hockey player, who gave his life fighting with the terrorists and prevented the plane from hitting a target that could have killed other hundreds or thousands of people.

How on earth were they able to respond united as one human being? Imperceptibly, with every word and musical note, the memory of some turned into a modern myth of tragic heroes. And with every phone call, millions and millions of dollars were put in a collection aimed at rewarding not a man or a family, but a spirit, which no money can buy.

What on earth can unite the Americans in such a way? Their land? Their galloping history? Their economic Power? Money? I tried for hours to find an answer, humming songs and murmuring phrases with the risk of sounding commonplace. I thought things over, but I reached only one conclusion;

Only freedom can work such miracles.

APPENDIX B:
WHO WAS LUCIFER, NOW KNOWN AS SATAN?

I saiah 14 begins with a prophecy against the king of Babylon (probably Sennacharib, king of Assyria who subjugated Babylon—2 Kings 18, 19; Isaiah 37) who though powerful when he assailed Israel would eventually become humiliated before his contemporaries (verse 10). Beginning with verse 12, we have a description of a potent individual that the Christian church has generally applied to Satan, rather than to a specific earthly monarch.[1157]

Lucifer, son of the morning, is described as one who has "fallen from heaven" (verse 12); who said in his heart, "I will exalt my throne above the stars of God" and will "sit on the mount of the congregation on the farthest sides of the north" (verse 13). Further, "I will be like the Most High" (verse 14) yet his end shall be in "Sheol, to the lowest depths of the Pit" (verse 15).

The name *Lucifer* comes from the Latin Vulgate translation ("light bearer") of the Hebrew *helel,* meaning "shining one." "The name *helel,* and its equivalent in related languages, was commonly applied to the planet Venus as a morning star because of its unrivaled brilliance. Venus is the brightest of all the planets, and at maximum brilliance shines more than seven times brighter than Sirius, brightest of all the fixed stars. ... The LXX renders *helel* as *heōsphoros,* 'morning star,' literally. 'bringer of the dawn' ... Compare the Hebrew, *helel ben-shachar,* 'Lucifer, son of the morning,' literally, 'shining one, son of dawn.'" —*SDABC,* vol. 4, 170.

CHRIST'S RIVAL

It is more than interesting that Peter (2 Peter 1:19) refers to Christ as the *phōsphoros,* "light bearer," or "day star." And the Revelator (22:16) calls Jesus "the bright and morning star [literally, "dawn star"]. What seems to be going on here? Apparently, we are getting a sense of Satan's "high position he once held in heaven, next to Christ, and to imply that he is, even now, a rival of Christ." —*Ibid.*

In Ezekiel 28, the King of Tyre is extolled for his pride and arrogance (verse 1–10) but then Ezekiel does what Isaiah did in reference to the King of Babylon—he uses the king as an earthly foil, a reflection of Satan. In other words, God says, "Do you want to know what Satan is like? Look at the King of Tyre."

Ezekiel describes Satan as "the seal of perfection, full of wisdom and perfect in beauty. You were in Eden, the garden of God. ... The workmanship of your timbrels and pipes was prepared for you on the day you were created. You were the anointed cherub who covers; I established you; you were on the holy mountain of God; you walked back and forth in the midst of fiery stones, you were perfect in your ways from the day you were created till iniquity was found in you . ... Your heart was lifted up because of your beauty; you corrupted your wisdom for the sake of your splendor; ... You have become a horror, and there shall be no more forever" (28:12–19).

[1157] See Alden Thompson's excellent analysis of Isaiah 14 and Ezekiel 28 in *Who's Afraid of the Old Testament God?* (Grand Rapids, MI: Zondervan, 1989), 56–59.

Locating Satan in "Eden, the garden of God" points in a larger sense to heavenly dwellings before this world was even created (See *Patriarchs and Prophets*, 35). He was created perfect in wisdom and beauty but Lucifer, not God, created a devil, whom we know as Satan. His astonishing role as the "covering cherub" illustrated by the "cherubim overshadowing the mercy seat in the Jewish Temple" (*SDABC, op. cit.*, 676) highlights how far Satan has fallen.

THE MYSTERY OF INIQUITY

"Till iniquity was found in you" may be the saddest words every penned. What was that "iniquity"? Part of that iniquity was pride "lifted up because of … beauty" and perverted "wisdom." Isaiah noted that Lucifer wanted to be "like the Most High," a created being, so arrogant, so proud, that he would convince himself that he deserved the prerogatives of his Creator! Of course it is a mystery! That is what the Bible means by the "mystery of inequity"! Sin cannot be explained, it can only be observed and resisted. "It was a new element, strange, mysterious, unaccountable" (*Patriarchs and Prophets*, 39).

When one understands Ezekiel 28 and Isaiah 14 as background for the origin of sin and the downfall of Lucifer, the first among angels and created beings, we have a believable picture of the rise of evil in a perfect universe. Later references to Satan provide insights (Luke 4:5,6; 10:18; John 8:44; 1 John 3:8; 2 Peter 2:4; Jude 6; Revelation 12:7–9, etc.) into his character and devices but do not add to the essential facts of his origin and fall.

APPENDIX C:
"THE HEART OF POWER"

I read some years ago that power is the "modern idolatry," that it is a "god, and a heady intoxicating one; success is its creed." Further, "the promises of power are hard to resist, and few of us do."[1158]

My mind drifted immediately to Lucifer, prototype of the power machine that drives men and women to be Number One at all costs: "I will ascend … I will exalt … I will be like the Most High" (Isaiah 14:13, 14). The lust for power, to be recognized, to be in charge, became the original sin.[1159] And, fueling this lust, the mysterious feelings of jealousy, then envy, then hatred, imperceptibly entered his heart and the universe.[1160]

[1158] Cheryl Forbes, *The Religion of Power* (Grand Rapids, MI: Zondervan Publishing House, 1983), 73. I am indebted to Forbes for prompting some of the following insights.

[1159] *Patriarchs and Prophets*, 35. "Little by little Satan came to indulge the desire for self-exaltation. … Not content with his position, though honored above the heavenly host, he ventured to covet homage due alone to the Creator. … And coveting the glory with which the infinite Father has invested His Son, this prince of angels aspired to power that was the prerogative of Christ alone." —*Sermon and Talks*, vol. 1, 387, 388.

[1160] *Early Writings*, 145.

COMPULSION TO BE NUMBER ONE

What is this alien force that started the "war ... in heaven" (Revelation 12:7)? Is it possible that this same compulsion to be Number One, to be recognized as someone "important," that seems to drive the secular world, may also be the Christian's Number One temptation? Or should Christians look at "power" differently than a non-Christian, crave it differently, and use it differently?[1161]

Let us first look at secular power.

In 1975, Michael Korda, editor-in-chief at Simon & Schuster for many years, authored a book that became overnight a blockbuster—*Power! How to Get It, How to Use It.*[1162] It fit the times! Riding those coattails in 1977, Korda authored another best seller, *Success!*[1163] Two "powerful" books that are quoted often. Korda seemed to harness the roaring '70s and anticipated the momentum of the '80s and beyond.

Note some of the credo that millions bought into: "To succeed, you have to learn to follow our natural instincts and appetites ... that what you want is O.K. You should start out by not feeling guilty about what is a perfectly natural and healthy ambition. ... Before you read any further, stop and tell yourself:

"It's OK to be greedy.
It's OK to be ambitious.
It's OK to look out for Number One.
It's OK to have a good time.
It's OK to be Machiavellian
     (if you can get away with it).
It's OK to recognize that honesty is not always the best policy
     (provided you don't go around saying so).
It's OK to be a winner.
And it's *always* OK to be rich."[1164]

Further, "*how* you become a success is, of course, your business. Morality has very little to do with success. ... This is a book about success, after all, not morality."[1165]

NEVER ENOUGH

A key principle is to recognize that "the fastest way to succeed is to look as if you're playing by other people's rules, while quietly playing by your own. ...

[1161] Dave Hunt & T. A. McMahon, *The Seduction of Christianity* (Eugene, OR: Harvest House Publishers, 1985) in chapter entitled, "The Temptation of Power," highlights the deceptiveness of power that has misled and will continue to mislead modern Christians: "Unfortunately, Christians who have tasted genuine miracles often succumb to the temptation to be able to control the occurrence and increase of God's power through methods, principles, and laws ... The fact that they may have stepped over the line into the occult without realizing it doesn't help either them or their followers to escape the consequences." 105.

[1162] New York: Ballantine Book/Random House, 1975.

[1163] New York: Random House, 1977.

[1164] *Success!*, 4.

[1165] *Ibid.*, 5.

Nobody minds ruthless, egocentric careerism and self-interest, provided they are suitably screened."[1166] Another, "too much is not enough."[1167]

The rest of this fascinating book is a manual on how to be "successful" by playing with Korda's rules. It became a handbook of how to be noticed as a successful person—your clothing, your car, your office, or where you sit at the conference table.

How does this play out? For instance, a bank president does not dress or talk like a college professor (they each have their own dress code and manner of speech). A deputy vice-president's office is not the same size or in the corner office as the vice-president's. The examples of symbols that signal power are endless, even to the kind of cufflinks or jewelry worn; the color, size, and quality of a briefcase; tie styles or a person's height and slimness.

These symbols "name" a person. They are power signals. Besides, they become self-intoxicating and eventually self-destructive![1168]

Authority and power are not the same. We sense in most every relationship that someone must "rule." Or at least have the "last word." But authority is never a personal attribute; it is, or should be, conferred on a person who has certain responsibilities. Even Jesus, while on earth, had "conferred authority": "I can of Myself do nothing" (John 5:30); "I have come down from heaven, not to do My own will, but the will of Him who sent Me" (6:38). He did not use unilateral power. Authority and its use depend on the person or group conferring the authority.

However, the misuse of authority blurs into power and power (in the secular sense) always ends up controlling, coercing, or destroying someone else. The underlying force of the U. S. Constitution is that it recognizes this lust for power. Its struggle to get the three branches of government in place took years. Its separation of these three powers was a first in the history of government. James Madison and others saw the problem historically and experientially—"If men were angels, no government would be necessary."[1169]

In Christian circles, is it possible to slip from "responsible authority" into forcing a person to "do it my way" by threats, bribes, manipulation and perhaps sheer violence. How easy it is for "the boss" to marginalize an employee until he or she feels worthless, or just fire the employee for no other reason than he or she may be a threat to his own survival. Whistleblowers, for example!

How does secular power infect Christians so that they reach for the same symbols of "success" that permeate the secular world? Not many will admit that deep

---

[1166] *Ibid.*, 13.

[1167] *Ibid.*, 47.

[1168] "The main thing that traps people into spiritual emptiness is some sort of berserk ego. Says Psychologist Shirley Sugerman, in *Sin and Madness: Studies in Narcissism*: "The ancient wisdom of both East and West [tells] repeatedly of man's tendency to self-idolatry, self-encapsulation, and its result: self-destruction." —Frank Trippett, *Time*, June 8, 1981.

[1169] *The Federalist*, No. 51. "The conception of human nature stated ... in *The Federalist* is pessimistic or, ... realistic. Men are not to be trusted with power, because they are selfish, passionate, full of whims, caprices, and prejudices. Men are not fully rational, calm, or dispassionate. Moreover, the nature of man is a constant; it has had these characteristics throughout recorded history. To assume that it will alter for the better would be a betrayal of generations unborn." —Benjamin Fletcher Wright, "Introduction" to *The Federalist*, 1, 27 (John Harvard Library Edition, 1961).

within, almost unconsciously, are germs of greed, pride, and selfishness.[1170] And these germs are only ways that the lust for power expresses itself. It is the area that Jesus was aiming at when He included in "the Lord's prayer" the phrase, "deliver us from evil."[1171] And what John heard the angel say, "Because you say, 'I am rich, have become wealthy, and have need of nothing'—and do not know that you are wretched, miserable, poor, blind, and naked."[1172]

THE "INNER RING"

In other words, unless we catch ourselves, we mask these deep-seated germs with the visible signs and symbols of Christian service. In the sanctuary of power, we all recognize those who are "in the inner ring," as C. S. Lewis described it.[1173] And we all know the temptation to "belong" in that "ring." We have observed, perhaps even experienced, those who are "left out." What do I mean? Think of the committees not appointed to or the president's secret "kitchen cabinet," or not making the nominating committee's "small list." What about last week's party you just heard about? To be "left out" can be crushing to anyone who does not see the difference between secular power and Christian power.

Lewis does not mince words: "My main purpose in this address is simply to convince you that this desire is not of the great permanent mainsprings of human action. It is one of the factors which go to make up the world as we know it—this whole pell-mell of struggle, competition, confusion, graft, disappointment, and advertisement, and if it is one of the permanent mainsprings then you may be quite sure of this: unless you take measures to prevent it, this desire is going to be one of the chief motives of your life, from the first day on which you enter your profession until the day when you are too old to care. ... But whether by pining and moping outside Rings that you can never enter, or by passing triumphantly further and further in—one way of the other—you will be that kind of man. I have already made it fairly clear that I think it better for you not to be that kind of man. ...

"Of all the passions the passion for the Inner Ring is most skilful in making a man who is not yet a very bad man do very bad things. ... As long as you are governed by that desire you will never get what you want. You are trying to peel an onion: if you succeed there will be nothing left. Until you conquer the fear of being an outsider, an outsider you will remain. ...

"You yourself once you are in, want to make it hard for the next entrant, just as those who are already in made it hard for you. ... Your genuine Inner Ring exists for exclusion. There'd be no fun if there were no outsiders."[1174]

The lure of the Inner Ring is antithetical to Christianity. Yet it is probably the most "respected" temptation within Christian circles. To be worthy, we think, we must make ourselves visible with the tokens of "success" (translation: "power").

[1170] McCullough, *John Adams*, quoting John Adams: "Ambition is one of the more ungovernable passions of the human heart. The love of power is insatiable and uncontrollable." 70.

[1171] Matthew 6:13 KJV.

[1172] Revelation 3:17.

[1173] "The Inner Ring" was the Memorial Lecture at King's College, University of London, 1944. It eventually was included in *The Weight of Glory* (Grand Rapids, MI, William B. Eerdmans Publishing Company, 1979).

[1174] *Ibid.*

Titles, assistants, secretarial help, size of office, perks, access to those who "really know what's going on,"—these all add up. The more one has, the more power others sense you have, right or wrong.

The subtlest part of the corridors of power[1175] that Christians slip into almost unconsciously, almost like breathing, is that it is most often assumed that "power" is necessary to promote Christianity around the world. Right and wrong! We will discuss later the kind of "power" with which the Christian church as been endowed. But for now, we can observe that most Christians believe that they are justified in using power "to get the work done."

USING THE GOD CARD

How do we do this? Beyond the typical displays of "success" already mentioned, the Christian often uses the God card: "I thank the Lord for His guidance in this matter," "If I know my heart, I believe that … ," or "I have been impressed that. …"

Further, we use the call to prayer to avoid confrontations, or use guilt to get others to do the Lord's work free or at a greatly reduced stipend—while we hold hefty salaries and perks. We tell the world (and ourselves) that this "call" is from the Lord, after we have made judicious phone calls to those who could "work something out." We look carefully for those on the "winning side." The "winning side," of course, must be the most "spiritual." How often then do we add to our saviors! Jesus isn't enough, so we add to our pantheon persons here and there with whom we confide as we seek closer relationships with those who are visibly pious, knowing that in some way this gets closer to the "inner ring."

All this is perfectly understandable, but questions must be asked: What difference is there between the "visibly pious" and the Pharisees Jesus called "hypocrites" who were known for their scrupulous tithing, but not for their sense of "justice and the love of God"? They "love the best seats in the synagogues and greetings in the marketplaces" (Luke 11:42, 43; 20: 46, 47).

In many of Christ's teachings, He seems to advise anonymity and quiet caring for others. Righteousness and power don't march to the same drummer, if I read James correctly: "The wisdom from above is first pure, then peaceable, gentle, willing to yield, full of mercy and good fruits, without partiality and without hypocrisy. Now the fruit of righteousness is sown in peace by those who make peace" (3:17).

Perhaps, in all this emphasis on power, we too often confuse authority with power and surround ourselves with others who are beholden to our "appreciation"—that is, the tokens of power we can deal out. And the rest in the organization learn quickly when to speak, when to be silent, or when and how to vote. Is there anyone who has not felt the breath of power when one in authority, sensing that others are not quickly "recognizing" his or her authority, soon resorts to manipulating, threats, or coercion in what we may call "spiritual violence?"[1176] The self-destruct virus is already working.

[1175] C. P. Snow, *Corridors of Power* (London: Macmillan, 1964).
[1176] Forbes, 89.

SUCCESS?

Another way we mask our lust for power is to rename it—call it "success." Or, perhaps, "achievement." Think of the many books on the market with "success" in their titles! But what is most astounding: think of the many religious programs on radio and television that promise "success" in your business, health, or marriage. Blatantly, they promise "health and wealth" by putting your hand on the television set, by sending for some gift—and the list goes on. In other words, God is always in the success business, never into failures. Makes me wonder about John the Baptist and Jesus Himself. Or James, His brother, the first to be martyred.

Think of Norman Vincent Peale's long career in publishing and as a radio preacher, emphasizing "the power of positive thinking." With a slight twist but with the same wand, Robert Schuller emphasizes "the power of possibility thinking." But then we use words such as "the power of the blood" and the "power of the Holy Spirit." Are we talking about two different worlds here? More about that later.

I like Cheryl Forbes' questions: "Where did we ever get the idea that the Bible holds the key to success? How did we decide that Christianity 'does' something for us? By our words and deeds, we proclaim that the only reason Christ came was to 'give' us things—and we don't really mean eternal life but the life that is eternally pleasurable here and now. Somehow, we have forgotten that Christ said His peace is not like the world's. However, if it's not like the world's, we don't really want it."[1177]

Is it possible that we somehow have turned everything upside down when we tell the world that the evidence of God's leading is reflected in our magnificent churches and imposing schools and hospitals, our three-car garages, and in our remarkable record for supporting humanitarian causes?

Is it possible that we identify with the most handsome, the most famous, the most prosperous when we seek leadership or look for the most photogenic for our PR media? Would Jesus have approved our categories for the "successful" person? Did Jesus package Christianity so that the world would recognize the symbols of success?

PACKAGING CHRISTIANITY

Is it a fair and honest "piece of goods" to use the "good life, and gracious living" as Christian witnessing? In other words, "if you want the good life, join up with us!" In our appeals for donations, do we use the guilt principle as well as highly effective direct-mail techniques (excellent power tools)? But where is the power of the Holy Spirit involved?

Do we ever stand before a terrific offer, a once-in-a-life time opportunity, and have a sense of rightness tug at us so that we turn away, knowing that the price of success would be too high, too costly?

Look over the book market for books on "what to do when you fail!" Of course, there are none! One fails because he or she has not learned the rules of success, that is, they need to learn how to develop power! We want success because it gives us power. And then we pause and look over the landscape at the hundreds of thousands of "powerful" people who seem to have it all—wealth, fame, reputation,

---

[1177] Forbes, 63.

or trophy wives. And the closer we look, too often we see suicides, divorces, the addicts, the lonely—all smothered in their symbols of success!

Is the price of "reaching the top" too costly for so many? What happens to many the day after they retire, or the day after someone younger has replaced them? What is left in the center of their lives after "power" vanishes?[1178]

But it is not only the powerful who exhibit the symbols of power. What about the powerless, those who find their moment of importance with graffiti, with their super-loud radios as they drive slowly through city streets, with their own clothes styles (zoot-suiters of the '50s) that often become the next fad of the powerful, those who find acceptance in their neighborhood gangs with their symbols of success—such as jackets or tattoos. All momentary power! The urge to be "somebody" may take many different tracks. Is there a better way to be "somebody"?

WHAT CAN JESUS TEACH US ABOUT POWER?

Think of it: What were the disciples thinking about most during the last week they had with Jesus before Calvary? Listen to James and John, on the side, *telling* Jesus how they wanted to help Him in His kingdom (on earth): "Grant us that we may sit, one on Your right hand and the other on Your left, in Your glory" (Mark 10:37).[1179] They wanted to be CEO and CFO! Three years with Jesus and His disciples can only think of "power"! Even during the Last Supper, "There was also rivalry among them, as to which of them should considered the greatest" (Luke 22:24)!

Note that Judas understood the corridor of power—he sat on the Lord's left, the usual place of honor, and John was on His right.[1180]

Ted Engstrom, President Emeritus of World Vision (with that organization for 50 years) and currently vice chairman of Focus on the Family, and author of more than 40 best-selling books on Christian leadership and management, believes that power ought to have a *negative* connotation for Christians. Engstrom is a voice crying in the wilderness. He goes on to say that we too often "equate power with influence money and position."

Further, Engstrom says that "organizations as well as individuals must evaluate whether it will play a servant role, which is a very difficult thing to do, or whether it will continue down the power path." He urges Christians to seek their role models in the Scriptures rather than elsewhere.[1181]

LEARNING FROM BIBLICAL LEADERS

So how do we do that? We find spiritual leaders in the Old Testament who left a record of learning the difference between using 1) power to "get ahead" and 2) power of trusting God and His promises. Think of Abraham before He learned the habit of trusting God implicitly for His inner power. He used his wife's beauty to

---

[1178] Bernard Loiseau, one of France's most celebrated chefs committed suicide after his flagship restaurant (Cote d'Or in Burgundy) was downgraded by Gault-Millau, a restaurant guide. He had said to another three-star chef, "If I lose a star, I'll kill myself." The power of "success" is full of delusions. —BBC News, February 25, 2003.

[1179] Matthew said that "the mother" of James and John made this request and that when the other disciples heard of it, "they were moved with indignation against the two brothers" (20:20–24).

[1180] *The Desire of Ages,* 644.

[1181] Forbes, 100–102.

protect himself against Egypt's Pharaoh (Genesis 12:11–20). It worked once, so he tried it again with Abimelech (Genesis 20:2–18).

Think of Jacob and Esau, both struggling for power and note the aftermath of it all (Genesis 29–33). Ah, but consider Joseph and how he was a servant-leader, not only for the land of Egypt, but for his brothers who wanted to destroy him for "his dreams" (Genesis 37:5). He really understood the power that serves, not the power that enjoys the pride of office.

Think of Moses and his journey from the power of doing God's work his own way (Exodus 2:14) to the power of a servant-leader where he was willing to sacrifice his own life if it meant the saving of his ungrateful church members (Exodus 32:11–14; 32:32). God exchanged Moses' shepherd's rod for "a rod of power which he could not lay down until God should release him."[1182] This kind of power the world knows nothing of!

When we think of Saul and David, we watch the mingling of secular power and God-given power—but David often showed his ambivalence concerning power. Observe his flagrant abuse of power in taking Bathsheba for his wife and causing her husband to be killed! The lust of power takes many forms!

Think of those cameo-like temptations that Jesus faced in the wilderness after His baptism—they were all about power, especially the second. Satan used the God card by implying that Jesus could do far more good with power than without it. His forever answer is unfolded in His Beatitudes (Matthew 5:3–12).

If we make Jesus our Lord, we should listen to Him talk about power. He didn't hold up material possessions as a sign of their loyalty or His favor (Matthew 6:25–34; Luke 10:3–8). In fact, He offered them a life of self-denial, a life of turning the other cheek (Matthew 5:38–44; 10:38, 39; 16:24).

Remember when Christ's brothers tried to reason with Him regarding how best to make His way in the world, doing good in wider circles, so that they could really be proud of Him (and ride His coattails to fame). But Jesus had retired to Galilee because He saw the thunderclouds developing in Judea—the storm of a gigantic power struggle.

His brothers urged Jesus: "Depart from here and go into Judea, that Your disciples also may see the works that You are doing. For no one does anything in secret while he himself seeks to be known openly. If You do these things, show Yourself to the world" (John 7:3, 4). How did Jesus answer? "My time has not yet come, but your time is always ready" (verse 6). Is there anywhere a better distinction between how God measures success and the world's view?

SOUND PRINCIPLES

At the same time Jesus gave us sound principles regarding how to be good managers; that is, stewards of the responsibility entrusted to us. For example, think through the implications of His parable of the Businessman who entrusted his assets to his employees (Matthew 25:14–30). His main point was that the amount of "money" entrusted to each employee was commensurate with the natural and cultivated capabilities that each had. And that the responsibilities given to all of us depend on our ability to handle each level of increasing responsibility—increasing power.

[1182] *Patriarchs and Prophets*, 396.

In other words, "The development of all our powers is the first duty we owe to God and to our fellowmen." For what purpose? "No one who is not growing daily in capability and usefulness is fulfilling the purpose of life."[1183] That sounds like a recipe for "success" as God would define it.

Before we leave Jesus, think of His face-to-face with Pilate. Pilate had power! "Are You not speaking to me? Do You not know that I have power to crucify You, and power to release You?"

Jesus answered, "You could have no power at all against me unless it had been given you from above" (John 19:10, 11). Jesus had power but all those who measured power and success with self-centered goals (the original sin) misunderstood it. Jesus gave His followers power by which they could overcome power—and show Satan wrong again.

That one man who seemed to embrace and spread Christ's message of genuine power was once a "company man," a paradigm of what the world generally means by success and power. Paul really had the credentials and all the trappings of a highly "successful" man (Philippians 3:4–7). But after the Light and Voice along the Damascus Road (Acts 9:3–8), Paul turned the game of power upside down. He became a servant-leader—the power of a Spirit-filled life.

But his fellow workers had not learned as fast as Paul had. Think of Peter (Galatians 2); the Jerusalem council (Acts 15); old-covenant troublemakers (Galatians 4:16–19); the confused Corinthians (1 Corinthians 1:10–17).

In his second letter to the Corinthians, Paul highlighted the difference between secular power and spiritual power: "If the Lord is willing, however, I will come to you soon, and then I will find out for myself the power which these proud people have, and not just what they say. For the Kingdom of God is not a matter of words but of power. Which do you prefer? Shall I come to you with a whip, or in a spirit of love and gentleness?" (4:19–20, GNB) In other words, are my opponents all talk or do they really have the power they only talk about?

The unconverted Paul would have come with all the force and symbolism of miffed authority; after conversion, Paul lived under the power of Love and Gentleness.

HOW DOES GOD MEASURE SUCCESS?

I am reminded of an unexpected paragraph in a recent *Newsweek* article (May 6, 2002, 32): "Christianity was never supposed to be easy. The contradictions in Jesus' legacy are thick and epic. In defeat there is victory; in humility, strength; in surrender, gain; in darkness, light. All counterintuitive ideas, and all promise reward later, not now—beyond time and space. It is not a creed of comfort. ... But the price of the journey, however steep, is worth paying, for in the Christian imagination the ultimate sacrifice has already been made. 'Be of good cheer,' Jesus says, 'for I have overcome the world.' Amid the storm we may at least take comfort in that."

It may be that Jesus summed up the power/success problem with these "counterintuitive" words: "If anyone desire to come after Me, let him deny himself, and take up his cross, and follow Me. For whoever desires to save his life will lose it, and

---

[1183] *Christ's Object Lessons*, 329, 330.

whoever loses his life for My sake will find it. For what is a man profited, if he gains the whole world, and loses his own soul" (Matthew 16:24–26)?

Losing one's life for Jesus does not mean that we should seek martyrdom or become the doormat for everyone else. Losing one's life means that we no longer thirst for recognition or lust for power. In order to save one's life, we must reject any temptation that promises power at the expense of compromised integrity, which is another way of saying, losing one's soul.

HOW DO ENDTIME CHRISTIANS MEASURE POWER?

We measure power by the evidences of the Spirit of Power. The Spirit's power makes a huge difference in any life, similar to the change that Paul experienced after conversion.

Paul talked about this power throughout His letters to various churches. Note the plain-spoken difference between the Spirit-led life and the natural man or woman (Galatians 5:16–25).

To the Ephesians, Paul wrote: "Now to Him who is able to do exceedingly abundantly above all that we ask or think, according to the power that works in us ..." (3:20). What a legacy, what a promise!

Peter, out of his own experience, could write: "His divine power has given to us all things that pertain to life and godliness, through the knowledge of Him who called us by glory and virtue" (2 Peter 1:3).

Ellen White has nailed down how the power of the Spirit gives us "all things that pertain to life and godliness. The impartation of the Spirit is the impartation of the life of Christ. It imbues the receiver with the attributes of Christ." Further, "Christ has given His Spirit as a divine power to overcome all hereditary and cultivated tendencies to evil, and to impress His own character upon His church."[1184]

It is interesting to note that the promise of the gifts of the Holy Spirit for which Jesus told His disciples to wait after His ascension came in that Jerusalem upper room when the disciples "were no longer striving for the highest place."[1185] And the latter rain, which will surpass the events of the first-century church, will not fall "when the work of others is discounted, that the workers may show their own superiority."[1186] Further, no one will receive the latter rain "unless they obtain the victory over every besetment, over pride, selfishness, love of the world, and over every wrong word and action."[1187]

Let us be completely clear: Genuine Christians will *possess* power, on one hand, and be *used* by Power, on the other. Christians are not meant to be wimps.

Their power is summarized in one word—"character."[1188] They have placed a check on "the inordinate love of property and power,"[1189] resisted the "danger of trying to exercise a controlling power upon others" and "the power of an unsanctified will."[1190]

[1184] *The Desire of Ages*, 805, 671.
[1185] *Testimonies*, vol. 8, 20.
[1186] *Selected Messages*, vol. 1, 175.
[1187] *Early Writings*, 71.
[1188] *Christ's Object Lessons*, 340.
[1189] *Patriarchs and Prophets*, 534.
[1190] *Testimonies*, vol. 6, 397.

They have been educated to "value power" but "above power, goodness, above intellectual acquirements, character." They have learned to make "the best use not only of one but of all our powers and acquirements; ... [that] in true education the selfish ambition, the greed for power, the disregard for the rights and needs of humanity, that are the curse of our world, find a counter-influence. ... In God's plan there is no place for selfish rivalry."[1191]

Ellen White puts the right touch on genuine power when she notes that "the lust of the flesh, the pride of the eye, the display of selfishness, the misuse of power, the cruelty, and the force used to cause men to unite with confederacies and unions ... all these are the working of Satanic agencies."[1192]

So we end up where we started—the Power of our Creator was shared with His created intelligences. No limit was put on creativity and service. But power was "misused" when Satan used his great mind to exalt himself, when he lusted for prerogatives that never could have been his.

In the grand work of the gospel, when the image of God is restored in those who are safe to save, all the seeds of misused power will be worked out of the human mind. They have seen the horrific consequence of misused power. For them, rebellion will never arise again.

APPENDIX D:
THE DEVOLUTION OF ENVY

We say it so casually, "I sure do wish I had your luck (talent, good looks, or whatever). I envy you." It's a compliment, not an insult. Something more like flattery, not even jealousy.

We normally think of envy as jealousy. But jealousy is more like covetousness. Someone looks at what you own and says: "I wish I had that. Maybe I can save some money to buy it." This we all understand, but jealousy is not nearly as devilish as envy.

Envy is different. It runs along these lines: "He's got it. I don't have it. I'd like it, but I know I can never get it. Maybe I'll steal it. Nobody ought to be allowed to have it if everyone can't have one just like it. I'll destroy it. I'll have the government make it illegal to own one."[1193]

Girls often have a problem in that few girls feel that they are pretty! So they resent what they think are better-looking girls. But no matter what they do, they will never get those good looks transferred! Jealousy is not applicable here. Envy is the problem. How does the ugly girl, in her opinion of course, vent her wrath? By throwing acid in the face of the better looking girl. Or by using a razor blade. Or something less obvious like lies about her character. A book has been written about this sort of envy: *Facial Justice*, 1960, a 1984-type book about a future society in which beauty is made illegal, and good-looking people are required by law to get face lifts to make all women look average.

[1191] *Education*, 225, 226.
[1192] *Evangelism*, 26.
[1193] Gary North, *Successful Investing in an Age of Envy* (Sheridan, IN: Steadman Press, 1982), 4.

Let's look at arson. Most arsonists resent the property of others. They may get joy out of the fire itself, but we must ask why? Most arsonists get joy seeing other people's property, hopes, and visible signs of success being consumed.

Terrorism is another envy-created phenomenon. Terrorists do not think they are bringing in peace on earth with their destruction. The terrorist uses terror because he hates the existing order. Destruction becomes a blessing because envy is driving the terrorist to destroy what he does not have.

Governments always move from freedom to chaos because of the permeating system of envy. Especially when we realize that there are only two kinds of voters: those who vote, and those who live to vote. Those who produce and those who consume. And those who consume always increase to the point that there are fewer and fewer producers to support all the consumers. We call it the redistribution of wealth.

But envy is not driven by hoping to have as much money as everyone else. His basic motivation is that nobody should have what he doesn't have, that it is unfair and somehow, arbitrary. Envy doesn't want to "get his" at your expense. Envy tries to "smash yours" at your expense. His motivation is perverse: It's the act of taking away yours, destroying yours, which gives him his kicks.

In August 1959, Stephen Nash was executed (after murdering 11 people). His defense: "I never got more than the leavings of life, and when I couldn't even get those any more, I started taking something out of other people's lives."[1194]

Envy is rampant in the land. Politics of envy is running loose in government. In the coming economic disruptions and final crises, no restraints on envy.

The awful truth about envy is that it can never be satisfied or placated. Every time someone tries to buy off envy, the envious are repulsed. And every sign of success makes you a potential target of someone's envy. On so many levels, envy wants what another has and resents him for having it![1195]

A familiar quote (La Rochefaucald): "Few are able to suppress in themselves a secret satisfaction at the misfortune of their friends."[1196] Everyone on earth knows or has known the truth of that observation.

Aristotle said that envy grows most naturally in relationships between equals. But that is not generally so. We live in a world, a universe, of unequals against unequals. And we pretend that everyone should be equal, or is equal. This is the breeding ground for envy. The idea that we are all equal has been perverted into the idea that we are identical—that we all have the same capabilities and like to do and experience the same things. Those who look around and see those enjoying experiences they aren't or can't achieve, they tend to be envious. What requires hard work and natural talent is not something to respect, but to destroy.[1197]

Gossip is a form of envy, perhaps the most common. Another is any appeal to socialism. It isn't the hope of raising the income of everybody to make everyone even or equal that motivates; it's really the inner envious drive to wipe out the signs of success in others.

[1194] Ibid., 5.

[1195] Alfie Kohn, No Contest (Boston: Houghton Mifflin Company, 1986), 141.

[1196] Ibid., 6.

[1197] Henry Fairlie, The New Republic (September 17, 1977), cited in Ibid., 6.

Envy is great on blaming others. As we saw earlier in chapters 33 to 35, envy will be a driving passion in the endtime. Envy resents anyone who seems to have more peace or more solid reasons for what one does. Resentment leads to seeing the envied one as a threat. Envy leads to ways of getting even! And when real trouble happens, those envied will be blamed.

In the endtime, those who understand these unparalleled times, those who have peace in the midst of great distress, will be a special target. Why? Because your peace in the face of disaster will further enrage the envious, especially when they note that you were the ones who had been warning them of these troubles—that you are prepared and they are not! Such is Satan's final strategy as he orchestrates a perfect setup for the envious to destroy, in some way, the troublers of their conscience.

APPENDIX E:
THE COSMIC CONFLICT IMBEDDED IN EXTRA-BIBLICAL MATERIALS

I continue to be amazed, the longer I live, to keep learning about the widespread "awareness" of extraterrestrial forces battling on a cosmic level for control (or demise) of this planet or even of the entire universe. You will find this awareness in ancient civilizations as well as among modern primordial tribes in Africa, South America, and India.

For example, the older the inscriptions found in Sumerian digs, the more monotheistic they tend to be.[1198] This rather significant prevailing belief in a "high God," however, does not rule out lesser gods, even as we see often in the Old Testament. As time went on, the troubles that beset men and women everywhere were attached to these lesser gods—the "high God" generally is no longer involved in human affairs. This we see in all kinds of literature, including the Old Testament, men and women praying to the gods of rain, various animals, the sun, and the seasons for relief. But these lesser gods are "never portrayed as mere puppets of Yahweh."[1199]

In fact, the appeal throughout the Old Testament is for the Israelites to recognize the superiority of Yahweh above all lesser gods that permeated the thinking of their contemporaries.[1200] They were instructed that no other god could threaten the well-being of Yahweh, even though it might appear at times that the lesser god

---

[1198] Argued by Assyriologist and Sumerologist, Stephen Langdon in "Monotheism as the Predecessor of Polytheism in Sumerian Religion," *Evangelical Quarterly*, (April 1937), 136–146, cited by Gregory A. Boyd, *God at War* (Downers Grove, IL: InterVarsity Press, 1997), 124. Boyd has provided an overview of ancient and modern examples of spiritual warfare as reflected in various primordial peoples. He catalogs the Halakwulups of Tierra del Fuego, the aborigines of southeast Australia, the Bambuti pygmies of Central Africa and Andaman Island in the Gulf of Bengal, virtually thousands of African tribes, and many more. His references and bibliography are exemplary.

[1199] Boyd., *op. cit.,* 129.

[1200] Exodus 12:12; 2 Samuel 7:23.

was winning the war.[1201] At the headwater of those Ten Commandments that God wrote with His own finger (Exodus 31:18), God (Yahweh) put everything in perspective: "I am the Lord your God, who brought you out of the land of Egypt . ... You shall have no other gods before Me" (Exodus 20:2, 3).

THE WORLD IN BETWEEN

In other words, from the earliest of times, whether biblical or extrabiblical, that "world in between," the realm of spiritual forces between God and humanity, was generally assumed. Those forces were either good or evil. Moses, in his valedictory, sharpened this picture of spiritual forces that had enormous influence on the Israelites as well as their contemporaries: "You shall not go after other gods, the gods of the peoples who are all around you" (Deuteronomy 6:14). But reflecting after 40 years, he sadly noted: "They [Israelites] went and served other gods and worshiped them, gods that they did not know and that he [Yahweh] had not given to them" (Deuteronomy 20:26). In fact, Moses referred to these "gods" as "demons" (Deuteronomy 32:17).[1202]

One of the endless discussions through the years has been whether these "gods" or "demons," or spiritual agencies in general, were animate or inanimate, free-willed or mindless beings. Were they products of creative imaginations or free-willed, spiritual beings of the "world between?" The Old Testament has no problem identifying these spiritual beings as being either loyal to God or rebellious and part of the Evil Empire.

For example, Psalm 82 refers to the rebel angels: "God stands in the congregations of the mighty; He judges among the gods. How long will you judge unjustly, And show partiality to the wicked? ... I said, You are gods, And all of you are children of the Most High. But you shall die like men, And fall like one of the princes" (verses 1, 2, 6, 7).

Psalm 103, to loyal angels: "Bless the Lord, you His angels, Who excel in strength, who do His word, Heeding the voice of His word" (verse 20, see also Psalm 148:2).

DANIEL 10

One of the classic illustrations of the interaction of spiritual beings, between "good and bad angels" is found in Daniel 10. For three weeks Daniel was in great distress over a message of last-day events that God had given him (10:1, 2, 14). The vision troubled him and he became ill, thinking of its implications that he could understand only slightly. Suddenly, a heavenly being appeared, giving Daniel the assurance that his prayers had been heard and also the remarkable information that

---

[1201] For example, note how the drought in Elijah's time was interpreted by the priests of Baal and probably by most of the Israelites, 1 Kings 18.

[1202] "The evidence from the Old Testament is that the people in general had a difficult time focusing their attention on the one true God. Even when they were right with him, the threat of neighboring deities was a real one. Thus, for practical reasons, God treated Israel very much as a wise father might treat a young son if the two of them were to set out on a jaunt through the woods. To warn a small lad of wildcats, bears, and snakes, could be quite unsettling. So the father simply says: 'Trust me. Whatever happens, I will take care of you.'" —Alden Thompson, *Who's Afraid of the Old Testament God?* (Grand Rapids, MI: Zondervan Publishing House, 1989), 48.

he (the angel) had been detained, prevented from coming to Daniel for the past 21 days, because "the prince of the kingdom of Persia withstood me" (verses. 10–13)!

Further, the angel informed Daniel that he would not have been able to break through this evil angelic cordon except for the arrival of "Michael, one of the chief princes ... for I had been left alone there with the kings of Persia" (verse 13).

What could this possibly mean? We are witnessing a cosmic struggle, a very real battle going on behind the scenes that directly affected events on earth. In fact, the angel goes on to inform Daniel that the "prince" (evil angel) of Persia is defeated in his attempt to thwart God and His plans to use Daniel. However, another evil angel, "the prince of Greece will come" (verse 20) and the only other power (on earth or heaven) that can vanquish these powerful evil agencies is "Michael your prince" (verse 21).[1203]

Conclusion: These demonic angels are free-willed, powerful, and determined to frustrate the will of God and to torment His loyal people.

SATAN IN JOB ONE

Another reference to these spiritual agencies, both good and evil, that roam freely throughout the universe is found in Job 1:6. Although many translations of the Hebrew text say, "the sons of God," the Septuagint reads, "angels of God." In one sense, angels as created beings can be referred to as "sons of God."[1204] However, Satan is not in the same class as the other angels in this divine council (2:1) for he is God's antagonist (1:9–12; 2:4–7). The story of Job dramatically pulls back the curtain on the "real" world. We see how malignant is the power of evil. Further, we see how in this world of free-willed intelligences, both angelic and human (who can choose their own destiny), how those choices directly affect the well being of others. We also see that God is not the instigator or cause of pain, suffering, or death, a concept that has not been given enough thought, even among Christians.

Probably the cameo clarity of the beginning of evil is portrayed by Isaiah (14:12–15) and Ezekiel (28:12–17)[1205] that many feel gave shape to much of the dualisms that appeared in heathen philosophers after their time.[1206] In Appendix B, we examined these two chapters that provide the anatomy of a brilliant mind that

---

[1203] Jude 9 refers to Michael as the archangel who contended with the devil over the body of Moses. Strong evidence suggests that Jesus is Michael, the "archangel," who calls for the righteous dead at His second coming (1 Thessalonians 4:16). Revelation 12:7–9 points to "war ... in heaven" wherein "Michael and his angels fought against the dragon ... and his angels. ... The great dragon was cast out, that serpent of old, called the Devil and Satan, who deceives the whole world."

[1204] "The Scriptures declare that upon one occasion, when the angels of God came to present themselves before the Lord, Satan came also among them, not to bow before the Eternal King, but to further his own malicious designs against the righteous." —Ellen G. White, *The Great Controversy Between Christ and Satan* (Mountain View, CA: PPPA, 1948), 518. (PPPA now in Nampa, ID).

[1205] See "Appendix B: Who Was Lucifer, now Known as Satan?"

[1206] José M. Bertoluci, "The Son of the Morning and the Guardian Cherub in the Context of the Controversy Between Good and Evil," Th.D. Dissertation, 1985, Andrews University. Dr. Bertoluci reviews (1) the various interpretations of Isaiah 14:12–15 and Ezekiel 28:12–17 beginning in the early church fathers to the present (1–54); (2) the parallel materials found in Sumerian, Akkadian, Hittite, Greek, Ugaritic, as well as biblical literature, which show common "terms and expression" in Near East "documents" (although the author finds that these materials "cannot support the view " of Isaiah and Ezekiel "directly borrowing from other ancient myths" (144–145). The

nurtured seeds of rebellion. And we will observe how those seeds sprout up whenever certain misplaced ideas about the character of God are indulged in by other beings beside Lucifer and how these principles of Evil have permeated the social fabric of human history.

APPENDIX F:
WIFE OF BATH PRINCIPLE (ARE THERE THINGS WE SHOULD NOT KNOW ABOUT?)

Chaucer, in his Canterbury Tales, had the Wife of Bath tell her story of why she had so many husbands. Chaucer demonstrated his deep insights into human nature as he analyzed the psychological contours of a shrewd lady who always seemed to get what she wanted. He had one lightning line where the Wife of Bath confessed a deep human mystery: "Forbid a thing, and that thing covet we."[1207]

Wrapped up in these few words is the essence of what happened to Eve in the Garden, to the builders of the Tower of Babel, and to about every person who has ever lived. Is it possible to want to know too much? Is it possible to confuse the "thirst" for knowledge with the pursuit of truth? Is it possible that curiosity for a "new experience" can be the subtlest human weakness? What is there about curiosity that is wonderful and dynamic, on one hand, but the doorway to new problems that we may not have solutions for, on the other? And in many cases, curiosity for too many is the door to hell.

Samuel Johnson said that "curiosity is one of the permanent and certain characteristics of a vigorous mind."[1208] Watch any baby, any bright student, and you see curiosity at work. Review the past century of medical advances, of technological wonders that have made life much more comfortable and interesting—and one senses the enormous power of curiosity.

Others can see that "contrasting threats like overpopulation and AIDS appear to be traceable to the effects of 'progress.' One powerful reading of history points out that the most advanced nations on Earth have produced unthinkable weapons of destruction at the same time as they have developed a media culture that revels in images of destructive violence. Can such a combination fail to propel us toward barbarism and self-annihilation?"[1209]

---

remainder of this laudable contribution examines the two passages in their immediate context and then exegetes them in the light of the whole Bible (146–293). He ends his study of these two passages with these final words: "God, through his prophets, chose the expressions, *King of Babylon* and *King of Tyre* to portray the being who was the originator of evil and the propelling force behind every effort to disturb order in God's universe. These two passages also prophetically give us the certainty that evil is destined to be exterminated, and Satan and his followers will be no more forever" (303).

[1207] "Look out a thing we may not lightly have, And after that we'll cry all day and crave, Forbid a thing, and that thing covet we."

[1208] *The Rambler,* March 12, 1751.

[1209] Roger Shattuck, *Forbidden Knowledge* (New York: St. Martin's Press, 1996), 1.

PROBLEMS OF UNIMPEDED RESEARCH

Mortimer Zuckerman, editor-in-chief, *U.S. News & World Report,* reflected on our marvelous high-tech world that leaves us vulnerable to a wide range of threats. "The tragedy is that the very science and technology that have enriched life have also put more potent tools in the hands of evildoers. In a single strike, terrorists can wreak havoc costing thousands of lives and billions of dollars. ... But what can we do to stop one disaffected loner? More research? ... The questions raise delicate issues: the rights of unimpeded science, the rights of privacy. Against them now we must set the very right to survive. Can we, in this vulnerable new world, where evil runs rampant, live forever relying on the good sense of millions of individual biologists? ... In the 21st century, the risk is the perversion of knowledge."[1210]

Back to Eve for a moment. Ellen White described Eve's slippage when she looked upon the fruit of the forbidden tree with "curiosity and admiration."[1211] But then her fall—the next step in a "spirit of irreverent curiosity."[1212]

Let's examine the "spirit of irreverent curiosity," because here we have the genesis of all sin or iniquity (Ezekiel 28:15) as Bernard of Clairvaux noted many centuries ago.[1213] This mysterious compulsion permeates and motivates much of the literature from the earliest of written history.

Robert Louis Stevenson highlighted "irreverent curiosity" in his story of Dr. Jekyll and the scoundrel, Mr. Hyde. As the last chapter reveals, Jekyll and Hyde are the same person. Hyde is the evil side of Dr. Jekyll but the time comes when the doctor's drugs could not suppress Mr. Hyde, his own creation. Shattuck sees Stevenson unfolding not a "'strange case' but the common temptation to lead two lives"[1214] Further, the emphasis is not primarily on the monstrous Hyde but on Dr. Jekyll, who "discovers evil by succumbing to the allurements of his own genius."

Dr. Jekyll is a modern parable of those who confuse the pursuit of knowledge with the pursuit of truth. Jekyll discovered that his pursuit of what he thought was truth "unstrung his moral character."[1215]

This, of course, could open up the door to the world of academic freedom or to freedom of expression in the arts. But such is not the theme of this appendix. There has always been a tension between "liberalism and limits."[1216] Our concern here is more limited, focusing on how far is too far when we enter the field of unlimited research, into the world of forbidden knowledge.

DANGER IN PRESSING CURIOSITY TOO FAR

From earliest poets and philosophers we can trace this *leit motif*—that there is unanticipated danger in pressing curiosity too far, unanticipated consequences in the world of forbidden knowledge. For example, Hesiod (early 8th-century B.C. Greek poet/philosopher) introduces us to Prometheus, one of the Titans who ruled

---

[1210] September 1, 2003.
[1211] *Ibid.,* 54.
[1212] *Patriarchs and Prophets,* 55.
[1213] Shattuck, 70.
[1214] *Ibid.,* 4.
[1215] *Ibid.,* 4.
[1216] *Ibid.,* 6.

the world. Zeus gave him the task of making a man out of clay mixed with water and shaped like an image of the gods.

Then Prometheus thought, "What gift shall I give this man so that he can be superior to the animals?" And with lightning speed, he thought of fire. With fire, man could make weapons and subdue the beasts, make tools, and keep his home warm. So back to heaven Prometheus went, lit his torch at the sun and brought fire back to earth rejoicing.

But Zeus felt betrayed. He now saw man with fire, not only a match for the animals but perhaps equal to the gods. So to get even, Zeus made woman, a very captivating woman, and called her Pandora—Gift of all. He presented her to Prometheus who immediately cautioned his brother Epimetheus to beware of the gifts of Zeus.

As you would guess, Epimetheus was beguiled by Pandora and took her to his home. But in his home he had kept a special box in which he had kept some special gifts that he had not passed out to the animals when he had created them. He told Pandora never to touch this box, warning her that she must never, ever open it.

PANDORA'S BOX

But what Prometheus and Epimetheus did not know is that Zeus had endowed Pandora with the gift of curiosity. As soon as Epimetheus left, she was driven by unrestrained curiosity. She picked up the box, telling herself that surely just one peek could do no harm. And you know the rest of the story. As soon as she lifted the cover, out came a host of diseases, plagues, envy, spite, and rage—all manner of Evil. She slammed down the cover, leaving only one gift in the box—hope. Hope is all that mankind has left

So as Zeus had planned, he had nothing more to fear from mankind who now had women and enough troubles to keep them busy. But still Zeus would not forgive Prometheus for stealing fire and giving it to men. He chained Prometheus to the highest rock on Mt. Caucasus where the sun would forever scorch him and where a vulture would eat out his liver, and as soon as the liver was eaten it would grow back again.[1217]

We say, that is some story! But it became a theme that has been woven in and out of literature ever since. What is that theme? *The power and consequences of unrestrained curiosity.* Pandora's box is a metaphor known by most any elementary school student, and Pandora herself has become an allegorical figure for "beautiful evil."[1218]

DAEDALUS AND ICARUS

Think of Daedalus, the fabled inventor, sculptor and artist of ancient Athens. Events forced him to flee to Crete where King Minos was the mighty ruler. The King was delighted with his visitor and made great plans for Daedalus. He commissioned him to build a mighty labyrinth, a place that has such twisted paths that nobody who entered could ever find his way out. The labyrinth was to be the final

---

[1217] Anne Terry White, *The Golden Treasury of Myths and Legends* (New York: Golden Press, 1959), 11, 12.
[1218] Shattuck, 15.

prison for the Minotaur—the half-bull, half-man beast. Even Daedalus almost lost himself in building it. But the King had it all figured out. He would not let Daedalus leave the island, fearing that he might reveal the secret of the labyrinth. Daedalus was a prisoner on Crete!

Time passed, and the restless inventor began to study birds. He said the King controlled the sea but not the air. He watched the birds so well that he thought that he could make wings that would fly. Patiently he found little feathers, then bigger feathers, and finally the feathers of the eagle; patiently he imbedded them into warm wax; having dried, the wax became very strong. Eventually he did fly.

His young son Icarus wanted a set for himself. And the day came when Daedalus and his son were ready to fly together. But father gave his son a warning: "Don't be reckless! Take a middle course between heaven and earth. For if you fly too high, the sun will scorch your feathers. If you fly too low, the sea will wet them. Take a middle course, I will be your guide, follow me and you will be safe."[1219]

Icarus had the time of his life. He soared and swooped over the Mediterranean, they could see Athens. With each swoop, Icarus went higher and higher. "I am flying higher than the eagles." And then he felt a warm glow. He had come too close to the sun. He hurtled downward into the sea. His father saw only feathers floating on the sea.

Daedalus landed on an obscure island and cursed the skill that had wrought his son's destruction. Two lessons: Icarus did not "fly the middle course" and Daedalus cursed his own skills that created such a disaster. Unintended consequences in pursuing unrestricted freedom—some things are not safe to pursue.

EVE'S CURIOSITY

The story of Eve in the Garden parallels mythical Pandora in her reach for the "box"—the forbidden fruit. Opening that "box" has indeed given this planet the horror of all human diseases, the malignity of distrust and envy, and everything else under the folder called Evil.

This *leit motif* of unrestrained curiosity moves inexorably through the Bible, chapter after chapter. Eve's box of forbidden fruit produces exactly what God said it would—humanity would get to know evil firsthand. God commissioned Noah to call a halt to the prevailing "imagination of man's heart," which is "evil from his youth" (Genesis 8:21). In fact, "every intent of the thoughts of his heart was only evil continually" (Genesis 6:5). Men and women still retained much of Adam and Eve's vigor and skills. Their technological achievements would be astonishing by our modern standards; their curiosity knew no bounds. And if God had not intervened, the plan for this world to be part of God's answer to Satan would have collapsed. In comes Noah and his family, and the promise of Genesis 3:15 was given a fresh start.

Now let's look at the Tower of Babel (Genesis 11). The *leit motif* moves from the Garden to the Ark to the "plains of Shinar." Here also we have a reflection of Satan's move in heaven when he too said of himself, let me "make a name" for myself (Genesis 11:4; Isaiah 14:13, 14; Ezekiel 28:2). The builders of the Tower not only wanted to make a name for themselves, they wanted to "build ourselves a city,

---

[1219] Anne Terry White, 50.

and a tower whose top is in the heavens" (Genesis 11:4). Now that is truly curiosity unrestrained!

Again God saw the line of truth in deep trouble because the people of Shinar were still exceptional in technology and all manner of skills and "nothing that they propose to do will be withheld from them" (Genesis 11:6). They were united by a universal language, with great skills and great imagination (curiosity) to defy the faint call of reason and truth. And God chose, for the sake of truth, to scatter them "over the face of all the earth" (Genesis 11:9), frustrating their plans for a world empire with a universal language and unified plans to build their tower. So we see again how "overheated imagination, the dark side of curiosity, calls down punishment on itself."[1220]

UNINTENDED CONSEQUENCES

One can go through the Bible and rarely miss an example of unintended consequences when men and women push the envelope of curiosity into forbidden fruit. Results are often fatal. "Remember Lot's wife—do not look behind you" (Luke 17:32; Genesis 19:17).

In 1987, Nicholas Reschar, a keen historian and philosopher of science, wrote an essay on "forbidden knowledge" that incorporates the general theme of this appendix:

> "Some information is simply not safe for us—not because there is something wrong with its possession in the abstract, but because it is the sort of thing we humans are not well suited to cope with. There are various things we simply ought not to know. If we did not have to live our lives amidst a fog of uncertainty about a whole range of matters that are actually of fundamental interest and importance to us, it would no long be a human mode of existence that we would live. Instead we would become a being of another sort, perhaps angelic, perhaps machine-like, but certainly not human.

> "There is a more deeply problematic issue, however. Are there also moral limits to the possessions of information per se—are there things we ought not to know on moral grounds?"

Reschar went on to say that "it is the basically correct moral of [the Garden of Eden] story that we may well have to pay a price for knowledge in terms of moral compromise."[1221]

MILTON'S *PARADISE LOST*

Milton ends *Paradise Lost* with Adam responding to Michael's picture of the earth remade: "Greatly instructed I shall hence depart [from Eden] which was my folly to aspire, Henceforth I learn that to obey is best, And love with fear the only God, to walk As in his presence, ever to observe His providence, and on him sole depend."[1222]

[1220] *Ibid.*, 17.
[1221] Nicholas Reschar, *Forbidden Knowledge and Other Essays on the Philosophy of Cognition* (Dordrecht: Reidel, 1987), 9. Cited in Shattuck, 43, 44.
[1222] Book XII, *Harvard Classics*, vol. 4, 359.

Shattuck devotes an entire chapter to "Milton in the Garden of Eden," and concludes that "this immense poetic and theological testament, devoted to restaging the greatest story ever told, incorporates warnings against proud knowledge as stringent as the Tower of Babel episode and Candide's 'Let us cultivate our garden.'"[1223]

Shattuck agrees with Milton that curiosity and the pursuit of knowledge is not to be rejected but the limits of curiosity should be recognized, especially when Milton has Raphael reminding Eve, "Heaven is for thee too high To know what passes there. Be lowly wise; Think only what concerns thee and thy being; Dream not of other worlds, what creatures there Live, in what state, conditions, or degree—Contented that thus far hath been revealed Not of Earth only, but of highest Heaven."[1224]

LOWLY WISE

To be "lowly wise" is not a condemnation of the pursuit of knowledge! Jesus Himself said, "You shall know the truth, and the truth shall make you free" (John 8:32). But the pursuit of knowledge should not be confused with the pursuit of truth. Jesus refers to revealed truth, knowable and eternal. Knowledge and experience, according to the insights of poets, philosophers, and historians, do have limits when the contours of morality are included in the equation of life.

All we need for further examples of "unrestrained curiosity" is to contemplate the results of contemporary demands for unrestrained sexual expression, in speech, film, and modern art. The Marquis de Sade syndrome has reached its zenith, it seems, chiefly because one wonders how much more liberty there is left to express or discover. Just look at any local magazine rack for some idea of what is available at more secreted outlets. And to think that such porno materials, whether magazine, videos, or Internet sites are kept from "minors" is ludicrous.[1225]

Pandora's box, Icarus' flight too near the sun, Dr. Jekyll's unrestrained curiosity, and Eve's "curiosity"—all suggest that there is merit in "taking the middle course" and being "lowly wise." And listening to the Voice of Truth rather than the clamor for "experience."

APPENDIX G:
PROVIDENTIAL MOMENTS IN WORLD HISTORY

Obviously, any reference to "providential moments in world history" would appear to some as mere personal opinion; they would look at the same event and see nothing "providential" or unusual, while others see enormous significance. Those working from the standpoint of the Great

---

[1223] Shattuck, 75.

[1224] Book VIII, *Harvard Classics*, vol. 8, 251.

[1225] "Following the liberating sweep of the 1960s, a series of major government reports and court decisions during the 1970s, in Europe and the United States, removed virtually all restriction on obscene and pornographic materials except for their distribution to minors. The U. S. Supreme Court decision in *Miller v. California* (1973) has stood for more than twenty years and makes prosecuting of obscenity close to futile." —Shattuck, 228.

Controversy, however, would expect God to intervene in the affairs of Planet Earth. Although we cannot predict when those "moments" would be, neither could Satan foresee them.

Among several seminal books that have looked at history noting that a contrary event would have essentially changed the way history books would have been written, two have had special significance: *The Fifteen Decisive Battles of the World from Marathon to Waterloo*[1226] and *What If? The World's Foremost Military Historians Imagine What Might Have Been.*[1227]

In his introduction, Creasy wrote: "When I speak of causes and effects, I speak of the obvious and important agency of one fact upon another, and not on remote and fancifully infinitesimal influences. … When I speak of cause and effect, I speak of those general laws only by which we perceive the sequence of human affairs to be usually regulated, and in which we recognize emphatically the wisdom and power of the supreme Lawgiver, the design of the Designed."[1228]

Among Creasy's 15 decisive "moments" (until A.D. 1815) were: The Battle of Marathon, 490 B.C.; Defeat of the Athenians at Syracuse, 413 B.C.; Battle of Arbela, 331 B.C.; Victory of Arminius over the Roman Legions under Varus, A.D. 9; Battle of Chalons, 451; Battle of Tours, 782; Battle of Hastings, 1066; Joan of Arc's Victory over the English at Orleans, 1429; Defeat of the Spanish Armada, 1588; Battle of Blenheim, 1704; Victory of the Americans over Burgoyne at Saratoga, N.Y., 1777; Battle of Valmy, 1792; and The Battle of Waterloo, 1815.

After describing in detail these historical events, Creasy quoted contemporaries who also saw in these "moments" extraordinary circumstances and consequences that changed the direction of world events into unforeseen paths. Many called these events (as did Hegel) times "when world's history hung trembling in the balance."[1229] At this point, a lover of history is always tempted to expand the details of these "trembling" moments—but space forbids.

Cowley's book worked from the opposite point of view: What would have happened at these critical, pivotal "moments" in history if the victors were losers and losers were victors! What if the Persians had beaten the rowers of Athens in 480 B.C.; or the Spanish Armada had won, 1588; or the Germans had repulsed the Allied invasion, 1944; what if Hitler had not invaded Russia, 1941; what if that mysterious plague had not destroyed Sennacherib's army outside of Jerusalem in 701 B.C.; what if the Japanese with its superior naval fleet had won at Midway, 1941; or what if the U.S. Civil War could have turned out differently, 1865.

Standing before the Court of the Areopagus, Paul proclaimed what God had been revealing to him regarding the history of Planet Earth: "God, who made the world and everything in it, since He is Lord of heaven and earth, does not dwell in temples made with hands. Nor is He worshiped with men's hands, as though He needs anything, since He gives to all life, breath, and all things. And He has made

---

[1226] E. S. Creasy (New York: A. L. Burt Company, Publishers, 1851).
[1227] Edited by Robert Cowley (New York: G. P. Putnam's Sons, 1999). Contributing authors included Stephen Ambrose, John Keegan, James M. McPherson, David McCullough, Alistair Horne, William H. McNeill, etc.
[1228] Creasy, *op. cit.*, 9.
[1229] Cowley, *op. cit.*, 17.

from one blood every nation of men and has determined their preappointed times and the boundaries of their habitation" (Acts 17:24–26).

Ellen White commented on this understanding of history: "Every nation that has come upon the stage of action has been permitted to occupy its place on the earth, that it might be seen whether it would fulfill the purpose of 'the Watcher and the Holy One.' Prophecy has traced the rise and fall of the world's great empires— Babylon, Medo-Persia, Greece, and Rome. With each of these, as with nations of less power, history repeated itself. Each had its period of test, each failed, its glory faded, its power departed, and its place was occupied by another. While the nations rejected God's principles, and in this rejection wrought their own ruin, it was still manifest that the divine, overruling purpose was working through all their movements. ... We need to study the working out of God's purpose in the history of nations and in the revelation of things to come."[1230]

Ellen White's appeal can be especially rewarding if we should consider the various battles listed above from the standpoint also of how God intervened on each occasions. For instance, consider what would have happened to His cause on earth, either through the Israelite nation or the Christian church, if the winner were the loser! Take each "providential moment" and examine the alternatives, such as Catholic Spain overwhelming the ill-prepared Protestant Britain in 1588! Or if Christian Martel with his much fewer soldiers had been beaten back by the Muslim hordes in 732! And on we could go!

APPENDIX H:
THE BIBLE REVEALS THE COSMIC CONFLICT BETWEEN CHRIST AND SATAN

From Genesis to Revelation, the conflict is highlighted as an intense struggle for the loyalties of men and women. John the Revelator quickly painted the picture of "war in heaven" (Revelation 12:7) even as Moses had quickly painted the picture of war in Eden (Genesis 3)

We are not left in darkness regarding how the conflict ends. John tells us that after millenniums of struggle, after Satan has done all he can to deceive the universe; the universe hears "the mighty voice of a great multitude in heaven crying, 'Hallelujah! Salvation and glory and power belong to our God, for his judgments are true and just'" (Revelation 19:1, 2).

In this affirmation lies a clue as to what the conflict was all about. We hear the echoes of Satan's charges: God has been unfair—He is severe and arbitrary.[1231] The Great Controversy ends only when God's created intelligences are convinced that He is worth loving and deserving of trust.

From Genesis to Revelation the story of the controversy unfolds, describing how God defends Himself and settles the questions that the Great Deceiver has raised. From one point of view, Christian theology is simply the story of

---

[1230] *Education,* 176, 177, 184.
[1231] See 38.

who gets what, and why, out of the controversy. Theology is the science of God's self-communication[1232] as it relates to the challenge of His antagonist, the first-born of His creation. The Bible, then, is the theater wherein we observe (1) the antagonist at work stalking his victims like a roaring lion (1 Peter 5:8), relentlessly subverting the God's government; and (2) the infinitely patient, gracious God telling His side of the conflict.

As we have already reviewed, the origin of Lucifer who became Satan and the circumstances relating to his rebellion in heaven is suggested in Isaiah 14 and Ezekiel 28.[1233] By turning the allegiance of the angels to himself, he usurped glory and authority that were God's. He especially coveted the place of that member of the Godhead we have come to know as Jesus Christ. Covetousness, jealousy, deception, rebellion—it was all there—even in heaven. He lied about God, charging that God's law of love was not really in the best interests of created beings; that God, who demanded loyalty and obedience from others, Himself exercises no self-denial or sacrifice. Eventually Lucifer through humans who bought into his lies charged that God's law could not be obeyed and that God was the author of sin, suffering and death (see the Book of Job, John 9:2).

How To Restore Rebels

How would God relate to rebellion? Would he forgive a rebel? How would He restore sinners who had been infected morally and depraved physically by their rebellion? How would He restore security to a questioning universe? By putting into effect what we have come to call the "plan of salvation." The first insight is found in God's promise in Genesis 3:15—Satan would be wounded unto death. And sinful men and women would have infused strength from God in the conflict.

Basic to this "plan" would be the demonstration made by Jesus of what God is really like. John made it clear that Jesus had come to reveal the truth about God (John 1:1–3, 14). Other New Testament writers, years after Jesus had returned to heaven, assessed the impact and difference His life and death had made (Romans 1:16, 17; Hebrews 1:1–3).

Why was more time needed after Jesus lived, died, and ascended? It would take time for men and women to grasp the leap of faith—the joining of fact and feeling as men and women responded to the gospel of Jesus Christ. Telling this story would bring a new dynamic to the human race "for it is the power of God to salvation for everyone who believes [has faith]" (Romans 1:16). This good news promised that "the God of peace will crush Satan under your feet shortly" (16:20).

These thoughts lead us to recognize why God now needed men and women of faith to witness, to prove, that what Jesus did as our Example, as well as what He had done as our atoning Sacrifice, nails Satan against the wall of universal scrutiny. In other words, what was yet to be made clear to men and women before God could close the curtains on the Great Controversy?

[1232] "If God's will to Lordship is his *self-affirmation* 'over against'… the creature, then his love—his will to fellowship—is his unconditional *self-communication* to the creature." —Emil Brunner, *Truth as Encounter*, Translated by Olive Wyon (Philadelphia: The Westminster Press, 1943), 97.
[1233] See 413, 414.

JOB DESCRIPTION OF THE CHRISTIAN CHURCH

Before Jesus ascended He laid out the job description for the Christian Church. John records part of our Lord's incredibly moving prayer to His Heavenly Father wherein Jesus said: "As you have sent me into the world, I also have sent them into the world" (17:18; see also 20:21).

Could it be that, in some important aspects, the plan of salvation depends on His disciples' doing faithfully what He did so faithfully! And if they do not, they would be His followers in name only! And some day such followers will hear those dreadful words, "I never knew you [for what you said you were]" (Matthew 7:23).

New Testament writers clearly focused on the purpose of the gospel. See Titus 2:11–14 NIV, 2 Peter 3:11–14 NIV and 1 John 1:9 NIV. For them and other biblical writers, the double purpose of the gospel included both forgiveness and restoration. Cleansing from the effects of sin was clearly understood. Augustus Toplady understood all this well when he wrote in his first verse of "Rock of Ages,"—"Be of sin the double cure, Cleanse me from its guilt and power."

The big issue continued to be: Can God be trusted? Does His Word produce the results that He promises? Can we truly draw on the same power Jesus depended on to overcome sin (Revelation 3:21)? In the larger sense, can fallen beings be rescued from sin so decisively that by the grace of God they can be trusted to be loving, honest, gracious, compassionate people in whom even the desire to sin will never arise again? In other words, will the power of the gospel truly restore men and women into reflecting the image of their Lord so that they are safe to save? Can they be trusted with eternal life?

Paul's song in Ephesians sets forth God's redemptive purpose in bold lyrics (Ephesians 1:4–12; 3:8–19). Paul grasped the Spirit's message: The Christian church was destined to be the living exhibit of God's wisdom, the handiwork of His enabling grace, the convincing testimony that His ways are "true and just" (Revelation 19:2).[1234] Ellen White's plea echoes throughout her writings: "If there was ever a people in need of constantly increasing light from heaven, it is the people that, in this time of peril, God has called to be the depositaries of His holy law, and to vindicate His character before the world. Those to whom has been committed a trust so sacred must be spiritualized, elevated, vitalized, by the truths they profess to believe."[1235]

[1234] "The Savior came to glorify the Father by the demonstration of His love; so the Spirit was to glorify Christ by revealing His grace to the world. The very image of God is to be reproduced in humanity. The honor of God, the honor of Christ, is involved in the perfection of the character of His people." —*The Desire of Ages,* 761. "The honor of Christ must stand complete in the perfection of the character of His chosen people." —*Signs of the Times,* November 25, 1890. See also *Testimonies,* vol. 8, 14–16. "It is God's purpose that His people shall be a sanctified, purified, holy people, communicating light to all around them. It is His purpose that, by exemplifying the truth in their lives, they shall be a praise in the earth. The grace of Christ is sufficient to bring this about. But let God's people remember that only as they believe and work out the principles of the gospel, can He make them a praise in the earth. ... Not with tame, lifeless utterance is the message to be given, but with clear, decided, stirring utterances. ... The world needs to see in Christians an evidence of the power of Christianity." —*Testimonies,* vol. 8, 14–16.

[1235] *Testimonies,* vol. 5, 746.

Jesus And The Church Are God's Witnesses

Further, "It becomes every child of God to vindicate His character. You can magnify the Lord; you can show the power of sustaining grace."[1236] (See Ezekiel 36:21–27, RSV.) Would any Christian who understands what Jesus did in the Garden and on the Cross want to do any less? Those who understand how much God needs their witness are on the way to hastening His return.[1237] Jesus and His Church are God's witnesses that what Satan has said about Him are lies! In a special sense, Christians as well as God "are on trial before the heavenly universe."[1238]

We can now more clearly understand why the purpose of the gospel has so much to do with helping God settle the Great Controversy with Satan. Did God place an impossible burden upon His followers when He exhorted them to walk as Jesus walked? (See 1 John 2:6; cf. Ephesians 5:1, 2; Philippians 2:1–5; 1 Peter 1:15, 16.) Did God ask too much when He sought a people who would "keep the commandments of God and the faith of Jesus" (Revelation 14:12; 12:17)?

Malachi points to the endtime and the final moments of the Controversy: "Who can endure the day of his coming and who can stand when he appears? For he is like a refiner's fire and like fuller's soap; he will sit as a refiner and purifier of silver, and he will purify the sons of Levi and refine them like gold and silver, till they present right offerings to the Lord. ... Then once more you shall distinguish between the righteous and the wicked, between one who serves God and the one who does not serve him" (3:2, 3, 18).

John the Revelator focuses on the same endtime when Satan's contends fiercely against God's loyalists "who will endure the day of His coming"—because their testimony completes God's case against him (Revelation 12:17). They have "endured" all of Satan's mightiest thrusts (Matthew 24:9). They have let God work out His plan in their lives and He endorses them with His approval—He writes His name in their foreheads (Revelation 14:1).

God pulls the final curtain on the Controversy when the harvest of the earth is "fully ripe" (Revelation 14:15, RSV). That is, when the wheat and the tares, God's loyalists and Satan's loyalists, are fully revealed in the endtime.

[1236] *Ibid.*, 317. "Like our Savior, we are in this world to do service for God. We are here to become like God in character, and by a life of service to reveal Him to the world. In order to be coworkers with God, in order to become like Him, and to reveal His character, we must know Him aright." —*The Ministry of Healing*, 409.

[1237] "It is the darkness of misapprehension of God that is enshrouding the world. Men are losing their knowledge of His character. It has been misunderstood and misinterpreted. At this time a message from God is to be proclaimed, a message illuminating in its influence and saving in its power. His character is to be made known. Into the darkness of the world is to be shed the light of His glory, the light of His goodness, mercy, and truth. ... Those who wait for the Bridegroom's coming are to say to the people, 'Behold your God.' The last rays of merciful light, the last message of mercy to be given to the world, is a revelation of His character of love. The children of God are to manifest His glory. In their own life and character they are to reveal what the grace of God has done for them. The light of the Sun of Righteousness is to shine forth in good works–in words of truth and deeds of holiness." —*Christ's Object Lessons*, 415, 416.

[1238] *Christ's Object Lessons*, 303.

God's loyalists have trusted His promises and are willing to follow Him wherever He goes—they have permitted Him to live out in their lives the principles of Jesus. Satan's loyalists have thrown their freedom away as they allowed Satan's principles to ensnare them in self-destructive habits.

NEURAL PATHWAYS SETTLED FOREVER

The neural pathways of God's loyalists are so settled into truth, intellectually and spiritually, that they will never want to say "no" to God ever again. Their choices became habitual responses to all that was good, beautiful, just, and loving. These habits now spontaneous and natural, have been etched forever in what we call character. They can be trusted with eternal life. God's plan is vindicated.

The neural pathways of Satan's loyalists are settled into selfish grasping, selfish justification, and hatred to all who represent the good, the beautiful, the just, and the lovable. Their habitual responses have also become spontaneous and natural; they are also etched into character that cannot be changed. They would not be safe to save.

The main issue in the Great Controversy has been whether God or Satan had the blueprint for a safe, secure, loving universe built on mutual trust of all parties.

When the last words are said (Revelation 15:3, 4; 19:1, 2) the universe will have all the evidence needed for the vindication of God's character and government. Not only will the faithful of earth help to vindicate God's character, but so will Satan and his loyalists—they will have demonstrated that rebellion against truth is always self-defeating, self-destructive, for "the wages of sin is death" (Romans 6:23). Just as God said in the beginning!

APPENDIX I:
WHY JESUS CAME!

The Christian Church has been long divided, often with dire results, over why Jesus became man. The question is often referred to under the term, the "atonement" (at-one-ment). Unfortunately, (1) no church is exempt from deep divisions caused by different answers to our question; (2) every church, most every theologian, has viewed the atonement in terms of why Jesus died[1239] without going back further and asking why Jesus became man;[1240] and (3) without asking first, why Jesus came, conventional theories of the atonement seem irreconcilable.

Fortunately, in asking first the question why Jesus came, we are better able to see the big picture of why Jesus died. In doing so, we find the ability to join together the key ingredients of the hitherto irreconcilable theories of the atonement.

PRIMARY REASON FOR THE INCARNATION

The answer to our question is best illuminated within the Great Controversy Theme. *Only when we understand the issues in the Controversy will we understand why*

[1239] See "*Appendix I: Why Jesus Died.*"

[1240] Anselm (1033–1109) may have come the closest with his attempt to answer *Cur Deus Homo* (Why a God-man?).

Jesus became man. All the accusations of Satan against God are essentially answered in our Lord's incarnation. In fact, that is the primary reason Jesus became man—to answer Satan's charges that God was unfair to make laws that created intelligences could not keep or, if they tried, would live a dreary, suffocating life without personal freedom and without the opportunity to reach one's full potential. In proving Satan wrong and God right, Jesus also showed, contrary to Satan's lie to Eve (Genesis 3:4) that sinners won't die, that sin ends in death—the awfulness of being separated from God and life forever.

Before we let the Great Controversy Theme shed light on our question, it would be helpful to review the four general answers that theologians have given to our question. Although each theory centers on the Cross, each differs as to what the Cross-event means—chiefly because they did not step back far enough to ask, "Why did Jesus come in the first place?"

- The *"ransom"* theory. (Sinners belong to Satan but God paid the price for their redemption through the death of Jesus. Satan accepted the "ransom," Jesus for sinners, but Satan could not hold Jesus in the grave. Jesus proved victorious over Satan, the hope of all Christians.)

- The *"satisfaction"* theory. (Most notably argued by Anselm, sin was considered a dishonor to God but Jesus on the Cross "satisfied" this dishonor. Protestant Reformers added a twist when they emphasized that Jesus paid the price [the penalty] incurred when sinners broke God's law, thus Jesus "satisfied" justice—a thoroughly objective event as far as sinners are concerned. The concept of "substitution" is thus linked to the "satisfaction" theory.)

- The so-called *"moral influence"* theory. (Abelard, 1079–1142, responded to Anselm by noting that the New Testament emphasized the enormous impact that the Cross makes on the believer—something happens in believers when they contemplate the death of Jesus. They are led to repent and their lives are transformed.)

- The *"family"* theory. (Probably set forth best by McLeod Campbell (1800–1872), the atonement was viewed from the standpoint of the family relationship, between God as Father and sinners as children and how this earthly dynamic can help us to understand the love of God for his earthly children.)

All these theories are saying something important, but by themselves they are incomplete and thus force an incomplete picture of why Jesus came and why He died. *I think the best way to answer our question is to review how Ellen White unfolded the big picture as she understood the question within the framework of the Great Controversy Theme* [note that some of the following references combine several categories]:[1241]

[1241] These references in this appendix are abstracted from a longer study paper prepared by the author. The categories, or reasons for His coming, here listed are: 1) Jesus came to vindicate the character of God before the universe; 2) Jesus came to represent the Father and reveal His character and love for us; 3) Jesus came to restore the image of God in man. 4) Jesus came to be both our Savior and Example; 5) Jesus came to give His church a legacy; 6) Jesus came to bring us back to harmony with God; 7) Jesus came to impart the Holy Spirit so that we could learn

- **Jesus came to vindicate the character of God before the universe.**

"The plan of salvation had a yet broader and deeper purpose than the salvation of man. It was not for this alone that Christ came to the earth; it was not merely that the inhabitants of this little world might regard the law of God as it should be regarded; but it was to vindicate the character of God before the universe." —*Patriarchs and Prophets*, 68.

- **Jesus came to represent the Father and reveal His character and love for us.**

"Satan led men to conceive of God as a being whose chief attribute in stern justice-one who is a severe judge, a harsh exacting creditor. He pictured the Creator as a being who is watching with jealous eye to discern the errors and mistakes of men, that He may visit judgment upon them. It was to remove this dark shadow by revealing to the world the infinite love of God, that Jesus came to live among men. The Son of God came from heaven to make manifest the Father." —*Steps to Christ*, 11.

"No verbal description could reveal God to the world. Through a life of purity, a life of perfect trust and submission to the will of God, a life of humiliation such as even the highest seraph in heaven would have shrunk from, God Himself must be revealed to humanity. In order to do this, our Saviour clothed His divinity with humanity. He employed the human faculties, for only by adopting these could He be comprehended by humanity. Only humanity could reach humanity. He lived out the character of God through the body which God had prepared for Him. He blessed the world by living out in human flesh the life of God, thus showing that He had the power to unite humanity to divinity" —*Manuscript Releases,* vol. 9,126

- **Jesus came to restore the image of God in man.**

"He came, not to break down the moral power of men, but to restore it. He came to break the power of oppression. His work was to release those who were in bondage to Satan. Those who say, I am a child of God, and yet do work which will grieve and oppress, executing cruel actions against their fellow men, are not following the Lamb whithersoever He goeth, but are followers of another leader. They develop the attributes of Satan, and make it manifest that they are participators and co-workers with him to bind, imprison, and condemn, to cause all the suffering possible to body and mind, because they cannot compel men to be untrue to God and dishonor His work and transgress His holy law." —*Manuscript Releases,* vol. 14, 93; *Signs of the Times,* Dec. 22, 1887.

---

how to love; 8) Jesus came to teach us how to live; 9) Jesus came to give us divine power to live overcoming lives; 10) Jesus came to break the power of Satan; 11) Jesus came to break down every wall of exclusion; 12) Jesus came to impart His righteousness; 13) Jesus came to bear the penalty of our sins; 14) Jesus became man so that He could truly sympathize and assist us overcoming sin; 15) Jesus came to be our Surety and Substitute so that we can be obedient; 16) Jesus came to prove Satan a liar regarding the possibility of obedience; 17) Jesus came to put man on vantage ground through whom the attributes of God could be revealed.

"Jesus came to our world to dispute the authority of Satan, who claimed supremacy over the earth. He came to restore in man the defaced image of God, to impart to the repentant soul divine power by which he might be raised from corruption and degradation, and be elevated and ennobled and made fit for companionship with the angels of heaven, to take the position in the courts of God which Satan and his angels lost through their rebellion." —*Review and Herald*, May 8, 1894.

"Jesus came to restore in man the image of his Maker. None but Christ can fashion anew the character that has been ruined by sin. He came to expel the demons that had controlled the will." —*Faith to Live By*, 142.

• **Jesus came to bear the penalty for our sins.**

"Jesus came to bear the penalty of man's transgression, to uphold and vindicate the immutability of the law of God, and the rectitude of His government. He came to make an end of sin, and to bring in everlasting righteousness. He can lift sinners from their low estate, and in so doing magnify the law of Jehovah. These thoughts make me almost forget my pain." —*Manuscript Releases*, vol. 8, 45.

"Christ came to die because not a precept of His Father's law could be altered to excuse man in his fallen condition. As this picture was presented before Moses, again an expression of grief and sadness came over his countenance." — *Manuscript Releases*, vol. 10, 57.

• **Jesus came to be both our Savior and Example.**

"This lamentable condition would have known no change or hope if Jesus had not come down to our world to be man's Savior and Example. In the midst of a world's moral degradation, he stands a beautiful and spotless character, the one model for man's imitation. We must study, and copy, and follow the Lord Jesus Christ; then we shall bring the loveliness of his character into our own life, and weave his beauty into our daily words and actions. Thus we shall stand before God with acceptance, and win back by conflict with the principalities of darkness, the power of self-control, and the love of God that Adam lost in the fall. Through Christ we may possess the spirit of love and obedience to the commands of God. Through his merits it may be restored in our fallen natures; and when the Judgment shall sit and the books be opened, we may be the recipients of God's approval." —*Signs of the Times*, Dec. 22, 1887.

"Our characters must reach the standard of holiness. Every thought and habit must be brought into harmony with the will of God. Jesus came to our world to be our Saviour and example, and it is in his name alone, that we may gain the victory over perverted nature. He overcame in man's behalf, and through his grace we may become 'partakers of the divine nature, having escaped the corruption that is in the world through lust.'" —*Signs of the Times*, Feb. 17, 1888.

"But sin has almost obliterated the moral image of God in man. Jesus came down to our world that He might give man a living example, that he might know how to live and how to keep the way of the Lord. He was the image of the Father. His beautiful and spotless character is before man as an example for him to imitate. We must study the copy and follow Jesus Christ, then we shall bring His loveliness and beauty into our character. In doing this we are standing before God through faith, winning back by conflict with the powers of darkness the power of self-control, the love of God that Adam lost. We are through Jesus Christ living and keeping the laws of God." —*Sermons and Talks,* vol. 1, 33.

"The young may have moral power, for Jesus came into the world that He might be our example and give to all youth and those of every age divine help." —*Child Guidance,* 167.

"As we see the condition of mankind today, the question arises in the minds of some, 'Is man by nature totally and wholly depraved?' Is he hopelessly ruined? No, he is not. The Lord Jesus left the royal courts and, taking our human nature, lived such a life as everyone may live in humanity, through following His example. We may perfect a life in this world [which] is an example of righteousness, and overcome as Christ has given us an example in His life, revealing that humanity may conquer as He, the great Pattern, [conquered]. Men have sold themselves to the enemy of all righteousness. Christ came to our world to live the example humanity must live, if they [are to] secure the heavenly reward. ... Theories that do not recognize the atonement that has been made for sin, and the work that the Holy Spirit is to do in the hearts of human beings, are powerless to save. Christ lived the unpolluted life in this world to reveal to human beings the power of His grace that will be given to every soul that will accept Him as his Saviour. Man's pride would lead him to seek for salvation in some other way than that pointed out in the Scriptures." —*Manuscript Releases,* vol. 9, 239.

- **Jesus came to give His church a legacy.**

"Jesus came to the world, lived a holy life, and died, to leave to the church His legacy in the valuable treasures He entrusted to them. He made His disciples the depositaries of most precious doctrines, to be placed in the hands of His church unmixed with the errors and traditions of men. He revealed Himself to them as the light of the world, the Sun of righteousness. And He promised them the Comforter, the Holy Spirit, whom the Father was to send in His name" —*Signs of the Times,* Nov. 16, 1891.

- **Jesus came to bring us back to harmony with God.**

"Joshua represents those who are seeking God and keeping his commandments. ... The infinite sufferings of the Son of God in Gethsemane and on Calvary were endured that he might rescue his people from the power of the evil one. ... It is through Christ's righteousness alone that we are enabled to keep the law. Those who worship God in sincerity and truth, and afflict their souls before him as in the great day of atonement, will wash their robes of character and make them white in the blood of the Lamb. ... Those who have manifested true repentance for sin, and by living faith in Christ are obedient to God's commandments, will have their names retained in the book of life, and they will be confessed before the Father and before the holy angels. ... Christ came to our world and died a shameful death because the precepts of the law could not be changed. ... He died to bring us into harmony with the law of Heaven." —*Signs of the Times,* June 2, 1890.

- **Jesus came to impart the Holy Spirit so that we could learn how to love.**

"Jesus came to impart to the human soul the Holy Spirit by which the love of God is shed abroad in the heart; but it is impossible to endow men with the Holy Spirit, who are set in their ideas, whose doctrines are all stereotyped and unchangeable, who are walking after the traditions and commandments of men as were the Jews in the time of Christ." —Manuscript Releases, vol. 5, 52.

- **Jesus came to teach us how to live.**

"Christ came to bring divine power to unite with human effort, so that although we have been debased by perverted appetite, we may take courage, for we are prisoners of hope. ... Everyone that is in harmony with Christ will bear the Christ-like mold. ... He came to our world to show us how to live a pure, holy life, and I have purposed in my heart that He shall not have lived and died in vain for me." —*Signs of the Times,* August 4, 1890.

"The great Teacher came into our world not only to atone for sin, but to be a teacher both by precept and example. He came to show man how to keep the law in humanity, so that man might have no excuse for following his own defective judgment. We see Christ's obedience. His life was without sin. His lifelong obedience is a reproach to disobedient humanity." —*Selected* Messages, vol. 3, 135, 136.

- **Jesus came to give us divine power to live overcoming lives.**

"Jesus came to our world to bring divine power to man, that through his grace, we might be transformed into His likeness." —*Signs of the Times,* June 16, 1890.

"Not until the life of Christ becomes a vitalizing power in our lives can we resist the temptations that assail us from within and from without. Christ came to this world and lived the law of God, that man might have perfect mastery over the natural inclinations which corrupt the soul. The Physician of soul and body, He gives victory over warring lusts. He has provided every facility, that man may possess completeness of character." —*Ministry of Healing,* 130, 131.

- **Jesus came to break the power of Satan.**

"Jesus has not changed; He is the same yesterday, today, and forever, and He still loves and pities the erring, seeking to draw them to Himself, that He may give them divine aid. He knows that a demon power is struggling in every soul, striving for the mastery; but Jesus came to break the power of Satan and to set the captives free." —*My Life Today,* 300.

"Christ came to cut us loose from the originator of sin. He came to give us a mastery over the power of the destroyer, and to save us from the sting of the serpent. Through his imparted righteousness he would place all human beings where they will be on vantage ground. He came to this earth and lived the law of God that man might stand in his God-given manhood, having complete mastery over his natural inclination to self-indulgence and to the selfish ideas and principles which tarnish the soul. The Physician of soul and body, he will give wisdom and complete victory over warring lusts. He will provide every facility, that man may perfect a completeness of character in every respect."—*Manuscript Releases,* vol. 7, 320.

- **Jesus came to be our Surety and Substitute so that we can be obedient.**

"The Son of God, the sinless One, the One perfect in obedience, becomes the channel through which the lost communion may be renewed, the way through which the lost paradise may be regained. Through Christ, man's substitute and surety, man may keep the commandments of God. He may return to his allegiance, and God will accept him." —*Manuscript Releases,* vol. 19, 352.

- **Jesus came to break down every wall of exclusion.**

"Jesus came to demolish every wall of exclusion, to throw open every wall in the temple where God presides, that every ear may hear, that every eye may see, that every thirsty soul may drink of the water of life freely." —*Our High Calling,* 245.

- **Jesus came to impart His righteousness.**

"He assumed human nature, and was tempted in all points like man is tempted, that we might know how to meet the foe. He waits to impart to each member of the human family power to become a partaker of the divine nature, power to overcome the corruption that is in the world through lust. [John 3:14–18, quoted.]" —*Manuscript Releases,* vol. 17, 83.

"He lived the law of God, and honored it in a world of transgression, revealing to the worlds unfallen, to the heavenly universe, to Satan, and to all the fallen sons and daughters of Adam that through His grace humanity can keep the law of God! He came to impart His own divine nature, His own image, to the repentant, believing soul." —*Manuscript Releases,* vol. 8, 40.

- **Jesus became man so that He could truly sympathize and assist us in overcoming sin.**

"Since Jesus came to dwell with us, we know that God is acquainted with our trials, and sympathizes with our griefs. Every son and daughter of Adam may understand that our Creator is the friend of sinners." —*The Desire of Ages*, 241.

"Jesus came to the world as a human being, that He might become acquainted with human beings, and come close to them in their need. He was born a babe in Bethlehem. He grew up as other children grow. And from youth to manhood, during the whole of His earthly life, He was assailed by Satan's fiercest temptations." —*Bible Echo*, September 3, 1900.

"Jesus came from heaven to earth, assumed man's nature, and was tempted in all points like as we are that he might know how to succor those who should be tempted. Christ's life is for our example. He shows in his willing obedience, how man may keep the law of God, and that transgression of the law, and not obedience of it, brings him into bondage." —*Signs of the Times*, August 1, 1878.

- **Jesus came to prove Satan a liar regarding the possibility of obedience.**

"In heaven Satan had declared that the sin of Adam revealed that human beings could not keep the law of God, and he sought to carry the universe with him in this belief. Satan's words appeared to be true, but Christ came to unmask the deceiver. He came that through trial and dispute of the claims of Satan in the great conflict, He might demonstrate that a ransom had been found. The Majesty of heaven would undertake the cause of man, and with the same facilities that man may obtain, stand the test and proving of God, as man must stand it. Christ came to the earth, taking humanity and standing as man's representative, to show in the controversy with Satan that he was a liar, and that man, as God created him, connected with the Father and the Son, could obey every requirement of God. Speaking through His servant He declares, 'His commandments are not grievous.' It was sin that separated man from his God, and it is sin that maintains this separation." —*Manuscript Releases*, vol. 6, 115.

"Satan had claimed that it was impossible for man to obey God's commandments; and in our own strength it is true that we can not obey them. But Christ came in the form of humanity, and by His perfect obedience He proved that humanity and divinity combined can obey every one of God's precepts." —*Christ's Object Lessons*, 314.

"Satan has declared that man cannot keep the law. I [Christ] will show that his statement is false, that man can keep the law. I have come to remove deception from the minds of men, to make plain that which Satan is trying to make obscure. I have come to establish the law that Satan is seeking to make void, to show how far-reaching are the principles of this law. I have come to strip from it the burdensome exactions with which man has loaded it down. I have come to show its length and breadth, its dignity and nobility. I will open before men the purity and spirituality of God's commandments. Not to introduce a new law have I come, but to establish the law which to all eternity will be the standard of obedience." —*Manuscript Releases*, vol. 18, 133.

- **Jesus came to put man on vantage ground revealing the attributes of God.**

"Christ came to this earth and suffered the sorrows, disappointments, and griefs of humanity, that man might stand on vantage ground before angels and before men, revealing to the world the attributes of God. Let us put self out of sight, and think more of Christ. People are longing to hear of the Saviour from those who have learned of Him His meekness and His lowliness, and who can therefore speak words of sincere experience. Such ones inspire faith and confidence. They show no coarseness of speech, no carelessness of attitude; for they realize that they are representatives of Christ" —*Manuscript Releases*, vol. 18, 97.

CONCLUDING THOUGHTS

Nowhere in theological literature will one find such a wide grasp of "why Jesus came." But these reasons are not like pearls on a string, to be studied independently of the other reasons. Each of them flows out of the purpose of the gospel—to restore in man the image of his Maker. The "everlasting gospel" is really the story of why Jesus became man and why He died. He came not only to offer forgiveness to a lost world, He came to give every sinner moral power to repent of and to turn from his sins, power to keep him or her from sinning so that they are ultimately safe to save. God and the angels will not and cannot permit rebels back into heaven. That attitude will be worked out of each sinner who is saved (within the time they had to live) before he or she dies or before earth's final probation is closed. That is why Jesus came—not to save His people in their sins but from their sins (Matthew 1:21). He is both our all-atoning Sacrifice and our all-powerful Mediator, our Savior and Example, our Teacher and Mentor. To Him be honor and glory forever!

APPENDIX J:
WHY JESUS DIED!

As we noted in *Appendix H: Why Jesus Came*, most problems and divisions within the Christian Church since the 1st century A.D. have centered on "why He came" and "why He died.' Usually, answers to these two questions are based on certain presuppositions that also determine the theologian's understanding of the gospel. If one has a limited understanding of the gospel or of a philosophically determined picture of God, then his understanding of why Jesus came and died is also limited—as we have discussed in this book.

When we step back and ask these two questions first before defining the gospel, then the gospel takes on a fresh, wide-angled scope that embraces the purposes of

God's side of the Great Controversy. Thus, the life and death of Jesus are means to a greater end, and not the end itself. Here follows a brief overview of Ellen White's larger view of why Jesus died (abstracted from a more extended study paper that I prepared).

- **That He might purify us from all iniquity.**

"Sanctification of soul, body, and spirit will surround us with the atmosphere of heaven. If God has chosen us from eternity, it is that we might be holy, our conscience purged from dead works to serve the living God. We must not in any way make self our god. God has given Himself to die for us, that He might purify us from all iniquity. The Lord will carry on this work of perfection for us if we will allow ourselves to be controlled by Him. He carries on this work for our good and His own name's glory." —*Manuscript Releases*, vol. 4, 348.

"Christ came to our world to elevate humanity, to renew in man the image of God, that man might become the partaker of the divine nature. Jesus gave Himself for us that He might redeem us from all iniquity, and purify unto Himself a peculiar people, zealous of good works. Christ dwelling in our hearts by faith causes us to become as a branch grafted into the true Vine. The Majesty of heaven gave His life to make us individually His own by bringing back the transgressor to his loyalty to God's law, by turning away the sinner from his iniquity. Oh, that men would love and fear God!" —*Manuscript Releases*, vol. 14, 85.

- **That we may be redeemed and restored.**

"As a remedy for the terrible consequences into which selfishness led the human race, God gave His only begotten Son to die for mankind. How could He have given more? In this gift He gave Himself. 'I and My Father are one,' said Christ. By the gift of His Son, God has made it possible for man to be redeemed, and restored to oneness with Him." —*Manuscript Releases*, vol. 7, 233.

"The precious revelation of God's will in the Scriptures with all their unfolding of glorious truth is only a means to an end. The death of Jesus Christ was a means to an end. The most powerful and efficacious provision that He could give to our world, was the means; the end was the glory of God in the uplifting, refining, ennobling of the human agent." —*Manuscript Releases*, vol. 7, 274.

"Christ gave His life to make it possible in our humanity to meet the conditions that will give all an entrance into that city whose builder and maker is God." —*Manuscript Releases*, vol. 16, 189.

"That His church will be capable of caring for others and carry out its commission Christ has given His precious life to make it possible to establish a church that will be capable of caring for sorrowful, tempted, perishing souls. He has bought us with His own life, shed His own blood in order that He might wash away the stains of sin, and clothe us with the garments of salvation." — *Manuscript Releases*, vol. 2, 277.

"Christ lived and suffered and died to establish a church capable of doing this noble work. He bought her, he cleansed her with his own blood, and clothed her with the garments of his salvation. He laid the corner-stone upon the blood-stained rock of Calvary. He made his church the depositary of his precious law, and transferred into her hands in a high and holy sense the work of carrying out his holy designs; that the church should take the work when he left it, and carry it forward to its consummation." —*Review and Herald*, June 7, 1887.

- **That we might be brought back to His loyalty and become obedient to His commandments.**

"Christ died that the transgressor of the law of God might be brought back to His loyalty, that he might keep the commandments of God, and His law as the apple of His eye, and live. God cannot take rebels into His kingdom; therefore He makes obedience to His requirements a special requirement." —*Manuscript Releases*, vol. 1, 112.

"Is the matter of gaining eternal life one to be trifled with? With His own life Christ paid the price of our redemption. He died to secure our love and willing obedience. All the blessings we enjoy come from Him. He calls upon us to remember that the humblest opportunity to serve Him is a consecrated gift. You need to become acquainted with your Bible. You will then see that age after age Jesus has been delivering His goods to men and women. Each generation has its special trust. Your future welfare depends on the use you make of your entrusted talents." —*Manuscript Releases*, vol. 18, 269.

- **That we would have sufficient grace and power to remove natural defects and tendencies.**

"We hear many excuses, I cannot live up to this or that. What do you mean by this or that? Do you mean that it was an imperfect sacrifice that was made for the fallen race upon Calvary, that there is not sufficient grace and power granted us that we work away from our own natural defects and tendencies, that it was not a whole Saviour that was given us? Or do you mean to cast reproach upon God? Well, you say, it was Adam's sin. You say, I am not guilty of that, and I am not responsible for his guilt and fall. Here all these natural tendencies are in me and I am not to blame if I act out these natural tendencies. Who is to blame? Is God?" —Sermon preached at Minneapolis General Conference, Sabbath, Oct. 20, 1888, cited in A.V. Olson, *Through Crisis to Victory*, 262.

"Believers are to represent in their lives, its power to sanctify and ennoble. … They are to show forth the power of the grace that Christ died to give men. … They are to be men of faith, men of courage, whole-souled men, who, without questioning, trust in God and His promises. …" —*Amazing Grace*, 247.

"When Christ gave His life for you, it was that He might place you on vantage ground and impart to you moral power. By faith you may become partakers of His divine nature, having overcome the corruption that is in the world through lust." —*Manuscript Releases*, vol. 14, 73.

"We need to be filled with all the fullness of God, and we shall then have life, power, grace and salvation. How shall we obtain these great blessings? Christ has died that we might receive them by faith in His name. He has freely offered us light and life. Then why should we persist in driving pegs on which to hang our doubts? Why should we fill the gallery of the mind with gloomy scenes of doubt? Why not let the bright beams of the Sun of righteousness shine into the chambers of heart and mind and dispel the shadows of unbelief? Turn to the Light, to Jesus the precious Saviour." —*Mind, Character and Personality*, vol. 2, 680.

"He who repents of his sin and accepts the gift of the life of the Son of God cannot be overcome. Laying hold by faith of the divine nature, he becomes a child of God. He prays, he believes. When tempted and tried, he claims the power that Christ died to give, and overcomes through His grace. This every sinner needs to understand. He must repent of his sin, he must believe in the power of Christ, and accept that power to save and to keep him from sin. How thankful ought we to be for the gift of Christ's example!" —*Selected Messages*, vol. 2, 224.

"How could he give you any stronger evidence of his love than he gave when he died for you on Calvary's cross? He died that you might have power to break with Satan, that you might cast off his hellish shackles, and be delivered from his power. Jesus paid your ransom with his own blood, and shall he have died for you in vain? How can you answer in the judgment for your neglect of his great salvation? O that God would open your eyes, that you might see how flimsy are the excuses you now think to present to God! Why have you not responded to his love? Why has he died for you in vain?" —*Youth's Instructor*, March 2, 1893.

• **That we could see that the law of God is unchangeable and eternal.**

"The light that I have is that God's servants should go quietly to work, preaching the grand, precious truths of the Bible—Christ and Him crucified, His love and infinite sacrifice—showing that the reason why Christ died is because the law of God is immutable, unchangeable, eternal. The Spirit of the Lord will awaken the conscience and the understanding of those with whom you work, bringing the commandments of God to their remembrance." —*Review and Herald*, April 6, 1911.

• **That the universe could view the character of God more fully.**

"What great and wonderful effects have come from the crucifixion of Christ! What a view of the character of God [and] His sacrifice has opened to the universe! His love for man, far surpassing all human love, has lifted the law of God to its own eternal dignity. The attributes of God have been revealed, and the holy requirements of His law have been vindicated. The effects of the sacrifice on the cross are still felt; but all who would be saved must themselves have an interest in the crucified One." —*Manuscript Releases,* vol. 18, 73.

"The Lord our Redeemer had not yet demonstrated fully that love to its completeness. After His condemnation in the judgment hall, His crucifixion on the cross, when He cried out in a clear, loud voice, 'It is finished,' that love stands forth as an exhibition of a new love—'as I have loved you'—is demonstrated. Can the human mind take this in? Can we obey the commandment given?" —*Manuscript Releases,* vol. 16, 190.

- **That His death would atone and "pay" for our sins.**

"Christ died because there was no other hope for the transgressor. He might try to keep God's law in the future; but the debt which he had incurred in the past remained, and the law must condemn him to death. Christ came to pay that debt for the sinner which it was impossible for him to pay for himself. Thus, through the atoning sacrifice of Christ, sinful man was granted another trial." —*Faith and Works,* 30.

"Such is the value of men for whom Christ died that the Father is satisfied with the infinite price which He pays for the salvation of man in yielding up His own Son to die for their redemption. What wisdom, mercy, and love in its fullness are here manifested! The worth of man is known only by going to Calvary. In the mystery of the cross of Christ we can place an estimate upon man." —*Amazing Grace,* 175.

- **That His life may be lived in us.**

"It is your privilege to become meek and lowly in heart; then angels of God will co-operate with efforts. Christ died that His life might be lived in you, and in all who make Him their example. In the strength of your Redeemer you can reveal the character of Christ, and you can work in wisdom and in power to make the crooked places straight." —*Gospel Workers,* 164.

"As a divine Saviour, Jesus died for us that we might live His life of purity, truth, and righteousness. He teaches us how to live. Our prayer should be, 'Create in me a clean heart, O God; and renew a right spirit within me.'" —*Manuscript* Releases, vol. 18, 277.

- **That the moral image of God should be restored.**

"All heaven is interested in the restoration of the moral image of God in man. All heaven is working to this end. God and the holy angels have an intense desire that human beings shall reach the standard of perfection which Christ died to make it possible for them to reach." —*In Heavenly Places,* 286.

"Christ died that the moral image of God might be restored in humanity, that men and women might be partakers of the divine nature, having escaped the corruption that is in the world through lust. We are to use no power of our being for selfish gratification; for all our powers belong to Him, and are to be used to His glory." —*Reflecting Christ*, 165.

"Christ has died that the moral image of God might be restored in our souls and might be reflected to those around us." —*Faith and Works*, 61.

- **That we could reach our personal potential.**

"But men have been satisfied with small attainments. They have not sought with all their might to rise in mental, moral, and physical capabilities. They have not felt that God required this of them, they have not realized that Christ died that they might do this very work. As the result they are far behind what they might be in intelligence and in the ability to think and plan." —*Testimonies*, vol. 5, 554.

"By the sacrifice of Christ every provision has been made for believers to receive all things that pertain to life and godliness. God calls upon us to reach the highest standard of glory and virtue. The perfection of Christ's character makes it possible for us to gain perfection." —*Manuscript Releases*, vol. 14, 351.

- **That we may see the sinfulness of sin.**

"He died that you might be led to see the sinfulness of sin and come unto Him that you might have life." —*Manuscript Releases*, vol. 17, 49.

- **That He might reclaim the kingdom that Satan has claimed since Eden.**

"It was to make an inroad on the territory of Satan, and dispute his usurped authority, and reclaim the kingdom unto Himself, that Christ died. With the shout of a monarch who has clothed himself with zeal as a cloak, will He fight His antagonist, the prince of darkness, and win back the kingdom Satan claims as his own rightful dominion." —*Manuscript Releases*, vol. 18, 54.

- **That He might save sinners from their sins.**

"Christ died to save sinners, not in their sins, but from their sins (Matthew 1:21)." —*Manuscript Releases*, vol. 19, 182.

APPENDIX K:
FAITH, THE WORD THAT DECIDES EVERYTHING

T he fundamental misunderstanding of faith is perhaps the core reason for the multiplicity of Christian churches because misunderstanding faith has created wide variances in the interpretation of almost every biblical doctrine.

Revelation 14:12 describes God's loyalists in the endtime as those "who keep the commandments of God and the faith of Jesus." Hebrews 11:6 challenges us all that "without faith it is impossible to please [God]." Faith is surely a word that decides everything.

Part of the confusion over the meaning of faith (English readers) is that we don't have a verb form for "faith." We do for most nouns, such as the swimmer swims, the hunter hunts, or the runner runs. But it is awkward to say, the faithful person faiths! In the Greek, the language of the New Testament, we have no problem! The noun is *pistis* and the verb, *pisteuin.* Unfortunately, at least in the King James Version, *pistis* becomes "faith" and *pisteuin* to "believe." The same awkwardness happened to *fides* and *credere* in Latin and *foi* and *croire* in French. Why this strange disconnect between noun and verb? This all happened because translators thought of faith as primarily a mental act.

PROBLEM SUBSTITUTING BELIEF FOR FAITH

When one recites John 3:16 in English, for example, the core disconnect is obvious and has led many into a very limited gospel: "For God so loved the world that He gave His only begotten Son that whoever believes in Him should not perish but have everlasting life." The verb "believes" should be translated "have faith" That goes for about every instance where "believe" is noted in the New Testament when it refers to a person's response to God. To miss this point is to misunderstand dozens of texts such as Hebrews 3:19: "So we see that they [the Israelites] could not enter in because of unbelief." "Unbelief" should have been translated, "lack of faith," a totally different direction of thinking.

In general, faith describes the mental process by which we believe something on the basis of evidence or authority. We place value on that evidence and act accordingly. Its value or worth depends upon the quality of person or concept that evokes conviction and commitment. It follows then that faith in error will not produce the fruit of truth no matter how sincere a person may be! That is why Ellen White wrote: "Faith is the medium through which truth or error finds a lodging place in the mind. It is by the same act of mind that truth or error is received, but it makes a decided difference whether we believe the Word of God or the sayings of men."[1242]

Biblical faith is unique and specific. It describes the person we choose to believe, trust, and obey—and that person is God. This principle is vital—the object of faith determines its value. Therefore, it is very important that what or whom we have faith in is really the truth and worth our confidence!

Biblical faith involves the intellect, the will, and commitment. But it is none of these in themselves. Biblical faith is simply the man or woman saying, "yes" to whatever God has said and wherever He wants to lead. Why? Because men and women of faith know that God is worth believing, worth trusting, worth obeying. Further, they have learned assurance by personally believing, trusting, and obeying God.[1243]

[1242] *Selected Messages,* bk. 1, 346.
[1243] *The Ministry of Healing,* 461.

FAITH IS A HAPPENING FAR MORE THAN BELIEVING

Such faith transforms men and women. It is more than an intellectual experience, more than an emotional high and warm, fuzzy feelings. Faith is more than believing—it is a happening. A new power, a new principle of action, takes over a person's life.[1244] Faith joins the head and heart; it is "inseparable from repentance and transformation of character. To have faith means to find and accept the gospel treasure, with all the obligations which it imposes."[1245]

Now we can easily see why faith is the only condition for salvation. It drives Paul's classic formula of salvation: "For by grace you have been saved through faith" (Ephesians 2:8) But because faith has been misunderstood since the 1st century A.D., we can better understand why Catholics, Lutherans, Calvinists, and Methodists have a difficult time explaining this text to each other.

Paul is telling us that salvation is not by grace alone or faith alone. Salvation is not all God's work nor is it all man's. The ellipse of salvation-truth with its two foci—grace and faith—must not be manhandled to fit someone's notion of salvation. To make the ellipse of salvation-truth into two circles, overemphasizing one focus or the other, destroys the truth. We would have "another gospel."

Paul is simply saying that faith is the condition that makes salvation possible. Faith is not the cause—grace is. Although faith does not possess merit in itself, the absence of faith frustrates grace. Grace is whatever God has done, is doing, and will do for men and women. Our human minds cannot fathom what it all means. But in God's great plan to restore everything damaged by sin, God looks for our response to His grace. Faith is our grateful response to God's grace.

Paul understood this grace-faith ellipse. His writings show the danger of making two circles out of the ellipse. But the history of the Christian church shows that Paul's counsel was misinterpreted. Two groups arose, each one emphasizing one side of the ellipse at the expense of the other. We call them either antinomians (God's grace trumps God's law) or legalists who believe that even worthy acts in some way either earn God's love and approval or helps to secure the assurance of salvation.

BONHOEFFER SAW THE PROBLEM

Dietrich Bonhoeffer spoke out plainly against these two perennial theological errors that exist whenever Christians misunderstand grace and faith: "The truth is that so long as we hold both sides of the proposition together they contain nothing inconsistent with the right belief, but as soon as one is divorced from the other, it is bound to prove a stumbling block. 'Only those who believe [have faith] obey' is what we say to that part of a believer's soul which obeys, and 'only those who obey believe [have faith]' is what we say to that part of the soul of the obedience which believes. If the first half of the proposition stands alone, the believer is exposed to the dangers of cheap grace, which is another word for damnation. If the second half stands alone, the believer is exposed to the danger of salvation through works, which is also another word for damnation"[1246]

[1244] *Christ's Object Lessons*, 24, 96–98.
[1245] *Ibid.*, 113.
[1246] *The Cost of Discipleship* (New York: The Macmillan Company, 1963, paperback), 74.

In many ways biblical writers recognized the ellipse of salvation-truth. Paul said it clearly: "Let us then with confidence draw near to the throne of grace, that we may receive mercy and find grace to help in time of need" (Hebrews 4:16). And John: "If we confess our sins, He is faithful and just to forgive us our sins and to cleanse us from all unrighteousness" (1 John 1:9).

In other words, grace comes with two hands providing pardon (mercy) and power. Faith extends its empty hands and gets exactly what it needs, the grace of forgiveness, on one hand, and the grace to empower the life to overcome hereditary and cultivated tendencies to sin, on the other. We are not describing two kinds of faith any more than two sides of a sheet of paper become two separate pieces.

This is why faith embraces all that a responsible person does in responding to God's grace. God gave all created beings the freedom of choice. All created beings are free to respond to His biddings or to go off listening to a different drummer. A responsible person is "able to respond," never unresponsible. Irresponsible yes, but that is a human choice, the downside of "faith."

After saying all this, we must emphasize that faith is not an end in itself. It is not only a passive response to God's grace. Paul was clear: "Faith working through love" (Galatians 5:6). The end of all God's plans for us is that we change our self-centered lives in every respect and become truly loving; to Him and everyone else we meet daily. Faith is the path, spontaneous love is the goal.

Understanding the meaning of faith and its goal helps us to sort out the deep crevices between various church groups. The Great Controversy keeps the ellipse of salvation-truth in the core of every theological discussion. God, who has watched the seeds of sin bearing bitter fruit, does not play word games with men and women. The issue has always been from the beginning— faith or rebellion, obedience or disobedience, love or self-centeredness. Thus, every key biblical word must be understood in the light of the purpose of the gospel.

For instance, note how "forgiveness" takes on a larger meaning when considered from the standpoint of the Great Controversy: "Forgiveness has a broader meaning than many suppose. ... God's forgiveness is not merely a judicial act by which He sets us free from condemnation. It is not only forgiveness for sin, but reclaiming from sin. It is the outflow of redeeming love that transforms the heart. David had the true conception of forgiveness when he prayed, 'Create in me a clean heart, O God; and renew a right spirit within me.'"[1247] (Psalm 51:10.)

PARDON INCLUDES RENEWAL

Also, "To be pardoned in the way that Christ pardons, is not only to be forgiven, but to be renewed in the spirit of our mind. The Lord says, 'A new heart will I give unto thee.' ... Without the transforming process which can come alone through divine power, the original propensities to sin are left in the heart in all their strength, to forge new chains, to impose a slavery that can never be broken by human power. But men can never enter heaven with their old tastes, inclinations, idols, ideas, and theories. Heaven would be no place of joy to them; for everything would be in

---

[1247] *Thoughts From the Mount of Blessing*, 114.

collision with their tastes, appetites, and inclinations, and painfully opposed to their natural and cultivated traits of character."[1248]

All this highlights the reasons why Jesus came to earth (See Appendixes I and J). For example, "God loved the world so dearly that He gave His only-begotten Son that whosoever would accept Him might have power to live His righteous life. Christ proved that it is possible for man to lay hold by faith on the power of God. He showed that the sinner, by repentance and the exercise of faith in the righteousness of Christ, can be reconciled to God, and become a partaker of the divine nature, overcoming the corruption that is in the world through lust.[1249]

Does all this add to the urgency of those living in the endtimes? Without doubt! We have looked earlier at Revelation 14:12 where John describes God's loyalists in the endtime—they have learned how to endure tough times (KJV, NKJV, "patience," but "endurance" more accurate), they have found that the "faith of Jesus" makes commandment keeping a joy and a privilege. The faith of Jesus is the mirror side of commandment keeping. How could one divide our Lord's faith and His commandment keeping? And that is the purpose of the gospel—"The gospel of Christ is the law exemplified in character."[1250]

God is waiting for men and women of faith, the ripening of His gospel harvest. When this growing harvest becomes truly ripe, then "He who sat on the cloud thrust in His sickle on the earth, and the earth was reaped" (Revelation 14:14–16). These fully developed men and women know through experience "the faith that works by love and purifies the soul from every stain of sin."[1251]

THE HARVEST OF FAITH

This harvest of faith will silence all those who depreciated or ignored God's commandments. They will shut Satan's mouth that has smothered Planet Earth with his lies that God has been unfair to expect obedience from freedom-loving people. Lies that said commandment keeping was unnecessary because Jesus kept the law for us. Lies that God will look at Christ's perfect life only and not ours in the judgment. Lies that said that any attempt to live out a commandment-keeping life was attempting to add to Christ's complete atonement on the cross and that was pure righteousness by works and sheer legalism.

Those who fulfill Revelation 14:12 will *silence all these lies.* Not a rebel among them! The proof will be recognized by the angels and inhabitants of unfallen worlds. And Satan himself will bow before Jesus, his formidable opponent in the Great Controversy, and join those who "confess that Jesus Christ is Lord, to the glory of God the Father" (Philippians 2:11).

[1248] *Review and Herald,* August 19, 1890.

[1249] *Selected Messages,* bk. 1, 223.

[1250] *Maranatha,* 18.

[1251] *Review and Herald,* June 10, 1890.

APPENDIX L:
THE ELLIPSE OF TRUTH

A n ellipse is a stretched-out circle. A football gives us the idea. A circle has one center or focus; an ellipse has two foci—perfectly separated so that if one focus is pushed too far from the other, the perfect ellipse no longer exists. Further, if one emphasizes one focus above the other, the ellipse becomes two circles.

Example: We get water because of the ellipse principle. Water does not exist unless the circles of hydrogen and oxygen are reformed into an ellipse. If one should ask, which is more important, hydrogen or oxygen, the answer would be, "Both are equally important if you want a glass of water."

Truth is like that! Truth in any area of thought, whether in theology, philosophy, law, music, or education, must be understood in the form of an ellipse rather than a circle. Remember, an ellipse has two foci and a circle has one.

In politics, we see the two foci as socialism (collectivism, communism) and democracy. In economics, the foci are Keynesian (government control) and free trade (capitalism). In education, content-centered versus student-centered. In epistemology, idealism versus naturalism. The truth is, each side of the ellipse has something helpful to say about the subject.

In theology, truth is the sum total of its objective and subjective elements: One focus is the emphasis on transcendence (revelation) and the other is immanence (human response, such as reason and feeling). For those on the objective side, to ignore or underemphasize the subjective elements would be to make two opposing circles out of the integrity of the ellipse. And vice versa. The problem in Christianity since the first century has been the bifurcating of the ellipse of truth into two circles with each circle continuing to battle its limited understanding of truth.

BIBLICAL TRUTH UNDERSTOOD BY THE ELLIPSE OF TRUTH

But biblical truth, as understood within the Great Controversy Theme, unites the two circles within the ellipse of salvation. Thus revelation (the authority of God's Word) meets our human need (for meaning and relevance). This interaction of the objective, external Word meets the subjective response of a person saying, "This truth is for me."[1252]

In other words, when someone appeals to the Bible as the "truth" without an equal emphasis on personal meaning and relevance, we know that the ellipse has

---

[1252] Edwin Gaustad wrote: "Religion that the head finds wholly agreeable the heart finds emotionally sterile. Western religion, having over many generations accommodated itself to scholasticism, to the Enlightenment, to the demands of the scientific method, and to the positivistic temper, has won an intellectual respectability—and little else. In rejecting all that, the cult land occult fanciers have turned hungrily to other kind of religion—to the Jack Kerouacs, then the Alan Wattses and the Allen Ginsbergs, still later to the tantras, the sutras, the *I Ching*, to all the eroticism and mysticism and immaterialism of the Orient. A world view that had not made a long series of concessions to modern technology and profane secularity proved to be, not repugnant to the emancipated young, but alluring and even nourishing." —*Dissent in American Religion* (Chicago: The University of Chicago Press, 1973), 146.

become two circles—and truth has been compromised. On the other hand, when one appeals primarily to reason or feeling as the test of truth (human autonomy), we also know that the ellipse has now become two circles at war with each other.

Salvation truth binds together the objective will of God and the subjective "yes" of a responsible (response-able) person. Even as water cannot be divided between hydrogen and oxygen and remain water, so the objective and subjective elements of salvation cannot be divided and yet remain "salvation." No one bothers to ask which side of the ellipse is more important!

For example, grace fulfills its task only when men and women of faith respond. Likewise, pardon/forgiveness comes only to those who comply with its conditions such as a sincere desire for divine power to overcome the evil for which pardon is sought—thus grace is offered as both pardon and power.

HERESIES

When one of the foci in the ellipse of salvation-truth becomes a "circle of truth," we surely have partial truth, a heresy. For example:

- An overemphasis on objective justification leads to human passivity, with faith becoming primarily a matter of mental assent to revelation. This often leads to a *careless* use of such phrases as "Jesus paid it all." Or "the atonement was completed on the cross."

- An overemphasis on subjective sanctification leads to warm feelings, or reason, or good works as the test of faith. This often leads a person to *minimize* the primary authority of God and to make predominant such words as, "It's not truth for me unless I feel it, or until it makes sense to me." Or people may place primary weight on visual "evidence" such as faith-healers, glossalalia (speaking in tongues), charismatic speakers, hugging, or laughing in religious meetings. Or on the quiet satisfaction that they have dutifully "kept" the commandments.

- An overemphasis on objective justification tends to make imputed righteousness the most important element in salvation.

- An overemphasis on subjective sanctification (imparted righteousness) tends to make human performance the basis of salvation.

- An overemphasis on Christ's ministry on the Cross tends to eclipse the essential importance of Christ as our all-powerful Mediator/High Priest and/or to minimize the essential work of the Holy Spirit.

- Those who overemphasize free grace tend to seek assurance in the security of legal adjustments in heavenly books without a corresponding adjustment in the penitent's life; genuine repentance becomes mere confession. On the other hand, many who do not place proper emphasis on grace tend to seek their assurance in legalistic behavior. Neither group sees the larger picture of a gracious, forgiving Lord who extends His personal power to the penitent so that the sin that needed forgiveness can be overcome.

To sum up, to espouse and emphasize only one focal point in the ellipse is to distort truth. Even though each focus in the ellipse emphasizes truth worth dying for, arguments will never end until a person accepts the total picture of the truths emphasized in both foci. This understanding of truth is as inescapable as the joining of hydrogen and oxygen to make water.

FOG OF MISCOMMUNICATION

In practice, those who intensely defend one focus of the ellipse tend to not see the truth in what they are denying, which only increases the fog of miscommunication. This standoff often leads to each side denying the integrity of the other. Only with the ellipse of salvation-truth can an observer note that both sides are right in what they affirm but wrong in what they deny.

The writings of Ellen White transcend the contending circles of Methodists (human responsibility) and Presbyterians (God's sovereignty), for example, by seeing truth as the embracing ellipse rather than a tug of paradoxes and constant tensions. In hundreds of instances, she employs the ellipse of salvation-truth without using the phrase such as: "To talk of Christ without the Word leads to sentimentalism. And to receive the theory of the Word without accepting and appreciating its Authors makes men legal formalists. But Christ and His precious Word are in perfect harmony."[1253]

Ellen White saw clearly the ellipse of salvation truth:

> "The progress of reform depends upon a clear recognition of fundamental truth. While, on the one hand, danger lurks in a narrow philosophy and a hard, cold orthodoxy, on the other hand there is great danger in a careless liberalism. The foundation of all enduring reform is the law of God. We are to present in clear, distinct lines the need of obeying this law. Its principles must be kept before the people. They are as everlasting and inexorable as God Himself.

> "One of the most deplorable effects of the original apostasy was the loss of man's power of self-control. Only as this power is regained can there be real progress."

> "The body is the only medium through which the mind and the soul are developed for the upbuilding of character. Hence it is that the adversary of souls directs his temptations to the enfeebling and degrading of the physical powers. His success here means the surrender to evil of the whole being. The tendencies of our physical nature, unless under the dominion of a higher power, will surely work ruin and death.

> "The body is to be brought into subjection. The higher powers of the being are to rule. The passions are to be controlled by the will, which is itself to be under the control of God. The kingly power of reason, sanctified by divine grace, is to bear sway in our lives."[1254]

[1253] *Manuscript Releases*, vol. 20, 308.
[1254] *The Ministry of Healing*, 129, 130.

Note the clear relationship between the objective/subjective nature of God dealing with men and women; law/responsive will and reason; and grace/responsive will and reason. Note also what happens to truth when either side of the ellipse is emphasized at the expense of the other: cold orthodoxy/careless liberalism.

The goal of the Great Controversy cannot be achieved unless the ellipse of salvation-truth is understood, revealing how God and men and women work together in restoring men and women to be reflections of their Maker.

APPENDIX M:
RECOVERING TRUTHS HIDDEN FOR AGES

The Great Controversy Theme implicitly challenges those in the endtime who want to embrace all the truths that the New Testament teaches. In view of the clash and counterpunches of doctrinal controversies from the first century onward, it seems obvious that we should look at what has happened to Paul's mandate to Timothy: "Hold fast the pattern of sound words which you have heard from me, in faith and love which are in Christ Jesus. That good thing which was committed to you, keep by the Holy Spirit who dwells in us. ... And the things that you have heard from me among many witnesses, commit these to faithful men who will be able to teach others also" (2 Timothy 1:13, 14; 2:2). In Paul's second letter to the Thessalonians, he foretold that the church would experience a "falling away" (lit. "apostasy") that would cloud truth in the days ahead (2:3).

Let's examine some of the ways we can dissect what Paul may have been talking about relative to biblical doctrines that had been compromised and what we ought to do about these compromises and errors that are still fastened to the tree of truth today:

FALSE DOCTRINES BECOME "FLOATING GERMS" AND "PARASITES"

"Satan has wrought with deceiving power, bringing in a multiplicity of errors that obscure the truth. Error cannot stand alone, and would soon become extinct if it did not fasten itself like a parasite upon the tree of truth. Error draws its life from the truth of God. The traditions of men, like floating germs, attach themselves to the truth of God, and men regard them as a part of the truth. Through false doctrines, Satan gains a foothold, and captivates the minds of men, causing them to hold theories that have no foundation in truth. Men boldly teach for doctrines the commandments of men; and as traditions pass on, from age to age, they acquire a power over human mind. But age does not make error truth, neither does its burdensome weight cause the plant of truth to become a parasite. The tree of truth bears its own genuine fruit, showing its true origin and nature. The parasite of error also bears its own fruit, and makes manifest that its character is diverse from the plant of heavenly origin."[1255]

[1255] *Evangelism*, 589.

GREAT TRUTHS HAVE LAIN UNHEEDED

"Great truths that have lain unheeded and unseen since the day of Pentecost, are to shine from God's word in their native purity. To those who truly love God the Holy Spirit will reveal truths that have faded from the mind, and will also reveal truths that are entirely new. Those who eat the flesh and drink the blood of the Son of God will bring from the books of Daniel and Revelation truth that is inspired by the Holy Spirit. They will start into action forces that cannot be repressed."[1256]

OLD TRUTHS, LONG HIDDEN UNDER RUBBISH
OF ERROR, WILL BE RECOVERED

"These are God's agencies for communicating the knowledge of truth to the world. If through the grace of Christ his people will become new bottles, he will fill them with the new wine. God will give additional light, and old truths will be recovered, and replaced in the framework of truth; and wherever the laborers go, they will triumph. As Christ's ambassadors, they are to search the Scriptures, to seek for the truths that have been hidden beneath the rubbish of error. And every ray of light received is to be communicated to others. One interest will prevail, one subject will swallow up every other, 'Christ our righteousness.'"[1257]

IN THE ENDTIME, THE LIGHT OF TRUTH WILL EXPOSE
SYSTEMS OF ERROR SO LONG IN SUPREMACY

"As the end approaches, the testimonies of God's servants will become more decided and more powerful, flashing the light of truth upon the systems of error and oppression that have so long held the supremacy. The Lord has sent us messages for this time to establish Christianity upon an eternal basis, and all who believe present truth must stand, not in their own wisdom, but in God; and raise up the foundation of many generations. These will be registered in the books of heaven as repairers of the breach, the restorers of paths to dwell in. We are to maintain the truth because it is truth, in the face of the bitterest opposition."[1258]

GEMS OF TRUTH WILL BE SEPARATED FROM ERROR

"Gems of thought are to be gathered up and redeemed from their companionship with error; for by their misplacement in the association of error, the Author of truth has been dishonored. The precious gems of the righteousness of Christ, and truths of divine origin, are to be carefully searched out and placed in their proper setting, to shine with heavenly brilliancy amid the moral darkness of the world. Let the bright jewels of truth which God gave to man, to adorn and exalt his name, be carefully rescued from the rubbish of error, where they have been claimed by those who have been transgressors of the law, and have served the purposes of the great deceiver on account of their connection with error.

"Let the gems of divine light be reset in the framework of the gospel. Let nothing be lost of the precious light that comes from the throne of God. It has been misapplied, and cast aside as worthless; but it is heaven-sent, and each gem is to become the property of God's people and find its true position in the framework of

---

[1256] *Fundamentals of Christian Education*, 473.
[1257] *Review and Herald*, December 23, 1890.
[1258] Selected Messages, bk. 3, 407.

truth. Precious jewels of light are to be collected, and by the aid of the Holy Spirit they are to be fitted into the gospel system. God has poured his Spirit upon his servants, and qualified them to use their ability and talent in revealing truth to those who sit in darkness; but the very ability God has given by which to reveal truth to others, men, perverting their talents, employ to deceive; for they use their gifts as did Satan when he deceived the angels of heaven, and exalt self, causing their God-given abilities to administer to their own glory.

"These become confused by error, their minds are darkened by the enemy, and the truths which God imparted to them are buried by them in a mass of error, or basely perverted to serve the cause of evil. But these heaven-given rays of light are not to be lost to the world. These truths are to be as a lamp unto our feet, and as a light unto our path. It is these gems that will give attractiveness to the gospel plan, and they are to shine as stars amid the moral darkness of the world."[1259]

GOSPEL PLAN NOT YET FULLY UNDERSTOOD

"The great plan of human redemption is as yet but faintly understood, because men do not place themselves in the divine channel of light. There is too much following of men, and limiting the light by men's opinions and traditions. The wonderful truth of God is to be sought out by every mind, and the results of many minds are to be brought together from many sources as God's hereditary trust, and the divine power will work in such a way that true harmony will exist. In the revelation of Christ to the world the necessity of men will be met, and the work of God will move forward with beautiful harmony, as truth is disclosed to the world. Through careful study, through prayerful meditation, men will be enabled to place the truth before men in simplicity, so that the humblest minds can comprehend it, can receive it, and become elevated through its sanctifying influence, if they will but appropriate it, and practice its principles in their daily lives."[1260]

"Through all ages God has spoken and worked by human instrumentalities. God has given to men their faculties, and he expects them to use them and by use to improve their abilities. They are to employ these faculties in rescuing truth from the rubbish of error where it has been made to serve the cause of the great adversary. The gems of truth are imperishable, and the Lord would have them gathered up and placed in their proper relation, that they may embellish and adorn the doctrine of Christ our Saviour."[1261]

MORE LIGHT YET TO SHINE YET IT IS OLD LIGHT

"The question has been asked me, 'Do you think that the Lord has any more light for us as a people?' I answer that He has light that is new to us, and yet it is precious old light that is to shine forth from the Word of truth. We have only the glimmerings of the rays of the light that is yet to come to us. We are not making the most of the light which the Lord has already given us, and thus we fail to receive the increased light; we do not walk in light already shed upon us."[1262]

[1259] *Review and Herald*, October 23, 1894.
[1260] *Ibid.*
[1261] *Ibid.*
[1262] *Selected Messages*, bk. 1, 401.

"Although great and talented authors have made known wonderful truths, and have presented increased light to the people, still in our day we shall find new ideas, and ample fields in which to work, for the theme of salvation is inexhaustible. The work has gone forward from century to century, setting forth the life and character of Christ, and the love of God as manifested in the atoning sacrifice. The theme of redemption will employ the minds of the redeemed through all eternity. There will be new and rich developments made manifest in the plan of salvation throughout eternal ages."[1263]

FAITHFUL REFORMERS MADE MISTAKES; NOT OUR CRITERION EXCEPT AS MODELS OF STRENGTH

"As we read of Luther, Knox, and other noted Reformers, we admire the strength, fortitude, and courage possessed by these faithful servants of God, and we would catch the spirit that animated them. We desire to know from what source they were out of weakness made strong. Although these great men were used as instruments for God, they were not faultless. They were erring men, and made great mistakes. We should seek to imitate their virtues, but we should not make them our criterion. These men possessed rare talents to carry forward the work of the Reformation. They were moved upon by a power above themselves; but it was not the men, the instruments that God used, that should be exalted and honored, but the Lord Jesus who let His light and power come upon them. Let those who love truth and righteousness, who gather up the hereditary trusts given to these standard-bearers, praise God, the Source of all light."[1264]

APPENDIX N:
THE TWO COVENANTS

The controversy over the two covenants has troubled the Christian Church since the first century. The difference between the two covenants was first seen in the story of Cain and Abel. Cain brought his own offerings rather than listen carefully to the Lord. Abel listened to God, who had showed them a better way to signify their total reliance on the animal sacrifice that represented the death of a Savior. The difference between trusting God implicitly and serving Him in some other more convenient way is the difference between the new and the old covenant.

The primary focus on Paul's thoughts on the covenants is found in Galatians 4:21–31. For an illustration, Paul compared Abraham's two wives, Sarah and Hagar. Hagar's son, Ishmael, was a product of Abraham working out his way of serving God; Sarah's son, Isaac, was the son of promise, God's promise. Paul said that we have here two examples of how men and women follow God's leading: 1) By trusting in God's promises, not our own works; 2) By trusting in our own works to please God. Ever since, men and women have chosen between listening to God's

---

[1263] *Ibid.*, 403.
[1264] *Ibid.*, 402.

promises and acting accordingly or responding with their own promises to please God, promises that are as "ropes of sand."[1265]

The new (or everlasting) covenant was expressed anew in the seven promises that God spoke to Abraham in Genesis 12:1–3. Paul made clear that nothing can be "added" to that Covenant for God had ratified it (Genesis 15:7–17; Galatians 3:15–19). God asked no return promises from Abraham; his part was to believe God's promises. That is, have faith in God's promises. But after receiving these seven promises, Abraham stumbled into the future and into Old Covenant thinking. He listened to Sarah's unbelief and took Hagar as a second wife in order to get a baby boy, thus "helping" to fulfill God's promise of a host of descendants. God tested Abraham again on Mount Moriah when He asked for Abraham to slay Isaac, his true bloodline. Abraham did not stagger under this command this time— he had learned how to trust.

Ellen White recognized that "as the Bible presents two laws, one changeless and eternal, the other provisional and temporary, so there are two covenants."[1266] The first was made in Eden (Genesis 3:15), the "covenant of grace" which "offered pardon, and the assisting grace of God for future obedience through faith in Christ."[1267] "This same covenant was renewed to Abraham" (Genesis 22:18); Abraham's faith in God's promises and his obedience to the authority of God's law (Genesis. 26:5, 17:7) "accounted it to him for righteousness" (Genesis 15:6; Galatians. 3:6). This Edenic-Abrahamic covenant was called the *new* covenant in the New Testament because "it could not be ratified until the death of Christ"; that is, "sealed after the blood of the [old] covenant."[1268]

WHY ANOTHER COVENANT AT SINAI

In answer to the question, "Why was another [old] covenant formed at Sinai?" Ellen White noted that the Israelites, after their Egyptian bondage, "had to a great extent lost the knowledge of God and of the principles of the Abrahamic covenant."[1269] They "had no true conception of the holiness of God, of the exceeding sinfulness of their own hearts, their utter inability, in themselves, to render obedience to God's law, and their need of a Saviour. All this they must be taught."[1270]

Before giving the Ten Commandments at Sinai, God promised Moses and Israel: "Now therefore, if you will indeed obey [Lit: listen carefully to] My voice and keep my covenant, then you shall be a special treasure to Me above all people; for all the earth is Mine" (Exodus 19:5). But "the people did not realize the sinfulness of their own hearts, and that without Christ it was impossible for them to keep God's law." Not realizing their inability to keep God's law, "they readily entered into covenant with God" declaring, 'All that the Lord has said we will do, and be obedient.'"[1271] This impulsive covenant is now known as the "old" covenant.

[1265] *Steps to Christ*, 47.
[1266] *Patriarchs and Prophets*, 370.
[1267] *Ibid.*
[1268] *Ibid.*, 371.
[1269] *Ibid.*
[1270] *Ibid.*
[1271] *Ibid.*, 372; Exodus 24:7.

However, after a few weeks, "they broke their covenant with God, and bowed down to worship a graven image. They could not hope for the favor of God through a covenant that they had broken; and now, seeing their sinfulness and their need of pardon, they were brought to feel their need of the Saviour revealed in the Abrahamic covenant and shadowed forth in the sacrificial offerings. Now by faith and love they were bound to God as their deliverer from the bondage of sin. Now they were prepared to appreciate the blessings of the new covenant."[1272]

CONTRAST BOTH COVENANTS

Ellen White clearly contrasted both covenants: "The terms of the 'old covenant' were, Obey and live. ... The 'new covenant' was established upon 'better promises'—the promise of forgiveness of sins and of the grace of God to renew the heart and bring it into harmony with the principles of God's law. 'This shall be the covenant that I will make with the house of Israel; After those days, saith the Lord, I will put my law in their inward parts, and write it in their hearts. ... I will forgive their iniquity, and will remember their sin no more'" (Jeremiah 31:33, 34).[1273]

Thus, the difference between the two covenants is not time duration but to different religious experiences. The so-called new covenant, the Edenic covenant and Abrahamic covenants are the same; they describe God's promises of pardon and power to those who trust Him in faith to perform His promises. Echoing the concept that E. J. Waggoner presented in 1888, Ellen White emphasized that the *old* covenant describes the experience of those who do not understand that the *everlasting* covenant "is simply an arrangement for bringing men again into harmony with the divine will, placing them where they could obey God's laws."[1274] Thus, the *old* covenant does not describe a time period, from Sinai to the Cross, but an attitude that reflects reliance on external obedience to law without the heart's transformation that produces "the fruits of the Spirit."[1275] Thus, the experiences of the *new* and the *old* covenants are like parallel tracks (experiences) running from Abel and Cain to the Second Advent.

The "Sinaitic" law is the same law "written by the Holy Spirit upon the tables of the heart" (Jeremiah 31:33, 34). The same provisions of the Edenic and Abrahamic covenants—the *new* covenant—apply today: the gospel precedes obedience. Accepting Jesus as our Savior, "His blood atones for our sins, His obedience is accepted for us [not instead of], then the heart is renewed by the Holy Spirit. ... Through the grace of Christ we shall live in obedience to the law of God written upon our hearts."[1276]

[1272] *Ibid.*
[1273] *Ibid.*
[1274] *Ibid.*, 371.
[1275] *Ibid.*, 372.
[1276] *Ibid.*

APPENDIX O:
THE GREAT CONTROVERSY
IN THE TEACHINGS OF JESUS

Anyone reading the words of Jesus in the four Gospels should be impressed with His blazing forthrightness regarding the Great Controversy that has affected the whole universe. On many occasions he pointed his finger at the cosmic forces that interfaced on a daily basis with Him as well as His contemporaries.

He explained the forces behind the scenes when sin, suffering and death stared men and women in the face. A personal devil and his crew of subordinate devils were intent on creating confusion and strife, whether it be in storms, sicknesses, or evil surmisings.

JESUS NAILED SATAN

Jesus boldly declared that God was not the author of sin, suffering or death—"an enemy has done this" (Matthew 13:28). "The fall of our first parents, with all the woe that has resulted, [Satan] charges upon the Creator, leading men to look upon God as the author of sin, and suffering, and death. Jesus was to unveil this deception."[1277] Jesus nailed Satan for what he was and is: "He [Satan] was a murderer from the beginning and does not stand in the truth. ... He is a liar and the father of it" (John 8:44).

Jesus faced up to Satan shortly after His baptism in the Jordan. For 40 days, Satan used every deceptive wile in his playbook to encourage Jesus to compromise His mission on earth. After more than a month, Jesus said to him, "Away with you, Satan!" (Matthew 4:10).

Satan was no philosophical concept. He was a very real person who has only one aim—to destroy the kingdom of God. Jesus was not play-acting when He faced the devil as if Satan were merely a mythological notion. It was always a contest between light and darkness on a very personal level (John's favorite metaphor).

Jesus and His apostles conceded that Satan was the "god of this world" (2 Corinthians 4:4; see Ephesians 2:2). Jesus did not dispute this claim (Matthew 4:9). But Jesus did let Satan know that He came to set up a beachhead in the devil's kingdom. Further, Jesus warned Satan that the day would come when Christ's followers would be the secret underground, if need be, but preparing for the day when the Evil Empire would be no more!

Throughout Christ's ministry, it was kingdom against kingdom! Jesus made this clear to Pilate: "My kingdom is not of this world" (John 18:36). At the same time, Jesus announced that His kingdom was invading Satan's kingdom—D-Day had arrived: "The time is fulfilled, and the kingdom of God is at hand!" (Mark 1:15).

PARABLES NAILED SATAN'S INTERVENTIONS

We could trace out His kingdom's attack on Satan's kingdom by observing Jesus commanding the devils to leave possessed people (Mark 5:1–27;

[1277] *The Desire of Ages,* 24.

Luke 11:21–22; etc.). But for our purposes here, let's take a quick look in a different direction—at some of our Lord's parables.

- *The Sower and Different Types of Soil.* Jesus referred to His parables as "the mysteries of the kingdom of heaven" (Matthew 13:12; see also 13:24, 31, 33, 44, 45, 47). In explaining this parable, He said: "When anyone hears the word of the kingdom, and does not understand it, then the wicked one comes and snatches away what was sown in his heart" (13:19).

- *Wheat and Tares.* When Jesus explained the growth of tares (weeds) He said: "An enemy has done this" (Matthew 13:28). Further, "The enemy who sowed them is the devil, the harvest is the end of the age, and the reapers are the angels" (13:38).

- *Mustard Seed.* Our Lord's message is obvious. His little beachhead into Satan's territory seemed a lost cause in A.D. 31. But the seeds He planted would some day launch a movement that would encircle the earth, against all odds when first planted.

- *Leaven.* Again Jesus pointed out the small beginning of His kingdom's forces (Matthew 13:33). Wherever the leaven of the gospel is given a chance, transformations take place—in the personal life, in the home, in the community, in the church. Satan's kingdom has no defense against the leavening of truth.

- *Hidden Treasure* and *Pearl of Great Price.* Here Jesus looks at the motivation that drives His gospel forces into the field of the enemy. The field of the world is worthless as far as eternity is concerned; the gospel truths (hidden treasure and the pearl) are the highest goals one can seek (Matthew 13:44–46).

- *Dragnet.* Jesus ties all His parables together with his illustration of the fisherman's dragnet (Matthew 13:47–52). Satan's kingdom with his many subjects will exist until the end of the world, resisting madly the march of God's loyalists. But in the end Jesus will have the last word: everybody will be brought to that final moment when inhabitants of the Evil Empire will be separated from God's loyalists—forever.

- *The Narrow Way.* Starkly, Jesus compares the road of the Evil Empire and that of our Lord's loyalists (Luke 13:24). The road to hell is wide, easy, and comfortable with theologies that appeal to the heart rather than the head, to what a person wants, not to what God has made clear.

- *Wedding Garment.* Jesus compares His kingdom to a king who arranges a wedding reception for his son (Matthew 22:1–14). But Jesus warns, His kingdom is not for everybody. Although everyone is invited, only those who are willing to commit themselves to His kingdom's constitution will be allowed in. God, as King, has provided the invitation and whatever the invitee needs to respond. There should be no excuse; all excuses reflect preoccupation with personal desires. The devil wins by inciting rebuff to the King's invitation but in the end, the devil and his followers will be destroyed.

- *Wise and Foolish Virgins.* Here Jesus compares those who profess to be His followers and those who are truly His loyalists (Matthew 25:1–13). Time matters. Judgment day happens sooner than any of us think—especially the sleep of death. In the last days, probationary time will surely end. In this parable, we see the bleak future that awaits those who are more committed to evil principles than to Christlike principles. No matter what excuse the foolish person may use, Jesus will say, "I never knew you for whom you say you are."

When Jesus sent out the first 70 evangelists, He told them that they would be "lambs among wolves" (Luke 10:3). In addition to proclaiming the gospel, they would have power to heal the sick. Their credentials would be: "The kingdom of God has come near to you" (Luke 10: 9, 11). Satan is losing!

When they returned with their bubbling reports, Jesus said: "I saw Satan fall like lightning from heaven" (Luke 10:18). Satan is losing.

Contrary to so much theological and historical misfires, Jesus was more than a great moral teacher or even a creditable defender of human rights that cost Him His life. He didn't appeal to His hearers to view His life and miracles as merely a demonstration of God's mysterious providences. He was God Himself meeting face to face with Satan, the Prince of this world. And He will have the last word as He "grows" His earthly army until the whole universe can say, "Great and marvelous are Your works, Lord God Almighty! Just and true are Your ways" (Revelation 15:3).

APPENDIX P:
COMPARING THE END OF THE WORLD AND NOAH'S FLOOD

In Matthew 24, Jesus gives us a heads-up as to when He will return to this earth: "But as the days of Noah were, so also will the coming of the Son of Man be. For as in the days before the flood, they were eating and drinking, marrying and giving in marriage, until the day that Noah entered the ark, and did not know until the flood came and took them all away, so also will the coming of the Son of Man be" (Matthew 24:37–39).

What comparisons was Jesus referring to?

Peter helps us with our first clue: He said that Noah was a "preacher of righteousness" (2 Peter 2:5). Noah really knew what righteousness by faith was all about. He called on his neighbors to honor their Creator and to stop rebelling. Here is how God described those who refused to listen: "Every intent of the thoughts of his heart was only evil continually" (Genesis 6:5).

Clue #2 tells us what world conditions will be like: They will be "as were the days of Noah" (Matthew 24:37). Noah preached a clear message on righteousness by faith when "the earth was corrupt in God's sight, and ... filled with violence" (Genesis 6:11).

That must have been a horrid time to live when God Himself could no longer take it. But a violent society is not enough to convince people that they are living in the last days. Men and women are not frightened for long by the so-called breakdown of society, as long as the slide is gradual. Satan is smarter than we are. He knows that he can take over anything and anybody, not with a frontal attack but gradually. Think about what you see on television these days compared to only 30 years ago!

What Did They Not Know?

Clue #3: Noah's generation "did not know" (Matthew 24:39). What did they not know? They thought they knew more than Noah did. They "knew," on the basis of anything that could be seen or heard, there was no reason to expect doom. True, the world was a mess, society was in constant upheaval and wars were always breaking out. But what's new? People get used to tension and horror. For Noah's generation, the future never looked brighter; after all, that is what their teachers, religious leaders and scientists were telling them. But they refused to know the truth—the truth about righteousness by faith.

So Clue #4, comparing Noah's day to ours: When the door of probation is shut, on the basis of anything that can be seen or heard, this world will look safe enough to last for generations to come—and Satan will make sure of that!

Peter reminds us that "scoffers will come in the last days, walking according to their own lusts, and saying, 'Where is the promise of His coming? For since the fathers fell asleep, all things continue as they were from the beginning of creation" (2 Peter 3:3–4). Just as with Noah's generation, the last generation will scoff because the future never looked brighter!

Now just to make sure that we are on track, let's listen to the writer that we have learned to trust: "Come when it may, the day of God will come unawares to the ungodly. When life is going on in its varying round; when men are absorbed in pleasure, in business, traffic, in moneymaking; when religious leaders are magnifying the world's progress and enlightenment, and the people are lulled in a false security—then, as the midnight thief steals within the unguarded dwelling, so shall sudden destruction come upon the careless and ungodly, 'and they shall not escape.'"[1278]

Refuse To Know

What are we learning here? Those unprepared for the close of probation will not "know" the truth about transpiring events because *they refuse to know*. They prefer to "know" what best supports their own personal desires and selfish ambitions. We all see what we look for—it's all a matter of presuppositions and prejudices.

How can all this be? Our bookstores are loaded with books about the end of the world. Our supermarket tabloids almost always have a feature story with some fantastic reason why Jesus is soon to come. We can't say that nobody cares about the return of Jesus.

[1278] *The Great Controversy*, 38.

But most of the books on the Second Advent that we see everywhere are focused on the wrong signs. What are the signs that many Christians are looking for these days?

1. The end is near when Israel is restored as a nation.

2. The end is really near when the Israelites rebuild their temple in Jerusalem.

3. The end is near when natural disasters increase.

4. The six thousand years should soon end.

5. Asteroids will hit the earth soon.

6. The Bilderbergers, One-Worlders, the Illuminati, are working with the world's politicians and financial giants to create a world government which will set the stage for the mark of the beast and the emergence of the man 666.

7. Microchips will soon be placed in foreheads, or imbedded in credit cards, so that no one will be able to buy or sell—which in some way is connected with the mark of the beast, and on it goes.

Of course, there is plenty to be concerned about. But all these so-called signs are all focused on fighting the battle where it isn't. All these so-called signs are Satan's decoys to divert our minds from where the real battle of the last days is being fought. Where is that? In the minds of men and women where God is trying to place His seal and signature before the winds blow. Don't forget Revelation 7 and 14.

Which leads to Clue #5 in comparing Noah's day with ours: World conditions prior to the close of probation will give the last generation no more direct warning than world conditions gave to Noah's hearers, prior to the Flood.

THE DILEMMA

How can this be? It is the dilemma of the half-full and half-empty glass of water.

On the pessimistic side, it is the paradox of horror. When we get repeated doses of outrage and disasters, we tend to become inoculated into insensitivity. Yet the dreariness remains. After generations of unprecedented global horrors and the mind-numbing statistics describing ethnic cleanings by the many millions (Armenians, the Holocaust, Cambodia, Bosnia, Uganda, Iraq) and the millions on starvation level or those plagued by pollution disasters, we just flip the channels or turn the pages as casually as we do the weather report.

On the optimistic side, it is the addiction of good news. Think of transistors, the Pentium chip, Salk vaccine (polio), MRIs and CAT scanners, Teflon, lasers, polymers, and the list seems endless.

In the days just before the close of probation, the world will appear to be on the verge of removing its dreaded physical diseases, of solving polluting problems, of eliminating hunger and poverty. The stock market will be hovering at 25,000 or more—all the while the diplomats are putting in place an unprecedented world peace federation. Earth's billions will be listening for the latest from the Vatican, with the

Pope as the Master Peacemaker and with Mother Mary with her phenomenal assurance that all is well. With all that happening around us, dire warnings of the end of the world will sound as ridiculous and unbelievable as the words of lonely Noah as he implored his neighbors to enter the ark.

EMOTIONAL FATIGUE

Let us keep the whole picture in front of us. As far as observable data are concerned, and with the numbness that comes after a half-century cycle of unrelenting tensions and periodic relief, emotionally drained men and women may think of good reasons to scoff at the warnings of Seventh-day Adventists. Furthermore, hearing the cry of "wolf, wolf" too many times has already given emotional fatigue to too many Adventists. Too many Adventists, once hot in believing Jesus is coming soon, are now on a cool spiritual holiday—no deep sense of urgency, no deep sense of what God is waiting for.

Let's listen again to one with deep insight: "Christ declares that there will exist similar unbelief concerning His second coming. … When the professed people of God are uniting with the world, living as they live, and join with them in forbidden pleasures; when the luxury of the world becomes the luxury of the church; when the marriage bells are chiming, and all are looking forward to many years of worldly prosperity—then, suddenly as the lightning flashes from the heavens, will come the end of their bright visions and delusive hopes."[1279]

And again: "The crisis is stealing gradually upon us. The sun shines in heavens, passing over its usual round, and the heavens still declare the glory of God. Men are still eating and drinking, planting and building, marrying, and given in marriage. Merchants are still buying and selling. Men are jostling one against one another, contending for the highest place. Pleasure lovers are still crowding to theaters, horse races, gambling halls. The highest excitement prevails, yet probation's hour is fast closing, and every case is about to be eternally decided. Satan sees that his time is short. He has set all his agencies at work that men may be deceived, deluded, occupied, and entranced, until the day of probation shall be ended, and the door f mercy be forever shut."[1280]

Let's get some reality into all this: The pessimists are wrong—the future is not hopeless. The world will not end in either a whimper or a bang. World nuclear powers will not incinerate the earth; we will not drown or be suffocated in our own garbage, nor shrivel up in mass starvation.

And the optimists are wrong—the future is not in the hands of ingenious men and women who, up to now, have always come up with the "just in time" solutions. Technology will not cure, for example, the self-interest of family members or neighbors or nations, as they grab for what they have not earned, trampling others in their path. Technology may recycle used glass, paper and metals but not the rising tide of moral garbage that mocks the rising standards of living everywhere.

[1279] *The Great Controversy,* 338.
[1280] *The Desire of Ages,* 636.

STRIKINGLY SIMILAR TO NOAH'S MISSION

The Adventist mission is strikingly similar to that of Noah's prior to the Flood. That is why we must listen carefully to Jesus in this 24th chapter of Matthew: Adventists are to do for our generation what Noah did for his.

Strange as it may seem, world conditions did not shake up Noah's neighbors enough so that they flocked to his evangelistic meetings. Much to the contrary, they scoffed!

Perhaps the sliest, most sinister plan Satan has will not be cloaked in pessimism with all kinds of evidence that the world is falling apart. It will be the air of optimism that will finally choke those who are scoffing at the proclamation of the return of Jesus—just "as were the days of Noah."

Many religious people helped Noah build the ark. They even thought he was a great neighbor. He was always out somewhere helping somebody in need. They trusted his ethics but wished he wasn't such a fanatic about his religion.

Religious teachers even debated him because they thought his brand of "righteousness by faith" was too hard, too legalistic. After all, they observed, "God knows we are only human. He wants us to have a good relationship with Him—and all that stuff about conduct and behavior and character determining destiny is not where it's at. Noah, lighten up!"

But Noah's neighbors were soon to see that belief and behavior cannot be separated. If one's theology is not right, whatever one calls relationship is not right. They discovered too late that Noah alone had the truth about how to be in the right relationship with God. No room for diversity.

APPENDIX Q:
THE DIFFERENCE BETWEEN THE NEUTRAL AND MORAL CONCEPTS OF HELL

Four positions on the meaning of "hell" have emerged through the years: 1) Pure speculation; 2) Symbol of despair;[1281] 3) Literal punishment in terms of eternal hell-fire; 4) Annihilation, especially in the past 50 years.[1282]

Positions on the afterlife fall within one of two choices: 1) neutral death or 2) moral death. Neutral death advocates believe that the good and bad live on after death without any distinction between them. Moral death advocates contend that in some way the good are rewarded and the wicked are punished.

KIND OF GOD ENVISIONED

How one decides depends on a basic presupposition—what kind of God is envisioned. Does He reward the good and punish the wicked? Or does He keep working on those who have "died" until all eventually concede to His graciousness and thus "saved." We call that position "universalism."

[1281] Including J. L. Packer, Kenneth Kantzer, Robert Schuller, Billy Graham, and John Paul II.

[1282] Including Carl Braaten, F. F. Bruce, Edward Fudge, Andrew Greeley, Hans Kueng, Richard Neuhaus, Clark Pinnock, John A. T. Robinson, John R. W. Stott, and Helmut Thielicke.

At this time I am not doing an exegesis of the biblical texts that refer to "life after death," the punishment of the wicked, or the reward of the saints. I only want to highlight the basic differences in how people have understood "life after death." However, I can't ignore Augustine's remarkable understanding of God when he wrote that the ability of the lost to endure an eternity of a fiery hell is "a miracle of the most omnipotent Creator."[1283]

Neutral death is described most colorfully in Greek mythology—all the dead are somewhere together, no differentiation between the good and the wicked.

In the Jewish Bible, Deuteronomy gives us the classic description of justice that some call the neutral position.[1284] The blessings and cursings, especially in chapters 27 and 28, are unforgettably dramatic in their explicit descriptions of the blessed and the cursed. But through the years it became obvious that not all the liars, the greedy, and the oppressors seemed to be cursed—they seemed to live very well! I am not saying that Moses did not believe in an afterlife wherein true justice will be meted out, he just did not refer to it in this book.

The Book of Job, however, depicts the struggle of an honest man who is confused by what appear to him as grave injustices in life. As the struggle continues, it is apparent that he refuses to accept the neutral view of the afterlife. He boldly states that the afterlife should have some measure of compensation, for the good and the bad (13:15–18; 14:13–15).

Daniel is perhaps the clearest example in the Old Testament of a moral view of the afterlife: "At that time your people shall be delivered, everyone who is found written in the book. And many of those who sleep in the dust of the earth shall awake, some to everlasting life, some to shame and everlasting contempt" (12:1, 2).

AFTER THE MILLENNIUM

New Testament writers are much clearer regarding the moral view of the afterlife, that is, after the resurrection of the just and unjust (Matthew 25:46; John 5:29; Revelation 20:4–15). When biblical writers look into the future, after the return of Jesus, the redeemed are in heaven for at least 1,000 years. At the end of the millennium, this renewed planet becomes the eternal home of those trusted with eternal life.

The Great Controversy Theme gives us the truth about God and His government. This theme provides the framework for understanding the purpose of the gospel and how its fulfillment embraces the moral view of what happens in the after life (that is, after one is resurrected).

[1283] *De Civitate Dei*, transl. by Marcus Dods, *The City of God* (New York: Random House, 1950), 778–79.

[1284] Alan E. Bernstein, *The Formation of Hell* (Ithaca, NY: Cornell University Press, 1993), 146–153.

BIBLIOGRAPHY

Periodicals

"Bush Meets With Catholics on Faith-based Initiatives," *National Catholic Register*, February 11-17, 2001.

Baker, Peter, *Washington Post Foreign Service*, Friday, April 4, 2003.

Barnhouse, Donald Grey, *Eternity*, September, 1956.

Bennett, William J., "Count one blessing out of 9/11 tragedy: moral clarity," *Houston Chronicle*, October 7, 2001.

Blumenthal, Sidney, "Christian Soldiers," *The New Yorker*, July 18, 1994.

Boortz, Neal, "The war on individualism," October 1, 2002, ©2000 WorldNetDaily.com

Bork, Robert H., "No Court Can Save Us," *Wall Street Journal*, December 5, 2000.

Christianity Today, May 16, 1994, November 14, 1994, October 25, 1999, September 11, 2000.

Conn, Joseph L., "Papal Blessing?" *Church and State*, November 1995.

Cowell, Alan, *New York Times*, August 18, 1993.

Davidson, Richard M., "In Confirmation of the Sanctuary Message," *Journal of the Adventist Theological Society*, vol. 2, no. 1, 1991.

"The Good News of Yom Kippur," *Journal of the Adventist Theological Society*, vol. 2, no. 2, 1991.

"The Meaning of Nitsdaq in Daniel 8:14," *Ibid.*, vol. 7, no. 1, 1996.

DiMascio, William, "DNA evidence exposes system flaws," *The Philadelphia Inquirer*, August 7, 2002.

Dobbs, Lou, "The Dobbs Report," *U. S. News & World Report*, July 21, 2003.

Douglass, Herbert E., "Spirit of Prophecy Perspectives: Education's Grand Theme." —*Journal of Research on Christian Education*, vol. 10, Summer 2001, Special Edition.

Edwards, James R., "The Jesus Scandal," *Christianity Today*, February 4, 2002.

Fredericks, James, The Cross and the Begging Bowl: Deconstructing the Cosmology of Violence." *Buddhist-Christian Studies* 18 (1998).

Friedman, Thomas, *New York Times*, November 27, 2001.

George, Robert P., "Freedom and Its Counterfeit," *Imprimis*, August 2003.

Gibbs, N., "Angels Among Us," *Time*, Dec. 27, 1993.

Graham, Billy, "John Paul II, Man of the Year." *Time*, December 26, 1994/January 2, 1995.

Grimaud, Gerald , attorney in Tunkhannock, PA, a personal letter, January 18, 2002.

Grounds, Vernon, "Getting Into Shape Spiritually," *Christianity Today*, February 2, 1979.

Henderson, Mark, "IBM starts work on computer to rival the human brain," TIMESONLINE, Nov. 19, 2002.

Heston Charlton, *America 1st Freedom*, December 2001.

Istook, Rep. Ernest, RS-Okla., *The Sacramento Bee*, August 18, 1997.

Kahn, Chris, "Robertson, Falwell: U.S. Vulnerable," Associated Press, September 14, 2001.

Kjos, Berit, *The Front Page*, Tulsa, OK, August, 1995.

Leo, John, "Coercion on campus," *U. S. News & World Report*, May 15, 2000.

"Color me confounded," *U.S. News & World Report*, February 4, 2002.

"Deaf to good sense," *U.S. News & World Report*, March 25, 2002.

"Playing the bias card," *U. S. News & World Report*, January 13, 2003

"Creeping transnationalism," *U. S. News & World Report*, July 21, 2003.

Life, December 1989.

Mandel, Michael J., *Business Week*, February 25, 2002.

Mathewes-Green, Frederica, "Whatever Happened to Repentance?" *Christianity Today*, February 4, 2002.

Massing, Michael, "As Rabbis Face Facts, Bible Tales Are Wilting," www.nytimes.com. 2000/03/09.

McCloskey, Pat, "Washington's New Pope John Paul II Cultural Center," *St. Anthony Messenger,* April 2001.

Medved, Michael, "Admit terrorism's Islamic link," *USA TODAY,* June 24, 2002.

Morrow, Lance, "Is it Enough to Be Sorry?" *Times,* March 27, 2000.

"Has Your Paradigm Shifted?" *Time,* November 19, 2001.

"Who's More Arrogant?" *Time,* December 10, 2001.

"Awfully Ordinary," *Time,* December 24, 2001.

National Catholic Register, January 9, 16, 1994, December 11, 1994, October 16, 1994.

Newsweek, May 8, 2000, cover story, "What Teens Believe."

Olasky, Marvin, *Christianity Today,* December 14, 1992.

Ostling, Richard, *Time,* November 15, 1993

Packer, J. I., "Why I Signed It," *Christianity Today,* December 12, 1994.

Paschal, Rodl, "Spies and Secret Missions, A History of American Espionage," *Sacramento Bee,* April 4, 2003.

"Poll: Compared to allies, U. S. is more devout," *Sacramento Bee,* December 12/20/02.

Roberts, Steven, "Open arms for online democracy," *U. S. News & World Report,* January 16, 1995.

Sacks, Oliver, "Mendeleev's Garden, " *The American Scholar,* Autumn, 2001.

Safire, William "Threat of National ID," *The New York Times,* December 24, 2001.

"You Are A Suspect," *New York Times,* November 14, 2002.

Sartwell, Crispin, *Orlando Sentinel* (FL), January 4, 2002.

Siegel, Josh, "Concept of true freedom is found far beyond American ideal," *The State News,* MSU's independent voice, February 22, 2002.

Shea, William H., "When Did the Seventy Weeks of Daniel 9:24 Begin? *Journal of the Adventist Theological Society,* vol. 2, no. 1, 1991.

Taylor, LaTonya, "The Church of O," *Christianity Today,* April 1, 2002.

The National Catholic Register, October 26-November 1, 1997.

Time, December 4, 1989, February 24, 1992, October 5, 1992.

Time, Newsweek, and *U. S. News & World Report,* April 9, 1996.

Tolson, Jay, "All Thought Out?" *U. S. News & World Report,* March 11, 2002.

"The New American Empire?" *U. S News & World Report,* January 13, 2003.

U. S. News & World Report, June 24, 2002, August 12, 2002.

USA TODAY, March 30, 1994, October 31, 1997, October 29, 1998, September 24, 2001, March 7, 2002, May 6, 2002,

Vazsonyl, Balint, "Four Points of the Compass: Restoring America's Sense of Direction," *Imprimis,* November, 1997.

Weiss' *Safe Money Bulletin,* Mid-February, 2003.

Wertheimer, Ron, "Cronkite on Famine, Pestilence and Death," *The New York Times,* March 4, 2003.

Wieland, Robert J., *Dial Daily Bread,* September 10, 2001.

Dial Daily Bread, February 4, 2003.

Woodward, K. L., "Angels," *Newsweek,* Dec. 27, 1993.

Books

Abbot-Smith, G., A *Manual Greek Lexicon of the New Testament* (Edinburgh: T. & T. Clark, 1954).

Ambrose, Stephen E., *Citizen Soldiers* (New York: Simon & Schuster, 1997).

D-Day (New York: Simon & Schuster, 1994).

Augustine, The Confessions of Saint Augustine, (New York: Random House—*The Modern Library,* 1949).

Bacchiocchi, Samuel, *Hal Lindsey's Prophetic Jigsaw* (Berrien Springs, MI: Biblical Perspectives, 1987).

Barna, George, *The Second Coming of the Church* (Nashville, TN: Word Publishing, 1998).

Bennett, William J., *The Death of Outrage* (New York: Simon & Schuster, 1998).

Berlin, Isaiah, *Liberty*, ed. Henry Hardy (Oxford: Oxford University Press, 2002).

The Power of Ideas (Princeton, NJ: Princeton University Press, 2000).

Bernstein, Alan E., *The Formation of Hell* (Ithaca, NY: Cornell University Press, 1993).

Black, Robert W., *Rangers in World War II* (New York: The Ballantine Publishing Group, 1992).

Blanshard, Paul, *American Freedom and Catholic Power* (Boston: The Beacon Press, 1949).

Bloom, Allan, *The Closing of the American Mind* (New York: Simon & Schuster, Inc., 1988).

Bloom, Harold, *The American Religion* (New York: Simon & Schuster, 1992).

Boozer, Jack & William A. Beardslee, *Faith to Act* (Nashville, TN: Abingdon Press, 1967).

Bork, Robert H., *Slouching Towards Gomorrah* (New York: HarperCollins*Publishers*, 1996).

Boyd, Gregory A., *Cynic, Sage or Son of God?* (Wheaton, IL: Bridgepoint, 1995).

God At War (Downers Grove, IL: InterVarsity Press,1997).

Satan and the Problem of Evil (Downers Grove, IL: InterVarsity Press, 2001).

Brunner Emil, *Truth as Encounter* (Philadelphia: The Westminster Press, 1943).

The Christian Doctrine of Creation and Redemption (Philadelphia: The Westminster Press, 1952).

Bultmann, Rudolf, "New Testament and Mythology," in H. W. Bartsch (ed.), *Kerygma and Myth* (London: SPCK, 1952).

Jesus Christ and Mythology (New York: Charles Scribner's Sons, 1958).

Theology of the New Testament, vols. I, II, (New York: Charles Scribner's Sons, 1951–1955).

Casalini, Tom and Timothy White, *Ordinary Heroes* (Zionsville, IN: Sweet Pea Press, 2000).

Castiglioni, Arturo, M.D., "The Serpent As Symbol," *Ciba Symposia*, vol. 2, (March 1942).

Chalmers, Elden M. and Esther L., *Making the Most of Family Living* (Nampa, ID: PPPA, 1979).

Chandler, Russell, *Doomsday* (Ann Arbor, MI: Servant Publications, 1993).

Chaucer , Geoffrey, *Internet Medieval Source Book, Canterbury Tales*, gopher:// gopher.vt.edu

Clive, John, *Not By Fact Alone* (New York: Alfred A. Knopf, 1989).

Cobb, John, *Living Options in Protestant Theology* (Philadelphia: The Westminster Press, 1962).

Cowley, Robert, ed., *No End Save Victory* (New York: G. P. Putnam's Sons, 2001).

Cranfield, C. E. B., *The International Critical Commentary, The Epistle to the Romans,* vol. 1 (Edinburgh: T & T Clark Limited, 1973).

Crier, Catherine, *The Case Against Lawyers,* (New York: Random House (Broadway Books), 2002).

D'Aubigné, J. H. Merle, *History of the Reformation of the Sixteenth Century* (New York: Robert Carter and Brothers, 1875).

Damsteegt, P. Gerard, *Foundations of the Seventh-day Adventist Message and Message* (Grand Rapids: William B. Eerdmans Publishing Company, 1977).

Dante, *The Divine Comedy,* Canto V (Harvard Classics, vol. 20)

Douglass, Herbert E., *Faith, Saying Yes to God* (Brushton, NY: TEACH Services, Inc., 2002, Review and Herald Publishing Association(RHPA), 1978).

Rediscovering Joy (RHPA, 1994).

Messenger of the Lord (Nampa, ID: (Pacific Press Publishing Association,) 1998). (PPPA).

The End (Brushton, NY: TEACH Services, Inc., 2001; PPPA, 1979).

Why Jesus Waits (PPPA, 2001).

How To Survive the 21st Century (RH, 2000).

Fleming Thomas, *Liberty! The American Revolution* (New York: Viking, the Penguin Group, 1997).

Flynn, Ted and Maureen, *The Thunder of Justice* (Sterling, VA: Maxhol Commitments, 1993).

Foner, Eric, *The Story of American Freedom* (New York: W. W. Norton & Company, 1998).

Fowler, John M., *The Cosmic Conflict Between Christ and Satan* (PPPA, 2001).

Frazee, W. D., *Ransom and Reunion* (Nashville, TN: Southern Publishing Association, 1977).

Froese, Arno, *How Democracy Will Elect the Antichrist—The Ultimate Denial of Freedom* (West Columbia, SC: The Olive Press, 1997).

Fromm, Erich, *Escape From Freedom* (New York: Avon Books, 1941).

Froom, Leroy Edwin, *The Conditionalist Faith of Our Fathers,* vol. II (RHPA, 1965).

Movement of Destiny (RHPA, 1971).

Gallagher, Jonathan, *Is God To Blame?* (Grantham, England: The Stanborough Press, 1992).

Gane, Roy, *Altar Call* (Berrien Springs, MI: Diadem, 1999).

Gaustad, Edwin Scott, *Dissent in American Religion* (Chicago: The University of Chicago Press, 1973).

Geiermann, Peter, *The Convert's Catechism of Catholic Do*ctrine, (St. Louis: B. Herder Book Co., 1957).

Gingrich, Arndt &, A *Greek-English Lexicon of the New Testament* (Chicago: The University of Chicago Press, 1957).

Girard, Rene, *Violence and the Sacred* (Baltimore: The Johns Hopkins University Press, 1977).

Girdlestone, Robert, *Synonyms of the Old Testament* (Grand Rapids, MI: Wm. B. Eerdmans Publishing Company, 1956).

Goldstein, Clifford, *Day of the Dragon* (Boise, ID: PPPA, 1993).

One Nation Under God? (Boise, ID: PPPA, 1996).

Grenz, Stanley J., & Roger E. Olson, *20th Century Theology* (Downers Grove, IL: InterVarsity Press, 1992).

Guy, Fritz, "The Universality of God's Love," in *The Grace of God and the Will of Man,* ed., Clark H. Pinnock (Minneapolis, MN: Bethany House Publishers, 1989).

Hawking, Stephen, *A Brief History of Time* (New York: Bantam Books, 1988).

Hegstad, Roland, *God's Got to Look Good* (PPPA, 1986).

Heppenstall, Edward, *Our High Priest* (RHPA, 1972).

Holbrook, Frank, *The Atoning Priesthood of Jesus Christ* (Berrien Springs, MI: Adventist Theological Society Publications, 1996).

Horn, Siegfried and Lynn Wood, *The Chronology of Ezra 7,* 2nd Edition (RH, 1970).

Seventh-day Adventist Bible Commentary [SDABC] (RH, 1953-).

Hunt, Dave & T. A. McMahon, *The Seduction of Christianity* (Eugene, OR: Harvest House Publishers, 1985).

How Close Are We? (Eugene, OR: Harvest House Publishers, 1993).

Hutchins, Robert M., and Mortimer J. Adler, *The Great Ideas Today 1973* (New York: Encyclopedia Britannica, Inc, 1973).

Jenkins, Philip, *The Next Christendom* (Oxford: Oxford University Press, 2002).

Kelly Alfred H., & Winfred A. Harbison, *The American Constitution: Its Origins and Development,* rev. ed. (New York: W. W. Norton & Company, Inc., 1948, 1955).

Kierkegaard, Soren, transl. David F. Swenson, *Philosophical Fragments* (Princeton, NJ: Princeton University Press, 1969).

Klemperer, Victor, *I Will Bear Witness* (New York: Modern Library Paperback Edition, 1999).

Kübler-Ross, Elisabeth, *The Wheel of Life* (New York: Scribner, 2001).

Kyle, Richard, *The Last Days Are Here Again* (Grand Rapids, MI: Baker Books, 1998).

Lewis, C. S., *God in the Dock* (Grand Rapids, MI: William B. Eerdmans Publishing Company, 1970).

Mere Christianity (San Francisco: Harper San Francisco, 1952, 1980).

The Great Divorce (San Francisco: Harper San Francisco, 1946, 1973).

The Problem of Pain (London: Collins, Fontana Books, 1957).

The Screwtape Letters San Francisco: Harper San Francisco, 2001).

Lossing, B. J., *Biographical Sketches of the Signers of the Declaration of American Independence* (New York: George F. Coolidge & Brother, 1848; reprinted, Aledo, TX: WallBuilder Press, 1998).

MacArthur, Jr., John F., *Faith Works, the Gospel According to the Apostles* (Dallas: Word Publishing, 1993)

The Vanishing Conscience (Dallas: Word Publishing, 1994).

Macquarrie, John, *Twentieth-Century Religious Thought* (New York: Harper & Row, Publishers, 1963).

Martin, Malachi, *Hostage to the Devil* (San Francisco: HarperCollinsSan Franciscos,1976, 1992).

The Decline and Fall of the Roman Church (New York: G. P. Putnam's Sons, 1981).

The Keys of This Blood (New York: Simon & Schuster, 1990).

Maxwell, A. Graham, *Can God Be Trusted* (Nashville, TN: Southern Publishing Association, 1977).

Maxwell, C. Mervyn, *God Cares,* vol.1 —*The Message of Daniel for You and Your Family* (PPPA, 1981).

God Cares, vol.2—*The Message of Revelation for You and Your Family* (PPPA, 1985).

McCullough, David, *John Adams* (New York; Simon & Schuster, 2001).

McKeon, Richard, ed., *The Basic Works of Aristotle* (New York: Random House, 1941).

McPherson, James M., ed., *To the Best of My Ability* (New York: Dorling Kindersley Publishing, Inc., 2000).

Meerloo, M.D., Joost A. M., *The Rape of the Mind* (New York: Grosset & Dunlap, 1956).

Melady, Thomas P., *The Ambassador's Story—The United States and the Vatican in World Affairs* (Huntington, IN: Our Sunday Visitor, Inc., 1994).

McFarland, Ken, *The Lucifer Files* (PPPA, 1988).

Mikaelian, Allen, *Medal of Honor* (New York: Hyperion, 2002).

Milton, John, *Paradise Lost,* bk. 1, (Harvard Classics, vol. 4).

Morgan, Douglas, *Adventism and the American Republic* (Knoxville, TN: The University of Tennessee Press, 2001).

Murray, Iain, *The Forgotten Spurgeon* (Edinburgh: The Banner of Truth Trust, 1978).

Neall, Beatrice S., "Sealed Saints and the Tribulation," *Symposium on Revelation,* (Silver Spring, MD: Biblical Research Institute, 1992).

Nelson, Dwight K., *Countdown to the Showdown* (Fallbrook, CA: Hart Research Center, 1992).

Neufeld, Don, editor, *The Seventh-day Adventist Encyclopedia,* Revised Edition (RHPA, 1976).

North, Gary, *Successful Investing In An Age of Envy* (Sheridan, IN: Steadman Press, 1982).

Olson, A. V., Thirteen *Crisis Years,* (RHPA, 1981).

O'Reilly, Bill *The No Spin Zone* (New York: Broadway Books, 2001).

Orwell, George, *1984,* (Hammondsworth, England: Penguin Books, 1954).

Parker, Geoffrey, *Success is Never Final* (New York: Basic Books, Perseus Books Group, 2002).

Patterson, James and Peter Kim, *The Day America Told The Truth* (New York: Prentice Hall, 1991).

Paulien, Jon, *What the Bible Says About the End-time* (RHPA, 1994).

Peck, M. Scott, M.D., *People of the Lie* (New York: Simon & Schuster, Inc., 1983).

Peth, Howard, *Vanishing Saint: Is the Rapture Real?* (Roseville, CA: Amazing Facts, 1987).

Phillips, J. B., *Making Men Whole* (London: Fontana Books, 1952).

Polkinghorne, John, and Michael Welker, eds., *The End of the World and the Ends of God* (Harrisburg, PA: Trinity Press International, 2000).

The God of Hope and the End of the World (New Haven: Yale University Press, 2002).

Pope John Paul II, "Ut Unum Sin" (That They May be One). www.vatican.va/ holy_father/John_Paul_II/encyclicals/ document

Pope, Alexander, *Essay on Man* (Harvard Classics, vol. 40).

Postman, Neil, *Amusing Ourselves to Death* (New York: Penguin Books, 1985).

Reid, G. Edward, *Sunday's Coming!* (Fulton, MD: Omega Publications, 1996).

Restak, M. D., Richard M., *The Brain* (New York: Bantam Books, 1984).

The Mind (New York: Bantam Books, 1988).

Ringer, Robert J., *How You Can Find Happiness During the Collapse of Western Civilization* (New York: QED/ Harper & Row, 1983).

Robbins, John W., *Ecclesiastical Megalomania, The Economic and Political Thought of the Roman Catholic Church* (The Trinity Foundation, U.S.A., 1999).

Robinson, John A. T., *The Human Face of God* (Philadelphia: The Westminster Press, 1973).

Robertson, Pat, *The New World Order* (Dallas: Word Publishing, 1991).

Sample, Tex, *U.S. Lifestyles and Mainline Churches* (Louisville, KY: Westminister/John Knox Press, 1990).

Shattuck, Roger, *Forbidden Knowledge* (New York: St. Martin's Press, 1996).

Shea, William H., *Selected Studies on Prophetic Interpretation* (Washington, DC: RHPA, 1982).

Smith, David L, *A Handbook of Contemporary Theology* (Wheaton, IL: Victor Books, 1992).

Smith, Page, *The Shaping of America*, vol. 3 (New York: McGraw-Hill Book Company, 1980).

Spalding, A. W., *Christ's Last Legion* (RHPA, 1949).

Strommen, Merton P., *et al, A Study of Generations* (Minneapolis: Augsburg Publishing House, 1972).

Teel, Jr., Charles W., ed., *Remnant and Republic* (Loma Linda, CA: Loma Linda University Center for Christian Bioethics, 1995).

Vick, Edward W. H., *Is Salvation Really Free?* (RHPA, 1983).

Vincent, Marvin R., *Vincent's Word Studies in the New Testament* (Peabody, MA: Hendrickson Publishers, n.d.).

Wallenkampf, Arnold V, Richard Lesher, Frank B. Holbrook, editors, *The Sanctuary and the Atonement* (Silver Spring, MD: Biblical Research Institute, 1989).

Walton, Lewis R., *The Lucifer Diary* (Glennville, CA: Aralon Press, 1997).

Walvoord, John V., *Armageddon, Oil and the Middle East Crisis* (Grand Rapids, MI: Zondervan, 1990).

Wesley, John, *The Works of John Wesley*, Third Ed. (Kansas City, Mo: Beacon Hill Press, 1978).

Wills, Garry, *Under God* (New York: Simon and Schuster,1990).

Wohlberg, Steve, *Exploding the Israel Deception* (Fort Worth, TX: Amazing Discoveries, 1998).

Truth Left Behind (PPPA, 2001).

Wynkoop, Mildred Bangs, *A Theology of Love: The Dynamic of Wesleyanism* (Kansas City, Mo: Beacon Hill Press, 1972).

Yancey, Philip, *Disappointment With God* (Grand Rapids, MI: Zondervan, 1988).

The Jesus I Never Knew (Grand Rapids, MI: Zondervan, 1995).

The Bible Jesus Read (Grand Rapids, MI: Zondervan, 1999).

Rumors of Another World (Grand Rapids, MI: Zondervan, 2003).

Yankelovich, Daniel, *New Rules* (New York: Random House, 1981).

Yallop, David A., *In God's Name, an Investigation into the Murder of Pope John Paul I* (New York: Bantam Books, 1984).

Zurcher, J. R. *What Inspiration Has to Say About Christian Perfection,* transl. Edward F. White (RH, 2002).